D0709264

Wilford J. Eiteman
Professor of Finance
Graduate School of Business Administration
The University of Michigan

Charles A. Dice
Professor Emeritus of Business Organization
College of Commerce and Administration
The Ohio State University

David K. Eiteman
Associate Professor of Finance
Graduate School of Business Administration
University of California, Los Angeles

THE STOCK MARKET

Fourth Edition

McGraw-Hill Book Company

New York, St. Louis, San Francisco, Toronto, London, Sydney

The Stock Market

Library of Congress Catalog Card Number 65-22105

14 15 16 17   K P K P   7 9

PREFACE

The first edition of *The Stock Market*, written by Professor Charles A. Dice of Ohio State University, appeared in 1926. At that time stock trading was viewed with suspicion, and the operation of exchanges was a mystery. Furthermore, common stocks were not considered a proper medium for investment by persons of limited means. Consequently, the first edition addressed itself to the inquiring layman; it explained in simple, straightforward language how the stock market was organized and how it operated. The description included such supplementary matters as the construction of stock market indexes, the forecasting methods then in vogue, and the services offered by advisory agencies.

Significant changes in the economy took place in the ensuing years: the growing popularity of common stocks, induced by Edgar L. Smith's *Common Stocks as Long-term Investments*; the great bull market of 1928–1929; the spectacular crash of 1929. These historic happenings were followed by a prolonged economic depression. Gradually the concept of a market changed from a place in which to gamble to a place in which to acquire and dispose of securities at prices related to intrinsic values. The Securities Exchange Act of 1934 drastically altered many practices of the exchanges. These changes in philosophy and procedure led to the 1941 revision of *The Stock Market*. The third edition (1951) updated the material but preserved the style, approach, and coverage of the earlier editions.

During the fifteen years that have passed since the appearance of the third edition, common stocks have become widely accepted as desirable investments. In fact, owing to years of continuous inflation, they are now considered by some to be the *only* safe medium of investment for the long-term investor. Today, too, the man on the street is increasingly aware of the effect of international events, an awareness which has brought with it an interest in foreign investment. At the same time automation has introduced many innovations in trading procedures. This fourth edition of *The Stock Market* covers all these new developments.

Chapter 1 describes the function of the market—what an exchange is supposed to do. Chapters 2 to 4 show how the principal exchanges of the world have evolved to perform that function.

Chapters 5 to 18 give a detailed description of the organization and operation of the New York Stock Exchange. Chapters 19 to 28 deal with the use of market facilities by speculators and investors. They cover such matters as the assumptions that underlie various investment programs, the methods of analyzing financial statements, the use of advisory services and forecasting statements, and the theories of stock values. Chapter 29 reviews the events that led to regulation and the elimination of undesirable practices.

The authors acknowledge their obligation to the many institutions that have so willingly cooperated with them. The following organizations deserve special mention:

The New York Stock Exchange
The American Stock Exchange
The Midwest Stock Exchange
The Pacific Coast Stock Exchange
The National Association of Securities Dealers
The Paris Bourse
The London Stock Exchange
The Tokyo and Osaka Securities Exchanges
Babson's Reports, Inc.
Dow Jones & Company, Inc.
Moody's Investors Service, Inc.
Standard & Poor's Corporation
Value Line Investment Survey

Without the assistance of Sylvia C. Eiteman, who also edited the manuscript, this fourth edition would not have been completed.

Wilford J. Eiteman
Charles A. Dice
David K. Eiteman

contents

part 1

GENERAL CHARACTERISTICS OF STOCK MARKETS

1 the work of a stock exchange

Stock exchanges are elaborate systems that enable investors to acquire or dispose of securities at prices that are "fair and equitable." That such systems are convenient to those who wish to buy or sell securities is obvious. That such systems perform a function of importance to society is less obvious. By increasing the investment options available to individuals, a securities market enlarges the aggregate amount of funds available to finance production and promotes a desirable allocation of the funds among the several industries.

Economic Function of Finance

The supreme objective of an economy based on freedom of choice is maximization of consumer satisfactions. Attainment of this goal requires that industry produce the right quantity of the right type of goods and have them available for consumption at the right time. Deciding what constitutes "right" is a prerogative of consumers. Consumers exercise this prerogative when they purchase or refuse to purchase the goods offered to them by producers. Often their decisions are whimsical—they may change their minds at any moment. This makes it difficult for producers to adjust production to consumer demand. Nevertheless, producers are financially rewarded or punished by the economy on the basis of the accuracy of their predictions of consumer whims.

In a less-developed economy consumer wants are so few that the cooperative arrangements into which producers must enter are relatively simple. But in a highly developed economy the constant stream of new inventions and the apparent insatiability of consumer appetites complicate the productive process. Under such conditions the coordinated activities of hundreds of thousands of persons are required to produce even the simplest articles in the quantities demanded by consumers. This leads to large-scale production.

Large-scale production makes it necessary for each producing organization to have vast amounts of financial capital for the purpose of acquiring land, buildings, equipment, and raw materials and of employing labor. No individual or small group of individuals is rich enough to provide the amount of capital required by a large manufacturing establishment. Giant enterprises such as the American Telephone & Telegraph Company and the United States Steel Company are forced to draw on the savings of thousands of persons.

The corporate form of organization is well adapted to the task of raising capital from many persons. By issuing different types of securities, it can offer to each investor a means of productively employing funds suited to his need and temperament.

Some investors want safety of principal and stability of income. To them the corporation offers its bonds—a form of investment contract promising to return the investor's funds on a specified date and to make periodic payments of interest in the interim.

Other investors desire stability of income but are willing to commit their savings for an indefinite period and to assume a greater degree of risk than the bondholder. To them the corporation offers its preferred stock— a form of investment contract promising to pay annual dividends of a stated amount provided that earnings (after income taxes) are adequate for the purpose.

Still other investors are willing to shoulder the residual risks that must be borne by the ultimate owner of any business venture. This is in the hope that the profit realized will be adequate compensation for the risks involved. To such investors the corporation offers its common stock. In theory, common stockholders are the owners of all the corporate earnings left after payment of income taxes and the prior claims of the other classes of investors.

The three types of securities described, issued by corporations and sold to the investing public by investment bankers, provide corporate enterprises with the funds they need to obtain the land, buildings, equipment, raw materials, and labor required to produce the goods demanded by consumers. The first three of these are classified by accountants as "fixed assets" and the rest as "current assets." Figure 1–1 is a flow chart giving a visual summary of the process.

At the beginning of a productive period the manager of each enterprise estimates how much of his firm's product will be demanded by consumers. Then he arranges for the firm to acquire the estimated quantity either by manufacture or by purchase. The expenses incurred in the procurement of the goods constitute the firm's "operating costs." The aggregate sum received from the sale of the goods is its "gross revenue." The amount by which gross revenue exceeds operating costs (excluding interest, dividends, and income taxes) is the firm's "operating profit." This is the sum that is available to pay income taxes and to compensate those who provide the firm with the capital it uses. The amounts of the gross revenue, the operating costs, and the operating profit and the disposition of the last of these are reported to investors on a firm's income statement (see Table 1).

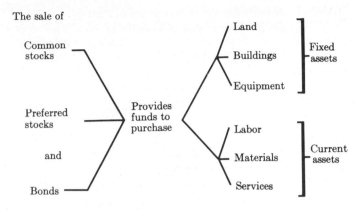

Fig. 1–1   A flow of funds chart.

The amount of capital being used by a firm and the sources of the capital are revealed on the balance sheet (see Table 2).

Investors use the data revealed on balance sheets and income statements as a basis for their opinions regarding the desirability of the several types of corporate securities as a media for investment. To analyze the statements, investors frequently compute and interpret ratios. (A ratio is the figure

TABLE 1   Income Statement of a Hypothetical Company (as an investor should visualize it)

Gross revenue
The aggregate sum received from customers in payment for the goods delivered to them $100,000

Operating costs
The total cost of acquiring the goods which have been delivered to customers. The various types of costs—material, labor, and overhead—are usually itemized   60,000

Operating profit
The sum available to pay income taxes and to compensate those who provided the firm with its capital $ 40,000

Disposition of operating profit
Interest paid to bondholders	$ 5,000
Income taxes paid to government	18,200
Preferred stock dividends	7,000
Common stock dividends	5,000
Retained for reinvestment	4,800
Total	$40,000

TABLE 2   Balance Sheet of a Hypothetical Firm
(as an investor should visualize it)

Assets (capital employed)

Current assets		
Cash	$ 50,000	
Inventories	185,000	
Receivables	50,000	$285,000
Fixed assets		
Land (at cost)	$ 15,000	
Buildings (net)	85,000	
Equipment (net)	115,000	215,000
Total		$500,000

Liabilities (sources of capital)

Bonds, 4%, ten-year, $1,000 par	$125,000
Preferred stock, 7% dividends	100,000
Common stock (original investment)	100,000
Surplus, earnings of past years reinvested in the firm	175,000
Total sources	$500,000

obtained when one number is divided by another.) Ratio analysis is treated in detail in Chapter 25. Here it is sufficient to mention one ratio that has significance to the economy as well as to the individual investor—the rate of return on capital invested ratio.

If the operating profit of a firm is divided by the total of its assets, the resulting ratio is the rate of return earned by the firm on its productively employed capital. The rate of return earned by the hypothetical firm whose accounting reports were given above is 8 per cent ($40,000 ÷ $500,000).

If consumers demand more of a product than an industry has produced, competition among buyers tends to raise the price. This higher price increases the operating profits of the firms within the industry, raises their rate-of-return ratios, and encourages them to expand their scales of operation. The reverse is also true. If consumers are slow to accept the goods produced by an industry, competition among sellers tends to depress the price. The reduced price decreases the operating profits of the firms within the industry, lowers their rate-of-return ratios, and encourages them to curtail their scales of operation. Thus, the average rate of return of an industry acts as a barometer to indicate the desirability of expanding or contracting production.

An identical rate of return for all industries (of equal risk) would suggest that the capital employed by each is producing equal amounts of consumer satisfactions.[1] A discrepancy in the rates of return of two industries would suggest that too much capital is being employed by one and not enough by the other. In this event, an equalization of rates of return would be most easily accomplished by shifting capital from one productive use to the other.

Although current assets can be transferred from one industry to another, fixed assets cannot be transferred so easily. Thus, if an equilibrium of rates of return is to be achieved, it must be done by guiding the flow of *new* savings toward investment in those industries where a high marginal rate of return suggests that additional capital is desirable.

Economic Function of a Securities Market

Many persons believe that a *good* securities market contributes to economic well-being by (1) *increasing the quantity* of funds available to finance industry and (2) *directing the flow* of new savings toward investment in industries where expansion of facilities is most desirable.

Increasing the Quantity of Funds Available.　When an investor purchases a newly issued bond or a newly issued share of stock, his money passes into the hands of a corporation to be dispensed in the acquisition of productive equipment. If the properties acquired by the issuing corporation are fixed assets, the expended funds are recovered from customers by means of depreciation charges spread over many years. If the properties are current assets, the expended funds are recovered when goods are sold to customers but the funds are immediately reexpended in the acquisition of more merchandise. Hence, in neither case are they available for return to the investor who initially supplied them. The conclusion is obvious: Personal savings used to purchase new security issues are irrevocably committed to productive uses—if not forever, at least for a long time.

If there were no way of avoiding this situation, individuals would be hesitant about committing their savings to productive uses and the total amount of funds available to finance industry would be much smaller than it is. The stock market offers an avenue of escape for an *individual* investor but not for investors in the aggregate. A person who purchases a new security that is listed can recover his funds by selling it on an exchange.

[1] Actually the equilibrium is achieved at the margin; that is, each company within an industry would expand its scale of operations until the last unit of capital employed by each is earning an identical rate of return. Also one must draw a distinction between rates of return which are temporarily high and those which are consistently higher than average. It is the latter that signify the desirability of expansion of capital employed in an industry.

Knowledge that a ready market exists reduces the hesitancy of investors to acquire securities when they are first issued and so causes the total quantity of funds available to finance industry to be greater than it otherwise would be.[2]

Directing the Flow of New Savings.   Other things being equal, potential investors prefer to place their funds in the securities of companies which consistently earn higher than average rates of return. As emphasized earlier, companies with higher than average rates of return are the ones in which expansion is most desirable from the point of view of maximizing consumer satisfactions. Investors, attracted by the high rates, compete for the outstanding securities of such companies on a stock exchange and cause their prices to be higher in comparison with earnings than are those of companies with lower rates of return.

Consequently, when the former companies seek new capital to finance expansion, they are able to obtain more funds at lower costs than would otherwise be the case. In this way the price-setting activity of exchanges contributes to an economically desirable allocation of capital resources among the several industries.

Determination of a Fair and Equitable Price

The economic benefits of a securities market described above accrue to society only if the market that exists can be said to be a good market. What, then, are the criteria of a "good" market? An important attribute of a good market is that its quotations deviate as little as possible from "true investment value." The statement raises two questions: What is true investment value? How does a market set prices that approximate this value?

The Concept of True Investment Value.   In a stock exchange transaction a purchaser acquires what the seller relinquishes, that is, the ownership of a stream of future earnings per share.[3] The other privileges acquired by the purchaser do not weigh heavily in determining investment value.[4] Thus investment value may be defined as the present worth of a stream of expected earnings per share.

---

[2] Marketability also increases the attractiveness of securities to investors by making securities acceptable to lenders as collateral for short-term loans.

[3] Some theorists consider dividends rather than earnings per share to be the basis of true investment value. Since dividends depend in the long run upon earnings per share and since the payout ratio (dividends to earnings) tends to stabilize around 60 per cent, discounting dividends at a low rate gives the same value as discounting earnings at a higher rate.

[4] These other privileges are the right to vote, the right to a certificate, the right to information, the preemptive right, and the right to share in residual assets in case of liquidation.

When each component of a stream is specific as to amount and certain to be paid (as is the case with the interest payments of a high-quality bond), the present worth of the stream is computed by a formula in which the discount rate is the only variable. But when some of the components of a stream cannot be predicted with certainty (as is true in the case of earnings per share of a common stock), the formula for computing present worth has two variables: the discount rate and differences in individual estimates of the components of the stream. It is not surprising, therefore, that there are as many opinions about the present worth of a particular stock as there are persons making evaluations. The important point is that opinions of value depend upon expected earnings even though estimates of earnings vary widely.

Determination of Market Price. Obviously, a single market quotation cannot reflect a number of divergent opinions concerning the present worth of a particular issue. But a single market quotation can reflect a consensus of investor opinion regarding present worth. Most organized markets operate on the assumption that the price that results in the maximum volume of trading approaches closest to the price that represents a consensus of investor opinion. Therefore, they have established procedures designed to determine this price objectively. The procedure for determining fair prices works in the following manner:

Each investor first decides independently the present worth of the stream of earnings as he anticipates its components to be. Having arrived at a quantitative value, he compares this value with the current quotation of the issue. If he is already a holder of shares and if the current quotation exceeds his opinion of present worth, he may decide to sell. If he has funds and if his opinion of present worth exceeds the current quotation, he may decide to purchase. In either case, his decision leads to the placing of an order with a broker.

Orders originating in this way are of two types. Some (market orders) call for execution "at the best price immediately obtainable," and others (limited orders) call for execution "at a specified price" or better. If all the orders of a given period involving a particular issue could be concentrated in the hands of a single exchange official, it would be a simple task for him to array them in such a way as to reveal the number of shares offered and wanted at each prospective price and to discover the price at which the number of shares wanted is exactly equal to the number of shares offered. He would then find that the price that equates supply and demand is the same price that maximizes turnover of ownership.

An illustration, based upon foreign stock exchange practices, will clarify the procedure. Assume that during a given week brokers receive market orders to purchase 3,000 shares and market orders to sell 2,000 shares of a particular issue. Assume further that brokers also receive limited orders to buy and sell shares at the specific prices listed below:[5]

Buy orders	Sell orders
Buy 100 shares @ 19¾	Sell 100 shares @ 20
200 shares @ 19½	200 shares @ 19¾
300 shares @ 19¼	300 shares @ 19½
400 shares @ 19	400 shares @ 19¼
400 shares @ 18¾	800 shares @ 19
300 shares @ 18½	600 shares @ 18¾
200 shares @ 18¼	400 shares @ 18½
100 shares @ 18	200 shares @ 18¼

If the market price is 20, the total number of shares wanted is 3,000—the number ordered "at the market." If the market price is 19¾, the total number of shares wanted is 3,100—the market orders plus the first limited order. If the market price is 19½, the total number of shares wanted is 3,300—the market orders plus the first two limited orders. If this type of tabulation is continued for both buy and sell orders, an array showing the number of shares wanted and offered at each possible price would appear as follows:

Shares wanted	Possible prices	Shares offered
3,000	20	5,000
3,100	19¾	4,900
3,300	19½	4,700
3,600	19¼	4,400
4,000	19	4,000
4,400	18¾	3,200
4,700	18½	2,600
4,900	18¼	2,200
5,000	18	2,000

It will be noted that, if the price is 19, the number of shares wanted and offered is exactly equal and that this is not true of any of the other prices. The price of 19 is then the "fair and equitable" price that would prevail if all the persons who placed the orders assembled and bargained skillfully for themselves.

[5] Limited orders to buy are to be interpreted as meaning at the price specified or *lower*. Thus an order to buy at 19¾ is also an order to buy at 19½. Similarly, orders to sell at a specified price are to be interpreted as meaning at the price specified or *higher*. Thus an order to sell at 18¼ is also an order to sell at every higher price.

The situation depicted in the above series is frequently shown in diagram form. In such a diagram the number of shares wanted at each possible price is represented by a line sloping downward to the right and called the "demand curve" (see *DD'* in Figure 1–2). The number of shares offered at each price is represented by a line sloping upward to the right and called the "supply curve" (see *SS'* in Figure 1–2). As noted, the two curves intersect at the price of 19.

The mechanical procedures actually employed by different stock exchanges vary, but the purpose of these procedures is the same throughout: to disclose the price that maximizes turnover. Some exchanges operate a continuous two-way auction market in each issue. On other exchanges, brokers buy from and sell to "dealers," who carry inventories and merchandise shares of stock in much the same manner as if shares were groceries or hardware items. On still other exchanges, orders to buy and to sell shares are handed over to "specialists," who enter the orders in their books and periodically determine what price maximizes turnover. Although the methods may vary, the goal is always to discover a fair and equitable price.

The Economic Role of Speculation

It is difficult to distinguish between an investor and a speculator. In general, an investor buys and sells securities on the basis of dividend income or of expected increases in investment value. By contrast, a speculator buys and sells securities to obtain a profit from anticipated changes in market price (as distinguished from investment value).

Speculation is defended on three grounds: (1) it minimizes deviations

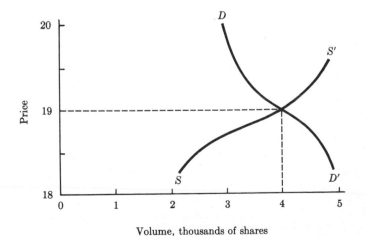

Volume, thousands of shares

Fig. 1–2 Supply and demand for a hypothetical issue.

of prices from investment values; (2) it causes quotations to be continuous; and (3) it enables prices to reflect future as well as current events. These functions, each of which contributes to investor welfare, are discussed in turn.

Speculation Minimizes Deviations from Fair Prices. A fair price has been defined as the price that maximizes turnover when all the buy and sell orders for a particular period of time are accumulated for execution as of some one moment. Unfortunately, orders originating during a period of time—such as an hour, a day, or a week—are not executed simultaneously. Instead they flow into the market at irregular intervals and are executed immediately. This sporadic inflow causes actual market quotations to deviate from the "fair" price for the period. The deviations are technical rather than fundamental in nature, since they are the result of timing.

An illustration will clarify the problem and its solution. Let us recall the earlier illustration, in which a price of 19 was determined to be fair when all the accumulated orders of a week were executed as of one moment. Retaining the assumption regarding the number of buy and sell orders originating during the week, let us change the assumption regarding the number of trading moments in the week from one to five—one each day. Obviously, daily determined prices will coincide with or deviate from a single weekly determined price according to how the week's orders are distributed among the five days.

The five dots on the horizontal line in Figure 1–3 are daily prices if the week's orders are distributed evenly over the five days. The dots on the curved line are daily prices if buy orders are distributed among the five days in the ratio of 2:1:2:3:2 and sell orders are distributed in the ratio of 2:3:2:1:2.

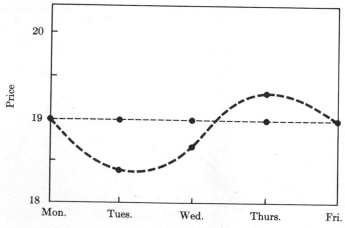

Fig. 1–3 Result of sporadic distribution of orders.

If the assumptions are relaxed to allow a number of trading moments in each day (say, one each hour) and if the orders for each day are distributed unevenly among these trading moments, then hourly prices will deviate about the price that results from a single daily execution of orders. Note that this fluctuation of prices within the day results purely from the "timing" factor and not from any change of investor opinion regarding the investment worth of the shares being traded during the week.

When the period of time during which investors' orders are accumulated is long enough to make the demand and supply situation representative of investor opinion, the price-determining mechanism of the market sets prices that approximate investment worth. In such cases successive market quotations of an issue change up or down in conformity with changes in investor opinion. Price changes of this type are economically *desirable*.

But, as has been illustrated, the immediate execution of orders as they appear in the market frequently causes actual prices to deviate from investment worth. Price changes that originate from an irregular flow of orders might be characterized as *unnecessary*. Regardless of whether price changes are the result of the irregular appearance of orders or signal a beginning of a change in investor opinion, they appear on the tape and are called to the attention of any who may be watching. Deciding whether a change reported on the tape is desirable or unnecessary is difficult at the time it is observed; its true character can be known for certain only in retrospect. Nevertheless, an ideal market would minimize the number and extent of unnecessary price changes.

A trader who can distinguish immediately between the two types of price changes can make a fortune in short order by taking a market position in opposition to unnecessary price changes and in conformity with desirable price changes. The reverse of this is also true: one who fails to distinguish between the two can lose a fortune equally quickly. Thus, the only true measure of the judgment of a speculator is the amount of annual income tax he has to pay. From a social point of view, the contribution of successful speculation to the market is the minimization of the number and reduction of the magnitude of the unnecessary price changes and the time acceleration of the desirable price changes.

For example, in the illustration used earlier, the fair price for the week on the basis of investor opinion was determined to be 19. The price on Tuesday as shown in Figure 1–3 was lower than this price because of a *temporary* excess of sell orders and a *temporary* lack of buy orders. This disequilibrium arose from the irregular flow of orders into the market, and the price change that resulted would be classed as unnecessary. A sensitive speculator would attempt to make a profit from the situation by buying 400 shares at the market on Tuesday for resale on Thursday. Had such an order been placed, the price on Tuesday would have dropped only to $18\frac{3}{4}$, and on

Thursday it would have risen only to 19. Thus the effect of the speculative transaction would have been to lessen the deviation of daily prices about the weekly determined fair price.

If the price decline on Tuesday had been due to a change in investor opinion and not to the irregular flow of orders into the market and if the speculator had mistaken it for an unnecessary change, the effect of his order on Tuesday's price would have been the same but he would have been forced to liquidate on Thursday at a price lower than anticipated. Thus uninformed speculative activity has the effect of retarding desirable changes in market prices. Only wise or successful speculation performs its economic role of stabilizing prices.

Speculation Increases the Continuity of Prices. A market is said to be "continuous" when successive quotations vary by $\frac{1}{8}$ point. Other things being equal, an investor would prefer such a market.

After execution of a transaction in a very active issue, there remain many unfilled orders to buy at slightly lower prices and many unfilled orders to sell at slightly higher prices. Consequently, if a seller exhausts all the orders to buy at a given price, he has only to lower his offer to sell by $\frac{1}{8}$ point to encounter another tier of unexecuted buy orders. Similarly, if a buyer exhausts all the orders to sell at a given price, he has only to raise his bid by $\frac{1}{8}$ point to encounter another tier of unexecuted sell orders. The existence of many unfilled orders at each $\frac{1}{8}$ above and below the most recent quotation means that successive quotations will move up or down by $\frac{1}{8}$-point intervals.

The situation is quite different in the case of an inactive issue. To illustrate, suppose that the most recent quotation for an issue is 121 and that the following unfilled orders are all that remain on the specialist's book after the execution:

Sell 100 shares @ 124	Buy 100 shares @ 117
Sell 100 shares @ 126	Buy 100 shares @ 114

If, now, the next order to come into the market happened to be an order to buy 100 shares at the market, it would be executed at 124 (the lowest standing unfilled offer to sell). If this order were followed by an order to sell 100 shares at the market, it would be executed at 117 (the highest unfilled order to buy). If then an order were received to buy 100 shares at the market, the price would jump to 126. The ticker tape would report the following successive prices of the issue:

$$121 \ldots 124 \ldots 117 \ldots 126$$

Obviously, quotations of an inactive issue have only historic significance and should not be taken as indicative of its market value; by contrast, quotations of issues that enjoy a continuous market suggest the price at which additional shares in reasonable quantities could be sold. A continuous market is not due to speculation; it is due to the existence of many unfilled orders to buy and sell shares at slightly higher and lower prices. A continuous market could exist without any speculative orders. However, speculation does *contribute* to the continuity of quotations by increasing the number of orders to be executed.

Speculation Causes Prices to Discount Future Events.   True investment value, to which market prices should correspond, has been defined earlier as the present worth of future earnings. If, as some believe, investors are not adept at forecasting, are too often preoccupied with other matters, and are prone to view the future as a continuation of the present, their notions of value are likely to deviate from true investment worth. If speculators are as expert at forecasting as reputed, their opinions of value should correspond more closely to investment values. Therefore, informed speculation in an issue should act as a corrective influence on the tendency of prices to deviate from investment worth.

Thus, if investors underestimate the effect of a prospective increase in earnings, current prices will tend to be lower than true investment worth. Speculators, perceiving the situation, will purchase shares for resale later at higher prices. The effect of their purchases will be to raise prices immediately and so to bring the current level of quotations closer to that of long-run investment value.

Similarly, if investors are unduly optimistic about a prospective improvement in earnings, current prices will tend to be higher than long-run investment worth. This will encourage speculators to sell short. The effect of the short sales will be to depress prices immediately and so again to bring the current level of quotations closer to that of long-run investment value.

The whole argument, however, is predicated upon the assumption that speculators are better at forecasting the effect of change than are investors. If this assumption is true, speculative activity does have the moderating influence claimed. But many deny the assumption and argue that speculators spend most of their time trying to predict the behavior of other speculators and very little time trying to forecast long-run investment value. If so, it is doubtful that speculative activity has the effect on prices claimed by its defenders.

Evolution of Organized Securities Markets

The promotion, establishment, and successful operation of an organized market for securities presupposes certain environmental conditions. One of the most important of these is the existence of large-scale business enterprises that employ processes requiring enormous amounts of capital. This need forces companies to fragment their liabilities: that is, to divide them into thousands of identical units each of which is evidenced by a transferable certificate.

If the stocks and bonds issued by enterprises are held by the government or by a few wealthy persons, a central trading place for securities is not necessary, since the number of ownership transfers is likely to be low. In this situation, buyers and sellers find their counterparts and arrange details concerning prices, deliveries, and payments by personal negotiation. But if ownership of stocks and bonds is widely distributed, the number of transfers increases to such an extent that it is possible for a few persons to earn their livelihood by acting as intermediary agents for a fee. This relieves buyers and sellers of the burden of locating their counterparts and arranging the transfer details. The existence of intermediary agents also tends to localize trading activity.

As the volume of trading mounts, the number of intermediaries increases and speculators begin to appear. The speculation is frequently accompanied by some socially undesirable practices. To curb these practices, limited membership associations of brokers are organized to establish professional standards of behavior. At first the trading of the associated brokers is usually conducted in the open—in a courtyard, on a balcony, on a street in the financial district, or in or near a coffeehouse—but after a time the traders acquire a building and conduct their activities indoors.

As soon as a group limits the trading of its members to specified (listed) issues, unlisted issues begin to be traded by nonmembers. It is not unusual for the volume of this off-the-exchange trading to become so heavy as to warrant the organization of another group of brokers. In this way two and three exchanges have been established in some cities. Sometimes a new exchange is merged with an older one.

To minimize misunderstandings and facilitate rapid handling of transactions, members of an exchange must come to an agreement on certain routine matters. The following questions suggest the nature of the problems that need to be solved:

How are new members to be chosen to take the place of those who die or wish to retire?

What are the responsibilities of the companies whose securities are listed?

Are members to be permitted to trade for their own account, or must they confine their activities to acting as agents for the investing public?

Shall each member execute orders in all the issues listed, or shall some be assigned to specific issues in which they act as specialists?

May members extend credit accommodations to their customers (margin trading)?

May members execute sales for customers who do not own the shares they are selling (short selling)?

What is the unit of floor trading to be?

What is to be the standard routine by which members determine contract prices?

How are deliveries of securities and payments of contract sums to be effected?

The various stock exchanges of the world do not give the same answers to these questions. The lack of uniformity arises from the fact that each exchange evolved from a local situation and its members solved their problems without knowing what was happening elsewhere. Not until long after local practices became traditions was effective communication between exchanges established.

Chapters 2 to 4 describe how the leading exchanges of the world have organized to perform the work of a stock exchange as presented in this chapter.

2 the new york stock exchange

The New York Stock Exchange is the dominant market for securities in the United States. No one can pretend to understand the organization of the American capital market without a fairly comprehensive knowledge of the history, organization, and mode of operation of this exchange. This chapter gives a general description of its operations, and Chapters 10 to 13 go into great detail concerning certain aspects of these operations.

Brief History of the Exchange

During the colonial period of American history there was no pressing need for an organized securities market, for there were no securities to be bought and sold. Most capital financing was handled in London, and the securities arising from it were traded there also. The outbreak of the Revolutionary War cut off access to the British capital market. Henceforth funds had to be raised within the Colonies.

The Continental Congress and the 13 states issued bonds and notes to raise money to finance the war. For a while trading in these securities was very active, but when their value declined almost to zero, they disappeared from circulation. In 1781 the Bank of North America was established in Philadelphia with an initial capital of $400,000. Four years later this was increased to $2 million. In 1784 shares of the Bank of New York were offered for public subscription, and in 1791 the First Bank of the United States was chartered with a capital of $10 million divided into 25,000 shares.

The first Secretary of the Treasury, Alexander Hamilton, asked Congress to assume the war debts of the Continental Congress and of the 13 states. Congress agreed to the first at once and refunded the debt with bonds of the United States government at par. Later it passed a second act doing the same for the state debts, but it spread the refunding over a period of five years. As a result of these two acts, bonds with a par value of $77.5 million were added to the floating supply of securities.

The Formative Period. Before security trading can become a business, there must be an adequate supply of securities widely enough distributed to assure frequent and numerous exchanges.

The bonds issued by the Federal government and the shares of the several banks mentioned above furnished the media needed for the beginning of organized security trading in this country.

Philadelphia was the first commercial and financial center of the nation. It was also the political capital during this period. Two of the country's largest banks, the Bank of the United States and the Bank of North America, were located there. Under the circumstances, it is not surprising that the first organized stock exchange in America was established in this city.

There was some trading in securities in New York City, but the volume was small, and the activity was unorganized. Those interested in buying or selling stocks or bonds gathered under a buttonwood tree at 68 Wall Street to consummate their deals. The first move to organize trading was made in May 1792, when 24 brokers met in Corre's Hotel and pledged themselves "not to buy or sell from this day for any person whatsoever, any kind of public stock at a less rate than one quarter per cent commission on the specie value and that we will give preference to each other in our negotiations." On sunny days the now "associated" members traded on the street; but in inclement weather they retreated to the shelter of the nearby Tontine Coffee House to conduct business in a private office "high up under the eaves."

During the years that followed, the nation's economy developed rapidly, and many new banks and business concerns were organized, thus supplying the investing public with additional stocks. Prominent among the newcomers were fire and marine insurance companies and water companies. The War of 1812 added millions to the Federal debt, and the supply of bonds was augmented. Although the charter of the First Bank of the United States was not renewed by Congress when it expired in 1811, the Second Bank of the United States was organized in 1816, with a capital of $35 million.

Period of Development and Growth. As a result of the multiplication of stock and bond issues, the increasing number of persons engaged in the brokerage business, and the enlarged public interest in the securities market, the simple agreement made under the buttonwood tree in 1792 became inadequate to maintain the brokers' sense of their responsibility to the public and to each other. Accordingly, in 1817, the New York group sent a representative to observe the operations of the stock exchange in Philadelphia. After his report, a similar association was formed in New York, with a constitution and bylaws. This group adopted the name New York Stock and Exchange Board. Quarters were rented at 40 Wall Street, and market activities were moved to this location. Membership in the new organization was limited. New members were required to pay an initiation fee of $25 and to receive the affirmative vote of all but two existing members.

The next two decades saw a great development in canal building and in railroad construction. In 1821 the stock of the Morris Canal Company was sold to the public, and in 1830 the shares of the Mohawk and Hudson Railroad were listed for trading. In 1835 the first corner in the history of the young exchange occurred in the shares of the Morris Canal Company. The years 1836 and 1837 were full of surprises, rumors, and scandals. Shortly after the Morris corner, the volume of sales in Harlem Railroad was nine times the number of shares issued. Alarmed by these happenings, the Exchange appointed a committee to investigate cornering and the practice of selling for future delivery. By the middle of 1836 daily sales reached a volume of 8,000 shares, a figure that was considered by the press at the time to be very unusual. The market broke in October of that year.

The growth of stock trading activity was centered in government, bank, canal, and insurance securities. Then railroad stocks took the lead and held it until 1913. The *New York Herald* reported sales of 3,631 shares on May 13, 1835, of which 3,160 were rail shares.

The growth of stock trading in the years to follow paralleled the growth of the nation's economy. The invention of the telegraph in 1842 made possible closer contact between the market and the business world. The panic of 1857 had its counterpart in the stock market; the uncertainties of the Civil War were accompanied by wild speculation; the depreciation of the currency led to the "Gold Conspiracy" and Black Friday.

During the Civil War, speculation was so extensive that many traders spent their days at the Exchange and their evenings at the Fifth Avenue Hotel, buying and selling. Many speculators attempted to become members of the Exchange but could not gain admittance because of the exclusive character of the membership. In 1864 these men organized a more liberal association called the "Open Board of Brokers." At about the same time a "Gold Exchange" was formed to trade in gold.

The outstanding speculative event in the history of the Gold Exchange was Black Friday, September 24, 1869. For several years the country had been on a paper money basis, with gold running at a premium. The fluctuations in the gold price of paper money caused much speculation in gold. Congress had made laws aimed to restrict speculation in gold, but these resulted only in higher premiums and did not stop the speculation. The restrictions were repealed in 1864. Gold dealers were then free to establish an organized market for gold. The market functioned until 1877, when it was dissolved.

It was during the year 1869 that Jay Gould and James Fisk attempted to engineer a corner on gold. Gould had employed more than forty brokers; a pool had been formed to put up gold; and President Grant had been lavishly entertained and carefully instructed as to the desirability of maintaining a relatively high premium on gold for the good of the export business, of the country in general, and of the farmer in particular. It was Gould and Fisk's plan to buy all the gold available. On September 24, their brokers were instructed to buy as much gold as possible. Gold was run up to $162\frac{1}{2}$, when President Grant learned what was happening and instructed the Treasury to sell gold. This burst the bubble as men scrambled to sell. The price tumbled to 133. The gold transactions of the day amounted to well over $400 million. Losses were tremendous. Many brokerage houses failed.

Gambling and irresponsible speculation were not limited to gold. The same thing was going on in regard to all stocks. The twenty years ending with 1872 were years of struggle between Daniel Drew, Commodore Vanderbilt, Jay Gould, and James Fisk for domination of the Harlem, the Hudson, the Erie, and the New York Central railroads. Courts were bribed, legislatures were bought, trickery of the most subtle kind was employed, stocks were watered, and railroads were milked. It was the day of the free-booter in big business and in the stock market.

The Open Board of Brokers operated as a distinct exchange until 1869, when it was consolidated with the New York Stock Exchange. The Exchange now owned its own building, having erected a small structure in 1865 on the site still occupied by the older part of its present quarters.

After the Atlantic cable was laid in 1866, arbitrage between New York and London became of some importance. The industries that had grown up as a result of the demand for war materials were fast shifting into the production of goods for consumption. The securities of these industries, together with those of the expanding railroads, offered the public a speculative medium and formed the basis of a "new era" philosophy. By 1873 the New York Stock Exchange had become a permanent institution in the business life of the nation. Its purpose was to furnish an open, free market to its members and to guard against anything that might be considered against their interests from the long-time point of view. During the period much progress was made in developing high standards of business morality, but fundamentally the Exchange remained a private institution, operating primarily as a marketplace for its members and only secondarily or indirectly for the benefit of society.

The Contemporary Period.   The passage of the Securities Exchange Act of 1934 marks the beginning of the modern period of the Exchange's history and a reversal of the hitherto dominant philosophy regarding its purpose.

The old Exchange was a voluntary association of 1,375 members existing for the purpose of providing themselves a place for the purchase and sale of securities. The Exchange was not a legal entity. It was neither a partnership nor a corporation. It had a constitution and bylaws but no capital, and it had issued no property rights of any kind to its members. Each member voluntarily entered the association by its permission. Since a member acquired no profit rights in the association and since the association had asked no special favors from the state, it had the right to discipline and expel its members as it saw fit.

Consequently, the courts were inclined to reason that the business of the old Exchange was not "affected with a public interest" like that of a corporation that deals with the public. Thus the Exchange was protected in its right to use its own discretion as to membership and to grant or withhold any of its services and privileges. As an example, it could grant or deny the use of its quotation service to whomever it chose.

The language of the Securities Exchange Act of 1934 reflects a different view The act declares that transactions in securities upon security exchanges and in over-the-counter markets affect the national public interest: (1) because a large volume of such transactions are carried on for the public, who find the mails a convenient means of effecting their ˙exchanges; (2) because a large part of the transactions originate outside the states in which the markets are located and thus constitute an important part of the current of interstate commerce; (3) because the company whose security is traded in is often itself engaged in interstate trade; (4) because security transactions involve the use of credit, thereby affecting the financing of trade, industry, and transportation, not to mention the national credit; and (5) because the prices established on the exchanges are disseminated and quoted throughout the world and are used as a basis for determining the amount of certain taxes owed the Federal and state governments and as collateral for bank loans.

The law further declares that the prices determined on the exchanges are susceptible to manipulation and control and that their dissemination gives rise to excessive speculation and unreasonable fluctuations. This causes unreasonable expansion and contraction of credit, obstructs the effective operation of the banking system, intensifies and prolongs national emergencies, and produces widespread unemployment and dislocation of industry.

For these reasons, stock exchanges were held to be proper subjects for government regulation. Whether one agrees with the logic or not, the fact is that stock exchanges are now subject to the control of a commission set up by the Securities Exchange Act of 1934.

The Organization of the Stock Exchange

The New York Stock Exchange is registered as a "national securities exchange" in accordance with the provisions of the Securities Exchange Act, which denies the use of the mails or any "instrumentality of interstate commerce" to unregistered exchanges. Since the term instrumentality of interstate commerce probably covers every interstate use of the telephone, the telegraph, the radio, the railroads, the express companies, and the airlines, this amounts to an ultimatum to exchanges to register or cease to exist.

As is explained elsewhere in more detail, an exchange achieves registration by filing an application with the Securities and Exchange Commission, setting forth such information about its organization and activities as is required and agreeing to cooperate with the Commission in the enforcement of the act and to comply with such rules and regulations as the Commission may from time to time deem it desirable to make.

On December 10, 1937, the president of the New York Stock Exchange appointed a special committee to study the organization and administration of the Exchange and to make recommendations for improvement. On January 27, 1938, this committee made its report, and shortly afterward a new constitution embodying the recommendations was adopted by the members. Three years later the constitution was again revised. The government and administration of the Exchange were altered to eliminate the committee system and to vest authority in a board of governors, the administration of the constitution and the policies of the board being in the hands of a president and the members of his staff. This revision became effective on September 30, 1941.

In 1955 the Committee on Banking and Currency conducted an investigation of the stock market. The Committee's principal concern was with the current high level of stock prices and the possible effect upon the economy of the nation. Questionnaires were mailed to brokers, dealers, investment advisers, and economists; and oral testimony was taken of many high-ranking officers in the fields of finance, industry, and government. But no conclusions were reached, and so no new laws or regulations resulted from the study.

In recent years the New York Stock Exchange has instigated a number of changes in its procedures. The length of the trading day has been extended by one-half hour, to compensate for the market closing on Saturdays. Membership has been reduced from 1,375 to 1,366 by the purchase and retirement of 9 seats. Prior to 1953 members of the Exchange could not incorporate their firms; now this is permitted.

In 1962 and 1963 an external review of all aspects of the stock market was conducted by a special staff assembled by the Securities and Exchange Commission for the purpose. The recommendations of the study have led to many proposals and much discussion. The pros and cons of the recommendations are treated at appropriate places in later chapters.

Membership on the Exchange. A membership on the New York Stock Exchange is often referred to as a "seat." The term seat had its origin years ago, when the number of members was small and each member sat at a desk to transact business. Now the variety of stocks traded, the size of active membership, and the volume of business done require so much activity of members on the floor as to make seats impractical. Nevertheless the term survives.

The number of memberships on the Exchange is limited by its constitution to 1,366. Prior to 1929 the limit was 1,100. Then in 1929 at the height of market activity it was felt that more members were needed to handle the heavy volume of transactions. The plan of enlargement adopted by the Exchange involved giving each existing member a transferable right to purchase one fourth of a new seat. The transfer and execution of these rights increased the membership to 1,375. During the next two decades the volume of trading shrank to such an extent as to make 1,375 members excessive. So in 1952 members approved a ten-year plan to reduce the number of memberships by authorizing the officials to purchase seats for permanent retirement at prices not to exceed a stated maximum. Nine seats were purchased and retired before the market value of seats rose above this maximum. The expiration in 1962 of the retirement authorization stabilized membership for the time being at 1,366.

Only natural persons may be members or allied members of the New York Stock Exchange. But members may associate together as partners or as stockholders in a corporation. In such cases, the partnership or corporation is known as a "member firm." Individuals who are neither regular nor allied members of the Exchange may be limited partners or nonvoting stockholders in a member firm, but they may not exercise a voice in policy making or in the administration of the firm. Their function is merely to provide capital as an investment, in return for which they may receive interest on their money, a percentage of the firm's profits, or their proper share of any dividends distributed.

A membership on the Exchange is not property freely alienable but is of the nature of a franchise, subject to restrictions imposed at the time it is created. One of these restrictions is that it may be transferred only with the approval of the Board of Governors of the Exchange. Another restriction is that the proceeds of a transfer shall be paid to the Exchange and shall be disbursed for the following purposes and in the following order of priority:

First,   in the payment of such sums as the Board of the Exchange shall declare are due to the Exchange from the retiring member, and

Second, in the payment of such sums as the Board of the Exchange shall declare are due to the Stock Clearing Corporation from the retiring member, and

Third,   in payment of such sums as the retiring member may owe to other members of the Exchange arising out of business relationships, and

Fourth, as reimbursement of any unusual expenses incurred by the Exchange in the process of disposing of the proceeds of the sale, and

Fifth,   the balance (if any) may be paid to the retiring member or to his legal representative and is available under the law to outside creditors of the retiring member.

The courts have consistently upheld the Exchange in its contention that it and its members have prior claims against the proceeds which result from a transfer of membership.

There are two prerequisites for becoming a regular member of the Exchange. First, one must prove his eligibility; second, he must arrange to acquire a vacant seat. An applicant for membership must be twenty-one years of age or over, must be a citizen of the United States by birth or naturalization, must be sponsored by two members or allied members of the Exchange, and must present letters of recommendations from at least three responsible persons. In addition, he is required to sign a personal statement giving minute details of his business affairs and to arrange for a physical examination by the medical clinic located in the Exchange building.

Notice of a proposed transfer of membership must be posted on the bulletin board of the Exchange for ten days before the Board of Governors may ballot on his application. The applicant and his sponsors must appear personally at the time the application is being considered. Approval of the application requires an affirmative vote of two thirds of the governors present at the meeting.

At the same time an applicant must arrange to acquire a vacant membership by gift or purchase. Members wishing to dispose of their seats on the Exchange notify the secretary of the fact and of the price that they are asking.[1] The secretary maintains a file of written bids and offers for seats. If an applicant for membership finds the lowest offer satisfactory, he may simply accept it. If he is not satisfied with the offer, he may negotiate for a membership. However, final arrangements for transfers made elsewhere must be consummated in the office of the secretary. To indemnify the seller for costs arising from a buyer's failure, an applicant must deposit 20 per cent of the agreed price with the secretary at the time the agreement is reached. The balance is payable to the Exchange at the time the transfer is effected.

The acquisition of a seat may be financed by any one of four methods. The simplest is for the applicant to pay for the membership with his own funds. In this case, there is no question of the seller or a lender having a lien on the seat.

---

[1] If a member of the Exchange dies, the ownership of his seat passes to his estate, which may offer it for sale at once, hold it for sale at a later date when the price may be higher, or hold it until an heir of the deceased becomes eligible for membership. The Exchange does not object to an estate holding a membership as long as the dues continue to be paid.

A second method is for the applicant to receive a membership as a gift—from a relative or from the estate of a relative. As a condition for approving such a transfer, the Exchange requires that donee to obtain a written release from the donor to evidence the fact that the donee is under no obligation to make any payment to the donor.

The third method is used when the applicant borrows funds to pay for his membership and the lender is secured by a lien on the seat. In this case the Exchange does not approve of the transfer until the lender agrees in writing to subordinate his claim against the member to all claims of the Exchange and its members. The purpose of this subordination agreement is to preclude a lender from asserting any claim against the proceeds of a later transfer of the membership. Thus the Exchange safeguards further its claims of priority for itself and its members.

The fourth mode of payment is more complicated, requiring detailed explanation. Frequently a member firm wishes to enable one of its partners or stockholders to become a member of the Exchange. The individual concerned applies and is made a member, the firm paying the purchase price of the membership. The firm and the member sign an "a-b-c" agreement as follows: First, the firm releases the member from any obligation to reimburse it for the funds it has invested. In return, the member agrees that in case of dissolution of the firm, or his withdrawal from the firm, or his death he or his legal representative will do one of the following:

a. The member or his estate will retain the membership and pay the firm a specified amount.
b. The membership will be sold and the proceeds (remaining after prior claims of the Exchange and its members are met) will pass to the firm.
c. The membership will be transferred for a nominal consideration to some person designated by the firm.

It is the intention of this agreement that the member shall decide as to whether or not provision (a) shall be implemented. If his decision is that it shall not, then the firm is to have the option of choosing between (b) and (c). It will be noted that the firm and not the member bears the risk of loss from the investment in the seat.

If a new and inexperienced member is to be active on the floor, he must be guided by an experienced floor member for such a period as may be necessary to acquaint him with floor procedures. If a neophyte is to do business with the public and has not had the experience to qualify him for such contacts, he must do one of three things: (1) serve as a trainee in the office of a member firm for a period of six months; (2) pass an examination prescribed by the Exchange; (3) take and pass a special course of study approved by the Exchange.

Becoming a member of the New York Stock Exchange may prove to be a costly process. The price of purchasing a seat in 1963 varied from a low of $160,000 to a high of $217,000. Besides, the new member must pay an initiation fee of $7,500 and such quarterly dues as the Board of Governors may levy from time to time. (At the time of writing, the aggregate amount of dues assessed to members in any one year may not exceed $2.1 million.) Furthermore, he must pay the Exchange each year an amount equal to 1 per cent of the commissions that he earns on transactions executed on the floor. Finally, he must make an initial contribution of $15 to a gratuity fund (from which benefits of $20,000 are paid to families of deceased members) and an additional contribution of $15 whenever a member dies.

The price paid for seats has varied from $500 in the 1860s to $625,000 in 1929. Table 3 shows high and low prices of seats for the last eighty-nine years. The prices vary with the activity of the market. When security prices are rising rapidly and the volume of transactions is high, seats are in demand and prices rise. The opposite conditions in the stock market bring a slackening demand for seats and falling prices.

A membership on the Exchange has many advantages. The prestige that attaches to it brings rewards in many ways. The member can do his own trading without commission charges and can secure the services of other members at rates below those charged nonmembers. To protect the interests of the investing public, however, trading by members for their own account is controlled by rules of the Exchange and of the Securities and Exchange Commission.

When it is noted that a seat purchased at the highest price of 1942, $30,000, was worth $190,000 at the lowest price of 1964, the attractiveness of a seat as an investment is readily apparent, regardless of the other advantages mentioned. On the other hand, the rapid decline in the value of a seat from 1929 to 1932 ($625,000 to $68,000) which accompanied the slackening of stock market activity emphasizes the speculative nature of such an investment. Purchase of a membership as an investment or speculation is not permitted by the Exchange.

The constitution of the Exchange also provides for an unlimited number of "allied" members. To become an allied member, one must be a general partner or a voting stockholder in a member firm, make a written pledge to abide by the rules and regulations of the Exchange, and be approved by the Board of Governors. An allied member does not have the right to go upon the floor of the Exchange.

Government of the Exchange.   The government of the New York Stock Exchange is vested in a board of 33 governors, 29 of whom are elected by the members. The composition of the board is as follows:

TABLE 3   Membership Prices

Year	High	Low	Year	High	Low
1875	$ 6,750	$ 4,250	1920	$115,000	$ 85,000
1876	5,600	4,000	1921	100,000	77,500
1877	5,750	4,500	1922	100,000	86,000
1878	9,500	4,000	1923	100,000	76,000
1879	16,000	5,100	1924	101,000	76,000
1880	26,000	14,000	1925	150,000	99,000
1881	30,000	22,000	1926	175,000	133,000
1882	32,500	20,000	1927	305,000	170,000
1883	30,000	23,000	1928	595,000	290,000
1884	27,000	20,000	1929*	625,000	550,000
1885	34,000	20,000	1929†	495,000	350,000
1886	33,000	23,000	1930	480,000	205,000
1887	30,000	19,000	1931	322,000	125,000
1888	24,000	17,000	1932	185,000	68,000
1889	23,000	19,000	1933	250,000	90,000
1890	22,500	17,000	1934	190,000	70,000
1891	24,000	16,000	1935	140,000	65,000
1892	22,000	17,000	1936	174,000	89,000
1893	20,000	15,250	1937	134,000	61,000
1894	21,250	18,000	1938	85,000	51,000
1895	20,000	17,000	1939	70,000	51,000
1896	20,000	14,000	1940	60,000	33,000
1897	22,000	15,500	1941	35,000	19,000
1898	29,750	19,000	1942	30,000	17,000
1899	40,000	29,500	1943	48,000	27,000
1900	47,500	37,500	1944	75,000	40,000
1901	80,000	48,500	1945	95,000	49,000
1902	81,000	65,000	1946	97,000	61,000
1903	82,000	51,000	1947	70,000	50,000
1904	81,000	57,000	1948	68,000	46,000
1905	85,000	72,000	1949	49,000	35,000
1906	95,000	78,000	1950	54,000	46,000
1907	88,000	51,000	1951	68,000	52,000
1908	80,000	51,000	1952	55,000	39,000
1909	94,000	73,000	1953	60,000	38,000
1910	94,000	65,000	1954	88,000	45,000
1911	73,000	65,000	1955	90,000	80,000
1912	74,000	55,000	1956	113,000	75,000
1913	53,000	37,000	1957	89,000	65,000
1914	55,000	34,000	1958	127,000	69,000
1915	74,000	38,000	1959	157,000	110,000
1916	76,000	60,000	1960	162,000	135,000
1917	77,000	45,000	1961	225,000	147,000
1918	60,000	45,000	1962	210,000	115,000
1919	110,000	60,000	1963	217,000	160,000

* To Feb. 18, 1929.
† Ex rights.

13 Governors are members of the Exchange residing and having their principal places of business within the metropolitan area of the City of New York. Not less than seven must be general partners or voting stockholders in a member firm engaged in business involving direct contact with the public and not less than ten must spend a substantial part of their time on the floor of the Exchange.

6 Governors are members of the Exchange, residing and having their principal places of business within the metropolitan area of the City of New York, and are general partners or voting stockholders in member firms engaged in a business involving direct contact with the public. Five of this group must be allied members.

9 Governors are regular or allied members of the Exchange residing and having their principal places of business outside the metropolitan area of the City of New York, and are general partners or voting stockholders in member firms engaged in a business involving direct contact with the public. At least two of this group must be regular members of the Exchange.

All the above are elected by the members of the Exchange for three-year terms and may not serve for more than two consecutive terms. They are then ineligible for election, except as chairman of the board, until an interval of at least two years has passed. The terms of office of approximately one third of these governors expire each year.

3 Governors are representatives of the public. These are elected by the Board upon nomination of the President of the Exchange and serve for a term of one year.

2 Governors are ex-officio members. One, the chairman of the Board, is elected by members of the Exchange for a term of one year, and the other, the president of the Exchange, is elected to serve at the pleasure of the Board. The chairman must be a member of the Exchange. If the president is a member of the Exchange at the time of his election, he must dispose of his membership.

The Board of Governors is vested with all the powers necessary for the government of the Exchange, the regulation of the business conduct of members and allied members, and the promotion of the welfare, objects, and purposes of the Exchange. It has control of the property and finances of the Exchange. It has power to try charges against members and allied members and to punish such as are found guilty and to prescribe rules for making and settling contracts on the Exchange, the formation and continuance of member firms, the business connections of members and allied members, and the capital requirements for members and member firms. The board may delegate many of its powers to the president, officers, or employees of the Exchange or to committees it may authorize. Subject to policies laid down by the Board of Governors, the board has made a broad delegation of some of its powers to the president of the Exchange, who in turn has redelegated some of these powers to the executive staff. Members, allied members, and member firms affected by any decision rendered under this delegation of authority may appeal the decision to the Board of Governors.

Internal Organization of the Exchange.   The president is the chief executive officer of the Exchange and represents it in all public matters. He is selected by the board and serves at its pleasure. Subject to the approval of the board, he appoints the officers of the Exchange and fixes their duties and terms of employment.

Under the president there are six executive officers who report directly to him. Three of these are line officers—an executive vice president in charge of operations, a vice president in charge of administration, and a vice president in charge of public relations—and three are staff officers—a vice president in charge of governmental affairs, an economist, and a special assistant to the president. (See Figure 2–1.)

Listing Requirements.   Only listed securities may be traded on the floor of the New York Stock Exchange. To be listed, a company must meet certain requirements of the Exchange and be willing to keep the investing public informed about its affairs, and it must be a going concern at the time of applying. In determining eligibility for listing, the Exchange pays particular attention to such matters as (1) the degree of national interest in the company, (2) its relative position and stability in the industry, and (3) whether or not it is engaged in an expanding industry with prospects of maintaining its relative position in the economy.

While each case is decided on its merits, the Exchange generally requires (1) demonstrated earning power of more than $2 million under competitive conditions, (2) net tangible assets or aggregate market value of common stock in excess of $12 million, and (3) at least 1,000,000 shares of common stock outstanding and held by not fewer than 2,000 persons (after substantially discounting the number of holders of less than 100 shares). A detailed description of listing requirements and routines will be found in Chapter 10.

The Exchange may delist an issue at any time if the board feels that continued dealings in the issue are not advisable. For example, the board would normally consider removing an issue from the list if:

1. The number of stockholders in the company should be reduced to 800 or less (after substantially discounting the number of odd-lot holders).
2. The number of shares outstanding should become less than 300,000.

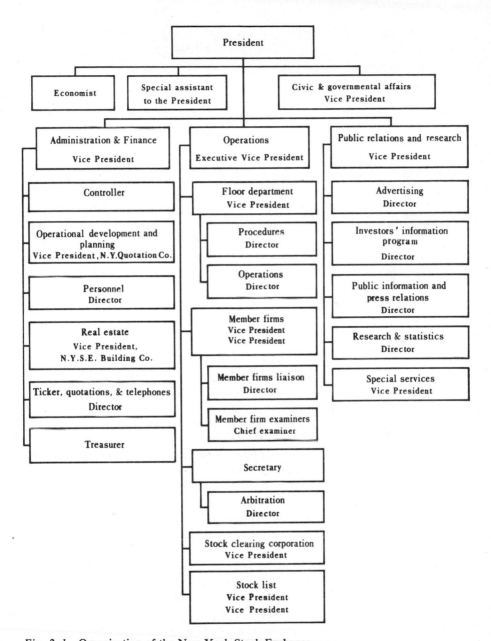

Fig. 2–1 Organization of the New York Stock Exchange.

3. The aggregate market value of the outstanding shares should decline below $5 million, exclusive of concentrated holdings.

4. The company's net earnings after taxes should be less than $400,000 for three consecutive years.

At the beginning of 1964, there were 1,188 domestic companies and 26 foreign companies with common stock issues listed on the New York Stock Exchange. In addition, 893 domestic bond issues and 38 foreign corporate bond issues were listed, and 254 government or foreign bank bond issues.

Operations of the Exchange

Customers' instructions are communicated to brokers in the form of "orders" to buy or to sell securities. When a broker receives an order, he proceeds to execute it in accordance with these instructions. Execution and performance of orders involve three steps: (1) the making of a contract on the floor of the Exchange, calling for the delivery of a given number of shares of an issue in exchange for the payment of a specified sum of money; (2) actual delivery of the shares; (3) settlement of the money obligation.

Type of Orders.   The unit of trading on the New York Stock Exchange is 100 shares, and contracts made on the floor imply "regular way" performance unless otherwise specified; that is, delivery and payment are to be completed on the third trading day following the date of the contract. If a broker receives an order to buy or to sell less than 100 shares, he gives the order to an odd-lot dealer for execution. This dealer stands ready to buy or to sell odd lots at a price $\frac{1}{8}$ or $\frac{1}{4}$ point away from the price at which the next full-lot transaction is executed on the floor. The practices of odd-lot dealers are explained in detail in Chapter 12.

Members of the Exchange accept and execute three types of customers' orders. The first type is known as a "market" order by which is meant that the shares are to be bought or sold immediately at the best price obtainable. The second type of order is known as a "limited" order, by which is meant that the shares are to be bought or sold at a price specified on the order or at a better price. A limited order is good for the time the customer indicates: for a day, for a week, for a month, or until canceled. The third type of order is known as a "stop" order. A *buy* stop order becomes a market buy order when the price of an issue rises to a specified level. A *sell* stop order becomes a market sell order when the price of an issue declines to a specified level.

Sell orders received from customers may also be classified as "long" or "short." The first term (long) applies to a situation in which a customer actually owns the shares which he has ordered to be sold. The second term (short) applies to a situation in which the customer does not own the shares which he has ordered to be sold. In the latter case, the broker must borrow shares to make delivery and, until the customer "covers" his position by ordering the shares purchased, he is said to be *short* the shares which he has sold and which the broker has borrowed. The right to sell short is limited by rules imposed by the Exchange and by the Securities and Exchange Commission. The reader will find a complete description of all the technical aspects of short selling in Chapter 15.

Customers' orders may also be classified as "for cash" or "on margin." The first term means that the customer intends to pay for the shares which he is buying. The second term means that the customer intends to pay only a portion of the purchase price and to remain indebted to the broker for the balance. Members of the Exchange are permitted to extend credit to their customers, but the extent of such credit accommodation is limited by (1) an *initial* margin requirement set by the Federal Reserve Board and (2) a *maintenance* margin requirement specified by Exchange rules. According to the first of these, a broker may not execute an order for a customer if the execution would cause the customer's debt to the broker to exceed the loan value of the customer's collateral. The loan value of securities set by the Federal Reserve Board has varied from 50 per cent of market value to zero. The limitation imposed by the Exchange requires that a customer's collateral exceed the amount of his debt at all times by 25 per cent. The practice of trading on margin and the effects of the two types of limitations are explained more fully in Chapter 14.

Contract-making Procedure. Fair and equitable prices, as defined in the preceding chapter, are determined on the New York Stock Exchange by what might be called a two-way auction. When a broker receives an order to buy a particular issue "at the market," he goes at once to the post on the Exchange floor where the issue is traded and inquires of the specialist standing there as to what the existing "bid" and "ask" prices are. A bid price is the *highest* price at which there is an unfilled limited order to buy. An ask price is the *lowest* price at which there is an unfilled limited order to sell. Obviously, ask prices will be higher than bid prices, or the unfilled order would have been executed. But the difference between the bid and ask prices may be very small, perhaps only $\frac{1}{8}$ or $\frac{1}{4}$ point.

The broker with the order to buy at the market knows that he can obtain the shares for his customer at the ask price. He also knows that it is useless for him to try to obtain them at the bid price, for an unfilled order at this price having priority over his order already stands in the market. If the spread between the bid and ask prices is $\frac{1}{8}$ point, he will simply accept the specialist's offer to sell at the ask price. If the spread is more than $\frac{1}{8}$ point, he may try first to obtain a better price. In this event he will start by proclaiming a willingness to buy at $\frac{1}{8}$ point above the specialist's bid price. If no one accepts, he will raise his bid $\frac{1}{8}$ point at a time until either the specialist or some other broker says, "Take it."

If a broker receives an order to sell a particular issue at the market, he behaves in exactly the same way except that he begins the bargaining process by offering to sell at a price $\frac{1}{8}$ point below the specialist's ask price and continues to lower his offer $\frac{1}{8}$ point at a time until someone accepts.

Limited orders to buy or to sell securities are given to the specialist in the issue for execution. The specialist enters such orders in his "book" and strives to execute the buy order specifying the highest price or the sell order asking the lowest price. These two orders, as explained, constitute his bid and ask prices for the issue.

Delivery of Securities.   In theory, every share sold on the floor is delivered by the seller to the buyer. In practice, this is not done. The members of the New York Stock Exchange deliver the shares that they sell to the central delivery department of the Stock Clearing Corporation, and they receive from it the shares that they have purchased. Before attempting deliveries, however, members "clear" their purchases and sales and then deliver only the balances that do not cancel out. To illustrate, suppose that a particular broker has made the following contracts on the floor during a particular day:

Purchase contracts			Sales contracts		
Shares	Issue and price	Money sum	Shares	Issue and price	Money sum
300	Greyhound @ 47	$14,100	100	U.S. Steel @ 45	$ 4,500
200	U.S. Steel @ 46	9,200	300	Burroughs @ 29	8,700
200	Burroughs @ 26	5,200	200	Chrysler @ 85	17,000
100	Dana @ 42	4,200	100	Dana @ 43	4,300
800		$32,700	700		$34,300

It will be noticed that the broker has purchased and sold 100 shares of Dana Corporation. A literal performance of the terms of his contracts would require him to deliver a stock certificate for 100 shares of this issue to the central delivery department and then to receive from it a certificate for 100 shares of the same issue, perhaps even the identical certificate he delivered. Obviously this is unnecessary. Instead each broker offsets his obligations to deliver particular issues against his right to receive the same issues and delivers or receives the share balances which do not offset.

If the purchase and sale contracts listed above are cleared in this manner, the broker will be obligated to deliver 100 shares of Burroughs and 200 shares of Chrysler, and he will have a right to receive 100 shares of

U.S. Steel and 300 shares of Greyhound. He will deliver the first and receive the second from the central delivery department of the Stock Clearing Corporation on the fourth full business day following the day of the trades. The details of stock clearing are explained in Chapter 13.

As soon as a purchasing broker receives the certificates for the shares to which he is entitled, he takes them to the transfer agent of the company to be canceled and to have new certificates issued and registered (1) in the name of the purchasing customer, (2) in the name of the brokerage firm, or (3) in "street name," that is, in bearer form. The exact procedure to record a transfer of ownership on the books of a transfer agent is explained in Chapter 5.

Cash Settlements.   The purchase of a security gives rise to one broker's obligation to pay and another broker's right to receive payment. Thus the aggregate obligations of all members to pay is exactly balanced by the rights of all members to receive payments. For this reason, the cash settlement department of the Stock Clearing Corporation is willing to assume all the obligations to pay in return for all the rights to receive payment. As a result, the broker in the illustration above can settle his entire day's transactions by drawing a draft for $1,600 against the cash settlement department. Had the total value of his purchase contracts exceeded the total value of his sale contracts, he would have been able to settle the day's contracts with a single check to the Stock Clearing Corporation.

Volume of Trading.   In 1964 the number of shares sold on the New York Stock Exchange was 1,236,565,000. This compares with 1,124,800,410 shares sold in 1929, the largest sales of any year prior to 1963, and with 170,603,000 sold in 1941, the smallest sales of any recent year. Bond sales in 1964 amounted to $2,524,500,000 par value as compared with $4,132,-731,558 par value in 1922, the highest total of all time. In 1964 daily volume of shares traded fluctuated from a low of 3,051,000 on August 10 to a high of 6,851,000 on April 2.

The record of sales shows that only eight 3-million-share days occurred prior to July 1, 1926. After this date, however, 2-, 3-, 4-, and 5-million-share days became a common occurrence, with even larger volumes at times. The year 1929 had twenty-two days in which volume exceeded 6 million shares, eight days in which it exceeded 7 million shares, and three days in which it exceeded 10 million shares. The largest daily volume on record is 16,410,000 shares on October 29, 1929.

3 other american exchanges and markets

Most American investors think of the stock market in terms of the New York Stock Exchange, but actually a total of 18 separate stock exchanges exist in the United States. Fourteen of these are registered stock exchanges, and 4 are exempt stock exchanges as defined by the Securities Exchange Act of 1934.

The two largest stock exchanges are truly national organizations. In 1963 the New York Stock Exchange accounted for about 85 per cent of the dollar volume of all transactions on registered exchanges. In the same year the American Stock Exchange, which is the second largest, handled over 7 per cent of dollar volume. The remaining registered exchanges are regional, with two exceptions. One is the Chicago Board of Trade, which although formally registered with the SEC as a stock exchange no longer provides for trading in stocks. All trading on the floor of the Chicago Board of Trade now is in commodities. The second is the National Stock Exchange, organized in New York City in 1962 with hopes of becoming a third national exchange. Trading in this market has not yet developed sufficient volume to warrant its consideration as a major exchange.

The 14 registered stock exchanges in the United States are listed in Table 4, with 1963 data on dollar volume and share volume. Trading on the Spokane, Salt Lake, and San Francisco Mining exchanges is primarily in mining stocks rather than in stocks in general.

Four stock exchanges in the United States are exempt from registration with the Securities and Exchange Commission because their volume of transactions is small. Altogether the four exempt exchanges have a dollar volume equal to 0.03 per cent and a share volume equal to 0.07 per cent of the volume on all registered exchanges. As can be seen from Table 5, 96 per cent of the dollar volume on these four exchanges takes place on the Honolulu Stock Exchange.

There is yet another major securities market in the United States—the over-the-counter market. This market is an informal

TABLE 4   Sales Volume of Stock Transactions, Registered Stock Exchanges, 1963

	Dollar volume (at market prices)	Share volume	Dollar volume, % of total	Share volume, % of total
New York Stock Exchange	$54,886,500,727	1,350,885,007	85.3	73.5
American Stock Exchange	4,755,285,747	336,260,742	7.4	18.3
Midwest Stock Exchange	1,755,658,788	43,773,297	2.7	2.4
Pacific Coast Stock Exchange	1,539,647,605	51,292,538	2.4	2.8
Philadelphia-Baltimore-Washington Stock Exchange	688,438,392	15,770,516	1.1	0.9
Detroit Stock Exchange	334,883,198	8,775,368	0.5	0.5
Boston Stock Exchange	274,085,531	5,595,436	0.4	0.3
Cincinnati Stock Exchange	40,767,940	833,798	0.1	*
Pittsburgh Stock Exchange	33,368,409	796,512	0.1	*
Spokane Stock Exchange	6,126,711	5,490,435	*	0.3
Salt Lake Stock Exchange	4,765,818	13,802,101	*	0.7
National Stock Exchange	408,221	388,712	*	*
San Francisco Mining Exchange	255,662	4,855,043	*	0.3
Chicago Board of Trade	0	0	*	*
All registered exchanges	$64,320,192,749	1,838,519,505	100.0	100.0

* Less than 0.05 per cent.
SOURCE: *Statistical Bulletin,* SEC, February 1964.

collection of brokers and dealers connected by nationwide telephone, teletype, and telegraph services. Securities traded in the market include almost
all Federal, state, and municipal securities, almost all bank and insurance
stocks (although the passage of the Securities Acts Amendments of 1964 is
expected to cause many banks and insurance companies to list their shares

TABLE 5   Sales Volume of Stock Transactions on Exempt Stock Exchanges, 1963

	Dollar volume (at market prices)	Share volume	Dollar volume, % of total	Share volume, % of total
Honolulu (Hawaii) Stock Exchange	$20,131,814	770,800	96.0	63.8
Richmond (Virginia) Stock Exchange	390,272	8,869	1.8	0.7
Wheeling (West Virginia) Stock Exchange	373,539	13,059	1.8	1.1
Colorado Springs (Colorado) Stock Exchange	84,524	415,744	0.4	34.4
All exempt exchanges	$20,980,149	1,208,472	100.0	100.0

SOURCE: *Statistical Bulletin,* SEC, February 1964.

on an organized exchange), the stocks of many industrial and utility companies ranging in size from small to large, and all mutual fund shares.

Allocation of Stocks to the Various Exchanges and Markets.   Stocks of the very largest and best-known American corporations are usually listed and traded on the New York Stock Exchange. "Listing," a legal step required to obtain SEC and Exchange approval for trading of a stock on a registered exchange, is usually initiated by a corporation which seeks the benefits of an organized market for its shares. The nature of listing requirements on the New York Stock Exchange is explained in Chapter 10. Stocks of many additional large American corporations are listed and traded on the American Stock Exchange, which in general provides a national market for securities of companies not yet large enough to list their stock on the New York Stock Exchange.

One might presume that regional stock exchanges would function primarily as a marketplace for stocks of regional corporations which have not yet grown to the national stature required for listing and trading on one of the exchanges in New York City. At one time this was in fact the major function of the regional exchanges, but with the passage of time trading in regional stocks has diminished until it is a minor facet of the operation of the regional exchanges.

The various regional exchanges developed in the last half of the nineteenth century and in the early twentieth century primarily as places for effecting transactions in stocks of local interest. At this time, the sale of new issues as well as continued trading in already outstanding shares took place on these exchanges, which, however, gradually lost their function of providing a primary market for local stocks. The reasons for this were many. The development of efficient communications via telegraph, telephone, and teletype enabled the major exchanges in New York City to serve investors from coast to coast with equal efficiency. Companies which had been regional in nature expanded into national concerns and wanted national markets for their stocks. Improved communication also enabled the over-the-counter market to compete with regional exchanges, and the less stringent public reporting requirements for stocks traded in the over-the-counter markets encouraged many managements to avoid formal listing on local exchanges. (At the time of writing, the signing of the Securities Acts Amendments of 1964 by President Johnson appears to be creating a move by many companies to transfer their securities from the over-the-counter markets to the organized exchanges. Under the amendments, large publicly owned companies must make more information available to the public and their stockholders than required heretofore, regardless of whether or not the company is listed on an exchange.)

Regional exchanges responded to the loss of primary markets in local issues by developing competing markets for stocks traded on the New York exchanges. At present over 90 per cent of the trading on regional stock exchanges is in securities also traded on a New York exchange, and less than 10 per cent is in securities traded solely on regional exchanges.

Statistics for each of the seven nonmining regional exchanges are shown in Table 6. These statistics reveal, by way of illustration, that 95.8 per cent of the issues traded and 94.8 per cent of the dollar volume of sales of securities on the Boston Stock Exchange are from issues also traded on either the New York or the American Stock Exchange.

At present, stocks traded on a regional stock exchange fall into one of three classifications:

1. Solely listed securities are stocks of companies which have taken the initiative with the Securities and Exchange Commission and with a regional stock exchange to list their stocks on a regional exchange. A solely listed stock is traded on only one stock exchange.

2. Dually listed securities are stocks of companies which have formally listed

TABLE 6   Sole Trading and Dual Trading on Major Regional Exchanges, 1961

| | Number of issues | | | |
	All stocks	Solely traded	Dually traded*	Dually traded, %
Boston	451	19	432	95.8
Cincinnati	155	22	133	85.8
Detroit	239	12	227	95.0
Midwest	513	85	428	83.4
Pacific Coast	578	60	518	89.6
Philadelphia-Baltimore	634	88	546	86.1
Pittsburgh	118	9	109	92.4
	Dollar volume of sales, thousands of $			
Boston	$ 318,520	$ 16,501	$ 302,019	94.8
Cincinnati	46,539	6,245	40,294	86.6
Detroit	240,532	11,622	228,910	95.2
Midwest	1,761,746	113,832	1,647,914	93.5
Pacific Coast	1,275,110	144,790	1,130,320	88.6
Philadelphia-Baltimore	663,320	8,179	655,141	98.8
Pittsburgh	35,400	3,347	32,053	90.5

* Dually traded on either the New York Stock Exchange or the American Stock Exchange.

SOURCE: *Report of Special Study of Securities Markets of the Securities and Exchange Commission,* 88th Cong., 1st Sess., House Document 95, 1963, part 2, p. 1084. (Hereafter referred to as *Special Study.*)

their stocks on two or more exchanges. Again the initiative for each listing came from the company, which had to apply for the privilege. In many cases dual listings occur when a company that is listed on a regional exchange applies for listing on one of the New York exchanges but does not terminate its regional listing.

3. The third classification is stocks which are granted "unlisted trading privileges" on one of the regional exchanges. Under the provisions of the Securities Exchange Act of 1934 securities which have been listed on one registered securities exchange may be granted unlisted trading privileges on another exchange. The initiative for unlisted trading privileges comes from an exchange rather than from the company, usually because the regional exchange wants to broaden the number and quality of issues traded. In general, dually traded stocks (including dually listed issues and issues with unlisted trading privileges) are the more active stocks on the New York Stock Exchange.

In the pages that follow, the American Stock Exchange, the Midwest Stock Exchange, the Pacific Coast Stock Exchange, and the over-the-counter market are considered in detail.

The American Stock Exchange

The American Stock Exchange, sometimes called Amex for short, is the second largest securities exchange in the United States. Like the London Stock Exchange and later the New York Stock Exchange, the predecessor of the American Stock Exchange began out of doors; and just as both the New York and the London stock exchanges finally sought more comfortable and convenient quarters by going indoors, so the American Stock Exchange, as it grew older and more respectable, withdrew into large and modern quarters in its own building at 86 Trinity Place in New York City.

The Old Curb Market.   Prior to adopting its present name in 1953, the American Stock Exchange was called the New York Curb Exchange, a name reflecting the colorful history of trading carried on by brokers and dealers standing in the streets and on the sidewalks of lower Manhattan. In the earliest years trading occurred in William Street, between Exchange Place and Beaver Street. In the 1890s the market moved to Broad Street (just below Wall Street), and later it shifted south on Broad Street below Exchange Place. The Curb market finally moved off the streets and into its Trinity Place building in 1921.

No one knows for certain when the American Stock Exchange was started, but most authorities trace its beginnings to the 1849 discovery of gold in California. In the last half of the nineteenth century there was little or no formal organization. Then in 1908 the New York Curb Agency was formally organized. The report of the Hughes Commission in 1909 so severely criticized frauds practiced on the Curb market and so strongly recommended reformation that in 1911 a new organization called the New York Curb Market Association was formed. The association was governed by a board of representatives of 15 members, who undertook to eliminate questionable trading practices, establish a dues-paying membership, organize a listing department, and maintain public records.

Members of the Curb market transacted business in the open street, in good weather or bad. Writing in the *New Republic* as late as August 19, 1920, A. G. Gardiner described Curb trading thus:

> In the street a jostling mass of human beings, fantastically garbed, wearing many-colored caps like jockeys or pantaloons, their heads thrown back, their arms extended high as if in prayer to some heathen deity, their fingers working with frantic symbols, their voices crying in agonized frenzy, and at a hundred windows in the great buildings on either side of the street little groups of men and women gesticulated back as wildly to the mob below. It is the outside market of Mammon.

The quotation is colorful but possibly overdrawn. Brokers whose hands were extended "as if in prayer to some heathen deity" were actually signaling market information to clerks perched above the streets in nearby windows. The many-colored caps were the means by which clerks spotted their brokers in the tangled mob. In the last years of outdoor trading the association had about 550 members, and memberships were selling at $5,000 to $7,000 each.

The American Stock Exchange.   In 1921 the New York Curb Market Association moved indoors and shortened its name to New York Curb Market. Another name change to New York Curb Exchange was made in 1929; and the present name, American Stock Exchange, was adopted in January 1953 in recognition of the Exchange's national and international character.

The trading floor of the American Stock Exchange is a vast, air-conditioned room five stories high, without supporting columns. It is 152 feet long and has an area of 20,023 square feet. On the floor are 21 trading posts, plus a special bond post, where over 1,000 listed and unlisted stock and bond issues are traded. Each post is an open, octagonal desk having the most modern equipment. Suspended from the ceiling before the visitors' gallery at the north end of the room is a projection screen, which reproduces in enlarged form transactions as they appear on the stock tickers of both the American and the New York stock exchanges. Two large annunciator boards, which serve notice when a particular member is wanted by his telephone clerk, are located on the north and south walls. On the east and west sides of the floor are tiers divided into sections from which members' telephone clerks maintain liaison between the member firms and the floor brokers. A rostrum from which official announcements are made is located in the center of the southern end of the room.

In May 1964 the American Stock Exchange became the first stock exchange in the world to put into operation a computerized telephone quotation service. The Exchange's Am-Quote service, able to answer 1,200 telephone inquiries a minute, is part of an electronic data-processing system leased from Teleregister Corporation to record and report all exchange transactions. Members and member firms of the Exchange may subscribe to its service. To obtain a quotation, one dials a code number and receives the following information: stock symbol, bid, offer, last sale, net change from previous close, volume, open, high, and low. The reply is selected and assembled in proper sequence by the computer from a prerecorded vocabulary of 60 letters, numbers, and words.

In addition to information provided by the Am-Quote service, transaction information on American Stock Exchange stocks is available on 1,880 stock tickers in operation in 395 cities throughout North America and on some 6,588 desk inquiry units of the type described in Chapter 6.

Organization. The American Stock Exchange was entirely reorganized in 1962 after two specialists were expelled for violating Exchange and SEC rules. In the months that followed, detailed studies of the Exchange were made by the Securities and Exchange Commission and by a special committee of Exchange member firms.

The study by the Exchange committee led to the drafting and approval of a completely overhauled constitution which provided for a new 32-member board of governors as the sole policy-making body and for a much enlarged professional executive staff with increased responsibility for administering day-to-day operations. The membership of the new board was set up so as to eliminate a major criticism that the Exchange had been dominated by floor members, mostly specialists, who perpetuated their control through an outmoded committee system. The new board of governors is composed of 12 members chosen from among the floor members of the Exchange (at least 6 of whom may not be from specialist firms), 10 members from New York offices, 5 members from out-of-town offices, 3 representatives of the public, and the chairman and the president of the Exchange.

During the period of reorganization, the Exchange's administrative staff was grouped into six major divisions. The operations division administers floor and office rules and policies. It also maintains surveillance over the market with a view to detecting unusual activity and bringing about the immediate release of information in which investors have a warrantable interest. A market procedures division provides closer liaison between members and floor officials, assembles data for use in allocating stocks to specialists, and helps train new specialists. An office procedures division oversees admissions procedures, including approval of registered representatives; administers rules on margins, capital, and commissions; and conducts field examinations of member firms.

A securities division supervises the listing and delisting of securities. An administration and finance division controls Exchange expenditures, reviews personnel performance and salaries, and retrains and relocates personnel whose positions have been eliminated by automation. Lastly, a public affairs division provides the news media and the public with information about the Exchange. For financial analysts and the public, the Exchange publishes the *American Investor* magazine and various brochures.

The American Stock Exchange also operates its own clearing corporation, with offices at 12 Albany Street in New York City. In 1963 the American Stock Exchange Clearing Corporation joined with the National O-T-C Clearing Corporation to help clear approximately 1,400 over-the-counter securities in addition to the securities traded on the American Stock Exchange.

Membership.   For many years the American Stock Exchange has had both regular members, who possess all the rights and responsibilities of full membership, and associate members. Associate members are not entitled to trade on the floor but may transmit orders through regular members for execution at a smaller commission than is charged nonmembers. Associate memberships are held by securities firms, many of whom belong to the New York Stock Exchange or to one of the regional exchanges. By this device American Stock Exchange facilities are made available to securities firms whose Amex business itself might not warrant investment in regular membership even though the firm meets all Exchange standards. It is estimated that in recent years about 25 per cent of the volume of the American Stock Exchange has come through its associate members.

The new constitution of the American Stock Exchange retained the associate member classification and in addition provided for 151 new regular memberships to be offered to qualified representatives of associate member organizations. This constituted the first increase in membership in forty-three years. The first 101 new seats were offered in 1963 at a discount of $5,000 from the last sale price in the regular seat market, with a minimum price of $40,000. In the regular market, sales of memberships in 1963 ranged from a low of $52,500 to a year-end high of $66,000. By the beginning of 1964, 89 new members had been admitted, increasing total regular membership from 499 to 588; and an additional 5 new memberships were waiting approval by the board of governors. During 1964 and 1965 an additional 57 new memberships are to be offered at the same discount but at a minimum seat price of $55,000. At the beginning of 1964 there were 298 associate member firms in addition to the 588 regular member firms.

Listing Requirements. Shortly after the adoption of the new constitution, higher listing standards and new delisting criteria were adopted. The Exchange now looks for net tangible assets of over $1 million (as compared with the $12 million required by the New York Stock Exchange) and for net aftertax earnings of at least $150,000 in the fiscal year preceding the listing, with an average of at least $100,000 annually for the previous three years. (The New York Stock Exchange expects earning power of $2 million after taxes.) Companies seeking to list their common stock are expected to have 200,000 shares publicly distributed among no fewer than 750 stockholders, including at least 500 holders of 100 shares or more. (The New York Stock Exchange seeks 1 million shares outstanding among no fewer than 2,000 holders of round lots.) Outstanding shares should have a minimum market value of $2 million, with the publicly distributed shares being worth at least $1 million. (The New York Stock Exchange expects an aggregate market value for the common stock of $12 million.)

As is apparent, requirements for listing on the American Stock Exchange are similar to but less stringent than those for listing on the New York Stock Exchange. Thus the American Stock Exchange serves to provide a national trading forum for securities of companies that are generally younger or smaller than those traded on the New York Stock Exchange. With the passage of time some of these companies will grow and move their listings to the larger exchange. Many others will remain on the American Stock Exchange, satisfied with the market created there for their shares. No issues are listed on both the American and the New York stock exchanges.

To improve the quality of its listings, the American Stock Exchange also adopted new delisting criteria in 1962. Issues may now be considered for removal from trading if the company has not operated at a net profit for at least one of the last three years; if fewer than 70,000 shares are held by the public; if the total number of shareholders has fallen below 250 or if the number of round-lot holders has dropped below 150; if the aggregate market value of all outstanding common shares is less than $1 million or if the aggregate market value of publicly held shares is less than $500,000. Under these policies, some 63 issues were removed from trading in 1962 and 1963.

At the beginning of 1964 there were 841 issues of stock, common and preferred, listed on the American Stock Exchange. Foreign (non-Canadian) issues totaled 33, of which 24 were American depository receipts. An additional 162 issues were traded on an unlisted basis, raising the total number of issues traded to 1,003.

The Midwest Stock Exchange

The largest stock exchange in the United States outside of New York City is the Midwest Stock Exchange, located in Chicago. It is the descendant of several earlier Chicago and other Midwestern exchanges.

History.   The first Chicago Stock Exchange originated on January 5, 1865, four months before the end of the Civil War, when a group of brokers in grain, gold, and securities met to organize an exchange. Since prices of the commodities bought and sold on the Chicago Board of Trade at that time were quoted in gold dollars, it was necessary that operators in that market also deal in gold. In addition, the Board of Supervisors of Cook County had issued several million dollars of scrip to finance the sending of equipped soldiers to the front. A market where this gold and scrip could be traded was desirable. There existed also considerable interest in Chicago city bonds and in the securities of local banks and the People's Gas Light & Coke Company.

When the end of the war brought an end to active trading in gold and scrip, the members of the new Exchange one by one allowed their memberships to lapse. An attempt was made in 1869 to revive the Exchange, but without success. In January 1882, however, a mutual association of brokers was set up "to be known as the Chicago Stock Exchange, each member to have a voice in the management and an interest in the funds." The new organization had the approval of New York Stock Exchange officials and received 3,000 applications for membership. Two hundred and fifty of these were accepted in March, but by May 6, 1882, the roll of members had increased to 749. Membership on the new Exchange did not prove so profitable as at first anticipated. Five years later a seat could be purchased for $40, and many memberships were allowed to lapse. Only 25 votes were cast at the annual election in 1887. Thereafter, the affairs of this Exchange prospered with the growth of speculation and the increased interest in the ownership of equity securities by the general public.

In 1928 the Chicago Stock Exchange moved into a building at 120 South LaSalle Street, a location that now is the home of its successor, the Midwest Stock Exchange. The trading floor, on the second and third floors of the building, is 96 feet long and 59 feet wide and has seven trading posts. An electronically controlled quotation board 50 feet long by 6 feet high now occupies the north wall and displays the full range of prices for 330 issues. In planning the room, special attention was paid to acoustics so that an ordinary speaking tone can be heard distinctly throughout the room. The lighting is indirect, and an electric paging and announcing system is used.

A desire to reduce overhead and to compete more effectively for new issues led to the merger on December 1, 1949, of the Chicago Stock

Exchange with stock exchanges in Cleveland, Minneapolis–St. Paul, and St. Louis, to create the present Midwest Stock Exchange. The New Orleans Stock Exchange joined the group in 1960. The Detroit, Cincinnati, and Pittsburgh stock exchanges have been invited to join but have not yet done so.

Membership.   When the Midwest Stock Exchange was formally created in 1949, 400 memberships were authorized and subsequently issued. Three hundred of these went to members who had belonged to the Chicago Stock Exchange. Fifty-eight memberships went to members of the Cleveland, Minneapolis–St. Paul, and St. Louis exchanges, and the remaining 42 memberships were sold to persons who had not belonged to any of the four merged exchanges. Since 1949 seats on the Midwest Stock Exchange have been sold in the open market at prices ranging from $2,500 to $20,000. The last sale as of December 31, 1963, was at $10,000.

The Chicago Stock Exchange had 183 member firms just before the merger. Consolidation added 42 more, and since then newly elected firms have brought the total to 311. These firms have more than 2,100 offices scattered over 49 states and 20 foreign countries.

Trading Methods.   At the beginning of 1964 there were 522 issues listed or admitted to trading on the Midwest Stock Exchange. Represented in this total were 471 corporations, 370 of which have stock issues listed on the New York Stock Exchange as well. Of the 522 issues, 389 were fully listed.

In general, trading procedures on the Midwest Stock Exchange parallel those used on the floor of the New York Stock Exchange. However, for many issues which are traded on both the New York and Midwest exchanges, a dual trading system has been developed. An odd-lot order is filled on the Midwest Stock Exchange based on the proper round-lot transaction on the New York Stock Exchange or on the basis of Midwest round-lot prices if so designated by the customer. The odd-lot differential in all dual listings conforms with that of the New York market. When the New York round-lot price is used, a lapse of three minutes plus the number of minutes the New York tape is late is applied before the odd-lot order is effective. Of the 396 issues traded on both the New York and Midwest exchanges, 276 are included in the dual trading system. The remaining 120 issues are smaller in size and are traded at an inactive post.

As part of the original consolidation which created the Midwest Stock Exchange two branch offices were established: one in Cleveland and one in St. Louis. These offices are connected by private telephone with most of the member offices in the respective cities and in turn are connected by private wire with the trading floor of the Exchange. In addition to these facilities, the Exchange maintains six private teletype wires to other areas of the country, as well as one to Toronto, Canada. Other members have access to the trading floor through the use of public teletype machines, three of which are maintained on the trading floor.

In its drive to compete with other securities markets, the Midwest Stock Exchange has introduced a number of innovations. It was the first exchange to permit the corporate form of securities firm, as contrasted with the partnership form, to become an exchange member. It was the first exchange to offer "clearing by mail" to out-of-town members, thus enabling them to earn the same commissions as in-town members by transacting business in their own name rather than through a Chicago correspondent. It was the first exchange to provide specialists with a mechanized and complete bookkeeping and cashier service. The Midwest Stock Exchange was also first in utilizing a computer to improve clearing services for members, in providing members with a complete centralized bookkeeping service, and in clearing all over-the-counter stocks for any member firm regardless of location.

The Pacific Coast Stock Exchange

California is now the most populous state in the United States and the origin of some 12 per cent of the nation's securities transactions. It is only natural, then, that California and the West in general are served by a dynamic regional exchange. The Pacific Coast Stock Exchange, with dual trading floors in San Francisco and Los Angeles, is the second largest regional exchange in terms of dollar volume and the largest regional exchange in terms of share volume.

History.   The Pacific Coast Stock Exchange was formed in 1957 by the merger of the San Francisco Stock Exchange and the Los Angeles Stock Exchange. The origin of the San Francisco Stock Exchange dates back to 1882, when 25 brokers met to organize a market for the securities of nonmining corporations. The first list published by this Stoc and Bond Exchange, as it was then called, included the shares of nine local street railway companies, a number of insurance stocks, several bank stocks, some water company stocks, and a group of powder-manufacturing issues. Mining stocks were not listed because an ample market for them already existed in the separate San Francisco Mining Exchange, previously organized to specialize in the shares of mining companies. During its seventy-five years of separate existence, the San Francisco Stock Exchange kept pace with developments in the securities markets. It established a clearing house for stocks in 1923. Two years later clearing was extended to include money payments. In 1928 the present system of odd-lot trading was instituted, and in 1938 the San Francisco Curb Exchange was absorbed.

Between 1887 and 1897 three separate stock exchanges were formed in Los Angeles for the purpose of trading in stocks, particularly those of the various mining and land development companies then being formed in that part of the state. By late 1899 all three exchanges had ceased to function; but in that year a new exchange, the Los Angeles Oil Exchange, was formed for the primary purpose, as its name implies, of trading in stocks of the expanding oil companies of southern California. Memberships, limited to 50, were sold at $50 apiece, and regular trading sessions began early in 1900. In its first year of operation, the Oil Exchange broadened its outlook to include all types of stocks, and in 1907 its name was changed to the Los Angeles Stock Exchange.

Soon afterward the Exchange expanded its stock list by absorbing competitive Los Angeles exchanges with such descriptive names as the California Oil and Stock Exchange, the Los Angeles Miners Exchange, and the Los Angeles–Nevada Mining Stock Exchange. By 1909 it had eliminated all rivals for its position of supremacy in southern California. In 1929 the Exchange adopted the post system of continuous trading, to replace the old call method then in use. In 1930 it moved into a new building housing what is now the Los Angeles trading floor of the Pacific Coast Stock Exchange.

The unification of the two California exchanges into the Pacific Coast Stock Exchange (PCSE) on January 2, 1957, was the result of over a quarter of a century of discussions, plans, and hopes for a unified Western securities market which would serve investors and industry more efficiently. Initially, the merger provided for the Los Angeles and San Francisco exchanges to operate as divisions of PCSE, membership in PCSE being acquired through either division. Each division had its own governing board, its own officers, and separate assets, while PCSE operated as a parent organization whose constitution and rules took precedence over those of the divisions. The PCSE board of governors was composed of representatives of each division's board. Subsequent steps toward unification were taken as the provisions of each division's constitution and rules were brought into agreement, dropped from the division rules, and added to the rules of PCSE.

In 1961 a single constitution and set of rules was adopted for PCSE, and those of the divisions were eliminated. This new constitution provided for a single governing board and a single president. The representatives of each division on the PCSE board of governors constituted a management committee for their respective division and acted on its internal fiscal affairs. The assets of each division remained separate.

Each division originally operated a clearing department. In 1960 the Los Angeles division transferred its clearing functions to a wholly owned subsidiary, the Los Angeles Stock Clearing Corporation, which also provided accounting and cashier functions for various members on its data-processing equipment. Similar work was performed for the San Francisco division by its clearing department. In 1945 the Los Angeles division had sold its land and building and leased them back for operating purposes. The San Francisco division's land and building were owned by the San Francisco Stock and Bond Exchange, a wholly owned subsidiary of the San Francisco division.

One result of this complicated structure was that, during the early years of unification, membership was tied to a particular division so that prices of seats in San Francisco and in Los Angeles were not necessarily the same.

In January 1964 additional steps were taken toward complete unification. The clearing department of the San Francisco division and the Los Angeles Stock Clearing Corporation were merged into the Pacific Coast Stock Exchange Clearing Corporation, a wholly owned subsidiary of the Pacific Coast Stock Exchange equally owned by each division. The Pacific Coast Stock Exchange Clearing Corporation conducts similar activities in both cities.

Final unification steps, scheduled for completion by January 1965, are a spin-off of the San Francisco Stock and Bond Exchange to the San Francisco division members and a lease-back of the physical plant for use by the San Francisco operations. This step will equalize the assets of both divisions and enable a transfer of all assets to PCSE, thereby eliminating the division entities. By 1965, then, both the San Francisco division and the Los Angeles division will be merged into the parent PCSE, to create a truly homogeneous unit.

Membership.   At the time of the merger in 1957, the San Francisco division of the Pacific Coast Stock Exchange had 80 members. The Los Angeles division had 60 members, but by 1959 this number was raised to 80. At present the PCSE has 160 members and 131 member firms which operate more than 800 offices throughout the world. Some two thirds of these offices are located in the 13 states west of the Rocky Mountains. Cost of membership in 1963 ranged from $5,500 to $7,500.

The Pacific Coast Stock Exchange, along with the Detroit and Honolulu exchanges, is unique among American regional exchanges in permitting member firms to split fees with banks and with nonmember securities firms belonging to the National Association of Securities Dealers. A fee of $100 is charged for this privilege. The Pacific Coast Stock Exchange permits members to "give up" as much as 25 per cent of the commission on a transaction received from such nonmember securities firms. (The Honolulu exchange also permits up to a 25 per cent give-up. The Detroit exchange permits up to a 40 per cent give-up.) In 1963 some 420 nonmember securities firms availed themselves of the PCSE's commission-sharing rules to execute orders on that exchange. The competitive advantage of commission sharing for regional exchanges lies in the fact that orders for dually traded securities placed with nonmember securities firms about the country tend to be sent to the regional exchange, so that the nonmember firm (of the New York Stock Exchange) may earn a portion of the commission, rather than to the New York Stock Exchange, which does not permit commission sharing with nonmembers.[1]

Trading Methods.   The Pacific Coast Stock Exchange is unique among exchanges in that it operates on two trading floors over 400 miles apart. The two floors operate as a single unit, and buy or sell orders may be filled in either city.

A unique direct-voice communication system makes this possible. Specialist posts on each floor are connected with the other trading floor by special full-time telephone circuits. Each circuit attaches to low-volume speakers and to telephone-type handsets, which in seconds enable a seller on one trading floor to locate a buyer on the other.

The system works as follows: A commission broker on the Los Angeles floor receives an order to sell 300 shares of XYZ stock at 25. He proceeds to the Los Angeles specialist in XYZ, who perhaps will take 200 shares at that price. To help the broker sell the remaining 100 shares, the Los Angeles specialist lifts his handset and presses a "talk" button, connecting himself instantly with the San Francisco floor. He utters the symbol of the stock, XYZ, and his voice emerges from speakers at all specialist posts on the San Francisco floor.

In San Francisco, the specialist in XYZ hears the symbol called and picks up his handset. The Los Angeles specialist says, "There are 300 shares of XYZ offered at 25. I'll take 200. How about you?" The San Francisco specialist may reply, "I'll take the other 100." All 300 shares have been sold in a few moments.

Each floor of the Pacific Coast Stock Exchange has 17 specialists, who also act as odd-lot dealers in the stocks assigned to them.

The Pacific Coast Stock Exchange is unusual in another respect. Located three time zones to the west of New York, its trading session runs

---

[1] The *Wall Street Journal,* on July 23, 1964, pointed out that many New York Stock Exchange member firms were using regional exchanges to circumvent the rigid commission-cutting rules of the New York Stock Exchange, especially as the rules apply to large-volume orders of institutional investors. The *Journal* described how a large institution owing a nonmember securities firm for previous brokerage services might decide to sell a stock traded on both the New York Stock Exchange and the Detroit Stock Exchange. By placing the order with a member firm having seats on both exchanges to sell the securities on the Detroit Exchange and give up a portion of the commission to the nonmember firm, the institutional investor might satisfy its debt to the nonmember firm without paying any more money than it would have on a regular commission. The Big Board member, in turn, obtains an order which otherwise might have gone to the so-called "third market"—an over-the-counter market in listed securities in which New York Stock Exchange members may not deal.

from 7 A.M. to 2:30 P.M., Pacific time. Thus, while its opening coincides with the 10 A.M., Eastern time, opening of the New York Stock Exchange, its closing is two hours after all Eastern securities markets have shut for the day. From 12:30 to 2:30 P.M., Pacific time (3:30 to 5:30 P.M., Eastern time), it is the only principal stock exchange in the nation remaining open. If important news breaks in the East after the close of the markets there, investors around the nation and the world are able to execute orders which would otherwise have to be held overnight for the next morning's New York opening.

Round-lot orders placed on the Pacific Coast Stock Exchange for dually listed securities may be given "primary market protection" by the specialist, guaranteeing a price in line with the New York price. As on the Midwest Stock Exchange, odd-lot orders in dual stocks are filled at the regular odd-lot differential away from the first effective round-lot price reported on the New York tape, after a lapse of three minutes from the specialist's receipt of the order. Tape lateness is added to the three minutes. Other rules apply to odd-lot and round-lot stop orders and limit orders to ensure that they also receive as good a price as they would in New York.

Some 619 issues of Eastern, Western, Hawaiian, and Philippine companies are traded on the Pacific Coast Stock Exchange. Of these issues, 43 are traded exclusively on this Exchange. The remainder are dually traded issues also handled on one of the Eastern exchanges. In general, standards for listing on the Pacific Coast Stock Exchange include at least 750 stockholders, at least 250,000 shares issued and outstanding (exclusive of concentrated or family holdings), demonstrated earning power of $100,000 annually after taxes, and total assets of $1 million.

The Over-the-counter Market

The first securities issued by the Federal government and private commercial enterprises were bought and sold in the offices of banking houses. These houses actually had counters over which investors bought and sold by negotiation and over which they paid for and accepted delivery of the securities in which they were dealing. Such purchases and sales were known as "over-the-counter" transactions, to distinguish them from those executed on the organized exchanges.[2]

The SEC estimates that in 1961 approximately 38 per cent of the

[2] For a more detailed account of this market, the reader is referred to Irwin Friend, D. Wright Hoffman, and Willis J. Winn, *The Over-the-counter Securities Market,* New York: McGraw-Hill Book Company, 1958; and to chaps. VII and XII(G) of the *Report of Special Study of Securities Markets of the Securities and Exchange Commission,* 88th Cong., 1st Sess., House Document 95, 1963. (Hereafter referred to as *Special Study.*)

dollar value of corporate stock sales took place in the over-the-counter market.[3] Approximately 14,000 domestic stocks and 3,340 governmental and corporate bonds were advertised for sale in the over-the-counter market during a sample ten-month period in 1961–1962. By comparison, in the same period, 3,041 stock issues and 1,284 bond issues were traded on all exchanges in the United States.[4]

Methods of Trading.   Buyers and sellers of *listed* securities meet, through their agents, the brokers, in concentrated spots (i.e., the exchanges) and arrive at their prices by the auction method. Over-the-counter transactions are effected within or between the offices of securities houses, prices being established by individual negotiation. Moreover, the over-the-counter dealer usually buys and sells as principal. The method by which a transaction is executed in the over-the-counter market will be made clearer by an illustration.

Assume that Mr. Leonard of Chapel Hill, North Carolina, wants to buy 100 shares of the common stock of Southern Consolidated Toy Company, an issue that is traded exclusively over the counter. Leonard informs his broker, Weatherspoon & Company of Durham, North Carolina, of his interest in the stock and requests a quotation on it. The broker, upon checking the market, discovers that Petry, Lundeberg & Company of Charlotte, North Carolina, is currently quoting the issue at 42 bid, offered at $43\frac{1}{2}$. The prices quoted Weatherspoon are "inside," or wholesale, prices at which securities dealers will sell to each other. Weatherspoon & Company adds about a 5 per cent markup to the price and informs Leonard that the stock could probably be obtained at about $45\frac{5}{8}$. If this price is agreeable to Leonard, he gives instructions to buy 100 shares of Southern Consolidated Toy common at $45\frac{5}{8}$, or better. Weatherspoon & Company immediately telephones Petry, Lundeberg & Company. A conversation similar to the following takes place:

Weatherspoon: What is your market in Southern Toy?
P., L. & Co.:   Forty-two bid, offered at $43\frac{1}{2}$.
Weatherspoon: What is the size of your market?
P., L. & Co.:   Two hundred shares either way. (*This means that they stand willing to buy or to sell this number of shares at the extreme quotations.*)
Weatherspoon: I will pay $42\frac{3}{4}$ for 100.

---

[3] Over-the-counter sales of corporate stock in 1961 were estimated at $38.9 billion and sales on all exchanges at $63.8 billion. *Special Study,* part 2, p. 547.

[4] *Special Study,* part 2, p. 548. These figures for the over-the-counter market represent primarily actively traded issues. Because the over-the-counter market is the residual market for all stocks not listed on an exchange, many additional thousands of issues are traded on an infrequent basis.

P., L. & Co.:	(*not being willing to sell at this price but yet being willing to make some concession*) I will sell 100 at 43.
Weatherspoon:	I will take 100 at 43.
P., L. & Co.:	I have sold you 100 shares of Southern Toy common at 43.

By negotiation Leonard's broker has been able to obtain the stock for him at a more favorable price than that first quoted. Adding about a 5 per cent markup to its wholesale cost of 43, Weatherspoon & Company charges Leonard about $45\frac{1}{8}$.

In transacting orders for customers in the over-the-counter market securities firms usually act as dealers; that is, they buy in the wholesale market and resell to the customer at a retail price. However, if Leonard had so specified, Weatherspoon & Company would have purchased the stock as an agent, charging Leonard 43 per share plus a commission.

In the above example, both Weatherspoon & Company and Petry, Lundeberg & Company acted as dealers. Weatherspoon & Company acted for a customer, however, while Petry, Lundeberg & Company was making a regular market for the stock. When a dealer makes a regular market for a security, he continually announces the fact that he is willing to buy the stock at the bid price or to sell it at the offer price. He is thus a "merchant" in securities. Not only must he be ready to pay for the shares he buys, but he must be prepared to deliver those he sells. This necessitates his keeping an "inventory," or supply of the issue, on hand. This inventory is spoken of as the "position" of the house. The profit of the dealer is derived, of course, from the difference between the price paid and the price received.

At first glance it would appear that a dealer makes the price as well as the market. This is not so, however. No dealer could afford to buy continually without sometimes selling, and to sell continually without buying would be impossible. In the long run, therefore, purchases and sales must balance. For this reason, if a dealer raises his bid and ask prices, he finds his inventory growing too large. A lower price for an issue has a tendency to increase his sales and decrease his purchases. Similarly, if too many of the public are buying and not enough are selling, he can bring purchases and sales into a better balance by raising his bids and offers. Thus he does not make the price but, rather, is the medium through which supply and demand over a period of time set the price.

Prices in the Over-the-counter Market.   As the above example shows, there are two sets of prices for stocks traded in the over-the-counter market—the inside, or wholesale, price and the outside, or retail, price. Inside prices are the prices at which one securities firm will sell to another securities firm, while outside prices are those which the public must pay for the stock. If a customer places an order, he usually pays the outside price, the broker (acting as a dealer) having purchased the stock at the inside price and resold it at a profit. In such a transaction, the customer pays no commission as such but simply pays the net price charged by the broker-dealer.

Brokers are free to mark up the wholesale price as they see fit, subject only to the suggestion of the National Association of Securities Dealers that a 5 per cent markup is reasonable under normal conditions. According to the 1963 *Report to Members of the National Association of Securities Dealers,* typical markups in 1963 were as follows:

Per cent of markup	Per cent of transactions
Under 3.0	44.7
3.1– 5.0	37.7
5.1– 7.0	7.8
7.1–10.0	3.8
Over 10.0	6.0
	100.0

Over-the-counter Quotations. By means of the telephone, telegraph, and teletype, investment dealers and brokers in all parts of the country are linked together in one immense securities market. Wholesale (inside) prices for this market are collected and disseminated daily by the National Quotation Bureau, Inc. (a subsidiary of Commerce Clearing House) with offices at 46 Front Street, New York City. On a normal business day the bureau publishes quotations on some 8,000 separate stock issues and on some 2,000 bond issues in its *National Daily Quotation Service.* The Eastern Stock Section of this service, commonly called the "pink sheets" because of the paper on which it is mimeographed, contains about 200 pages of quotations. The Eastern Bond Section is printed on "yellow sheets" and runs about 30 pages. The Western Section, published in Chicago and called the "green sheets," usually contains about 32 pages; and the Pacific Coast Section, published in San Francisco and called the "white sheets," runs to about 42 pages. Subscription to the service is limited to securities dealers and brokers registered with the SEC. Only these subscribers have the right to advertise their prices in the sheets.

When a subscriber wishes to insert a bid or an offer in the daily service, he makes out a ticket giving the firm name, its telephone and teletype numbers, the date, the number of shares wanted or the number offered, and a bid or ask price for at least half the issues which he stands willing to buy or to sell. In New York these quotations are collected about noon by a squad of messengers. Quotations are received from out-of-town dealers via telephone, telegraph, teletype, or air mail. Between 2 and 5 P.M. the quotations are sorted alphabetically according to issue and are then stenciled. By 6 P.M. the pages have been printed, assembled into sets, placed in pre-addressed envelopes, and shipped to various financial communities for distribution. The next morning thousands of dealers throughout the country will have the quotations ready to serve their customers. It was by means of a service such as this that Weatherspoon & Company, in our illustration above, discovered that Petry, Lundeberg & Company of Charlotte was quoting the issue in which Leonard was interested.

Each month the quotations that have appeared in the daily service are summarized in *The National Monthly Stock Summary* and *The National Monthly Bond Summary,* both published by the National Quotation Bureau.

Municipal bond offerings in the over-the-counter market are listed daily in *The Blue List of Current Municipal Offerings,* published by the Blue List Publishing Company, now a subsidiary of Standard and Poor's Corporation, with offices at 130 Cedar Street in New York City.

The National Association of Securities Dealers.   Prior to the stock market crash of 1929, many abuses developed in the securities business, the extent of which was not known or understood even by those involved. As a result of the investigations carried on during the Depression of the 1930s, the extent of the abuses became apparent. To many it appeared that everyone connected with the securities business was dishonest.

The NRA and the Investment Bankers Code were advanced by leaders as a chance to eliminate the unscrupulous, to reaffirm professional standards, and to regain public esteem. But the Supreme Court outlawed the Investment Bankers Code along with others. During the period from October 1935 to October 1939, the Investment Bankers Conference Committee and later the Investment Bankers Conference, Inc., spent more than $350,000 trying to maintain high standards of professional conduct.

The Maloney amendment to the Securities Exchange Act was born out of the negotiations between these industry representatives and the Commission. The amendment, passed by Congress in 1938, authorized investment bankers to form associations for the purpose of self-regulation. Association rules limit price concessions, discounts, and allowances to members and withdraw membership privileges for failure to abide by the rules. The National Association of Securities Dealers, Inc., was the first and to date the only such organization to be formed.

The NASD is a nonprofit corporation organized under the laws of the state of Delaware. It is managed by a board of 21 governors. Any broker or dealer engaged in the investment banking business is eligible for membership, provided, in brief, that he has never been expelled from a national securities association or from a national securities exchange and has never been convicted of a felony or misdemeanor involving the purchase or sale of any security. Membership is obtained by application to the board of governors and by agreement to abide by the rules of the organization, to pay the necessary dues and assessments, and to supply essential information. Such an application must have the approval of the district committee of the district in which the applicant has his place of business. An applicant who has been refused membership has the right to a hearing before the board and may if necessary carry an appeal to the Securities and Exchange Commission.

For the purpose of administration, the country is divided into 13 regional districts, which have the initial responsibility for enforcing the rules of fair practice. Local administration in each district is under a district committee, composed of 6 to 18 members who are elected for a three-year term by member firms and branch offices within the district. Major duties of the district committee (sitting as its District Business Conduct Committee) are to review all examination reports submitted by NASD examiners, to investigate all complaints made by the public against NASD members, to file charges against members and registered representatives for violations of the laws and rules of the association, to act as a judge in disciplinary proceedings, and to assess penalties. Penalties may range from censure or fine to suspension or expulsion from the NASD.

The National Association of Securities Dealers has four stated objectives:

1. To promote through cooperative effort the investment banking and securities business, to standardize its principles and practices, to promote therein high standards of commercial honor, and to encourage and promote among members observance of Federal and state securities laws

2. To provide a medium through which its membership may be enabled to confer, consult, and cooperate with governmental and other agencies in the solution of problems affecting investors, the public, and the investment banking and securities business

3. To adopt, administer, and enforce rules of fair practice and rules to prevent fraudulent and manipulative acts and practices, and in general to promote just and equitable principles of trade for the protection of investors

4. To promote self-discipline among members, and to investigate and adjust grievances between the public and members and between members

NASD Rules of Fair Practice. Members of the National Association of Securities Dealers must abide by the association's 28 rules of fair practice. Among the responsibilities pinpointed by these rules are those which require a member to observe high standards of commercial honor and to follow just and equitable principles of trade. Recommendations for the purchase or sale of securities must be suitable for the customer on the basis of whatever information about his other security holdings and financial circumstances he has revealed. Charges made for services performed must be reasonable and not unfairly discriminatory between customers. Markups or commissions charged on over-the-counter orders must be fair, all the relevant circumstances surrounding the transaction being taken into consideration. Reports of transactions must represent bona fide transactions, and quotes of bid and ask prices must be bona fide unless clearly indicated to be only nominal. Members must notify customers whether they filled orders by acting as brokers for the customer, by acting as dealers for their own account, or by acting as dealers for some other party. Members must deal with nonmember brokers and dealers at the same prices, for the same commissions or fees, and on the same terms and conditions as they deal with the general public.

The Third Market.   Recent years have witnessed a rapid expansion of over-the-counter trading in stocks listed and traded on the New York Stock Exchange and, to a lesser extent, on other organized exchanges. Because this market is competitive with the organized exchanges, it differs from the normal over-the-counter market in unlisted securities and has come to be called the "third market."

Sales in the third market, according to estimates made by the SEC's *Special Study,* run to about 3.3 per cent of the volume and 3.8 per cent of the dollar value of sales on the floor of the Exchange.[5] Since the stocks traded in the third market are apt to be the more active listed ones, the per cents cited probably underestimate the importance of this market.

Most transactions in the third market are between large institutional investors and securities firms which do not belong to an organized exchange.[6] However, it now appears that individual investors are using this market more than was realized. The major motivation for institutional use of the market is to save costs. Commissions on the New York Stock Exchange are computed on the value of a single round lot, with no reduction for increased number of round lots in a single order. The commission on a 100-share transaction in a stock priced at $50 on the Exchange would be $44. The commission on a 10,000-share transaction in the same stock would be $4,400; but frequently dealers in the third market will charge less than the Exchange commission rates for buying or selling the larger block of stock. In studying the participants in the third market, the *Special Study* reported that both pension funds and insurance companies did a larger proportion of their trading in NYSE listed stocks in the third market than they did on the Exchange itself.

[5] *Special Study,* part 2, p. 1063. See pp. 870 to 911 for the most detailed study of the third market made to date.

[6] The seven largest dealers in the third market in 1961 were American Securities Corp.; Blyth & Company; A. W. Benkert & Company; The First Boston Corporation; J. S. Strauss & Company; Weeden & Company; and Stewart, Miller & Company. *Special Study,* part 2, p. 872, note 121.

4 foreign stock exchanges

Regardless of the country in which an exchange is located, its basic function is the same even though the form of securities traded, the organization of the market, and the mechanical procedures differ. The present chapter describes the history, organization, and routines of several of the leading stock exchanges located outside the United States.

The Paris Bourse

The Paris Bourse had its beginnings in 1138, when the activities of the money lenders of the city were concentrated near what is now the central produce market. During the next two centuries these activities shifted to the Pont au Change, a bridge crossing the Seine near the Palace of Justice. From 1305 to 1797 the Bourse occupied successively a courtyard of the Palace of Justice, the Palace Vendôme, the Halle aux Blés, the site of the present National Library, and the apartments of Anne of Austria in the Louvre. Then for ten years trading took place at several points near the present site of the Bourse. On May 24, 1808, the market moved into a building copied from the Temple of Vespasian at Rome and constructed specially for the Bourse by Napoleon I. The Bourse still occupies this building, which is located on the Rue du Quatre Septembre about five streets east of the Place de l'Opéra.

The early Bourse was not exclusively a stock exchange, since commodities and instruments evidencing debts were also traded. Some years after the market moved into its present quarters, the trading in commodities was transferred elsewhere.

For a time Paris had three markets for securities: the Parquet, or official market; the Coulisse, or semiofficial market; and the Hors Cote, a market dealing in unlisted securities without governmental supervision.

The Parquet market derived its authority from an 1808 government decree recognizing an association of brokers (*agents de change*) with membership limited to 70 persons. This association was given a monopoly in the trading of listed securities. Its members were forbidden to engage in any business other than acting as intermediary for investors. Thus, they could not trade for their own account, invest capital in outside enterprises, advise investors, or make recommendations regarding the purchase and/or sale of securities.

Partly as a result of these restrictions and partly as a result of an increase in the number of unlisted issues, a second market evolved—the Coulisse. At first this second market was an unofficial one dealing only in unlisted issues; so its members were free to trade for their own account, give advice, and loan money to customers. Gradually its activities encroached upon the privileges reserved for the Parquet. The word *coulisse* means "hall" and dates back to the time when the *agents de change* met in the grounds of the Convent of the Filles de St. Thomas d'Aquin and the members of the unofficial group met in the hall leading to the official premises. When the Parquet market moved into its present building, the Coulisse moved into an adjoining veranda.

In 1898 a law was passed clarifying the monopoly rights of the Parquet and curbing the activities of members of the Coulisse by depriving the latter of the possibility of dealing in shares of any issue listed on the official market. By 1961 the membership of the Coulisse had declined to 18. A reorganization effected in this year merged the 18 Coulisse members with the 68 *agents de change,* and the Coulisse ceased to exist.

The Hors Cote was a market without organization or control. Members dealt mostly in the shares of small, inactive companies. Trading took place at unusual hours and in various places; quotations lacked reliability and authenticity. A number of scandals associated with the market during the 1920s brought it into general disrepute; so, beginning on January 21, 1929, it was subjected to government regulation. At this time trading was moved to the veranda of the Bourse, and quotations appeared on three designated boards. Gradually the market lost its identity as its activities merged with those of the Coulisse, which, as explained, was later absorbed into the Parquet.

Membership.   Members of the Paris Bourse are semigovernmental officials charged with the responsibility of supervising the process of exchanging security ownership in France. The routine work of executing orders, making prices, delivering securities, and settling money sums may be performed by employees, but members of the Bourse are jointly and severally responsible for the outcome. This responsibility is the reason why the Bourse has been given a legal monopoly of security exchange transactions and why its members are prohibited from trading for their own account, advising investors, or financing customers.

Membership in the Bourse is limited to 85. An applicant must be nominated by a retiring member or by the heirs of a deceased member. He must take an examination to prove that he has a suitable technical and cultural background. He must have the approval of the 11-member council and an affirmative vote of the membership. If he meets these requirements, he is appointed to his post by the Minister of Finance.

The nomination by a retiring member or by the heirs of a deceased member probably involves a monetary settlement. The amount of the settlement varies, but in a recent transfer it was 250,000 francs ($50,607). If a new member becomes a partner of a brokerage firm, he must contribute to the firm's capital. A firm of four partners is required to have a minimum capital of 1 million francs ($202,428) and must make a contribution of 600,000 francs ($121,457) to the guaranty fund. The new member must contribute one fourth of each of these sums.

Continental-type Stock Certificates. The type of stock certificate used in France and in other continental European countries is unknown to investors in the United States. It is customary for European companies to issue *bearer certificates with dividend coupons attached.* When an issuing company declares a dividend payable, the holder of the certificate detaches the proper coupon and presents it to a bank for payment. Since a company does not know who its stockholders are, it cannot notify them individually of dividend declarations. Consequently, each holder of European shares must watch newspapers constantly for notices of dividend payments.

Certificates of stock in European companies may be registered in the name of the owner, but this does not obviate the necessity of watching for dividend notices, since to collect a dividend a holder of registered shares must take his certificates to a bank to have them stamped as evidence of payment. An alternative to the watching process is to shift the burden to an institution by depositing the certificates with it for safekeeping. In fact, France has a special stock deposit bank called SICOVAM which is designed for this purpose.

Each depositor in SICOVAM has an account in his name. When he deposits shares of a given company, his account is credited and his shares are grouped with other shares of the same company. If the company declares a dividend, the bank collects for all the shares held by it and credits the accounts of the various shareholders for their proportionate amounts. The concentration of so many shares in a single depositing institution greatly simplifies the making of deliveries. If broker A wishes to have shares of a listed company delivered to broker B, he has merely to request SICOVAM to debit his account and to credit the account of broker B for as many shares as are to be delivered. This procedure makes it possible to transfer *ownership* of shares without moving the certificates.

Types of Orders. In France a market order is called *au mieux,* which means "at the best," and a limited order is called *order lie.* But the French have one type of order not to be found in the United States—*à appréciation.* This type of order is used when a trader wishes to buy or to sell a relatively large quantity of shares in a market that is thin. The order permits the broker to divide the total quantity of shares to be purchased or sold into smaller quantities for execution as if they were separate orders.

To illustrate, suppose that an order of this type is given to buy 75 shares of an issue that was last quoted at 70 francs. Assume also that there are no unfilled buy orders in the market and that the following sell orders are all that await execution:

Sell   50 shares @ 82
       25 shares @ 76
       25 shares @ 71

If the broker bids for all 75 shares at one time, he would be forced to pay 82. But if he bids first for 25 shares, he would get them for 71. If, after completion of this transaction, he bids for another 25 shares, he would get them for 76. If then he bids for still another 25 shares, he would get them for 82. Thus he would acquire the 75 shares at an average cost of 76.

Comptant and Terme Transactions.   Contracts made on the floor of the Paris Bourse contemplate delivery on the next scheduled delivery date. In France delivery dates are scheduled for a year in advance and occur about once a month. Two types of contracts are made on the floor: *comptant* (cash delivery) and *terme* (future delivery). The distinction between the two has to do with *when title to the shares passes* from buyer to seller, and not to when the certificates are to be delivered. In a *comptant* transaction title passes at the time the contract of sale is made. In a *terme* transaction title passes at the next delivery date.

There are two situations in which the difference between the two types of transaction becomes important. The first is when a dividend is declared during the interval between the date of a contract and the date of delivery. Since an *owner* of shares is entitled to the dividend, the moment that title passes determines who owns the shares and who gets the dividend. In a *comptant* transaction it is the buyer; in a *terme* transaction it is the seller.

The difference between a *comptant* and a *terme* transaction is also of importance to a trader who wishes to profit from an expected decline in the price of an issue. To circumvent the prohibition against short selling, a French trader must engage in a complicated maneuver involving both a *terme* and a *comptant* transaction.

To illustrate, assume that a particular issue is selling at 91 on October 4 and that the next delivery date is October 25. Monsieur Pelet, who does not own any of this issue, expects the price to decline. So, on October 4, he orders his broker to sell 100 shares for future delivery. The sale is executed at 91, and delivery is to occur on October 25. Thus M. Pelet has sold shares which he does not have at the moment, but the period of time during which he can maintain this *de facto* short position is limited by the approaching delivery date to 21 days.

If the market price of the issue declines to, say, 75 before the delivery date and if M. Pelet does not expect the price to decline further, he may order 100 shares purchased in the *comptant* market. These shares will be delivered to his broker on the same day that the broker is obligated to make delivery on M. Pelet's *terme* transaction. Thus M. Pelet sold shares at 91 that he purchased (later) at 75 and has profited the same as though he had been permitted to make a short sale.

If M. Pelet does not close out his short position by October 21 and if he expects the price to continue to decline still further, he can prolong his *de facto* short position by the following procedure, possible only on the third day preceding a delivery day: First, he makes a purchase in the *comptant* market to obtain shares to make delivery on his October 4 *terme* sale. This purchase closes out his short position. Then he sells 100 shares of the issue in the *terme* market, specifying delivery, say, on November 21 (the delivery date following October 25). The second transaction reestablishes his *de facto* short position.

Trading with Buyers' Options.   An option is a contract between two persons in which the maker of the option agrees to deliver a specified number of shares at a specified price to the holder of the option on a delivery date that is one, two, or three months away when and if the holder of the option requests a delivery to be made. As noted, the terms of the contract allow the holder, but not the maker, to cancel the option. It is understood that the holder will notify a maker on "answer day" if he intends to request delivery. Answer day is the fourth trading day preceding a delivery day.

If the maker of an option holds shares at the time when the holder calls for delivery, he has only to deliver the shares which he holds. If the maker of an option does not hold shares at the time the holder calls for delivery, he must buy the shares in the *comptant* market. Trading in sellers' options is not permitted on the Bourse.

The existence of buyers' options makes it possible for a French trader to do indirectly what he is not permitted to do directly—that is, to trade on margin. If M. Pelet expects the market price of an issue to rise, he may buy an option for a small cash outlay. Then, if the price does rise, he sells shares in the *comptant* market and makes delivery with shares acquired through the exercise of the option. If the price of the issue does not rise, he merely allows the option to expire, thus losing only the small amount he paid for it.

Price-determining Procedures.   Three methods for determining "fair and equitable" prices are employed on the Paris Bourse. They are (1) *cotation à la criée* (quotation by cry), (2) *cotation par opposition* (quotation by opposition), and (3) *cotation par casiers* (quotation via boxes). Each of these three methods is different from any employed in the United States and so requires extended explanation.

1. Trading in the more active issues is carried on under the auspices of

auctioneers at five or six posts located at various spots on the floor of the Bourse. One of these, the *parquet* (meaning "basket"), appears as a circular fence located in the center of the trading floor. Only members of the Bourse may participate in the activity at this post. The other posts are rectangular enclosures at one end of which sits an auctioneer with a microphone strapped to his chest. The microphone enables him to communicate with two clerks who stand at a blackboard on a scaffold above and behind him. The blackboard contains the names of the issues traded at that post.

Representatives of brokers who have orders to buy or sell one of the listed issues assemble within the enclosure. When the bell rings to signal the opening of the market, the auctioneer notes the price at which the first issue on the list closed the previous day. For illustration, assume this price to be 26. If the auctioneer thinks that this might be a good price at which to start the day's bargaining, he informs the clerk on the scaffold, who then writes the figure on the blackboard. All the brokers in the enclosure who have orders to buy at this price or at a higher price or who have orders to sell at this price or at a lower price now begin to make arrangements with each other to deliver or to accept delivery of shares at the price of 26.

If it happens that supply and demand equate at 26, each broker is able to arrange deliveries and receipts for all the orders held and the hubbub soon dies down. In this case, the auctioneer proclaims his tentative price of 26 to be the official price.

However, if supply and demand do not equate at 26, all the brokers on one side of the market are able to arrange deliveries satisfactorily but some of the brokers on the other side are still clamoring for counterparts. The auctioneer, noting the situation, knows that his tentative price did not equate demand and supply. If the brokers left are buyers, the auctioneer instructs the clerk to erase the 26 on the blackboard and to write 27 in its place. This means that all the arrangements to deliver and to receive shares at the previous tentative price (26) are to be fulfilled at a contract price of 27. The shift in the contract price divides the brokers into two groups: those who are satisfied with the price change and those who are unhappy about it.

The first group (those who are satisfied) includes (1) all who executed orders *at the market* (whether to buy or to sell) and (2) all who executed *limited sell* orders. Customers who ordered shares purchased at the market want the shares regardless of the price, and all sellers at a price of 26 are happy to receive 27. Thus this group of brokers remains silent when the contract price is changed from 26 to 27.

The second group (those who are unhappy about the price change) includes those who executed buy orders for customers who set a top limit at 26. These customers will not accept the shares at a price of 27, but the broker has obligated himself to accept delivery, and now he must pay 27. He can extricate himself from the situation (1) by selling an equal number of shares at 27 or (2) by shifting his obligation to accept delivery to another broker. Brokers in this position reenter the market on the selling side at the price of 27 and are joined by brokers with limited orders to sell at 27.

Thus, the auctioneer's change in price augments supply and so makes it possible for the brokers unable to arrange deliveries at the previous price to find their counterparts. When the auctioneer finds the price that minimizes bargaining activity, he knows that he has located the price that comes closest to equating supply and demand. He informs the clerk on the scaffold that the last tentative price announced by him is to become the official price of the issue. The clerk draws a line under the price on the blackboard to indicate that for the moment trading in this particular issue is completed. The auctioneer then announces a tentative price for the second issue on the list, and the process is repeated.

2. Quotation by opposition is used to determine contract prices for less active issues. A clerk of the Bourse sits within a small enclosure with a big book in front of him. Five or six lines are devoted to each of the six or seven issues assigned to him. As brokers receive orders to buy or to sell shares of an inactive issue, they go to the appropriate clerk and report the price, but not the number of shares, at which they are willing to buy or sell. The clerk enters the price and the initial of the firm on the records, which are open for all to view. A clerk's records of orders to buy and sell a hypothetical issue might appear thus:

	XYZ common shares										
	Buy orders						Sell orders				
Price	42	44	—	41	40	43	41	43	—	42	45	44
Firm	A	B	C	D	E	F	M	N	O	P	Q	R

This record would be read and interpreted as follows: Firm A is willing to buy the issue at 42 or better, firm B is willing to buy at 44 or better, firm C is willing to buy at the market, and so on.

Periodically, an official of the exchange calls at the clerk's post to note the names of the firms wishing to trade and the prices at which they are willing to buy or sell. He then locates the representative of each firm and asks how many shares he wishes to buy or sell. This information is arranged in a table as follows for purposes of determining the price that maximizes turnover:

Shares wanted	Possible price	Shares offered
100	40	50
85	41	60
75	42	65
72	43	75
60	44	95
40	45	110

If the exchange official were to set the price at 42, 75 shares would be wanted but only 65 shares would be offered and turnover would be the smaller of the two figures. Prospective buyers willing to trade at the price would be unable to obtain 10 shares. If the official price were set at 43, 72 shares would be wanted and 75 shares would be offered. Thus there would be 72 shares traded, and prospective sellers willing to trade at this price would be unable to dispose of 3 shares. Under the circumstances the official would set the price at 43, since more shares would be exchanged at this price than at 42.

3. The quotation-via-boxes method of setting official prices is essentially the same as quotation by opposition. The difference lies in the fact that the clerk of the Bourse sits in a cage, and brokers hand him slips of paper indicating the number of shares and the prices at which they are willing to trade. The slips are assembled by issue, and periodically a price that maximizes exchange of shares is determined and announced by the clerk.

One post in the Bourse is devoted to trading in unlisted issues. Representatives of brokers with orders to buy or to sell unlisted issues proceed to this post and make a public offer to buy or to sell. If the offer is accepted, an exchange is effected. If the offer is not accepted, the broker is free to cross a buy and a sell order if he has both.

Settlements between Member Firms.   Settlement periods on the Bourse are scheduled one a month and require six trading days. The first day of the period is called "answer day." On this day holders of options must inform makers whether or not it is their intention to exercise the option and to demand delivery during the current settlement period.

The second day of the period is known as "settlement day." Contracts made on settlement day must specify whether delivery and payment are to be effected in the current settlement period or in the subsequent settlement period.

The third day of the period is "report day." On this day each firm must report all its obligations to make deliveries or payments to the clearinghouse.

The fourth and fifth days are "delivery days." On the first of the two delivery days brokers deliver registered certificates, and on the second they deliver bearer certificates. If the shares to be delivered are on deposit with SICOVAM, the selling broker has only to notify that agency to debit his account and to credit the account of the purchaser for the proper number of shares. If the shares to be delivered are in the selling broker's possession, he has only to deliver them to SICOVAM for deposit to the credit of the buying broker's accounts.

On the sixth day of the period brokers settle money obligations by means of checks drawn against the Bank of France.

Publication of Quotations.   The Paris Bourse publishes a daily *Bulletin de la Cote* containing "authentic and official" quotations established during the previous day's trading. Statistics of volume are not given. Each issue of the bulletin is divided into two parts, part 1 containing quotations for forward transactions (*terme*) and part 2 reporting the prices of cash transactions (*comptant*).

Brokerage Fees and Taxes.   French brokers charge a fee of $\frac{7}{10}$ per cent of the amount of a purchase or sale of shares on forward transactions and a fee of $\frac{5}{10}$ per cent on cash transactions. Both buyer and seller must pay a transaction tax amounting to $\frac{6}{10}$ per cent on cash transactions and $\frac{3}{10}$ per cent on forward deals. There is no French capital gains tax but the income tax rate applicable to dividends is 24 per cent.

French Trading in American Shares.   Visitors in Paris will find a modern brokerage office with a quotation board on the Avenue des Champs Elysées near the Clemenceau Metro station. This office is operated by a well-known American firm. Another, less elaborate office, also operated by an American firm, will be found on the Place Vendôme. These offices are operated for the benefit of foreigners living in Paris. They do not normally buy or sell securities for French citizens, and they do not purchase French securities for foreign citizens.

If a foreigner in France wishes to purchase or to sell French shares, he may place his order with one of these American brokers, who will then relay it to a French broker for execution. Payment for such purchases can be made in foreign currency, but the funds are given to the Bank of France, which pays the French broker in francs. If a French investor wishes to purchase United States shares, he pays the Bank of France in francs and the bank pays the American broker in dollars. If a French investor places an order with a French broker to buy United States shares not listed on the Bourse, the order is relayed to an American brokerage firm for execution in New York. Payment would have to be effected through the Bank of France in the same manner.

Shares of a number of non-French companies are listed on the Bourse. For example, the *Bulletin* for October 21, 1963, lists *terme* quotations for 56 issues, among them the following United States companies:

American Tel. & Tel.
Ford
General Electric
General Motors
Goodyear
International Nickel
International Tel. & Tel.
Procter & Gamble

The shares of these non-French companies are on deposit with SICOVAM and are registered on the books of the several companies as belonging to that institution. Actual ownership of the shares vests in the persons whose accounts are credited for their deposit.

The London Stock Exchange

The London Stock Exchange had its beginnings in the seventeenth century, when the British government and certain trading enterprises began to raise money by the sale of stocks and bonds to the public. As trading in these securities increased, it became possible for some persons to make a living by acting as agents for buyers and sellers. Trading at first took place at the Royal Exchange but later moved to the coffeehouses located near Exchange Alley. The uniformed attendants seen on the floor of the Exchange today are still called waiters, a survival from those early days.

In 1773 the company of stockbrokers decided to acquire a house of its own. The new building stood on the corner of Threadneedle Street and Sweetings Alley, where the Exchange is still located. A part of the present structure dates back to 1802 and the remainder to 1885.

Membership.   The London Stock Exchange has 3,460 members. New members are admitted only as old members retire or die. Acquiring membership is called "nomination." The cost of nomination has fluctuated over the years from £1 ($2.80) to £2,000 ($5,600). In addition to this cost, new members must pay an entrance fee of £1,050 ($2,940) and an annual subscription of £250 ($630).

Applicants for membership must be twenty-one years of age and must (as a rule) be native-born British citizens. Obviously, they must be men of high character and sound credit standing, for the motto of the Exchange is *Dictum meum pactum* (my word is my bond). To ensure high professional standards, an applicant for membership must be proposed and seconded by two members who have known him for at least four years and who are willing to vouch for his character. However, neither proposer nor seconder assumes any financial liability for an applicant's subsequent default. In addition, applicants must receive the approval of not fewer than three fourths of the council and must have spent at least two years working for a member firm of the Exchange.

Government.   Members of the Exchange are regulated by 200 rules made and administered by a council of 36 members. One member of the council is the government broker, and the rest are elected from and by the members to serve for a period of three years. Twelve members of the council retire each year but are eligible for reelection. Members serve without compensation and are aided in the execution of their duties by a permanent staff headed by the secretary of the council.

Listing Requirements.   The main functions of the London Stock Exchange are (1) to provide a means for raising permanent capital and (2) to maintain an efficient market for the purchase and sale of securities. Members of the Exchange are quite conscious of the fact that an efficient market can operate only if all who use it have confidence that, within reason, they and the investor concerned possess the same facts as their opposite number in the floor contract. For this reason the Exchange requires that, before listed securities may be traded, specific requirements must be met. These requirements include the following.

1. A filing of profit and loss figures of the company and its subsidiaries (if any) for a period covering the preceding ten years
2. A complete description of the type of activities in which the company and its subsidiaries are engaged and of its management
3. A report of the firm's assets and liabilities certified by a firm of public accountants

These requirements are not exhaustive: the committee on admissions may demand whatever additional information it feels to be important. These details together with full particulars of the share issue to be listed are written into a prospectus, which must be placed in at least two national daily newspapers.

After providing the Exchange with the initial information required, an applicant company must sign a "general undertaking" contract in which it agrees to inform the Exchange on all matters of importance which may occur in the future. The Exchange feels that, when such information is available to all, rumors cease to have influence and both parties can deal with reasonable assurance that neither has special information denied to the other. This ideal is difficult to achieve, but it is the objective used as a guide in determining what information must be revealed by listed companies. In the interests of investors the Exchange can and frequently does suspend trading in a particular security if it feels that insufficient information has been made available to the public.

Members of the London Stock Exchange can deal in unlisted securities provided that the security is listed on a recognized stock exchange elsewhere in the world. Since 1962 members have been allowed to open branch offices abroad with the permission of the council and subject to the Exchange's rule concerning advertising. (Stockbrokers are not permitted to advertise as a firm.)

Trading Procedures.   The trading floor of the London Stock Exchange is divided into areas called "markets." Each so-called market is a section of the floor where a particular class of securities is traded. Thus, there is a market for gilt-edged bonds (governments), a market for oil stocks, a market for mining stocks, and so on. The "pitches" (locations) of jobbing firms that deal in the various classes of securities are found in the appropriate markets. A jobber hangs a price list of the issues in which he specializes on the wall or column near his pitch and remains in the vicinity during trading hours to accept orders. Large jobbing firms deal in several markets, but smaller firms frequently confine their trading to one or two.

Trading on the Exchange begins at 9:30 A.M. (except for gilt-edged securities, which starts at 10 A.M.) and continues until 3:30 P.M. on every day except Saturday, Sunday, and holidays. At 2:30 P.M. loud rattles are sounded. This notifies the members that no more transactions will be entered on that "day's list"—the record of transactions executed, from which are compiled the prices reported in next morning's newspapers. Trading on the Exchange continues, but transactions executed after the first rattles are included in the next day's list.

Rattles sound again at 3:15 P.M., this time to inform members that they may smoke during the last quarter of an hour's trading if they wish. At 3:30 P.M. the closing of the house is announced by a third rattle. Closing of the Exchange does not mean the end of a day's trading; members are permitted to execute transactions in their offices or over their telephones at any hour of the day or night.

Brokers and Jobbers.   Members of the London Stock Exchange may act as jobbers or as brokers, but they may not serve in both capacities. A jobber is one who buys and sells securities for his own account and risk. He deals with brokers and with other jobbers but never with the public. In a particular market he chooses certain issues in which to deal, but he is not obligated to buy or to sell these issues unless and until he announces bid and ask prices. Once a jobber announces a price, he is obligated to buy a *reasonable* quantity of the issue at the bid price or to sell a *reasonable* quantity of the issue at the ask price. Normally there are a number of jobbers dealing in each security. Since brokers usually secure quotations from more than one jobber before trading and since jobbers compete for the patronage of brokers, the resulting prices are set competitively.

A jobber makes his profit by buying at prices that *average* lower than those at which he sells. It is obviously to his advantage to maximize his trades while still keeping his inventory of each issue within reasonable limits. If his bid and ask prices are too low, he will find his sales to brokers exceeding his purchases from them and his inventory shrinking. On the other hand, if his bids and asks are too high, he will find his purchases exceeding his sales and his inventory mounting. Although it is customary to speak of a jobber as "making a price," it is evident that the price is really made for him by supply and demand. All that the jobber does is to adjust his bid and ask prices up or down in keeping with market conditions so that his inventory remains at a more or less constant level in the long run.

A broker, unlike a jobber, deals with the public. As agent on a commission basis, he accepts buy and sell orders from customers for execution on the trading floor. When a broker receives a buy order, he goes to the market where the security is traded and looks for a jobber in the issue. When he finds a jobber, he asks the price without revealing whether he intends to buy or sell or even to trade. The jobber replies by quoting his current bid and ask prices. If the broker is not satisfied with these quotes, he moves on to other jobbers in the same issue, hoping to discover a better price for his customer. When he is satisfied that he has found the best possible price, he merely informs that jobber that he will take so many shares at his offering price. Broker and jobber each make a note of the agreement in their notebooks, and the deal is completed.

Settlements between Customer and Broker.   A customer's ownership of shares begins or ends at the moment when his broker enters into an agreement with the jobber. As soon as a transaction is executed, the broker makes out a "contract note" and sends it to the customer (see Figure 4–1). This contract note recites the following:

1. The number of shares bought or sold for the customer.
2. The name of the issue traded and the price at which the transaction was executed.
3. The amount of the broker's commission. The amount is determined by a scale of fees but approximates $1\frac{1}{4}$ per cent of the money value of the transaction.
4. The amount of the transfer stamp tax to be paid by the buyer, currently 1 per cent of the money value of the transaction.
5. The amount of the registration fee charged by the company to record the change of ownership of the shares. The amount varies, but 2 shillings sixpence ($0.35) is typical.
6. The amount of the contract note stamp tax. This will approximate $\frac{2}{10}$ per cent of the money value of the transaction and must be paid by both buyer and seller.
7. The "account" date upon which the customer pays the broker for a purchase or receives payment from him for a sale.

Settlements between Members.   Members of the London Stock Exchange divide a year into 20 "account periods" of two weeks' duration and 4 account periods of three weeks' duration. Each account period begins on a Monday and ends on a Friday; it is followed by an "account day," which is the first Tuesday following the last Friday of the account period. Settlement for all transactions executed during a given account period begins on the account day following the period. There are two exceptions to this rule:

ANOTHER BROKER & CO.

Stock & Share Brokers

A. B. JONES   E. F. JONES
C. D. SMITH   G. H. SMITH

TELEPHONE: LONDON WALL 8888 (6 LINES)
TELEGRAMS: BROTHER LONDON E.C.2.

99 Throgmorton Street,
(AND STOCK EXCHANGE)
London, E.C.2.   10th Jan. 1964

Bought
by Order &
for Account of?

Miss A. Buyer,
The Cottage,
Buckhorn,
Wessex.

Subject to the regulations and practice of the Stock Exchange, London

Stock or Share	Stock Code	Price	Consideration	Transfer Stamps	Transfer Fees	Contract Stamp	Brokerage	Total
A. Public Company Ltd. 150 Ordinary Shares	909090	23/3	£174-7-6	£1-15-0	2/6	2/-	£2-3-7	£178-10-7

For Settlement 21st January, 1964

ANOTHER BROKER & CO.

CONTRACT STAMP 2/-

MEMBERS OF THE STOCK EXCHANGE, LONDON

BUDGET 1962.
WE WOULD SUGGEST THAT YOU RETAIN
THIS CONTRACT NOTE FOR TAX PURPOSES.

E. & O. E.

Fig. 4-1 A contract note.

1. Transactions executed on the last two days of an account period (that is, on the last Thursday and Friday) may, by mutual consent, be on a "new time" basis, which means that settlement is postponed until the account of the subsequent account period.

2. If a buyer wishes to delay payment of a purchase or a seller wishes to delay delivery of a security beyond the proper account day, this can be arranged. Normally a delay in payment calls for the debtor to pay interest to the creditor. Sometimes, however, the reverse is the case—the creditor pays interest to the debtor. The British call the first arrangement "contango" and the second "backwardation."

Customers settle their contract obligations with brokers at the end of each account period on the basis of the terms recited in their contract notes, described earlier. Money obligations between members of the Exchange are settled by check on the proper account day. This means that a situation occasionally arises in which a broker finds that he has paid for shares that he has not received or has received payment for shares which he has not delivered. Such situations are adjusted by the activities of the "buying-in–selling-out" department of the Exchange and are described later.

Delivery of Securities. The procedure for accomplishing deliveries of securities is rather complex. It is more readily understood if the reader bears in mind the problems that must be solved. To illustrate the nature of these problems, assume that A sells stock to B, who sells it to C, who sells it to D, and so on, until finally Y sells it to Z. All these transactions are assumed to have been executed within a single account period. The fact that they were executed at different prices is of no consequence, for each of the 26 participants knows who owes him, and whom he owes, and how much. Thus money settlements present no problem, for each debtor can pay his creditor.

But delivery of the shares presents a more difficult problem. Only one certificate is available for delivery, and it is in the possession of A. If A were to deliver it to B, and B were to deliver it to C, and so on, until Y delivers it to Z, an unreasonable amount of time would be consumed in the process and the certificate might be lost or stolen during the transfer. The whole procedure would be simplified if A (the original seller) would merely deliver the certificate to Z (the final buyer). This cannot be done, however, because A sold the shares to B and does not know anything about Z. Obviously, a simple solution requires that A learn about Z's existence. On the London Stock Exchange this is accomplished by the following routine.

At the end of each account period, a broker who has purchased shares *which he did not resell* during the period wants delivery. This broker makes out a "ticket" for each block of stock for which he expects to take delivery. Among other things the ticket reveals the name of the buying broker. The broker who makes out the name ticket takes it to the "settling room" of the Exchange and deposits it in the box that belongs to the jobber from whom the stock was bought. The box mentioned is one of a series on the wall of the settling room, each jobbing and brokerage firm having its own box. The jobber who receives the ticket examines his records and passes the ticket on to the broker or jobber from whom he purchased the shares. The process is continued until the ticket reaches the hands of the broker who first sold the shares. This broker then learns the identity of the broker to whom the shares are to be delivered.

In the illustration used earlier, Z originates the ticket and places it in Y's box. When Y gets the ticket, he passes it on to X, who passes it on to W, and so on, until finally B drops it in A's box. Thus A, who is already aware that he must deliver shares, learns to whom he is to deliver them. The procedure is simple in theory, but sometimes complications arise. Consider, for example, what happens if A sells 300 shares of an issue to B, who sells 200 of the shares to C and 100 of the shares to D. Obviously, C makes out a ticket for 200 shares, and D makes out a ticket for 100 shares, and both are passed to B, who passes both tickets on to A. Thus A knows that he is to deliver 200 shares to C and 100 shares to D.

The following transaction involves one degree more of complexity: Suppose that A sells 100 shares of an issue to C and that B sells 200 shares of the same issue to C, who sells all 300 shares to D. Now D makes out a ticket calling for the delivery of 300 shares to himself. He passes this ticket to C. It becomes necessary for C to split the ticket into two, one ticket for 200 shares to be passed to B and another for 100 shares to be passed to A. However, C puts D's name on both the new tickets. Thus A delivers 100 shares to D, B delivers 200 shares to D, C makes no deliveries, and D receives 300 shares.

All that this system of tickets accomplishes is to reveal to whom and by whom shares are to be delivered. The actual delivery remains to be effected. This is more difficult to accomplish in Great Britain than it is in the United States.

An American stock registering agency transfers the ownership of any stock certificate (1) if it is endorsed by the retiring owner and (2) if the authenticity of the endorsement is guaranteed by the broker. The situation is different in Great Britain. There a registrar may not make a change in the register of a company except on the authority of a duly completed "transfer form," which must be signed by the seller and must bear a revenue stamp. The buyer must also sign if the shares are partly paid (see Figure 4-2).

When the broker of the original selling customer (T. H. E. Seller, Esq., in Figure 4-2) receives a ticket, he fills out the details on a transfer form and sends it to his customer, who must sign it. The transfer form is then returned to the broker, who attaches it to the ticket. If the broker holds a certificate

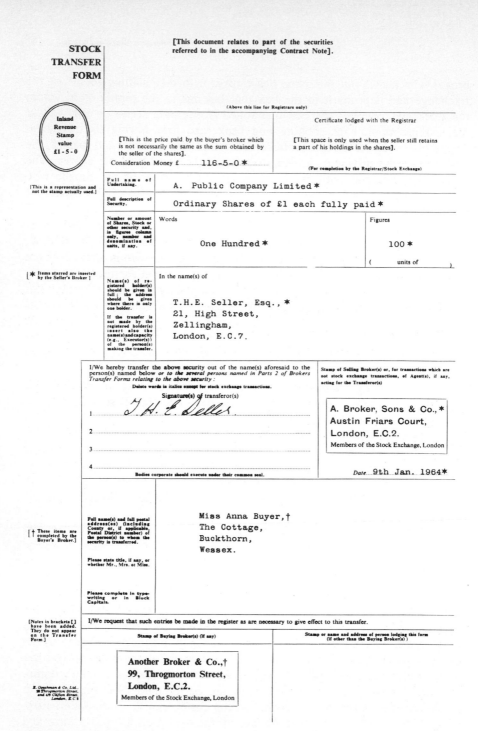

STOCK TRANSFER FORM

[This document relates to part of the securities referred to in the accompanying Contract Note].

Inland Revenue Stamp value £1 - 5 - 0

[This is a representation and not the stamp actually used.]

(Above this line for Registrars only)

Certificate lodged with the Registrar

[This is the price paid by the buyer's broker which is not necessarily the same as the sum obtained by the seller of the shares].

Consideration Money £ ....116~5~0.*........

[This space is only used when the seller still retains a part of his holdings in the shares].

(For completion by the Registrar/Stock Exchange)

Full name of Undertaking.   A. Public Company Limited *

Full description of Security.   Ordinary Shares of £1 each fully paid *

Number or amount of Shares, Stock or other security and, in figures column only, number and denomination of units, if any.

Words

One Hundred *

Figures

100 *

(units of)

[* Items starred are inserted by the Seller's Broker]

Name(s) of registered holder(s) should be given in full; the address should be given where there is only one holder.

If the transfer is not made by the registered holder(s) insert also the name(s) and capacity (e.g., Executor(s)) of the person(s) making the transfer.

In the name(s) of

T.H.E. Seller, Esq., *
21, High Street,
Zellingham,
London, E.C.7.

I/We hereby transfer the above security out of the name(s) aforesaid to the person(s) named below *or to the several persons named in Parts 2 of Brokers Transfer Forms relating to the above security :*
Delete words in italics except for stock exchange transactions.

Signature(s) of transferor(s)

1 *T.H.E. Seller*

2

3

4

Bodies corporate should execute under their common seal.

Stamp of Selling Broker(s) or, for transactions which are not stock exchange transactions, of Agent(s), if any, acting for the Transferor(s)

A. Broker, Sons & Co., *
Austin Friars Court,
London, E.C.2.
Members of the Stock Exchange, London

Date....9th Jan. 1964*

[† These items are completed by the Buyer's Broker.]

Full name(s) and full postal address(es) (including County or, if applicable, Postal District number) of the person(s) to whom the security is transferred.

Please state title, if any, or whether Mr., Mrs. or Miss.

Please complete in typewriting or in Block Capitals.

Miss Anna Buyer, †
The Cottage,
Buckthorn,
Wessex.

[Notes in brackets [] have been added. They do not appear on the Transfer Form.]

I/We request that such entries be made in the register as are necessary to give effect to this transfer.

Stamp of Buying Broker(s) (if any)

Stamp or name and address of person lodging this form (if other than the Buying Broker(s))

E. Couchman & Co. Ltd., 18 Throgmorton Street, and 6/8 Clifton Street, London, E.C.2

Another Broker & Co., †
99, Throgmorton Street,
London, E.C.2.
Members of the Stock Exchange, London

Fig. 4–2 A transfer statement.

74

for the proper number of shares, he sends the stock certificate, the transfer form, and the ticket to the broker of the final purchaser (Miss Anna Buyer in Figure 4–2). This broker then adds the name and address of and other particulars on the buying client to the transfer form. The delivery of the stock certificate, together with a completed transfer form, constitutes authorization to a stock registrar to cancel the old certificate and to make out a new certificate in the name of the new owner.

If the selling broker holds a stock certificate for a larger number of shares than were sold, he deposits the stock certificate with the stock registrar, who marks on the transfer form that this has been done. Then the selling broker delivers the transfer form to the broker named on the ticket. After details concerning the new owner have been added by the buying broker, the form is presented to the registrar, who is thereby authorized to cancel the old certificate and to issue two new certificates—one to the new stockholder for the number of shares purchased and the other to the old stockholder for the number of shares remaining in his name.

Buying-in–Selling-out Activities.   Occasionally a broker who expects to take delivery of shares and who has issued a ticket in the proper manner does not receive the transfer form ten days after account day. If he is not willing to wait longer, he may request the buying-in–selling-out department of the Exchange to purchase the shares for him for immediate delivery. If this happens, the original seller has to find a new buyer for his shares and also has to pay the departmental charges. Similarly, if a broker is obligated to deliver shares but does not receive a ticket within a reasonable time after the proper account day, he may request the buying-in–selling-out department to sell the shares for immediate delivery. If so, the issuer of the delayed ticket must complete a fresh bargain and bear the departmental charges.

Sale of New Issues.   The London Stock Exchange does not permit listed companies to sell new issues for cash except by the issuance of rights to existing shareholders. A listed company may issue new shares for property provided that control of the company is not affected by the issue and that full details are revealed to existing shareholders. By special permission a new issue of shares in an existing company may be offered to the public without first being offered to existing shareholders.[1] This is done by two arrangements, "prospectus" and "offer of sale."

In the first case (by prospectus) all the shares in the new issue are offered for public subscription, and in the second case (by offer for sale) the entire issue is purchased by a broker of a banking house for resale. In both cases the place or places where applications to purchase the new shares

[1] The same procedure is used when an issue of shares in a newly constituted company that has no shareholders other than subscribers is to be sold on the market for cash.

may be made must be specified in an advertisement printed in no fewer than two leading newspapers.

There is a third method of issuing new shares. This is called "placing" and also requires the permission of the Exchange. In a placing deal the broker or banking house purchases the entire issue and offers not more than 75 per cent of the shares to its own clients and the remainder to jobbers, who offer them to the public through other brokers. The practice is contrary to the philosophy of British finance, which is that, when a new issue is advertised, every member of the public reading the advertisement should have an *equal* chance of getting some of the new shares. Consequently, the Exchange is considering a reduction of the proportion of the new issue that may be reserved for the clients of the placing broker or banking house to something less than the 75 per cent figure mentioned above. Another suggestion under consideration is to have investment houses guarantee to purchase all the shares unsold after an issue has been offered to the public for ten days.

The Federation of Stock Exchanges.   In addition to the London Stock Exchange, there are a number of other, less important exchanges in Great Britain. An attempt is being made to promote a cooperative arrangement between these exchanges and the London Stock Exchange, looking to a greater degree of unification, for their mutual benefit and that of the investing public.

Japanese Securities Exchanges

Although individual procedures employed on Japanese exchanges are similar to those found elsewhere, the particular combination of practices used by the Japanese exchanges is unique. The exchanges in New York, Paris, and London evolved from an early need of these communities for a place in which to trade securities. As security trading grew in importance, new methods were needed to handle the volume, but innovations were adopted reluctantly. As a result, vestiges of outmoded practices are still found on the three big exchanges. Their existence is defended on the basis of tradition.

By contrast there are few if any traditions on a Japanese stock exchange. Exchanges in Japan were closed at the end of World War II by order of the authorities, and their procedures were completely overhauled before the markets were allowed to reopen. Apparently, the criterion for this reorganization was: What is the simplest and most direct method for accomplishing that which must be done? A visitor to one of the older exchanges notes great confusion; an observer of the operations of a Japanese exchange is impressed by its orderliness.

The nine stock exchanges of Japan are located in Tokyo, Osaka,

Nagoya, Kyoto, Kobe, Hiroshima, Fukuoka, Niigata, and Sapporo. Their organizations and procedures are similar; their differences relate mostly to size and importance.

History. The first organized markets for securities in Japan came into existence in 1878, when exchanges were founded almost simultaneously in Tokyo and in Osaka. Very shortly thereafter, smaller regional markets sprang up in numerous other cities. All the early exchanges were joint-stock companies operating for the personal profit of their members.

When Japan entered World War II, the several exchanges were consolidated into a single large corporation called the Japan Securities Exchange. The government supplied one fourth the capital (200 million yen) and appointed all the governors. On August 10, 1945, trading on the Japan Securities Exchange was suspended.

A new Securities Exchange Act was enacted in April 1948. This act formally dissolved the Japan Securities Exchange and provided for the establishment of new exchanges on a nonprofit membership basis. Promotion of the public interest and protection of investors were declared to be the prime considerations of the new act.

The Tokyo, Osaka, and Nagoya securities exchanges were approved and allowed to open on May 14, 1949. One month later exchanges opened in Kyoto, Kobe, Fukuoka, Hiroshima, and Niigata. A year later the ninth exchange opened in Sapporo.

Membership. A member of a Japanese stock exchange must be a business *establishment* organized as a joint-stock company and conducting a business in securities. In Tokyo and Osaka a member firm must have a minimum paid-in capital of 50 million yen ($140,000). In Nagoya the minimum capital requirement is 25 million yen ($70,000), and elsewhere it is 15 million yen ($40,000).

There are two kinds of members: regular and *saitori,* or *nakadachi.* A regular member is a securities company whose principal activity consists in buying and selling securities on the floor of an exchange for customers or for its own account. Regular members are permitted to engage in underwriting, to promote mutual funds, and to act as depositories for customers' securities.

A *saitori,* or *nakadachi,* member is a company whose principal activity is that of serving as an intermediary between regular members. Each *saitori,* or *nakadachi,* member is assigned to a trading post to act as a specialist for particular issues. Specialists are not allowed to trade for their own account.

The Tokyo Securities Exchange has 112 members, of which 12 are *saitori* members and 100 are regular members. The Osaka Securities Exchange has 77 members, of which 11 are *nakadachi* members and 66 are regular members. The Nagoya Securities Exchange has 8 *saitori* members and 37 regular members. All members of the other six Japanese exchanges are regular members.

Listing Requirements. For several years only companies that met the "first section" requirements described below were permitted to have their shares traded on the floor of the Tokyo, Osaka, and Nagoya stock exchanges. As a result, shares of moderate-sized and of small companies could not meet the requirements for listing and so were traded in localized over-the-counter markets. By 1960 the turnover in the unorganized markets had reached significant volume. Accordingly, the three largest exchanges each established "second sections" in order to bring over-the-counter trading under control. Requirements for listing on a second section of an exchange are similar in nature but much less stringent than those for listing on a first section.

A company applying for listing on the first section must have been in existence for three years, must have a paid-in capital in excess of 1 billion yen ($2,800,000), and must have more than 3,000 stockholders. Presumably such a company has been listed previously on one of the smaller exchanges or on a second section of one of the larger exchanges. If so, to qualify for listing on the first section, its daily average volume of trading must have exceeded 200,000 shares. Finally, a company seeking listing on a first section must have paid cash dividends of not less than 10 per cent (of its par) for two consecutive years and must offer evidence of being able to continue paying dividends of like amount for the foreseeable future.

A company applying for listing on one of the smaller exchanges or on the second section of one of the larger exchanges must have been in existence for two years, must have a paid-in capital in excess of 100 million yen ($280,000), and must have no fewer than 250 shareholders. In addition, 5 per cent of its outstanding shares must be held by small investors (defined as those holding less than 5,000 shares). Such companies must have paid dividends of not less than 5 per cent (of par value) for three consecutive half years and must offer evidence of being able to continue payments at this rate for the foreseeable future.

Trading Procedure. There are 13 horseshoe-shaped posts on the first section trading floor of the Tokyo Securities Exchange and 11 on the first section floor of the Osaka Securities Exchange. Employees of *saitori* or *nakadachi* members stand at assigned points inside the posts, while representatives of regular members and employees of the exchange move about the area between the posts. (Altogether there are about 1,200 persons on the floor when trading is in process.)

When a clerk of a member firm receives an order from a client to buy or to sell a certain number of shares of a particular issue, he transmits the order by telephone to another clerk on the floor, who relays it by means of hand signals to one of the firm's representatives. The representative goes at once to the post where the particular issue is traded and places the order with the *saitori* or *nakadachi* member. The latter enters the details (number of shares, price, type of order, etc.) on his order sheet.

If the order is a market order, it is executed immediately at the lowest ask price if it is a buy order and at the highest bid price if it is a sell order. If the incoming order is a limited buy order, it is executed as soon as an offer arrives to sell the issue either at the market or at a specified price as low as the limited buy order. If the incoming order is a limited sell order, it is executed as soon as an offer arrives to buy the issue at the market or at a specified price as high as the limited sell order.

The opening price of each issue is established by the so-called "Itayese method." Under this method buying and selling orders are arrayed on a sheet, and a price is established that permits all market orders to be executed. The process is similar to *cotation par casiers* on the Paris Bourse.

The opening and closing prices of certain specific issues are set by the "Gekitaku method." Regular members with orders to buy or to sell these specific issues gather at a post located at the end of the floor. There a trained employee of the exchange conducts a two-sided auction of each issue in turn. When a price equating supply and demand is reached, he closes the trading in that issue by striking the desk with a wooden clapper. The procedure is somewhat similar in operation to the auction methods used at the posts on the trading floor of the Paris Bourse.

Unit of Trading. The issues on the Tokyo Securities Exchange are classified as (1) first section, first group; (2) first section, second group; and (3) second section. The unit of trading for the first classification is 1,000 shares and for the second and third classification 500 shares. The unit of trading for shares having a par value of 500 yen or more is 100 shares regardless of classification. First group shares are those which a securities financing corporation (of which there are three) accepts as collateral for loans.

The unit of trading on the Osaka Securities Exchange is 1,000 shares for the first section and 500 shares for the second section except for shares having a par value of 500 yen or more, in which case the unit of trading is 100 shares.

The unit of trading for all the other Japanese stock exchanges is 1,000 shares except on the Sapporo Securities Exchange, where it is 500 shares.

Purchasing by Foreigners. Foreigners who reside outside of Japan may purchase Japanese shares and make payment in certain foreign currencies.[2] However, purchasers using these currencies should authorize their brokers to validate the purchase. "Validation" grants a foreign purchaser a right to

[2] The following foreign currencies are acceptable: Austrian, Belgian, British, Canadian, Danish, Dutch, French, German, Italian, Norwegian, Portuguese, Swedish, Swiss, and United States.

withdraw dividends and the proceeds of a future sale in the currency in which payment was made. Shares purchased and validated may be transferred to other foreign investors without restriction and without loss of the withdrawal-of-funds privilege.

American owners of Japanese shares may not subscribe to new shares offered by rights financing unless the Japanese company registers the issue with the Securities Exchange Commission. Since it would rarely pay a Japanese issuer to register an issue merely for the convenience of a few shareholders residing in the United States, the effect is to force American holders to sell their holdings cum rights and to repurchase them ex rights.[3] This involves a double brokerage commission.

Foreigners residing in 17 specified countries are permitted by Japanese law to purchase securities and to pay for them in yen.[4] Such foreigners are free to sell their securities when they choose, but they may not withdraw dividends or the proceeds of sales by converting the funds into a foreign currency.[5]

Clearing.   All contracts executed on the floor of the Tokyo and Osaka securities exchanges are settled through a clearing department. The procedures used are not sufficiently different from those employed on the New York Stock Exchange to warrant separate description.

Margin Trading.   Regular members of Japanese stock exchanges are allowed to extend credit to customers on securities acceptable as collateral by stock financing corporations. This means that a broker may lend money to those who buy the specified issues and may lend shares of the specified issues to those who sell short.

Margin requirements are set by the Minister of Finance. There are two types of margin requirements: cash margins and equity margins. The cash margin requirement has varied since 1953 from 30 to 70 per cent of market value, and the equity margin requirement has varied from 50 to 70 per cent of market value.

An example may render the concepts of cash and equity margins clearer. Suppose that a trader purchases shares worth 100,000 yen at a time when the cash margin requirement is 30 per cent and the equity margin requirement is 70 per cent. The trader may choose one of two alternatives. He may deposit 30,000 yen in cash with his broker, in which case he has a debit

[3] Rights issued by Japanese companies are not transferable as they are in the United States; hence a shareholder cannot protect his equity by selling rights.

[4] The countries of residence are: Finland, France, Germany, Great Britain, Greece, India, Malaya, Norway, Pakistan, Sweden, Switzerland, Taiwan, Thailand, United States, Uruguay, and Yugoslavia.

[5] There are some exceptions to the right of foreigners residing outside the country to buy Japanese stocks with yen. Shares in banks, cement factories, chemicals, fisheries, mining, shipbuilding, transport industries, and public utilities may be purchased with yen only with governmental permission.

balance of 70,000 yen secured by collateral worth 100,000 yen. Or he may purchase the stock without cash by depositing other shares having a market value of 43,000 yen. In this case he has a debit balance of 100,000 yen secured by collateral worth 143,000 yen.[6] It will be noted that in both cases the market value of the collateral is 140 per cent of the debit balance.

In Japan margin traders must liquidate debit balances within a limited period of time. In Tokyo this period is ninety days; in Osaka and Nagoya, three calendar months. Traders pay interest on debit balances and are entitled to receive interest on credit balances.

When a customer purchases shares on margin, his broker borrows the necessary funds from a securities finance corporation, using the customer's shares as collateral. Similarly, when a customer sells an issue short, his broker borrows the shares from a securities finance corporation.[7]

Share Prices.   Japanese securities are quoted in yen; 3.6 yen at current rates of exchange are worth 1 cent in United States currency. Prices of shares quoted on the Tokyo Securities Exchange vary from 30 to 500 yen per share. For example, Yawata Iron & Steel Company shares closed at 58 on January 13, 1964. This price is the equivalent of 16 cents in United States money. The company earned 4.22 yen per share (1.3 cents) and paid a dividend of 4 yen (1.1 cents). If a United States investor were to purchase 1,000 shares of this issue, he would be committing funds of only $160. Thus a small United States investor in Japanese stocks must become accustomed to thinking of values in terms of cents and of volume in terms of thousands or tens of thousands of shares.

The Japanese have a stock market average, and like that in the United States it is called the Dow-Jones index. It is computed daily from the quotations of 225 leading issues. During 1963, the Japanese Dow-Jones index varied from a high of 1,634 to a low of 1,200.

Other Foreign Stock Exchanges

The histories, organizations, and practices of the stock exchanges located in Paris, London, and Japan have been presented in some detail. Stock exchanges exist also in most of the major cities of the world. Space does not permit a description of each of these. In most respects these exchanges resemble the ones described. Such minor differences as exist are the result of adaptation to local conditions.[8]

[6] The collateral consists of the shares deposited plus the shares purchased. It will be noted that 70 per cent of 43,000 yen is 30,000 yen, the amount of cash margin required on a purchase of 100,000 yen.

[7] There are three such corporations: Japan Securities Corporation, Osaka Securities Corporation, and Chubu Securities Financing Corporation.

[8] For a detailed description of some of these exchanges, see *Leading World Stock Exchanges,* by David K. Eiteman and Wilford J. Eiteman, vol. 1, 1964, and vol. 2, 1966 (Ann Arbor, Mich.: University of Michigan Bureau of Business Research).

part 2 THE INVESTOR
AND THE MARKET

5 types of securities

When economic organization was simple and the tools and machinery employed by business were few, the individual businessman could furnish all the capital that he needed out of his savings and his borrowing power based on his property, character, and ability. But as population increased and as better transportation made possible wider markets, more funds had to be provided to take care of the extensions of plant and of machinery required in order to meet the greater demands. The first step was for several men to pool their funds to secure the necessary increase in capital. Such cooperation, under proper restrictions and agreements, constituted a partnership. As population grew, as markets became more extensive, and as more complicated and more expensive machinery was invented, still more funds had to be assembled for the use of a single operating unit. The partnership type of organization served very well as long as only limited amounts of funds were needed, but it had serious limitations when large amounts had to be collected. Thus many persons with varied interests had to be induced to give funds to the organization. But these persons would not contribute their funds if they were required to become partners and, as such, to assume full responsibility for the acts of all other partners. In addition, many would refuse to put their funds into an organization so constituted that they could not withdraw them at will, without difficulty or expense; and this is the situation if their funds were put into a partnership. Moreover, large business units require continuing existence whereas partnerships have to be reorganized each time one of the partners dies or wishes to withdraw.

The development of the corporate organization was a long step forward in the economic organization of society. The corporation is an entity with indeterminate life. Ownership of its assets is represented by stock certificates which have been issued by the corporation to persons who have contributed funds or services as part owners. The principle of limited liability applies to the stock of all corporations. The stockholder's financial responsibility to the company is strictly limited to the par value of the stock he holds or to the amount he paid for the stock if it has no par value.

The corporation may borrow money and issue to its creditors its own obligations, usually in the form of certificates called bonds.

Both bonds and stocks can be transferred without difficulty from holder to holder so that both the stockholder and the bondholder can readily sell their rights in the company to other investors. This is especially true of those corporate stocks and bonds for which a wide and active market has developed.

Stock certificates may be written for any number of shares so that the man with small means may own stock. Corporate bonds usually come in $1,000 denominations, although smaller denominations are sometimes issued for the convenience of small investors.

As an instrument of production the corporate organization is exceedingly efficient. Its main features are relatively simple. The stockholders elect a board of directors to whom are delegated all questions of management except such general matters as increases or decreases of authorized capital stock, mergers, and liquidation. The directors elect the president, vice presidents, and other officers of the company, who carry out the plans of the directors.

The corporate organization is an efficient productive instrument, has indeterminate life, offers its owners limited liability, and issues bonds and certificates of stock that can be transferred from holder to holder without difficulty. It thus makes a wide appeal to all types of investors.

Capital and Capital Structure

Every corporation has a certain amount of wealth in the form of land, buildings, machinery, tools, raw materials, finished goods, patents, franchises, goodwill, investments, cash, and so forth, which it uses to produce goods or services. The object of the corporation and the technical processes required to accomplish its purpose determine whether land or buildings or perhaps patents, formulas, or goodwill shall constitute a large part of the wealth or supposed wealth employed by corporate management in production. These items appear as assets on the corporation's balance sheet, and the sum total of their marketable value, considering the corporation as a going concern, may be called the "capital" of the corporation. Such material goods as the corporation owns have been contributed by the owners and by the creditors. The wealth contributed by the owners is represented by certificates for the shares of stock which the owners hold. The total number of shares owned by the stockholders constitutes the total capital stock issued and outstanding. The number of shares of stock owned by stockholders multiplied by the par, or stated, value of the stock gives the "stock capitalization" of the corporation.

The fact that the par, or stated, value of the capital stock of a corporation amounts to $5 million is no guarantee that the actual land, machinery, and other property represented by the capital stock could be sold for such a sum. As a matter of fact the assets counterbalancing the stock may never have been worth the par, or stated, value of the stock; or, if they once did, bad management may have resulted in great decreases in their value.

After the formation of the corporation, the amount of stockholders' investment will change because of the retention of earnings. Stockholders' reinvestment of earnings is as much an investment in the business as their initial investment, but it is not reported as part of the par, or stated, value of the capital stock. Rather it is called "retained earnings," "reinvested earnings," or sometimes "earned surplus." After a time the retained earnings portion of the stockholders' investment may come to exceed the par, or stated, value of the original investment. The total stockholders' investment, which is the sum of the stated value of the capital stock, the capital surplus, and the retained earnings, constitutes the "stockholders' equity," or "net worth," of the business.

In many corporations a considerable part of the wealth indicated on the asset side of the balance sheet has been contributed by the creditors of the company. An important characteristic of a creditor's contribution of funds to a corporation is that the funds must be returned to the creditor sooner or later. If the date of return is near, the creditor's claim against the assets of the corporation will appear among the liabilities as a bill, note, or account payable. If the date of return is more distant, the creditor's claim will appear as a mortgage or bond payable. The sum of the par value of the capital stock and the par value of the mortgages, bonds, certificates, and notes may be called the "total capitalization" of the corporation.

It may be said, then, that the capital of a corporation is the plant, machinery, raw material, goods in process, goodwill, patents, and so forth— the total amount of wealth, tangible and intangible, employed by the corporation as a going concern. All the items on the asset side of the balance sheet, considered apart from their valuation in dollars, are the company's capital. The stock capitalization of the company is the sum total of the par, or stated, value of the stock outstanding, evidenced by stock certificates in the possession of stockholders. The total capitalization of a corporation is the sum of the par, or stated, value of all the capital stock outstanding and the mortgages, bonds, and notes—i.e., the relatively long-term debt. The sum of the investment of all long-term creditors and the stockholders' equity, including retained earnings, represents the total recorded value of the permanent investment in the company. This sum is usually called "capital structure" or "invested capital."

Stock and Bonds Distinguished

There are many differences between stock and bonds, some of which are described here.

Ownership versus Indebtedness.   Certificates of stock represent ownership in the corporation; bonds represent long-term debt. A stockholder is a part owner of the corporation. A bondholder is a creditor who has a claim against the corporation equal to the face value of his bond. If the claims of bondholders are paid off, whatever assets remain belong to the stockholders as a class. A share of stock indicates ownership of a fraction of the total value accruing to stockholders as a class. Ownership carries with it responsibility for the management of a company and presents a possibility of making a profit or a loss.

Security of Principal and Income.   A bond is a formal document obligating a corporation to pay a specific sum of money (called the "principal") on a specified date (known as the "maturity date") and to make periodic interest payments until the principal sum is paid. Bonds are usually issued in $1,000 denominations, although par values of $500 and $100 are not uncommon. Interest payments are usually semiannual.

A bondholder is almost certain to receive his interest payments when due and to recover his principal at maturity, because the failure of a company to make any one of these payments constitutes an act of insolvency.

By contrast a share of stock has no maturity date, and the issuing company does not bind itself to pay dividends. A shareholder's money remains in a company until the company is liquidated. A share of stock simply entitles its owner to a vote at the annual stockholders' meeting, to equal treatment on a share-for-share basis in any dividend distribution that may be made, and to receive a pro-rata portion of the residual assets of the company in case of liquidation. Thus a stockholder's welfare depends on the fortunes of the company. If net earnings available to common stock are large, the shareholder will find his investment profitable because of increased dividends and/or enhanced market value of the stock. On the other hand, if earnings available to the common stock decline, a stockholder may expect the dividend rate to be reduced and the market value of his share to shrink. The legal obligation of a company to pay the interest and the principal of a bond places the bond investor in a more secure position than the stockholder. This does not mean, however, that the common stock of one company may not be a better investment than the bond of another company.

Preferred stock is in a position midway between common stock and bonds. Preferred stock is not a debt obligation of a company, as is a bond, but it does usually have a prior claim to a fixed rate of dividends if a company has earnings and to assets equal to its par value if the company is liquidated. These claims are prior to those of common stockholders. However, a failure to pay dividends is not in itself an act of insolvency leading to bankruptcy.

Control.   Stock owners of a corporation control it. They take the major risks of the business and have the right to elect the directors of the company and to vote on fundamental policies of management. Bondholders, who are frequently large financial institutions such as banks and insurance companies, want an assured income. They do not want or expect to share in the work of management. Only if management by the stockholders fails to provide ample protection to the bonds do bondholders demand and receive a voice in management.

Reorganization. In the reorganization of a company after failure, bonds are likely to fare better than stock. Existing common stock may be wiped out. Preferred stockholders may be compelled to give up their preferred stock and to accept new common stock; junior bondholders may have to accept preferred stock for their bonds. The first mortgage bonds will suffer the least.

Common Stock

"Capital stock" refers to the aggregate equity ownership of a corporation. If several classes of capital stock exist, "common stock" is used to indicate that class of stock possessing the residual ownership. The term common stock is also frequently used to refer to capital stock when there is only one type of stock outstanding.

Certificates of Stock. The total ownership in a corporation is represented by the total amount of stock outstanding. The outstanding stock is divided into equal units, known as shares. Each share is interchangeable with every other share and carries with it the rights to income, property, and control that every other share does. Some stockholders own many shares, others few. As evidence of their rights in the corporation, each owner is issued one or more certificates of stock. A certificate may evidence one or many shares. The number of shares so evidenced is always written on the face of the certificate. A specimen stock certificate is shown in Figure 5–1.

A stock certificate attests that a specified holder is the owner of a certain number of shares of the common stock of the company, such shares being transferable on the books of the company on surrender of the certificate properly endorsed. The certificate is signed by the president or a vice president and one other of the following officers: secretary, assistant secretary, treasurer, and assistant treasurer. The certificates of most large corporations are not valid unless countersigned by a transfer agent and a registrar. The transfer agent is usually a bank or trust company that receives the certificate from the holder, cancels it, and issues a new certificate in the name of a new owner. Smaller corporations often act as their own transfer agents, designating the secretary or an assistant secretary to perform the work. The registrar is a bank or trust company separate from the transfer agent that registers the fact of the transfer and certifies that only the proper number of shares have been issued.

Fig. 5–1 A specimen stock certificate.

Authorized and Outstanding Stock. At the time of organization, promoters may plan for growth of the business by getting authorization in the corporate charter for an amount of stock larger than is needed at the moment. Suppose that the charter authorizes an issue of 200,000 shares of stock but that the corporation sells only 150,000 shares to stockholders; then 50,000 shares remain authorized but unissued. (Such unissued stock is not treasury stock.) At a later date the remaining 50,000 shares may be sold and issued to buyers and the proceeds used for expansion. Once the full 200,000 authorized shares have been issued and sold, the corporation must amend its charter before it can issue and sell additional shares.

By "outstanding stock" is meant such stock as has been issued and is now held by owners other than the corporation itself. A corporation may buy and hold part of its own stock and by so doing reduce its stock outstanding. In addition, the amount of outstanding stock may be reduced through the return by some stockholder of a part of his stock to the corporation. Such stock is usually called "treasury stock." The corporation may sell its treasury stock, in which case it again becomes outstanding; or it may cancel it, thus reducing the amount of issued stock. Canceled stock remains authorized.

Par Value of Stock. Today par value is of little practical significance to investors. Half a century ago a share of stock commonly had a face amount called "par value." Par value was supposed to represent the amount of capital originally paid in to the company for each share of stock, and if a share of stock were issued for less than par value, the directors had the right to assess the stockholder for the difference between purchase price and par value. The par value of all the shares of a company was regarded as a trust fund for the safety of the firm's creditors.

The intent of par value as a legal certification of the amount of original investment was easily circumvented. In many promotions shares of stock would be issued in return for property, patents, or trademarks alleged to be equal in value to the par value of the issued shares. In fact the property might be worth considerably less. Par value also ceased to reflect the original investment when subsequent expansion of a firm was financed by the sale of new shares of stock at a price which, because it reflected the past growth of the company, was above the par value of the shares.

For these reasons, plus the fact that transfer taxes were frequently levied on the par value of stock, a trend developed in the 1920s for corporations to change from par-value to no-par-value stock. No-par-value stock would be carried on the corporation's records at an arbitrarily stated value. In recent years the trend has been back to par-value stocks having an arbitrarily low par value, such as $1 per share. Par value may be regarded as arbitrarily low when the shares of stock are sold initially at a price substantially in excess of par value. The additional investment in the company above par value is carried on the books under some title such as "Capital Surplus" or "Shareholders' Investment in Excess of Par Value."

Fortune magazine's July 1963 list of the 500 largest United States industrial corporations included 432 firms with shares listed on a national exchange. The par value of the shares was as follows:

	Number of companies	Per cent of total
No-par stock	65	15
Par value less than $1	19	5
Par value of $1	112	26
Par value between $1 and $10	169	39
Par value of $10	40	9
Par value above $10	27	6
	432	100

The range of par values was from as low as 25¢ per share for Merganthaler Linotype to as high as $50 per share for Anaconda Company.

It is now common for stock certificates to have the inscription "fully paid and nonassessable" on their face. This ensures that stockholders' shares of stock were not originally sold to the public for less than par value and that there is no possibility of additional assessment.

Stock Rights.   When for any reason directors and stockholders decide to increase the amount of capital stock of their company, it is customary to give each stockholder the privilege to subscribe to his portion of the new shares. At times this is required by the corporate charter. If there are 200,000 shares outstanding and 50,000 new shares are to be issued, then each group of 4 old shares carries the right to subscribe to 1 new share. The corporation issues to each stockholder a certificate giving him a number of rights equal to the number of shares he holds. In this case a stockholder with 4 rights would be able to buy 1 new share of stock from the company at a price which would be somewhat lower than the market price of the stock outstanding. If the old shares were selling for $40 per share, the subscription price might be set at $35 per share. In such a case a stockholder possessing 4 rights clearly has a document of value—in this case the value of the 4 rights would be $5 and the value of a single right $1.25.

If the investor did not choose to invest in the new shares of stock, he might sell his rights on the market. The bundle of 4 rights would bring at least $5 as long as the stock was valued at $40, but the rights would bring more or less if the market value of the stock rose above or fell below $40. The mechanical aspects of issuing rights and of trading them in on the market are treated fully in Chapter 17.

Dividends.   A dividend is a distribution of corporate earnings among stockholders. A dividend may be paid in cash or in property, or it may be in the form of issuance and distribution of additional shares of stock.

When the board of directors of a company decide to pay a dividend, they announce the amount of the dividend on a per share basis and select a "date of record." Each shareholder will thus receive an amount equal to the per share dividend multiplied by the number of shares he holds. The dividend is sent to the person whose name appears on the records as the owner of the shares on the date of record.

Cash dividends are usually declared and paid on a quarterly basis, but semiannual and annual payments are not unusual. As mentioned, a dividend may be made payable in stock. In such a case the dividend is paid by issuing one new share of stock to the shareholder for each specified number of old shares held. For example, a 10 per cent stock dividend means that 1 new share will be issued for each 10 shares outstanding. A problem arises about what to do with fractional shares. For example, if a shareholder holds 12 shares at the time when a 10 per cent stock dividend is declared, he is entitled to receive $1\frac{1}{5}$ new shares. Some companies solve the problem by issuing certificates for the fractional shares and permit shareholders to accumulate the fractions until they equal a full share. Other companies purchase the fractional shares for cash and sell them on the market as whole shares. By the latter plan, the stockholder mentioned above receives 1 new share and cash equal to one fifth the market value of a share.

The declaration of a stock dividend does not increase the net worth of a corporation. All that happens is that each share of outstanding stock henceforth represents a smaller proportion of the aggregate net worth, which has not changed.

As mentioned, dividends are occasionally made payable in property other than cash. After World War I several companies declared dividends payable in the Liberty bonds they had purchased during the course of the war. A company engaged in promoting real estate might declare a dividend payable in lakeside lots. At the time of passage of the Eighteenth Amendment several distilleries declared dividends payable in liquor. A dividend payable in shares of stock of a subsidiary company is called a "spin-off."

Dividends are classified as "regular" and as "extra." The fact that a dividend is labeled regular implies that the stockholder may expect to receive the dividend periodically. If a dividend is labeled extra, this probably means that the directors do not want the stockholders to consider the increased dividend rate as permanent. A declaration of a large extra dividend is generally known as "cutting a melon." Extra dividends may be paid in cash or in property or in stock. Stock dividends are frequently extra dividends.

The board of directors of a company has the sole power to declare a dividend payable on both the preferred and the common stock. The policy may be to pay dividends each year equal to most of the earnings or to pay small dividends or no dividends and to retain the undistributed earnings for reinvestment.

On the New York Stock Exchange shares are traded ex dividend on the third business day before the date of record set by a company's board of directors. Thus, if one buys a share of stock on a Tuesday when the following Friday is the date of record, one acquires the stock without the right to receive the dividend. If the same stock is purchased on Monday, the purchaser receives the dividend.

Transfer of Stocks.   On the back of a stock certificate is found a form for assignment of the stock to a new holder. The New York Stock Exchange requires that the following form be used on all listed stocks:

> For value received................hereby sell, assign, and transfer
> unto ....
> ....
> ....shares of the capital[1] stock
> represented by the within certificate and do hereby irrevocably consti-
> tute and appoint...
> ....attorney to transfer the said

---

[1] On certificates without nominal or par value the word "capital" may be omitted.

stock on the books of the within named company with full power of
substitution in the premises.

Dated................................. 19....

....

In presence of

....

NOTICE: The signature of this assignment must correspond with the
name as written upon the face of the certificate in every particular
without alteration or enlargement, or any change whatever.

The transfer of title, according to this assignment, is without condition,
and the power of attorney cannot be recalled once it is given. The notice
calls attention to the fact that the Exchange requires that the signature of
the holder as signed to the assignment blank conform in every particular
to that written on the face of the stock certificate.

From the point of view of the company, title to ownership is not transferred by the present holder to a new holder until the old certificate has
been canceled and a new certificate has been issued to the new owner in
his own name and until the name has been changed on the books of the
company.

If a holder of a certificate for 100 shares of stock sells his stock, the
buyer will want the stock put in his name on the books of the company
and will want a certificate attesting his ownership. The seller correctly endorses his certificate and hands it to the buyer, who sends the certificate to
the company or to the company's transfer agent. The agent makes out a new
certificate in the name of the new owner, has the appropriate signatures
attached, and sends the new certificate to the new address. The old certificate
is canceled and attached to the proper stub in the stock book.

If the owner of the 100-share certificate sells only 50 shares, then he
endorses the certificate, signifying that 50 shares are to be transferred to
the name of the buyer, and sends it to the transfer agent, who makes out
two certificates, one for 50 shares in the old owner's name and the other
for 50 shares in the new owner's name. After the proper signatures have
been attached, the agent sends the two certificates to their respective owners.
The old certificate for 100 shares is canceled and attached to its stub, and
the books are changed to show that the old owner now holds only 50 shares
and that a new stockholder has been added to the family of proprietors,
with an interest in the company amounting to 50 shares of its stock.

Suppose that an owner of stock has sold or desires to sell his stock
through broker A. How shall he fill in the assignment blank? In order to
avoid the difficulties connected with lost or stolen certificates, a good plan
is to mail the stock certificate unendorsed and to mail separately a detached
assignment form endorsed in blank. If the separate assignment form is lost
or stolen, the holder can do nothing with it unless he also has the relevant

stock certificate. This is unlikely, especially if the two envelopes are sent by different mails. Moreover, if the stock certificate unendorsed is lost or stolen, nothing can be done with it by the finder or thief unless he has the relevant detached assignment form.

If the owner writes the name of the broker in the blank space conferring the power of attorney, then the latter must attach a form which substitutes another person to act as his attorney for the purpose of transferring title. For example, if a broker sold the stock represented by a certificate so endorsed as to grant him power of attorney, on delivering the certificate he would be required to attach a substitute power of attorney signed in blank or signed with the purchasing broker's name given as the substitute attorney. A common form of a power of substitution is as follows:

I (or we) hereby irrevocably constitute and appoint. . . . .
. . . . my (or our) substitute to transfer the within named stock under the foregoing power of attorney, with like power of substitution.
Dated. . . . .   19. . . .
. . . .

In the presence of
. . . .

The simplest form of endorsement is the endorsement in blank, which consists of the signature of the owner, with the spaces for the name of the new owner and the attorney left blank. When this form of assignment is properly witnessed, the certificate may pass from hand to hand without further endorsement, as if it were currency or a bearer credit instrument such as a coupon bond or bearer check. Whenever a holder desires to have the certificate recorded in his own name, he signs it in the first blank space at the top of the assignment form, leaving the space for the name of the attorney empty. On receipt of the certificate the transfer agent will insert his own name into this space.

The signature of the owner to the assignment "must correspond with the name as written upon the face of the certificate in every particular without alteration or enlargement, or any change whatever" to meet the requirements of the New York Stock Exchange and exchanges generally. An unmarried woman should have the word "Miss" prefixed to her name on the face of a stock certificate. It must then be endorsed with the same prefix for transfer.

If the name of the stockholder has been misspelled or otherwise incorrectly entered on the face of the certificate, an endorsement made by writing first the name as it stands on the certificate followed by the name correctly written as is done in the case of checks makes the certificate nondeliverable. The certificate must be returned to the corporation, which must write in the words "correct name is . . . ," with the correct name entered. The transfer agent who countersigned the certificate as originally written must sign the correction.

The assignment provides a space for the name of a witness to the signature. Anyone may act as witness except that in a few states a married woman's assignment of a stock certificate must be acknowledged before a notary public.

It is the custom of members of the New York Stock Exchange to guarantee the execution of the assignment of stock received by them from their clients for sale on the Exchange. A proper representative of the firm writes his name below that of the witness. This means that the firm guarantees to the future holder that the signature is genuine and that the person making the assignment has full right to do so. The law holds the firm responsible if the signature is a forgery or if the assignment is not made with the proper authority. If there is uncertainty about the signature, the assignment should be guaranteed by the customer's bank or acknowledged by a notary public.

A certificate in proper form, properly witnessed and guaranteed by a member of the Exchange, is good delivery on the Exchange and may pass from hand to hand without modification.

Suppose that an owner of stock takes out a loan at his bank and pledges shares of stock as collateral. To protect itself against loss, the bank requires him to put the stock into transferable form. How shall he proceed with the assignment?

Since the certificate will be held by a bank, it is probable that a blank endorsement will involve the least inconvenience to all concerned. If the endorsement is placed on the stock certificates, then, when the loan is paid, the bank will return the collateral to its owner, endorsed in blank. In order to avoid the risk involved in holding endorsed certificates, the custom is to have the borrower endorse in blank detached assignment forms, which are destroyed upon payment of the loan and return of the collateral.

Preferred Stock

Many corporations have both common stock and preferred stock outstanding. Preferred stock gives investors a larger return than bonds and at the same time offers them greater safety than common stock. From the legal point of view, preferred stock constitutes an ownership interest which has been given certain preference over common stock. From an investment point of view, preferred stock resembles a weak bond investment.

Preferred stock is characterized primarily by its prior claim to income. A 7 per cent preferred stock means that the stockholder will receive a 7 per cent dividend annually before any dividends can be paid on the common stock. The dividend rate may be expressed as a per cent of the par value of the preferred stock, as for example, the 7 per cent cumulative preferred stock of United States Steel Corporation, which has a par value per share of $100. In this case the annual dividend is $7. Frequently, the dividend rate of preferred stock is expressed in dollar terms, as, for example, the $5 cumulative preferred stock of General Motors Corporation. This stock has no par value. The holder receives a $5 dividend per share per year.

Preferred stock may or may not possess a number of other preferential characteristics, depending upon provisions in the corporate charter. The more important of these possible characteristics are described here.

Cumulative Dividends.   Most modern preferred stock is cumulative, meaning that the stock retains the right to receive all back dividends which have not been paid. Preferred dividends are payable only on order of the board of directors. Failure to pay a preferred dividend does not constitute a breach of contract. Directors may stop paying preferred stock dividends when the earnings of the company are insufficient or even when they prefer to retain funds in the company for expansion. The only pressure on the directors to pay is the fact that dividends on the common stock cannot be paid until after the payment of preferred dividends. If the preferred stock is cumulative, all past unpaid dividends as well as current dividends must be distributed before dividend payments to the common stockholders can begin. If preferred dividends are passed for many years, a large accumulation can exist. For example, as of June 1964, the accumulated arrearage on the $7 cumulative preferred stock of Eastern States Corporation was $110.25 per share. The stock was selling at about $190 per share.

If preferred stock is not cumulative, the board of directors can manipulate dividend payments so that the preferred stock loses most of its income preference over the common stock. To illustrate, assume that a company just earns the dividend on a noncumulative preferred in a lean year but that in the next year it earns more than is needed for the preferred. If the directors pass all dividends in the first of the two years, they may pay a single preferred dividend in the second year and distribute the remainder of the earnings of the two years to the common stockholders. In this way, the dividends not paid to the preferred stockholders in the first year are added to the potential dividend of the common stockholders in the second year. Clearly a noncumulative preferred stock is relatively unattractive. Most currently outstanding issues of noncumulative preferred stock were created during reorganizations, at which time the holders had little choice as to the form of salvage they would accept on their original investment.

Participation in Residual Earnings.   Most preferred stock is nonparticipating, meaning that the preferred stockholder receives only his stated dividend and no more. The theory is that the preferred stockholder has surrendered any claim to the residual earnings of his company in return for the right to receive his dividend before dividends are paid to common stockholders. Occasionally an issue of preferred stock is made participating. After the participating preferred stock receives its stipulated dividend, it shares additional earnings in some fashion with the common stockholders. An example of a participating preferred stock is Arden Farms Company's $3 cumulative preferred stock. This stock has the prior claim to cumulative dividends of $3 per share; and, in addition, whenever a dividend is declared on the common, there must be declared upon each preferred share an amount equal to one-fourth the dividend declared on each common share. However, additional dividends on the preferred are limited to a maximum $1 per share in any calendar year.

Voting Rights.   Preferred stock does not normally confer voting rights on the owners. However, votes may be provided by the corporate charter, and companies incorporated in Illinois and Mississippi must provide voting rights for holders of preferred stock under the laws of those states. In general, though, the voting right is regarded as having been surrendered by the preferred stockholders in return for a prior claim to dividends. In the event that preferred dividends are passed, however, preferred stockholders are frequently given certain voting rights. Since 1940 the listing requirements of the New York Stock Exchange have required that preferred stockholders be given the right to elect two directors if as many as six quarterly dividends are passed.

Redemption Provisions.   Preferred stockholders may recover their principal from the company either by sharing in the assets when the corporation is liquidated or by having their shares called. Almost all preferred stock has preference as to assets in liquidation, meaning that if the corporation is dissolved the preferred stockholders will recover their invested principal before the common stockholders receive a liquidating dividend. This preference, however, must be stated in the corporate charter; otherwise preferred stock will share equally with the common in the proceeds of liquidation. The amount that preferred stock receives when it has preference to assets in liquidation is usually either the par value, if the stock has a par value, or a stated value for no-par shares, plus any accumulated dividend arrearage.

Preferred stock may be redeemed during the life of the company if the corporate charter provides for calling the stock and if the directors decide the stock should be called. Most modern preferred stock is callable, at the option of the directors, at a price stated in the charter. This price is usually 5 to 10 per cent above the par value or the stated value in liquidation. The premium is to compensate the investor for the disadvantage of having his stock called away from him.

Directors may call the preferred stock with general funds at their disposal, or a sinking fund may have been provided which earmarks a certain portion of yearly earnings for the purpose of retiring preferred stock. Preferred stock is equity capital, however, and the failure of the company to earn money with which to retire the preferred stock does not constitute an act of insolvency. Money available for the retirement of preferred stock is used either to call the stock or to purchase the stock on the market when its price is below the call price. For example, if the preferred stock of XYZ Company is callable at $108 per share and is selling at $102 per share, it is advantageous for the company to purchase the stock in the market until such time as the price rises above $108. When the stock is priced below $108, the retirement program operates to the investors' advantage, for the additional demand tends to support the price. However, the existence of a call price also acts to the investors' detriment, for the price cannot go above $108 without investors risking the immediate loss of part of their investment. Prices will sometimes rise slightly above the call price because investors believe the company is not likely to call the stock.

In Great Britain the term "preference stock" is used to mean preferred stock.

American Depositary Receipts

American depositary receipts, commonly called "ADRs," are negotiable receipts of a New York bank for foreign securities held by that bank in a foreign country. ADRs provide a convenient way for American residents to buy, hold, and sell foreign stocks.

Americans who choose to buy foreign securities directly encounter a number of difficulties. Physical transfer at the time of purchase and again at the time of sale is delayed by the many miles over which the securities must be sent. Postage and insurance add to the cost of making international deliveries. The bearer form of common stock certificate used on the European continent is unfamiliar to American investors, and American investors frequently have difficulty in learning about dividends and in presenting the appropriate dividend coupon to the proper bank for collection. Complicated forms are frequently required to avoid paying foreign taxes on dividends or sales proceeds. If the stocks are registered, the transfer office will be in a foreign country and the transfer process may involve complicated forms in an unfamiliar language. When dividends or sales proceeds are received, there may be a currency exchange problem. If a stockholder dies while holding foreign securities, it may be necessary to go through probate procedure in a foreign country as well as in the United States before title to the security can be transferred. In many cases married women are under certain legal disabilities with regard to the ownership of foreign securities.

Because of these complications several New York banks issue American depositary receipts in this country against foreign securities held in their depositaries abroad. These receipts are occasionally called "American shares" or "New York shares" instead of ADRs. Ownership of such a receipt provides an American investor with an American-type certificate evidencing ownership of shares of foreign stock. The underlying foreign security is held abroad in the bank's depository, and the bank collects dividends in the foreign country, converts them to United States dollars, and sends dollar dividend checks to the American ADR holders.

Thus the American investor in foreign securities receives a familiar and convenient type of security. ADRs are quickly and easily transferable in this country, for the seller need only endorse his certificate in blank and deliver it in order to bring about a change of the registered holder on the books of the New York bank; no change in legal title to the underlying securities abroad is necessary. The bank provides further service by looking after subscription rights, enabling the American investor to exercise his rights if they are registered with the SEC, or selling the rights abroad and remitting the proceeds in dollars to the investor. Depository banks also supply annual reports and proxy forms to American investors on request.

Physical Form of ADRs.   ADRs are engraved certificates, much like stock certificates. They indicate on the face the name of the issuing depository, the terms of the depository arrangement, the name of the registered holder, and the number of ADR shares which the certificate evidences. Both 100-share certificates and odd-lot certificates are used. One ADR share may be equivalent to one foreign share, or the ratio may be changed to give the ADR a convenient value for American investors. For example, one share of the Simca ADR is equivalent to $\frac{1}{2}$ share of capital stock in the French company, while one share of the Sony ADR is equivalent to 10 shares in the Japanese company. Most ADRs are issued by five large New York banks: Morgan Guaranty Trust Company, Chase Manhattan Bank, Irving Trust Company, Chemical Bank–New York Trust Company, and First National City Bank.

Market for ADRs.   ADRs are traded in the regular markets in the United States. Seven are listed on the New York Stock Exchange, and 24 are listed on the American Stock Exchange. Over 180 ADRs are traded in the normal over-the-counter market in the United States.

An American holder of ADRs who wishes to sell his securities will do so in the United States market. However, if he wishes, he may sell the underlying securities in the foreign stock market, surrender his ADRs to the New York bank which created them, and instruct the New York bank to release the underlying securities in the foreign country. This release may be accomplished by air mail or by cable. The procedure permits international arbitrage in foreign securities and tends to keep the American price of ADRs in line with the price of the same securities abroad.

Cost of ADRs. New York banks charge certain fees for their handling of American depositary receipts. Typical fees are given here:

1. For the issuance of an American depositary receipt, or for the surrender of such receipt and the delivery of the underlying shares, for each 100 American depositary shares or fraction thereof:

   If the market price of the ADR
   share is: The fee is:

$5 or less	$3
$5.01 to $10	$4
$10 or over	$5

2. For transferring an ADR, the fee is $1.50 for each receipt of 100 shares or fraction thereof.
3. For splits or consolidations not involving transfer, the fee is $1 for each receipt issued.
4. For disbursing dividends to holders of ADRs, the fee is 1 cent per ADR, plus taxes and charges.

Bearer Depositary Receipts. Morgan Guaranty Trust Company of New York also issues bearer depositary receipts for the benefit of continental European investors who want bearer certificates to represent their investment in American stocks. A BDR issued through the European office of the bank represents the purchase and deposit in New York of the shares of certain American companies. These shares are registered in the name of the Morgan Guaranty Trust Company. A European investor obtains the same advantages as does an American holder of ADRs, including having his securities in a form which fits continental European customs and practices. A BDR has an appropriate number of coupons attached, and when dividends are declared in the United States, the fact is advertised in newspapers both in the United States and abroad. BDR holders receive their dividends, either cash or stock, by depositing their BDRs temporarily with the designated depository abroad or by surrendering a designated coupon. Subscription to additional shares and voting are handled in the same way.

As with the ADR, bearer depositary receipts enable international arbitrage to take place between the security markets of the world.

Other Types of Stock

Class A and Class B Stock. Common stock may be divided into two or more classes. The distinction between classes may be the same as that between preferred and common stock, the class A stock being in effect preferred stock and the class B stock being ordinary common. More often the distinction between classes lies in the voting rights, class A having a vote and class B having no vote. The combinations of rights as between classes is limited only by the imagination of those who organize the companies.

The stock structure of the Ford Motor Company is a good example of the use of classified common stock. Common stock of Ford Motor Company is divided into three classes as follows:

Class A stock	50,558,070 shares equaling	46% of the total
Class B stock	12,583,360 shares equaling	11% of the total
Common stock	47,170,826 shares equaling	43% of the total
Total capital stock	110,312,256 shares equaling	100% of the total

All classes of capital stock share equally on a per-share basis in dividends and in the event of liquidation of assets. The class A stock is entirely owned by the Ford Foundation and is nonvoting. It may be converted into ordinary common if sold to the general public. The class B stock is entirely owned by the Ford family or their trusts or corporations and by the Edison Institute. The stock receives a number of votes per share such that the voting power of the class B stock as a whole is equal to 40 per cent of the total voting power of all voting stockholders. Class B stock may also be converted into ordinary common if sold to the general public.

The common stock is owned by the general public and receives one vote per share, the total voting power of the common stock being limited to 60 per cent of the total vote.

It will be seen that the Ford family, which owns 11 per cent of the total stock outstanding and 21 per cent of the voting stock, is able by the device of classified stock to have 40 per cent of the vote in the corporation.

Guaranteed Stock.   This term refers to the common or preferred stock of a company that has been leased or that has become subsidiary to another company through some form of combination. The guarantor company contracts to pay an amount that will provide a regular stated dividend to the stockholders of the company whose stock is guaranteed. The amount of the guarantee is an unconditional fixed charge of the guarantor company.

Guaranteed stocks are found in industrials and rails; in the latter, they usually arise as the result of the lease by a larger railroad of a smaller one. The lessee company agrees to pay interest charges on funded debt, taxes, and an annual rental in cash equal to an agreed rate on the outstanding common stock. A large industrial company may likewise lease the property of another industrial and guarantee to pay its taxes, fixed charges, and a specified dividend on its stock.

An example of guaranteed stock is the common stock of Beech Creek Railroad Company, listed on the New York Stock Exchange. The entire railroad was leased to the New York Central Railroad effective October 1, 1890, for 999 years for a rental which included payment of 4 per cent per annum dividends on the par value of the common stock of the railroad. The bid and ask for Beech Creek common stock was $37\frac{1}{2}$ to 39 on June 8, 1964.

Debenture Stock.   The term "debenture stock" is not in common use in the United States. Because of its infrequent use, no well-defined meaning of the term has developed. For many years E. I. du Pont de Nemours & Co. had outstanding approximately 1,100,000 shares of 6 per cent cumulative stock which it called debenture stock but which was in effect preferred stock. This stock had a par value of $100, was callable at $125, and in case of liquidation had preference as to assets over the common up to par value plus accumulated dividends. In case of default of dividends for six months, the debenture stock, which was otherwise nonvoting, assumed sole control of the company to the exclusion of the common stock. In October 1939, the company offered to exchange $1\frac{1}{8}$ shares of $4.50 cumulative preferred no-par stock. About 97 per cent of the holders of the old debenture stock accepted this offer. The balance of the debenture stock was called at $125.

In Great Britain the expression debenture stock is used to refer to a debt type of obligation which may or may not be secured by a mortgage. Unsecured debt is also called "unsecured loan stock." For example, Dunlop Rubber Company, Ltd., has outstanding £3,169,000 of $3\frac{1}{2}$ per cent first mortgage debenture stock.

Voting Trust Certificates.   One of the methods of concentrating control of a company is the creation of a voting trust, whereby stockholders deposit their stock with a group of persons acting as trustees. The stock is transferred on the books of the company to the trustees so that they become the stockholders and have full right of voting the stock. The trustees issue to the stockholders, in exchange for their stock, certificates of beneficial interest called "voting trust certificates." These certificates entitle the holder to receive the dividends paid on the stock and, upon the termination of the voting trust, to receive the number of shares of stock of the company held by the trustees in exchange for the certificates. Voting trust certificates are listed on the New York Stock Exchange and other exchanges and are actively traded.

Bonds

The bondholder, like the stockholder, aids in financing a corporate enterprise. However, the funds that he contributes to the enterprise must be returned to him on the maturity date of the bond, and in addition he must receive an annual, semiannual, or quarterly interest payment. Failure of a corporation to meet any one of these obligations leads it into immediate financial difficulties. Obviously, the bondholder should be considered a *creditor* rather than an owner of a corporation.

Bonds have par value, generally $1,000, although pars of $500 and $100 are not uncommon. The interest rate specified on a bond refers to its par value. Thus a 5 per cent, $1,000-par-value bond sold to an investor for $926.50 and having 10 years to run would pay $50 interest each year, but the yield to the investor would be 6 per cent. The yield of a bond is the annual interest payment, plus a portion of the discount or minus a portion of the premium, divided by the investment in the bond. The interest payment in the above case is $50. The theoretical increase in value of the bond during the first year would be $5.59. The sum of these two items, $55.59, divided by the price, $926.50, gives 0.06; thus the yield is 6 per cent.

The names attached to bonds are usually intended to be descriptive of the bondholder's contractual rights in the corporation. Thus a "first mortgage" bond means that the bondholder's claim is secured by a mortgage against the corporation's assets. Similarly, a "second mortgage" bond means that the bondholder's claim against the assets is subject to the prior lien of a first mortgage. A "divisional mortgage" bond might mean that the bondholder was secured by a first mortgage on one division of the corporation's assets, whereas a "general mortgage" bond would mean that the bondholder's claim was junior to one or more underlying bond issues. A "debenture" bond is a general claim against the corporation, no particular assets being pledged as security. The title "collateral trust" bond suggests that the assets pledged are stocks and bonds of other corporations placed in the possession of a trustee. In an "equipment trust" bond the bondholder's security is the *title* to movable equipment which the corporation "rents" until the rent payments pay for the property. In such a case the failure of a corporation to pay an instalment when due enables the bondholder to seize his property and to sell it to some other corporation.

Sometimes a part of the name attached to a bond issue refers to the method of paying it off. Thus a "sinking fund" bond probably means that the corporation is periodically setting aside funds with which it will ultimately redeem the bonds. A "serial" bond issue is one in which a certain number of bonds mature each year. If a bond issue is "callable," it may be paid off at any time convenient to the corporation prior to maturity. "Convertible" bonds may be exchanged at the option of the bondholders for preferred or common stock in some specified ratio.

A whole list of names—refunding, expansion, consolidation, and the like—refer to the purpose of the issue. Other descriptive terms are occasionally added to the title merely to increase its sales appeal. For example, an issue subject to a number of small junior issues might be called a "first consolidated." If this were the first bond issue sold since the company had consolidated, the title would be literally true but the real purpose in choosing such a title might be a hope that investors would confuse "first" with "first mortgage." Since the passage of the Securities Act of 1933 it is unlawful for issuers to use a name the effect of which is to mislead investors.

6 brokerage offices

A young man accompanies a friend to a brokerage office. It is the first time he has made such a visit. On entering, he finds himself in a large room filled with the din of persons talking, telephones ringing, and the irregular buzzing of an electric quotation board that covers one entire wall. The major portion of the room is given over to a number of cubicles, where conservatively dressed men of various ages work at desks. Some of these men are conversing with customers, while others are talking on the telephone. They glance at the quotation board frequently. In the center of the board is a long, narrow screen, called a "Trans-lux," across which a series of letters and numbers are moving. Placed around the office are a dozen or more comfortable chairs for customers to occupy while they focus their attention on the symbols projected on the screen.

Some of the persons in the room appear excited; others are calm. Many are smoking; some are reading the newspaper. The normal impression is of a very busy place, although on some days this is not true. Impressed by the din and bustle, the young man may well imagine that fortunes are being made and lost in the room before his eyes. He may also imagine that the men sitting and standing about are very shrewd and very rich. The whole scene appears mysterious, confusing, and unintelligible. But later visits will enable the young man to analyze this confused whole into its parts, and it is these parts which this chapter attempts to describe.

The Member Firm

The brokerage office which the young man entered probably belongs to a firm that is a member of the New York Stock Exchange. On January 1, 1964, there were 670 such member firms, having over 3,400 offices in some 859 cities in the United States and 24 foreign countries. Member firms are private partnerships or corporations with offices to contact and serve the public. They receive orders from customers and transmit them to the New York Stock Exchange for execution. The Exchange supervises and regulates its member firms to ensure that they maintain adequate capital and that they conduct their business in the interests of the general public. Some firms have only one office in one location, while others operate a large number of offices scattered throughout the country. One large firm, for example, maintains 137 offices in 35 states, plus branches in 13 foreign countries. Large national firms are frequently called "wire houses" because of the large communications network they must maintain.

Upon entering a brokerage office, a customer is usually greeted by a smiling woman receptionist, who offers to help him or to direct him to a registered representative. The customer may talk to the registered representative, or if he prefers, he may simply browse in the office library or sit and watch the quotation board. In many instances he will find himself ignored unless he asks for attention.

The Registered Representative

The employee of a brokerage firm with whom a customer has most contact is known as a "registered representative." Some customers refer to him as their "broker." In some firms he is called an "account executive," a "customer's man," or a "stock salesman." Regardless of what he may be called, he is the firm's contact with the public; he solicits and processes orders for listed and unlisted securities.

A registered representative must be at least twenty-one years old and a person of good character and business repute. In addition, he must have received adequate training in the securities business and must have passed the examinations given by the New York Stock Exchange and by the National Association of Security Dealers. He must have filed a signed statement with the New York Stock Exchange, agreeing to abide by its rules relating to ethics and business conduct. A violation of any of these rules is grounds for loss of registration and expulsion from his position with the member firm.

The Quotation Board

Most brokerage offices operated by members of the New York Stock Exchange have a quotation board. On this board transactions in the different issues traded on the floor of the Exchange are reported, sale by sale, as they occur. The board is a complicated affair, but an experienced board watcher can at a glance get a comprehensive view of the day's market. Some brokerage offices rely upon electronic data-giving machines in place of quotation boards, on the theory that the quiet atmosphere created by these recently invented machines is more conducive to the kind of investment activity which they wish to encourage among their clientele.

Electric Quotation Boards.   Quotation boards are of two types: the modern electric board and the old chalk board. Electric boards are manufactured by and may be leased from Teleregister Corporation or Scantlin Electronics, Inc. The boards consist of several hundred or more black and gray panels placed adjacent to each other along one wall of a brokerage office. Each panel reports on transactions in a particular issue. A typical bank of panels appears in Figure 6–1.

The ticker symbol for each issue appears at the top of each panel in large white letters. For example, the AMR in the first panel in Figure 6–1 refers to American Airlines. To the right of this symbol appear two prices in small white letters. The uppermost of the two, $27\frac{1}{8}$ in the case of American Airlines, is the highest price and the lowermost, $19\frac{3}{8}$ in the case of American Airlines, is the lowest price at which the stock has traded during the current calendar year.

Below this information are five sets of numerical indicators not dissimilar to the price mechanisms on a modern cash register. Each set of indicators appears as a two- or three-digit price in white. This number represents the price of the stock in whole dollars. Following the two- or three-digit number is another figure in orange. This orange digit represents a fraction of a dollar in eighths. (Prices in the stock market are always expressed in eighths.) Thus, a figure of 204 where the 2 and the 0 are in white and the 4 is in orange indicates a price of 20 and $\frac{4}{8}$ dollars, or \$20.50.

The topmost of the five prices shown in each column of Figure 6–1 is the closing price of the previous day. The second from the top is the price at which the first sale of the current day was executed and is referred to as the "open." Note that American Airlines (AMR) opened at $20\frac{5}{8}$, or up $\frac{1}{8}$ point from the previous close, while Braniff Airways (BNF) opened at the same price as on the previous day. (In stock market parlance a point is a dollar.)

The third price in the column is the highest price and the fourth price in the column is the lowest price at which the stock has traded during the day. The bottom price is the price at which the last transaction was executed.

While watching the board, an observer will hear a whirring noise caused by the revolutions of the electric price indicators. When trading is active, the noise is continuous and distracting. When trading is slow, the noise is sporatic and barely audible. Habitual brokerage-office traders have instinctively come to accept the intensity of the din as a rough indicator of market activity.

The panels of an electric board may be arranged alphabetically by company name or by ticker symbol, but sometimes they are grouped by industry classifications. The panels shown in Figure 6–1 are an example of the latter. Frequently a portion of a board is reserved for the most recent

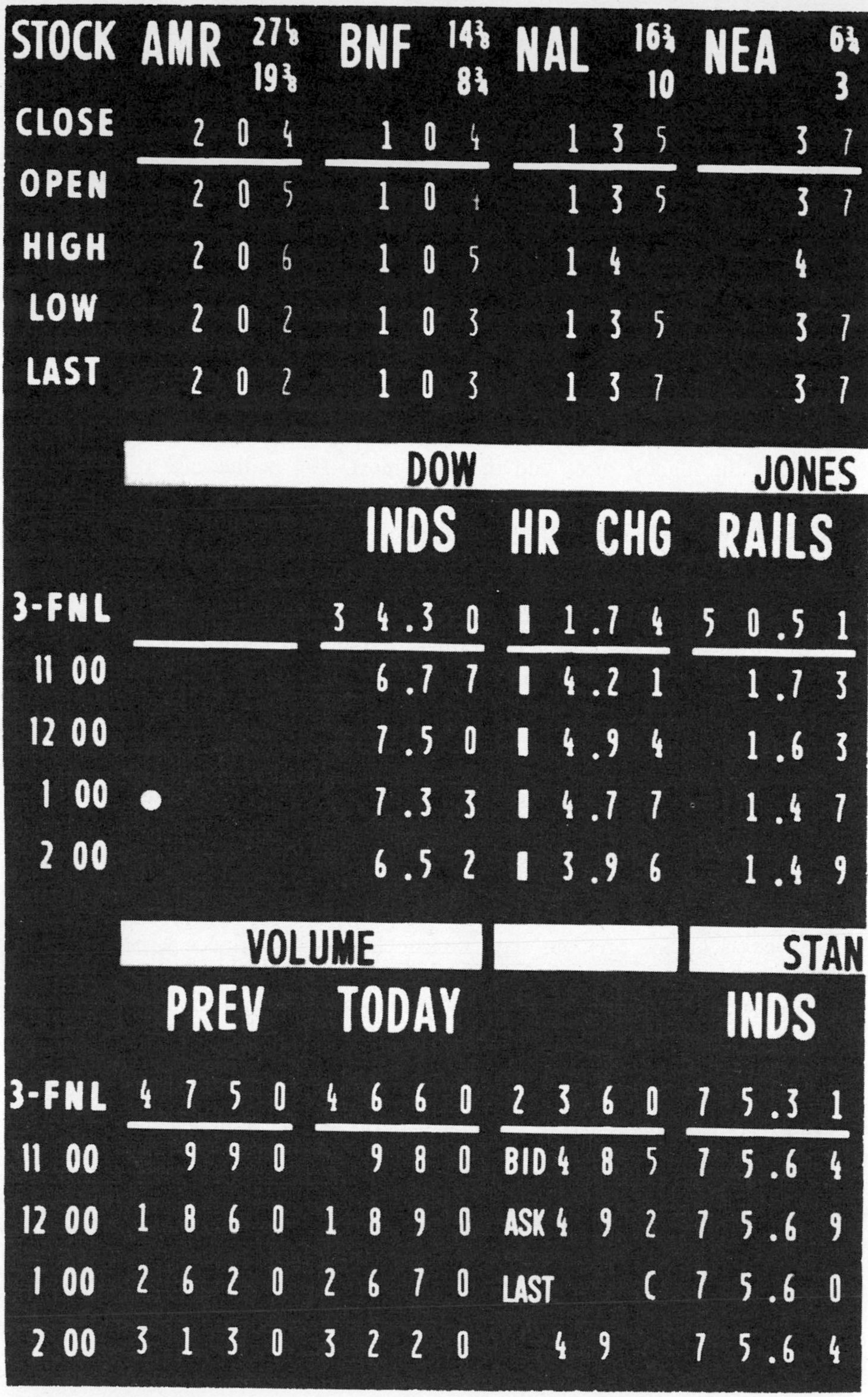
STOCK AMR 27⅛ 19⅜ BNF 14⅜ 8¾ NAL 16¾ 10 NEA 6¾ 3
CLOSE 2 0 4 1 0 4 1 3 5 3 7
OPEN 2 0 5 1 0 4 1 3 5 3 7
HIGH 2 0 6 1 0 5 1 4 4
LOW 2 0 2 1 0 3 1 3 5 3 7
LAST 2 0 2 1 0 3 1 3 7 3 7
DOW JONES
INDS HR CHG RAILS
3-FNL 3 4.3 0 1.7 4 5 0.5 1
11 00 6.7 7 4.2 1 1.7 3
12 00 7.5 0 4.9 4 1.6 3
1 00 7.3 3 4.7 7 1.4 7
2 00 6.5 2 3.9 6 1.4 9
VOLUME STAN
PREV TODAY INDS
3-FNL 4 7 5 0 4 6 6 0 2 3 6 0 7 5.3 1
11 00 9 9 0 9 8 0 BID 4 8 5 7 5.6 4
12 00 1 8 6 0 1 8 9 0 ASK 4 9 2 7 5.6 9
1 00 2 6 2 0 2 6 7 0 LAST C 7 5.6 0
2 00 3 1 3 0 3 2 2 0 4 9 7 5.6 4

Fig. 6–1 A typical bank of panels.

prices of less active issues (see Figure 6–2). As will be noted, this portion of the board gives only the ticker symbol and the last price of each issue. For example, the last price of American Radiator and Standard (AST) was $11\frac{6}{8}$. Frequently, a portion of an electric board is set up to reveal information on stock price indexes, volume of trading, and commodity prices.

The data shown on an electric board are taken from the ticker tape in New York City at central stations and transmitted by private wire to the more than one hundred cities in the United States where electric boards are now used. Thus, in each brokerage office that subscribes to the electric board service, a customer interested in a particular stock can view the pertinent data moments after actual transactions occur on the floor of the Exchange. Electrically operated boards are available also for American Stock Exchange and regional exchange transactions.

Chalk Quotation Boards. Some brokerage offices maintain quotation systems on chalk boards. Although arrangements differ in detail, a typical chalk board might appear as in Figure 6–3. The large blackboard is divided into sections headed "Chemicals," "Steels," "Oils," "Aerospace," and so on. Under Chemicals one will recognize columns for Allied Chemical, American Cyana-

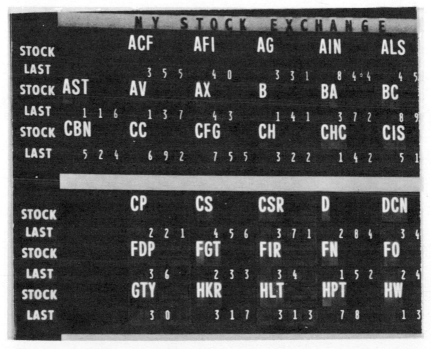

Fig. 6–2 A portion of a board.

mid, Dow Chemical, and so forth. In Figure 6–3 the companies are indicated by their ticker symbols.

Above the industry designations are several lines of figures that give previous quotations. Notice the illustrative data given on these lines for DOW (Dow Chemical). According to this board, the stock sold as high as 70 and as low as 55 in 1963. In 1964 the price ranged from $73\frac{7}{8}$ to $66\frac{5}{8}$. The price on the previous day opened at $72\frac{1}{2}$, rose as high as $72\frac{5}{8}$, dropped as low as 72, and closed at $72\frac{3}{8}$. The stock pays an annual dividend of $1.80 per share.

The vertical columns just below the horizontal line giving the company ticker symbols are where the board boy marks up the quotations in order, sale after sale, as they are reported on the ticker tape. For example, the data in the DOW column indicate that the first sale was at a price of 72. The next sale was at $71\frac{7}{8}$, and subsequent sales were at $71\frac{3}{4}$, $71\frac{5}{8}$, $71\frac{1}{2}$, and $71\frac{3}{4}$. The three tiny slashes indicate three more sales with no change in price, after which sales at $71\frac{5}{8}$ and $71\frac{3}{4}$ followed.

When the whole column is filled, the data are erased and a notation of the open, high, and low prices to that time is recorded at the top of the column. A horizontal line is drawn under these quotations, and subsequent prices are recorded in the same fashion as previously.

New York Stock Exchange Quotations									
1963	High			70					
	Low			55					
1964	High			$73\frac{7}{8}$					
	Low			$66\frac{5}{8}$					
Previous day									
	Open			$72\frac{1}{2}$					
	High			$72\frac{5}{8}$					
	Low			72					
	Close			$72\frac{3}{8}$					
Dividend				1.80					
Chemicals									
	ACD	ACY	DOW	DD	MTC	MC	OLM	UK	
			72 71 7 6 5 4 6 ≡ 5 6						

Fig. 6–3 A chalk quotation board.

The Ticker Tape and the Trans-lux

Almost all brokerage offices have a ticker tape machine, and many of these also have a Trans-lux on which the ticker tape is projected. A ticker tape is a mechanical printer that records the pertinent details of stock exchange transactions on a narrow strip of paper $\frac{3}{4}$ inch wide within a minute or two of the time when the transactions occur on the Exchange floor. Information is sent over private telegraph wires directly from the Exchange building. The Trans-lux is a long, narrow screen located high on the wall of a brokerage office, where it is visible from all corners, thus enabling many persons to read the tape at the same time. The Trans-lux transfers the information given on the ticker tape to a plastic film, which is then projected onto the screen. Ticker tape information is available for transactions in stocks on the New York Stock Exchange, the American Stock Exchange, and most of the regional exchanges. Ticker tape information for bond transactions on the New York Stock Exchange is also available.

As an alternative to the traditional ticker tape and Trans-lux, some brokerage offices use the Lectrascan device developed by Ultronics Systems Corporation of New York City. Information from the ticker telegraph line is fed directly into a transistorized control unit, which instantly activates a series of alphanumeric tubes to display the price information on an electronic panel. Ticker symbol and transaction information remain stationary until succeeded by new transactions.

The present stock ticker was installed in 1964 to provide the American financial community with rapid stock quotations. Banks that extend loans based on stocks and bonds as collateral or that sell securities directly want to know the market price and trend at any given moment; such banks are generally more liberal with securities-based credit when there is a continuous market with constant quotations. Persons buying in one market to sell in another must work quickly to take advantage of price fluctuations and differences in various markets. The speculator who depends on quick turns must have immediate and accurate information.

The new ticker system, developed by Teletype Corporation in conjunction with the Exchange staff, prints at speeds varying with market activity of 500, 600, 700, 800, or 900 characters per minute. Printing speed is changed automatically to keep pace with trading. At the maximum speed of 900 characters per minute, the tape should not be late provided that the volume of trading does not exceed 10 million shares a day.

The old ticker (in operation from 1930) could print only 500 characters a minute, with the result that in a very active market quotations could not be put on the tape as rapidly as sales were being made. This was particularly evident during the break and recovery that occurred in May 1962, when transmission fell behind as follows:

Day	Share volume for day	Tape delay at 3:30 p.m.	Time last sale reported
Mon., May 28	9,349,110	1 hr 9 min	5:58 p.m.
Tues., May 29	14,746,200	2 hr 23 min	8:15 p.m.
Wed., May 30	(Exchange closed on Memorial Day)		
Thurs., May 31	10,706,970	1 hr 46 min	5:25 p.m.

The volume of 14,746,200 shares traded on May 29, 1962, was second in history only to the volume of 16,410,030 shares traded on Thursday, October 29, 1929. On Tuesday, November 11, 1963, the first day of trading after the assassination of President John F. Kennedy, the volume was 9,323,960 shares.

Reading the Ticker Tape. The tape is a narrow ribbon of paper on which the abbreviations of the names of many different stocks, the number of shares sold, and the price per share are printed by the ticker instrument, either for reading from the tape or for projection on the Trans-lux screen. A representation of a piece of tape and the abbreviations for some of the leading stocks is shown below:

$$A \quad T \quad\quad GM \quad\quad CN$$
$$51\tfrac{1}{2} \quad 2s124 \quad 3s78\tfrac{1}{2} \quad 2s22\tfrac{5}{8} \quad 3s\tfrac{1}{8}$$

$$IBM \quad\quad\quad XRX \quad DOW$$
$$2s458\tfrac{1}{4} \;\tfrac{1}{4} \quad 284\tfrac{1}{2} \quad 60$$

This tape shows that 100 shares of Anaconda (A) were sold at $51\tfrac{1}{2}$ per share; 200 shares of American Telephone and Telegraph Company (T) at 124 per share; 300 shares of General Motors Corporation (GM) at $78\tfrac{1}{2}$; 200 shares of New York Central (CN) at $22\tfrac{5}{8}$, followed by another sale of 300 shares at $22\tfrac{1}{8}$; 200 shares of International Business Machine (IBM) at $458\tfrac{1}{4}$, followed by an additional 100 shares at the same price; 100 shares of Xerox (XRX) at $284\tfrac{1}{2}$; and 100 shares of Dow Chemical (DOW) at 60.

The letters printed on the top half of the tape are symbols for the various stocks. One, two, or three letters may be used to designate each stock listed on the Exchange. Volume and price are reported on the bottom half of the tape—volume appearing before the small letter s and price after. If no volume is given before a price, 100 shares have been sold. When 200, 300, 400, and so on, up to 900 shares are sold, only the digits 2, 3, 4, and so on, up to 9 are printed before the letter s. If the volume is 1,000 shares or more, it is printed in full. Thus a sale of 2,500 shares of General Motors would appear

When stocks are traded in 10-share units instead of 100-share units, the volume is indicated in full before the symbol ss. Thus a sale of 20 shares of Superior Oil of California at $1,372 per share would appear

Normally odd lots are not printed on the ticker tape, but on special occasions and with the approval of a floor official they may be reported. In such cases the letters SHRS are used to designate an odd-lot transaction. Thus a sale of 25 shares of International Business Machines at $459 per share would appear

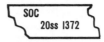

Sometimes errors are made on the tape. They are corrected as follows:

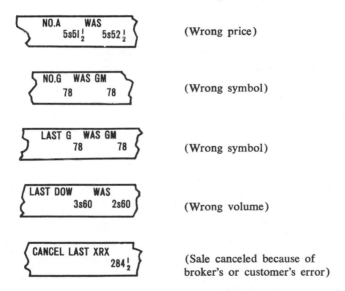

If a sale is not printed in its proper sequence, the letters SLD are placed after the symbol and before the price. Thus, if a sale of New York Central was reported late, the ticker would indicate

When it seems likely that the tape will fall behind because of great activity on the floor, DIGITS DELETED appears on the tape. Thereafter volumes of 1,000 shares and more are reported with the last two digits deleted; i.e., the number of 100-share round lots are reported in the manner done for volumes ranging from 200 to 900 shares. Also only the last digit and the fractional portion of the price are reported. Thus, a sale of 2,500 shares of General Motors at $78\frac{3}{8}$ appears as

$$\text{GM} \quad \text{25s } 8\frac{7}{8}$$

Exceptions to this procedure are opening sales and sales where the price ends in zero. When the tape is late, transactions of most 10-share units are omitted. When conditions permit, DIGITS RESUMED appears on the tape, and transactions are reported in the normal manner. If 10-share unit sales have been omitted, DELAYED SALES appears on the tape, followed by the previously unreported sales.

If the tape is five minutes late, the word FLASH appears, followed by the reporting of prices in certain selected stocks. In June 1962, the list of FLASH stocks was extended to include 100 stocks which are now reported in two groups of 50 stocks each at approximately five-minute intervals. Only the ticker symbol and the price are reported in FLASH tapes; the sale will be reported again later in its regular order. The purpose of the FLASH system is to provide investors with current information about the most important issues when volume is so heavy that complete up-to-the-minute reporting is not possible.

The letter Q is placed before the symbol of any company in receivership or bankruptcy. Thus the following quotation

$$\text{QZX} \quad \text{2s3}\frac{1}{4}$$

means that 200 shares of stock of the ZX Company, now in bankruptcy, sold for $3.25 a share.

When the market is dull, the ticker tape has no difficulty staying abreast of operations on the floor. On very dull days there are moments when the Trans-lux stands still. It is the practice of the Exchange to print the bid and ask prices of issues following each sale whenever sufficient excess capacity exists. Thus, on a dull day one might see

$$\text{X} \quad \text{2s55}\frac{3}{8} \quad ..\text{B.55}\frac{3}{8}..\frac{1}{2}$$

which would be interpreted to mean that 200 shares of United States Steel common sold at $55\frac{3}{8}$ and that $55\frac{3}{8}$ is bid for another 100 shares (at least) but that $55\frac{1}{2}$ is demanded by the lowest remaining unfilled selling order.

Other Sources of Stock Price Data

An order to buy or to sell a stock at a stated price stands in the market (1) until it is executed or (2) until it is withdrawn by the person who gave it. A standing order to buy 300 shares of Y Company at 32 takes precedence over all orders to buy at lower prices. Similarly, a standing order to sell 200 shares of this stock at 33 takes precedence over all orders to sell at higher prices. It is obvious that the highest standing buy order (called the "bid") and the lowest standing sell order (called the "ask") are very significant to a potential purchaser or seller.

The ticker tape normally provides only "last sale" transaction information. There are several ways, however, by which a broker may obtain current bid and ask prices on a given issue. Unfilled standing orders are usually in the possession of the specialist in the issue, and a broker may request that the floor member of his firm go to the specialist's post, ascertain the bid and ask, and report back. As an alternative he may cause the New York office of his firm to telephone the quotation service of the Exchange, obtain the desired information, and relay it to him. In recent years new electronic desk inquiry units which provide this information have been developed and are in use in many brokerage offices.

The Telephone Quotation System.   Early in 1965 a new computer-based quotation processing system was installed by the New York Stock Exchange to replace the old quotation room service. The equipment was developed jointly by International Business Machines Corporation and the New York Telephone Company to take advantage of the many technological developments in data processing.

Immediately after each transaction on the floor of the Exchange, a reporter at the trading post marks the details on a special card with an ordinary lead pencil. Cards are preprinted with the ticker symbols of those stocks for which that reporter is responsible and have spaces where the reporter indicates volume, the price for as many as three transactions, and the most recent bid and ask price.

As soon as the reporter marks the card, he places it in an optical data reader, which instantly transmits the information to one of the Exchange's two high-speed random access computers. At the same moment last sale information is sent out on the high-speed ticker system installed in 1964. Under this system, last price information is available on ticker tapes and Trans-lux screens across the country in about one half of a second after being "read" on the floor. (The old ticker involved a normal lag of one or two minutes between the moment a transaction occurred and the time it appeared on the national ticker network.)

In addition to being almost instantaneously reported on the ticker system, last sale information is returned to each of the floor trading posts by loudspeaker and by special printers for the benefit of odd-lot dealers, who base their prices on the price of the last round-lot transaction.

Bid and ask information, as well as last price data, is used by the Exchange's quotation service to provide brokers with current information through the Telephone Quotation Service. Subscribers (all members of the Exchange), who used to dial either a quotation girl or a tape-recorded quotation system, now obtain up-to-the-minute bid, ask, and last sale information by dialing a four-digit code number and obtaining a "spoken" reply assembled by the computer.

This "voice assembly" unit contains a vocabulary made up of 126 key words, syllables, digits, and letters recorded on various tracks of a revolving magnetic drum. Electronic reading heads play back these sounds in a sequence determined by the computer to form an easily understandable voice reply. A request for a quote on XYZ stock might produce a "spoken" reply as follows: "X-Y-Z forty-one and three-quarters-to-two—last—forty-one-and-seven-eighths." That is, someone is willing to buy at least 100 shares at $41\frac{3}{4}$; someone else is willing to sell at least 100 shares at 42; and the last sale was at $41\frac{7}{8}$.

If the broker also wants to know the "extent" of the market, he must ask his firm's floor member to go directly to the specialist on the floor, who might reply "41 and $\frac{3}{4}$ to 2, 300, 200" meaning that $41\frac{3}{4}$ is bid for 300 shares and 200 shares are offered at 42.

A response from the computer can be delivered in about six seconds. The system is capable of providing voice responses to as many as 400,000 telephone inquiries a day. (The record number of inquiries under the old system was 243,000 calls during the market break of May 29, 1962.) Special high-speed telephone equipment capable of handling 300 calls simultaneously is used.

The new computer-based quotation system also provides current information on about eight hundred most active stocks to private quotation services for transmission directly to their member firm subscribers. This information is fed to the services on a separate direct telegraphic circuit.

The quotation system also provides other services, such as inquiry stations on the floor, where members may obtain current information on volume, ranges, last sales, previous sales, and bid and ask quotes on all stocks and continuous compilation of market statistics on the securities market in general.

The Old Quotation Room.   The efficiency of the new quotation service can be appreciated only by comparing it with the previous system, which in its time was also regarded as highly efficient but which now seems antiquated in a world of instantaneous electronic data processing.

Under the old system, member firms had direct telephone wires to a central quotation room located in the Exchange building. On a large electric quotation board in this room were posted the current bid and ask of all but 300 of the securities listed on the Exchange. Every change in the bid or ask price on the floor of the Exchange was reported to one of a number of operators in this room by direct telephone from the floor of the Exchange. Each operator controlled a section of the quotation board in front of her and changed the bid and ask prices electrically as she received them. A number of quotation clerks also sat in front of the board. To obtain a quote on XYZ stock, the New York office of the brokerage firm dialed the code number of XYZ on a private wire that connected the firm's office with the quotation room. The quotation girl taking the call reported back the current bid and ask price, information which then was relayed by the firm's New York office to the inquiring broker.

Quotations for about three hundred of the most active stocks were maintained on a separate quotation system, which provided the quote from a tape recorder. The New York office of the member firm simply dialed the indicated number for the stock and heard a recorded voice, which repeated the bid and ask twice. When the bid and ask price changed on the floor, the quotation clerk dialed the automatic quotation system and recorded the new quote on the tape, wiping out the old tape in the process.

Private Quotation Systems. In addition to the Quotation Service of the New York Stock Exchange, member firms may subscribe to several privately operated data dissemination systems. In general, these systems work by means of desk-top inquiry units located in various brokerage offices throughout the country. Besides current market data the systems provide a variety of basic information about a stock, including per share earnings and dividends. In all cases the current market portion of the data is obtained directly from the quotation facilities of the Exchange.

In many brokerage offices the desk inquiry units are located so that customers can operate them directly. Three such units will be described briefly: the Quotron II, the Telequote III, and the Stockmaster. The three items are pictured in Figure 6–4.

The Quotron was first introduced in 1960 by Scantlin Electronics, Inc., of Los Angeles. Within two years over twenty-two hundred desk units were installed in over seven hundred brokerage offices throughout the country. The current version of this device, Quotron II, provides up-to-the-second data on any stock by printing the information on a $\frac{3}{4}$-inch-wide paper tape, which may then be torn off and retained as a permanent record. Quotron II provides information on last sale, net change from previous sale, up or down tick from previous sale, previous close if the stock has not yet opened, open, high, and low for the day, cumulative volume, bid and ask, identification of ex-dividend and flash price stocks, dividend rates and yields, earnings, and price-earnings ratios plus market aggregate information and stock price indexes. Inquiry is made by pressing alphabetical keys for the stock symbol and then pressing

Fig. 6–4   The Quotron II, the Telequote III, and the Stockmaster (bottom to top).

the appropriate request button. The Quotron II system also provides port-folio valuation information and confirmation of transactions as to principal, taxes, commissions, SEC fee, and final amount.

Teleregister Corporation of Stamford, Connecticut, first introduced its Telequote device in 1961. The initial desk-top device was about the size of a telephone and contained a telephone-type dial. By dialing a code number for a particular stock, the current bid, ask, and last price data appeared either on a small panel above the dial or on a special panel on the Tele-register quotation board in the office. The current improved version of this device is Telequote III. By punching the appropriate stock symbol into the machine a broker can obtain for any listed stock the bid, ask, last price, price trend since previous sale, previous close, open, high, low, volume for the current day, time since last sale, price-earnings ratio, and dividend. Addi-tional information is available on stock price indexes, New York Stock Exchange volume, and lateness of the ticker tape. The information appears on a small television-type screen, $2\frac{1}{8}$ inches wide and $2\frac{1}{2}$ inches high, located on the unit. Another model of Telequote III prints information out on a paper tape.

The Stockmaster was introduced in 1961 by Ultronics Systems Corpora-tion of New York City. To make an inquiry of this unit one pushes the stock symbol buttons and then an interrogation button for the information desired. The answer appears in three numerical indicators located above the key-board. A complete range of information on listed and unlisted stocks and on commodities is available.

Other Services

Large brokerage houses offer their customers many other free services. For example, most of them provide a news ticker service, a ticker which prints the latest news on ribbons of paper about 5 inches wide. This private wire service carries almost immediately all the news that is available from New York to all the branches throughout the country. A constant stream of news items flows over the wires. As soon as they are received these items are posted in typewritten form on bulletin boards or they may be projected on large screens in a fashion similar to the projection of the ticker tape onto the Trans-lux so that everyone in an office may read the news as it is first reported.

The latest tips and rumors, the hard facts, the gossip, the advice and the warnings, the gloom and the optimism of Wall Street and the country come in ceaseless, irrepressible streams. A jump in the price of grain when the prosperity of the farmer is considered to be an important factor arouses the lounging traders in a New York office and in an Omaha office at about the same time. A sharp break strikes fear into the hearts of traders throughout the country at the same moment.

Not only does the brokerage house provide a wire service to furnish up-to-the-minute information on all matters pertaining to the market; it also provides a statistical staff who gather data on the earnings and movements of particular stocks and of stocks grouped by industries and on the market as a whole. Corporation reports are analyzed, and the financial and business prospects of a great variety of corporations are studied. The results of these analyses and studies are always available to clients of the house free of charge and are frequently put into pamphlet or book form for distribution to such persons as are interested.

Because of the need and demand for information gathered from all possible sources and analyzed by a responsible and disinterested statistical group, a number of nationally and internationally known organizations have been formed to offer facts and advice about the stock market. One need only read through the advertisements in *Barron's* or in the financial section of the Sunday *New York Times* to see how many such services are available. Every brokerage house subscribes to several services of this kind and makes them available to its clientele. In many respects these services are much like human beings: one service may be bullish at the very same time that another is bearish.

7 the relation of broker and customer

The relation between broker and customer should be one of confidence and goodwill. At times the broker will have relatively large amounts of his customer's property in his keeping. At other times the customer will be in debt to his broker. Custom, law, and good business policy regard certain standards as fundamental to a satisfactory relationship between the customer and the broker. It is the purpose of this chapter to point out accepted standards to which both parties should make an earnest effort to conform.

In general an investor speaks of the man at the brokerage house with whom he deals as "his broker." Technically, this man is a representative of the broker (hence his official title, "registered representative"), while the partner or voting stockholder of the firm who executes orders forwarded by his representatives is the broker.

Selecting a Broker

The investor's first step in establishing a satisfactory relationship is to choose a firm that is suitable for his needs and to select a representative of the firm with whom he can work. In practice it is hard to separate the two choices, for if one has chosen a satisfactory firm but is unhappy with the representative, it is embarrassing to shift one's account to another representative within the same firm.

Although thousands of new investors select brokers each year, it is doubtful that many of them devote as much thought to finding the best representative as the size of their financial commitment warrants. What follows are some pointers in making a wise selection.

Membership on an Exchange. An inexperienced investor should place his account with a firm that is a member of the New York Stock Exchange. Few investors have the time or ability to make a detailed study of the financial strength, standards of business practice, or technical competence of a brokerage firm. The advantage of selecting a New York Stock Exchange member firm is that the investor knows that the Exchange is maintaining constant surveillance over the firm to ensure compliance with its rigorous standards. One or more partners or voting stockholders of a member firm must be members of the Exchange. Before acquiring membership, these persons are screened in respect to their business history, previous residence, educational background, military service, and bank and brokerage house accounts; they are also screened in respect to any involvements in securities violation, criminal indictment and conviction, financial difficulty, and litigation. A person may become a member of the Exchange only if his past record is without blemish.

The Exchange also administers tests to ensure a certain level of ability. Members planning to engage in activities on the floor must pass an examination dealing with floor procedures and rules. Members and allied members who expect to work in a firm's office must take another examination dealing with Exchange rules and procedures, responsibilities of proprietors in member organizations, and supervision of offices, salesmen, and accounts. Representatives of brokers must have had six months' experience and must have passed an Exchange examination before being allowed to handle customers' orders. These examinations help to ensure that persons in member firms are competent in the fields in which they work.

The New York Stock Exchange imposes additional rules on member firms as such. Net capital is required to be at least $50,000 for any member organization carrying accounts for customers and at least $25,000 for all other member firms. In addition, an Exchange rule (as well as an SEC rule) prohibits aggregate indebtedness of any member firm from exceeding twenty times net capital.

The New York Stock Exchange requires that member firms doing business with the public carry fidelity bonds covering general partners or officers and all employees. These bonds, which vary in size depending upon the net capital of the firm, insure against losses from dishonest or careless acts but not against losses from insolvency. The Exchange itself carries a blanket bond of $10 million covering all Exchange member firms to the extent that fidelity losses exceed a firm's own bonds.

The sum total of these requirements for New York Stock Exchange members and member firms is that the probability of loss from dishonest or careless acts is minimal. Although other organized exchanges and the National Association of Securities Dealers impose somewhat similar requirements on their members, these are generally less stringent and less rigorously enforced. Since orders that must be executed on regional exchanges or in the over-the-counter market can always be efficiently handled by NYSE member firms, either through a partner's membership on a regional exchange or through a correspondent firm, there remains little reason to select other than an NYSE member firm.

Another reason for choosing a New York Stock Exchange member firm is the attitude which the Exchange has taken in matters dealing with confidence in the securities business. The biggest Wall Street scandal in a generation unfolded in November and December of 1963, when it became apparent that Ira Haupt and Company, a highly regarded old-line brokerage firm, was insolvent as the result of the inability of one of its customers, Allied Crude Vegetable Oil and Refining Company, to answer a margin call for $18 million. The loss resulted from the bad judgment of Ira Haupt in extending credit to Allied for commodity purchases. Because Exchange member firms are permitted to mix their commodities and securities business, investors for whom Ira Haupt held securities in street name or to whom Ira Haupt owed money on account of security transactions were threatened with large losses. To relieve the situation, the New York Stock Exchange made available up to $12 million to pay the debts of Ira Haupt to its more than twenty thousand customers. The Exchange also arranged for certain banks to defer collection of loans made to Ira Haupt. In announcing the arrangement on November 25, 1963, Keith Funston, President of the New York Stock Exchange, said, "While the Exchange has no legal obligation for the debts of member firms to their customers, it is hoped that this plan will prevent loss to the securities customers of Ira Haupt and Company. The Board [of Governors of the New York Stock Exchange] took this unusual step on the basis of the exceptional facts surrounding this particular case, and it should not be considered a precedent."[1]

Even though the Haupt case cannot be considered a precedent, it is apparent that the Exchange is concerned with more than just its bare legal obligations. This fact in combination with the rigid scrutiny given the financial condition, standards of business practice, and technical competence of its members is why, on the whole, we recommend here that the brokerage firm selected by a customer be a member of the New York Stock Exchange. It must be observed, however, that there are many houses of high standing that are not NYSE members. If such a house belongs to the National Association of Securities Dealers, if the investor knows that the management is capable and honest, if he can make himself reasonably familiar with the financial condition of the house, and if he finds a broker whose advice and opinion he trusts completely, then it may be advisable to choose such a firm in preference to one about which he knows very little, even though it is a member of the New York Stock Exchange.

A Well-known Institution.   The brokerage firm selected should be a well-known and long-established institution. One of the first steps for an investor to take is to ask for recommendations from his bank or from friends whose opinions he trusts. All partners, brokers, and employees of the firm should

[1] Quotation from New York Stock Exchange press release, Nov. 25, 1963. The amazing story of the Haupt scandal is explained in some detail in "Lessons from the Haupt Affair," *Fortune,* January 1964, pp. 74–78.

be above suspicion and should have a reputation for ability and honesty. Partners and senior employees should have experience in the securities business. If there is reason to suspect any person associated with the firm, it is better to take one's business elsewhere rather than to run even a slight risk of loss due to questionable dealings.

The SEC's *Special Study* showed that disciplinary action against members of the National Association of Securities Dealers in the years 1959 to 1961 was heavily concentrated on firms which had only recently entered the securities business and which were not members of an organized exchange. Securities firms newly established had a distinctly higher incidence of violations of net capital rules and of rules on the maintenance of books and records than did older firms. These difficulties were most often attributable to lack of familiarity with the technical and financial aspects of the securities business.[2]

Type of Clientele Sought.   Brokerage houses differ enormously in the type of clientele they attempt to build up. Some try to develop a large business with investors of modest means who are primarily interested in buying and selling odd lots; others seek wealthier customers; some are interested primarily in soliciting institutional business.

These differences are apparent in the public advertising of brokerage firms. One large house continually stresses the need for caution about buying stocks without having adequate savings and life insurance, thus suggesting that it is interested in the new investor of modest means. Another member firm styles itself a "private banker" to attract professional and institutional investors. Some brokerage firms emphasize fundamental long-run investing in their sales literature, while others seek to develop a clientele interested primarily in short-term speculative trading. Some emphasize growth stocks; others, income stocks.

The research reports of certain houses are obviously written for general public reading, while other houses turn out detailed and sophisticated evaluations aimed primarily at analysts for large institutions. Some houses emphasize mutual funds for individual investors of modest means, while others avoid selling mutual funds and advertise the New York Stock Exchange's monthly investment plan. Brokers in some houses are glad to work with investment clubs, helping them to organize and offering suggestions for study by club members, while brokers of other houses concentrate almost entirely on the more affluent investors in the community.

In short, while almost all brokerage firms welcome all types of investors, some houses are keyed to a particular type. In choosing a brokerage firm that will serve his needs best, an investor should try to judge the type of clientele sought in relation to the type of investor he is.

[2] *Report of Special Study of Securities Markets of the Securities and Exchange Commission,* 88th Cong., 1st Sess., House Document 95, part 1, pp. 65–66.

Services Available.   At first glance it might appear that most New York Stock Exchange member firms offer about the same services. Commissions on Exchange orders are identical, and, to the average investor, all firms appear equally efficient in executing orders. Differences between firms relate more to the availability of a special service which an investor may or may not want. A particular brokerage office may or may not have an electric quotation board, a Trans-lux screen, or a Dow-Jones news ticker. If these are of importance to an investor, he should select a firm that possesses them. If an investor is in the habit of telephoning his order to his broker, the availability of these facilities will not interest him.

Most brokerage firms have research departments. These vary from large groups of full-time, highly competent analysts to relatively uninformed persons who process the analytical work of others and in effect turn out "second-hand" analyses. A measure of professional competence in the security analysis field is the designation of "Chartered Financial Analyst" (C.F.A.). Holders of this degree have studied for and passed a series of three rigorous examinations on investment principles, applied security analysis, and investment management decision making. A recipient of the degree must be a member in good standing of one of the 34 societies of financial analysts located in the United States, must have had a minimum of three years of experience as a financial analyst, and must possess a bachelor's degree from an accredited academic institution or the equivalent in training. An investor selecting a brokerage firm on the basis of its research department should know the size of the department and the number of C.F.A.s on the staff. Also he should read some of their reports and compare them with similar ones published by other brokerage houses.

Some investors are interested in commodities and will want to choose a firm with a representative who understands commodity trading and who can efficiently transmit orders to the various commodities exchanges. Other investors interested only in stocks may wish to avoid a brokerage house which does a heavy business in commodities on the basis that the house's interests and attention are not concentrated on the stock market. As was mentioned above, it was the commodity business of Ira Haupt and Company that caused its failure and froze the accounts of many investors who were themselves concerned only with stocks.

A great many firms combine their regular brokerage business with a volume of activity as underwriters of new corporate securities. For an investor who is interested in purchasing new issues such a house is desirable; but one who is inclined to be annoyed when a broker telephones him about each new offering would want to make his attitude clear. Brokers at a few houses tend to recommend newly underwritten securities in preference to listed securities in order to earn the larger commissions. If an investor suspects he is being sold securities primarily because the broker wants a commission rather than because the security is best for the investor, he should close his account with that firm.

Many brokerage offices maintain a research library for their customers to check on companies in which they have developed interests. If these facilities are important to an investor, he should certainly investigate their availability.

The Registered Representative.   The person within the brokerage office with whom an investor will have most contact is the registered representative. As was pointed out in the previous chapter, this man may be called an account executive, a customer's man, or a stock salesman. A registered representative should be congenial and a person in whom the investor feels confidence. At a minimum, the representative is an order taker who processes orders involving large sums of money. At the other extreme, the representative may function as an investment adviser making recommendations that the investor follows blindly. Most cases lie somewhere between: the representative giving the investor information on the market and on specific securities and the investor deciding whether or not to follow the advice proffered.

One can evaluate a representative by inquiring into his business and educational background and his investment philosophies and goals. A representative consumed with a burning desire to engage in technical trading is hardly the best person for an investor wanting to buy on fundamentals, and vice versa. An investor should also assure himself that the representative is available at all times during business hours and is not so overburdened with other accounts that he cannot give the investor as much attention as he needs. The representative should be able to furnish the investor at all times, on reasonable notice, information on any company whose securities interest the investor.

The representative should not be the type who is always trying to sell the investor something. On the other hand, he should be aware of the securities held by the investor and should inform him of any news that is relevant to the investor's holdings. Basically the function of the representative is to give service and information to the investor so that the latter can make investment decisions and can have them executed properly and swiftly. A share of the responsibility for a mutually satisfactory business relationship between the two lies with the investor, for he must make his own philosophies and desires quite clear so that the representative is able to offer the type of service sought.

Opening an Account

Many small investors who would like to buy common stocks do not do so simply because they do not know how to go about it. Some persons are under the impression that only those who have business to transact dare walk into a brokerage office. If you are one of these persons, the authors suggest that you make five consecutive visits to five different brokerage offices. If anyone notices you or speaks to you, it will be unusual.

A great many people have the idea that brokers do business only with persons who invest thousands or tens of thousands of dollars. To such the following statement taken from an advertisement of one of the largest brokerage establishments will be revealing: "In our 127 offices, we're proud and happy to do business with people who talk in hundreds of dollars as well as people who deal in four and five figures." The New York Stock Exchange's *1965 Census of Shareowners in America* estimated that as of early 1965 over 20 million Americans owned stock in the nation's publicly held companies. The *Census* estimated that 16 per cent of all shareowners had incomes of less than $5,000 per year and that an additional 38 per cent of all shareowners were in the $5,000 to $10,000 income bracket.

Now let us suppose that you want to buy 100 shares of Sperry Rand common and that you have never before purchased stock. How do you proceed? First, you may, if you wish, make the purchase through your bank. To do this, you need only communicate your wishes to your banker, who will handle all the details for you. This is sometimes the simplest procedure if you contemplate only one isolated transaction, for it is not necessary to open a brokerage account.

Most of the time, however, a person will open an account at a brokerage house and place his order in person or by telephone. Opening an account at a brokerage office is as easy as opening a charge account at a department store or a savings account at a bank. Perhaps a friend or a bank has recommended a particular brokerage firm; or perhaps you simply choose a firm from the yellow pages of the telephone directory. In either case all you have to do is to walk into the office and inform the receptionist that you would like to open an account. You will be introduced at once to one of the broker's representatives. (The various representatives in an office usually rotate in receiving "walk-ins.") If you prefer, you may discuss your particular investment needs with a resident partner or with the office manager, who will then introduce you to a representative who seems most suited to your particular needs.

As a new customer, you will be asked to fill out a "signature and identification" card similar to that appearing in Figure 7–1. A rule of the New York Stock Exchange requires every member firm to use "due diligence to learn the essential facts relative to every customer, every order, every cash or margin account. . . ." This is generally interpreted to mean that each broker should know his customer and should obtain information on his residence, occupation, citizenship, social security number, and references.

Accounts may be either "cash accounts" or "margin accounts." The procedure for opening an account described above applies to cash accounts. Should you desire to open a margin account, an arrangement that will permit

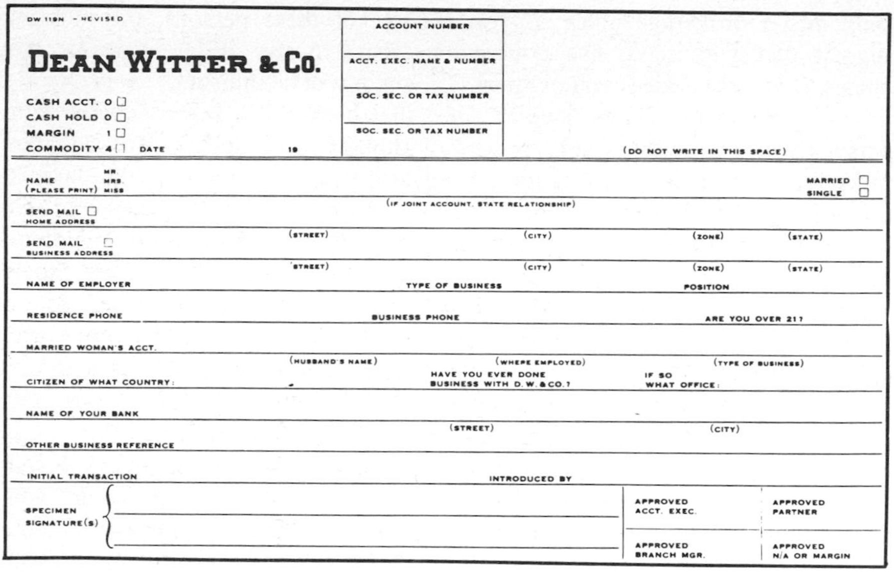
DW 119N - REVISED

DEAN WITTER & CO.

ACCOUNT NUMBER

ACCT. EXEC. NAME & NUMBER

SOC. SEC. OR TAX NUMBER

SOC. SEC. OR TAX NUMBER

CASH ACCT. 0 ☐
CASH HOLD 0 ☐
MARGIN 1 ☐
COMMODITY 4 ☐ DATE 19

(DO NOT WRITE IN THIS SPACE)

NAME (PLEASE PRINT) MR. MRS. MISS — MARRIED ☐ SINGLE ☐

(IF JOINT ACCOUNT, STATE RELATIONSHIP)

SEND MAIL ☐ HOME ADDRESS — (STREET) (CITY) (ZONE) (STATE)

SEND MAIL ☐ BUSINESS ADDRESS — (STREET) (CITY) (ZONE) (STATE)

NAME OF EMPLOYER — TYPE OF BUSINESS — POSITION

RESIDENCE PHONE — BUSINESS PHONE — ARE YOU OVER 21?

MARRIED WOMAN'S ACCT. — (HUSBAND'S NAME) (WHERE EMPLOYED) (TYPE OF BUSINESS)

CITIZEN OF WHAT COUNTRY: — HAVE YOU EVER DONE BUSINESS WITH D. W. & CO.? — IF SO WHAT OFFICE:

NAME OF YOUR BANK — (STREET) (CITY)

OTHER BUSINESS REFERENCE

INITIAL TRANSACTION — INTRODUCED BY

SPECIMEN SIGNATURE(s)

APPROVED ACCT. EXEC. — APPROVED PARTNER

APPROVED BRANCH MGR. — APPROVED N/A OR MARGIN

Fig. 7–1 A signature and identification card.

you to buy securities and borrow part of the purchase price from the brokerage firm, you will be asked to sign a "customer's agreement and loan consent" form. The purpose of this form is to authorize the brokerage office to retain your securities as collateral against the loan, to sell the securities if necessary under certain circumstances, and to loan the securities held in the account to other parties.

There are other types of accounts which may be opened in certain circumstances. Short sales may be handled in a separate account. In some states special forms are needed for a married woman to have an account. Joint accounts may be opened in two or more names. Corporations and partnerships may have accounts for which special forms are required. The same is true with regard to investment club accounts and accounts in which agents or attorneys have authority to place orders. Accounts may be opened in which a broker is given limited or full discretion in the handling of the account. However, every discretionary order entered by the broker must be approved at the time of the order by a general partner or voting stockholder of the member firm.

Should an investor have accounts with more than one brokerage firm? An investor on margin should stay with one firm, because his gains in some securities can be credited against his losses in others, thereby maximizing his purchasing power. Stockbrokers frequently provide extra services to their more active customers, perhaps by sending them monthly stock guides or more detailed analytical reports. If an investor's entire business goes to one broker, the volume of business done may be large enough to warrant special attention, whereas if he divides it among several brokers, the volume may not warrant such services from any. Furthermore, the investment advice given by a broker is valid only if he knows the investor's entire portfolio. If an investor's business is scattered among several firms, no one broker can properly make suggestions as to the balance in the portfolio.

On the other hand, if the volume of his business warrants it, the investor will receive more ideas and suggestions if he deals with several brokers. Also, he will be in a better position to appraise the service being rendered by a particular broker. He may find a broker at one firm who is particularly well informed on growth stocks and a broker at another firm who knows more about bonds. Under such circumstances he might well decide to open accounts at both firms.

Placing an Order

After an investor has opened an account, he is ready to place an order. He may do this over the telephone or in person. The agent of the broker who takes the order will make a notation of the details on a prepared form similar to those shown in Figures 7–2 and 7–3.

In Figure 7–2 the customer has ordered the broker to sell 100 shares of General Motors at the market. The cross in the upper left-hand corner indicates that the order is to be executed on the New York Stock Exchange. The order expires at the end of the current day. The customer's name is John Jones, and his account number is 240–17297. The account executive's (representative's) number is 19. The proceeds of the sale are to be held in the customer's account. These details are all noted on the order form.

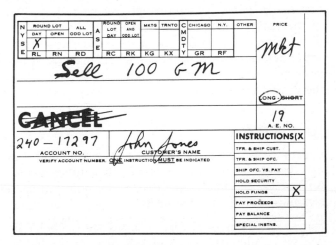

Fig. 7–2   A market sell order.

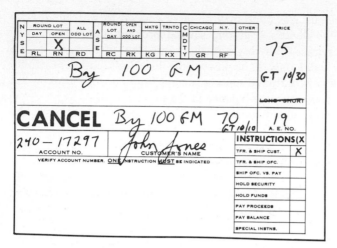

Fig. 7–3   A limited buy order.

In Figure 7–3 John Jones has instructed the broker to buy 100 shares of General Motors at a price not to exceed 75 a share. It is an open order, meaning that it does not expire at the end of the current day. The GT 10/30 below the price indicates that the order is to remain good through October 30. This buy order is to take the place of an earlier order to buy 100 shares of General Motors at 70, which was to remain good until October 10. (This is the meaning of the notations after the word "cancel.")

If the representative with whom a customer normally places his order is out of the office, the order may be given to any of his associates. If the investor wishes to place an order while he is traveling in an area where his firm has no offices, he may simply enter any brokerage firm, place the order in the normal fashion, and instruct the broker to "give up" the order to his own firm. The order will be executed the same as if it had been placed with the investor's firm, the amounts will be debited or credited to the customer's account with his broker, and the two brokerage houses will share the commission.

Types of Orders

Orders are of two types: to buy and to sell. Both buying and selling orders may be (1) at the market or (2) at a price specified. Selling orders may furthermore be either long or short. All orders at specific prices have certain expressed or implied time limits.

Market versus Limited Orders.   An investor calls his broker on the telephone and says, "Buy 100 shares of U.S. Steel at the market." The broker understands this to mean that he shall buy the stock named as soon as he can reasonably transmit the order to his man on the floor of the New York Stock Exchange, who is to buy at once at the price then quoted at the Steel post. If the order were given, "Buy 100 shares of U.S. Steel at 55," the order would be known as a "limited" order. Since a definite price has been specified, the broker will not buy except at a price of 55 or lower. A limited order to sell at 55 would be executable only at 55 or higher.

Stop Orders.   A stop order is a special type of limited order. Stop orders were formerly called "stop-loss" orders, but the name was changed because use of the order limits only the amount of loss—it does not guarantee avoidance of loss. Stop orders may be either buy or sell orders. A unique characteristic of a stop order is that it is not executed until after the stock sells at or goes through the price specified. Then a stop order becomes an ordinary market order.

To illustrate, suppose that Texaco is selling at 75 and that a short trader places a buy stop order at a price above the current price, say, at 78. The stop order will be held in abeyance until a transaction in Texaco is executed at 78. Then it will be treated as an ordinary order to buy the issue at the market. Or suppose that a trader holds Texaco on margin when the price is 75. He might place a stop order to sell the issue at 73. The order would not be executed as long as the price remains at $73\frac{1}{8}$ or higher. But if the price touches 73, the stop order would be "elected" (market parlance for becoming a market order) and would immediately become an order to sell the issue at the market.

There are four possible uses of a stop order.

1. To Limit a Loss on the Long Side of the Market.   After a careful study of the factors involved, Mr. Brown believes that the common stock of National Steel will advance. He buys 100 shares at 60, putting up 30 points' margin. The market, however, may not move as Brown expected, and he is not ready to take much of a loss. Brown, therefore, at the time he buys the stock puts in an order to sell at 58 stop. If Brown has misjudged the market for National Steel, he will be stopped out at 58 and will lose $2 per share plus his commissions, tax, and interest.

If the price next falls to 52 and conditions still seem favorable for a rise, Brown can buy at 52, or 8 points lower, and after the price has gone up about $2\frac{1}{2}$ points all further rise will be clear profit, the former loss having been retrieved. The market may now go to 65 or 70, as Brown expected, and his profits will be much better than if he had not used the stop order but had held the stock through the reaction.

If the stock did not come back, Brown would suffer a small loss but would have 28 points of his margin free for dealing in some other issue. If he had not used the stop order but had held on, his account would have shown a large paper loss, all his margin would have been tied up, and he would have been in danger of being called for more.

There is another side to this story. If the price had dropped to 57 and had then turned upward, Brown would have been sold out at a loss of over 2 points, and unless he was watching closely, he probably would not have gone into the market before the price had reached 60 again. If Brown had not used the stop order, he would not have suffered the loss of $2 per share plus commissions for buying and selling, tax, and interest.

2. *To Limit a Loss on the Short Side of the Market.*   After a careful study of the relevant facts concerning United Fruit, Brown decides that there are critical factors in the market and the position of the company which indicate a decline. He therefore sells short 100 shares at 24. To protect himself against mistaken judgment and a rise in the market, he places a stop at 27. If the price now rises to 32, Brown must take a loss of 3 points, plus commissions for buying and selling and tax; but he can sell short again at 32 if he wishes, and any subsequent decline below 29 will be profit. Assuming that the price declines to 20, Brown will gain 5 points more than if he had held his short position through the rise. If the stock had not declined, he would have limited his loss and would have the remainder of his margin free for further trading.

Here, as on the long side of the market, there is always the contingency of being stopped out at the turning point of the market price. If the price goes to 27 or 28 and then begins the expected decline, the stop order will probably mean nothing but loss. It may be said that such a loss, however, is relatively cheap insurance and should be taken on the same theory that the thrifty householder insures his property year after year although he never has a fire.

3. *To Protect a Gain on the Long Side of the Market.*   Let us assume that Brown bought 100 shares of United Airlines common at 60 and that the price has gone to 65. By placing a stop at 61 he protects himself against a sudden decline. On the other hand, the price can run to 70 and upward. As the price moves up, the stop can be placed at 62, 63, 64, and so on, until a satisfactory gain is realized or until the price seems to have discounted the favorable factors of the situation, when a stop can be put close up to the market. If the price goes further, well and good, but if it declines, a figure very near the top is realized.

4. *To Protect a Gain on the Short Side of the Market.*   Brown has sold 100 shares of Westinghouse Electric short at 35 because he believes after careful investigation that the price will decline. Sometime later the price has declined to 30. A stop now entered at 33 will protect him against a loss. As the price declines, the stop can be moved down, a reasonable distance above the market always being kept, until a satisfactory profit is shown or until the price seems to have discounted the unfavorable factors. When this happens, the stop can be moved down near the market, and if the market continues to decline, the additional profits are again protected.

If the price rises, the stop will be caught but a satisfactory profit has been realized. In all these efforts to protect against a loss and make certain of a gain there is always the danger that the stop will be placed too close to the market and the stock sold out on the long side or bought in on the short side just at the point where the expected movement really begins.

Stop Limit Orders.   An ordinary stop sell order for Texaco at 70, entered when the stock was selling at 75, would become a market order as soon as Texaco sold at or below 70. An investor placing this type of order would expect it to be executed at 70 or $69\frac{7}{8}$ because under ordinary circumstances stock prices do not vary from transaction to transaction by more than $\frac{1}{8}$ or $\frac{1}{4}$ point. But suppose that a market crisis, such as occurs from time to time, develops just after a sale at 70 causes the stop order to become a market order. Owing to the crisis, the bid price might fall immediately to, say, 64. Since the stop order is now a market order, it would be executed immediately at the best price obtainable, which is now 64. The investor would, to say the least, be unhappy; but this is what he ordered.

To avoid the possibility of the market price running away after the stop order is elected, stop buy and stop sell orders may be entered with a price limit. Thus the above order might have been placed as: Sell 100 Texaco, 70 stop, 69 limit. This tells the broker to sell Texaco as soon as possible after there is a transaction on the floor at or below 70, but not to sell it for less than 69. A stop limit order is thus a stop order that becomes a limited order instead of a market order after it is elected.

Time Limits on Orders.   Suppose that the customer placed a limited order to buy 100 shares of U.S. Steel at 55. If the price does not decline to 55, shall the broker consider the order good for tomorrow also? Upon taking the order, the broker should ask, "Do you want that an open order?" or simply, "Open order?" A limited order with nothing specified about the time of expiration is good only for the day on which it is given. If open order is specified, the order remains in force until executed or canceled. In ordering a broker to buy or sell at a specified price, the time of expiration should always be stated, even if the order is intended to be good for one day. If nothing is said, the broker must interpret the order as good only for the day, but he might be uncertain as to what was really intended.

Orders at the market have no time limit, for they are to be executed immediately at the best price obtainable. For orders with a price limit, the following time periods are customary: (1) "Day order"—good for the day on which the order is given, and if not executed to be canceled at the end of that day. (2) "G.T.C." (good 'til canceled) order—an open order that stands until filled or until canceled by the customer. G.T.C. orders placed with the specialist automatically expire as of the last business day of April and October unless confirmed or renewed on the date of expiration. Individual brokerage-house practice varies in maintaining confirmation of outstanding G.T.C. orders. Some houses mail "in force notices" periodically to inform the customer that his order is still in force. Other houses require a positive confirmation at periodic intervals, such as every thirty days. (3) "Good through May 5"—automatically void after the specified date. Such orders are placed with the specialist on the Exchange floor as G.T.C. orders; it is up to the individual brokerage firm to cancel the order at the appropriate time if it has not been filled.

When the stock for which a broker holds an open order to buy, an open stop order to sell, or an open stop limit order to sell is traded ex dividend or ex rights, the price indicated on the order is reduced by the amount of the dividend or right. The broker will inform the customer of this action, and if the customer does not approve, he may cancel or change the order. Open orders to sell, open stop orders to buy, and open stop limit orders to buy are not changed when a stock sells ex dividend or ex rights.

Immediate Orders.   Two types of orders may be used when immediate execution is desired. In an inactive market the difference between successive sale prices may amount to several points. There may be only one sale a day or only two or three a week. A limited order to buy at 25 may never be executed; while the trader is awaiting a further decline in price, a turn may come and the price may jump to 27 or higher. In such circumstances either a "fill or kill" order or an "immediate or cancel" order may be entered.

A "fill or kill" order for 500 shares at 25 would be executed *in its entirety* as soon as it reached the trading floor, or if the market price were $25\frac{1}{2}$ so that no purchase could be made or if only 200 shares were available at 25, the entire order would be canceled and a report of the condition of the market sent to the customer. An "immediate or cancel" order is similar except that any portion of the order that could be filled at the specified price would be filled and the unfilled portion of the order would be canceled. Thus, if 200 shares were available at 25, 200 shares would be purchased and the remaining 300-share portion of the order would be canceled. Stopping stock with a specialist (see Chapter 11) is considered an execution of a "fill or kill" or of an "immediate or cancel" order.

Not-held Orders.   A "not-held" order is an order to buy or to sell a specified stock in which the broker is *relieved of all responsibilities* with respect to the time and the price or prices of execution. That is to say, the broker is not held responsible for executing the order, nor is he liable for missing the market. A broker handling a not-held order on the floor of the Exchange is free to use his own judgment. A not-held order differs from a purely discretionary order in that neither the particular stock to be traded nor the decision whether to buy or sell it is entrusted to the broker's discretion. Not-held orders are handled by floor brokers and commission brokers.

Other Order Types.   Several other kinds of orders may be used when particular results are desired. An "alternative" order or an "either/or" order signifies that one of two alternatives is to be accomplished. For example, a customer's instructions might be: "Buy a particular stock at a limited price, or if this cannot be done, buy it on a stop order." Or the instructions might read: "Buy 200 shares of General Motors at 93, or if this cannot be done, buy 400 shares of Ford at the market."

An order marked "at the close" is to be executed at or as near to the close of the market as possible. An order marked "at the opening" or "at the opening only" is to be executed at the opening of the stock or not at all. An order marked "do not reduce" (DNR) indicates that a stop order to sell or a stop limit order to sell is not to be reduced by the amount of a cash dividend on the ex-dividend date. DNR instructions apply only to cash dividends; the order price would still be reduced if the stock goes ex-stock dividend or ex rights.

A "percentage" order indicates that a stated amount of a specified stock is to be purchased at the market or at the limited price after a fixed number of shares of such stock has been traded. A "scale" order specifies the amount of stock to be bought or sold at specified price variations. For example, a scale order might call for 200 shares to be purchased at 40, 200 more shares to be purchased at 38, and 200 more shares to be purchased at 36. Scale orders must indicate the total amount to be purchased as well as the quantities to be purchased at the various price variations.

A market sell order marked "sell plus" indicates that the stated amount of stock is to be sold only if the price obtained is either (1) not lower than the last sale if that sale was above the last previous sale at a different price, or (2) not lower than the last sale plus the minimum fractional change in price if the last sale was below the last previous sale at a different price. A limited price order marked "sell plus" would have the additional restriction of stating the lowest price at which the order could be executed.

A market buy order or a limited price buy order may be marked "buy minus" to indicate that the stock should be purchased only if the price is either (1) not higher than the last sale if the last sale was below the last previous sale at a different price, or (2) not higher than the last sale minus the minimum fractional change in price if the last sale was above the last previous sale at a different price.

A "switch," or a "contingent," order is an order for the purchase of one stock and the sale of another stock at a stipulated price difference. A "time" order becomes a market or limited price order at a specified time, such as 12 noon.

The Significance of an Order.   While the form and wording used in placing an order are very simple, their implications are many and far-reaching. An order to buy or sell is a contract between two parties. On the one hand, it states that the customer proposes to buy (or sell) a specified number of shares of a given stock at the market or at a stated price; on the other hand, it gives the broker full power to act for the customer in carrying out the transaction. It implies that, since the broker is a member of an exchange with a constitution and bylaws and with settled modes of procedure, in carrying out the transaction he will proceed in accordance with the rules of the exchange and that he will violate none of them. (See *Clews v. Jamieson,* 182 W.S. 461.) The broker in accepting the order agrees to execute it in good faith with the due diligence and reasonable care that would ordinarily be expected of a broker and in accordance with all the rules and customs of the exchange of which he is a member.

Many firms have their order blanks printed to read, "Buy for my account and risk." When this phrase does not appear, it is implied as one of the customs of the business. The phrase signifies that all risk is assumed by the customer as long as the broker uses due care and diligence. The broker does not guarantee the value of the stock, nor does he guarantee the genuineness of the stock certificates, although he does keep careful watch for forgeries and illegalities. If it is shown that he has not taken reasonable care to detect forgeries, he is responsible for all loss due to his negligence. In this connection it must be noted that no loss accrues to the broker if in good faith he has made a contract to buy or sell, as the case may be, but, because of circumstances over which he has no control, the party with whom he made the contract fails to deliver or to accept the stock and pay for it. The order does not imply that the broker agrees to buy or to sell, but it does imply that he agrees to make the contract to buy or to sell with due diligence and in good faith.

If the second party to the contract fails, it is up to the customer to take such legal steps as seem wise. The Exchange has provided ways and means to compel members to keep their contracts. It also protects members from loss due to default of contracts by other members insofar as practicable.

If it is the intention of customers not to deliver stock sold or not to receive stock bought, so that the transaction involves no transfer of stock, New York laws hold that such customers are gambling in differences and that such transactions are invalid. Brokers knowing that the parties to the transaction do not intend that there shall be a transfer of stock cannot legally enforce their commissions or recover any advances of funds they may have made. The order by the customer implies an intention that stock shall be transferred from seller to buyer.

Executing the Order

Although a customer is not concerned with the details of executing his order, he may nevertheless be curious as to how his order is executed. To illustrate, let us assume that Jones has given an order to buy 100 shares of Eversharp

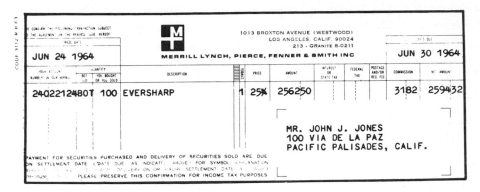

Fig. 7–4   A broker's confirmation form.

at the market. As soon as the broker in the Los Angeles–Westwood office receives this order, he forwards it by private wire to the New York office of his firm. From there it is transmitted to the floor of the Exchange by telephone. A messenger takes the call and contacts the firm's floor trader by having his number flashed on a large annunciator board. The floor trader takes the order and goes immediately to the post where Eversharp is bought and sold to inquire (of the specialists in the issue) as to the bid and ask price.

The bid is the highest standing order to buy, and the ask is the lowest unfilled order to sell. Suppose that the bid for Eversharp is $25\frac{1}{2}$ and the ask is $25\frac{3}{4}$. Jones's broker knows that he cannot obtain the stock for $25\frac{1}{2}$, because an order at this price stands unfilled at the moment. He knows that he can fill Jones's order immediately at $25\frac{3}{4}$, for an unfilled offer to sell at this price exists. Before filling the order at this price, however, he will make an oral bid at $25\frac{5}{8}$, and if no one accepts his bid, he will accept the existing offer to sell at $25\frac{3}{4}$.

Let us suppose that Jones's order is executed at $25\frac{3}{4}$. The broker on the floor telephones the information to his New York office, who relays it on to the Los Angeles–Westwood office. If Jones is still in the office, the broker will inform him that his order has been executed. In any case, Jones will receive, perhaps the next day, a written confirmation of the execution of his order. This confirmation may appear as shown in Figure 7–4.

Commissions, Interest, and Taxes

In accepting the customer's order, the broker agrees to attend to all the technical details involved in the buying or selling of stock on the Exchange. For this service he receives a commission. If the stock is to be carried on margin, he borrows the money at his bank to pay for the stock. In borrowing he regularly pledges the customer's stock for the loan of funds. He must pay interest on the borrowed funds, and therefore he charges his customer a rate of interest on the accommodation.

Commissions.   The constitution of the Exchange requires its members to charge a commission for every order to buy or sell that they execute, regardless of whether the order is executed for a member or a nonmember. The amount of the commission must be that prescribed by the constitution. No rebates, returns, discounts, or allowances in "any shape or manner," direct or indirect, are allowed. The scale of commissions in effect in 1965 is shown in Figure 7–5.

Interest Charges.   The broker charges interest on debit balances, a debit balance being the net amount owed to the broker by the customer as of a given moment. Since an active trader is buying and selling frequently, his debit balance changes frequently, perhaps even several times a day. For this reason interest is computed on the balance as it stands at the close of business each day. If a customer's debit balance on May 1 is $10,000 and on May 2 he sells $4,000 worth of stock and on May 4 he buys stock worth $6,000, then $10,000 will run at interest for one day, $6,000 for two days, and $12,000 until the next transaction occurs. At times an account will show a credit balance, meaning that at that moment the firm owes money to the customer. A broker may permit a reduction in the interest charged on debit balances if the customer has maintained a credit balance for part of the month. Interest, usually at a very low rate, is sometimes allowed a customer on credit balances left with the broker for reinvestment; however, a rule of the Exchange expressly prohibits the payment of interest on credit balances left with the broker for the purpose of receiving interest.

A flat rate of 6 per cent is customarily used to compute the interest. At the end of the month, the actual interest charges are adjusted to the rate to be charged. Suppose that at the end of the month the interest on the debit balances amounts to $120 and on the credit balances $24, both computed at 6 per cent. If the broker charges 5 per cent and pays 1 per cent, the adjusted interest items will be $100 and $4, respectively, and the customer's account will be charged the difference, $96.

The rate at which the adjustment is made is ascertained by finding the average rate the broker has paid on all his borrowed money. To this average rate he adds a small charge for his service in managing the loan, perhaps $\frac{1}{4}$–$\frac{1}{2}$ per cent. Suppose that a broker finds that the average cost of his money is $4\frac{1}{2}$ per cent and he adds $\frac{1}{2}$ per cent for his services. Then his rate to the customer would be 5 per cent. The rate allowed on credit balances is the result of many competitive factors, which need not be taken up at this time. When the market rate of interest is very low, brokers cannot afford to allow interest on credit balances.

NEW YORK, AMERICAN AND
OTHER MAJOR STOCK EXCHANGES

Non-Member Minimum Commissions on Stocks, Rights and Warrants

SELLING AT $1.00 AND ABOVE

On single transactions not exceeding 100 shares based upon the amount of money involved the minimum rates apply:

ROUND LOTS

(A *unit of trading, a combination of units of trading, or a combination of a unit or units of trading plus an odd lot, amounting to 100 shares or less.)

Money Value	Commission
Under $100	As mutually agreed
$100 to $399	2% plus $ 3.00
$400 to $2,399	1% plus $ 7.00
$2,400 to $4,999	½% plus $19.00
$5,000 and above	1/10% plus $39.00

ODD LOTS
(Less than a *unit of trading)

Same rates as above, less $2, but in any event not less than $6 per single transaction.

Notwithstanding the foregoing:

(1) when the amount involved in a transaction is less than $100, the minimum commission shall be as mutually agreed;

(2) when the amount involved in a transaction is $100 or more, the minimum commission charge shall not exceed $1.50 per share or $75 per single transaction, but in any event shall not be less than $6 per single transaction.

To determine the commission charge to be made on a transaction involving multiples of 100 shares, e.g., 200, 300, 400, etc. shares, multiply the applicable 100-share commission by 2, 3, 4, etc., respectively, as the case may be.

In the case of stocks with a 100 share unit of trading, on an order entered for a combination of a round lot and an odd lot, the commissions for the round lot and the odd lot must be computed separately and totaled to determine the commission charge for the entire order.

In the case of stocks with a unit of trading of less than 100 shares, on an order not exceeding 100 shares, the commission shall be computed on the basis of the money value of all shares executed in the transaction. For one or more units of trading, with or without an odd lot, the commission shall be computed from the round lot formula. When there is only an odd lot (less than the unit of trading) the commission shall be computed from the formula using the odd lot deduction.

SELLING BELOW $1.00 PER SHARE

On stocks selling below $1.00 per share commissions shall be on a per share basis and shall be not less than the following:

Price per Share	Rate per 100 Shares
1/256 of $1	$0.10
1/128 of $1	0.15
1/64 of $1 and above but under 2/32 of $1	0.50
2/32 of $1	0.50
Over 2/32 of $1 but under 8/32 of $1	1.00
8/32 of $1 and above but under 1/2 of $1	2.00
1/2 of $1 but under 5/8 of $1	3.00
5/8 of $1 but under 3/4 of $1	3.75
3/4 of $1 but under 7/8 of $1	4.50
7/8 of $1 but under $1	5.25

Notwithstanding the foregoing, when the amount involved in a transaction is less than $100, the commission shall be as mutually agreed; when the amount involved is $100 or more, the minimum commission shall be not less than $6 or the rate per share, whichever is greater.

*100-share and 10-share units on New York Stock Exchange; 100, 50, 25, and 10-share units on American Stock Exchange.

_____

Fig. 7–5

On a short sale, the broker must deliver the stock sold to the buyer on the fourth day after the date of the sale. To do this, he borrows the stock from someone who has stock on hand and is willing to lend it. The lender of the stock requires the borrower to deliver to him cash to the market value of the stock lent. The broker allows no interest on the credit as long as the short transaction is not covered by buying in the stock and delivery to the lender. The credit on the broker's books due to a short sale, therefore, does not serve to reduce an otherwise debit balance and does not enter into the computation of interest.

Stock Transfer Taxes.   Beginning in 1905, the state of New York levied a tax of 2 cents on each $100 or fraction thereof of par value of stock sold or transferred to another person, the seller paying the tax. Since many corporations then issued stock without par value, the law was subsequently amended to levy a tax of 2 cents per share on a transfer of no-par stock. At present the New York state tax is levied on the sales price of the stock, regardless of par or no par, as follows:

On shares selling at less than $5 per share	1¢ per share
On shares selling from $5 to less than $10	2¢ per share
On shares selling from $10 to less than $20	3¢ per share
On shares selling at $20 or more	4¢ per share

The rate on transfers not involving a sale is 2 cents per share. New York levies no tax on sales or transfers of subscription rights or warrants.

During World War I the Federal government placed a 2-cent tax on stock transfers. Over the years this tax has been changed from time to time and at present is as follows:

Tax rate: A tax at the rate of 4 cents on each $100 or major fraction of the actual value of the stock, rights to subscribe to stock, or warrants involved in the sale or transfer is levied. The sale or transfer of rights to subscribe to bonds is not taxed.

Limits: There is a maximum tax rate of 8 cents per share and a minimum tax rate of 4 cents per transaction.

Exemptions: Certain transactions are exempt from the Federal tax, including the sale by an odd-lot dealer of shares to any broker, pursuant to an order from a customer of that broker. Prior to the addition of this provision to the Internal Revenue Code in 1959, odd-lot transactions were taxed twice—once when the shares were sold to the odd-lot dealer by the public and again when they were resold by the odd-lot dealer.

The SEC also imposes a fee on a transaction on any registered exchange. At the present time the fee is 1 cent for each $500 or fraction thereof of money involved.

The New York state and Federal taxes described above as well as the

SEC fee apply only to sales of stock. There are no taxes on purchases. Thus only the seller has a tax to pay.

Shares of stock sold on the various regional exchanges outside the state of New York do not have to pay the New York state tax. This is sometimes advanced by the regional exchanges as a reason for doing business with them rather than in the state of New York; members of the New York Stock Exchange, believing they are losing trade to out-of-town exchanges, have at times sought tax relief from the New York state legislature.

The Broker's Reports to Customers

It is customary for brokers, especially members of the New York Stock Exchange, to keep customers fully informed about the status of their accounts. At the end of each day, the broker sends each customer a confirmation of all purchases and sales during that day on a form such as was shown in Figure 7–4. This notice contains the number of shares purchased or sold, the price, commissions, taxes, and the net charge to the customer's account. Another slip confirming open orders not executed is also sent to customers following the placing of such an order. Open orders are confirmed periodically, perhaps once a month, thereafter.

A third type of notice has to do with ex-dividend and ex-rights dates of stocks for which there are outstanding limited orders to buy or sell. If Mr. Smith has an open order with his broker to buy Greyhound at 26 and in a few days Greyhound sells ex dividend 25 cents, the broker informs his customer that on the day when Greyhound sells ex dividend the order to buy will be adjusted to $25\frac{3}{4}$. If the customer does not agree, he can so inform his broker. Open sell stop orders are similarly reduced. If the order were a sell order or buy stop order, the customer would be notified but the order price would not be adjusted.

It is also customary for the broker to render a monthly statement of account. Such statements are made as of the close of business on the last day of the month. They give an itemized report of all buying and selling transactions, of all cash or securities received or delivered, of commissions charged, of interest due, of the debit or credit balance, and of the stocks held by the broker or perhaps the stocks on which the customer is short at the close of business on the last day of the month. Forms used differ with different firms. A typical statement is given in Figure 7–6.

It shows that Smith maintains three accounts with his broker: a cash account, in which he buys and sell securities for cash; a general account, in which he buys and sells on margin; and a short account, in which he engages in short selling. In his cash account, Smith purchased 200 shares of Technicolor, Inc., during the month and had it delivered to the transfer agent to be registered in his own name. He also sold 120 shares of Boston Edison,

	BOUGHT RECEIVED OR LONG	SOLD DELIVERED OR SHORT	DESCRIPTION	PRICE	DEBIT	CREDIT	BALANCE	TYPE
DUPLICATE STATEMENT								
AUG 28 1964							◄ 1 23456	
			ROBERT A. SMITH					
			315 WOLFSKILL DRIVE					
			LOS ANGELES, CALIFORNIA					
DATE								
JUL 31			BAL FWD JULY 31 1964			4649 91		1
AUG 5	200		TECHNICOLOR INC	21	4256 00			1
AUG 10		200	TECHNICOLOR INC	DEL TO TFR				1
AUG 13		100	BOSTON EDISON CO	42 1/4		4179 10		1
AUG 13		20	BOSTON EDISON CO	42		825 46		1
AUG 17	100		BOSTON EDISON CO	RECEIVED				1
AUG 17	20		BOSTON EDISON CO	RECEIVED				1
AUG 20			CK NO 65432	CHECK	5000 00			1
			CASH ACCT BALANCE				398 47CR	
JUL 31			BAL FWD JULY 31 1964		4680 80			2
JUL 31			JULY INTEREST	D 6	31 11			2
AUG 3		DV 100	UNITED FRUIT CO	DIVIDEND		15 00		2
AUG 6	50		GULF OIL CORP	47 3/8	2368 75			2
AUG 10			CASH REC 222			3000 00		2
AUG 10		DV 100	STANDARD OIL OF CALIF	DIVIDEND		50 00		2
AUG 12		100	STANDARD OIL OF CALIF	67 1/4		6672 45		2
AUG 24	100		INT'L HARVESTER	81	8147 10			2
			GENERAL ACCT BALANCE				5490 31	
JUL 31			BAL FWD JULY 31 1964		3100 20			4
AUG 10		100	DELTA AIR LINES	79 3/4		8029 34		4
			SHORT ACCT BALANCE				11129 54CR	

PAINE, WEBBER, JACKSON & CURTIS
MEMBERS PRINCIPAL STOCK AND COMMODITY EXCHANGES
ESTABLISHED 1879

PLEASE MENTION YOUR FULL ACCOUNT NUMBER ON ALL CHECKS AND COMMUNICATIONS AND REPORT ANY DIFFERENCES IMMEDIATELY TO THE OFFICE SERVICING YOUR ACCOUNT INDICATED ON REVERSE SIDE

LONG	SHORT	POSITION
200		OWENS ILL GLASS
100		FORD MOTOR CO
20		INT'L BUSINESS MACHINE
100		UNITED FRUIT CO
50		GULF OIL CORP
100		INT'L HARVESTER
	50	COLGATE PALMOLIVE
	100	DELTA AIR LINES

Fig. 7–6 A customer's monthly statement.

delivered the securities to the brokerage firm a few days later, and took proceeds of $5,000 out of his account. At the end of the month he had a credit balance of $398.47 in his cash account, indicating that on balance his brokerage firm owed him this amount.

In his general account, Smith was charged interest on his debit balance for the previous month and received dividends on the shares of United Fruit and Standard Oil of California held in his account for him by the brokerage firm. During the course of the month he purchased 50 shares of Gulf Oil and 100 shares of International Harvester, and he sold his 100 shares of Standard Oil of California. Also during the month he deposited an additional $3,000 cash in the account. At month end Smith's general account showed a debit balance of $5,490.31, indicating that on balance he was in debt to his broker by this sum.

In his short account, Smith sold 100 shares of Delta Air Lines short during the month and ended the month with a credit balance of $11,129.54.

At the bottom of the statement, all shares in the accounts which are being held for Smith by his broker are listed. Shares which Smith purchased and had delivered to himself, such as the Technicolor stock, are not listed because they were not retained by the brokerage firm.

Margin Requirements

When Smith signs an order to buy 100 shares of a stock, he thereby agrees either that he will pay in full or that he will provide funds or stock in sufficient amount to meet the margin requirements of his broker. If Smith pays in full, the broker will attend to all the details of transfer into his name and will deliver the stock to him; or if Smith so desires, the broker will take the stock for safekeeping, collect dividends, and credit his account.

If Smith decides to trade in listed stock on margin, he must meet the initial margin requirements established by the Board of Governors of the Federal Reserve System and the initial and maintenance requirements of the New York Stock Exchange. Most brokers will not accept margin orders for unlisted securities.

At the present writing, the initial margin requirement of the Federal Reserve System is 70 per cent. Thus, to buy 100 shares of a stock at $60 per share, Smith would have to put up 70 per cent of the total $6,000 purchase price, or $4,200. He could borrow the remainder from his brokerage firm. If the Federal Reserve Board's initial margin requirement had been only 50 per cent, Smith would have had to put up only $3,000 and he could have borrowed the remaining $3,000.

The initial margin requirement of the New York Stock Exchange is that the equity in an account must be at least $1,000. The Exchange's maintenance margin requirement is 25 per cent. Once the stock is purchased, Smith will have to put up additional equity if his margin drops below this maintenance margin requirement. In the above example, if the stock were originally purchased at $60 per share on a 70 per cent initial margin, the margin would not decline to this maintenance margin level until the stock dropped to $24 per share. At this point, the stock is worth $2,400, but Smith's debt to his broker is still $1,800. His equity is the difference, $600, which is 25 per cent of the $2,400 value of the stock. If the stock had originally been purchased on 50 per cent margin, additional equity would have to be deposited if the stock fell to $40 per share. The stock would be worth $4,000; the debt would remain at $3,000; the equity would be $1,000; and the equity as a per cent of the value of the stock would be 25 per cent.

The above example points out both the advantage and the risk of low margin requirements. The advantage is that the investor needs fewer funds to purchase a given number of shares. The disadvantage is that, as the price declines, additional equity has to be deposited sooner (or the investor will be wiped out more quickly) if the initial margin is small.

A brokerage firm may impose its own margin requirements, either initial or maintenance, in excess of the minimum standards set by the Federal Reserve Board of Governors and the New York Stock Exchange, if it believes for some reason that the nature of the stocks held or the level of the market makes the commitment too risky otherwise. In so setting more stringent requirements the brokerage firm is acting with the customer in mind, for it is in effect saying that it does not believe the customer is safe on a smaller margin.

Margin trading is treated in detail in Chapter 14.

Pledging of Stock

Pledging of Stock by the Customer. We have thus far considered the broker as the agent of the customer. When, however, the customer asks the broker to furnish him with funds required in addition to the margin provided by the customer and pledges the stock bought, a new relationship arises in that the broker and customer now stand in the relation of pledger and pledgee and customs and laws pertaining to this relationship apply. In the case of *Markham v. Jandon,* 41 N.Y. 235, now famous as having laid down the basic principles upon which later law has developed, the brokers contended that in furnishing the funds on a margin transaction they were simply carrying out their functions as an agent of the customer. The plantiff contended that in the execution of the order to buy stocks the brokers acted as agent but in supplying funds in behalf of the customer the brokers became creditors of their customer and insofar as they held collateral as a pledge for the payment of the loan the new relation of pledger and pledgee had arisen. The court denied the claim of the brokers and held for the plaintiff, the customer, and pointed out that the law defining the relationship between pledger and pledgee applied. The court summarized the law on the point at issue in a sentence: "The creditor may resort to judicial process, or he may sell, without judicial process, upon giving notice to redeem, and giving notice of the time and place of sale." In enlarging upon the phrases "giving notice to redeem" and "giving notice of the time and place of sale," the court said, "To authorize the defendants to sell the stock purchased, they were bound first to call upon the plaintiff to make good his margin, and, failing in that, he was entitled, secondly, to notice of time and place where the stock would be sold; which time and place, thirdly, must be reasonable."

The broker thus has no right to sell pledged stock (1) unless the margin becomes impaired;[3] (2) unless he gives notice of such impairment and demands a specific sum or gives such facts as indicate the specific sum that

---

[3] See also *Taylor v. Ketchum,* 35 How. Pr. 289.

must be provided;[4] (3) until a reasonable time has elapsed during which the pledger might make good the impaired margin; (4) unless notice be given of a definite time and place of sale; and (5) unless the time and place be reasonable. In another connection, the New York courts stated the reason for requiring notice of a definite time and place of sale as follows: "The object to be attained by giving the notice is to afford the debtor opportunity to redeem, and to be present at the sale to see and know that it is fairly conducted and the property disposed of to the best advantage."[5]

But suppose that the broker were able to comply with all these conditions. May he sell the stock on the New York Stock Exchange or on some other well-organized exchange? The courts have consistently held that exchanges are private markets because they permit none but members to trade on the floor of the exchange. The same reasoning which requires that notice of a definite time and place be given and that the time and place be reasonable also makes it mandatory that the sale be public and open to anyone in order that bidding may be freely competitive and that the debtor may be present "to see and know that it is fairly conducted and that the property is disposed of to the best advantage."

In the case of *Markham v. Jandon,* mentioned above, a minority of the judges gave a dissenting opinion which pointed out the fact that under the rapidly fluctuating conditions that frequently exist in the market for stocks it would be next to impossible for brokers to live up to the law without frequently suffering severe losses. And since the customer had not kept his part of the contract in maintaining a proper margin, the brokers should not be held for loss that has accrued to the customer because of the action of the brokers in selling securities held in pledge for the customer's debts. The majority opinion gave due weight to these points but replied that if the nature of the brokerage business involved special hazards the broker should protect himself by a contract between himself and his customer which gave him such rights as would afford proper protection. This opinion has been reiterated in one form or another again and again by the courts and forms the basis of the contract, written or implied, which the broker's customer assumes at opening his account and with each order to buy or sell that he gives his broker.

Pledging of Customer's Stock by the Broker.   That the broker carrying stock purchased by a customer on margin may pledge such stock with a bank or banker has long been held as a fixed principle by the courts. The pledgee bank or banker obtains a "good" lien on the pledged stock and can sell the pledged stock without giving notice to the customer who is the owner of the stock.

[4] See *Boyle v. Henning,* 121 Fed. 376.
[5] See *Wheeler v. Newbould,* 16 N.Y. 392; also *Small v. Housman,* 208 N.Y. 125.

The broker, however, must stand ready to meet certain conditions. First, he must have on hand or under his control an equal number of shares of the same stock so that if the customer tenders to the broker payment in full the broker can deliver the stock without going into the market to buy it in. In *Mayer v. Monzo,* the court gives a summary of preceding decisions on this point as follows:[6]

> It is settled that a broker who buys stocks for a customer on margin, and to whom the customer still owes a part of the purchase price, is entitled to pledge the stocks so bought for so much of the purchase price as his customer still owes. The broker's whole duty to his customer under such circumstances is either to have on hand or under his control the stocks which he is carrying for his customer, but he is not required to do both, that is, to have the amount of stocks under control and also, an equal amount on hand.

In the second place, he must not pledge the stock for an amount larger than is owed him on the stock by the customer without the customer's consent.

The New York court saw in its decision in the case of *Mayer v. Monzo* that it would be almost impossible for a broker to attend to the details involved in maintaining the ruling in previous cases,[7] that a broker may not pledge stock held for a customer for a loan larger than the amount still owed him on the stock. A broker with hundreds of active accounts, each buying and selling, switching from one stock to another, depositing and withdrawing funds, would have to keep the stock of each customer separate from all other pledged stock and make incessant changes both in the stock pledged and the amount borrowed. The New York court, therefore, ruled that the necessary control of the same amount and kind of stock as that owned by the customer did not require that the stock be not pledged for an amount larger than the customer's indebtedness but that "if the broker has the stock under his control (even if it be pledged), and can resume possession by paying the amount borrowed thereon, not exceeding the amount which the customer owes on account of the purchase, there has been no conversion."

This decision was given in 1912, previous to the New York law of 1913 which makes it a felony punishable by a fine of not more than $5,000 or by imprisonment for not more than two years or both when a broker pledges securities held by him on a margin transaction for an amount greater than that owed by the customer.

Third, if his pledgee sells the stock without giving notice to his customer

[6] 151 N.Y. App. Div. 866 (1912).
[7] See *Douglas v. Carpenter,* 7 N.Y. App. Div. 329, and *Strickland v. Magorn,* 119 N.Y. App. Div. 113.

so that the customer cannot exercise his right to put up more margin, the broker is responsible for loss accruing to the customer.

On all these points the laws and rulings of the courts of the several states differ. We are here concerned only with the law as it applies to brokers in the state of New York.

Brokers, following the suggestion of the courts that they should make special contracts with their customers so as to protect themselves against the hazards of their business, have placed in their order blanks, confirmation blanks, signature cards, and so forth, such conditions as give them adequate protection and simplify the necessary technique of the transaction. Below is given an illustration of such an agreement.

IT IS AGREED BETWEEN BROKER AND CUSTOMER:

1. That all orders are received and executed subject to the rules and customs of the market or exchange (and its clearinghouse, if any) where order is executed;

2. That actual receipt of securities purchased and actual delivery of securities sold is contemplated by both parties;

3. That all securities purchased or received for the customer's account and not paid for in full may be loaned by the broker, may be used by him in making deliveries or substitutions, or may be pledged either separately or together with other securities, either for the sum due thereon, or for a greater sum, without retaining for delivery a like amount of similar securities, all without further notice to the customer, and with his consent, which is hereby specifically given;

4. That the broker may, whenever in his judgment it appears necessary for his protection, and without any further notice to the customer, close out the customer's account or accounts, in whole or in part, by selling the securities therein held at public or private sale without any tender to the customer of the securities sold, or by buying at public or private sale any or all securities sold but not received from the customer for delivery;

5. That all statements of accounts current as rendered the customer from time to time are acknowledged by the customer to be correct unless written notice or exception thereto be given the broker within four days after their receipt.

BLANK & CO.

The Rights of a Customer in Bankruptcy

Considerable uncertainty exists in the average investor's mind in regard to a customer's rights should a broker become insolvent. The 1963 failure of Ira Haupt and Company, and the confusion that it engendered, is a case in point. A clear concept of the various types of property that a broker ordinarily holds and of the legal claims that stand against that property is essential to an understanding of the rights of the customer in bankruptcy proceedings.

The assets of a broker are of three general types: (1) securities of customers, (2) amounts due from customers, and (3) cash. The securities of customers may be further subdivided into three groups. In the first sub-group are the securities that a broker has purchased for his margin customers. In actuality such securities are the property of the customers, but since margin customers do not pay for their securities in full, the certificates are registered in the broker's name; so they appear to be property of the firm against which the rightful owners merely hold a claim.

The second group of securities includes those purchased for customers who have paid for them in full but who have left them in the broker's possession for safekeeping or for resale at a later date. This group would also include the securities held for margin traders whose debit balances at the moment are amply secured by other collateral. Theoretically, securities of this group are segregated from those of the first type. However, to facilitate purchases and sales, borrowing, deliveries and transfers, and for economy reasons, it is the custom for brokers to keep such certificates in street name. This practice makes it difficult for a customer to point to some one certificate and say, "That is the certificate which belongs to me." Consequently, securities of this class also appear to be the property of the firm against which the rightful owners merely hold a claim.

The third group of securities comprises the certificates registered in the name of a customer and deposited with a broker. Even here, if a broker should lend the certificates to a short seller for delivery and then neglect to have the new certificates registered in the customer's name when they were returned, the securities would thereby take on a legal appearance of property of the firm, and the customer's rightful title would be reduced to a mere claim against this property. The fact that the broker's lending of the securities was illegal in this instance would not protect the customer from loss of his title.

The claims against a broker's property also fall into three general classifications: (1) loans from banks, (2) obligations to deliver securities belonging to his customers, and (3) sums of money owed to customers with credit balances. Loans from banks are secured of course by rehypothecation of customers' partially paid stocks. Theoretically, a broker must not borrow on a customer's securities more than the customer owes him, but in practice this limitation applies to the total loans of a broker in relation to the aggregate indebtedness of his customers since it is not practical to apply it to each individual customer's transactions.

The rights of customers to call for deliveries of fully paid securities are supposed to be secured by the actual segregation of the securities for which they may call. As we have seen above, such securities, even when segregated, are generally registered in the broker's name. Customers cannot, therefore, call for delivery of their securities if the broker becomes insolvent.

Theoretically, customers' credit balances, which represent their rights to withdraw cash, are protected by the cash holdings of brokers. Actually, however, at no time since 1935 have brokers ever held as much cash as customers have the right to withdraw. Furthermore, the cash so held is the property of the firm and not of the particular customers who deposited it.

The chart in Figure 7–7 offers a visual summarization of the property and claims described above and will aid the reader in understanding the discussion which follows.

Section 10 (*e*) of the Federal Bankruptcy Act, as amended in 1938, reads:

> All property at any time received, acquired, or held by a stock-broker from or for the account of customers, except cash customers *who are able to identify specifically their property* (italics added), shall constitute a single and separate fund; and all customers, except cash customers shall constitute a single and separate class of creditors, entitled to share ratably in such a fund on the basis of their respective net equities as of the date of bankruptcy.

According to this, a customer who at the date of bankruptcy has a debit balance of $1,000 secured by collateral valued at $10,000 cannot get delivery

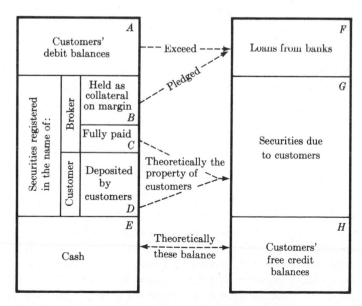

Fig. 7–7   Assets and claims of a typical brokerage firm.

of his stock by paying the $1,000. Instead, the amount of his debit balance will be deducted from the value of his collateral on the date of bankruptcy, and he will receive a "net equity" claim for $9,000 against the assets of the brokerage firm after liquidation.

If a bankrupt broker held fully paid securities of a customer, the position of that customer would depend upon whether his securities were of the type represented by C or D in the chart. Securities registered in a customer's name and left on deposit with a broker can be claimed immediately because the customer is able to trace the identical certificates that he owns. But if the broker rightfully or wrongfully transferred the shares to his own name for pledging as security for a loan or to some other individual (perhaps for lending), the customer would discover that he had only a general claim against the assets of the broker.

The condition of the customer who has deposited cash or left the proceeds of a sale with his broker is still more perilous. Such a customer would have a "free credit balance" (H in the chart). Theoretically the broker is holding his cash, but as was pointed out above the custom is for the brokers to commingle such cash with cash received from other sources and use it to finance the business. In this fashion the "depositor of cash" with a broker becomes an ordinary creditor of the firm. If the assets of the firm prove only sufficient to pay 63 cents on a dollar, such customers will receive back 63 per cent of what they deposited. This is true even if brokers actually segregate and hold available the cash belonging to customers with credit balances.

The Moral Relations of Broker and Customer

The broker should be interested in raising the standard of the brokerage business and in educating the community in the science and art of investment. While it is not the province of the broker to decide whether the customer shall buy this or that security, nevertheless he should make his influence constantly felt on the side of the careful, intelligent use of funds. He should point out the risks as well as the attractive points in the several stocks; should insist on safe margins; should not permit the customer to overbuy or oversell; and should show the customer the best methods to build up his credit standing with the firm and in the community. These moral obligations put the broker in a critical position in relation to his customer. The rules of the Exchange require the broker to execute the customer's order as it is given by him. On the other hand, the broker knows that the customer is often inexperienced, is acting without proper investigation, has been influenced by interested parties, or is simply taking a chance. If the broker advises the customer, later he may find the customer censuring him as incompetent; if he does not advise him and the customer loses, the customer will take his business to another house because he will feel the first broker did not take the proper interest in him.

The broker must not intentionally make any false statement as to the facts about any stock or its value, either orally or by mail or in an advertisement. Nor may he make a false statement of any transaction executed for his customer. All such acts of intentional falsehood are held by many states as felony punishable by a fine or imprisonment or both.

The customer, on his part, should not expect too much from his broker. Brokers are fallible in their judgment, as are other men, and may not always interpret the market correctly. It is the broker's business to supply information and give efficient service, but it is not his business to make decisions for customers as to what they should buy or sell.

8 reading the financial news

The space devoted to strictly financial news varies from a few columns on local securities in the smaller newspapers to many pages in the great dailies covering the financial news of the world. One newspaper, the *Wall Street Journal,* specializes in business news alone. It typically devotes 20 to 26 pages to facts about government activity; notes on the affairs of the leading corporations; statistics summarizing current production, marketing, and the money situation; security quotations for all the leading exchanges; and brief summaries of market opinion. Proper reading of the *Wall Street Journal* or the financial sections of the large general newspapers requires a systematic plan of reading.

Purpose in Reading

Few businessmen have the time to read the *Wall Street Journal* from cover to cover. In order to economize on time, they must devise a plan and read with a purpose. That purpose is to relate the information gained to changes in prices of securities that have already occurred or that can be expected to follow.

The man who reads about a strike or a late frost in the wheat belt simply to keep informed and to appear intelligent in company is largely a spectator on the sidelines of an interesting game. He knows many interesting facts, and he gets many thrills from his understanding of what is happening, but he is not a part of the action itself. Only if he interprets each news item as a cause of a fluctuation in interest rates, as the basis of a rise or decline in bond prices, or as the reason for a change in the market value of stocks, and only when a right or wrong interpretation of these movements means gain or loss to him, is he in the vital stream of things.

At first it seems impossible always to ask: What effect will this or that have on prices? But soon a habit is created, and almost automatically the mind relates all sorts of information to the security market as cause or effect. Consistent, systematic reading, with cause and effect on the market always in mind, soon gives one the power to remember all manner of relevant data without great effort. Moreover, the power to interpret the effect of events on the market grows with one's memory and experience.

System in Reading

Each reader should mark out for himself a systematic method of reading the daily newspapers and the weekly magazines. The outline of topics here proposed is one of many that might be set down. The order in which the topics appear should not be considered inflexible. It might easily happen that the subject of agricultural prosperity is, at a given moment, so vital that it should be put first for the time being. At another point, perhaps, exports and imports stand out. The reader must adapt himself to the outstanding current interest. The general topics here proposed are: (1) governmental matters; (2) production; (3) trade and transportation; (4) consumption; (5) the price level; (6) corporate conditions; (7) banking conditions; (8) the technical condition of the market.

Government Matters.   Since 1940, international affairs have had such an important effect upon trade and industry as almost to dominate the total picture. Obviously, if the productive resources of a country are going to be diverted to foreign aid or to preparation for war, employment possibilities within the country, the demand for consumers' goods, the amount and distribution of gross income, the allocation of raw materials and the rate of production achieved, as well as the earnings of corporate stocks, are all going to be affected. In some cases the effect will be favorable to stock ownership; in other cases it will be adverse.

Of late years, the front pages of all newspapers have presented a great variety of such news. The discerning reader will pick out the significant events and follow them through, asking all the time, "What effect will this have upon business, trade, profits, and security prices?" The front page of the *Wall Street Journal* for June 29, 1964, supplies an interesting illustration of this sort of thing.

The right-hand column contains an article on the advent and effect of younger managers in Wall Street securities firms, and the left-hand column reports on a rising trend in the use of carpeting in such places as elementary schools and hospitals. "What's News," two columns devoted to concise summaries of major news items in business and finance and in the world at large, contains brief items on bargaining between General Motors Corporation and the United Auto Workers, on the latest Communist military offensive on the Laotian Plain of Jars, on racial strife in St. Augustine, Florida, and on the contest between Governor Scranton of Pennsylvania and Senator Goldwater of Arizona for the Republican nomination for President. Other short reports deal with monetary "guidelines" for the Federal Reserve Board, the cost of living, the Treasury's plans to alleviate the coin shortage, and the publication in Dallas of the diary of Lee Harvey Oswald, the accused assassin of President John F. Kennedy. In the center of the paper appears a full-column story on the flight of Whites from Kenya and on the economic effect this is having on the African country. Column five is devoted to its regular

Monday subject, an appraisal of current trends in business and finance. Other topics in this column appearing regularly each week are reports on commodities, on taxes and tax laws, on the background of trends in industry and finance, and on events in Washington, D.C. All these happenings are significant to the economic activity that will take place in the nation in the months that lie ahead. They will affect corporate earnings and so cause stock ownership to be more or less desirable.

New laws, state and national, are vital to prosperity in one way or another. Court decisions may promote one industry and hurt another. Public improvements or their neglect, conservation of public funds or their extravagant use by officials, all react favorably or unfavorably on the security market.

Front-page news has an influence on security prices in two ways. In the long run, the trend of stock prices is probably determined by the trend of per share earnings. Each of the items recounted in a financial newspaper has a large or small effect upon the future earning power of some corporations. As a result it will have some influence upon the ultimate level of security prices. But the announcement that an event has taken or is about to take place may have an immediate psychological effect upon market traders. Sometimes this immediate effect may be in the opposite direction of the long-run effect. For example, suppose that the United States is suddenly involved in a war. Some traders, visualizing the disrupting effect of a war upon our economy, will sell their holdings. This panic selling will tend to depress stock prices. Yet the ultimate effect of the war may well be to bring inflation, augmented per share earnings, and higher stock prices.

Obviously a reader of the financial pages must distinguish between the possible immediate and the likely ultimate effect of the news presented to him.

Production.   Without production there can be neither trade nor consumption. Efficient production is the basis of large earnings. On the other hand, over-production in individual lines often brings disaster to large groups of persons. The various types of business activity, although seemingly unrelated, are in reality highly interdependent. This is because the volume of production in each industry influences the costs of production and the demand for the finished products of other industries. To illustrate, increases or decreases in the wages paid to the workers in iron and coal mines not only affect the costs of the raw materials used by automobile manufacturers but directly and indirectly augment or diminish consumer demand for automobiles. With such a high degree of interdependence, it becomes evident that no one great industry can long be depressed or prosperous without having a like effect upon all others. The security market is extremely sensitive to such changes in basic conditions.

The production of the farm, the mine, and the factory must be noted separately as well as in conjunction. The buying power of millions of agricultural workers is important to manufacturing and to trade and is dependent largely upon the volume and the prices of cotton, wheat, corn, cattle, and hogs. Sugar and tobacco are also basic to a number of the larger industries. For example, the retail price of cigarettes tends to remain stable, but the price of tobacco fluctuates with the amount grown; as a consequence, profits of the tobacco companies, and so the market prices of their stocks, tend to fluctuate inversely with the price of raw tobacco, due allowance being made for tax rate changes.

The unprecedented development in the use of electric power and electrical appliances throughout the world in the last half century and the tremendous possibilities that seem just ahead not only center attention on the development of electrical and electronic manufacturing concerns but also on the copper-producing industries. These have acquired a position of extraordinary economic importance as copper has become an international necessity. The outlook for future development seems unlimited. In the study of this great industry, the copper resources, the surplus copper on hand, the average daily production, and the average daily consumption statistics are vital. Exports of copper are of great significance when there is a large surplus on hand. Since silver is produced along with copper by the copper-producing companies, a high price for silver may be the source of a substantial part of the company's net earnings. There are high-cost and low-cost producers of copper. A fall of $\frac{1}{2}$ cent in the price of copper may change black figures to red on the income statements of high-cost producers. An unexpected discovery of a new body of copper ore may alter the industry overnight and triple the value of the company that found the ore.

The oil industry has long been a source of extraordinary profits, but the business is still highly risky. There are all grades of stock, from investment quality to the merest wildcat speculation. Financial success may depend on success in striking oil, on the vagaries of Middle East politics, or on changes in American tax laws. Statistics of daily production of crude oil, surplus oil stored, average daily gasoline production and stock on hand, average daily consumption, the season of the year, and probable consumption figured on the output of cars and trucks are points of interest. The production activities and market operations of the great international integrated companies, Gulf, Mobile, Royal Dutch Shell, Standard of New Jersey, Standard of California, and Texaco, and the prices quoted by them are very significant for the oil situation.

Industrial activity is basic to stock prices. The National Bureau of Economic Research has found that stock prices are one of the leading indicators of changes in the level of business activity.[1] Statistics on the relation-

[1] From 1879 to 1958 the bureau found that stock prices led business cycles, measured from trough to trough, by an average of 6.3 months. The range was from a lead of 21 months to a lag of 9 months. Julius Shiskin, "Signals of Recession and Recovery," *Occasional Paper* 77, National Bureau of Economic Research, New York, 1961.

ship between stock prices and industrial activity are published monthly in the U.S. Department of Commerce's *Business Cycle Developments*. The investor's problem is to anticipate changes in business activities before they are generally reflected in stock prices. The volume of business activity is indicated by indexes computed weekly and monthly by various statistical agencies. These indexes, an example of which is shown in Figure 8–1, are reported on the financial pages of newspapers and in business magazines.

There is no lack of pertinent statistical material for the student of business activity; more frequently the problem is to sort that which is pertinent from that which is not needed. Typical of the business data available are *Business Week's* figures of the week, an example of which appears in Figure 8–2. Because steel is a basic material for all industry, production figures

Business Index Fell in the Week

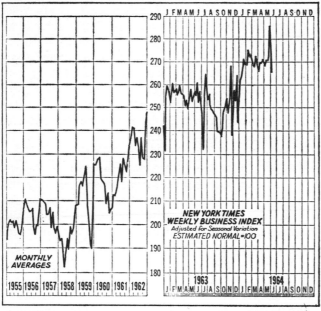

The New York Times   June 14, 1964

The New York Weekly Index of Business Activity fell to 265.7 in the week ended June 6 from 285.6 in the preceding week. A year ago the figure was 255.5.

All six components of the index fell.

The table below gives the index and its components, each of which has been adjusted for long-term seasonal trends:

	June 6 1964	May 30 1964	June 8 1963
Combined Index	265.7	285.6	255.5
Misc. carloadings	103.7	111.0	106.7
Other Carloadings	62.5	66.9	66.2
Steel	167.8	169.0	174.4
Electric	434.9	463.6	430.6
Paperboard	389.5	437.8	357.9
Lumber	106.1	124.8	98.7

Fig. 8–1   New York Times business index chart.

BUSINESS WEEK index chart..........................	1957-59 average	Year ago	Month ago	Week ago	Latest week
	100	123.8	129.1	129.6r	129.7*

1957-59=100
seasonally adjusted

Year ago

J A S O N D | J F M A M J J A S O N D | J F M A M J J A S O N D | J F M A M J
1961   1962   1963   1964

Figures of the week

Production

	1957-59 average	Year ago	Month ago	Week ago	Latest week
# Steel ingot [thous. of tons].....................................	1,860	2,426	2,511	2,417r	2,349
# Automobiles	102,264	170,543	172,493	179,821r	176,634
# Electric power [millions of kilowatt-hours].....................	12,385	17,369	18,277	18,938	19,233
# Crude oil, refinery runs [daily av., thous. of bbls.]..................	7,852	8,647	8,684	8,940	8,881
Bituminous coal [daily av., thous. of tons].......................	1,437	1,618	1,527	1,568r	1,607
# Paperboard [tons] ....:............	284,346	372,507	394,239	399,730	380,642

Trade

	1957-59 average	Year ago	Month ago	Week ago	Latest week
# Carloadings: miscellaneous and l.c.l. [daily av., thous. of cars].........	61	56	55	54	55
# Carloadings: all others [daily av., thous. of cars]....................	44	46	43	43	47
Retail sales [unadjusted, in millions of dollars].....................	$3,947	$4,964	$5,045	$5,149	$5,051
Department store sales [unadjusted, in millions of dollars]...........	††	N.A.	$328	$336	$335
Business failures [Dun & Bradstreet, number]......................	276	274	255	252	238

Prices

	1957-59 average	Year ago	Month ago	Week ago	Latest week
Industrial raw materials, daily index [BLS, 1957-59=100].............	100	93.2	100.6	101.5	101.6
Foodstuffs, daily index [BLS, 1957-59=100].......................	100	93.0	87.9	86.9	86.9
Print cloth [spot and nearby, yd.]...............................	18.3¢	18.5¢	18.1¢	18.1¢	18.0¢
Finished steel, index [BLS, 1957-59=100].........................	100	102.1	103.0	103.0	103.0
Scrap steel composite [Iron Age, ton]............................	$41.82	$25.83	$31.83	$32.83	$33.17
Copper [electrolytic, delivered price, E&MJ, lb.].....................	29.241¢	31.000¢	32.000¢	32.000¢	32.000¢
Aluminum, primary ingot [U. S. del., E&MJ, lb.]....................	25.0¢	22.5¢	23.5¢	24.0¢	24.0¢
Wheat [No. 2, hard and dark hard winter, Kansas City, bu.]..........	$2.11	$2.02	N.A.	N.A.	$1.56
Cotton, daily price [middling, 1 in., 15 designated markets, lb.]..........	33.94¢	33.82¢	33.36¢	33.30¢	33.28¢
Wool tops [Boston, lb.]...	$1.86	$1.84	$1.83	$1.83	$1.83

Finance

	1957-59 average	Year ago	Month ago	Week ago	Latest week
500 stocks composite, price index [S&P's, 1941-43=10].............	47.00	69.98	80.52	80.10	80.92
Higher medium-grade corporate bond yield [A issue, Moody's].....	4.34%	4.45%	4.60%	4.60%	4.60%
Treasury bill rate [new issue, 91 days]............................	2.837%	2.979%	3.475%	3.496%	3.478%
Demand deposits adjusted † [$ millions]...........................	††	62,191	60,692	63,140	63,286
Total loans and investments † [$ millions].........................	††	131,935	139,185	140,053	142,013
Commercial, industrial and agricultural loans † [$ millions]...........	††	37,039	39,954	39,789r	40,448
U. S. Govt. guaranteed obligations held † [$ millions].................	††	29,791	26,488	26,391	26,500
Total federal reserve credit outstanding [$ millions].................	28,011	33,498	36,179	36,597	36,811
Free reserves [$ millions].......................................	**	214	109	40r	134
Gold stock [$ millions]...	20,982	15,798	15,462	15,460	15,461

Monthly figures of the week

		1957-59 average	Year ago	Month ago	Latest month
Housing starts [in thousands]...............................	May......	††	169.5	150.5	156.9
McGraw-Hill indexes of New Orders [1957-59=100]					
New orders for machinery, except electrical [seasonally adjusted]..	May......	100	147	193	186

Used in computing Business Week Index [chart]; other components [not listed] are machinery, other transportation equipment, construction
* Preliminary, week ended June 20, 1964   †† Not available. Series revised   r Revised   † Reporting member banks
** Not applicable   N.A. Not available

The pictures: Cover, Tibor Hirsch; 31, WW; 38, (top) Tibor Hirsch, (bot.) Joan Sydlow; 42, American Can Co.; 51, General Electric; 58, 59, 60, 62, J. Edward Bailey; 66, Douglas Fir Plywood Co.; 70, 72, Eiji Miyazawa; 88, Herb Kratovil; 96, Herb Kratovil; 98, Hat Corp. of America; 100, Ed Malsberg; 104, 105, Mike Shea; 115, Herb Kratovil; 118, Joan Sydlow; 139, 140, Leonard Nadel; 148, (lt.) Herb Kratovil, (rt.) Don Uhrbrock; 152, 153, Berni Schoenfield.

Fig. 8–2

are considered very good, if not the best, simple barometer of increasing or declining prosperity. Automobile production, which is closely tied to automobile sales, is a sensitive barometer of consumer behavior and thus of the level of economic activity. Electric power production, refinery runs of crude oil, coal output, and paperboard production are all important measures of production in the country.

It is difficult to separate the indicators of production from those of trade and finance. Carloadings, volume of retail sales, trends in department store sales, and Dun & Bradstreet's figures on business failures all may be used to predict changes in the business climate. Changes in the yield on corporate bonds or on treasury bills indicate shifts in the demand for money, as do statistics on loans and investments of the commercial banks. Net free reserves of the Federal Reserve System show the relative ease or tightness of credit in the country. Changes in the gold stock are a measure of the relative strength of the United States dollar in the world economy.

Trade and Transportation.   Not only must goods be produced, but they must be passed along in a constant stream to the consumer. To this end a great structure of railroads, highways, waterways, and airlines has been built up to supply the great wholesale and retail market structure. Public opinion, favorable legislation, mergers, adequate rates and earnings, proper maintenance, and constructive financing are all necessary to the prosperity of the transportation industry and of business generally. A relatively small number of failures among wholesalers and retailers, good earning figures, large volume of sales, and small inventories show a sound condition in domestic trade. Weekly carloadings and debits to individual accounts or check transactions are indicators of trade activity.

International business is an important factor. Businessmen and government officials like to see a favorable balance of trade. The uncertainty of foreign competition may put a damper on initiative in domestic trade. A great corporation becomes unable to compete against foreign imports, and its stock begins a prolonged slump. A great corporation expands production abroad, and its stock rises in anticipation of increased earnings from international operations.

Consumption Conditions.   If the consumption of goods is not maintained at a high rate, all production must soon slow down. On the other hand, when consumption is increasing rapidly, industrial production will be increased and maintained. Here, then, is another of the fundamentals that affords a center about which to group many facts.

The Department of Commerce publishes an index of wholesale trade and one of retail sales each month. Department store sales and department store stocks are reduced to index form, and an index for each is published by the Federal Reserve banks. Carloadings are published weekly, with comparisons for the same week of the preceding year. Less-than-carload shipments are particularly indicative of the movement of merchandise from the factory to the store. A proper combination of the statistics on carloadings, wholesale and retail trade, department store sales, and department store stock on hand gives a pretty fair conception of the movement of goods into the consumers' hands. The volume of savings deposits, increases or decreases in wages, and the statistics of employment indicate the buying capacity of the consuming public. The balance of exports and imports of consumable goods also has significance in evaluating consumption.

Businessmen know how decisive an excessive inventory may be in causing breaks in prices. Production must be balanced by consumption. Unduly large stocks of finished goods in the hands of manufacturers, wholesalers, or retailers suggest a slowing down of consumption and so serve as indicators of trouble. Various reports from trade associations and the indexes of the Federal Reserve banks mentioned above deal with this problem. The weekly reviews of trade by Dun & Bradstreet and the report on trade conditions in the *Commercial and Financial Chronicle* comment upon and reveal the current inventory situation.

Prices.   The general price level, wholesale and retail, is measured by a number of carefully constructed indexes. Most of these indexes are published monthly in the *Federal Reserve Bulletin* and the *Survey of Current Business,* and they are frequently noted on the financial pages of the newspapers. The most notable American indexes of wholesale prices are the Bureau of Labor Statistics indexes of wholesale prices by commodities.

Indexes of retail food prices and of the cost of living in the United States, England, France, Germany, Netherlands, and Switzerland are published by various foreign agencies. *Iron Age* publishes weekly composite indexes of the price of pig iron and scrap steel per ton and of finished steel per pound. Daily price quotations on all the leading commodities are found regularly. Cotton, wheat, corn, oats, rye, pork, lard, short ribs, sugar, cocoa, coffee, and rubber are traded on organized exchanges like the Chicago Board of Trade, the New York Cotton Exchange, the New York Coffee and Sugar Exchange, the New York Produce Exchange, and the New York Cocoa Exchange.

Corporate Conditions.   With the country as a whole prosperous, one industry may be depressed. Again, with a given industry as a whole booming, one unit of the industry may be having a hard struggle. The investor studies the corporation reports of a number of units of an industry to get a view of the industry as a whole. The situation in any one plant is in part arrived at by an analysis of its reports. While corporation reports are not final by any means, they are one factor which carries much weight. It is certain that a conservative investor will not place his money with a corporation on which he cannot get full information. The primary risk taker aims to take as little risk as possible, and the better he knows the facts the more nearly he accomplishes his aims. If, then, information exists but is not made available by the management to the investor, an attitude so adverse to sound business is displayed that the investor should withhold his funds and put them with a management who can see the investor's point of view. The United States Steel Corporation has an enviable record of giving the public full and carefully assembled data on the company's business and condition.

Probably no single institution has done more to persuade industrial corporations to publish adequate reports than the New York Stock Exchange. The standards of reporting established by the Securities and Exchange Commission have given impetus to the movement for revealing data which once were available only to those in control.

Nearly all leading industrial corporations publish quarterly, semiannual, or annual reports consisting of a financial statement, income account, and general statement of the condition of the corporation. The railroads make monthly reports of earnings to the Interstate Commerce Commission and an annual report to the stockholders. All corporations listed on the New York Stock Exchange make at least one full report each year to the Exchange.

Banking Conditions.   Banking conditions are studied from two points of view: (1) the probable outlook for the supply of credit and its cost in interest rates to the business community, and (2) the probable supply of credit and its cost to the purchaser of securities.

The Board of Governors of the Federal Reserve System publishes a weekly report for each Reserve bank and a consolidated report for the System. The report includes a statement of changes in member bank reserves, which is frequently used as an indicator of changes in Federal Reserve policy. The Board of Governors also releases a report on the condition of reporting member banks in New York and Chicago and a report on the condition of member banks in leading cities throughout the country. Items of special note in these reports are increases or decreases in loans and discounts, government securities, currency in circulation, float, gold stocks, and demand deposits.

Technical Position of the Market.   The investor is interested in knowing whether the market has been very extensively bought or sold. How do present security prices compare with prices of previous years? Is there great enthusiasm, or are all market operators gloomy? What are big financial institutions doing? Is there a large short interest? Is there a large supply of stock overhanging the market, or is stock scarce? The situation in the market itself, regardless of fundamental conditions, may be decisive for some weeks.

Summary.   The plan of reading here set forth would lead to systematic reading by the investor under several general topics: (1) governmental affairs; (2) production; (3) trade and transportation; (4) consumption; (5) prices; (6) corporate conditions; (7) banking; and (8) technical condition of the market. Other schemes may be suggested, but if the above plan is carried out, the reader will soon feel a vital interest in the affairs of the world, and the amount of available information that he will soon have at his fingertips will be greater than he ever imagined.

Stock Quotations

Our next task is to explain the presentation of facts on the financial page. The method of quoting stocks and bonds is always a mystery to the uninitiated. However, quotations are now well standardized, and wherever they are published, the method of presentation is practically identical.

Listed Stocks.   In Figure 8–3 is shown a portion of the list of stock quotations taken from the *Wall Street Journal,* Monday, June 29, 1964, giving the market of Friday, June 26. The first two columns give the highest and the lowest prices at which a sale was made in each issue during the year 1964. The third column gives the name of the company and its dividend in dollars on an annual basis. Some corporations, Celotex for example, pay no dividends on their common stock. Dividend rates are in dollars and represent an annual disbursement based on the last quarterly or semiannual declaration.

An "a" indicates that a company has paid an extra dividend. For example, the regular dividend of Fruehauf Trailer Company is $1.50, but the company has paid an extra dividend within the past year. If all shares of stock were $100 par value, the dividend rate could be given in percentages of par. This is frequently done in foreign countries. However, since the par of shares varies from $100 to no-par value, the only consistent and simple way to give the dividend is in terms of dollars.

Other abbreviations commonly used by the *Wall Street Journal* and their meanings include the following:

cld–called	wi–when issued
x–ex dividend	pf–preferred stock
y–ex dividend and sales in full	nd–next day delivery
x-dis–ex distribution	vj–in bankruptcy or
xr–ex rights	receivership
xw–without warrants	fn–foreign issue subject
ww–with warrants	to interest
wd–when distributed	equalization tax

New York Stock Exchange Transactions

Friday, June 26, 1964

--1964-- High	Low	Stocks Div.	Sales in 100s	Open	High	Low	Close	Net Chg.
15⅛	12⅝	Carlisle .50	4	14	14	14	14	.....
106½	103	Caro C&O 5	z30	105½	105½	105½	105½	−1
38	36½	Caro PwLt 1	33	37¾	38⅜	37¾	38¼	+ ½
56¼	51	CaroT&T 1.60	6	51	51	51	51	.....
39⅞	31½	CarpStl 1.20a	8	35⅝	35⅞	35½	35⅞	+ ⅜
58½	41¾	Carrier 1.60	5	53½	53½	53⅛	53¼	− ⅝
34½	32⅛	CarrGen .30e	1	34⅛	34⅛	34⅛	34⅛	− ⅜
22⅛	16⅝	CarterPd .40	31	17¼	17⅝	17⅛	17½	+ ⅜
17¼	10⅛	Case JI	10	15⅝	15⅞	15⅝	15⅝	...
131	84	Case 7 pf	z10	126	126	126	126	+ ½
7	4⅜	Case 2nd pf	7	6¾	6¾	6⅝	6⅝	− ⅛
37¾	35¾	CastleCk 1.40	13	36¼	36¼	36	36	− ½
65⅞	48¼	CaterTr 1.60	59	65⅝	65⅞	64½	65¼	− ⅝
33¼	30	CaterTrac wi	60	33⅛	33⅛	32⅝	32⅞	− ¼
29	24⅞	Ceco Stl 1.20	2	27⅜	27⅜	27⅜	27⅜	+ ⅛
72¼	57¼	Celanese 1.60	153	65¾	65½	64⅞	65¼	+ ¼
32½	25	Celotex	9	28	28	28	28	.....
18½	17¾	Celotex pf1	1	18¾	18¾	18¾	18¾	.....
55	42	CencoInst .50	10	46⅞	47¼	46¾	47	+ ⅛
37⅛	26	CentAg 1.60a	2	27¼	27¼	27⅛	27⅛	− ¼
19¼	17¼	Cent Fdy 1b	2	17¼	17¼	17¼	17¼	..
35¾	32½	Cen Hud 1.12	8	33¼	33¼	33¼	33¼	+ ⅜
53¾	46½	C IllLt 1.80b	3	53	53½	53	53½	+ ⅜
99½	96	C IllLt pf4.50	z80	97¾	97¾	97¾	97¾	− ¼
25⅝	23	C IllP Sv .84	20	24⅛	24½	24⅛	24½	+ ⅛
50	43½	Cent SW 1.28	17	48½	49	48½	48⅞	+ ⅜
29⅝	26	CenSoya 1.30	11	29	29¼	29	29¼	.
48	28¼	CerroCp 1.60	226	47	48½	47	48½	+1⅛
18¼	14⅛	Cer-teed .60	120	16	16½	16	16½	+ ¾
29⅝	22¾	CessnaAirc 1	29	26	26¼	25⅞	26⅛	..
3⅜	2½	Chad Goth	4	2⅞	2⅞	2⅞	2⅞	+ ⅛
36½	29½	ChampP 1.20	17	33⅜	34	33⅜	34	+ ½
42	36¼	ChampSpk 2	82	40	40⅛	39¾	39¾	...
38½	33	Chmplin 1.20	30	37¾	38⅛	37¾	38	+ ¼
20¼	15⅝	Checker Mot	3	15⅞	16	15⅞	16	+ ⅜
30⅜	25⅛	Chemetn 1	22	28⅜	29	28⅜	29	+1⅛
11¼	8⅛	Chemway .20	16	8⅜	8⅜	8¼	8¼	− ⅛
44¾	39¾	ChesVa 1.20b	1	41¼	41¼	41¼	41¼	+ ½
80¼	68½	Ches Oh 4	42	79½	79⅞	79½	79⅝	+ ⅜
59¾	51¼	Chesebr 1.40	36	55⅛	55¼	55	55¼	+ ¼
26¼	15¾	Chi&E Ill	3	24⅛	24⅛	24⅛	24⅛	− ⅛
33¾	18¼	ChiGtWn .50e	11	32¼	32⅜	32¼	32⅜	+ ⅛
47	36¼	ChGW pf2.50	5	45	45	44¾	44¾	− ¾
26¼	13¾	ChiMil St P 1	68	25⅞	25⅞	25¾	25⅞	− ¼
75	59½	ChMSPP pf5	5	70½	71	70½	71	.....
26¾	18⅞	ChiMusic .60	10	20½	20¾	20¼	20¼	− ⅛
49⅞	25⅝	Chi & NWest	17	49	49½	48¾	49¼	+ ½
72	47⅜	Chi&NW pf 5	19	70	70⅜	70	70	....
37¾	31⅛	ChPneu 1.40a	14	35	35½	35	35⅛	+ ½
35⅞	23¾	CRI Pacif 1	50	32⅛	32⅛	31⅞	31⅞	− ⅛
49	43	Chi Title 1.80	3	43	43	43	43	.....
19½	18	Chick C 1.20	5	18½	18¾	18½	18¾	.....
14⅝	10⅜	ChockFN .40	44	10⅞	11	10⅞	11	+ ⅛
18½	12⅜	ChrisCrft .66t	16	15½	15⅝	15½	15½	− ¼
52	37⅝	Chrysler 1	454	49¼	50	49¼	49⅜	+ ¼
27¼	24¾	CinGasEl .92	23	26⅞	27	26¾	27	.....
105¼	102¾	CinGE pf4.75	z10	105	105	105	105	+1
55½	40¾	Cin Mill 1.60	13	54½	54⅝	54½	54½	+ ½
40½	34⅜	CIT Fin 1.60	114	35	35	34⅝	34¾	− ⅜
71¾	62¾	CitiesSv 2.60	67	70½	71⅜	70⅜	71⅜	+ ⅞
119½	109¾	CitSv pf 4.40	3	117½	117½	117¼	117¼	+ ¼
65¼	57½	CitS cvpf2.25	12	64	64⅝	63½	64⅝	+ ⅝
26⅜	19¾	City Inv .50b	2	20	20	19⅞	19⅞	− ⅜
38⅝	32	CityProd 1.50	9	35⅞	35⅞	35½	35¾	.....
9	8	City Stores	3	8⅜	8⅜	8⅜	8⅜	.....
54¾	40¾	ClarkEq 1.60	18	54⅞	54⅞	54⅛	54½	− ¼
65¾	49⅞	ClevCliffs 2a	3	61¾	61¾	61¼	61⅝	+ ⅜
35⅞	31	ClevElIll 1.20	47	33½	33½	33	33⅛	− ⅜
41½	38⅝	Clev P spl 2	z10	40	40	40	40	.....
48½	38	Clevite 1.40b	24	48⅛	48⅛	47⅝	47⅝	− ⅛
55½	49	CluettP 1.70	6	53⅜	53¾	53⅜	53½	+ ½
146	137¾	CluettP pf 7	z100	138½	139	138½	139	+ ½
38½	29	Coast St Gas	88	32½	32⅞	31¾	32	− ½
132½	111¾	Coca Cola 3	22	129¾	129⅞	129	129¾	+ ¼
28	22	CocaBt NY 1	17	23	23½	23	23½	+ ⅞

--1964-- High	Low	Stocks Div.	Sales in 100s	Open	High	Low	Close	Net Chg.
33½	25½	Fifth Ave L	8	29⅞	29⅞	29¼	29¼	− ½
39¾	31⅝	Filtrol 1.80	20	37¼	37¼	36½	36½	− ½
68⅝	45⅜	FinFed 2.57t	13	48½	48⅞	48¼	48⅞	+ ⅜
44⅜	37⅛	Firestne 1.10	41	41¼	41¾	41¼	41½	− ⅛
47⅛	33	FstChrt 1.97f	40	34⅛	34¼	33½	34	.....
52	46½	FstNatStr 2a	4	49½	49½	49½	49½	.....
22	18¾	Fischbach 1	5	19⅛	19⅛	19	19	− ¼
28¾	23	Flintkt .80	40	25	25⅛	24¾	24⅞	+ ⅛
90	86½	Flintkt 4pf 4	z100	87½	87½	87½	87½	− ½
14⅞	8½	Fla E Coast	25	13¼	13⅜	13	13	− ¼
48½	43	Fla Pw 1.12	17	46⅛	46½	45⅝	46	− ⅛
78¾	71	Fla PL 1.40	29	78	79½	78	79½	+1½
19	15⅜	Fluor .78t	25	19	19¼	19	19⅛	+ ⅛
24¾	19⅛	FoodFair .90	85	23⅜	23⅜	22¼	23	− ¼
18⅞	15½	FdGMkt .33t	13	18⅝	18⅝	18½	18⅝	+ ¼
58⅞	51½	FMC Corp 1	28	57¾	58	57½	58	+ ⅜
22¼	15⅜	FoodMart .70	12	21¾	21⅞	21⅝	21⅝	− ⅛
16⅛	10⅞	Foote M .15g	31	15⅜	15¾	15¼	15½	− ¼
58⅞	48⅞	Ford Mot 2	195	51¾	52	51⅝	51⅞	+ ⅜
11⅞	9¾	Forem D .40	79	11¾	11⅞	11⅝	11⅝	− ⅛
32⅜	23⅞	Fost Wheeler	6	30¾	31	30½	31	...
50	35	Foxboro .80	2	46¾	46¾	46¼	46¼	− ¾
33½	28⅝	Fram 1.20b	x5	31	31¼	31	31¼	+ ⅝
39⅝	33	FreeptS 1.20	54	35⅜	35⅜	35⅛	35⅛	− ⅛
45¾	38	Frito Lay .70	10	43½	43½	42¾	42¾	−1
32½	28	Fruehf 1.50a	x71	31⅜	31⅜	31	31⅛	+ ⅛
89	86	Fruehauf pf4	z100	87½	87½	87½	87½	+ ½
		G						
35½	25⅞	GambSk 1.20	9	32½	33	32¼	33	+ ¾
4⅞	3⅞	Gar Wood	2	4	4⅛	4	4⅛	+ ⅛
48⅜	36¼	GardDen 1.75	24	45½	45¾	45	45¾	+ ¼
17¾	15½	Garlock .60	1	16⅛	16⅛	16⅛	16⅛	..
22¼	17⅞	G Accept 1	4	20½	20½	20⅛	20⅛	− ¼
32	28½	GAmIn 2.15e	3	30⅞	30⅞	30⅝	30⅝	− ⅛
36	30⅛	GAmOil .40b	39	32⅜	33⅜	32	32	...
78	69⅞	GATran 2.50	22	76¼	76½	75⅞	76	− ¼
11⅜	8½	Gen Baking	2	8⅝	8⅝	8½	8½	− ⅛
94	90	GenBak pf6	z600	90¼	90⅜	89¼	89¼	−1⅛
11	9	GenBanc .48	4	10¼	10⅜	10¼	10⅜	..
31½	26½	Gen Cable 1	15	27⅞	28⅝	27⅞	28⅝	+ ⅞
73½	38¼	Gen Cig 1.20	11	72½	73	72¼	73	+ ½
7	5	Gen ContFin	28	6⅞	6⅞	6¾	6⅞	...
31⅝	23½	Gen Dynam	74	27½	27⅝	27¼	27½	...
90⅝	78¾	GenElec 2.20	196	79	79¼	78¾	79	− ¼
21½	19¼	GenFinan .80	9	20¼	20⅜	20¼	20¼	..
92⅜	82	Gen Foods 2	48	87⅝	88	87½	87¾	− ⅛
16⅝	11½	Gen Instrum	147	13	13⅜	13	13⅜	+ ⅜
42⅜	36	G Mills 1.20	34	39¾	39⅞	39⅛	39⅜	− ⅜
115½	112¾	G Mills pf5	z40	114	114	114	114	−1
90⅝	77¼	GenMot 1.80e	277	86½	87¾	86⅜	87⅝	+1⅛
116¾	112½	G Mot 5pf 5	4	115¼	115¼	114⅝	114⅞	− [illegible]
90⅛	86½	G Mot pf3.75	5	90⅛	90¼	90⅛	90¼	+ ¼
28¾	22⅜	GPCem 1.20	17	25¼	25½	25¼	25¼	+ ⅛
32⅜	25½	GPrecn 1.20	13	27	27	26¾	26⅞	− ⅛
6	5½	GPubSvc .33e	43	5⅞	5⅞	5¾	5¾	..
36	31½	GPubUt 1.28	24	36¼	36¼	36	36	+ ⅛
18½	13¾	GRefrac .60a	69	15¼	15⅜	15¼	15¼	+ ⅛
34½	26¾	Gen Sig 1.20	7	32¾	32⅞	32½	32⅝	.
27⅞	22½	G StlInd 1.20	208	27¾	28¾	27¾	28¾	+1⅛
35⅝	31⅜	GTel&El .88	334	32⅜	33⅛	32¼	33	+ ¾
14¼	11¼	GenTime .25	143	12⅛	12⅝	12⅛	12¼	+ ⅛
28¼	21⅜	GenTire .50	99	22⅝	22⅞	22⅝	22⅝	+ ⅛
40¼	36	Genesco 1.60	8	39¼	39¼	39⅛	39⅛	....
104¾	101¾	Genes pf4.50	2	104¾	104¾	104¾	104¾	....
54	49¾	Ga Pac n1	32	53¾	53⅞	53¼	53¾	[illegible]

--1964-- High	Low	Stocks Div.	Sales in 100s	Open	High	Low	Close	Net Chg.
70¼	58¼	KimbClark 2	71	58¼	58½	58⅛	58½	− ⅜
51¾	40½	King S 1.60a	2	50¾	50⅞	50¾	50⅞	+ ⅛
23¾	15¾	Kinney Svc	9	16¼	16¼	16⅛	16⅛	− ⅛
23½	18¾	KirkNat .40	12	19½	19½	19½	19½	...
24½	14⅜	KLM Airline	1	19	19	19	19	− ¼
49¾	39¾	Koppers 2	5	46½	46⅞	46½	46⅞	+ ⅛
37	27½	Korvette	63	34⅝	35⅜	34⅝	35	....
40½	28⅞	Kresge 1.20	77	40⅞	41⅜	40⅞	41	+ ½
30⅝	21	KressSH .25g	1	26¾	26¾	26¾	26¾	...
22	16⅞	Kroehler .40e	2	21¼	21¼	21¼	21¼	+ [illegible]
34⅜	26½	Kroger 1.10	16	33¾	34	33⅝	33¾	− ⅜
32	28¾	KVPSu 1.40a	12	30⅛	30¾	30⅛	30¾	+ ⅝
		L						
9¼	6	Lab Electron	26	6	6¼	6	6	....
28⅛	23⅜	LacGas 1.05b	9	24½	24¾	24½	24¾	+ ⅜
31¼	25	Lane Bry 1b	4	29½	29½	29½	29½	....
18⅞	15	Lanv Ritz .40	39	17⅞	17⅞	17½	17⅝	− [illegible]
21¾	18½	Lanvin pf.80	2	20¾	20¾	20⅝	20⅝	+ [illegible]
15¼	11¼	Lear Sieg .50	19	12¼	12¾	12⅛	12⅝	+ [illegible]
24¼	18¼	Lee Nat Cp	4	19¼	19⅜	19¼	19⅜	...
54⅞	31⅝	Leesona .50	45	47½	48⅜	47⅜	48¼	+ [illegible]
18⅞	15	Leh Port 1	8	15⅞	16	15⅞	16	+ [illegible]
3¼	1¼	Leh Val Ind	16	2½	2½	2⅜	2⅜	− [illegible]
28¾	21⅛	LVInd pf1.50	1	26	26	26	26	....
30¾	28⅝	Lehman 1.59e	14	29½	29½	29⅛	29½	+ [illegible]
31⅞	27⅞	Lehn&Fink 1	14	29⅞	29⅞	29¾	29⅞	+ [illegible]
11½	9⅞	LeonardR .60	2	10	10⅛	10	10⅛	+ [illegible]
58¾	51⅞	LOFGls 2.60	43	56	56⅞	55¾	56⅞	+1[illegible]
19½	14	Lib McN .35t	241	19⅛	20¼	19	20	+1
85¼	70	Liggett&M 5	24	74⅝	75¼	74⅝	75	+ [illegible]
154	151½	Ligg&My pf7	z10	152¼	152¼	152¼	152¼	[illegible]
40¼	30⅛	Lily Tulip 1	46	34⅜	34⅜	34	34¼	+ ¼
20¼	14½	LingTVgt .50	45	18¼	18¼	18⅛	18¼	..
68½	55½	LinkBlt 2.40a	10	62	62	61½	61½	− [illegible]
5¼	3¾	Lionel Corp	21	4⅛	4⅛	4	4⅛	...
79⅝	58¼	LittonIn 1.98f	101	64¾	65	64⅜	64⅜	..
93	83¼	Litton cvpf 3	14	89¾	90	89½	90	+ [illegible]
40⅞	31¾	LockAirc 1.60	303	34⅝	35¼	34½	35	+ [illegible]
24¾	17¼	Loews Thea	8	18⅝	18¾	18½	18¾	...
24⅜	18⅞	LoneSCem 1	37	21	21¼	21	21⅛	+ [illegible]
23⅞	21⅝	LoneS Gas 1	86	23	23	22⅝	22¾	− [illegible]
35¼	30⅛	LongIslLt .92	29	31⅞	31⅞	31½	31⅝	− [illegible]
9¾	6⅛	Loral Electr	14	6⅝	6⅝	6½	6⅝	..
50⅜	40⅛	Lorillard 2.50	55	42⅜	42¾	42⅛	42⅝	+ [illegible]
37⅞	33½	LouisGE .98	8	34⅞	34⅞	34½	34½	− [illegible]
94¾	81¾	Lou Nash 3a	2	83½	83½	83½	83½	+ [illegible]
15⅛	12	Lowenstein	4	14⅞	15	14⅞	15	+ [illegible]
25	19¼	LuckySt .80b	17	24⅜	24¾	24¼	24½	+ [illegible]
79	40⅞	LukensSt 1.60	140	78	80½	77¾	80¼	+2
21⅜	18½	Lykes SS .80	4	19⅛	19⅜	19⅛	19⅜	...
		M						
33½	23	MacAnd 1.20	2	32⅛	32⅛	32⅛	32⅛	− [illegible]
48	36¾	MackTr 1.80	46	46⅞	47¼	46⅞	47⅛	+ [illegible]
84½	74½	MacyRH 2.20	7	78⅜	78¾	78⅛	78¾	+ [illegible]
95	91½	Macy pf 4.25	z350	94	94	94	94	+1[illegible]
22⅞	18¾	MadFd 1.28e	49	19½	19¾	19⅜	19¾	+ [illegible]
1⅞	1½	Mad Sq Gar	14	1½	1½	1½	1½	..
46	31	MagmaC .50e	9	37	37¼	37	37	+ [illegible]
43⅞	29¾	Magnavx .90	69	32½	32¾	32⅛	32⅝	...
34½	28⅛	Mallory 1.20	2	29	29	29	29	...
26½	21	MnShirt .70b	6	22½	22½	21¾	21¾	...
28	24	Manning 1.40	1	25¼	25¼	25¼	25¼	...
68⅞	55¾	Marathon 2	29	65	65	64⅜	64½	− [illegible]

Fig. 8–3 NYSE stock quotations (from the *Wall Street Journal*), circles added by authors. All *Wall Street Journal* excerpts in this book are reproduced by permission of the copyright holder, the Dow Jones & Company, Inc.

Column 4 gives the volume of sales in hundreds for the day. For example, on June 26, 1964, 27,700 shares of General Motors were sold. Odd-lot sales (less than 100 shares) are not included in these figures. The leaders of the market can usually be identified by glancing down this column to locate the stocks with large volumes. Of course, before any final judgment can be given, volume must be checked against the number of shares of the company listed and the rise of the price per share. In respect to the volume of trading, the leaders of the market change from time to time. At one point chemical stocks may be popular; at another manufacturers of data-processing equipment are volume leaders. Increased tension in the Cold War may cause volume in the aerospace companies to rise. Perhaps a single stock, such as Chrysler, will become popular when its products are well accepted.

A leader of six months ago may not be popular today. Stocks have their periods of youth and activity, after which they leave the stage, settle down to a normal, conservative growth pattern, or emerge again, through some technological innovation, to the forefront of the public's attention.

The fifth, sixth, seventh, and eighth columns give the price at which the first sale was made, the highest price for the day, the lowest price for the day, and the price paid on the last sale of the day. If only one sale were made, the opening, high, low, and closing prices would all be the same, as in the example of 100 shares of Kress (S.H.) at $26\frac{3}{4}$. The first, or opening, price of the most conservative investment stocks is usually about the same figure as the closing price the previous day. This is not necessarily true, however, especially with widely fluctuating values. Many things can happen between 3:30 P.M., when the Exchange closes, and 10 A.M. the next morning. A customer's inquiry as to how the market opened may be answered, "The market opened up." This means that the leading stocks opened higher than the close of the previous day.

On Friday, November 22, 1963, the New York Stock Exchange was closed shortly after 2 P.M. following the news of the assassination of President John F. Kennedy in Dallas. In the last few minutes of trading after the tragic news reached the floor the market dropped 18 points to close at 711.49. By the time the market opened on the following Tuesday morning, selling orders had accumulated, and the market opened at 738.43, a rise of 26.94 points, or about 3.8 per cent above Friday's close.

On the day on which a stock is sold ex dividend the opening, if nothing of importance has happened since the previous day's close, will probably be lower than the previous close by the amount of the dividend. The quotation for a share of stock includes in the price the accrued dividend up to the ex-dividend day, which is the third business day before the company's books are closed. If a company pays $1.50 quarterly, the price of the stock on the fourth business day before the company's books are closed will include the dividend; on the next day the dividend is not included. Thus a purchaser of the share on the day before the ex-dividend day would be willing to pay $1.50 more for the share than he would on the following day. Bonds, with a few exceptions like income bonds or defaulted bonds, sell "plus accrued interest." The quoted price of a bond does not change at the time of interest payments. The buyer of a bond pays the quoted price plus the amount of interest that has accrued from the date of the last interest payment to the date of purchase.

The column headed "Net Change" compares the closing price of the day with the closing price of the previous day on which there was a sale. Liggett & Meyers closed at 75, which was up $\frac{5}{8}$ from Thursday's close. Thursday's close must have been $74\frac{3}{8}$. Note that Friday's opening at $74\frac{5}{8}$ was $\frac{1}{4}$ point above Thursday's close.

In some papers ninth and tenth columns are added to give the bid, or buying, price and the offer, or selling, price quoted by brokers at the close.

There may be no actual sale for some time before the close, but brokers are willing to buy each stock at some price. The bid is, of course, lower than the offer price. The bid and ask prices relative to the closing sale indicate the strength of the market at the close. For example, suppose that the last sale of Texaco was at $79\frac{1}{4}$, that the bid price was also $79\frac{1}{4}$, but that the ask price was up $\frac{1}{4}$ from the last sale. In this event, Texaco closed strong, for had an additional buy order come to market, the price would have risen to $79\frac{1}{2}$, whereas had an additional sell order come to market, the price would not have declined. On the other hand, Curtiss-Wright might close at the high for the day and up $\frac{1}{8}$ from the previous day, but its bid and ask prices might indicate that had an additional sell order come to the market just before the close the price would have declined $\frac{1}{8}$ point.

The term "spread" is used to designate the difference between the bid and ask prices. The spread on the New York Stock Exchange cannot be less than $\frac{1}{8}$ point. The activity of a stock can generally be judged by the width of the spread between the bid and the offer. Activity narrows the spread. Of two stocks having the same degree of activity, but one widely fluctuating and the other hardly fluctuating at all, we expect to find the spread of the former much greater than that of the latter. Again, in a rapidly rising or falling market spreads will be wider than in a steady market. The spread then finally depends on the activity of the stock, the width of its fluctuations, and the steepness of up-and-down movements of prices in the market as a whole.

Each day there are many stocks on the New York Stock Exchange for which there are bid and ask prices but in which no actual sales take place. Such stocks with the bid and ask quotations are reported separately, not in the same place with sales.

Those who wish to inform themselves on what the market is doing but who do not have time to study the long list of quotations reported on the financial page can make use of the numerous summaries now printed in most of the nation's newspapers. For example, the *Wall Street Journal* displays in a box the open, high, low, close, net change, and volume of the 10 most active issues each day. On another page it also gives the total number of issues in which trading occurred, the number of stocks that advanced, the number that declined, the number of new highs, and the number of new lows. Thus, if 1,383 issues were traded and if 84 issues made new highs, while only 14 made new lows, the reader would quickly conclude that the course of the market was upward. Frequently, the number of new highs and new lows, or advances and declines, indicate a different direction for the market than do the Dow-Jones averages. Figure 8–4 is a reproduction of summaries of this nature published by the *Wall Street Journal*.

Full lists of sales and prices on the American Stock Exchange are also quoted, but only leading stocks are given in the quotations for regional exchanges such as the Toronto, Philadelphia-Baltimore-Washington, Mid-

22 THE WALL STREET JOURNAL,
Monday, September 21, 1964

Friday's Volume, 6,160,000 Shares

Volume since Jan. 1:	1964	1963	1962
Total sales	889,243,657	801,926,753	687,848,352

MOST ACTIVE STOCKS

	Open	High	Low	Close	Chg.	Volume
Ford Mot	59	59⅜	57⅜	57⅞	− ¾	156,200
Chrysler	66⅛	66⅜	64⅛	65	−1⅛	147,700
Ch MSP Pac	27¼	30¾	27¼	30¾	+3¾	110,700
Am Motors	18	18	17½	17½	− ½	91,000
Xerox Corp	118¾	119⅛	115⅝	117⅝	− ¾	78,300
US Steel	63¾	63¾	61½	62⅝	−1	71,200
Brunswk	8⅛	8⅝	8	8¼	+ ¼	69,100
Sperry Rd	14½	15	14½	14⅝	+ ¼	68,800
Am Photo	7⅝	8⅝	7⅝	8	+ ⅜	63,600
Beth Steel	43	43¼	40⅛	42½	− ⅜	61,300

Average closing price of most active stocks: 42.47.

MARKET DIARY

	Fri.	Thur.	Wed	Tues.	Mon.	Fri.
Issues traded	1,354	1,383	1,332	1,371	1,347	1,368
Advances	392	691	582	472	478	605
Declines	687	431	470	660	605	488
Unchanged	275	261	280	239	264	275
New highs, 1964	63	84	58	59	77	82
New lows, 1964	14	14	23	27	26	12

Fig. 8–4

west, Salt Lake City, Detroit, Pittsburgh, Boston, Cincinnati, Pacific Coast, and Honolulu exchanges. Local newspapers and local editions of national newspapers frequently carry a full account of local exchanges. Thus the West Coast edition of the *Wall Street Journal* carries a full list of Pacific Coast Stock Exchange transactions.

Over-the-counter Stocks. An extensive over-the-counter market for securities also exists. Under the Maloney Act of 1938, brokers selling stocks and bonds over the counter may organize into national associations. The only such organization existing is the National Association of Securities Dealers, and the *Wall Street Journal* devotes practically a full page to reporting bid and ask prices obtained from the NASD. Quotations are supplied for industrial and utility stocks, bank stocks, insurance stocks, and foreign stocks. Corporate bonds and public authority bonds are also quoted, as are mutual funds. Additional over-the-counter stock quotations are supplied in a weekly list in Monday's *Wall Street Journal.*

Bid and ask prices in the newspapers are "retail" prices, i.e., prices that are generally available to the public. These prices are usually determined by marking up the "inside," or "wholesale," ask price at which NASD members trade among themselves. Customary markups are as follows:

Stocks priced under \$25 per share:	5.0%
Stocks priced from \$25 to \$70:	3.6–5.0%
Stocks priced from \$70 to \$135:	2.5–3.6%
Stocks priced above \$135:	2.0%

New York Stock Exchange quotations are usually accompanied in most newspapers by an article describing the day's market and explaining the different factors that influenced it. The column is headed "Abreast of the Market" in the *Wall Street Journal*. The headlines indicate the outstanding movements of the market, while the paragraphs that follow give more detail on the factors affecting individual stock prices.

Bond Quotations

Bond Quotations on the New York Stock Exchange. The quotation of bonds takes quite a different form from that of stocks. In the *Wall Street Journal,* bonds traded on the New York Stock Exchange are classified as follows: (1) corporation bonds, (2) foreign bonds (governmental), (3) New York City bonds. The American Stock Exchange and leading regional exchanges also quote bonds but have smaller lists.

Bonds are regularly quoted "plus accrued interest," meaning that the purchaser pays the price quoted for the bonds plus the accrued interest from the last interest date to the date of purchase. If a bond paying interest on January 1 and July 1 were purchased on May 1, the buyer would pay to the seller the indicated purchase price plus interest on the principal amount for four months (January through April). On July 1 the buyer would receive interest for a full six-month period, a portion of which would reimburse him for the accrued interest paid to the seller and the remainder of which would compensate him for his investment in the bond during May and June. Income bonds and bonds in default are quoted "flat," meaning that no accrued interest is paid. The seller surrenders all claim to interest due him.

Prices on corporation bonds and foreign government bonds are quoted in $\frac{1}{8}$ points and are expressed as a per cent of par value. The unit of trading on the New York Stock Exchange is bonds of $1,000 par value; so a price of $92\frac{7}{8}$ quoted for an American Telephone & Telegraph Company bond means that the bond was sold at 92.875 per cent of par, or $928.75, plus accrued interest.

A few United States government, New York state, New York City, and International Bank bonds are listed on the New York Stock Exchange, but most trading in these bonds takes place in the over-the-counter market. These bonds are quoted in $\frac{1}{32}$ points, a decimal being used to separate the fractional from the dollar portion of the price. A price of 92.26 for a New York City bond means that the bond sold at $92\frac{26}{32}$ of par, or $928.125 per bond.

The interest rate on bond quotations is also given as a percentage of par; thus $4\frac{1}{2}$s means that interest payments are 4.5 per cent of the par value of the bond per year. Portions of the New York Stock Exchange bond quotation section from the *Wall Street Journal* are shown in Figure 8–5.

Corporation Bonds
Volume, $8,530,000

New York Stock Exchange Bonds

Friday, June 26, 1964

Volume, All Issues, $8,750,000

Dow Jones Bond Averages

New York City Bonds

Foreign Bonds
Volume, $220,000

Fig. 8–5 NYSE bond quotations from the *Wall Street Journal.*

Bond Quotations in the Over-the-counter Market. The over-the-counter market is the principal market for United States government bonds, notes, certificates, and bills; for bonds and notes of such semigovernmental organizations as the Federal Home Loan Bank, the Federal National Mortgage Association, and the Federal Land Bank; for bonds of the International Bank for Reconstruction and Development; for municipal bonds; and for a great many corporate bonds. Over-the-counter bond quotations for many of these bonds appear daily in the financial pages. A complete list of over-the-counter corporate bond quotations is published in the Bond Section of the National Daily Quotation Service. The *Blue List,* published by a subsidiary of Standard & Poor's Corporation, carries a complete list of municipal bond quotations.

Some bonds are quoted in the over-the-counter market on a yield basis rather than on a price basis. Both bid price and ask price are expressed in terms of the percentage yield obtained by the buyer if the bond is held to maturity. For example, if the XYZ 3¾ per cent municipal general obligation bonds, due in 30 years, were quoted at a bid of 3.95 and an ask of 3.85, a potential seller would look in a bond table and find that the bid price was $965. A potential buyer would be interested in the ask price, which he would find to be $982.30. Note that the ask price in dollars is higher than the bid price, as would be expected, but that when prices are expressed on a yield basis the ask price is a lower percentage yield than the bid.

Quotation changes on a yield basis vary by 1 "basis point," which is a change of $\frac{1}{100}$ percentage point in the yield. If a bond quoted on a yield basis of 3.67 per cent were to rise in price 2 basis points, the yield would fall to 3.65 per cent.

Stock and Bond Price Indexes

An integral part of stock and bond quotations in the financial pages is an understanding of stock and bond price indexes and averages. The next chapter is devoted entirely to this topic.

Dividend Declarations

The policy of a board of directors regarding dividend disbursements is closely watched. Rumors of extra cash dividends or of stock dividend payments often affect the market for the stock in question very materially. Every trader will be guessing what the board of directors will do at the next meeting. If the stock has been active, with an upward tendency, "insiders" are presumed to be buying because they know that the dividend will be increased or that there will be an extra.

The *Wall Street Journal* has a column entitled Dividend News, in which it informs its readers of the companies whose boards of directors have voted on the matter of dividends. Announcements of dividends are presented as shown in Figure 8–6.

New Offerings

The Securities Act of 1933 requires that an organization wishing to sell new issues of stocks or bonds in interstate commerce must first file with the Securities and Exchange Commission a statement containing information about the securities which it plans to offer. This statement, called a "registration statement," must remain on file for a period of not less than twenty days before the issuer sells or even makes an offer to sell a new security. Announcements of the filing of registration statements by corporations are

Corporate Dividend News

Fearn Foods, Inc., put its common stock on a quarterly dividend basis and declared a payout of 25 cents, payable July 15 to stock of record July 3. The company's latest payment was a semiannual dividend of 30 cents plus a year-end extra of 40 cents in January.

Eaton Manufacturing Co. raised its quarterly dividend to 50 cents a share from 45 cents, payable Aug. 25 to common stock of record Aug. 5.

Packer's Super Markets, Inc., declared a 4% stock dividend on common, payable July 23 to stock of record July 6. The company's last previous payment was a similar stock payout in June 1962.

Emery Industries, Inc., a producer of chemicals, raised its quarterly dividend to 12½ cents a share from 10 cents, payable Sept. 1 to stock of record Aug. 14. The increase is the third for the company in 14 months.

Dividends Reported June 26-27

Company	Period	Amt	Payable date	Record date
Appalachian Pwr 4½% pf.	Q	1.12½	8–1–64	7–6
Avco Corp	Q	.25	8–20–64	7–31
Arkansas Louisiana Gas	..	z.30	9–15–64	8–21

Company	Period	Amt.	Payable date	Record date
Axe Houghton Fund B		j.08	7–24–64	7–3
j-from income.				
Bergen Drug Co. Cl. A	Q	.12½	7–30–64	7–15
Campbell Machine Inc	Q	.08	11–15–64	10–30
Campbell Machine Inc	Q	.08	2–15–65	1–29
Campbell Machine Inc	Q.	.08	5–15–65	4–30
Central Hudson G&E		z.28	8–1–64	7–10
Computer Sciences Corp		z.03	7–31–64	7–15
Delaware Pwr & Lt	Q	.39	7–31–64	7–7
du Pont of Canada Ltd		z.20	7–31–64	7–3
Eaton Mfg Co		c.50	8–25–64	8–5
Eaton Mfg Co 4¾% pf	Q	.29	8–23–94	8–8
Emery Industries		c.12½	9–1–64	8–14
Exchange Fund Boston	S	n.29	7–15–64	6–30
n-from investment income.				
Fearn Foods Inc		h.25	7–15–64	7–3
h-First dividend on a quarterly basis.				
Fidelity Bk, Beverly Hills S	.15		7–31–64	7–15
Fidelity Bk, Beverly Hills Stk	2½%		7–31–64	7–15
First Nat'l Bk, San Diego	Q	.36	7–31–64	7–20
First Nat'l Bk, San Diego	Q	.30	11–1–64	10–20
Kroger Co	Q	.27½	9–1–64	7–31
Lincoln Rochester Trust	.	.70	8–3–64	7–17
McGregor-Doniger cl A	Q	.25	7–31–64	7–15
Monongahela Pwr4.40% pf	Q	1.10	8–1–64	7–15
Monongahela Pwr4.80% pf	Q	1.20	8–1–64	7–15
Monongahela Pwr 4.50% pf	Q	1.12½	8–1–64	7–15
New Hampshire Ball Brg In		.05	8–20–64	7–20
Northwestern Glass Co		.25	8–1–64	7–20
Packer's Super Markets	Stk	4%	7–23–64	7–6
Parke Davis & Co		.25	7–31–64	7–7
Pepsi-Cola Gen'l Btl	Q	.15	8–1–64	7–20
Porter (H. K.) Cu. 5½%pf	Q	1.37½	7–31–64	7–15
Reliance Elec & Eng		z.45	7–31–64	7–16
Republic Corp	Q	.15	8–14–64	7–31
Scott Aviation Corp		z.10	7–31–64	7–15
Security Columbian Bknt	Q	.07½	7–31–64	7–15

Company	Period	Amt	Payable date	Record date
Seligman & Latz Inc		z.20	7–30–64	7–10
Sierra Pacific Power	Q	.25	8–1–64	7–17
k-from net investment income.				
United Bond Fund		k.08	7–31–64	7–9
Universal Cont cl A	Q	.07½	7–15–64	7–7
Yates-American Machine	Q	.35	7–31–64	7–15

Stocks Ex-Dividend June 30

Company	Amount	Company	Amount
Amer Mfg	.50	Harb-Walker pf	1.50
Appalchn Pw 4½% pf	1.12½	Hoover Ball&Rear'g	.30
Atlantic Refining pf B	.93¾	Montana Power	.28
Bklyn Un Gas	.33	Owns-Corning Fbrgls	.25
Bullard Co	.15	Swingline Inc cl A	.30
Calgon Corp	.30	Tubos deA DeM 'A'	.12
Cont'l Motors	.10	Tubos deA DeM 'B'	.12
Frito-Lay	.17½	United Fruit	.15
Gen Mot $5 pf	1.25	Upjohn Co	.25
Gen Mot $3.75 pf	.93¾	Warner Co	.30

z-Unchanged from previous quarter. c-Increased dividend. d-Reduced dividend.

A, annual; Ac, accumulation; E, extra; F, final; G, interim; In, initial; Liq, liquidation; M, monthly; Q, regular quarterly; R, resumed; S, semi-annual; Sp, special.

Fig. 8–6 Wall Street Journal corporate dividend news.

news and are reported on the financial page. Investors looking for small companies going public for the first time can often find them in such listings, an example of which appears in Figure 8–7.

Changes in Insider Stockholdings

An insider may on occasion have access to confidential information which would permit him to trade in the market to the detriment of stockholders generally. To prevent such dealings, the Securities Exchange Act of 1934 provides that any person owning, directly or indirectly, more than 10 per cent of any class of stock listed on a national exchange, or who is an officer or director of the company issuing the stock, must report the amount of stock owned to the stock exchange and to the SEC. In addition, changes in the amount of holdings must be reported within ten days of the end of each month. The law also tries to prevent insiders from profiting from their position by providing that any profits derived by them from purchase and sale, or sale and purchase, within a six-month period shall be recoverable by the issuing company. The public is presumed to be protected by making changes in insider stockownership public information. Leading newspapers regularly carry information obtained from the SEC on changes in insiders' stockholdings. A typical report is shown in Figure 8–8.

Short Selling

If a person believes a stock is about to fall in price, he may sell the stock short in anticipation of buying it back at a later date. Short selling is ex-

```
┌─────────────────────────────────────────┐
│           SEC Calendar                    │
└─────────────────────────────────────────┘
```

Proposed new issues named below were filed with the
Securities and Exchange Commission on the dates shown.
Included in the list are issues with a dollar value of $2
million or more and, in the case of stocks, a share value
of at least $10. Issues may be cleared for sale by the
SEC in anywhere from a few weeks to several months.
Chief underwriter's name, where known, appears at the
right of the filing date.

BONDS

Jade Oil & Gas Co., cv. debs.		$2,500,000
Oct. 28, 1963		Hannaford & Talbot
Province of Santa Fe, Argentina, bonds		$3,000,000
Dec. 17, 1963		No Underwriting
IMC Industries, Inc., cv. debs.		$2,500,000
April 24, 1964		White & Co.
Airport Parking Co. of America, cv. debs.		$2,500,000
May 11, 1964		Burnham & Co.
Baltimore Gas & Electric Co., bonds		$30,000,000
June 1, 1964		Competitive
New Jersey Power & Light Co., debs.		$6,000,000
June 2, 1964		Competitive
Milwaukee Gas Light Co., bonds		$18,000,000
June 12, 1964		Competitive
Montana-Dakota Utilities Co., bonds		$12,000,000
June 12, 1964		Competitive
J. C. Penney Credit Corp., debs.		$50,000,000
June 19, 1964		First Boston Corp.
Northern Illinois Gas Co., bonds		$20,000,000
June 19, 1964		Competitive
Northern States Power Co. (Wis.), bonds		$15,000,000
June 22, 1964		Competitive

STOCKS

Research Capital Corp., com.		400,000 shs
Sept. 3, 1963		Hensberry & Co.
Life Holding Corp., com.		75,758 shs
Nov. 29, 1963		Ralph B. Leonard S Sons
Salant & Salant, Inc., Class A com.		250,000 shs
March 13, 1964		Kidder, Peabody & Co.
Northern States Power Co. (Minn.), $100 pfd.		150,000 shs
June 1, 1964		Competitive
Fabri-Tek, Inc., com.		200,000 shs
June 3, 1964		Kidder, Peabody & Co.
Melnor Industries, Inc., com.		225,000 shs
June 4, 1964		Francis I. duPont, A. C. Allyn, Inc.
Industrial Life Insurance Co., cap.		15,000 shs
June 8, 1964		Kidder, Peabody & Co.
Nationwide Corp., Class A com.		2,000,000 shs
June 10, 1964		Paine, Webber, Jackson & Curtis
Professional Insurance Co. of New York, com.		129,990 shs
June 11, 1964		M. A. Schapiro & Co.
Loehmann's, Inc., com.		210,000 shs
June 19, 1964		W. C. Langley & Co.
Rayette, Inc., com.		250,000 shs
June 22, 1964		Smith, Barney & Co.
American Hoist & Derrick Co., com.		200,000 shs
June 22, 1964		Lehman Brothers
American Fidelity Life Insurance Co., com.		211,159 shs
June 23, 1964		Alex. Brown & Sons
Republic Foil, Inc., com.		150,000 shs
June 23, 1964		Laird & Co.
Public Service Co. of North Carolina, $25 cv. pfd.		120,000 shs
June 25, 1964		First Boston Corp.

Fig. 8–7 SEC calendar from the *Wall Street
Journal.*

plained in detail in Chapter 15. The short sale is considered by many as an
indicator of potential demand for the stock, as those who have sold short
must sooner or later buy back. Thus the amount of short interest in a stock
is a matter of public interest. If the short interest in a stock becomes too
large relative to the number of shares outstanding, a "short squeeze" may

develop, in which the shorts all try to purchase a limited amount of stock and the price is driven up very rapidly.

If the amount of short interest is 5,000 shares or more, or if there has been a change in the short position of 2,000 shares or more during a month, the short position is reported in the *Wall Street Journal* and other financial papers on or about the twentieth of the month. A portion of the story and report from the *Wall Street Journal* of June 19, 1964, appears in Figure 8–9.

Money Market Quotations

Salient features of the day's money market may be determined from a listing of money rates which appears in leading financial pages daily. Figure 8–10 is taken from the *Wall Street Journal* of Thursday, September 17, 1964.

Corporation Reports

The *Wall Street Journal* and other financial dailies publish a tabulation of corporate earnings reports, annual or quarterly, as they are released. A condensed and sometimes a full report may appear elsewhere in the paper. An example of a condensed report taken from the *Wall Street Journal* is given in Figure 8–11.

Insiders' Stockholdings

The New York and the American Stock Exchanges reported yesterday the changes carried below in the share holdings of officers, directors and controlling stockholders of listed companies.

These reports were prepared from filings made by the insiders with the Securities and Exchange Commission pursuant to the Securities Exchange Act of 1934.

NEW YORK STOCK EXCHANGE
CHRYSLER CORP.—E.C. Quinn, vice president, sold 4,000 shares, cutting his holdings to 20,170 shares.
DYMO INDUSTRIES, INC. — Robert A. Hummert acquired 3,090 shares, bringing his direct holdings to 14,111 shares.
FLORIDA EAST COAST RAILWAY—Jose A. Ferre, a director, indirectly acquired an initial 10,000 shares through Miami Caribe

Investments, Inc.
GENERAL BAKING CO.—Lewis C. Davis, vice president, liquidated his holdings of 4,000 shares.
OCCIDENTAL PETROLEUM CORP. — Lowell W. Berry, executive vice president and a director, sold 11,525 shares, cutting his direct holdings to 83,760 shares.
OLIN MATHIESON CHEMICAL CO.—John W. Hanes Jr., a director, indirectly acquired an initial 5,000 shares.
XEROX CORP.—E. Kent Damon, vice president, sold 5,000 shares, reducing his holdings to 21,270 shares.
AMERICAN STOCK EXCHANGE
CUBIC CORP.—Anderson Borthwick, a director, acquired an initial 1,000 shares indirectly.
INVESTMENT PROPERTY BUILDERS, INC.—Herbert B. Hendrick Jr., vice president and a director, sold 1,200 shares, cutting his holdings to 1,500 shares.
LEVITT AND SONS, INC.—Julius Silver, vice president and a director, sold 1,000 shares, liquidating his holdings.
RIO GRANDE VALLEY GAS CO.—Paul O. Koester, a director, bought 1,500 shares, raising his holdings to 34,000 shares.
PYERSON AND HAYNES, INC.—Harvey J. Campbell, a director, sold 3,206 shares, liquidating his holdings.

Fig. 8–8 Changes in insiders' stockholdings. (*From the New York Times.*)

Big Board Short Interest Declined 174,458 Shares in Month to June 15

Drop, to 6,378,677 Total, Was First in 4 Months; Curtis, Texas Gulf Led Decreases

By a WALL STREET JOURNAL Staff Reporter

NEW YORK—The short interest on the New York Stock Exchange dropped 174,458 shares to 6,378,677 in the month ended June 15, the exchange said.

It was the first monthly decrease in the short position in four months. The short position June 15 was less than 0.1% of all shares listed on the Big Board, the exchange said. On May 15 the total was 6,553,135 shares, revised downward from an original estimate of 6,572,235 shares.

Texas Gulf, Curtis Drops

The drop in total short interest in the month ended June 15 was exceeded by a combined 269,447-share decline in the short interest in Curtis Publishing Co. and Texas Gulf Sulphur Co. common stocks. In the month ended May 15, the short interest in these two issues had climbed a spectacular 627,844 shares following substantial price gains for both. The price gains had been sparked by announcement April 16 that Texas Gulf Sulphur had found an apparent major mineral lode in Ontario, Canada, and that Curtis owned land near the discovery.

Of the 1,597 individual stock issues listed on the exchange June 15, there were 268 issues in which a short position of 5,000 or more shares existed or in which there was a change in short position of 2,000 or more shares since the latest report. A list of these positions follows:

	6-15-64	5-15-64	Shares Listed
Abbott Laboratories	r-10,352	s-2,184	13,168,685
ACF Industries	5,730	3,735	2,991,880
Addressograph Multig	6,525	19,770	8,030,506
Admiral Corp	8,430	.7,875	2,454,421
Air Products & Chem	2,084	4,637	2,154,992
Aldens Inc	17,100	15,063	2,161,482
Alleghany Corp	20,020	21,550	10,101,571
Allegheny Prw System	r-3,240	s-850	18,677,178
Allied Chemical Corp	5,196	5,441	26,729,724
Allis Chalmers Mf g	14,620	8,670	9,101,388
Alside Inc	18,460	16,002	2,109,602
Amerada Petroleum	5,554	4,890	14,753,200
Amer Airlines	11,482	11,612	8,472,321
Am Bdcst Para Th	6,004	5,679	4,595,213
Amer Can	28,481	6,181	16,387,157
Amer Crystal Sugar	2,995	450	371,517
Amer Enka Corp	5,521	3,490	2,710,896
Amer Hospital Supply	22,158	17,586	8,854,802
Amer Machine & Fdry	22,104	18,194	17,253,989
Amer Motors Corp	60,919	47,346	19,209,390
Amer News	990	3,390	1,728,000
American Optical Co	5,742	4,727	928,864
Amer Photocopy Equip	115,894	134,857	7,959,159
Amer Rad & Stand San	5,315	2,300	11,709,936
Amer Telephone & Tel	24,500	19,064	257,228,134
Amer Tobacco	19,636	19,746	26,390,200
Ampex Corp	46,959	36,567	9,207,479
Anaconda Co	17,780	17,728	10,959,387
Anken Chemical & Film	38,381	42,581	1,072,832
Ashland Oil & Ref Co	4,469	z-7,684	7,685,404
Assoc Dry Goods	8,249	8,299	4,650,849
Atl Coast Line RR	4,058	1,258	2,672,231
Atlas Corp	15,300	14,200	10,554,138
Avco Corp	11,500	4,230	11,315,186

	6-15-64	5-15-64	Shares Listed
General Foods	15,086	11,622	25,090,156
General Motors	39,818	35,958	286,820,572
Genesco Inc	7,788	8,188	4,101,948
Gen Tel&Electronics	259,173	229,421	77,211,038
Gen Tire & Rubber	15,292	7,292	16,743,351
Gillette Co	77,532	65,586	28,436,232
Goodyear Tire & Rubber	11,276	10,176	35,596,547
Grace (W. R.) & Co	44,214	117,782	13,627,386
Great Atl & Pac Tea	6,421	5,221	24,260,023
Great Westrn Finance	9,492	11,102	8,584,705
Greyhound	91,417	90,574	14,833,120
Gulf Oil Corp	4,780	15,680	165,701,677
Hardeman (Paul), Inc	2,877		1,727,640
Haveg Industries Inc	17,145	19,576	1,024,972
Helene Curtis Indust	91,625	98,109	2,152,474
Hercules Powder	113,000	15,352	18,304,528
Hertz Corp	4,770	1,384	2,766,901
High Voltage Eng	45.868	34,572	2,341,814
Hilton Hotels Corp	5,450	4,636	4,533,777
Holt Rinehart&Winstn	4,400	400	3,563,489
Honeywell Inc	7,069	3,234	7,028,943
Houston Lighting&Pwr	6,275	5,075	20,252,127
Ill Central Indust	6,700	8,215	2,960,556
Indiana General Corp	2,450	5,300	1,169,002
Ingersoll Rand	11,296	10,213	6,726,598
Inland Steel	5,241	5,241	18,105,091
Inter Business Mach	r-11,566	s10,969	34,969,760
International Paper	5,455	3,223	43,668,202
International Silver	15,689	15,477	1,361,964
Inter Tel & Tel	12,948	12,938	18,580,771
Interstate Dept Strs	2,972	6,269	1,530,794
Jones & Laughlin Stl	5,958	7,031	7,896,040
Kerr McGee Oil	7,911	39,026	6,409,774
KLM Royal Dutch Arls	370	2,570	161,527
Korvette (E.J.) Inc	24,682	24,316	4,357,800
Leesona Corp	7,541	8,021	822,220
Lehigh Valley Indust	9,900	15,000	4,650,167
Libby McNeil&Libby	39,333	38,903	4,767,513
Ling-Temco-Voucht	4,775	2,375	2,835,398
Lionel Corp	15,570	22,370	2,071,837
Litton Indust	48,676	52,619	10,896,899
Lockheed Aircraft	17,333	17,783	10,781,942
Loral Elcctronics	14,114	16,214	2,502,334
Lorillard (P.)	7,280	11,103	6,575,848
Lukens Steel	13,431	9,825	953,928
Madison Fund Inc	37,361	37,461	8,552,662
Magnavox Co	9,260	10,003	7,369,701
Maremont Corp	5,220	11,970	1,574,172
Mattel Inc	5,460	4,171	1,940,632
McCrory Corp	14,064	14,264	5,977,367
McDermott (J. Ray) & Co.	1,430	3,675	3,868,380
McDonnel Aircraft	5,080	3,539	3,758,694
Merck &Co Inc	r-15,923	s-5,456	32,337,820
Mesabi Trust	12,050	11,450	13,120,010
Metromedia Inc	6,279	6,735	1,842,322
Minnesota Min & Mfg	30,950	22,168	53,050,377
Mo Kans Texas RR	9,900	9,800	1,475,976
Monsanto Co	13,280	11,171	30,153,935
Motorola Inc	9,512	9,718	4,030,722
National Airlines	14,636	13,042	1,846,567
Nat Cash Register	4,164	9,002	8,302,776
Nat Dairy Products	3,697	1,314	14,464,305
NY Central RR	20,060	06,318	6,607,722
Norfolk & Western Ry	5,880	6,430	7,413,563
Northwest Airlines	9,015	7,265	2,280,995
Occidental Petroleum	44,080	23,690	6,188,024
Owens Corning Fbrgls	18,663	19,010	6,718,299
Pacific Petroleums	2,155	5,738	20,816,748
Pan Amer World Airwy	37,889	44,272	7,013,688
Pan American Sulphur	5,220	4,433	2,351,818
Penney (J. C.)	7,367	8,447	24,931,460
Pen Power & Light		3,600	12,425,372
Pennsylvania R R	59,127	55,607	13,650,540
Pepper (Dr) Co	7,210	10,093	1,453,230
Pepsi Cola	5,530	3,865	6,540,235
Perkin Elmer Corp	7,671	9,421	1,310,334
Pfizer (Chas.)	13,667	17,074	19,630,568
Phila & Reading Corp	5,542	6,442	3,175,861
Pitney Bowes Inc	18,682	2,896	4,426,141
Pittsburgh Steel	6,030	6,030	2,776,542
Polaroid Corp	49,836	49,461	3,934,730
Procter & Gamble	7,452	7,270	43,745,560
Pub Service Colorado		7,900	13,738,049
Pure Oil	6,295	2,670	10,081,416
Radio Corp of Amer	51,598	64,354	52,640,329
Ralston Purina Co	4,400	2,870	15,256,539
Raytheon Co	8,343	10,805	4,135,671
Republic Aviation	16,692	13,400	10,081,416
Rexall Drug & Chem Co	7,036	6,914	4,840,978
Reynolds Metals	45,634	47,253	16,531,053
Reynolds Tobacco	14,033	15,425	40,941,533
Richardson Merrell	9,639	8,307	6,135,998
Rohm & Haas Co	5,139	3,477	4,979,320
Rorer (Wm. H.), Inc	796	3,400	3,373,658
Royal Dutch Petr Co	6,295	29,285	30,475,094
Royal Crown Cola Co	12,214	7,146	1,219,309

Fig. 8–9 Wall Street Journal report of short interest.

Money Rates

NEW YORK—Bankers' acceptance rates for 1 to 90 days, 3⅞% to 3¾%; 91 to 120 days, 4% to 3⅞%; 121 to 180 days, 4⅛% to 4%.

Federal funds in the open market: Day's high 3⅜%; low 1%; closing bid 1%; offered 1%.

Call money lent to brokers on stock exchange collateral, 4% to 4½%.

Call money lent to dealers on Governments, 3⅝% to 3⅞%; brokers 3⅞% to 4¼%.

Commercial paper placed directly by a major finance company was as follows: 30 to 179 days, 3¾%; 180-239 days, 3⅞%; 240-270 days, 4%.

Commercial paper sold through dealers, 90 days and four to six months' maturities, 3⅞% to 4⅜%.

Certificates of deposit, predominant rate at New York City banks. Three months, 3¾% to 3.80% five months, 3.90% eight months and longer, 4%.

Fig. 8–10

The Value of the Financial Page

This chapter has dealt almost exclusively with facts bearing on the movement of security prices and published as part of the financial news. But many expressions of opinion on business conditions in particular industries and companies are also published. It is difficult at times to discriminate between facts and opinions. The best financial writers make it a practice to indicate when they are reciting facts and when they are giving opinions, either their own or those of others. The American people are optimistic and are pleased by optimistic opinions. Thus an attempt is made by financial writers to keep the financial page full of good news. The pessimism that often

Pan American World Airways

PAN AMERICAN WORLD AIRWAYS, INC., reports for the five months ended May 31:

	1964	1963
Earned per share	$.18	
Total operating revs.	216,621,000	$201,783,000
Net before income taxes	2,355,000	d-3,033,000
Federal income taxes	c-91,000	c-1,577,000
Net income	2,446,000	d-1,456,000
Capital shares	13,930,214	a-13,365,940
Month of May:		
Total operating revs	$50,143,000	$45,008,000
Net income	2,856,000	723,000

a-Adjusted to reflect 2-for-1 stock split in May, 1964.
c-Credit. d-Loss.

Fig. 8–11

pervades business does not always get into print. Big businessmen know this. They know that the interviewer wants an expression of confidence. It is interesting to watch the newspapers to see who the big men are who do talk for publication and how they always see prosperity ahead. It seems that the greatest amount of talking is done precisely when business begins to become somewhat uncertain. This is not by intention but is a natural consequence of the public's desire for information. When business begins to falter after a period of prosperity, the reporters rush to interview the men whose opinions should be correct. But these men are busy planning for five, ten, twenty years ahead. They are planning for steady growth. Of course they are optimistic. The reader is at fault in interpreting the statements as applying especially to the immediate future. He is led to this interpretation by his own narrow outlook and by the suggestions of the interviewer, who is seeking to answer the questions raised by the immediate uncertainty.

A financial reporter is subject to the same emotions as any other man. He goes from brokerage house to brokerage house and in a period of great activity absorbs the enthusiasm of the crowd. He describes the situation as he sees it. The reader misinterprets the perfectly accurate description of an enthusiastic crowd of traders into a forecast of the market.

Should one read the financial page at all? Yes, for it contains much that is useful. One must, however, be on guard every minute for propaganda, crowd psychology, deliberate deception, half truth, long-time news interpreted as representing the immediate situation, gossip, rumor, ill-advised opinion, and facts which appear adequate but in reality cover up facts of opposite import.

It takes time to learn the fine art of discrimination, but, once it is acquired, the financial page yields much of value. Statistics on fundamental conditions, however, are the important bases of judgment. They are also the anchor which holds one steady when everybody is rushing either to buy or to sell, when the air is full of optimism or of gloom.

The reader who is able to pick from among the mass of news the facts that have a long-time significance has acquired the basis of good investment judgment. The daily ration of current news is for the most part shallow and likely to give the uncritical reader a false picture of the forces that really make the market. One who does not supplement his reading of the financial pages by a careful analysis and systematic study of fundamental facts and statistics will never have a sound basis for his opinions. But this is hard work and not in favor with many readers who prefer to read the attractively written news features on day-to-day events rather than do any solid thinking on the larger phases of business. Such reading may enable one to talk glibly, but it will unfit one to interpret soundly and to act wisely.

9 stock price indexes

An index is a single figure that sums up a number of factors in each time period, thereby facilitating the measurement of change that may have occurred since an earlier period. The value of indexes is so well realized today that one can obtain an index for almost any phase of human activity.

In the field of stock prices there are two types of indexes: (1) averages, and (2) indexes proper. Strictly speaking, the Dow-Jones averages, the *New York Times* averages, and the *New York Herald Tribune* averages should not be called indexes. They are merely averages of stock prices stated in terms of dollars and, therefore, are rightly named. On the other hand, the indexes published by Standard & Poor's Corporation and the Securities and Exchange Commission are abstract numbers scientifically weighted and are true indexes. In some cases true indexes are labeled "averages" by their publishers. An example of this is the Value Line's stock average, which is in fact a true index, with June 30, 1960, equal to 100.

The various averages and indexes will be taken up in this chapter, not for purposes of criticism but simply to explain the nature of the different series available for use by investors, traders, and economists.

The Dow-Jones Averages

Brief History. The *Wall Street Journal,* published by Dow, Jones & Co., Inc., made its first appearance before the financial public on July 8, 1889. Before this time Dow, Jones & Co. had been issuing a daily letter which had a large circulation in the financial district of New York and among men interested in business and finance in other cities. The Dow-Jones averages were first published in this daily letter in 1884 and consisted of a simple arithmetic average of the closing prices of 11 active representative stocks, 9 of which were rails. The original 11 stocks were:

Chicago & North Western	N.Y. Central
Chicago, Milwaukee & St. Paul	Northern Pacific pfd.
Delaware, Lackawanna	Pacific Mail
Lake Shore	Union Pacific
Louisville & Nashville	Western Union
Missouri Pacific	

Soon the prominence of the Delaware & Hudson warranted its addition to the list, making a total of 12 stocks. The computation of the average then consisted in finding daily the sum of the closing prices for the day of the 12 stocks named and dividing the total by 12.

As time went on, other stocks became active on the market and it became evident that a more comprehensive list of stocks was needed to represent properly the market as a whole. Acting on this idea, the *Wall Street Journal* extended the list to include 8 additional stocks, all rails.

During the 1880s and 1890s there were many developments in the field of the railroads. To keep the list of 20 stocks representative of the whole market, changes had to be made from time to time. Meanwhile the industrial field was expanding. The tobacco trust, steel trust, whisky trust, sugar trust, and oil trust were huge industrial projects that promised much to the interests concerned. Their possibilities, combined with the inevitably large risk and uncertainty involved, created an ideal field for the speculator. The stocks of these companies were being actively traded in and had to be recognized in an average supposed to be comprehensive. However, the industrials were hardly comparable with the railroads, either as to the stage of development or as to the definite factors that affected their prices. It was therefore thought best to construct an average for the industrials separate from that of the rails.

On June 5, 1896, there appeared in the *Wall Street Journal* two averages, one based on 20 railroad stocks and the other on 12 active, representative industrial stocks. The average in each case was constructed as before, being a simple arithmetic average of closing prices each day. No attempt was made at weighting.

In the industrial list, 18 substitutions were made from January 1897 to September 1916, when the number of stocks included in the average was increased from 12 to 20. In making the substitutions, a stock might be taken off the list and then in a year or more be restored. For example, Southern Pacific common was put on the railroad list in 1900, dropped in 1901, and put back again in 1904. General Electric was put on the industrial list in 1899, dropped in 1901, and replaced in 1907. A number of other stocks, both rails and industrials, have had a similar history.

In September 1916, a new list consisting of 20 industrials was made up. This list contained only 8 of the stocks of the preceding group. Twelve new stocks were included.

Up to this time industrial averages had been computed on a percentage basis, but on October 13, 1915, a new ruling by the Exchange put all stock transactions on a dollar basis; so all quotations since that time have been made in terms of dollars per share. The industrial average was therefore computed on a dollar basis. For example, Westinghouse had a par of 50, but the price was not doubled. It was treated exactly the same as the price of U.S. Steel with 100 par.

The average on a dollar basis for the new list of 20 stocks was computed back to December 12, 1914. Before that time the industrial average was computed from 12 stocks on a percentage basis, but since the stocks used were 100 par value, the average computed on the dollar basis would have resulted in the same figure. Moreover, the 12 stocks were very probably as representative of the market in the earlier period as the 20 stocks were in the later period.

Present Method of Computation.   On September 10, 1928, the method of computing the Dow-Jones industrial averages was changed. Prior to this date, the average had been obtained by dividing the aggregate market value of the issues by their number, 20. If a stock was split, its quoted price was multiplied by the number of shares into which it was split. Thus the quotations for American Tobacco and American Car and Foundry were multiplied by 2, those for General Motors by $2\frac{1}{2}$, those for General Electric and Sears, Roebuck by 4, and those for American Can by 6. This method of preserving the continuity of the index, however, had one unfortunate result. If the prices of the 6 issues for which adjustments were needed chanced to move in an opposite direction from the prices of the other 14 issues, the averages moved with the smaller rather than with the larger group. To correct this distortion and to render it easier to make substitutions in the future, the following device was used.

The sum of the 20 prices adjusted for split-ups on September 10, 1928, the date the change became effective, was $4,776.40. This figure divided by 20 gave an average for the day of 238.82. The sum of the 20 issues unadjusted for split-ups was $3,033.01. The quotient of this figure divided by the average for the day is 12.7. In other words, the sum of the actual quotations divided by 12.7 gave the same average as was obtained by dividing the sum of the adjusted quotations by 20. From this day on, the averages have been computed by using unadjusted quotations as a numerator and an adjusted divisor.

On October 1, 1928, the list of stocks used to compute the industrial averages was increased from 20 to 30 stocks and the divisor changed from 12.7 to 16.67. As was explained above, this change in the divisor made the new average comparable with the old.

On January 2, 1929, Dow, Jones & Co., Inc., began the publication of an average of public utility stocks. At first 20 issues were used, but on June 1, 1938, the number was reduced to 15.

By August 1965 the original divisor of 16.67 for the 30 Dow-Jones industrials had been reduced through stock splits and substitutions to 2.278.

The railroad average divisor had been reduced to 4.924 and the utility divisor to 4.125. Stocks now making the three averages include the following:

Industrial averages

Allied Chemical	General Electric	Sears, Roebuck
Aluminum Co. of Amer.	General Foods	Standard Oil of Calif.
American Can	General Motors	Standard Oil of N.J.
American Tel. & Tel.	Goodyear	Swift & Co.
American Tobacco	International Harvester	Texaco
Anaconda	International Nickel	Union Carbide
Bethlehem Steel	International Paper	United Aircraft
Chrysler	Johns-Manville	U.S. Steel
Du Pont	Owens-Illinois Glass	Westinghouse
Eastman Kodak	Procter & Gamble	Woolworth

Railroad averages

Atchison	Delaware & Hudson	Norfolk & Western
Atlantic Coast Line	Erie-Lackawanna	Pennsylvania
Baltimore & Ohio	Great Northern	Southern Pacific
Canadian Pacific	Illinois Central	St. Louis-San Francisco
Chesapeake & Ohio	Kansas City Southern Ind.	Southern Railway
Chicago & North Western	Louisville & Nashville	Union Pacific
Chicago, Rock Island & Pacific	N.Y. Central	

Utility averages

American Elec. Power	Consolidated Nat. Gas	Panhandle Elec.
Cleveland Elec. Illum.	Detroit Edison	Peoples Gas
Columbia Gas	Houston Light & Power	Philadelphia Elec.
Commonwealth Edison	Niagara-Mohawk	Public Service
Consolidated Edison	Pacific Gas & Electric	S. Calif. Edison

The fourth Dow-Jones stock average is a combination of 30 industrials, 20 rails, and 15 utilities. Prior to the reduction in the number of issues included in the utility average on June 1, 1938, this composite average contained 70 stocks and was obtained by dividing their aggregate market value by 70. At first no changes were made in the divisor of the composite average when substitutions occurred, since it was felt that the effect of such changes on an average of 70 issues would be insignificant. However, the dropping of 5 utility stocks in June 1938 resulted in a 3.6 per cent decline in the average if no adjustment were made. To preserve the continuity of the composite index, therefore, the market value of the 15 utilities was increased by 33 per cent and the divisor left at 70. On May 10, 1945, the method of figuring the composite average was changed to the variable-divisor method also. At the present time (August 1965) the divisor is 11.903.

Since July 8, 1963, the Dow-Jones averages have been reported eleven times daily at half-hour intervals. The first report is at 10:30 A.M., thirty minutes after the Exchange opens; the last report, including a complete range of the day's averages, is at 3:45 P.M. The reports are sent out over the Dow-Jones news ticker service within three minutes of the close of each half-hour's trading. Several private electronic stock quotation services compute "unofficial" Dow-Jones averages every five minutes during the trading day and report this value over their own facilities. The Dow-Jones averages are published daily by the *Wall Street Journal* and by leading newspapers throughout the country. The averages' earnings per share and dividends are reported every Monday in the *Wall Street Journal*.

Bond Averages.   Dow, Jones & Co., Inc., publishes daily bond averages as well as stock averages. These averages comprise a daily average of:

10 higher-grade railroad bonds
10 second-grade railroad bonds
10 public utility bonds
10 industrial bonds
40 bonds (a combined average of the four averages)
10 railroad income bonds
20 municipal bonds (on a yield basis)

With the exception of the municipal bond average the daily figures are simply arithmetic averages of closing prices. The railroad, utility, industrial, and composite averages were begun in January 1915. The railroad income bond average was begun in January 1947. Because municipal bonds are serial bonds with varying yields to maturity, the municipal bond yield average is based on responses from reputable municipal bond dealers as to what each of 20 bonds would yield if it had a twenty-year maturity.

Barron's Averages

Barron's averages are published by Dow, Jones & Co. and appear in the weekly issues of *Barron's National Business and Financial Weekly*.

Barron's 50-stock Average.   This average is based on the prices of 50 selected stocks. Instead of averaging one share of each of the stocks, however, this average makes use of identical dollar amounts of each of the 50 stocks used. Thus, one share of an issue selling at $100, two shares of an issue selling at $50, and four shares of an issue selling at $25 would be used in computing the average. As a result equal percentage changes in the various issues have an equal effect on the average, regardless of whether the price happens to be high or low.

For example, in August 1964, a 10 per cent increase in the price of Du Pont, selling at 261, would have the same effect upon *Barron's* index as a 10 per cent increase in the price of American Tobacco, selling at 35, but the increase in Du Pont would have seven times the effect upon the Dow-Jones industrial averages as the increase in American Tobacco would have.

Barron's 50-stock average has been published regularly since 1934 and projected backward to 1919.

An integral part of *Barron's* 50-stock average is current, projected, and historic data on earnings and dividends. The following are available:

1. Projected quarterly earnings, based on changes in *Barron's* index of industrial production and trade, which Barron's believes permits a reasonably accurate computation of earnings rates at any level of business activity. The projected quarterly earnings represent what earnings for the next three months are expected to be if business throughout that period continues at exactly the same pace as in the latest week.

2. Projected annual earnings, computed by multiplying the projected quarterly figure by 4 to put it on an annual basis.

3. Actual quarterly earnings, which are average profits of the 50 companies weighted in the same way as the price average.

4. Earnings for the year just ended, which are estimated earnings for the 12-month period ending on the date shown. Because data for the 50 stocks are reported quarterly, nine months of earnings are known, making it necessary to estimate only the most recent quarter.

5. Five-year average earnings, which are presented for historical perspective and are changed as new figures are made available quarterly.

6. Dividends paid in the year just ended. This figure is changed only once each quarter after all payments for the period are known.

From the above data, *Barron's* computes and presents with its information the following ratios: (1) price to projected annual earnings, (2) price to five-year average earnings, (3) price to earnings for the year just ended, (4) an earnings yield, based on the ratio of earnings for the year just ended to current price, (5) a bond-to-stock yield, based on the ratio of the yield on *Barron's* 10 highest-grade bonds to the earnings yield on stocks, (6) a dividend yield, based on the ratio of dividends paid in the year just ended to current average price.

Other Averages. *Barron's* also publishes an average based on the 20 most active stocks of the week. *Barron's* 20 low-priced stock index is intended for comparison of the market behavior of low-priced stocks with that of high-priced stocks. The latest version of this index, introduced in 1960, contains industrial stocks listed on both the New York and American stock exchanges. To qualify, a share must have a price of $15 or less, a current ratio of better than 2:1, a satisfactory earnings record, and a price substantially below its 1959 high.

Barron's also publishes an index based on the yields of 10 highest-grade corporate bonds. This index is used in computing *Barron's* confidence index, which is a ratio of the yield on *Barron's* 10 highest-grade corporate bonds to the average yield on Dow-Jones 40 medium-grade bonds. The theory behind the confidence index is that when bond investors are confident of the business outlook they invest in the higher-yielding medium-grade bonds and the ratio rises. But when investors are pessimistic they shift to the highest-grade bonds, causing the yield on these bonds to fall more rapidly than the yield on medium-grade bonds. This in turn causes the confidence index to decline.

Barron's also publishes a series of 33 industrial group stock averages.

The *New York Times* Averages

Stock Averages.   Since 1911 the *New York Times* has published daily an average of 25 industrial stocks, an average of 25 railroad stocks, and an average of 50 stocks. Each day the simple arithmetic average of the high, the low, and the closing prices is given in three figures. No weighting is attempted. The frequency of split-ups over the years has made it necessary, for the desired consistency of the record, to continue split-up stocks at their new prices multiplied by the number of shares into which each former share had been subdivided. It is the policy of the *Times* to eliminate as many of the multiples as possible by switching to other securities of equivalent value as soon as possible after a split-up. However, at the present time it is still necessary to multiply every price by a factor. For example, the daily price of Du Pont is multiplied by 14, Chrysler by 16, Caterpillar Tractor by 30, Sears, Roebuck by 12, Union Carbide by 9, and General Electric by 12. If these 6 issues were to move 1 point in one direction and the other 19 issues were all to move 1 point in the opposite direction, the average would move with the 6 rather than with the 19.

The following stocks were used by the *New York Times* in September 1963 (the number opposite the name of the stock indicates the weight given the price of each issue):

New York Times 25 industrials

Air Reduction	9	Goodrich	6
Alcoa	12	Ingersoll-Rand	6
Allied Chem.	8	International Harvester	12
American Tel. & Tel.	3	International Nickel	12
American Tobacco	8	Johns-Manville	6
Bethlehem Steel	12	Kennecott	1
Caterpillar Tractor	30	Penney, J. C.	9
Chrysler	16	Sears, Roebuck	12
Douglas Aircraft	6	Standard Oil of N.J.	6
Du Pont	14	Union Carbide	9
Eastman Kodak	10	U.S. Steel	6
General Electric	12	Westinghouse	8
General Motors	6		

New York Times 25 Railroads

Atchison	10	N.Y. Central	1
Atlantic Coast Line	3	Norfolk & Western	4
Baltimore & Ohio	1	Northern Pacific	2
Canadian Pacific	1	Pennsylvania	1
Chesapeake & Ohio	1	Reading	1
Chicago, Rock Island & Pacific	2	Seaboard Air Line	2
Denver & Rio Grande	9	Soo Line	1
Erie-Lackawanna	1	Southern Pacific	6
Great Northern	1	Southern Railway	5
Gulf Mobile & Ohio	1	Union Pacific	10
Illinois Central	2	Western Maryland	$2\frac{1}{2}$
Kansas City Southern Ind.	4	Western Pacific	3
Louisville & Nashville	1		

Changes in the list of stocks used to compute the *New York Times* averages are made when a stock is merged into that of another corporation so that it no longer exists or after a stock dividend that materially changes the value of the stock. A stock dropped from the list is replaced by one of approximately the same value and of similar affiliation.

Bond Averages. The *New York Times* also publishes a daily bond average from the prices of 40 domestic bonds. The figures are the unweighted arithmetic averages of the daily closing prices of the bonds used.

The composite average of 40 bonds includes not only bonds little affected by the business circumstances of the issuing corporation but also those much affected by the prosperity of the company. In other words, the average is made up of bonds whose prices may be very differently affected by the fluctuations of finance and business. To be of greatest value to the investor, the price movements of high-grade bonds should not be included in the same average with price movements of lower-grade bonds.

Standard & Poor's Indexes

Until now we have been considering stock averages. We shall next consider a stock price index. The Dow-Jones stock averages, for example, are merely a series of averages of the prices of stocks. The average rises $5 or falls $5, which means nothing relatively. A rise of 5 points when the average is $400 cannot be compared with a rise of 5 points when the average is $800. On the other hand, an index is an average of the relative changes in all the stocks used for the index stated with reference to a base—usually 100. Standard & Poor's use 10 as its base, for reasons explained later.

The following example illustrates the difference in computation of an average and a simple index:

Stocks	Base		Current	
	Price	Index	Price	Index
A	$ 50	100	$ 75	150
B	75	100	100	133.33
C	125	100	150	120
Average	$ 83.33	100	$108.33	134.44

The present index of this group of stocks is 134.44—that is, the base, 100, plus the average of the percentage increases of all the stocks employed in the index, 34.44. It will be noted that the average price (in dollars) of the three issues rose from 83.33 to 108.33—an increase of 30 per cent. The significant figure is not the increase of one average price relative to another but rather the average of the relative increases.

Another defect of averages is that they are not weighted or, rather, that they are improperly weighted. For example, in a simple average an increase of $5 in the price of an inactive issue is given the same weight as an increase of $5 in the price of an active issue. Yet a purchase of 5,000 shares of the inactive issue might be sufficient to raise its price $5, whereas a purchase of 100,000 shares of the active issues would be required to raise its price $5. If an average is to be a true index of the movement of the market as a whole, then a $5 price advance in an inactive issue should not be allowed to influence the index by as much as a similar advance in the price of an active issue.

The idea of a weighted index of stock prices is not new, for the construction of such an index had been discussed time and again, even before Standard & Poor's Corporation launched its series. Some advocates of weighted indexes proposed weighting on the basis of trading volume; others suggested arbitrary weights which would properly represent the various industrial groups. An index weighted by shares traded was developed about 1927, but it proved to be very erratic and in 1929 reached such misleadingly high levels that it had to be abandoned.

The Stocks Used.   In order that an index may truly represent the changes in value of the securities traded on the stock market as a whole, care must be exercised to maintain proper representation on an industry basis. The market value of the 500 stocks used in the daily stock price index of Standard & Poor's represents 85 to 90 per cent of the value of all common stocks listed on the New York Stock Exchange. Daily stock price indexes are available for the following groups:

500 stocks, combined
425 industrials
25 railroads
50 utilities

Indexes for these main groups are announced hourly during the day over various ticker and news services and are updated every five minutes on the electronic quotation services.

Standard & Poor's publishes four stock price indexes for (1) 124 capital goods companies, (2) 194 consumer goods companies, (3) 25 high-grade common stocks, and (4) 20 low-priced common stocks. In addition, Standard & Poor's computes and publishes many indexes for subgroups of companies, such as 9 aerospace companies, 5 air transport companies, 4 aluminum companies, 5 automobile companies, and similar indexes for 86 other subgroups.

A base of 10 is given the Standard & Poor's stock price indexes for the period 1941 to 1943. The years of the base period are neither normal (being war years) nor recent; and the base-period value is an unorthodox 10 instead of the customary 100. The base of 10 was set so that the resulting index number levels would closely approximate the true average prices of all common stocks listed on the New York Stock Exchange at the time of the base period.

Prior to 1957 the Standard & Poor's daily stock price indexes were based on 90 stocks (50 industrials, 20 rails, and 20 utilities). Extreme care was then taken to maintain proper representation of all stocks listed on the New York Stock Exchange. The earlier indexes were converted to the base for 1941 to 1943 and were added to the new series, giving a continuous daily record back to 1928. Correlation studies were made by Standard & Poor's at the time to determine the coefficient of correlation between the price index of 90 stocks and the discontinued, broader weekly stock price index of 416 stocks. The study proved that the index of 90 was an accurate measure of the market as a whole.

Method of Computation. The price of each issue used in the current index is multiplied by the number of shares outstanding to obtain a computed market value of the entire issue. The aggregate market value is then expressed in index number form with the period 1941 to 1943 equal to 10. As a result of this procedure stock dividends and split-ups do not affect the continuity of the index, the shares outstanding being increased by the distribution and the price being proportionally lower. There is no need for any adjustment to the base value. Other changes in capitalization, mergers and acquisitions, rights, and so on, and substitutions in the list of component companies are handled by making the necessary revision to the weighting factor (shares outstanding) and by making an offsetting adjustment to the

1941 to 1943 base-period value. The capitalizations of all component companies are continually being checked so that any changes necessary may be made at the proper time. Similarly, new companies and new industries are watched with a view to being incorporated into the index at such time as they are deemed to be of sufficient importance.[1]

Weekly Stock Price Indexes and Companion Series.   Detailed weekly price indexes for the separate classifications (mentioned earlier) are computed as of the close of every Wednesday. This breakdown into individual industrial groups is based on the same 500 stocks as are used in the daily stock price indexes and the method of computation is the same, i.e., price multiplied by the number of shares outstanding to obtain an aggregate value which is expressed in index number form with the period of 1941 to 1943 equal to 10.

In addition to the weekly stock price indexes, quarterly earnings and dividends are computed on a comparable basis for each of the 94 group classifications. These quarterly figures are the basis for a price-earnings ratio and yield series. For the individual industry groups the earnings and dividends are based on twelve-month periods ending with each quarter.

For the composite of 500 stocks and for the three main groups for which stock price indexes are published daily, the earnings are computed on a single-quarter basis. The result for the quarter is adjusted for normal seasonal variations and expressed as an annual rate. In computing price-earnings ratios, the seasonally adjusted annual rates are more timely than is the total for the latest available twelve months.

A weekly yield index based on the current dividend rate is computed for each of the four main groups. These current dividend rates are related to the price indexes as of the close every Wednesday, the record extending back to 1926.

Book value for the industrial stocks is also available on an annual basis back to 1929.

A complete record of all the weekly stock price indexes and the related series is published in Standard & Poor's *Long-term Security Price Index Record,* which is a part of their Trade and Securities Service. This book contains the price index record for the last ten years by weeks and the entire early record on a monthly average basis.

---

[1] The formula for Standard & Poor's base-weighted index is

$$\text{Index} = \frac{\Sigma P_1 Q_0}{\Sigma P_0 Q_0} \times 10$$

where P_1 represents the current market price, P_0 the average price in the base period, and Q_0 the number of shares outstanding in the base period, subject to adjustment when necessary to offset changes in capitalization. Σ is the Greek letter sigma, which always means addition, or sum of, and in this instance indicates the addition of all the market values of the individual companies comprising the group.

Most of the price indexes have been extended on a weekly basis back to the beginning of 1926. However, publications containing this weekly detail are out of print. Furthermore, prior to 1957 the indexes were based on the period 1935 to 1939 equal to 100. The Cowles Commission for Research in Economics adopted Standard's indexes and in its book, *Common Stock Indexes, 1871–1937,* has extended the price indexes, by groups, back to 1871 on a monthly basis. Standard & Poor's has converted the four main groups to their 1941 to 1943 base and shows them, by months, back to 1871 in its *Long-term Security Price Index Record.*

Preferred Stock Indexes.   The Standard & Poor's preferred stock indexes are based on 15 (currently 14) noncallable issues and consist of a price and yield index. Beginning February 1928, the yield index has been an average of 9 (currently 8) median yields of the individual issues. The group yield has then been converted into an equivalent price on the basis of a 7 per cent dividend. Prior to 1928 the price index was a single average of the component issues, the price of each being adjusted to a 7 per cent dividend basis. The yield was simply the dividend (7 per cent) divided by the average price. These indexes extend back to January 1900 on a monthly basis. Since January 1929, they have been computed on a weekly basis.

Bond Indexes.   The weekly bond indexes provide a complete coverage of bond prices and yields. The following are the present groupings:

Yield indexes

Industrials: four indexes covering AAA, AA, A, and BBB bonds
Rails: six indexes, one for each class of bonds as above, plus BB and B
Utilities: four indexes, one for each class, AAA, AA, A, and BBB bonds
Composite of above: four indexes, one for each class
Government bonds: long-term, intermediate-term, short-term
Municipal bonds: 15 high-quality twenty-year bonds

Price indexes

Corporate bonds: high-grade
Government bonds: long-term, intermediate-term, short-term
Municipal bonds: 15 high-quality twenty-year bonds

All Standard & Poor's bond indexes are computed weekly (as of Wednesday's close) and are based on yield to maturity. The corporate yields are an average of the individual yields to maturity of a representative list for each classification. Where possible, the bonds used are noncallable long-term issues having no conversion clauses. These indexes are available, by weeks, back to 1937 in out-of-print publications of Standard & Poor's.

Government bond yield indexes show the median yield to maturity of all eligible bonds for each classification. Use of the median automatically eliminates breaks in the series as bonds pass out of or into any maturity classification. The current series, based on taxable issues only, extends back to 1937. Discontinued tax-exempt series are available back to 1917.

Municipal bond yield indexes show an average of the yield to maturity of 15 top-quality issues, selected for geographic representation. All issues used are serial bonds; so a twenty-year maturity is maintained. The index is available on a weekly basis back to 1929 and on a monthly basis back to 1900.

Standard & Poor's bond price indexes represent a conversion of the composite yields, a representative coupon and period to maturity being assumed for each group.

Discontinued Bond Indexes.   The discontinued bond indexes tabulatéd below are significant only for the periods covered. The weekly corporate series were available on a monthly basis from January 1900 to 1940 and on a weekly basis from January 1929 to August 1941. The daily indexes covered the period from January 1928 to 1940, the year 1926–1927 being available weekly. The discontinued treasury (tax-exempt) bond index supplied monthly quotations from June 1919 to December 1930 and weekly quotations from January 1931 to March 1951.

Discontinued bond indexes, yield basis

15 industrials
15 rails
15 utilities
45 corporate
Tax-exempt treasury bonds

These discontinued weekly indexes represented a simple arithmetic average of the yield to maturity of the issues in the group, with price a conversion of the average yield. The daily indexes are a simple average of quoted prices, all prices being adjusted to a 6 per cent coupon basis.

The Standard & Poor's *Long-term Security Price Index Record* contains most of these discontinued indexes on a monthly basis. A weekly record of all current series with monthly averages extending back as far as available is also included.

Moody's Averages

Moody's Investors Service publishes a common stock price average for 200 stocks and for the following subgroups:

125 industrials
 24 electric power and light public utilities
 25 railroads
 15 New York City banks
 10 fire and casualty insurance companies

The 200 stock price average is based on all the above, plus American Telephone & Telegraph. This issue was excluded from the public utility average to avoid dominating that group.

The various averages are computed at week end and at month end. Figures are available back to 1951 on a weekly basis and back to 1929 on a monthly basis. Annual figures, based on adding Moody's series since 1929 to the Cowles Commission figures prior to that date, extend the series back to 1897.

For each of the 5 subgroups and for the main 200 stock price average, data are available on price, earnings per share, and dividends per share. Book-value figures are also available for the 125 industrials and the 24 public utilities. The basic information is published in the blue pages of Moody's *Manuals* and in other Moody's publications.

Origin of Moody's Averages.   Moody's common stock averages were originally constructed to reflect the size and importance of the various industry groups on the New York Stock Exchange and, to a degree, the Federal Reserve Board's index of industrial production. Once the relative sizes of the various industries were determined, stocks were selected to make up each group. Each company chosen had to be representative of its industry or a segment of its industry. Investor interest in the company was considered, and the stock had to be publicly held and, in the case of the 125 industrials, listed on the New York Stock Exchange.

Stock price averages are also available for the following classifications, which are not part of the basic 200 stock price average:

20 growth stocks
20 income stocks
30 natural gas stocks
10 gas transmission stocks (part of the 30 natural gas stocks)
10 gas distribution stocks (part of the 30 natural gas stocks)
10 small life insurance company stocks
 9 large life insurance company stocks
 7 finance company stocks
12 out-of-town (non-New York City) banks
10 mutual fund management companies
10 small business investment companies
10 savings and loan associations

Method of Computation.   Individual prices are weighted by the number of shares currently outstanding. (The exception is Ford Motor Company, for which the weight is the number of shares in the hands of the public only.) Each price is multiplied by its weight. Then the sum of these products, or aggregate market value, is divided by the sum of the shares in the average, adjusted for stock dividends and splits, the result being the average price per share. This may be expressed in the following way:

$$\text{Average price per share} = \frac{\Sigma(P \times Nac)}{\Sigma Nad}$$

where P stands for the price per share, Nac the actual number of shares, and Nad the adjusted number of shares.

In order to keep the averages undisturbed by stock splits or stock dividends, the following method is used: Assume that company X, which has a capitalization of 1 million shares and whose stock is priced at $100, declares a 2-for-1 split. There are now 2 million shares outstanding (this is the "actual" number of shares, or Nac in the above formula). Assume also that after the split the price of the new shares becomes $50. The aggregate value of the capitalization $(P \times Nac)$ will therefore remain at $100 million. But if this $100 million were divided by the actual number of shares (2 million), this would give an average price of $50 for the stock, which would show a sharp break from the previous $100. To prevent the average from being disturbed by such a change caused purely by the split, we divide the $100 million not by the new 2 million shares, but by the former 1 million shares, thus getting a comparable price of $100. This 1 million shares in the divisor is the "adjusted" number of shares, or Nad in the above formula. A similar procedure is followed in the case of stock dividends, regardless of size. However, whenever the number of actual shares outstanding is increased for reasons other than a stock dividend or split (e.g., issuance of new stock through rights, conversion, and the like) the adjusted number of shares is increased proportionately.

Occasionally substitutions are made in the averages to reflect mergers or breakups or to replace companies which become unimportant or inactive with those representing new industries or industries not adequately represented hitherto. In all these cases, the group divisor, i.e., the adjusted number of shares (Nad), is changed so that the level of the average at the joining point remained unaffected.

Earnings and Dividends.   For the industrial group, quarterly earnings on figures are arrived at by aggregating the net incomes of the companies in the group, multiplying by 4 in order to place them on an annual basis, subtracting the total annual preferred dividend requirements, and, finally, dividing by the adjusted number of shares (Nad). The result gives quarterly average per share earnings for the group, unadjusted for seasonal changes. Since a few companies report the results of their operations only annually, their quarterly earnings have to be estimated. This procedure, however, has only a small effect on the average. In the final correction of a year's figures, the quarterly rates of these few companies are brought into conformity with the actual reported earnings. Quarterly earnings at annual rates are compiled for the industrial, railroad, and utility groups. For the last, however, earnings for the quarter represent results for the twelve-month period just ended.

To arrive at the dividend per share for the average of 200 common stocks or for any of the subgroups, the current indicated annual cash dividend rate per share of each stock is multiplied by its actual number of shares, the products added up for the group, and the resulting aggregate of dividend payments divided by the adjusted number of shares of the group— the same procedure we found to be used in computing average prices per share.

The indicated annual cash dividend rate for each stock is the "going" annual rate based on the latest declaration of cash payments; i.e., the annual rate is equivalent to what would be paid in the next twelve months if the most recent declarations, including extras, were continued. The dividend rate for each stock is based on the above procedure, interpreted in the light of its dividend history, of any statement by the company, and of the judgment of Moody's analysts who specialize in the company's field. The indicated annual rate is not, in any event, a forecast of what the company will pay in the next twelve-month period but rather a *post facto* statement assuming continuity of the current dividend policy by corporate management.

In the simplest case, the dividend rate is based on the latest regular quarterly payment multiplied by 4, plus any established extra. When a company changes its quarterly declaration, the annual rate is revised to reflect this change. For example, if the quarterly dividend of $1 is raised to $1.25, with no extras involved, the annual rate is raised from $4 to $5.

Where an extra has been paid, it is usually carried unchanged until altered in the following year's declaration. Exceptions are cases in which the company apparently absorbs the extra into quarterly payments; sometimes there are announcements to this effect. Also, when the regular quarterly rate is reduced drastically, the extra is automatically dropped. In instances of highly erratic quarterly payments the annual rate tends to be equal or close to the last twelve-month total of payments or to the latest quarterly rate multiplied by 3 plus the latest total year-end payment.

The dividend rates represent cash payments only and do not include stock dividends or payments which are made in the form of other companies' securities.

Preferred Stock Series.   Moody's Investors Service publishes preferred stock yield averages on a monthly basis extending back to January 1919. In their high-dividend classfication they publish three averages:

    10 high-grade industrials
    10 medium-grade industrials
    10 speculative industrials

In their low dividend classification they publish four averages:

10 high-grade industrials
10 medium-grade industrials
10 high-grade public utilities
10 medium-grade public utilities

Bond Yield Averages. Moody's Investors Service publishes the following
bond yield averages, most of which are available on a monthly basis extending back to January 1919.

The following five series are published for all corporate bonds, for
industrial bonds, for utility bonds, and for railroad bonds:

Average of yields on Aaa bonds
Average of yields on Aa bonds
Average of yields on A bonds
Average of yields on Baa bonds
Composite average of yields on all bonds in the group

Utility bond averages are also published for the following subgroups:

Holding companies
Light, power, and gas companies
Telephone companies
Traction companies
Waterworks
Other utilities

The average price of new capital, which is a weighted average of yields
on newly issued domestic bonds, is calculated on an annual basis.

Federal government bond yield averages are available for the following
groups:

Average of long-term partly tax-exempt bonds (1919–1945)
Average of long-term taxable bonds (1941 to present)
Average of three-year treasury obligations
Average of five-year treasury obligations
Average of ten-year treasury obligations
Ninety-one-day treasury bill rate (average rate for last offering of month)

The following state and municipal bond yields are published:

Average of yields on Aaa municipal bonds
Average of yields on Aa municipal bonds
Average of yields on A municipal bonds
Average of yields on Baa municipal bonds
Composite average of yields on all municipal bonds
Average of yields on Aaa ten-year state bonds
Average of yields on Aa ten-year state bonds

Stock Price Indexes of the Securities and Exchange Commission

In July 1942 the Securities and Exchange Commission began the compilation and publication of a weekly index of common stock prices based upon the weekly closing prices of 300 issues listed on the New York Stock Exchange. Since 1960 this index used the average weekly prices of the 1957 to 1959 period as a base of 100. Comparisons with the prebase period were preserved by adjustments made to the earlier figures so that the index can be run back to 1939. In mid-1964, however, publication of the index was discontinued. Since the index covers a recent time period and has been used in a number of research studies, its description is included here.

The SEC index is available for the following major groups and subgroups:

    193 *Manufacturing*
        108 durable goods manufacturers
            11 stone, clay, & glass product
            12 iron & steel
            10 nonferrous metal
             9 fabricated metal product
            16 nonelectric industrial machinery
             4 agricultural machinery
             5 office machines
             7 electric machinery
            10 radio, TV, & communications equipment
             4 motor vehicle manufacturing
             6 motor vehicle parts & accessories
             8 aircraft & missiles
             6 scientific instruments
       85 nondurable goods manufacturers
            22 food & beverage
             4 tobacco product
            10 textile mill product & apparel
             9 paper & allied product
            12 industrial chemicals
             8 drugs
             8 other chemicals
             8 petroleum refining
             4 rubber product

    18 *Transportation*
       14 railroad
        4 air transportation

34 *Utilities*
    3 telecommunication
   31 electric & gas utility

45 *Trade, finance, & service*
   21 retail trade
    7 motion pictures & broadcasting
    7 closed-end management investment companies
   10 other finance & service

10 *Mining*
    4 crude petroleum production
    6 other mining (metal, coal, sulfur)

The industrial subgroups represented were based on the Standard Industrial Classification Code devised by the Bureau of the Budget. In selecting the industrial groups and stocks to be represented, all companies with common stocks listed on the New York Stock Exchange were classified according to the Standard Industrial Classification. Industrial groups which accounted for more than 1 per cent of the volume or value of common stock trading on the Exchange were selected for representation in the index. Within each selected industry, the most active stocks were then chosen to give a coverage of at least 60 per cent of the volume and value of trading within that industry. The entire list of industries and companies was reviewed each year, with new industries and stocks added as needed and others dropped.

In the major revision and expansion of the indexes which occurred in 1959, for example, five new industrial groups were added and two industrial groups were discontinued. The additions were: office machines, scientific instruments, other chemical, rubber product, and other finance and service. Indexes for household machinery and railroad equipment were discontinued because stocks in these groups accounted for less than 1 per cent of the volume and value of all common stock trading on the Exchange in 1959. Substitutions did not affect the continuity of the composite and major group indexes because of adjustments made in the method of computation.

Method of Computation. The composite index and each of the subgroup indexes measured the total current market value of the issues included; this was derived by multiplying the number of shares outstanding by their price, as a percentage of their average weekly total market value in the 1957 to 1959 base period. The indexes were based on the last sales price of the week for each stock as reported in the financial press. Monthly and annual figures were averages of weekly indexes.

Because the indexes were based on total market value, no adjustment was necessary for stock splits or stock dividends. The new market price times the new number of shares reflected exactly the same aggregate value as was expressed before the stock split or stock dividend. Changes in capitalization which result from the sale of new shares of stock, from capital distributions of either cash or stock of another company, or from the substitution of new stocks or industries in the list of components were made by appropriate changes in the base value so that the new index was the same as that which would have prevailed had there been no change in shares or substitutions. The new (adjusted) base value was derived from the following proportions:

$$\frac{\text{New current value}}{\text{New base value}} = \frac{\text{old current value}}{\text{old base value}}$$

Thus

$$\text{New base value} = \text{old base value} \times \frac{\text{new current value}}{\text{old current value}}$$

The SEC indexes were published weekly in an SEC statistical release and monthly in the SEC's *Statistical Bulletin*. The statistical release was available without charge from the Commission; information on the composite and major industrial group indexes in the release was reported in the Tuesday edition of the *Wall Street Journal* and in various other newspapers.

Other Averages and Indexes

The *New York Herald Tribune* Averages. The *New York Herald Tribune* began publishing daily stock price averages on January 1, 1923. The *Herald Tribune* average is a composite of 100 stocks consisting of 70 industrials and 30 rails. The 70 industrials, in turn, are composed of the following groups:

15 manufacturing	6 steels	10 motors
10 oils	4 railroad equipments	5 foods
8 utilities	5 stores	7 coppers

Although the eight utilities may appear out of place in a grouping of industrial stocks, when the averages were inaugurated in 1923 utilities had not reached their present position of importance in the economy.

It is the stated policy of the *Herald Tribune* not to reveal the exact weights or factors used in compiling the average. Its system calls for fairly frequent substitutions in stocks and changes in weights applied, and these changes are made without special announcement to readers. Prior to 1949, the *Herald Tribune* substituted stocks in the average in lieu of weighting. For example, if stock A in the average priced at 200 were split 2 for 1, either a new stock equal in importance and activity and priced about the same as the old A stock was substituted, or the new A stock was retained and the loss of 100 points made up by substituting stocks of higher prices for those of lower prices in the particular group. If neither of these two methods were possible, the new stock of A was used and the price differential, 100 in the example, was added directly to the total of the group. Since 1949 the *Herald Tribune* has been using weighted stocks.

The *Herald Tribune* also publishes a stock price average for 25 leading stocks listed on the American Stock Exchange, an average for 10 aircraft stocks, an average for 20 grade A railroads, and an average for 10 grade B railroads.

The National Quotation Bureau Over-the-counter Average.   In 1948 the National Quotation Bureau originated an over-the-counter industrial stock average which is now published daily in the bureau's service and in numerous newspapers. The average is based on the sum of the bids on 35 issues regularly quoted in the bureau's Daily Quotation Service. The initial average, on November 7, 1948, was derived by dividing the sum of the bids by 35. Since that time the divisor has been changed many times to adjust for stock dividends, stock splits, and the substitution of stocks in the same manner as in the Dow-Jones averages. The divisor on May 14, 1963, was 12.30.

The 35 stocks selected for the average are chosen from over-the-counter stocks with the largest market value, the largest number of stockholders, and the most substantial quotation records. None of the issues used in the index are listed or traded on any stock exchange.

At the time when the average was first published in 1948, it was computed backward to October 1, 1938, for the first, tenth, and twentieth of each month. Because the average is not available on a historic basis, monthly and annual averages from October 1, 1938, through 1963 are given in Table 7.[2]

The Value Line Stock Average.   The most recent addition to the list of published indexes and averages of stock prices is the Value Line 1,100 stock average, first announced in May 1963, with prices worked back to a starting point equal to 100 as of June 30, 1961. The Value Line average differs from other averages and indexes in that it measures the price behavior of a broad spectrum of actively traded stocks and gives equal weight to each. The 1,100 stocks used encompass nearly all actively traded issues on the New York Stock Exchange and a sizable cross section of stocks traded on the American Stock Exchange, the regional stock exchanges, Canadian stock exchanges, and the over-the-counter market.

The average is computed weekly, based on Friday closing prices.

[2] For the specific prices on the first, tenth, and twentieth of each month from 1938 through 1948 see *The Stock Market* by Charles A. Dice and Wilford J. Eiteman, 3d ed. New York: McGraw-Hill Book Company, 1952, pp. 345–347.

TABLE 7 Over-the-counter Industrial Stock Price Index (Monthly and Annual Averages of Index on 1st, 10th, and 20th of Each Month, October 1938 to December 1963, National Quotation Bureau)

	Jan.	Feb.	Mar.	Apr.	May	June	July	Aug.	Sept.	Oct.	Nov.	Dec.	Annual average
1938										18.60	19.84	19.18	
1939	19.07	18.42	18.81	16.96	17.26	18.40	18.30	19.17	19.41	20.57	20.94	20.88	19.02
1940	21.29	21.77	22.16	22.67	21.26	18.41	19.41	19.74	20.28	21.19	22.15	21.71	21.00
1941	21.69	20.99	20.92	20.56	19.76	19.78	20.56	20.76	20.67	20.07	19.73	18.44	20.33
1942	18.33	18.42	17.84	17.14	16.70	17.14	17.68	18.10	18.19	18.63	19.25	19.08	18.04
1943	19.72	20.78	21.51	22.28	23.00	23.25	23.72	23.59	23.81	24.17	23.96	23.44	22.77
1944	24.14	24.70	25.04	25.15	25.51	26.12	27.00	27.12	27.43	28.49	28.61	28.87	26.52
1945	29.28	30.34	30.57	29.87	31.04	31.85	31.87	31.91	33.95	35.81	37.60	38.87	32.75
1946	38.89	39.28	37.96	40.53	41.67	42.57	40.97	39.36	34.11	32.18	32.84	33.83	37.85
1947	34.89	36.11	34.58	34.45	32.84	33.30	35.34	35.88	35.62	36.81	37.23	36.04	35.26
1948	36.21	34.10	33.69	36.04	36.93	37.65	36.92	35.92	35.45	35.38	34.27	32.89	35.45
1949	32.85	32.32	31.48	31.80	31.11	28.53	29.65	31.52	32.16	33.26	34.24	34.34	31.94
1950	35.72	36.37	36.45	36.48	39.90	37.57	35.41	37.45	38.82	41.05	41.10	41.47	38.15
1951	45.17	48.05	47.84	46.97	47.81	46.91	45.83	48.14	50.17	50.14	47.56	47.77	47.70
1952	48.31	48.75	47.20	47.00	45.51	47.03	48.08	48.26	47.34	46.80	46.89	48.44	47.47
1953	48.81	49.39	49.22	48.30	47.30	45.75	46.22	47.31	45.45	45.41	46.77	47.04	47.25
1954	48.21	50.54	51.71	53.07	53.76	54.15	56.23	59.83	60.23	61.58	63.22	66.28	56.57
1955	68.58	70.20	70.93	72.78	74.65	75.91	78.36	78.11	78.36	75.47	77.40	79.26	75.00
1956	79.40	80.32	84.65	86.71	88.22	85.07	89.77	93.33	89.68	87.03	88.03	87.44	86.64
1957	89.06	87.22	86.75	89.78	91.86	92.20	93.34	92.63	87.42	79.03	74.20	73.71	86.43
1958	75.12	78.90	78.30	79.89	81.77	82.89	84.35	88.91	91.85	94.94	97.60	100.46	86.25
1959	105.03	105.95	108.18	106.18	109.06	106.92	107.79	108.85	105.62	103.54	104.44	106.94	106.54
1960	107.34	103.63	103.02	106.09	104.89	106.50	105.67	103.92	104.19	99.17	98.51	102.74	103.81
1961	110.74	118.49	124.05	127.49	124.73	123.99	122.54	125.33	126.70	130.35	138.46	142.94	126.32
1962	139.34	141.31	143.16	139.20	128.62	112.23	107.47	110.73	111.83	106.98	110.51	119.68	122.59
1963	122.92	125.77	125.11	131.09	134.77	137.12	136.53	138.89	144.16	140.93	142.92	141.75	135.16

Weekly fluctuations in the index are computed by averaging the Friday-to-Friday percentage change in the price of each issue, after allowance for stock splits and stock dividends. A geometric (or logarithmic) average is used to avoid distortions arising from the cumulation of successive plus and minus percentage changes. For example, if a stock rose from 20 to 40 (up 100 per cent) and then fell back to 20 (down 50 per cent), it would show a net increase of 25 per cent if averaged arithmetically, that is, $(100 - 50) \div 2 = 25$. A geometric average will show the result as unchanged.[3]

The Best Index

Nine indexes or averages of stock prices have been described in this chapter. The question logically arises: Which is best? The answer depends on the use to which the index is put, for an index can be "good" or "poor" only with reference to the meaning attributed to it.

Persons from many walks of life use stock price indexes. Economists and statisticians use a stock price index to study long-run growth patterns in the economy, to analyze and perhaps to anticipate business cycle patterns, or to relate stock prices to other time-series economic data. Long-run investors regard an index as a bench mark against which to evaluate the performance of their own or of an institutional portfolio or to determine the level of the stock market in relation to earnings or dividends per share. Stock price indexes are also used by some long-run investors as a guide to portfolio balance along the lines of the Keystone seven-point plan, developed by Keystone Custodian Funds, Inc., of Boston. Market technicians base short-run buy and sell decisions, in many instances, on market patterns which have become apparent from studying stock price indexes.

The needs of the three groups can be evaluated in terms of the following characteristics of indexes:

1. General availability of the index
2. Weighting of individual securities and industries within the index
3. Long-run growth characteristics of the index
4. Sensitivity of the index to fluctuations in market prices

---

[3] The geometric average, or geometric mean, is the nth root of the product of n numbers. If five stock prices were used to compute the geometric mean, the mean would be

$$\text{Index value} = \sqrt[5]{A \times B \times C \times D \times E}$$

For computational purposes, the geometric mean is more easily arrived at by taking the antilog of the arithmetic mean of the logarithms of the stock prices, i.e.,

$$\text{Log of index value} = \frac{\log A + \log B + \log C + \log D + \log E}{5}$$

Availability of the Indexes.   Information on the current state of the stock market is available for the Dow-Jones averages every half hour and for Standard & Poor's major indexes every hour, rendering one or the other indispensable to a trader who makes his buy or sell decisions within trading hours. As stated before, certain data-disseminating services provide values for the two indexes every five or ten minutes on brokerage office electronic equipment.

Both the Dow-Jones and Standard & Poor's indexes are carried in the financial pages of most important daily newspapers and are thus readily available to investors interested in daily market patterns. The *Wall Street Journal,* which owns and publishes the Dow-Jones averages, does not of course carry the competing Standard & Poor's index. The *New York Times* and the *New York Herald Tribune* publish their own indexes daily. The National Quotation Bureau's over-the-counter index is also available on a daily basis, but it is carried in relatively few papers. The remaining indexes are published weekly. *Barron's* 50-stock average is based on prices as of the close of Thursday's market and is available the following Monday morning. Moody's averages, the Value Line average, and the SEC stock price index are computed weekly from Friday's closing prices and are published in the releases of those organizations.

Economists, statisticians, and some long-run investors will want to assemble complete historical records of an index for research purposes. Historic details on Standard & Poor's indexes are available in its *Trade and Securities Service Statistics,* and a daily record of its four main series is available in booklet form from the corporation. Monthly averages for its four main groups are also published in the *Federal Reserve Bulletin* and in the *Survey of Current Business.*

Historic data on Moody's averages appear in the blue pages of the various Moody's *Manuals* as well as in the *Survey of Current Business.* Historic data on both Moody's and Standard & Poor's indexes, as well as on the Cowles Commission indexes (which extend back to 1871), appear in *Historical Statistics of the United States, Colonial Times to 1957* published by the Bureau of the Census, 1960.

Historic data for the Dow-Jones averages including quarterly earnings, price-earnings ratios, and dividends as well as prices for the last trading day of March, June, September, and December for the industrial, rail, and utility averages are frequently published in *Barron's.* The number of yearly data presented varies with the space available, but it is frequently fifteen years or more. *Barron's* also carries, from time to time, data on the book value of the Dow-Jones industrials extending back twenty years. The *Survey of Current Business* reports monthly closing prices for the four Dow-Jones averages for the most recent fourteen months. A complete historical record of the Dow-Jones averages, giving monthly and yearly highs and lows and extending back to 1897 for the industrials and rails, back to 1929 for the utilities, and back to 1933 for the composite average, is available in Standard & Poor's *Trade and Securities Service Statistics.*

Monthly reviews of the *New York Times* averages appear in that paper about the first of each month, and annual reviews appear early in January. From time to time the paper has published, on an irregular basis, a booklet giving a complete daily record of the *New York Times* averages since 1911. Historic data on the Securities and Exchange Commission indexes appear in a booklet available from the Commission and in issues of the *Federal Reserve Bulletin.* Historic series for the National Quotation Bureau's over-the-counter index and for the Value Line average are available only from their publishers; and historical data on *Barron's* 50-stock average can be assembled only by going through all back issues of that paper.

Relative Weighting in Daily Stock Price Indexes. Stock components of the Dow-Jones industrials are weighted in accordance with the size of their prices. On June 28, 1963, the Dow-Jones industrials closed at 706.88. On that day, Du Pont, the highest-priced stock in the average, closed at 245.00. Had Du Pont closed 5 per cent higher at 257.25, the Dow-Jones industrials would have closed 4.21 points higher at 711.09. On the same day Texaco closed at 70.50. Had Texaco closed 5 per cent higher at 74.25, the Dow-Jones industrials would have closed only 1.29 points higher, at 708.17. Because of its higher price, Du Pont was given 3.26 times as much influence in the average as was Texaco. Yet on June 23, 1963, Du Pont's total market value was $11,266.6 million, only a small amount above the market value of $9,080.3 million for Texaco. The Dow-Jones averages are occasionally criticized because of this weighting system.

Stock components of Standard & Poor's indexes are weighted in direct proportion to their contribution to total market value of all stocks in the index. Thus the most heavily weighted stock in Standard & Poor's industrials is General Motors, which also has the highest market value of any industrial on the New York Stock Exchange. The most heavily weighted stock in Standard & Poor's composite index is American Telephone & Telegraph, which has the highest market value of any stock on the Exchange.

Weighting in the *New York Times* industrial average results from a combination of magnitude of price and assigned weighting. The most heavily weighted stock in the *Times* average, Du Pont, had a weight, as of June 28, 1963, 47 times that given to Kennecott Copper. The market value of Du Pont was 14 times that of Kennecott. The *Times* weighting system has evolved over the years as adjustments were made to maintain the continuity of the index in the face of continued stock splits.

Table 8 shows the weight of each of the ten most heavily weighted stocks in the Dow-Jones industrials, the *New York Times* industrials, and Standard & Poor's composite index as of June 28, 1963. The rank of each of these companies by total market value on the New York Stock Exchange among industrials (American Telephone & Telegraph being classified as an industrial) and *Fortune* magazine's ranking by 1963 sales and 1963 assets are also shown.

Several significant observations can be made from these data. The *New York Times* industrials are heavily influenced by a few stocks. Six of the 25 stocks in the *Times* list constitute over half the weight in that average, while the first ten stocks constitute 71 per cent of the weight. By comparison, the top ten stocks in the Dow-Jones industrials constitute slightly over half the weight. Standard & Poor's composite index is also influenced more than one might suspect by the price behavior of the stocks of the largest corporations. Ten out of the 500 stocks in that index make up 38.8 per cent of the weight.

The validity of any weighting must be measured against some standard. Standard & Poor's intentionally weights each stock in accordance with its total market value. Dow-Jones does not specifically weight any stock, with the result that stocks are weighted according to the magnitude of their prices. The Dow-Jones list is intended to measure the price performance, rather than market-value performance, of the "blue chips" or better-known companies which make up its list. The *New York Times* weighting system has evolved over the years as component stocks have been split. Among the other indexes with yet other weighting systems, *Barron's* averages and the Value Line averages are designed specifically to give equal weight to each stock, regardless of either the level of the stock price or its relative market value.

Stock price indexes could also be evaluated in terms of "industry balance." For example, on June 28, 1963, automobile companies constituted 7.85 per cent of the market value of all stocks on the New York Stock Exchange. The proportional weight of the automotive industry in the three indexes was:

Dow-Jones   6.46%
New York Times   7.88%
Standard & Poor's   7.47%

Similar tests would have to be made of all industry groupings for a definitive conclusion on industry balance. Standard & Poor's index is designed to give industries weight in proportion to their contribution to total value. In the other indexes a deliberate attempt is made to include stocks from a variety of industries.

TABLE 8   Relative Weighting in Daily Stock Price Indexes (Based on stock prices of June 28, 1963)

	Weight, %	Cumulative weight, %	Rank among industrials by total market value on NYSE (mid–1963)	Fortune magazine's rankings for industrials 1963	
				Sales	Assets
Dow-Jones 30 Industrials					
Du Pont	11.9	11.9	5	11	11
American Tel. & Tel.	5.9	17.8	1	*	*
Eastman Kodak	5.3	23.1	11	47	30
Union Carbide	5.0	28.1	14	27	18
Sears, Roebuck	4.3	32.4	8	†	†
Owens-Illinois Glass	4.0	36.4	78	79	83
General Foods	4.0	40.4	20	36	70
General Electric	3.8	44.2	7	4	10
Procter & Gamble	3.7	47.9	13	28	32
Texaco	3.4	51.3	6	8	7
Remaining 20 companies	48.7	100.0			
New York Times **25 Industrials**					
Du Pont	20.3	20.3	5	11	11
Caterpillar	7.7	28.0	38	54	59
Eastman Kodak	6.5	34.5	11	47	30
Sears, Roebuck	6.4	40.9	8	†	†
Chrysler	6.0	46.9	39	7	16
General Electric	5.6	52.5	7	4	10
Union Carbide	5.4	57.9	14	27	18
Aluminum Co. of Amer.	4.6	62.5	28	51	25
International Nickel	4.4	66.9	21	‡	‡
International Harvester	4.1	71.0	55	19	22
Remaining 15 companies	29.0	100.0			
Standard & Poor's 500 Composite					
American Tel. & Tel.	9.5	9.5	1	*	*
General Motors	6.5	16.0	2	1	2
Standard Oil of N.J.	4.8	20.8	3	2	1
IBM	3.9	24.7	4	18	13
Du Pont	3.7	28.4	5	11	11
Texaco	2.9	31.3	6	8	7
General Electric	2.3	33.6	7	4	10
Sears, Roebuck	2.2	35.8	8	†	†
Gulf Oil	1.5	37.3	9	9	6
Standard Oil of Calif.	1.5	38.8	10	14	8
Remaining 490 companies	61.2	100.0			

* *Fortune* magazine classifies American Tel. & Tel. as a utility rather than as an industrial. For purposes of showing the rank among industrials by total market value on the New York Stock Exchange, American Tel. & Tel. has been regarded as an industrial.

† *Fortune* magazine classifies Sears, Roebuck as a merchandising firm rather than as an industrial.

‡ *Fortune* magazine classifies International Nickel as a foreign (Canadian) company.

Growth Characteristics of the Indexes.   Annual values for six important indexes are plotted on ratio-scale paper in Figure 9–1.[4] The average annual
compound rate of growth for these indexes for various time periods is
shown in Table 9.[5]

For the entire period 1926 to 1963, Standard & Poor's and Moody's
indexes have grown most rapidly, both showing a 5.4 per cent per annum
increase. The Dow-Jones industrials increased at an annual rate of 4.5
per cent, while the *New York Times* industrials rose only 3.8 per cent per
annum. In general, these relative relationships hold for the shorter periods
studied, the only exception being the eight-year period from 1956 to 1963,
when the Dow-Jones showed a greater average growth rate than Moody's.

In general the market-value-oriented indexes of Standard & Poor's,
Moody's, and the SEC show similar growth rates. This would be expected
because the same statistical theories are used in their construction. The main
differences between the three are in the relative weightings given to various
industries and to various companies.

For every period studied, the *New York Times* average showed the
smallest rate of growth. As was explained above, the *New York Times*
average tends, among the averages studied, to give the greatest proportional
weight to the fewest stocks.

The most interesting comparison is between the value-oriented indexes
of Standard & Poor's, Moody's, and the SEC and the blue-chip-oriented
average of the Dow-Jones. Except for the period from 1956 to 1963, the
market value indexes have shown more growth than the Dow-Jones. Perhaps
this is because the greater base of the value-oriented indexes includes many
small companies which in the aggregate have grown more rapidly over the
years than have the companies, already recognized as dominant in their
industry, which make up the Dow-Jones. A second reason might be the
method by which a rapidly growing stock within the index is treated. As a
single stock in the value-oriented indexes increases in price, its internal
weight in the index *increases* because the aggregate market value of the stock
increases relative to the aggregate market value of all stocks. Stock splits and
stock dividends have no effect on this continued increase in weight. In the
Dow-Jones averages, however, a growing stock will *decrease* in relative

[4] Annual data defined as follows: *New York Times* 25 industrials, average of
yearly high and low; Standard & Poor's 425 industrials, average of daily closing prices;
Dow-Jones 30 industrials, average of daily closing prices; Moody's 125 industrials,
average of end-of-month prices; SEC 193 manufacturing, average of weekly prices; and
NQB over-the-counter 35 industrials, average of price for the first, tenth, and twentieth
of each month in the year.

[5] The growth rate is the annual increase in the slope of a regression line plotted
through the logarithms of the annual index values. Computations were made on the
computer facilities of the Western Data Processing Center at the University of California at Los Angeles.

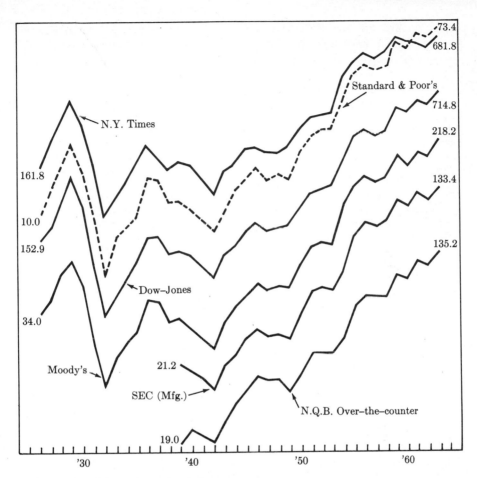

73.4
681.8

Standard & Poor's

714.8

218.2

161.8

133.4

10.0

152.9

135.2

N.Y. Times

34.0

Dow–Jones

Moody's

21.2

SEC (Mfg.)

N.Q.B. Over–the–counter

19.0

'30   '40   '50   '60

Fig. 9–1   Leading stock market indexes.

weight whenever there is a stock split because of the method of adjusting for splits in the divisor. When a stock split occurs, the Dow-Jones averages in effect retain one share of the split stock, sell the other shares, and reinvest the proceeds on a pro rata basis over the entire list. Since rapidly growing stocks tend to be split more frequently than do slower growing stocks, the Dow-Jones averages are continually shifting statistical weight from the former into the latter. On a long-term basis, this may tend to make the Dow-Jones averages grow less rapidly than Standard & Poor's, Moody's, or the SEC indexes.

Table 9 also shows correlation coefficients for the annual values of each index for the various time periods. The correlation coefficient indicates how well the actual data fit to a straight line growing at the indicated compound

TABLE 9   Average Annual Compound Rate of Growth for Yearly Data for Various
Stock Price Indexes, 1926–1963, 1939–1963, 1946–1963, 1956–1963.

	Average annual compound rate of growth	Correlation coefficient
1926–1963, 38 years:		
Dow-Jones 30 industrials	4.5%	0.77
Moody's 125 industrials	5.4	0.82
New York Times 25 industrials	3.8	0.75
Standard & Poor's 425 industrials	5.4	0.83
1939–1963, 25 years:		
Dow-Jones 30 industrials	8.7	0.97
Moody's 125 industrials	9.8	0.98
NQB over-the-counter index	9.1	0.98
New York Times 25 industrials	7.6	0.96
SEC 193 manufacturing	9.9	0.98
Standard & Poor's 425 industrials	9.8	0.97
1946–1963, 18 years:		
Dow-Jones 30 industrials	9.9	0.98
Moody's 125 industrials	11.0	0.98
NQB over-the-counter index	9.5	0.97
New York Times 25 industrials	9.0	0.96
SEC 193 manufacturing	11.1	0.97
Standard & Poor's 425 industrials	11.4	0.98
1956–1963, 8 years:		
Dow-Jones 30 industrials	6.2	0.91
Moody's 125 industrials	5.9	0.92
NQB over-the-counter index	7.4	0.95
New York Times 25 industrials	3.1	0.73
SEC 193 manufacturing	5.8	0.91
Standard & Poor's 425 industrials	6.5	0.93

growth rate. (A perfect correlation would be 1.00.) For the 1939 to 1963 period, the indicated growth rate is an excellent fit to the data, for all the correlation coefficients are above 0.96. The same general relationship holds for the 1946 to 1963 interval and for the 1956 to 1963 interval with but one important exception. In the last period the correlation coefficient for the *New York Times* 25 industrials dropped to 0.73. As can be seen from Figure 9–1, in recent years the growth rate of the *New York Times* 25 industrials has diminished considerably, relative to the other indexes.

When correlation coefficients for the entire period 1926 to 1963 are considered, the coefficients are much lower. The severe changes in the level of the market in the early 1930s have the effect of reducing the validity of summarizing market trends for that period in terms of an average growth rate.

Price Sensitivity among Indexes.   Market technicians, who use changes in stock price indexes as barometers of expected future fluctuations in the market, are primarily interested in having an index that is sensitive in reporting market changes. Data on price sensitivity in Table 10 show the annual high for various years as a per cent of the annual low, the percentage change in the various indexes during the market break of May 1963, and the percentage change in the various indexes over stock market cycles. When measured by the size of annual fluctuations, the *New York Times* average appears to be the most sensitive and the Dow-Jones average to be the least sensitive. However, the differences are not statistically significant at a 5 per cent level of confidence; hence it is more valid to conclude that there is no significant observed difference between the magnitude of the annual fluctuations of the three indexes.

During the critical market break of May 28 to 31, 1962, Standard & Poor's index fluctuated the most, its daily percentage change being greater than those of the other two indexes. During the first two days of the break, the Dow-Jones average changed percentagewise more than the *Times* average, but on May 30 the *Times* average recovered slightly more.

If sensitivity is taken to mean the percentage change between peaks and troughs of the stock market cycle, Standard & Poor's index appears the most sensitive, having changed the most percentagewise in six of the eight cycles since 1929. The Dow-Jones average appears the least sensitive.

These data indicate in a general fashion that Standard & Poor's index tends to fluctuate most during market changes and that the Dow-Jones tends to fluctuate least. Numerous exceptions exist, however, and perhaps the more obvious conclusion is that in general the three indexes give relatively parallel performances.

Conclusion.   In general, and quite surprisingly considering the different techniques by which they are created, the various stock market indexes and averages tend to perform in a similar manner. Economists and statisticians who want to study long-run growth patterns in the economy or to measure business cycle patterns will probably find one of the three market value indexes—Standard & Poor's, Moody's, or the SEC—best because of their weighting and easy availability. Users of these indexes must be sure that changes in aggregate market values are what they seek.

Long-run investors might be better advised to use either *Barron's* or the Value Line index as a quick measure of change in their own portfolios or as a standard against which to evaluate a portfolio's behavior. The logic behind this conclusion rests upon the authors' belief that a typical portfolio comes closer to being distributed evenly among the various stocks than it does to any other method of distribution. It would be an unusual portfolio that would hold twenty times as much General Motors stock as J. C. Penney

TABLE 10 Sensitivity of Daily Indexes—Industrials

	Dow-Jones	N.Y. Times	Standard & Poor's
1. Annual fluctuation—annual high as per cent of annual low:			
1929	192	212	179
1932	215	224	206
1937	171	168	186
1942	129	131	132
1946	130	135	136
1949	124	129	125
1950	120	121	126
1951	116	118	117
1952	114	193	115
1953	115	120	119
1954	144	154	150
1955	126	132	139
1956	113	116	117
1957	124	130	127
1958	134	136	136
1959	118	123	115
1960	121	134	117
1961	120	121	126
1962	135	144	137
1963	119	124	121
Fifteen years, 1949-1963			
Number times fluctuated most	0	10	5
Number times in middle third	2	5	8
Number times fluctuated least	13	0	2
2. Market break—percentage drop from previous day's close:			
Monday, May 28, 1962	−5.7	−5.4	−6.7
Tuesday, May 29, 1962	+4.7	+4.2	+4.6
Wednesday—market closed			
Thursday, May 31, 1962	+1.6	+1.9	+2.7
3. Stock market cycles—percentage change between peaks and troughs:			
1929 high to 1932 low	− 89.2	− 87.7	− 86.1
1932 low to 1937 high	+371.6	+314.3*	+414.2
1937 high to 1942 low	− 52.2	− 53.4*	− 58.3
1942 low to 1946 high	+128.7	+118.8	+145.8
1946 high to 1949 low	− 23.9	− 27.7	− 28.6
1949 low to 1956 high	+222.4	+238.7	+302.7
1956 high to 1957 low	− 19.4	− 23.8	− 21.2
1957 low to 1963 high	+ 82.8	+ 66.7	+ 88.8
Eight periods:			
Times changed most	1	1	6
Times changed in middle third	3	4	1
Times changed least	4	3	1

* The *New York Times* average reached a high in 1936 of 243.60. From its 1932 low to its 1936 high it rose 322.7%, and from its 1936 high to its 1942 low it fell 54.3%.

stock just because General Motors has twenty times the aggregate market value of J. C. Penney. Thus what happens to investors in the aggregate, as measured by the market value indexes, may not be as good an indicator of what might have happened to an individual portfolio as would an index constructed to give equal weight to each stock. The disadvantage of *Barron's* averages is that historical series are not available; and the disadvantage at present of the Value Line average is that it is relatively new and thus extends back only to mid-1961. It may be that the Dow-Jones average, in spite of its method of internal weighting, more closely approximates what one might expect from a diversified portfolio of good-quality stocks than does any other index of wide availability.

A long-run investor who wants to evaluate the level of the stock market in terms of its underlying characteristics of earnings, dividends, or book value per share will probably find the availability of information on the Standard & Poor's indexes the critical selection factor. Market technicians who desire to measure the market from hour to hour during a trading day will find either the Dow-Jones or Standard & Poor's indexes about equally efficient.

part 3

ORGANIZATION AND OPERATION OF THE NEW YORK STOCK EXCHANGE

10 listing requirements

An issue is listed when it is added to the list of securities in which trading on a particular exchange is permitted. The granting of listed privileges usually depends upon whether or not circumstances offer a reasonable assurance that an adequate auction market will exist if the security is admitted to trading. There is a technical distinction between "listing" and "admitted to trading" which should be borne in mind. A security is "authorized for listing" when an application is finally approved by the exchange. This is followed by registration with the Securities and Exchange Commission, and upon the effectiveness of that registration, the security is admitted to trading, i.e., actual trading begins on the floor of the exchange.

In theory, a stock exchange is a place where securities are bought and sold at "fair" prices. It is generally felt that a price arrived at by the competition of informed buyers and sellers is as near to a fair price as it is possible to come. Obviously, however, the bargaining of buyers and sellers will not result in fair prices if traders do not have the information necessary to judge the merits of the issues in which they trade, or if a sufficient number of buyers and sellers do not engage in the bargaining process so that the activity of many rather than of a few dominates the market. Most exchanges limit trading on their floors to those issues which meet these two requirements.

Until 1910 the New York Stock Exchange maintained both a listed and an unlisted department. Securities of corporations that refused to give "substantial" information about their business were carried in the unlisted department. In its report in 1909 the Hughes Commission recommended that the unlisted department be abolished, and this recommendation was put into effect the following year. Since that time only fully listed securities have been dealt in on the floor of the Exchange. The various regional exchanges admit to unlisted trading a number of securities listed and registered on other securities exchanges. In most cases these are securities of national interest already listed on the New York Stock Exchange.

General Requirements for Listing

Before a security may be admitted to trading, it must be approved for listing by the New York Stock Exchange and be registered under the Securities Exchange Act of 1934. Listing is a procedure separate and distinct from registration, effected by having an application to list approved by an exchange. Registration, however, requires (1) the filing of a registration statement with the Securities and Exchange Commission and with an exchange and (2) a certification by the exchange to the Commission that it approves the particular securities for listing. Registration becomes effective automatically thirty days after receipt by the Commission of this certification or sooner if requested by the company and approved by the Commission. The Commission does not have the power to prevent the listing of a security approved by an exchange unless the registration statement or the registrant fails to conform to the act or to some rule made by the Commission.

The New York Stock Exchange will want information about the management, property, business, and financial setup of the applicant corporation. Such data will be a part of the application proper. Because the specific data required for listing vary with industries and companies, the Exchange does not have a prepared form upon which to make application. Instead, the applicant presents the required data in the form of a coherent narrative, supplemented by financial statements. The Exchange employs a staff to assist and advise a company in the preparation of a listing application. When the application is ready, it is submitted to the Exchange, together with the signed agreements to be described later, a check to cover the listing fee, and other supporting documents. The Department of Stock List meets each Tuesday to consider applications. If the company applying does not have securities already listed on the Exchange, its application must be submitted to the Board of Governors for final action.

Companies contemplating listing may arrange for an informal, confidential, and preliminary review of their qualifications for listing prior to the preparation of the formal application. The Exchange will ask for as much of the following as is readily available:

1. A copy of the company's charter and bylaws
2. Copies of annual reports to stockholders for the last five years
3. The latest prospectus covering an offering under the Securities Act of 1933 and a proxy statement for the most recent annual meeting
4. A schedule showing the distribution of the company's stock, including a summary of stock owned or controlled by officers and directors, by their immediate families, and by large holders of 10 per cent or more of the outstanding stock
5. Information on situations in which officers, directors, or principal share-

holders have a personal interest in the affairs of the company in addition to their stock interest (as, for example, in the leasing of property to the company; in options from subsidiaries; or through an interest in competitors, suppliers, or customers of the company)

6. Specimens of bond or stock certificates

Such an informal preliminary review of eligibility is completed prior to any public announcement of a company's intention to file for listing.

If, after an informal review, a formal application for listing is made and approved, certification of approval is made to the Securities and Exchange Commission and thirty days after receipt of the certification by it the listing is automatically effective. The department announces when trading in the issue may begin upon acknowledgment of the receipt by the Commission.

The listing requirements of the New York Stock Exchange have two primary purposes: (1) they place before the Exchange the information essential to the "determination as to the suitability of the security for public trading on the Exchange"; and (2) they make available to the public "such information as [the public] may reasonably be presumed to require as an aid to its judgment as to the merits of the security." To be eligible for listing an applicant "must be a going concern, or be the successor to a going concern, and must have substantial assets or demonstrated earning power, or both." While the amount of assets and earnings is a consideration, the department places greater emphasis on such questions as the degree of national interest in the company, its standing in its particular field, the character of the market for its products, its relative stability and position in industry, and whether or not it is engaged in an expanding activity and has prospects of maintaining its position. In addition, the securities for listing must be sufficiently widely distributed to offer assurance that an adequate auction market will exist if they are listed.

Because the requirements described above are largely qualitative rather than quantitative in nature, the New York Stock Exchange has developed certain minimum criteria as guides. These yardsticks are intended to be applied in a flexible manner, for the listing decision is based on the suitability of the company as a whole and weight may be given to compensating factors. The guiding rules are:

Size.   The company's publicly held common stock should have an aggregate market value at the time of listing of at least $12 million.

Earnings.   The company should be earning under competitive conditions at least $2 million annually before corporate taxes and $1.2 million annually after corporate income taxes.

Stock Distribution.   The company should have at least 1 million shares outstanding and at least 700,000 shares publicly held. It should have a minimum of 2,000 stockholders of whom at least 1,700 hold round lots.

The Application for Listing of Stock

The following description of what should be included in the application is taken from *Listing Procedure and Directions for the Preparation of Applications for Original Listing* published by the Department of Stock List of the New York Stock Exchange. Applications for bonds are identical except that additional information on the bonds' indenture provisions must be included.

Heading.   At the beginning of the application the applicant must give the application number assigned by the Exchange, the date, the name of the company, the name and amount of securities covered by the application, the number of shares or principal amount of these securities presently issued, and the number of common stockholders of record as of the latest available date.

Description of Transaction.   If the application is an initial one for listing on the New York Stock Exchange, the company must so state. If the application is for the listing of unissued securities, a detailed statement of how the securities will be issued must be included.

Authority for Issuance.   The applicant must indicate the dates on which directors approved the issuance of any unissued securities covered by the application and the dates on which stockholder approval was or will be acquired.

History and Business.   Here the applicant gives in succinct narrative form a history of the corporation, stating where and when it was organized, the form of organization adopted, the duration of its charter, and an account of its development and growth in the particular line of business now conducted. If the company was organized as the result of merger, consolidation, or reorganization, the history of the predecessor companies must be traced. If it was organized as the result of reorganization, the circumstances of the reorganization must be described.

This is followed by a brief description of the present business of the applicant and its subsidiary or controlled companies, including principal products manufactured or services performed, principal markets for products and raw material, operations conducted, and merchandising methods. In general the statement must furnish such information as will serve to indicate clearly the growth and development of the particular industry in which the applicant is engaged and the growth and development of the applicant and the place it occupies in its field.

If a material part of the business is dependent upon patents, proprietary formulas, or secret processes, this must be so stated. The applicant must give the date of expiration of principal patents or of proprietary interests in principal formulas.

Highly specialized industries, such as utilities, oil-producing companies, and mining companies, are required to give such additional information as is necessary to present an adequate picture of the company.

Property Description.   This section calls for a brief description of the physical properties of the applicant and its subsidiary or controlled companies, stating location, character, condition of equipment, acreage, transportation facilities, etc. The applicant should state whether properties are owned or leased and if possible should indicate the normal capacity of plants in terms of units of production. In industries where properties are of vital importance, such as mining and oil companies, a report by an independent engineer is required.

Affiliated Companies.   Here the applicant lists all subsidiary or controlled companies, including companies in which the applicant owns or controls, directly or indirectly, 50 per cent or more of the voting power. A brief description of the capitalization of each company is required, together with an account of the part each such company plays in the business.

Management.   The applicant must reveal the names, titles, and addresses of all directors and officers and must state any other principal business affiliations they may have. A brief biographical outline for each of the principal officers of the applicant should supplement this part of the application.

Capitalization.   Under this caption a summary statement is given of changes in authorized stock and capitalization of the applicant since organization, with reference to dates of corporate actions effecting such changes. These data may be given in narrative form if desired, but if changes have been numerous, a tabulated statement is preferred.

A tabular form statement of substantial changes in the outstanding amounts of stock of the applicant over the past five years is also given, showing dates on which stock was authorized for issuance, the purposes of issuance, and consideration received. Such a statement should show shares reacquired by the applicant or its subsidiary or controlled companies. If there have been authorized for issuance any unissued shares, the amount authorized for issuance for each specific purpose should be shown, together with a statement as to the amount that will be credited, respectively, to capital and to capital surplus with respect to such shares upon issuance.

Funded Debt.   The applicant states here the aggregate amount of funded debt of the applicant company and subsidiary or controlled companies and gives a list of the outstanding issues and amounts, indicating amounts held by subsidiary or controlled companies. If this list is extensive, it may be appended to the application as an exhibit.

Stock Provisions.   Next the Exchange wants a summarized statement of the rights, preferences, privileges, and priorities of the class of stock applied for and of each class on a parity therewith or senior thereto.

If application is being made to list one or more senior classes of stock, the charter provisions attaching thereto are recited verbatim in an exhibit appended to the application in addition to the summarized statement. A full description of any provisions or indentures or other agreements restricting payment of dividends or affecting voting rights of the stock must be included.

Applications to list stock should state whether or not stockholders of any class have preemptive rights to subscribe to additional issues, either by charter provision or by statute.

Employees—Labor Relations.   Here the applicant states the total number of persons regularly employed and briefly describes current labor relations.

Stockholder Relations.   Under this heading the applicant must describe such relations as are over and above the Exchange minimum requirements as set forth in the listing agreements. This would include such matters as treatment of correspondence from stockholders, retention of public relations counsel, proxy solicitation policy, notice of dividend action either declared or passed, and the like.

Dividend Record.   This part of the application consists of a table showing the amount of dividends paid by the applicant (or its predecessors) each year for the five preceding years, per share and in the aggregate. Stock dividends are shown separately. The aggregate and per share amounts of any dividend arrearages are also stated.

Options, Warrants, Conversion Rights.   Here the applicant must reveal the terms and conditions of any options, purchase warrants, conversion rights, or other commitments pursuant to which the company may be required to issue any of its securities. If there are no such commitments, that fact should be stated.

Litigation.   The Exchange must be informed of all pending litigation of a material nature in which the applicant or any of its subsidiary or controlled companies may be involved which may affect its income from, title to, or possession of any of its properties.

Business, Financial, and Accounting Policies.   A number of items are called for under this caption. For example, if the applicant conducts a substantial portion of its business in leased premises, as is the practice of retail chain store organizations, a statement should be made of its policy with regard to such leases, i.e., whether in general the leases are long-term and whether rentals are at a flat rate or on a percentage of sales basis.

If the applicant's assets are subject to depletion, it should describe its policy about depletion, show the basis on which depletion is computed, and explain the theory underlying such basis.

The applicant should also give a reasonably detailed description of its depreciation policy and should state the method of depreciation followed, i.e., straight-line, etc. It should explain the theory underlying the method. Rates employed for major classes of property should be stated in tabulated form. The applicant should also state the policy followed with respect to those items which in ordinary practice are capitalized and amortized.

If it is the policy of the applicant to make future commodity commitments to an extent that may materially affect its financial position, it should so state. It should also indicate whether or not in the normal course of the business it is necessary to expand working capital to a material extent through short-term loans (or otherwise).

The practice followed in adjusting inventories to the lower of cost or market should be described; i.e., it should be stated whether "market" is considered as:

1. Replacement market, and whether or not in that event allowance is made for any decline in price of basic commodities in finished goods and work in process
2. Selling market, and whether or not in that event allowance is made for selling expense and normal margin of profit

The applicant should describe treatment of any intercompany profit on goods included in inventory. The method of computing cost of goods sold should be explained, i.e., whether computed on basis of "average cost," "standard cost," "last in, first out," "first in, first out," etc. If the amount of marketable securities held is considerable in proportion to the total assets, the method of computing profit or loss on sales of securities should be stated.

In the case of consolidation, the applicant must indicate the principle followed with respect to inclusion or exclusion of companies and should state whether or not all companies included in the consolidation employ the same principles of accounting. If not, it should indicate the nature of any substantial divergence.

The company must also supply information on the independent public accountants and on the chief accounting officer of the company.

Financial Statements.   The financial statements to be included in the listing application are as follows:

1. A summarized statement of consolidated earnings for the last ten fiscal years. This statement must show separately: sales; earnings before de-

preciation, interest, and Federal income taxes; amount of depreciation, interest, and Federal income taxes; and net earnings.

2. Consolidated income statements, balance sheets, and surplus accounts for the last two fiscal years, together with any statements for the period elapsed since the end of the last fiscal year. These statements should be in comparative form where practicable. Annual statements should be accompanied by the statement of the company's independent auditors, and interim statements should be certified by the company's principal accounting officer.

3. A pro forma, or "giving effect," consolidated balance sheet may also be required if there has been or is in prospect any major financing, recapitalization, acquisition, or reorganization.

If there are any subsidiary or controlled companies not included in the consolidated financial statements, the consolidated income account should carry a footnote reflecting the parent company's proportion of the undistributed profit or of the losses of such companies. There should also be a footnote to the consolidated balance sheet showing the amount by which the parent company's equity in the unconsolidated subsidiaries or controlled companies has increased or decreased as a result of profits, losses, and distributions.

The Exchange may require that separate financial statements of any such unconsolidated subsidiary or controlled company be furnished for inclusion in the listing application if the investment therein represents a substantial part of the assets of the applicant company. It may also require statements of the applicant as a separate corporate entity if in the department's opinion such statements are essential or desirable.

While there are no definite rules about the form or the degree of detail of the financial statements included in listing applications, it is the Exchange's aim to have such statements reasonably informative without being overburdened with detail. The accounting policies of the corporation must of course conform to accepted practice. All financial statements contained in the company's annual reports subsequent to listing must be in the same form as the statements in the listing application.

Opinion of Counsel.   A summary of the opinion of counsel is given here, together with the name and address of counsel rendering such opinion. This opinion must cover the incorporation of the applicant and the corporate steps taken for the issuance of the securities in question. It also must state that the stocks when issued are validly issued, fully paid, and nonassessable or, in the case of bonds, that they are valid and enforceable obligations of the company. If the counsel is an officer or director of the applicant, this fact must be disclosed also.

General Information.   Under this heading are given:

1. Date on which fiscal year ends
2. Principal business address of the applicant
3. Statutory address
4. Date and place of annual meeting. The percentage of voting stock that constitutes a quorum
5. Names and addresses of transfer agent and registrar

Signature.   The application must be signed by a properly accredited officer of the company.

Exhibits.   Data which it has been decided to include in the application as an exhibit rather than in the body of the application should be arranged in the same sequence as the data in which references to them occur in the application and should be alphabetically designated.

The exhibit section of the application follows immediately after the signature page and is introduced by a paragraph reading:

> These exhibits constitute an essential part of the application. The statements of fact contained herein are made on the authority of the applicant corporation in the same manner as those in the body of the application.

Supporting Papers.   Following this is a list of the papers required to be filed in support of the application. These papers are considered a part of the application, and it is the policy of the Exchange to make them available for public inspection at the office of the Department of Stock List upon request after the listing application is approved. They include:

1. A signed copy of the application in the form submitted to the Exchange.
2. A copy of the charter certified by the secretary of state of the state of incorporation.
3. A copy of the bylaws certified by a properly accredited officer of the applicant.
4. Resolutions: Certified copies of resolutions
   a. Of the board of directors authorizing the making of the application.
   b. Of the stockholders authorizing issuance (if such action was required) of any unissued securities included in the application.
   c. Of the board of directors authorizing the issuance of any unissued securities included in the application.
   d. Appointment of transfer agent and registrar.
5. Opinion of counsel.

6. Stock distribution schedule in the form prescribed and certified by the transfer agent.

7. Certificate of the registrar as to number of shares outstanding.

8. Specimens of stock certificates for 100 shares and fewer than 100 shares of each class proposed for listing. These should be accompanied by a letter from the transfer agent stating that an adequate supply of blank certificates is on hand.

9. Public authority certificates—if applicable.

10. Ten copies of any prospectus relating to the securities to be listed and issued during the past year.

11. Certified copies of the financial statements incorporated in the application.

12. A copy of the listing agreement.

13. A memorandum report on unpaid dividends and unsettled rights.

Mining companies and oil-producing companies must file reports by qualified engineers on property, reserves, equipment, etc. Under special circumstances additional papers may be required, as determined by the Exchange.

Listing Agreements

Of equal, if not of greater, importance compared with the information furnished in the application are the agreements entered into between the applicant and the Exchange. These provide for continuing relations between the two and are of such an elastic nature as to permit response to current changes in economic conditions. They do not have the force of law but have been the means over a period of years of securing improved relations between management and stockholders. Each provision has been promulgated as a result of actual experience. The contents of this agreement are contained in a formal printed contract. The general purpose of the agreement is not only to provide for the technical requirements to carry on trading but also to protect the members of the Exchange and their customers from fraud and to make available adequate current information. A brief summary of the provisions of this contract follows.

Changes in Corporate Setup.   Each corporation seeking listing privileges for its securities must agree to notify the Exchange of any change in the general nature of its business or of any disposal of property or collateral that might affect its financial position or the nature and extent of its operations. This provision also applies to similar changes in subsidiaries. The corporation must also promise to inform the department of changes in its certificate of incorporation or bylaws. In the event that it issues options or warrants, it is obligated to inform the Exchange promptly and to include the information in a report to its stockholders. Furthermore, the corporation promises not to repurchase its own stock at a price in excess of that at which the securities can be obtained in the open market and agrees to report promptly on any changes in the quantity of its stock held in its own treasury. It also agrees that, in redeeming any portion of listed securities, the particular shares or bonds to be redeemed will be chosen by lot or pro rata and that a fifteen-day advance notice of their redemption will be given to the authorities of the Exchange. The corporation must agree to furnish the Exchange on demand with such information about itself and its activities as the Exchange may reasonably require. Finally, on request the corporation agrees to provide the Exchange with the names of member firms which are registered owners of the corporation's stock if a need for such stock for loaning purposes develops. In addition, the corporation agrees to use its best efforts with known large stockholders to make reasonable amounts of their stock available in similar circumstances.

Corporate Publicity.   Each corporation whose stock is listed agrees to publish once each year and to submit to stockholders, not later than three months after the close of the preceding fiscal year and at least fifteen days in advance of the annual meeting of the corporation, a balance sheet as of the end of the fiscal year and an income and surplus statement for the fiscal year. These statements may be either (1) on a consolidated basis for the corporation and those subsidiaries in which it has a controlling interest or (2) on a nonconsolidated basis for the corporation as a single entity and in addition for each nonconsolidated subsidiary which the corporation controls. Control is taken to mean direct or indirect ownership of a majority of the equity stock of the subsidiary. The financial statements contained in the annual report must be audited by an independent firm of public accountants and must have the auditor's certificate appended. They must be in the same general form as the statements filed as a part of the original application for listing privileges.

Each corporation further agrees to make no substantial change in its accounting methods or in its policies relating to depreciation, depletion, or valuation of inventories and assets without notifying the Exchange and disclosing the effects of the changes to its stockholders in the next annual report. Each corporation must agree to issue quarterly statements of earnings based on the same degree of consolidation used in the annual reports. Furthermore, the corporation agrees that neither it nor subsidiaries controlled by it will make substantial charges against capital or surplus without notifying the Exchange and, if requested by the Exchange, without seeking stockholder approval or ratification.

Listed corporations are obligated to give to their stockholders and to the Exchange prompt notice of "any action taken by the corporation with respect to dividends or to the allotment of rights to subscribe or to any rights or benefits pertaining to the ownership of its securities listed on the Exchange." In all cases the corporation must allow its security holders a proper period within which to record their interest and to exercise their rights. The Exchange requires at least a ten-day advance notice of the closing of transfer books or the taking of a record of stockholders for any purpose.

Transfer and Registry Procedures.   Each corporation seeking listing privileges for a security must maintain two offices or agencies south of Chambers Street in the borough of Manhattan, city of New York, for the purpose of registering and transferring its listed securities. Each of these offices or agencies must be distinct from the other and acceptable to the Department of Stock List. The registrar must be a bank or trust company. When a company transfers stock at its own office, the transfer must be made by a person acceptable to the department. He must be specifically authorized by the board of directors of the company to countersign certificates and must be other than the officer authorized to sign certificates of stock. A company cannot be the registrar of its own stock. A corporation may be allowed to make transfer of its shares in cities other than New York, but in that case all certificates must be identical with those used in New York as to color and form and must be interchangeable with them. The total shares transferable in all such cities must be no greater than the amount listed.

Before being admitted to the stock list, all securities must be engraved and printed in a manner satisfactory to the department by an engraving company whose work the department is authorized to pass upon. The engraving must be done upon the premises of the bank note company, and the name of the manufacturer must appear upon the face of all securities and upon all instruments attached to them.

The face of a listed security must be fully steel-engraved and printed from at least two engraved steel plates, i.e., a border and tint plate from which a printing in color is made of the border and portions underlying the face of the security, and a hand-engraved faceplate containing the vignette and the descriptive or promissory portion of the security, printed in black. The combined impression of these plates must provide as effectual security as possible against counterfeiting. The printing of different classes and denominations of securities must be in distinctive colors, to make them readily distinguishable. The face text of all engraved listed securities should be in script lettering. To afford the maximum protection against counterfeiting, the Exchange recommends the use of the human figure with plainly discernible features as a part of all vignettes. A change in the design or form of a security cannot be made without the approval of the department.

The listing agreement further provides that transfer agents, registrars, fiscal agents, and trustees for any security of the corporation will be appointed only after prior notice to the Exchange. Registrars must be qualified with the Exchange to act as such, and trustees may not be appointed from among the corporation's own officers or directors.

The corporation further agrees to have an adequate supply of certificates on hand to meet demands for transfer and to supply to stockholders on request and without charge a printed copy of the preferences of all classes of stock if the preferences do not appear on the corporation's certificates. The corporation agrees to solicit proxies for all stockholder meetings and to issue new certificates to replace lost ones after notification of loss and receipt of proper indemnity.

Withdrawal from Listing and Registration

Section 12(d) of the Securities Exchange Act of 1934 provides as follows: "A security registered with a national securities exchange may be withdrawn or stricken from listing and registration in accordance with the rules of the exchange and, upon such terms as the Commission may deem necessary to impose for the protection of investors, upon application by the issuer or the exchange to the Commission; . . . ."

One of the factors which a purchaser of a security considers at the time he makes his purchase is whether the security is listed or not. If corporations were to be permitted to delist their securities at their own pleasure, a gross injustice to investors would result. Consequently, once a security is listed, the burden of proving that listing is no longer desirable or necessary and that security holders would not suffer if the security were to be removed from the list rests upon the corporation or upon the exchange seeking delisting. To delist a security, the exchange or corporation seeking delisting files with the Securities and Exchange Commission an application for permission to withdraw, citing the reasons for the request. After a hearing the Commission may grant or refuse the request.

The policy of the New York Stock Exchange in this respect is to refuse to delist a security which in its opinion is eligible for continued listing. However, if the proposed withdrawal is approved by $66\frac{2}{3}$ per cent of outstanding security holders and is opposed by fewer than 10 per cent of the bona fide individual holders, the Exchange will consider delistment.

The Board of Governors of the New York Stock Exchange will consider initiating action to suspend trading or to delist the stock of a company when the issue is held by fewer than 800 stockholders and by fewer than 700 holders of round lots, when the number of shares publicly held falls below 300,000, when the market value of these shares is reduced below $2.5 million, when the total market value of net tangible assets is less than $5 million, or when average net earnings for the three previous years are less than $400,000.

Mistaken Notions Concerning Listed Stocks

Many persons have the idea that the New York Stock Exchange sponsors every security listed and that if it does not it should not permit listing of the security. Nothing of this sort is possible, even if it were desirable. The Exchange cannot and does not recommend a security as of high investment value by admitting it to the list for trading. Moreover, it would be too costly for the Exchange actually to investigate the truth or correctness of the data furnished by applicant corporations. When it is realized that any guaranties against risk would involve a complete study of each corporation several times each year from the engineering, accounting, legal, financial, and business points of view, it is apparent that anyone who expects the Exchange to put its stamp of approval as to its investment position on any of the securities listed has a totally wrong conception of the functions of the Exchange.

The Exchange proposes to provide an open, free market for securities issued legally and without fraud and to give as full and as correct information as it reasonably can secure about such securities. The Exchange cannot even guarantee the information it receives. The matter of values and prices must always be left to the judgment of the individual investor and speculator. Everyone should know that some very weak securities are on the Big Board, that weak securities involve large elements of risk though they do sometimes develop into very strong investments, and that, on the other hand, some very strong investments that seem without risk will turn out to be failures.

The Value of Listing to the Investor

If the Exchange gives no guaranties and if very speculative stocks are on the stock list, why invest in listed stocks? There are several reasons. First, the fact that the security is listed gives an investor reasonable grounds to believe that the issue of securities was legal, that the concern was legally organized, and that at the time of listing it was a solvent, going concern with a relatively large issue of securities well distributed so that no single large interest had control of the market. He also knows that he is reasonably well protected against counterfeiting of the stock certificates and their overissue. Second, the investor knows that he can obtain at any time reasonably full and recent information about his securities from any member of the Exchange or from its secretary. Third, his securities have a much higher collateral value than if they had no open, continuous market. This is especially true of stocks. Bonds have a wide over-the-counter market, and listing does not mean so much in connection with their collateral value as in the case of stocks. Fourth, the investor has available constant quotations about the value of his securities and can convert them into cash at any time. Fifth, the investor is protected against unreasonable commissions and low standards of business practice. Sixth, the fact that his securities are traded on a highly organized market will protect him against the violent fluctuations to which he would otherwise be subject.

The Value of Listing to a Corporation

The authors have before them a prospectus describing a relatively large issue of stock by a syndicate of bankers and announcing that application will be made for the privilege of listing on the New York Stock Exchange. We have seen what listing may mean to the investor. The announcement of the intention to list is meant to appeal to the investor. But of what value is listing to the corporation issuing the stock? First, because of the benefits of listing, the corporation's securities will have better standing with investors and will on the whole command a higher price. Second, the securities will attain a wider distribution to owners, which will create a larger and wider interest in the prosperity of the company. Third, when securities are actively traded in and strong on the market, the company of issue receives a large amount of advertising through the market for its securities. This in turn has its effect on its employees and on the sale of its product. Fourth, future financing will be easier if a company and its securities are well known.

Not all companies are listed on the New York Stock Exchange. Some do not desire the wider distribution of stock required before listing or the wider distribution the market would create; others do not desire to make adequate reports and statements of their affairs; still others hesitate because they do not want their securities subject to the "uncertainties of speculation." Again, some companies cannot meet the requirements of the Exchange.

11 types of member activity

A visitor to the New York Stock Exchange looking down upon the floor from the visitors' gallery sees men gathered here and there in groups and others rushing about from group to group; but he cannot know that these men have widely different responsibilities and serve many varying, widely different purposes. Seldom are as many as two thirds of the total members of the Exchange present, and frequently as few as two fifths are in attendance.

Some of the men on the floor are brokers, some are dealers, and others combine the work of both. The technical difference between a broker and a dealer hinges upon whether the member acts as an agent or as a principal in a transaction. Brokers execute orders as agents for individual and institutional investors, security dealers, or other brokers. They are of two types, commission brokers and two-dollar brokers. Dealers, sometimes called "traders," buy and sell stocks for their own account, hoping to make a profit. There are also two types of dealers, registered traders and odd-lot dealers.

A third group of members—specialists—combine the work of broker and dealer. They buy and sell securities for others on commission, and they also buy and sell securities for their own account. Which activity they engage in at a particular moment depends upon the number of orders given them by other members, on the spread between the bid and ask prices, and on the activity of the market.

There is a group of members engaged in stock market activity who seldom if ever appear on the Exchange floor. These are partners or officers of member firms who own seats on the Exchange to enable their firm to obtain the commission rate advantages of membership. The orders of such firms are executed on the floor by correspondent firms. Finally, there is a small group of members who are inactive.

As of May 31, 1964, New York Stock Exchange members fell into these groupings:

Commission brokers and members not
    classified elsewhere*   648
Two-dollar brokers   150
Floor traders†   30
Odd-lot dealers   120
Specialists   357
Inactive members   61
    Total membership   1,366

    * Included 10 members who handle bond transactions exclusively.

    † The registered trader classification became effective Aug. 3, 1964. Prior to that date, similar activities were carried on by members classified as floor traders.

The Commission Broker

A commission broker is an Exchange member who is also a partner or officer in a commission brokerage firm that deals with private and institutional investors. The commission broker himself executes orders for his firm's customers on the floor of the Exchange. Commission brokerage houses frequently have more than one broker on the floor; Merrill Lynch, Pierce, Fenner & Smith, Inc., the largest commission house, has 10 such brokers. Some commission brokerage firms have many branches throughout the country, with private wire connections to all branches, so that they may serve a large segment of the nation. Other houses have no branches outside New York but depend on correspondents to furnish them a large amount of out-of-town business. Some commission houses that own a seat on the Exchange do not maintain a member on the floor of the Exchange but transact all their business through other member firms.

    Since a commission brokerage house deals with the public, it must maintain one or more brokerage offices to contact the public. Each such office must have reporting equipment to keep abreast of the market, access to bookkeeping and accounting services, and a well-trained sales force. The firm must have a research and statistical department from which salesmen and customers can obtain information about particular companies. Commission houses are the agencies that make it possible for small investors to buy the securities of the largest corporations. They pour a constant stream of buying and selling orders into the market, thereby contributing to a wide and deep continuous market that reflects every hope and fear of the investing public.

    The operation of a commission brokerage house and its relation to its customers were explained in detail in Chapters 6 and 7.

The Two-dollar Broker

This type of broker, whose formal name is "floor broker," transacts business for other members of the Exchange for a floor brokerage commission. For years this commission was $2 per 100 shares, hence the nickname. Since 1919 the commission has been increased several times so that at the present time it varies from $1.25 per 100 shares for issues selling at $1 per share to $5 per 100 shares for issues selling at a price above $200 per share. Nonetheless the nickname still persists.

When a commission broker or trader has orders which he cannot execute personally because of their number or because of the activity of the market, the services of a two-dollar broker are engaged. For example, if he has several market orders for different issues requiring his simultaneous presence at different posts on the floor, he hands such orders as he cannot execute to a two-dollar broker. If he has limited orders for stocks that are traded at different posts, he may need the services of a two-dollar broker to catch the market at the price set by his customer.

Some two-dollar brokers specialize in handling orders for large blocks of stock which would occupy too much of the commission broker's time. The fact that certain two-dollar brokers may know of possible buyers or sellers of such blocks, plus their ability to execute the orders quickly and without upsetting the market, makes their services desirable. Most such orders come to them through commission brokers, although occasionally a two-dollar broker may be contacted directly by a public institutional investor. Such public investors pay the regular nonmember commission.

The two-dollar broker's commission may seem low, but it should be remembered that he does not need an elaborate office and trained personnel. He deals directly with other brokers and dealers, and his responsibility beyond the execution of the order on the floor is not to be compared with that of the commission broker, who deals with the public, solicits orders, builds up a clientele, handles margin accounts, borrows money on collateral, collects dividends and interest, and performs the hundred and one services of a commission brokerage house.

The two-dollar broker performs an important function at times of peak volume when commission brokers are unable to handle orders as rapidly as they come to the floor. Peak loads of orders are thus handled immediately and efficiently, and the business of the Exchange flows along smoothly and without hindrance.

The Registered Trader

A new classification of membership, called "registered trader," was established in August 1964 to replace a group of members formerly called "floor traders." The new category was created to preserve the benefits to the investing public of the system of floor traders while eliminating some of the practices criticized in the Securities and Exchange Commission's *Special Study* in 1963.[1]

A registered trader is an Exchange member who buys and sells for his own account and profit or, perhaps, loss. He does not come into contact with the public, nor does he execute orders for other members of the Exchange. He is, in effect, a person who chooses to own his seat and pay the additional cost of membership in order to be able to execute transactions on the floor personally. Because a registered trader operates for himself, he must be discerning, alert, and self-reliant. His profits depend on the size and rapidity of his turnover of stock and on the accuracy of his estimate of future price movements. One moment he may buy, only to sell the next. Depending on how he senses that the market will turn, he may buy and sell an issue many times during the day and yet close the day without owning a single share. For this reason he is sometimes called a "daylight trader."

Registered traders are required to pass an examination to show their familiarity with the restrictions under which they must operate and the standards of performance expected of them. They are required to have at least $250,000 initial capital (as of January 1, 1965) and to maintain, on a monthly basis, a stabilization performance of at least 75 per cent in both acquisition and liquidation transactions. This means that at least 75 per cent of their purchases must be at prices below the last different price (in technical parlance, on a minus tick or on a zero-minus tick) and at least 75 per cent of their sales, except for liquidations at a loss, must be at prices above the last different price (i.e., on a plus tick or on a zero-plus tick). The purpose of this rule is to ensure that, on balance, registered traders retard rather than accentuate the trend of prices. In addition, registered traders are limited in their right to purchase stock at prices above the previous day's closing price.

Registered traders are also required to relinquish priority, precedence, and parity to off-floor orders when establishing or increasing a position in an issue or when liquidating a position. The rule of priority is that when two or more bids are made at the same price the bid clearly established as the first prevails. Precedence applies when no bid is clearly entitled to priority. For example, if all the various bids are for amounts of stock less than the amount offered, the bid for the largest number of shares has precedence over the others and will be filled first. Bids for amounts of stock greater than the amount offered have precedence over bids for amounts of stock less than the amount offered. If several bids are made for an amount of stock greater than the amount offered, the bids are considered to be on a parity with each other; that is, they are considered to have an equal claim, and the issue is

---

[1] *Special Study.* Floor trading is treated in part 2, pp. 203–242.

settled by tossing a coin. Parity also exists when bids are made simultaneously or when it is impossible to determine clearly the order of time in which they were made.

The effect of the rules which require registered traders to relinquish priority, precedence, and parity to off-floor orders is to prevent registered traders from using their potentially favored position on the trading floor to gain an advantage over the investing public.

Registered traders are denied the privilege of stopping stock and are prevented from executing, while on the Exchange floor, transactions for their own account on the same day in which they execute an off-floor order in the same stock. Transactions initiated off the floor by a registered trader are regarded as on-floor transactions, subject to all the rules for registered traders, if the trader has been on the floor during that day.

All Exchange members, while on the floor of the Exchange seeking to purchase stock for their own account, are forbidden to congregate at a particular post or to dominate the market of an issue. The new rules for registered traders clarify this by providing that no more than three registered traders may be in the trading crowd for one stock at the same time, unless written permission is given by a floor governor. Exceptions are permitted, however, whenever the floor governor believes the presence of a larger number of floor traders would be constructive. Brokers executing orders for registered traders must announce publicly that they are acting for them and must abide by all the rules imposed on registered traders.

As a member of the Exchange and executing his own orders, a registered trader pays no commissions and can afford to take much narrower margins than others. The SEC *Special Study*[2] estimates that a floor trader, the forerunner of the present registered trader, could make a profit buying 100 shares of a $25 stock and reselling later the same day if the stock rose as much as 8 cents a share. It estimates that member trading from off the floor (i.e., paying floor brokerage fees) would need a price rise of 15 cents per share just to break even and that a public (nonmember) investor would need a price rise of 68 cents per share to do as well.[3]

The Controversy over Floor Trading.   The registered trader position evolved out of controversy over floor trading, i.e., over the conditions under which members of the Exchange should be allowed to buy and sell stock for their own account. Over the years floor trading has been criticized many times

[2] *Ibid.*, p. 209.

[3] *Ibid.* These costs where applicable include brokerage fees, clearance fees, New York state and Federal transfer taxes, and the SEC fee. For the floor trader they do not include a return on his investment in a seat on the Exchange, his Exchange dues, floor privilege fees, initiation fee, or other incidental costs. The *Special Study* estimates that on the average these additional fixed costs were less than 2 cents per share.

as a vestige of a bygone era when the Exchange was a private club rather than an institution serving investors and the economy. The most recent critical evaluation of the floor trader function appeared in the 1963 SEC *Special Study*.[4] On the other hand, floor trading has been defended by the Exchange for providing a number of ancillary benefits which aid in the smooth working of a public marketplace.

The *Special Study* expresses the belief that the floor trader's privilege of access to the floor of the Exchange to execute personal orders gives him an unwarranted competitive advantage over the public at large. As described above, the cost of an in-and-out transaction for a floor trader is alleged to be substantially less than for a public investor. In addition the floor trader's position on the floor is claimed to provide him with a "feel" for the market not available to outsiders. The *Special Study* notes that trading activity can be observed minutes before it appears on the tape and that the floor trader is in a position to react more quickly than the general public in entering or withdrawing bids or offers. His intuition is strengthened by being able to listen to the observations and opinions of other floor members on general market conditions or on particular stocks when there is a notable change in the volume of orders, type of orders, or cancellations. The *Special Study* also observes that a floor trader's familiarity with the trading techniques of particular specialists or brokers, when combined with the knowledge that a large block of stock is being traded, can be of undue help in his trading activities.

The floor trader's position has been defended on the grounds that his ability and willingness to trade on small margins of profit and with rapid turnover help to provide (1) a continuous market, (2) liquidity, and (3) stability. It has been maintained that these conditions benefit all investors and warrant continuation of floor trading activity. The New York Stock Exchange provides a continuous market in that a market order in any stock can be executed immediately on the floor during trading hours. Because orders from customers of commission brokerage houses do not come in regularly, there might be at any moment a large number of sell orders but no buy orders, or vice versa. A scarcity of buy orders, for example, might lead to a temporary sag in the price at which a market order could be executed. Although the specialist is the party expected by the Exchange to provide continuity, the floor trader is also in a position to help, especially in periods of record-breaking activity or when large blocks of stock are offered. When the market starts to sag from a *temporary* excess of sell orders, the floor trader may see a chance to make a quick profit by buying. He may resell a few moments later or a few hours later, when buy orders in turn outnumber sell orders. His purchases provide a series of transactions at minimum variations in the price and enable the tape to report that the market is starting to drop. The

[4] *Ibid.,* pp. 203–242.

small sag reported on the tape may elicit additional buy orders from around the country and thus prevent the larger, unnecessary decline that would occur in the absence of floor trading. In addition, floor traders provide the only real competition with specialists, who, to dominate the market, keep their bids and offers close.

The floor trader's function has also been defended on the grounds that his participation increases liquidity. The larger the number of persons on the floor willing to buy or sell a particular stock on a small price variation, the greater the probability that when the number of shares offered or sought fails to balance it will still be possible to obtain an immediate execution. This is particularly true with blocks of stock slightly larger than the ordinary.

The third defense of floor traders is that they provide market stability so that prices change less rapidly from transaction to transaction than they would otherwise during a break or sudden rise of prices. It is maintained that floor traders act to stabilize a declining market by buying to cover short positions as the market declines. It is also maintained that floor traders frequently trade against the market trend as a whole or against the trend in individual stocks.

The *Special Study* concludes that floor trading is "inimical to the orderly functioning of the market" and "should not be permitted to continue. . . ."[5] Soon after release of the *Special Study,* the international consulting firm of Cresap, McCormic & Paget made a study of floor trading at the request of the Exchange. The Cresap firm recommended that the constructive aspects of floor trading be preserved in order to "materially assist in maintaining continuity and stability of prices and thereby provide support to the specialists when their particular stocks are subject to a major imbalance of supply and demand."[6] The report explains that the Exchange must be able to meet such widely differing needs as those of institutional and speculative investors and that floor traders are of material help in meeting these divergent objectives, on the one hand by helping to absorb the large blocks of stock typically offered by institutional investors and on the other by acting as a counterspeculative force to discourage the price trends and imbalances which characterize speculative activity. Indiscriminate abolishment of floor trading, the report concludes, would drive from the floor the large amounts of mobile, speculative, risk-taking capital needed for the orderly functioning of the Exchange as a marketplace serving the public.

The Cresap report recommends that a new classification of member be created to preserve the constructive aspects of floor trading. Negotiations between the New York Stock Exchange and the Securities and Exchange Commission, based in large part on the Cresap recommendations, ultimately led to the creation of the registered trader classification.

[5] *Ibid.,* pp. 240, 241.
[6] Cresap, McCormic, & Paget, *New York Stock Exchange Study of Floor Trading,* February 1964, p. VI-1.

The Odd-lot Dealers

Trading on the floor of the New York Stock Exchange is conducted in round, or full, lots of 100 shares each. (A few stocks, mostly preferred, are traded in 10-share units.) However, because there is a great demand for lots of less than 100 shares (i.e., for odd lots) from a multitude of small investors and speculators throughout the country, several Exchange members have developed the business of supplying commission brokers—the middlemen between the public and the odd-lot dealer—with any number of shares less than a full lot or, similarly, of buying from them. The general procedure of the odd-lot dealer is to sell odd lots and, when 100 shares or multiples thereof have been sold, to buy a round lot on the floor of the Exchange for delivery. Alternatively, they buy odd lots, accumulate them into 100-share units, and sell the resulting round lot on the floor.

The volume of odd-lot transactions has become so large and the business of the odd-lot dealer so important to the welfare of the small investor as to warrant devoting an entire chapter to a detailed description of odd-lot operations (see Chapter 12).

The Specialist

The specialist is a member of the Exchange who remains at a specific post on the floor, where he combines the work of broker and dealer by specializing in the issues assigned to him. As a broker he executes orders for the public which have been left with him by other members of the Exchange. As a dealer he buys and sells for his own account in order to "make a market" in the issues in which he specializes. Because he carries out all his work on the floor, he does not come into contact with the public and therefore, like the two-dollar broker and registered trader, he needs no elaborate office or expensive equipment. Since he cannot be at two different posts at the same time, the stocks in which he trades must all be located at one post on the floor of the Exchange.

History of the Specialist.   The origin and development of the business of the specialist are not very well known. According to tradition, a leg injury accounts for the first specialist. It is said that one of the members of the Exchange suffered a broken leg. Being unable to move about, he chose an issue in which there was much activity at the time, Western Union, and took up his position at the post where the stock was traded. As he sat there trading the issue, he became so expert at handling it that other brokers began to give him their orders for Western Union to execute. The execution of these orders and his own trading proved so profitable that, when his leg mended and he was able to get about again, he chose instead to remain at one post and to execute orders for and trade in only the few issues located there.

The development of a continuous auction market in the 1870s meant that market orders had to be executed as soon as a willing party could be located to take the opposite side of the transaction. Previously market orders could be held until the next "call" auction of the stock. Because buy and sell orders from the public seldom arrive on the floor at the same time, increased opportunity appeared for members to make a market in specific stocks by standing ready at all times to buy for their own account at one price or to sell for their own account at a slightly higher price. By so doing they provided the continuity needed in a good market. The modern specialist system came into being as a result of this need.

At first members became specialists on their own initiative and selected the stocks in which they wished to specialize. Competition among specialists in the more active stocks was not at all unusual. In recent decades, however, the specialist function has been increasingly formalized. Specialists are now registered with the Exchange and assume specific obligations for the making of a market. At the moment there are 357 specialists on the Exchange, organized into units composed of individuals, partnerships, and various other legal entities. As of February 1963, there were 110 such units made up of from one to nine specialists each.[7]

Issues are now assigned to specific specialist units by the Board of Governors of the Exchange. Most specialists carry between 6 and 15 issues; with a few exceptions, there is no competition between specialists. Since 1939 specialists have been required to maintain a specific minimum capital. At present a regular specialist at an active post must be able to assume a position of 1,200 shares in each 100-share unit stock and 120 shares in each 10-share unit stock assigned to him. A specialist at an inactive post must have net liquid assets of $50,000.

The specialist's life is not an easy one. He must stand at his post all day long, meeting all comers. The crowd about his post may be large, but he must know what each person in that crowd is doing. They are all watching him. Close observation, full knowledge, quick decision and action, and an attempt to deal squarely with all are the prerequisites of his position. It is to his interest to dominate the market at his post.

Types of Specialists and Their Functions.   The rules of the New York Stock Exchange provide for four types of specialists: (1) regular, (2) relief, (3) associate, and (4) temporary.

A regular specialist is a member who expects to act as the specialist in a listed issue and who is registered with the Exchange for that purpose. He agrees to execute efficiently all orders left with him and to maintain insofar as is reasonably practical a fair and orderly market in the issues for which he is the specialist. A "fair and orderly market" implies maintaining

[7] *Special Study,* part 2, p. 369.

price continuity so that each transaction is at as small a variation from the preceding transaction as is reasonable. The specialist is expected to minimize the effects of temporary disparities between supply and demand by dealing for his own account to the degree necessary. Dealings for his own account are prohibited if they are not reasonably calculated to "contribute to the maintenance of price continuity and to the minimizing of the effects of temporary disparity between supply and demand."

A relief specialist, as his name implies, is a member who will take over a regular specialist's work and service the market while the latter is absent. While a relief specialist serves, he is under the same obligations and responsibilities for the maintenance and stabilization of the market as a regular specialist.

An associate specialist is an assistant to a regular specialist. He is usually in training to become a regular or a relief specialist. As an associate specialist he may execute orders left with the regular specialist and render any other necessary assistance. He is not, however, responsible for maintaining or stabilizing the market through transactions for his own account.

A temporary specialist is appointed by a floor official to act in emergencies, as during the absence of regular or relief specialists or when volume becomes so great in a particular stock that the regular and relief specialists need assistance.

Specialists perform other tasks besides maintaining and stabilizing the market. Before trading starts in the morning, commission brokers sometimes forward market orders received overnight to the specialist. Using these orders and dealing for his own account to the extent necessary, the specialist establishes an opening price that clears the market and yet is as near as practicable to the previous day's close. In making the opening price the specialist considers the balance between buy and sell orders, the orders on his book that indicate the probable trend of the market, the general condition of the market, the opening of other key issues, and his own capital position. Overnight news of an unexpected nature may have a strong effect on the opening price or, indeed, on the ability of the stock to open without delay. If buy and sell orders at the opening are seriously out of balance, the specialist, with the approval of a floor governor, may delay the opening while additional orders are being sought. These may be solicited from floor traders or from the customers of commission brokerage firms. An opening bid and offer may be printed on the ticker tape to indicate the state of the market. Perhaps additional orders will be received or existing orders canceled. Then the specialist and the floor governor arrange an opening transaction that will be reasonable under the circumstances and yet will clear the market.

Because the activities of the specialists are at the very heart of a market system designed to enable any buyer or seller to locate an opposite number quickly and at a price reasonably close to the last sale, their work is carefully supervised by the Exchange. Some 40 floor governors and officials watch over floor trading, while an additional 200 staff members help police the market as a whole. Price and volume movements of all stocks are checked daily by a computer to reveal unusual variations. The Exchange investigates these variations carefully. Four times yearly the Exchange makes a surprise audit of specialist activity during a two-week period.

The Specialist's Book.   As a specialist receives orders from other members of the Exchange, he enters them in his "book." As orders are executed by him or canceled by the customers, he removes them from this book. Thus at any given moment the specialist's book summarizes the supply and demand situation for an issue with respect to standing orders. Orders to buy or to sell at the market are not entered in the book, of course, since they are executed as soon as they arrive at the post.

A specialist's book is usually a loose-leaf binder about 4 inches wide and 11 inches long. It may be rather thin or quite thick, depending on market activity and interest in the particular stock. It is a working tool of the specialist, who has one for each stock in which he specializes. He keeps all his books with him on the floor of the Exchange, either in his hand or on a shelf at his post, so that he can refer to them as needed in quoting a market for a stock. Usually a page in the book contains all recorded orders for an even dollar price and fractional variations of that price. Orders to buy are recorded on the left and orders to sell on the right.

Figure 11–1 shows a specialist's book opened to the pages recording his orders at a price of 35. On the left page our hypothetical specialist has recorded orders to buy 300 shares at a price of 35 for a broker named Martini and 100 shares at the same price for a broker named Beck. He also has orders to buy 700 shares for Pomeroy, 100 shares for Dignam, and 300 shares for Hutchinson, all at a price of $35\frac{1}{8}$. The specialist enters orders as received; the 700-share order from Pomeroy was the first received at this price and so has priority over the orders of Dignam and Hutchinson. At the present time the highest bid in this book is $35\frac{1}{8}$.

On the right page the specialist has recorded sell orders. An order to sell 100 shares at $35\frac{1}{4}$ for Reno was canceled, and orders to sell 200 shares for Harrington and 300 for Young have been executed. The buying broker's initials are indicated by ALM and TRC. The lowest unexecuted sell order on the book then is at $35\frac{3}{8}$, where the specialist has orders to sell 200 for Bartell and 100 for Woods. The order from Shelton was canceled, as was that from Brigham. There are also orders to sell 100 shares at $35\frac{1}{2}$ for Ricks and to sell 300 shares at $35\frac{5}{8}$ for Holtz.

If a commission broker on the floor were to receive an order to sell 100 shares of an issue at the market, he would hurry to the post where the issue is traded and ask the specialist for the market. The specialist would

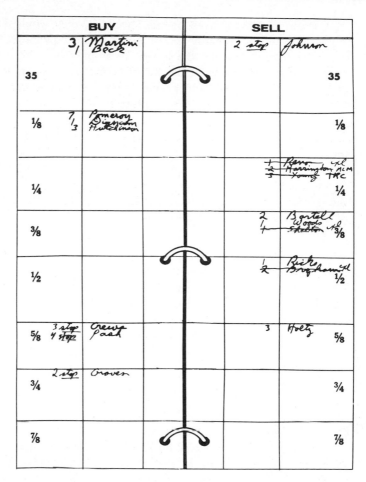

Fig. 11–1   Pages in a specialist's book.

not know whether the broker has stock to buy or to sell; so he would give his highest bid and his lowest ask prices. In the example above he would say, "$35\frac{1}{8}$ to $35\frac{3}{8}$" or, more simply, "$35\frac{1}{8}$ to $\frac{3}{8}$." This would mean that he is willing to buy at $35\frac{1}{8}$ or to sell at $35\frac{3}{8}$. (The broker would not know whether the bid and ask were for the specialist's own account or to execute orders on his book.) The commission broker might now offer his stock to the crowd at the post for $35\frac{1}{4}$ in the hope that someone would raise the bid price by $\frac{1}{8}$. If no one took his offer, he would offer to sell at $35\frac{1}{8}$, whereupon the specialist or some other broker or dealer in the crowd would call out, "Take it." The seller would respond, "Sold to you 100 shares A Company at $35\frac{1}{8}$," and the transaction would be completed. In the case above, if the

100 shares had been taken by the specialist, they would have been bought for the account of Pomeroy, whose order would now be reduced to 600.

The highest bid and the lowest offer prevail in all cases. However, if two or more men reply, "Take it," to a member's offer, the technical rules of priority, precedence, and parity determine who is entitled to the transaction. These rules have been explained already in connection with floor trading.

In many instances the contents of the specialist's book would be an important indicator of which way or of how far the market might move if a series of buy or sell orders suddenly engulfed the post. Because knowledge of the book's contents would be invaluable to anyone seeking to outguess the market or to take advantage of less well-informed investors, the rules of the Exchange prohibit specialists from disclosing the contents of their books.

Stop Orders.   One of the types of orders explained in Chapter 7 was the stop order, formerly referred to as a stop-loss order. Stop orders are in effect orders to buy or sell at the market which are to be held in abeyance until after there is a market transaction at a particular price. Because these orders are not executed immediately, they are given to the specialist and are entered in his book with the notation "stop." In Figure 11–1, stop orders to buy have been entered as follows:

300 shares at $35\frac{5}{8}$ for broker Crews
400 shares at $35\frac{5}{8}$ for broker Pash
200 shares at $35\frac{3}{4}$ for broker Graves

One stop order to sell 200 shares at 35 has been entered for broker Johnson.

Perhaps the customer of broker Crews believes that the market in this stock will suddenly start to rise. However, he does not want to put his money into the stock until he is sure of the rise; and besides, because he is going fishing, he will be out of contact with the market for several days. To be sure that he gets into the market if it should start going up, he enters a buy stop order at $35\frac{5}{8}$. This tells his broker and the specialist that he does not want to buy any stock at all *unless* the market price rises high enough for there to be a transaction at or above a price of $35\frac{5}{8}$. If such a sale occurs, the specialist is to treat broker Crews's order as a market order to buy 300 shares immediately at the best price obtainable (not necessarily $35\frac{5}{8}$). A stop order to buy may also be used to protect a short position in a stock. This is explained in more detail in Chapter 15.

A stop order to sell is the reverse. Perhaps broker Johnson's customer is also going fishing. He owns some of the stock and does not want to sell it unless it starts to drop in price. By entering a sell stop order at 35 he instructs his broker and the specialist to sell him out at the market if a transaction takes place at or lower than 35. The sell stop order can also be used in conjunction with short sales (see Chapter 15).

The advantage that knowledge of a specialist's book would afford the unscrupulous trader can now be illustrated by reference to Figure 11–1. Assume that the last transaction was at $35\frac{1}{4}$ and that the specialist sells only from his book. If a trader were to bid for 300 shares at the market, he would get the 300 at a price of $35\frac{3}{8}$. If he were to follow this purchase with another bid for 400 shares, he would buy 100 at $35\frac{1}{2}$ and 300 at $35\frac{5}{8}$. At this point the stop orders to buy for brokers Crews and Pash would be activated, and the trader could offer back at $35\frac{3}{4}$ all the stock he had purchased at lower prices on the way up. He would be safe in beginning this program if when he started he knew how much stock would have to be purchased to drive the price up to $35\frac{5}{8}$ and if he could be certain that he would touch off the stop orders at this level. He could be certain of these things only if he could see the specialist's book.

Such a program is not really so simple as it might appear, for as the trader tried to force the price up by buying, additional stock might be offered. The specialist, in his function of maintaining an orderly market, would be obligated to supply stock from his own account; and other sell orders might be in the hands of brokers or dealers in the crowd at the post. Thus the trader might have to buy a great deal more stock to push the price up than he could possibly unload at the higher price. In addition, because his actions were so obviously intended to manipulate the market, he would probably be detected and expelled from membership in accordance with Exchange rules.

Stopping Stock.   Another practice, not to be confused with stop orders is that of "stopping stock." Stop orders are placed by customers of commission brokerage firms. By contrast, stopping stock is a practice confined to members on the floor. The bid and ask price of PDX is $84\frac{1}{2}$ to 85. Broker X has an order to buy 100 shares at the market. He can execute this order at 85, but he would like to get a lower price if possible. At the same time he would not want to miss the market at 85. Therefore, he may ask the specialist, "Will you stop 100 for me at 85?" It will be noted (from the bid and ask quotations) that the specialist has an order to sell at 85. If he has two or more orders to sell at 85, he may say, "Yes." All this means is that he earmarks 100 shares offered at 85 for broker X if someone should take the other 100 shares at this price.

In the meantime broker X tries to fill his order at a lower price. If he succeeds, he cancels his stop. If he fails, he may change his stopped stock to an outright order to buy. It will be noted that the specialist might have refused to stop the stock for broker X if he (the specialist) had only one order to sell at 85. To have done so under such circumstances would have been to remove the offer from the market. Under certain restricted circumstances, however, a specialist may stop stock for his own account even when there is no executable order in his book at the stop price.

The Specialist's Conflict of Interest.   When a specialist acts as a broker, he is an agent of his customer. As such, his duty is to serve that customer as well as possible, and his compensation is the commission that he collects. When a specialist acts as a dealer, he acts for himself. Although his duty is to maintain a fair and orderly market, his compensation is the profit that he makes on the transaction. Because the broker and dealer functions are combined in the specialist, it is sometimes alleged that the personal interests of the specialist conflict with the interests of those to whom he owes a fiduciary duty.

Both brokerage and dealer activities are profitable for specialists. In 1960 the gross income of all New York Stock Exchange specialists was derived 55 per cent from commissions on brokerage business and 45 per cent from trading activities.[8] Great variety existed among the various specialist units. Of the 110 units, 14 derived all their gross income from commissions (they all experienced losses in their trading accounts), 56 derived over 50 per cent but less than 100 per cent of their gross income from commissions, 18 derived half their gross income from commissions, and 22 derived less than half their gross income from commissions.[9]

The conflict of interest inherent in one person's acting as both broker and dealer is most apparent when the specialist, acting to maintain a continuous market, elects to trade for his own account with an order in his book. A "proper" price is clearly a discretionary matter when the specialist serves two masters, his customer and himself. Yet if the specialist were not allowed to trade with his book, he would not be able at certain times to meet his public obligation of maintaining a fair and orderly market. This dilemma has been studied many times, most recently in the SEC *Special Study,* which concluded that the conflict of interest was tolerable "in view of the benefits which responsible dealer activities can confer on the market," but which added that such activities must be carried out "under a regulatory system which contains effective controls."[10]

The *Special Study* did identify other conflict-of-interest areas in specialists' activities which it said should be eliminated. These include acceptance of not-held orders, which give the specialist discretion as to the time and price of execution. Although such orders may be handled by commission brokers or by two-dollar brokers, their acceptance by specialists was deemed to involve too great a compromising of their fiduciary obligations.[11] The

[8] *Special Study,* part 2, p. 68.
[9] *Ibid.,* p. 371.
[10] *Ibid.,* p. 165.
[11] *Ibid.,* pp. 146–150, 169.

Special Study also criticized the stopping of stock against limited orders in the specialist's book on the grounds that the specialist then ceased trying to get the best possible price for that particular customer, even though such a stop was deemed to benefit the market as a whole.[12] Lastly, the *Special Study* expressed reservations about the practice of some specialist units of having a few public customers, usually institutions, friends, or officials of the companies in whose stock the specialist is registered, on the basis that serving two types of customers is a possible source of discrimination.[13] Accepting orders from such customers was forbidden by the Exchange in a new set of rules put into effect in September 1964.

Limitations to Member Activity on the Floor

Brokers and dealers are subject to numerous limitations and restrictions owing to the physical characteristics of the Exchange floor and the ticker service, the size of the crowds about the posts, the activity of the market, and the frailties of human nature. In order to trade effectively, numerous customs and rules of conduct have evolved, some of which have been considered important enough to be written into the constitution of the New York Stock Exchange. Below are outlined some of these customs, rules, and methods of transacting business.

Rules as to Bids and Offers.   In order to prevent the manipulation of bid and ask prices and to give all parties equal opportunity, the rules of priority, precedence, and parity, described earlier in this chapter, apply when bids or offers are made at the same price. Additional rules provide that (1) recognized quotations shall be public bids and offers in lots of one or more trading units. All bids and offers for more than one trading unit shall be considered to be for the amount indicated or any lesser number of trading units. For most stocks a trading unit consists of 100 shares. (2) A broker bidding for a large block of stock at a price above the market for 100-share lots cannot buy the large block in one lot unless the offering party has priority or precedence. Otherwise he must first accept all 100-share lots and multiples thereof being offered until he has accumulated the amount desired. (3) Similarly, a broker offering to sell a large block at a lower price than the market on 100-share lots, if his large block is taken, must first accept all bids of 100 shares and multiples thereof at the market price unless the buying party has priority or precedence.

Crossing Orders.   A broker having an order to sell 300 shares of American Can at 45 and also an order or orders to buy 300 shares of the same stock at the same price may not trade one order for the other until he has first

---

[12] *Ibid.*, pp. 150–154, 169.
[13] *Ibid.*, pp. 154–157, 170.

offered the stock at $45\frac{1}{8}$. If he cannot find a buyer at $\frac{1}{8}$ above the limited order, then he may close the 300 American Can to his customer at 45; i.e., a broker can cross orders only after the stock has been offered on the floor at $\frac{1}{8}$ above the selling price designated by the selling order.

Member Dealings for Their Own Accounts.   In general members may not trade for their own account when this would conflict with their responsibility to their customers. Specifically: (1) No member having an order for execution may fill that order by trading for his own account except (*a*) to rectify his failure to execute the order at the time it was received, or (*b*) in the case of an order to sell, after first offering the securities in the open market at a price $\frac{1}{8}$ point above his bid, or (*c*) in the case of an order to buy, after first bidding for the securities in the open market at a price $\frac{1}{8}$ point below his offer. In the last two cases, the price must be justified by the conditions of the market and the member who gave the order must accept the trade. (2) No member shall buy or sell for his own account any security in which he is directly or indirectly interested while he holds an unexecuted market order to buy the same security for a customer. (3) No member shall buy for his own account any security at or below the price at which he holds an unexecuted limited price order for a customer, nor shall a member sell for his own account any security at or above the price at which he holds an unexecuted limited price order for a customer. (4) No member originating an order on the floor for his own account is entitled to priority or precedence over or parity with an order which originated off the floor.

Discretionary Orders.   No member on the floor shall execute orders where he has been given discretion as to (1) the choice of security to be bought or sold, (2) the total amount of the security to be bought or sold, or (3) whether the transaction shall be a purchase or sale.

Prohibited Dealings and Activities.   Members are prohibited from offering publicly on the floor (1) to buy or sell securities "on stop" above or below the market, (2) to buy or sell securities "at the close," (3) to buy or sell dividends, (4) to bet upon the course of the market, (5) to buy or sell options to receive or deliver securities, and (6) to sell a security and at the same time agree to buy it back at a prearranged price, or to buy a security and at the same time agree to sell it back at a prearranged price.

12 odd-lot trading

The unit of trading for most active issues on the New York Stock Exchange is 100 shares. This is called a round lot. But many of the orders placed with brokerage houses involve fewer than 100 shares. An order calling for the purchase or sale of less than the unit of trading is an odd lot. American Telephone & Telegraph Company, the world's largest corporate enterprise in terms of assets, estimates that 75 per cent of its more than two million shareholders hold fewer than 100 shares. This figure suggests the importance of odd-lot investors and suggests that if brokers were to refuse orders for less than round lots they would lose a large proportion of their customers.

In terms of numbers, odd-lot orders account for 36.2 per cent of all orders, as shown by the following classification:

Size of order	Per cent of total
300 shares or more	9.3
200 shares	10.5
100 shares	44.0
Total round-lot orders	63.8
50 shares	6.1
25 shares	2.7
20 shares	3.0
10 shares	5.0
Units of other sizes	19.4
Total odd-lot orders	36.2
Total	100.0

In terms of number of shares exchanged, odd-lot transactions in recent years have accounted for about 13 per cent of total odd-lot and round-lot volume combined.

History of Odd-lot Trading

In the earliest years of trading on the New York Stock Exchange there was no official unit of trading, and thus there was no odd-lot business as such. Brokers accepted orders for whatever number of shares a customer wanted, issues were "called for trading" one at a time, and buying and selling brokers bid against each other until the market was cleared as much as was possible. When the Exchange first shifted to the continuous auction method (in which trading is carried on simultaneously in all issues), bids and offers were still made for varying numbers of shares. Very soon, however, the increased volume of trading forced the Exchange to designate 100 shares as the unit of trading in most issues.

As a result orders for *odd* lots (less than a unit of trading) were relegated to the offices of member firms for execution on an over-the-counter basis. With the growth of population, the rise in the wealth of the country, the increased popularity of common stocks with small investors, and the development of mass media for trading (ticker quotations, branch offices, and financial news reporting), the demand for odd lots grew tremendously. Soon it occurred to certain Exchange members that odd-lot orders could be handled more quickly by a dealer on the floor of the Exchange than by unorganized negotiation between several hundred brokerage offices. So evolved the odd-lot dealer.

At first transactions in odd lots were negotiated privately between dealer and commission broker. But as odd-lot transactions increased in number, this method became cumbersome and dealers began routinely to execute odd-lot orders at bid and ask prices. Thus, if a stock was bid 40 ask $40\frac{1}{2}$, an odd-lot customer could buy at $40\frac{1}{2}$ or sell at 40. This system resulted in odd-lot prices fairly close to round-lot prices. However, owing to the fact that there were no published records of prevailing quotations, the method created dissatisfaction among odd-lot customers and was abandoned in favor of the present system of trading on the next sale, plus or minus a differential which is added to the price per share paid (or deducted from the price received) by odd-lot customers. The operation of this system serves an enormous public demand for odd lots and at the same time permits the machinery of the Exchange to function efficiently on a uniform 100-share-unit basis.

Executing an Odd-lot Order

If William Carey wishes to buy 25 shares of Chrysler, he telephones his local commission broker and gives a buying order for this number of shares either at a price or at the market. His order is immediately transmitted to the New York office of the firm and from there to the floor of the Exchange. The firm's telephone clerk on the floor delivers the order to the tube station in his booth, where an Exchange employee inserts it in a cylindrical container and sends it through a pneumatic tube to the post where Chrysler stock is traded. At this post an Exchange employee time-stamps the order and places it under the odd-lot dealer's clip on the "odd-lot tree," a small rack which stands in the center of the open end of the horseshoe-shaped post.

At this point Carey's order becomes the responsibility of the odd-lot dealer. An associate broker employed by the odd-lot dealer takes the order from the tree and places it in a small handbook ready for execution after the next effective round-lot transaction in Chrysler. As soon as such a sale in Chrysler takes place, the associate broker makes a note that the odd-lot order is executed at a price equal to the round-lot price plus or minus the odd-lot differential. In executing Carey's order, the odd-lot dealer is selling from his own account (as principal) at a price determined automatically by the execution of a round-lot transaction on the floor. Notice of the transaction is time-stamped and returned by pneumatic tube to the booth of the commission broker who originated the order. The details are immediately wired to the branch office where the order originated, and Carey is notified that he has purchased 25 shares of Chrysler.

It will be noted that the commission broker himself does not execute odd-lot orders; rather he forwards them to an odd-lot dealer for execution. For his services the broker collects a regular commission from the customer. The odd-lot dealer gets no part of this commission but makes his profit on the difference between the prices at which he purchases shares and the prices at which he sells them.

Odd-lot Orders of Customers

When a customer places an order to buy an odd lot, it is understood that he will pay a price equal to the price of the next effective round-lot transaction executed on the floor, *plus the odd-lot differential*. Similarly, when a customer places an order to sell an odd lot, it is understood that he will receive a price equal to the price of the next effective round-lot transaction executed on the floor, *minus the odd-lot differential*.

If the price of a round lot of 100 shares is $40 or higher, this differential is $\frac{1}{4}$ point per share—a point is one dollar and so $\frac{1}{4}$ of a point is 25 cents. If the price of a round lot of 100 shares is $39\frac{7}{8}$ or lower, the differential is $\frac{1}{8}$ point per share ($0.125).[1] The size of the differential was originally determined by the odd-lot houses. However, since June 1, 1964, the New York Stock Exchange has assumed jurisdiction over the amount of the differential to be charged. From June 6, 1932, until 1951 the differential

[1] On stocks traded in 100-share units and selling at less than $12\frac{1}{2}$ cents per share, the differential is one half the price of the effective round-lot sale. For stocks selling in 10-share units, the differentials are as follows:

Round-lot sale price per share	Odd-lot differential per share
Above $75	$\frac{3}{4}$ point (75¢)
At $75	$\frac{5}{8}$ point (62$\frac{1}{2}$¢)
At 74\frac{7}{8}$	$\frac{1}{2}$ point (50¢)
25\frac{1}{8}$ to 74\frac{3}{4}$	$\frac{3}{8}$ point (37$\frac{1}{2}$¢)
$25 and below	$\frac{1}{4}$ point (25¢)

was $\frac{1}{8}$ point on all stocks traded in 100-share units. Higher operating costs after World War II led all odd-lot firms to raise odd-lot differentials to their present levels (effective August 1, 1951).

The round-lot sale that determines the price at which the odd-lot order is executed is called the "effective sale," or "triggering sale." In the case of market orders, the triggering sale is the next sale to take place after the odd-lot order is received at the odd-lot tree. For other types of orders, the triggering sale may be the next sale or a subsequent sale, depending on the conditions of the order, for the odd-lot customer like the round-lot customer may place several types of orders. Each of these is described below.

Market Orders.   Suppose that Mr. Stewart gives his broker an order to buy 25 shares of General Foods at the market. This order is transmitted to the proper odd-lot man on the floor of the Exchange in the manner described earlier. The odd-lot dealer interprets Stewart's order as follows: "Sell me 25 shares of General Foods common at a price $\frac{1}{4}$ point higher than the next effective price." Consequently, when he receives the order he waits until the next sale which gives him the price, to which he adds the $\frac{1}{4}$. If the next sale occurs at $85\frac{5}{8}$, the odd-lot dealer's price to Stewart would then be $85\frac{7}{8}$.

If Stewart had ordered a sale at the market instead of a purchase, the odd-lot dealer would have waited for the next sale and would have bought Stewart's 25 shares for his own account at $85\frac{3}{8}$, that is, $\frac{1}{4}$ below the round-lot price.

At the Open or Close.   Buying or selling at the open is subject to the same conditions as those enumerated above. If the market for U.S. Steel opens at 44, the odd-lot dealer sells at $44\frac{1}{4}$ and buys at $43\frac{3}{4}$ and the customer of the commission broker who handles the transactions gets $43\frac{3}{4}$ for his stock on a sale or pays $44\frac{1}{4}$ on a purchase.

Orders to buy or sell at the close are based on the final bid and ask price of the day. It is not possible to use the price of the last sale, which may have taken place an hour before the close, perhaps at a price several points away from the closing bid and ask prices. Under these circumstances, to use the last transaction sale as a basis of the price at the close would not represent the closing demand and supply situation at all. For these reasons the closing bid and ask prices are used. An odd-lot dealer, however, cannot fill an order to sell short at a bid price.

Limited Orders.   Stewart gives his broker an open order to buy 25 shares of Anaconda Copper at 36. The order is forwarded to the odd-lot dealer. At the time the order is received, Anaconda Copper is selling at 37; so the dealer enters the order in his book to await a drop in price. The drop comes after several days, following a report of the falling off of exports. Successive sales of the stock are made at $36\frac{1}{4}$, $36\frac{1}{8}$, 36, $36\frac{1}{8}$, 36, $35\frac{7}{8}$, $35\frac{3}{4}$, $35\frac{7}{8}$, 36. The order to buy at 36 signifies to the odd-lot dealer that the broker's customer is willing to pay 36 per share but not more and, therefore, that he must deliver the stock to the broker at 36. In order to safeguard his $\frac{1}{8}$, the dealer must buy at $35\frac{7}{8}$; thus the triggering sale is the first sale to occur at or below $35\frac{7}{8}$. When a full-lot sale is made at $35\frac{7}{8}$, he notes on his pad the fact that he sold 25 shares of Anaconda Copper at 36 ($35\frac{7}{8} + \frac{1}{8}$). If the price had not gone below 36, Stewart would not have had his stock. When Stewart sees $35\frac{7}{8}$ on the tape, he is sure that his order has been filled and that his account with his broker will shortly be debited for 25 shares of Anaconda Copper at 36 plus commission and taxes.

If Stewart had given an order to sell 25 shares of Anaconda Copper at 36 when the market price was below 36, then as soon as the price had risen to $36\frac{1}{8}$ his stock would have been taken by the odd-lot dealer at the post where it is traded. In other words, the odd-lot dealer would have bought the 25 shares at a price that would have allowed him a margin of $\frac{1}{8}$ point over the round-lot price. Stewart's broker, in this case, would have credited him with the price of 25 Anaconda Copper at 36 less commission and taxes.

There is no stock on which the market *always* varies by $\frac{1}{8}$ points between sales. Often the interval between one sale and the next is $\frac{1}{4}$ point. Sometimes the spread is as great as $\frac{1}{2}$ point, and occasionally it may be 1 or 2 points. Suppose that Stewart places an order to buy 50 shares of Gulf Oil at 50 when the stock is selling at, say, 51. Normally the odd-lot dealer would supply these shares at 50 when the round-lot price drops to $49\frac{3}{4}$. But suppose that in this instance the market declines precipitately from $50\frac{1}{8}$ to $48\frac{1}{2}$. At what price will the odd-lot dealer supply the stock? New rules, effective June 1, 1964, provide that all limited orders will be filled at the price of the effective sale plus or minus the appropriate differential. Thus Stewart would pay $48\frac{3}{4}$, the price of $48\frac{1}{2}$ plus a $\frac{1}{4}$ differential.[2]

If Stewart had wished, he could have added the words "immediate or cancel" (sometimes "fill or kill") to his order to indicate that, if the odd-lot dealer could not fill the order at its limit at once, the order was to be canceled.

Buy on Offer or Sell on Bid.   If for some reason Stewart did not want to wait for the next sale for his odd-lot order to be executed, he could have placed his order "buy on offer" or "sell on bid." A buy on offer order is executed at the round-lot offer price prevailing at the time the odd-lot dealer receives the order, plus the differential. A sell on bid order is similarly filled $\frac{1}{8}$ or $\frac{1}{4}$ point below the bid price. If Stewart had wished, he could have added a limit price to his buy on offer or sell on bid order so that he would be assured

---

[2] The new rules eliminated the $\frac{1}{2}$- and 1-point rule. Prior to June 1, 1964, if the first round-lot sale on the floor after receipt of the odd-lot order did not trigger the order, and if then the price dropped more than $\frac{1}{2}$ point below the limit on stocks selling at or below $39\frac{3}{4}$ or more than 1 point below the limit on stocks selling at 40 or above, the execution price was that of the effective round-lot sale plus $\frac{1}{2}$ point or 1 point. Under the old rules, Stewart would have paid $49\frac{1}{2}$ for his Gulf Oil stock. A similar rule had applied to limited sell orders.

that the price of his execution would not unexpectedly be out of the intended range. If such an order with limit attached could not be filled immediately, it would be canceled and Stewart notified.

Short Sales. Odd-lot short sales may be either at the market or at a limit. A market order marked "short" is filled at the price of the next round-lot sale minus the differential if the triggering round-lot price is above *the last different round-lot price*. If the next round-lot price is below the last different round-lot price, the odd-lot dealer must hold the short-sale order until a round-lot transaction does occur at a price above the last different round-lot price. In the language used on the floor of the Exchange, the triggering sale must be either a plus-tick or a zero-plus-tick transaction; minus-tick and zero-minus-tick transactions cannot trigger odd-lot short sales. The effect of these rules is to subject odd-lot short sales to the same limitations as round-lot short sales. These limitations are explained fully in Chapter 15.

To illustrate the working of an odd-lot short sale at the market, assume the following round-lot transactions to have occurred: 50, $49\frac{7}{8}$, $49\frac{3}{4}$. The odd-lot dealer has an order to sell 25 shares short at the market. The order may not be executed because the last round-lot price ($49\frac{3}{4}$) was not higher than the last preceding different round-lot price ($49\frac{7}{8}$). Assume now that the next round-lot transaction is effected at $49\frac{7}{8}$. The odd-lot dealer may now fill odd-lot short-sale orders because this price ($49\frac{7}{8}$) is higher than the last different round-lot price ($49\frac{3}{4}$). Assume further that four more round-lot transfers occur at $49\frac{7}{8}$. The odd-lot dealer can still fill odd-lot short-sale orders, since the last price, though the same as the previous price, is still higher than the last different price.

What this amounts to is to make odd-lot dealers "ineligible" to fill odd-lot short-sale orders at times. The ineligible periods are determined by the price sequence of round-lot sales. When the round-lot price is higher than the last different round-lot price, odd-lot short-sale orders are permissible. It should be noted that it does not matter whether the last different lower price occurred before or after the odd-lot dealer received the order to sell an odd lot short. For example, suppose that at 12 noon a dealer receives an order to sell an odd lot short at the market. The previous round-lot orders were $42\frac{1}{2}$, $42\frac{3}{8}$. The dealer is ineligible to fill the odd lot. At 12:20 P.M. a round-lot transaction is effected at $42\frac{1}{2}$. The odd-lot short-sale order may be filled.

A limited odd-lot short-sale order is, by definition, for execution after the round-lot market rises, since limited sell orders are placed at prices above the market. The effective transaction for a limited order to sell marked "short" is the first round-lot transaction which is above the specified limit by the amount of the differential, or by a greater amount, and which is also a plus-tick or zero-plus-tick transaction. The order will be filled at the price of the effective transaction, minus the differential.

Basis Price Orders.   A market, limited, or stop order for an odd lot entered at least half an hour before the close and designated as a "basis order" will be filled at the basis price if (1) there were no round-lot sales during the day and if (2) the closing bid and ask prices are more than two points apart. In this case the representatives of the odd-lot dealers meet after the market closes, compare their basis orders, and set a basis price between the bid and the ask prices. Odd-lot orders are then executed $\frac{1}{8}$ or $\frac{1}{4}$ point away from this. No short sales, cash, or sellers' options are executed on the basis price. Basis prices are printed on the stock ticker tape of the New York Stock Exchange, prefaced by "Basis Prices Established by Odd-lot Dealers," and followed by "Good Night."

Stop Orders.   A stop order for odd lots is an order to buy or sell fewer than 100 shares after a round-lot transaction takes place at or through a designated price, called the "stop price." Perhaps Stewart owns 20 shares of Texaco, which is selling at 75. He wants to hold this stock as long as it continues to rise, but he wants to sell if the market price starts to drop. As he is too busy with his daily work to keep an eye on the market, he enters a stop order to sell 20 shares at, say, 70 stop. If and when a round-lot sale occurs at 70 or below 70, Stewart's sell order becomes a market order. It will be filled at the price of the next round-lot transaction, less the $\frac{1}{4}$ differential. Similarly, a stop buy order becomes a market order to buy when a round-lot transaction occurs at or above the designated stop price, and it will be filled at the price of the next round-lot transaction, plus the differential.[3]

Stop orders may also have a limit attached. After the order is "elected" by a round-lot transaction at the stop price, the order becomes a regular limited order, to be filled as soon as it is possible to do so at a price equal to or better than the indicated limit. For example, Stewart might enter an order to sell his Texaco as follows: "Sell 70 stop, limit 69." The stock is to be sold after a round lot sells at or below 70, but the effective price must be at least $69\frac{1}{4}$ so that Stewart will receive 69 after deduction of the differential.

With or Without Sale Order.   It is possible for a customer to enter an odd-lot order limited as to price with the instructions "with or without sale" (W.O.W.). This is an order to buy or sell the specified number of shares

---

[3] This rule came into effect June 1, 1964. Prior to that date, stop orders were executed at the price of the round-lot transaction which "elected" the stop, plus or minus the differential. The effect of the old rules was to guarantee an execution at the price (plus or minus the differential) that elected the stop. Thus odd-lot stop orders possessed a degree of advantage over round-lot stop orders, which simply became market orders when elected and so could conceivably be filled at prices quite different from the stop price. The new rule results in odd-lot and round-lot stop orders being treated in the same way.

as soon as possible within the price limit, execution being based either (1) on the next effective round-lot sale or (2) on an effective bid or offer, whichever comes first. In execution on an actual sale, the rules for limited orders apply. In execution on the bid or offer, the rules for buy on offer or sell on bid orders apply. Short-sale orders may not be entered with the W.O.W. designation.

Odd-lot House Organization

The rules of the New York Stock Exchange prohibit any member from acting as an odd-lot dealer for an issue on the floor unless he is registered as an odd-lot dealer in that issue. Only two firms, Carlisle & Jacquelin and DeCoppet & Doremus, trade in all listed stocks other than those listed at Post 30 (where the unit of trading is 10 shares). Odd-lot dealers at Post 30 are Reuben Rose & Company, Inc., and R. S. Dodge & Company. Two other firms deal in odd lots—Scheffmeyer, Werle & Company at Post 6 and Zuckerman and Smith & Company at Post 2.

Each of the two principal odd-lot firms is represented on the floor by approximately 50 "associate brokers," who are themselves members of the Exchange but who give their full time to one of the odd-lot houses. These associate brokers own their own seats and their liaison with the odd-lot houses may be terminated at any time by either party. Each associate broker is assigned specific stocks to handle at specific posts. The associate brokers carry out the floor activities of the odd-lot firms by (1) executing for the firm orders to buy or sell odd lots at the proper price at each particular moment and (2) buying or selling round lots in the market so as to keep the inventory position of the firm in the issues assigned to them within the limits decided upon. The associate brokers get their income from floor brokerage fees paid to them by odd-lot dealers. They receive $1\frac{1}{8}$ cents per share on each odd-lot transaction priced below $10 per share, $2\frac{1}{4}$ cents per share on each odd-lot transaction priced at $10 or above, and a standard floor brokerage commission on round-lot transactions performed for the odd-lot firms.

Sources of Profit for Odd-lot Houses.   Odd-lot firms obtain their profit from the difference between the cost of the stock they purchase, either in odd lots or in round lots, and the proceeds of its sale, again either in odd lots or in round lots.

The odd-lot differential in conjunction with a round-lot price established on the floor of the Exchange sets a starting price from which an odd-lot firm may or may not make a profit, depending upon its ability to balance out the transaction at a gain. The final profit is not realized until every share of stock purchased as an odd lot has in turn been sold, either as an odd lot or as part of a round lot, or until every share of stock sold as an odd lot has been purchased, either as an odd lot or as part of a round lot.

To illustrate by a simple case, suppose that Hooper orders his broker to buy 35 shares of Tidewater Oil at $25\frac{1}{2}$, that Parker orders a second broker to buy 40 shares at the same price, and that Wisler orders still another broker to buy 25 shares of the issue at the same price. Suppose that these three orders all happen to go to the same odd-lot firm and simultaneously reach the associate broker who handles Tidewater Oil for that firm. This associate broker places an order with the specialist to buy 100 shares for his firm at $25\frac{3}{8}$. It happens that the specialist is able to fill the order immediately; so the round-lot transaction becomes the triggering sale causing the odd-lot orders to be executed. The odd-lot dealer notifies the brokers of Hooper, Parker, and Wisler that he has sold them shares at $25\frac{1}{2}$. The gross profit of the dealer would be computed thus:

100 shares sold to Hooper, Parker, and Wisler at $25\frac{1}{2}$ via their brokers (net)		$2,550.00
Less commission to associate broker		2.25
		$2,547.75
100 shares purchased at $25\frac{3}{8}$ from the specialist	$2,537.50	
Plus floor commission	3.65	2,541.15
Gross profit (i.e., before overhead)		$ 6.60

If the above orders placed by Hooper, Parker, and Wisler had been selling orders instead of buying orders, the same procedure in reverse might have been followed. In that case the associate broker might have asked the specialist to sell 100 shares at $25\frac{3}{8}$. Had this round-lot order been the effective order, the odd-lot dealer would have paid Hooper, Parker, and Wisler $25\frac{1}{2}$ for their shares. This time, however, the odd-lot dealer would have made less money on the transaction owing to the necessity of paying taxes on his round-lot sale.[4]

100 shares sold to specialist at $25\frac{5}{8}$		$2,562.50
Less floor commission		3.65
Less Federal and N.Y. state taxes		2.08
Less SEC fee		0.06
		$2,556.71
100 shares purchased at $25\frac{1}{2}$ from Hooper, Parker, and Wisler	$2,550.00	
Plus commission to associate broker	2.25	2,552.25
Gross profit (i.e., before overhead)		$ 4.46

The above examples are oversimplified in that they assume that odd-lot firms were able to offset exactly their odd-lot transactions with a purchase or sale of an identical number of shares in the round-lot market at the price

[4] Federal transfer taxes, New York state transfer taxes, and the SEC fee are paid by the seller of securities. The tax on odd-lot sales by customers to the odd-lot dealers is paid by the customer and so is ignored here. Odd-lot sales by dealers to customers are no longer taxed; prior to 1959 such sales were taxed, the tax being passed on to the buyer of the securities.

that triggered the odd-lot transactions. In reality a firm will be both buying and selling odd lots and will end up with a net residue of shares (either long or short) which it must dispose of or acquire. The price obtained for this residue bears no automatic relation to the prices at which the odd lots were bought or sold; during the interval between the odd-lot transactions and the offsetting round-lot transaction the market could have moved either to the advantage or to the disadvantage of the odd-lot firm.

From the odd-lot dealer's viewpoint, the most profitable situation would be one in which the accumulation of orders to buy happens to match exactly the accumulation of orders to sell. In such an event it would not be necessary for the odd-lot dealer to execute any round-lot transactions, since he could purchase stock from odd-lot sellers at $\frac{1}{8}$ or $\frac{1}{4}$ below round-lot prices and sell the same number of shares to odd-lot buyers at $\frac{1}{8}$ or $\frac{1}{4}$ above round-lot prices.

If odd-lot buy and sell orders matched in quantity between the time of each round-lot sale, the odd-lot dealer would make $\frac{1}{4}$- or $\frac{1}{2}$-point profit on each share handled. If odd-lot buy and sell orders matched only over a longer interval, say one hour or one day, the odd-lot dealer might make more or less than the amount of the differential, even though he could avoid making round-lot transactions entirely.

Consider the case of a stock quoted at 32 to a $\frac{1}{4}$. The odd-lot dealer is long 25 shares. He receives an order from a customer wishing to buy 50 shares at the market. There is no reason for him to make an offsetting transaction, for after this odd-lot order is executed, the odd-lot dealer will be short only 25 shares. Now assume that a round-lot customer enters an order to sell 100 shares of stock and sells at the bid price of 32. The odd-lot customer pays $32\frac{1}{8}$ for his stock. The market quote remains at 32 to a $\frac{1}{4}$, and the odd-lot dealer receives another order from a customer—this time to sell 50 shares at the market. A round-lot order comes into the market to buy 100 shares and is executed at the offer price of $32\frac{1}{4}$. The odd-lot dealer buys 50 shares from the customer for $32\frac{1}{8}$.

In this situation the odd-lot dealer bought 50 shares at $32\frac{1}{8}$ including the differential, and he sold the same 50 shares at the same price, $32\frac{1}{8}$, including the differential. He gained nothing from the presumed differential income available to him. Because market round-lot orders are most frequently filled at the respective bid or ask price, it is possible for an odd-lot dealer to net nothing from the odd-lot differential per se. It should be noted that, in the above example, both odd-lot customers received a price $\frac{1}{8}$ better than they would have received had they entered a round-lot market order at the same time, in spite of the fact that they paid an odd-lot differential.

Had the odd-lot orders arrived as above and the round-lot orders been reversed in sequence (round-lot customers first buying at $32\frac{1}{4}$ and then selling at 32), the odd-lot firm would have made $\frac{1}{2}$ point (twice the differential) on each share handled. The odd-lot customers would have paid more for their odd-lot purchase than they would probably have paid on a comparable round-lot order.

The potential profit received from odd-lot prices established by the round-lot market and the odd-lot differential may be increased or diminished by the degree of success achieved in offsetting round-lot transactions. Not often do orders to buy and to sell exactly offset each other. Usually a balance remains to be bought or to be sold. If this balance happens to be an even 100 shares, it may be acquired or disposed of in the round-lot market as in the case cited earlier. But should the number of shares in the balance not be divisible by 100, as is more likely to be the case, the odd-lot dealer must either purchase more shares than he needs or dispose of more than he has. An illustration will make this clearer.

Suppose that an odd-lot house has market orders to buy 1,432 shares and market orders to sell 1,175 shares. After crossing the orders to sell 1,175 shares with the orders to buy this quantity, the dealer will have a balance to acquire of 257 shares. Two round-lot purchases will provide 200 of these shares, possibly at a profit and possibly at a loss depending upon the direction of the market after the odd-lot orders were originally filled. The purchase of a third round lot will provide the dealer with the remaining 57 shares needed for delivery but will leave him with an inventory of 43 shares on hand. He may be able to dispose of these shares profitably at a later date, or he may be forced to take a loss on them if the market turns downward. If he expects the latter to occur, he may try to protect himself by selling a 100-share lot in the market and thus changing his position from that of being long 43 shares to that of being short 57.

The handling and timing of offsetting round-lot transactions involve substantial risks and may add either to the profits or to the losses of an odd-lot firm. The magnitude of the round-lot operation reveals its importance; in recent years round-lot sales and purchases of odd-lot firms have constituted about 25 per cent of the total share volume of the odd-lot firms and about 3.3 per cent of reported round-lot volume.[5]

From the odd-lot dealer's point of view, round-lot offsetting transactions are an integral part of the odd-lot operation. Odd-lot transactions cannot be carried out without the possibility of effecting a round-lot purchase or sale, and the profit (or loss) from the over-all operation cannot be attributed to either the odd-lot operation alone or the round-lot operation alone. Odd-lot firms regard the differential as a price-determining mechanism rather than as a commission-type charge against the odd-lot customer.

In general odd-lot firms now try to operate with as small an inventory as possible. In earlier years they frequently maintained a large long or short position based on their anticipation of the trend of the market.

---

[5] *Special Study,* part 2, p. 174; also *New York Stock Exchange Fact Book, 1964,* pp. 39, 46.

Regulation of Odd-lot Operations.   Section 19(b) of the Securities Exchange Act of 1934 provides that the SEC may alter or supplement the rules of the various national exchanges on a number of matters, including odd-lot purchases and sales. Supervision and regulation under this provision have been limited to the making of various studies, and the Commission has never made a formal decision as to the extent of its jurisdiction over odd-lot operations.[6]

The New York Stock Exchange possesses regulatory power over odd-lot operations, and it has adopted a number of rules applicable to the odd-lot business. Odd-lot dealers and brokers must be registered with and approved by the Exchange. They are prohibited from participating in any manner in the holding of puts, calls, straddles, or other options in stock in which they are registered. They are restricted in their participation in joint accounts, and they are required to report monthly their aggregate share volume of odd-lot purchases and sales. Odd-lot short sales are subject to rules similar to those on round-lot short sales. In addition, as was mentioned earlier, the Exchange has recently assumed jurisdiction over the amount of the odd-lot differential.

Additional rules of the New York Stock Exchange prevent an odd-lot dealer from executing a round-lot order himself when he has odd-lot orders for more than the amount of the round lot and when these odd-lot orders would be triggered by his round-lot transaction. Suppose that, on a stock bid at 30 and offered at 32, an odd-lot dealer has orders to buy a total of 150 shares at the market. He now holds 50 shares. If the dealer buys more shares at the offer price of 32, without trying to get a lower price, he triggers the orders for the total of 150 shares. Perhaps he could have bought the stock at 31 had he tried. By paying 32, he pays an extra $100 on the round lot. But he immediately recovers this on his odd-lot sales, as well as making an additional $50 on the 50 shares he sold from his own inventory. His differential is not affected.

To prevent such manipulation, the Exchange has ruled that round-lot orders which would trigger odd-lot sales or purchases of a number of shares greater than the round lot must be handed to the specialist for execution. That is, when an odd-lot dealer has more than a full lot to buy or sell and his own purchases or sales would fix the price, he will not execute his own order but will let the specialist make the purchase or sale under regular conditions. This strict rule prevents attempts to raise or lower prices to the profit of dealers.

Another effective hindrance to manipulation by odd-lot dealers is the watchfulness of the commission brokers. These brokers must keep the goodwill of their customers, and when customers feel that their orders are not properly handled and make complaints, commission brokers check up on

[6] *Special Study,* part 2, pp. 179–180.

the odd-lot dealers. The commission brokerage firms usually send all their odd-lot business to one odd-lot house at one time, shifting houses at regular or irregular intervals.

Service Activities of an Odd-lot House.   Although odd-lot firms do not compete pricewise through the differential, they do compete for the orders of commission brokerage firms by providing free services. This competition takes several forms. Through their order service department both the major odd-lot firms provide a last-sale service to their commission brokerage customers in the Wall Street area. By means of an elaborate telephone network and a large Teleregister board a number of telephone operators are able to supply the last-sale price for all stocks and rights listed on the Exchange, except for those at Post 30. The last-sale service also provides hourly and half-hourly market averages, hourly share volume, and information on tape lateness. The order service department also maintains sales recorders that compile a running record of individual round-lot transactions in each security, including the time of the transaction. Time is recorded by having the ticker tape time stamped every ten or fifteen seconds. The sales recorders can supply opening, high, low, and last-sale price information, as well as the time each transaction appeared on the tape.

Odd-lot firms also compete through a liberal adjustment policy. Each firm maintains an adjustment service, where claims on the part of commission brokerage customers can be investigated immediately and adjustments made when circumstances warrant. In general the odd-lot firms are very liberal in making adjustments.

The odd-lot firms help their commission brokerage firms' customers in still another way. Through their stock-borrowing activities, they in effect provide free financing to these firms. In order to meet delivery commitments and to "make change" from large lots to smaller lots, odd-lot firms borrow securities. Most of the stock borrowed comes from the unpaid margin accounts of commission brokerage firms. The loan of stock is matched by a 100 per cent cash collateral deposit by the odd-lot firm with the commission brokerage house. Since a commission brokerage house pays no interest on this money, the net result of stock-borrowing activities is to provide free capital to commission brokerage firms.

Evaluation of Odd-lot Operations by the SEC *Special Study*

In July 1963, the SEC released part 2 of its *Report of Special Study of Securities Markets,* one portion of which discusses and evaluates odd-lot procedures on the New York Stock Exchange.[7] The two main recommendations of the staff which carried out the study are that (1) the Exchange accept the responsibility of regulating odd-lot differentials and, as a first

[7] *Special Study,* part 2, pp. 171–202.

step, initiate a cost study of the odd-lot business; and that (2) the Exchange study the feasibility of automating the execution of odd-lot orders. In certain respects these two recommendations are interconnected.

The Odd-lot Differential and Costs of the Odd-lot Business.   As was mentioned earlier, the Exchange has now assumed responsibility for the odd-lot differential and for odd-lot trading rules, a step long advocated by the odd-lot dealers themselves. In addition, at the present writing the Exchange is sponsoring an independent cost study of the odd-lot business by Price Waterhouse & Company.

The essence of the *Special Study's* view is that some of the costs of the odd-lot business, such as the services provided to commission brokerage firms, could be reduced and thus open the way to lower odd-lot differentials. The *Special Study* observes that the size of the differential was originally established by the odd-lot firms and that at that time the major odd-lot firms were strong enough to cause the various regional exchanges about the country (which trade in dually listed stocks) to accept the New York Stock Exchange differential. The odd-lot investor, it is alleged, was not in a position to influence the amount of the differential because of a lack of price competition. The *Special Study* feels that if odd-lot firms would reduce some of their costs, which are incurred more for the benefit of the commission brokerage firm customers than for the benefit of the ultimate odd-lot investing public, the amount of the differential could be reduced.

The odd-lot firms have responded that the nature of the differential in a double auction market has been misunderstood and that it is in reality a pricing mechanism rather than a charge to the odd-lot customer. They have pointed out that in a double auction market the market value of a security can be expressed only by the bid and offer in the crowd at a particular time. The bid is the market value to those wanting to liquidate stock, and the ask is the market value to those wanting to purchase stock. The odd-lot firms believe that the only valid method of finding out whether or not the odd-lot differential is actually paid by the odd-lot customer is to determine the quote on the stock at the time the odd-lot order is received at the post and subsequently to compare the bid or offer, as the case may be, with the price of execution. If the odd-lot buyer paid in fact $\frac{1}{8}$ point higher than the offer price or received $\frac{1}{8}$ point lower than the bid price, then and only then, the odd-lot firms believe, can it be said that the odd-lot customer actually paid the amount of the differential. If the customer bought stock at or below the offer price or sold stock at or above the bid price, there is no real charge to the odd-lot customer.

Automation.   The *Special Study* goes into some detail in discussing plans for automation worked out for the Exchange in 1956 by Ebasco Services, Inc., an engineering consultant firm. In one suggested plan, data-processing equipment would have provided for odd-lot orders being entered into a computer, which would also receive reports of round-lot transactions. The computer would execute the order and fill out and route the necessary reports. This plan was based on the idea that the execution of an odd-lot order (certain "odd-ball" orders excepted) was an automatic matter which did not involve human judgment and so could be performed by machine. Ebasco estimated that under this plan the number of associate brokers could be reduced from 87 (in 1956) to about 14. The remaining associate brokers, according to the report, would be needed to execute offsetting round-lot transactions and to execute the "odd-ball" orders. The *Special Study* believes that computerized executions would lower costs and would contribute to the possibility of lower odd-lot differentials.

Computer technology is now far more advanced than it was in 1956. As of late 1964 the odd-lot firms and the Exchange were participating in a joint study of the feasibility of computer execution of odd-lot orders, and they hoped that by 1966 an experimental installation would be possible to test the reliability and economic feasibility of executing odd-lot orders by computer. The experiment would be run parallel with existing methods until the reliability of the computer system was sufficiently well established to justify entrusting the investing public's money to it.

If and when computer execution of odd-lot orders is accepted, it is estimated that the number of associate brokers will be reduced by only 10 to 20 per cent, rather than by the much larger amount indicated in the Ebasco report. The associate broker's economic function of managing the dealer's inventories will remain a vital part of the odd-lot operation. This trading function involves foresight, market sensitivity, and special aptitudes, as each associate broker must make hundreds of trading decisions daily. A typical broker's round-lot trading for inventory control purposes runs to tens of millions of dollars a year, and there is a limit to the number of issues one broker can handle effectively. It is difficult to hazard a worthwhile guess about what might in future years be a practical limit to the number of issues handled by each associate broker under computer operations and under projected Exchange volumes.

The Economic Function of the Odd-lot Dealer

The odd-lot system enables the small investor to buy or sell stock at within a fraction of the price at which large lots are traded. Moreover, odd-lot houses create a continuous market for small lots, so that any securities that the small investor wants to buy or sell are readily supplied or absorbed. Marketability and enhanced collateral value are thus assured for small lots on a footing equal to that of large lots.

The odd-lot business affords the means of diversification to the small investor. His funds are not adequate to buy in 100-share lots the stocks of a variety of corporations, but they are sufficient to buy 10-share lots of three or four or more companies and thus secure the benefit in safety of principal and income that diversification confers.

The odd-lot system makes it possible to distribute a corporation's stock to thousands of stockholders. The results of such a wide distribution are beyond calculation. In the first place, the small saver is given a chance to share in the growth of industry. In the second place, a wide distribution makes a stable market for a stock. It has been said that at the peak of a bull market a great number of small selling orders come into the market, helping to stop the upward movement, and that, on the other hand, during a decline many odd lots are bought, helping to keep the decline from going to extremes.

Widespread ownership of stock among the public does much to destroy the radical and destructive economic doctrines that appeal to those having no definite financial interest in the prosperity and dividend-paying power of any important enterprise. Widespread stock ownership creates an interest in the stability and prosperity of business generally and specifically in those of the companies whose stock is owned. It creates in the public general good will toward and understanding of industry. The education of the public in the problems of business and finance is stimulated by the actual ownership of shares.

13 clearing mechanisms

Broker A has an order to buy 100 shares of Coca-Cola at the market, and broker B has an order to sell 100 shares of Coca-Cola at the market. The two brokers meet on the floor of the Exchange and consummate a deal at, say, $97. After the customers who placed the two orders have been notified that their respective purchase and sale orders have been executed, everyone more or less assumes that the transaction is completed. Actually, if the situation is examined closely, it will be discovered that nothing has been accomplished other than that one broker has *agreed* to buy and another broker has *agreed* to sell 100 shares of Coca-Cola at $97 a share. Most of the real work connected with the transaction remains to be done. For example, according to the contract, the selling broker must *deliver a certificate* for 100 shares to the buying broker, and the buying broker must pay $9,700 to the selling broker. When and how are these obligations to be met?

Time of delivery and receipt of payment is a part of each contract executed on the floor of the Exchange. Floor contracts may be classified under one of three headings, according to the time of delivery contemplated.

Cash Delivery. If delivery is intended to occur on the day of the purchase or sale agreement, it must be so specified at the time of the offer and its acceptance. If a "cash delivery" contract is made before 2 P.M., delivery by 2:30 P.M. is contemplated. If a cash delivery contract is made after 2 P.M., delivery must occur within thirty minutes.

Regular Way. A "regular way" purchase and sale agreement calls for delivery of the securities and receipt of payment on the fourth business day following the day of the agreement. Thus shares sold on the floor regular way on Monday will be delivered on Friday if there are no intervening holidays. Odd-lot transactions between a broker and a specialist or an odd-lot dealer are an exception to this rule. Deliveries of odd lots are made on the fourteenth day following the day of the contract. Government bonds, sold regular way, must be delivered on the next business day. But an unqualified bid or offer for a full lot of stock assumes delivery regular way; that is, performance and settlement of the contract as between the buying and selling brokers will be effected on the fourth business day following the making of the agreement.

Seller's Options.   If a seller, by the terms of an agreement, has the right to deliver on a day of his own choice, the contract is said to be a "seller's option." Options involving listed shares of stock must run for not less than five or more than sixty days. If a specified delivery date is a day other than a business day, it is understood that delivery will be made on the next succeeding business day. Written contracts must be exchanged in all seller's options. Sellers, on a seller's option, may deliver sooner than agreed provided that they give buyers a one-day notice of intention. Delivery must be made on the last day of the contract if not made sooner.

Seller's options are a convenience to brokers dealing for foreign customers. If a New York broker sells 500 shares of an issue for the account of a customer in Paris, he may sell regular way and borrow stock for delivery or he may sell on a seller's option basis and make delivery one day after the shares arrive from Paris. The rules of the Stock Exchange permit option transactions because the agreement contemplates that securities will pass from buyer to seller. Only the exact date of delivery is uncertain. Seller's options differ from puts and calls in that whether the latter contracts do or do not require deliveries of shares depends on subsequent price movements.

Delivery When Issued.   A bid or offer "when issued" calls for delivery on a date determined by the Exchange. Sometimes a corporation announces a split-up of its stock and calls in its shares for reissue. During the interval when the old stock is unavailable for delivery, new shares may be bought and sold for delivery when issued. New shares to be issued as a result of rights financing are also sold in this way. One often sees price quotations for new stock marked "w.i." (when issued). Written contracts are required for all transactions executed on a when issued basis.

Delivery without Clearance

For a period of 100 years (to the day) deliveries of shares and cash settlements between members of the New York Stock Exchange were made directly between the brokers involved.[1] Under this "direct method" of settlement, the Coca-Cola sale cited above would have been settled as follows:

Comparison.   An employee of broker B (the selling broker) would call at the office of the buying broker before 4 P.M. on the day of the agreement, to compare his record of the transaction with that held by broker A. The

---

[1] On May 17, 1792, brokers recorded an agreement "neither to buy nor to sell at a commission less than one-fourth of one per cent" for the public. On May 17, 1892, the New York Stock Exchange Clearing House was established.

purpose of this comparison was to make certain that the two brokers were in agreement. Thus each brokerage firm had employees continually running about from office to office to eliminate differences in details of contracts made during the day so that deliveries might go on uninterrupted from the opening of business on the next day.

Delivery. On the morning of the day following the making of an agreement, a messenger of the selling broker would deliver the securities sold on the previous day to the office of the buying broker. If this broker had resold the securities on the previous day, his messenger would immediately rush them on to the office of the broker to whom they were resold. As might be expected, such a system of delivery works satisfactorily during periods of low normal trading but becomes cumbersome in a time of great activity.

Payment. When the messenger of the selling broker delivered the shares, he would receive the check of the buying broker. The messenger would take this check to the bank for certification, return it to his own office for recording, and then deposit it in a bank. As a result of this settlement procedure, large amounts of credit were tied up in stock market activity because all stock delivered was paid by certified checks on existing bank balances. One of the difficulties of the procedure was that a broker could not get his stock until he paid for it and frequently he could not pay for it until he had the securities to offer as collateral for a loan.

Two methods were used to circumvent this difficulty: overcertification of brokers' checks and morning loans. By the first method, the broker had an understanding with his bank whereby it would certify checks beyond his deposit balance provided that he gave the bank a note and deposited collateral immediately on receipt. By the second method, each morning before the Exchange opened the broker negotiated a bank loan based upon his unsecured note and his promise to send collateral to the bank as soon as it was received. Neither of the two practices was regarded favorably by banking authorities.

The Clearing Principle

Clearing is an operation that intervenes between the *making* of regular way contracts on the floor of the Exchange and the *performance* of the obligations of those contracts four days later (to deliver shares and make money payments). The clearance process greatly simplifies performance by eliminating many activities which make no positive contribution toward attaining the final objective of contracts considered in the aggregate.

Delivery Clearing. In a chain series of transactions involving the same quantity of shares of a particular issue, a terminal right to receive shares exists for each initial obligation to deliver shares. Interposed between the initial obligation and the terminal right are a series of intermediate obligations to deliver and rights to receive which balance in the aggregate and so may be canceled out. To illustrate, suppose that broker A sells 100 shares of X Company common to B, who sells it to C, who sells it to D, who sells it to E all on the same day. In this series A's obligation to deliver is *initial* and must be made. Similarly, E's right to receive is *terminal* and cannot be canceled. But the rights and obligations of B, C, and D are *intermediate* and cancel out since each is obligated to deliver and to receive the same number of shares of X Company (see Figure 13–1).

In the above example the situation begins with broker A in possession of 100 shares of X Company stock. The objective of the series of transactions is to leave broker E in possession of the shares. Performance of this objective can be achieved easily merely by having A deliver the shares to E. But A cannot make such a delivery because he has dealt with B and does not know about E's terminal right. A simple theoretical solution of the problem becomes practical if each participant reports all his obligations and rights to a central agency, which is thus in a position to eliminate the intermediate obligations and rights and to inform the member with the initial obligation as to the identity of the member with the terminal right. In effect this is what the machinery of the Stock Clearing Corporation attempts to accomplish.

Cash Clearing.   Although brokers B, C, and D in the example cited above bought and sold the same quantities of X Company shares and so are willing to cancel deliveries against receipts, they will not be willing to cancel money payments, since the prices at which they bought may not have been, and probably were not, identical with the prices at which they sold. Consequently, *two* clearing systems are needed, one to clear stock deliveries and the other to clear money payments.

Cash clearing is much less complicated than clearing deliveries. For every obligation of one broker to pay cash there exists a right of another

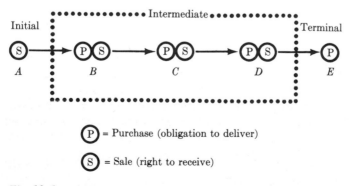

(P) = Purchase (obligation to deliver)

(S) = Sale (right to receive)

Fig. 13–1

broker to receive a similar amount of cash. Thus the obligations to pay off brokers in the aggregate are exactly equal to their aggregate rights to receive payment. There is no reason why a central agency should hesitate to assume the obligations to pay if it should be given all the rights to receive payment. This is what is done. Each broker makes all his payments to a clearing organization and receives from it all sums due to him. The transfer makes it possible for each broker to offset payments against potential receipts and to settle the balance with the clearing organization by writing or receiving a single check.

Adoption of the Clearing Principle.   A stock clearinghouse operating on the above principles was proposed repeatedly to the New York Stock Exchange, but the proposals were always rejected because of the fear that the clerks needed to do the routine work would divulge the business secrets of members of the Exchange. Finally, in 1892, a clearinghouse was established as a part of the Exchange under the management of a committee of five members appointed by the Governing Committee. This clearinghouse, as first established, cleared deliveries only in the more active (cleared) issues. Payments were still made by checks requiring morning loans or overcertification. Notwithstanding this limitation, stock clearing did greatly reduce the need for bank credit and, more important, created confidence among the members of the Exchange in the workability of the clearing principle.

The old clearinghouse scheme functioned quite satisfactorily until the beginning of World War I. Then the increase in market activity, together with the demand for funds for war financing, placed an unbearable burden on the New York City banks and led to their request that the Exchange take steps to reduce the demand of brokers for credit extension and certification. It was becoming increasingly obvious that a clearing system must be established that would clear money payments on balances of stock delivered and also that would handle the transfer of collateral loans from one party to another.

As a result, the constitution of the Exchange was amended on December 26, 1918, to provide for an organization distinct from the New York Stock Exchange, to be called the Stock Clearing Corporation.

The Stock Clearing Corporation

The Stock Clearing Corporation is a corporation organized under the laws of the state of New York. It is authorized to issue 5,000 shares of stock of $100 par value. Its charter provides that it shall be governed by a board of not fewer than five or more than nine directors.

The services of the corporation are available (1) to clearing members and (2) to nonmember banks who have been approved by the Stock Clearing

Corporation and who have entered into an agreement to comply with its regulations. A "clearing member" is a member of the New York Stock Exchange who has applied and been accepted for membership.

A clearing member must clear and settle every contract and transaction subject to clearing through the facilities of the Stock Clearing Corporation. A clearing member may clear contracts for other members of the Exchange, but in such cases the liability of the clearing member is the same as if the cleared contract were one of his own.

Each clearing member must make a contribution to the clearing fund of such an amount as shall be decided by the Stock Clearing Corporation. Ten thousand dollars of this contribution must be in cash; the balance may be in the form of a note secured by a deposit of bonds of the United States government, a state, or a political subdivision of a state.

If a clearing member fails to meet an obligation to the Stock Clearing Corporation, the amount of his default may be charged against his contribution to the clearing fund and he must restore the deficiency promptly. All the liabilities of the Stock Clearing Corporation are guaranteed by the existence of the clearing fund.

The expenses of the Stock Clearing Corporation are met by charges made for services rendered. Each clearing member pays a basic service charge of $40 a month, plus a charge based upon actual services received. Net annual earnings of the Stock Clearing Corporation in excess of 6 per cent of its capital stock are carried to its surplus until the surplus equals $500,000, after which any part of net annual earnings may be distributed as dividends.

The Clearing Mechanism

The following account of how the New York Stock Exchange's clearing organization operates is taken from the charter and bylaws of the Stock Clearing Corporation. The machinery and routine of the corporation are

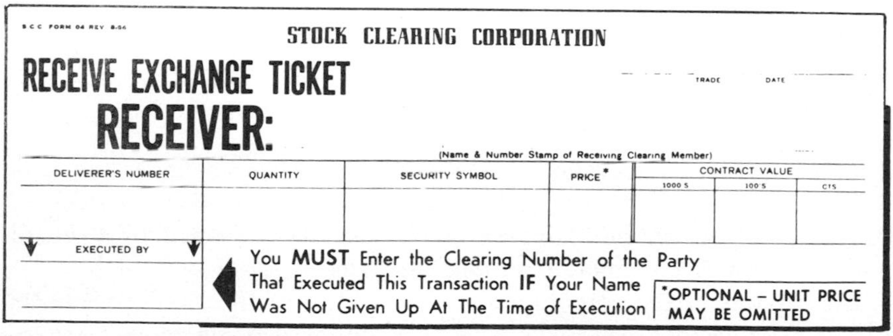
STOCK CLEARING CORPORATION

RECEIVE EXCHANGE TICKET

RECEIVER:

TRADE DATE

(Name & Number Stamp of Receiving Clearing Member)

DELIVERER'S NUMBER	QUANTITY	SECURITY SYMBOL	PRICE*	CONTRACT VALUE 1000 S	100 S	CTS

EXECUTED BY

You **MUST** Enter the Clearing Number of the Party That Executed This Transaction **IF** Your Name Was Not Given Up At The Time of Execution

*OPTIONAL – UNIT PRICE MAY BE OMITTED

Fig. 13–2 A receive exchange ticket.

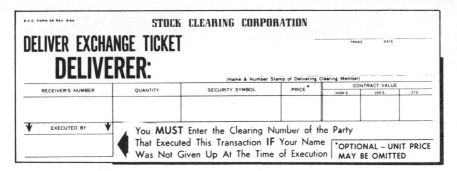

Fig. 13–3 A deliver exchange ticket.

devised to apply the principle of clearing explained earlier. In general the routine provides methods of (1) making certain that buyer and seller are in agreement; (2) offsetting obligations to deliver shares against rights to receive shares of the same issue, thereby determining the "balances to deliver" and "balances to receive"; (3) providing facilities for the delivery and receipt of these balances; and (4) canceling obligations to pay cash against rights to receive payment so that final settlement can be made with a minimum of check writing.

A round-lot transaction executed on the floor of the Exchange is a *verbal* agreement in which one member *promises* to deliver shares and the other member *promises* to pay money. The parties to the agreement do not exchange written confirmations of their promises but merely report the transaction to the office of the clearing member who consummates his trades.[2]

As soon as a clearing member's office is informed of the execution of a contract for a full lot on the floor of the Exchange, one of its clerks makes out a receive exchange ticket (Figure 13–2) or a deliver exchange ticket (Figure 13–3). The function of these tickets is to report the important details of each transaction to the Stock Clearing Corporation so that that agency can start the process of comparison and clearance. The information of importance to the clearing process is:

1. Identification of the buying member by his clearing number
2. Identification of the selling member by his clearing number
3. Identification of the issue traded by its ticker symbol
4. Number of shares traded
5. Total monetary consideration involved

Clearing members may present these data on punched cards in lieu of the exchange tickets if they so prefer.

[2] Every Exchange member need not be a member of the Stock Clearing Corporation, since he can make arrangements for his transactions to be merged (for clearing) with some other member who has clearing privileges.

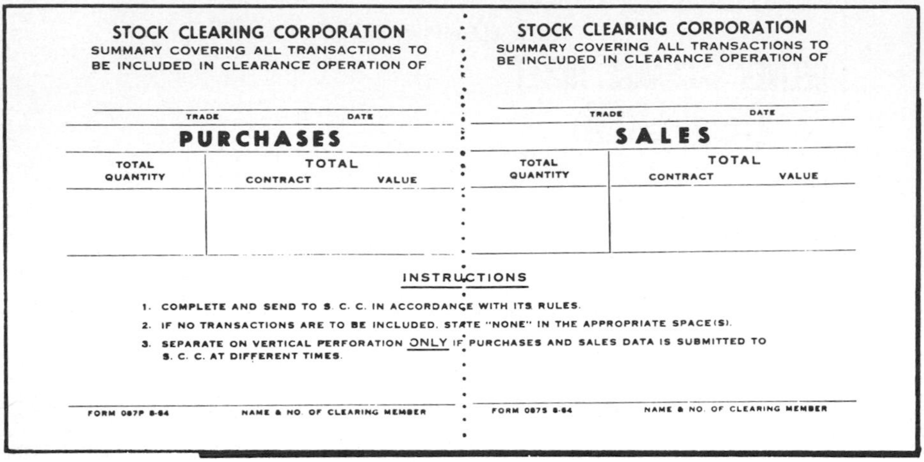

STOCK CLEARING CORPORATION
SUMMARY COVERING ALL TRANSACTIONS TO BE INCLUDED IN CLEARANCE OPERATION OF

TRADE	DATE

PURCHASES

TOTAL QUANTITY	TOTAL CONTRACT VALUE

FORM 087P 8-64 — NAME & NO. OF CLEARING MEMBER

STOCK CLEARING CORPORATION
SUMMARY COVERING ALL TRANSACTIONS TO BE INCLUDED IN CLEARANCE OPERATION OF

TRADE	DATE

SALES

TOTAL QUANTITY	TOTAL CONTRACT VALUE

FORM 087S 8-64 — NAME & NO. OF CLEARING MEMBER

INSTRUCTIONS

1. COMPLETE AND SEND TO S. C. C. IN ACCORDANCE WITH ITS RULES.
2. IF NO TRANSACTIONS ARE TO BE INCLUDED, STATE "NONE" IN THE APPROPRIATE SPACE(S).
3. SEPARATE ON VERTICAL PERFORATION ONLY IF PURCHASES AND SALES DATA IS SUBMITTED TO S. C. C. AT DIFFERENT TIMES.

Fig. 13–4 A summary report form.

Sometimes the member who made the floor contract is acting as an agent for another member. Formerly it was the custom for such an agent to reveal his principal by handing the other party to the contract a small green "give-up" slip. Thus, if X, acting for Y, sold 100 shares of an issue to Z, the green give-up slip informed Z that he would receive the shares from Y and not from X. However, the slips were small and easily lost or misplaced so that much unnecessary clerical work was involved in straightening out errors. Exchange tickets now contain a space for the agent's number, labeled "executed by." Thus, it no longer matters if Z thinks that he bought the shares from X (with whom he dealt), for the Stock Clearing Corporation can quickly eliminate X from the clearing process when it receives Y's sales exchange ticket.

Throughout each trading day clerks of clearing members prepare and accumulate exchange tickets (or punched tabulating cards) for all the contracts executed on the floor by their firms. Between 9 A.M. and 12 noon on the following day these exchange tickets are delivered to the central delivery department of the Stock Clearing Corporation, together with a summary report (Figure 13–4) covering all the transactions to be cleared for which exchange tickets are submitted. The summary report gives the total number of shares purchased and their aggregate contract value and the total number of shares sold and their aggregate contract value. This information appears later in the upper left-hand corner of the member's clearance statement.

It will be noted that the Stock Clearing Corporation receives two notices of each transaction: the first from the buying broker and the second from the selling broker. Except for a possible error, details of the transaction as shown by the two tickets should be identical. As soon as the tickets are received, the five important facts reported on them are punched onto tabulating cards that are fed into a machine, which transfers the data to a magnetic tape for processing by an electronic computer. Before processing the data, however, the computer performs a number of validating steps. First, to verify the contract price, it divides the total compensation of each trade by the number of shares, and then it compares this price with the high and low quotations of the issue to make certain that the contract price reported is within the range of prices for the day. Then it compares the data shown on the exchange ticket presented by the buyer with the data shown on the exchange ticket presented by the seller to make certain that the two are in agreement. The machine divides transactions into two categories, those which compare and those which do not. Four types of error are possible: (1) a member's clearing number may be entered incorrectly; (2) a stock symbol may be entered incorrectly; (3) the tickets may disagree about the number of shares traded; (4) a difference of opinion may exist about the price agreed upon.

The machine then prints a contract list of sales (Figure 13–5) and a contract list of purchases (on a form similar to the sales contract list but with the word "purchases" substituted for the word "sales"). Transactions that compare appear on that part of the form labeled A. Details of transactions that do not compare are reported in the section marked B of the contract list of the member who submitted the ticket and in the section marked C of the contract list of the member who is alleged to be the second party to the

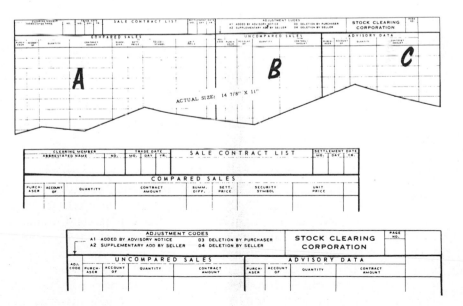

Fig. 13–5   A contract list of sales.

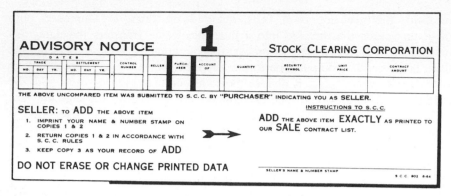

Fig. 13–6 An advisory form for sales.

contract. For example, suppose that member No. 660 reports that he sold 100 shares of XYZ to member No. 340 but that member No. 340 reports that he bought 100 shares of ABC from member No. 660. Since the details of the two exchange tickets do not agree, the information contained on No. 660's ticket will appear as an uncompared sale on his sales contract list and as advisory data on No. 340's purchase contract list. Similarly, the information given on No. 340's exchange ticket will appear as an uncompared purchase on his purchase contract list and as advisory data on No. 660's sales contract list. The leads contained in the "uncompared" and "advisory" columns make it a simple matter for the members to locate and correct the cause of the confusion.

Contract lists of purchases and sales consummated on the floor on a Monday are placed in the boxes of the members at 6 P.M. on Tuesday. Messengers pick up the forms the first thing on Wednesday morning and return them to the several brokerage offices for comparison with internal records.

As mentioned, each member is informed by his contract lists of the transactions for which he submitted exchange tickets that could not be matched with tickets submitted by the opposite party. The uncompared transactions of one member appear in the advisory column of some other member. If this other member knows the trade exactly as printed in his advisory data column and wishes to have the transaction added to the compared transactions, he merely fills out the proper form in triplicate (Figure 13–6 or 13–7) and sends two copies to the Stock Clearing Corporation. This agency transfers the transaction from the uncompared to the compared category and forwards one copy of the advisory form to the opposite party.

Uncompared transactions not corrected in this manner must be corrected by direct negotiation between the parties concerned. As soon as the detail that prevented comparison is located and corrected, the transaction

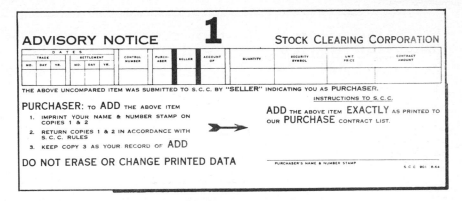

Fig. 13–7   An advisory form for purchases.

may be added to the list of compared transactions by filling out an add form (Figure 13–8).

Until 1 P.M. of the second business day following the date of trade (for example, Wednesday for contracts made on Monday), either the purchaser or the seller may have a particular contract deleted from the list of compared transactions. To accomplish such deletion, the initiating party must first contact the opposite party to obtain his consent to the submission of a single deletion form (Figure 13–9). This form is filled out in triplicate, the third copy being retained by the initiating party and the other two copies being sent to the Stock Clearing Corporation, which keeps one and forwards the other to the opposite party.

The computer then prepares a supplementary contract list of the original compared transactions with the requested additions and deletions. The situation is now ready for clearance, that is, for elimination of the transactions that cancel out.

S.C.C. FORM 090 8-64

ADD BY SELLER 1

STOCK CLEARING CORPORATION
EXCHANGE TICKET

TRADE DATE			SELLER'S	PURCHASER'S	QUANTITY	SECURITY SYMBOL	PRICE	AMOUNT		
MO.	DAY	YR.	NUMBER	NUMBER				1000'S	100'S	CTS.

SELLER — TO ADD AN ITEM: 1) ENTER REQUIRED DESCRIPTIVE DATA ABOVE; 2) IMPRINT YOUR NAME AND NUMBER STAMP ON COPIES 1 AND 2 AND SUBMIT TO S. C. C. IN ACCORDANCE WITH ITS RULES; 3) KEEP COPY 3 FOR YOUR RECORDS.

SELLER'S NAME & NUMBER STAMP   SELLER'S NAME & NUMBER STAMP

Fig. 13–8   An add form.

DELETION NOTICE   STOCK CLEARING CORPORATION

| TRADE DATE | | | PURCHASER'S NUMBER | SELLER'S NUMBER | QUANTITY | SECURITY SYMBOL | PRICE | AMOUNT | | |
MO.	DAY	YR.						1000's	100's	CTS.

TO **DELETE** AN ITEM:
a) ENTER REQUIRED DESCRIPTIVE DATA ABOVE
b) IMPRINT YOUR NAME & NUMBER STAMP ON
   COPIES 1 & 2 AND SUBMIT TO S. C. C. IN
   ACCORDANCE WITH ITS RULES.
c) KEEP COPY 3 FOR YOUR RECORDS.

S.C.C. FORM 905 8-64

INSTRUCTIONS TO S.C.C.

DELETE THE ABOVE ITEM FROM
THE CLEARANCE OPERATION

1

NAME & NO. STAMP OF CLEARING MEMBER REQUESTING DELETION

Fig. 13–9 A deletion form.

These cancellations are made by the computer. However, the nature of the process will be clearer if we describe a simple hypothetical situation cleared by the old method. Accordingly, assume that the sales contract list of clearing member No. 777 shows obligations to deliver the shares shown in column 1 and that his purchase contract list shows obligations to receive the shares shown in column 2 below. The net balance of shares in each issue to be delivered or received is obtained by subtracting obligations to receive from obligations to deliver, or vice versa. Clearing the transactions in columns 1 and 2 leaves the balances to deliver and receive shown in columns 4 and 5.

| Issues | Contract lists | | Eliminations (3) | Balance to receive (4) | Balance to deliver (5) |
	Purchases (1)	Sales (2)			
American Can	100	300	100		200
Burroughs		200	0		200
Chrysler	400	600	400		200
Dow Chemical	300	300	300		
General Motors	600	600	600		
Greyhound	400	400	400		
Johns-Manville	100		0	100	
L.O.F.	300	100	100	200	
Sears, Roebuck	600	300	300	300	
U.S. Steel	700	800	700		100
Total	3,500	3,600	2,900	600	700

The clearance process described in the paragraph above simplifies the delivery situation by removing (clearing out) all transactions in which mem-

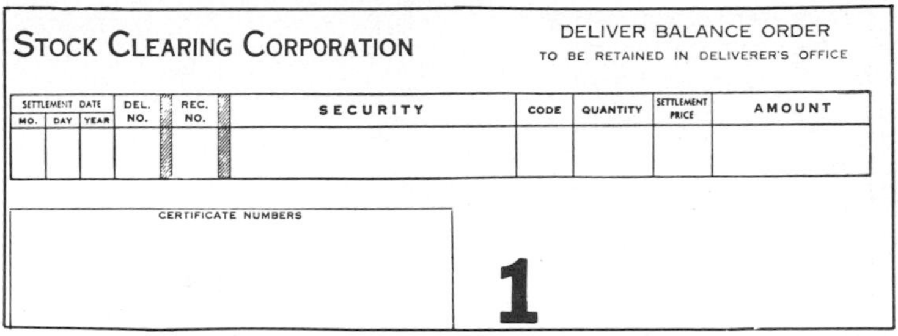

STOCK CLEARING CORPORATION

DELIVER BALANCE ORDER
TO BE RETAINED IN DELIVERER'S OFFICE

SETTLEMENT DATE			DEL. NO.	REC. NO.	SECURITY	CODE	QUANTITY	SETTLEMENT PRICE	AMOUNT
MO.	DAY	YEAR							

CERTIFICATE NUMBERS

1

Fig. 13–10 A deliver balance order form.

bers are obligated to deliver shares of the same issue as they are entitled to receive. The difficulty is that members still obligated to deliver shares do not know to whom to deliver them, since the purchaser with whom they dealt may have been "cleared" from the situation. This problem is easily solved.

The Stock Clearing Corporation makes out a "deliver order" for each issue in a member's balance to deliver (see Figure 13–10). Then it refers to members' balance-to-receive lists to find a member who is entitled to receive this particular issue and it makes out a "receive order" to this member (see Figure 13–11). The name (or number) of the receiving member is entered on the deliver order and the name (or number) of the delivering member is entered on the receive order. These forms are placed in the members' boxes, whereupon each member is fully informed about which certificate he must deliver (or receive) and to (or from) which members. The clearance of shares has been completed. What remains to be done is actual delivery of the shares and clearance of money payments.

Delivery of certificates is accomplished in the following manner. When a clearing member receives an order to deliver shares of an issue to a designated member, he places the certificates in a brown envelope, which he addresses to the receiving member by number. For each batch of 20 envelopes or fewer he prepares two copies of a credit list similar to that shown

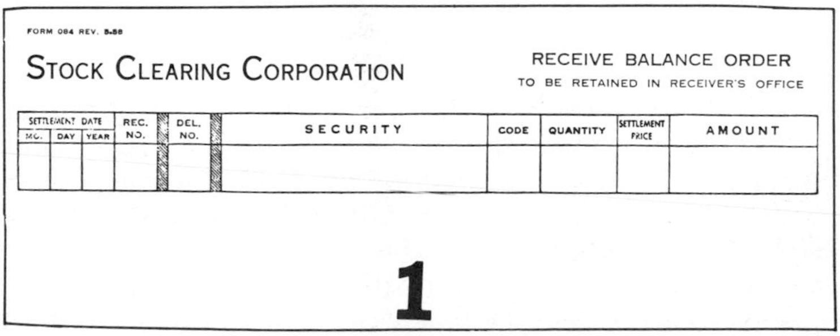

FORM 084 REV. 5-58

STOCK CLEARING CORPORATION

RECEIVE BALANCE ORDER
TO BE RETAINED IN RECEIVER'S OFFICE

SETTLEMENT DATE			REC. NO.	DEL. NO.	SECURITY	CODE	QUANTITY	SETTLEMENT PRICE	AMOUNT
MO.	DAY	YEAR							

1

Fig. 13–11 A receive balance order form.

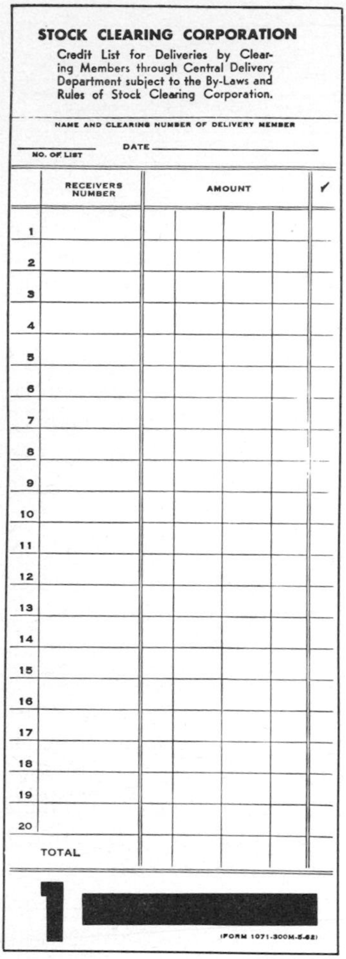

STOCK CLEARING CORPORATION

Credit List for Deliveries by Clearing Members through Central Delivery Department subject to the By-Laws and Rules of Stock Clearing Corporation.

NAME AND CLEARING NUMBER OF DELIVERY MEMBER

NO. OF LIST DATE

	RECEIVERS NUMBER	AMOUNT	✓
1			
2			
3			
4			
5			
6			
7			
8			
9			
10			
11			
12			
13			
14			
15			
16			
17			
18			
19			
20			
TOTAL			

1

(FORM 1071-300M-5-62)

Fig. 13–12 A credit list form.

in Figure 13–12. Each line on this list refers to one envelope and gives the name of the receiving member and the value of the contents *valued at settlement prices*. (The reason for valuation at settlement prices will be explained presently.)

Batches of envelopes containing stock certificates and the accompanying credit lists are delivered to the central receiving department before 12 noon on the fourth day following the date of sale (on Friday for sales made on Monday). The receiving clerk for the Stock Clearing Corporation verifies that there is an envelope for each item shown on the credit list. If so, one copy of the credit list is receipted and returned to the delivering member and the other copy is sent to the record-keeping division of the Stock Clearing Corporation. The brown envelopes containing the stock certificates are deposited in the lockboxes of the members to whom they are addressed, and the delivery and receipt of shares are completed.

There remains now only the matter of money clearance and settlement. Each member receives a clearance and settlement statement similar to the one shown in Figure 13–13. His name and number appear in the upper left-hand corner. Below this is given the number of shares purchased and sold. The dollar amount of the purchases and sales (at the contract prices) is shown to the right. Both the share totals and the dollar amounts of purchases and sales can be obtained from the contract lists of purchases and sales described earlier.

Shares to be delivered or received as specified on the deliver orders and receive orders are valued at settlement prices instead of at contract prices.[3] This results in each member's settlement account being debited or credited for an amount that is different from the amount he expected to

[3] The settlement price of each issue is the even dollar amount of the closing price, any fraction being disregarded. Thus, if an issue closes at 22⅝, the settlement price is 22.

SETTLEMENT DATE			CLEARING MEMBER		STOCK CLEARING CORPORATION			
MO.	DAY	YR.	NAME	NO	8 BROAD ST. — NEW YORK			

			AMOUNT		
CLEARANCE STATEMENT			DEBIT		CREDIT
	SHARES				
TOTAL CONTRACTS: PURCHASES (DR) SALES (CR)	PURCHASED	SOLD			
TOTAL BALANCE ORDERS: DELIVER (DR) RECEIVE (CR)	DELIVER	RECEIVE			
			DO NOT INCLUDE THE ABOVE IN TOTALS		
SETTLEMENT STATEMENT			DEBIT		CREDIT
CASH ITEMS:					
02 CLEARANCE ADJUSTMENT					
03 MEMBER TO MEMBER AND NON-MEMBER BANK					
05 NON-MEMBER BANK TO MEMBER					X X X X X X X X X X X
60 FEDERAL TAX					X X X X X X X X X X X
61 N.Y. STATE TAX					X X X X X X X X X X X
71 MARKS TO MARKET (ESCROW)					
78 MARKS TO MARKET (SPECIAL) (WHEN APPROPRIATE TAKE CREDIT FOR BONDS DEPOSITED)					
SUB TOTALS					
97 SUSPENSE					
98 DRAFT (DR) CHECK (CR)					
TOTAL					

Fig. 13–13 A clearance and settlement form.

pay or to receive. To adjust for this difference, the Stock Clearing Corporation computes the difference between purchases and sales at contract prices and the difference between receipts and deliveries at settlement prices. If the two differences do not agree (as they certainly will not), a clearance cash adjustment debit or credit is made to the member's settlement statement. The effect of this clearance cash adjustment is to cause the balance of the settlement account to be the same after it is debited for deliveries received and credited for deliveries made at settlement prices as it would have been had it been debited for actual purchases and credited for actual sales. The member does not care how the final balance is derived as long as it agrees with his expectations. The total of the clearance cash adjustment amount is given on line 02 of the form shown in Figure 13–13.

The credit lists which accompanied the brown envelope containing the stock certificates become the basis of a debit to the receiving member's account and a credit to the delivering member's account. The totals of these debits and credits are reported in line 03 of the form shown on Figure 13–13.

Members borrowing from banks may request the Stock Clearing Corporation to deliver shares they are entitled to receive to banks to be used as collateral for loans. The bank's loan is effected by debiting the bank's account at the Stock Clearing Corporation and crediting the member's settlement account. Such an entry will show on line 03 of the form shown in Figure 13–13.

Taxes payable to the Federal government and to the state of New York are also settled merely by having the Stock Clearing Corporation debit the settlement account of the member (on lines 60 and 61) and credit the account of the respective governments.

When all the appropriate debits and credits have been entered in the member's settlement account, they are subtotaled and a balancing debit or credit is computed (on line 98 of Figure 13–13). Clearing members whose account is balanced with a debit remit the amount to the Corporation in the form of a certified check. Firms having a credit balance present a draft on the Corporation for its signature.

The clearance operation just described eliminates about 35 per cent of the deliveries of securities and about 85 per cent of the money transfers called for by the agreements made on the floor of the Exchange.

A Stock Depository.   The New York Stock Exchange has established a central depository for stock certificates somewhat similar to those used by some European stock exchanges. This depository system, called the "central certificate service," was inaugurated on November 8, 1965; it will be in full operation by April 1966.

Under the new system, clearing members leave a designated number of shares of "eligible" issues with the Stock Clearing Corporation.[4] These deposited shares are combined into large-denomination certificates which are left with custodian banks in the name of the Stock Clearing Corporation.

A computer keeps a running record of the number of deposited shares belonging to each broker. When a participating broker wishes to make delivery of deposited shares to another broker, the computer merely subtracts the shares from the account of the delivering broker and adds them to the account of the receiving broker. This procedure will reduce the physical transferring of certificates by 75 per cent. If a customer calls for delivery of shares which a broker has deposited, the broker may withdraw the necessary certificates from the central depository.

[4] About 2 per cent of listed securities do not qualify for deposit because the issuing companies are incorporated in states or countries whose laws bar participation in such setups.

14 margin trading

Trading on margin refers to the practice of purchasing stocks with borrowed funds. One cannot purchase shares entirely with borrowed funds, since a broker always requires that a customer pay *some* portion of the costs with his own money. In stock market parlance the portion so paid is the customer's *margin*. Thus, if an investor buys shares worth $10,000 and advances $6,000 of his own funds, his margin is $6,000 in monetary terms, or 60 per cent if expressed as a percentage of the value of the shares purchased.

Purchasing property with borrowed money is a universal practice in business and industry. A retailer furnishes his own permanent capital and part of his working capital and borrows for the remainder of his needs at a bank. A wholesaler supplies a part of his capital needs and borrows the rest, hoping to pay back the borrowed funds when he has sold out the goods on which he borrowed. A manufacturer organizes a corporation; the stockholders furnish equity, and the bondholders and banks lend the additional funds needed to carry on the business. The head of a family of small means buys a modest house, paying down 20 per cent of the purchase price, and a savings and loan association lends the other 80 per cent, with a mortgage on the property as collateral. It is not surprising, therefore, to find investors and speculators making use of borrowed funds.

There are a number of advantages in having a margin account with a broker. For example, if one plans to buy and sell several times within a few days, having a margin account eliminates the necessity of making payment for each purchase and receiving payment for each sale. Instead transactions are recorded in the account as they occur, so that purchases and sales offset each other to some extent. It does not matter that the customer is "in debt" to the broker at times as long as the amount of the debt does not exceed certain prescribed limits.

Some customers use a margin account as a means of purchasing shares on an instalment basis. Perhaps a customer has $2,000 available to purchase stock. He deposits this with his broker, purchases, say, $3,000 worth of stock, and owes the broker $1,000. Each month thereafter he makes a payment into his account to reduce the debt. When this is liquidated, he may make another $3,000 purchase of shares, continuing to make monthly payments. Dividends received on the shares held as collateral offset the broker's charges of interest and may even accelerate liquidation of the indebtedness. From a broker's point of view such an account is a margin account; from a customer's point of view it is only a means of buying shares on an instalment basis. But the principal reason for having a margin account is to obtain the leverage advantage made possible by the practice of trading with borrowed capital.

The Use of Credit to Buy Securities

Assume that an investor with $10,000 of capital locates a stock which he is convinced will rise 50 per cent during the next three or four weeks. If he invests his $10,000 in this stock and if his prognostication is correct, he will be able to sell it for $15,000 and thereby earn a profit of $5,000, or 50 per cent, on his $10,000 all within a period of a month or less. But by means of margin trading he can do much better. For example, he might combine his original $10,000 of capital with an additional $10,000 borrowed from his broker or some other lender and purchase twice as many shares. Then, if the expected rise materializes, he will be able to sell his holdings for $30,000, repay the $10,000 loan, and have $20,000 of funds in place of the $10,000 with which he started. As a result of this financial maneuver he will make a profit of 100 per cent instead of 50 per cent on the funds committed by him to the venture.

Earning this additional profit involves added risk. If the investor had been wrong about the price movement, the story would have had a different ending. Suppose that the price of the stock unexpectedly declined 25 per cent. The trader's losses then would be $2,500 if he invested his own money as compared with $5,000 if he supplemented his funds with a loan of $10,000. In the latter case the shares for which he paid $20,000 would bring him only $15,000 when sold, and, after paying off the $10,000 loan, he would have left only $5,000 of his original capital.

In short, supplementing one's own capital with borrowed funds in order to buy more shares than would otherwise be possible is a two-edged sword that multiplies the amount of profits or losses to be obtained from a given market fluctuation. In the example used above, a 50-50 combination of equity and borrowed funds doubled the profit on a profitable transaction and doubled the loss on an unprofitable transaction. Had a larger proportion of borrowed funds been used, more shares could have been carried and a much greater leverage effect attained. The following table shows the effect upon profits and losses of using increased quantities of borrowed funds.

Customer's margin	Percentage return resulting if prices:	
	Advance 50%	Decline 25%
100%*	+ 50	− 25
75	+ 67	− 33
50	+100	− 50
25	+200	−100
12.5	+400	−200

* A margin of 100% is a cash transaction.

Clearly small margins pyramid profits at a rapid rate, a fact that does not escape the attention of speculative traders who tend to do most of their trading on margin. Conversely, when a trader misjudges the market and shares decline in value, his losses pyramid also.

The magnitude of risk involved in margin trading for both the customer and for the brokerage firm extending credit was dramatically illustrated in November 1963 by the failure of Allied Crude Vegetable Oil and Refining Company. Although the case involved commodities rather than stocks, the principles are identical. Allied had been purchasing soybean and cottonseed oil contracts on margins as low at 5 per cent (commodity margins are not so strictly regulated as stock margins), apparently in the hopes of cornering the market and also in anticipation of a price rise if negotiations to export American grains to the Soviet Union, then under way, worked out. Two New York Stock Exchange member firms, Ira Haupt and Company and J. Williston & Beane, Inc., supplied most of the credit, which they in turn obtained from banks by pledging warehouse receipts for the oil as collateral.

On November 15, 1963, wheat negotiations between the United States and the Soviet Union were suspended, and soybean and cottonseed oil contracts began to fall. By Monday, November 18, these drops had so reduced Allied's margin with its brokers that Haupt sent a margin call to Allied for about $18 million and Williston sent a call for about $610,000. Allied was unable to supply any additional equity and filed a petition in court for voluntary bankruptcy. Subsequently much of the oil pledged as collateral was found to have disappeared from Allied's tank farms. The affair promises to become one of financial history's leading scandals.

Allied's inability to provide more equity not only forced it out of business but also reduced the net capital requirements of Haupt and Williston below the minimum required by the New York Stock Exchange. Both firms were immediately suspended from membership. J. Williston & Beane, Inc., which had only about 10 per cent of the Allied business, was able to borrow additional capital and was quickly reinstated. Ira Haupt and Company, however, a well-regarded house which had been in business since 1927, was forced into voluntary liquidation with probable losses to its creditors and partners. The Exchange, to maintain public confidence in the investment community, authorized up to $12 million of Exchange funds for the purpose of reimbursing Haupt customers whose accounts had been frozen at the time of suspension. It is estimated that final liquidation of Haupt will take two years.

A Transaction Step by Step

If a broker lends money to a customer who wishes to trade on margin, he must keep a careful record of all transactions in order to be continuously informed of the amount of the customer's debt to him. The record is kept on a page in the broker's ledger. There purchases of stock are entered on the left (debit) side, sales of securities on the right (credit) side; deposits of cash by a customer are entered on the right side, withdrawals of cash on the left side. When the sum of the figures on the left side exceeds the sum of those on the right, the account is said to have a *debit* balance, i.e., a left-hand balance. A debit balance means that the customer is in debt to the broker. Conversely, if the sum of the figures on the right side exceeds that of the figures on the left side, the balance is a *credit* balance and indicates the amount that the broker owes to the customer.

In order to make certain that customers pay their debts, a broker requires each of his customers to leave in his possession readily salable property, i.e., stocks and bonds, having a market value in excess of the amount of the customer's debt. In the parlance of the Street this property is referred to as *collateral*. The excess of the value of the collateral over the customer's debt is the *equity* or *dollar margin*. The ratio of the dollar margin to the market value of the collateral is called the *percentage margin*. Thus the word margin may mean either a dollar sum or a percentage relationship.

Purchase of Stock.   Mr. Hoad of Columbus, Ohio, decides that Sears, Roebuck at $100 is a good buy. He has $5,000 available and so can buy 50 shares if he pays cash for them. (In all the examples in this chapter commissions and taxes are ignored.) Alternatively he can buy the stock on margin, putting up a portion of the purchase price and borrowing the remainder from a broker. He has already opened a margin account at the Columbus office of Thomas Moore & Company. The registered representative of this firm has informed Hoad that a 50 per cent margin is adequate; so Hoad can buy 100 shares with his $5,000 if he so chooses.

Hoad deposits his check for $5,000, and the bookkeeper credits his account for this amount (see entry *a* in the accompanying illustration). Hoad then signs an order to "Buy for my account and risk 100 shares of Sears, Roebuck common at the market," or he may give the order by telephone. In either case, the order is transferred immediately to the wire desk, where it is sent by private wire to the New York office for execution. Let us assume that the order is executed at 99¾. The details will be transmitted by wire to the Columbus office, and Hoad will be informed of the purchase. The bookkeeper will then debit Hoad's account for the purchase price of the stock, $9,975, as shown in entry *b*:

(Debit side)	W. A. Hoad, Columbus, Ohio	(Credit side)
(b) Purchase, 100 shrs. @ 99¾	$9,975.00	(a) Deposit of cash $ 5,000.00
(d) Interest on $4,975 @ 4%, 45 days	24.87	(c) Sale of 100 shrs. @ 112 11,200.00

The next day Hoad receives by mail a confirmation of his order to buy Sears, Roebuck at the market and also a statement giving the shares bought, the price, the commission, and the total debit made to his account as a result of the transaction.

At this moment, Hoad's account contains a debit of $9,975 and a credit for $5,000 and consequently has a debit balance of $4,975. In due course, Thomas Moore & Company receives the stock which was purchased for Hoad, but instead of delivering the certificates to Hoad it holds them as collateral to secure the $4,975 debt due the firm. Hoad's equity, or margin, is $9,975 minus $4,975 or $5,000, that is, the value of the 100 shares of stock minus the debit balance. Stated as the ratio of the equity to the value of the collateral, Hoad's margin is 50.13 per cent.

Sale.   After some weeks the price of Sears, Roebuck has gone to 110 and is still rising. For various reasons Hoad thinks he had better take his profit. He calls up the broker and orders him to sell 100 shares of Sears, Roebuck at 112, G.T.C. The routine of transmitting and recording a selling order is exactly the same as a buying order. On the floor of the Exchange the stock is selling at perhaps 110½. Under these conditions, the order will be handed to a specialist who stands all day at Post 9. Some days later the price goes to 112, and the specialist sells the stock. He informs Thomas Moore & Company's telephone clerk, who, as in the buying order above, starts the machinery that finally informs Hoad of the execution of his order.

Thomas Moore & Company credits Hoad with the value of 100 shares at $112 (less commissions and taxes, which we are ignoring), or $11,200 (see entry c). In addition, the account would be debited $24.87 interest on $4,975.00 for 45 days at 4 per cent (see entry d). At this point Hoad has a credit balance of $6,200.13. Thus his profit on the venture in which he risked $5,000 of his own funds is $1,200.13, or 24 per cent.

Short Sales. Hoad might expect that the price of the stock would drop instead of rise. If so, he could obtain a profit on the decline by selling short. Selling short would involve the following sequence of events: (1) Hoad would sell shares of stock which he does not own. (2) In order to deliver the shares sold, Hoad would borrow stock from or through his broker. His broker would require a deposit, usually cash, as security for this loan of stock. (3) At a later date, when the price of the stock had (hopefully) dropped, Hoad would buy the stock in the market and deliver this stock in repayment of the shares borrowed. If his analysis of a drop in the price of the stock were correct, Hoad would make a profit on the difference between the initial high sale price and the subsequent lower repurchase price.

The amount of deposit required as security for the loan of shares (step 2 above) is determined by the margin requirements in effect at the time of the short sale. Thus all short sales involve margin trading. Short selling is treated in detail in the following chapter.

Interest and Dividends

The broker charges interest on the amount of money he lends to the customer. In regular way transactions the broker must pay for stock by the fourth full business day following the date of sale. He borrows the funds in the morning at his bank and makes payment on receipt of the securities. Interest, therefore, begins to accrue on the day on which the stock is delivered. When the broker sells the long stock for his customer, he credits him with the net proceeds of the sale on the fourth day after the day of the sale. Interest on money borrowed to finance the margin purchase does not cease until the credit is entered on the books the fourth day after the sale.

The broker regularly collects all dividends and credits them to customers' accounts. The board of directors of a corporation meets and declares the regular quarterly dividend to the stockholders of record as of the close of business of, say, June 2, payable on July 1. The stock will sell ex dividend on May 30, but it will not be until July 1 that the dividend checks are received. If the stock is sold immediately before the ex-dividend date, the broker on receiving the stock has it transferred on the books of the corporation to his name. If there is not time to have the stock transferred, the selling broker will give the buying broker a "due bill," which is a form of promissory note by which the seller, who still has his name on the books of the company when they are closed, promises to pay the dividend to the broker who bought the stock too late to have it transferred. The broker's books will show these items as "due bills receivable." Stock dividends are credited as so many additional shares on the day on which they are received.

Margin Requirements

If the price of Sears, Roebuck in the example given earlier began to decline, Hoad's margin would shrink, since the amount of the debt is stationary. At a price of 90 his margin would be 45 per cent, at 80 it would be 38 per cent, at 70 it would be 29 per cent, and at 60 it would be 17 per cent. At prices lower than 49¾, Hoad's debt to the broker would actually exceed the value of his collateral. It is obvious that for its own protection Thomas Moore & Company must demand an initial margin adequate to absorb any reasonably expected losses and that it also must set some figure below which Hoad's margin must not be permitted to decline under any circumstances. As Hoad's margin approaches this minimum, he will be called upon to reduce his debit balance by depositing additional cash, or to increase the value of his collateral by depositing additional securities, or to do both. If more margin is not forthcoming, Thomas Moore & Company can sell him out to prevent a loss to itself.

Adequate margins, both initial and maintenance, are of interest to many parties besides the lending broker. Perhaps Hoad himself should be protected from taking on an undermargined position such that a slight fluctuation in the market would wipe him out. One's view on this depends primarily on how far one thinks that regulatory authorities should go in protecting persons from their own foolhardiness. A more compelling reason for rules requiring adequate margins is that the economic well-being of the entire nation is tied to the use of credit. Regulation of stock market credit is thus part of the over-all regulation of economic affairs carried on by the government to promote maximum employment, production, and purchasing power.

Maintenance Margin.   The requirement that a customer maintain a margin means only that the value of his collateral must at all times exceed the amount which he owes his broker. Thus, if his collateral is worth 10 per cent more than his debt, he has a 9 per cent margin; if his collateral is worth 35 per cent more than his debt, he has a 26 per cent margin; and so on. The existence of this margin, or excess value of the collateral, ensures the collectibility of the customer's account since the value of the collateral can shrink by the amount of the margin without endangering the balance owed the broker.

For years the percentage by which the value of a customer's collateral must exceed the amount of his debt to a broker was left to the discretion of the individual broker. As was to be expected, minimum margin requirements varied among brokers and among customers of the same broker. Also the requirement changed from time to time, more margin being required in times of high prices than in times of low prices.

In 1903 the New York Stock Exchange passed a rule prohibiting members from accepting or carrying an account for a customer "without proper and adequate margin," but the question of what constituted proper and adequate margin was left for the individual broker to decide. In 1933 the Exchange decided that accounts with debit balances of $5,000 or under must maintain a margin of not less than 50 per cent of the debit balance and that accounts with debit balances over $5,000 must maintain a margin of not less than 30 per cent of the debit balance.

The promulgation of this rule introduced an innovation in terminology. As was stated earlier, a margin is usually expressed as the ratio of a customer's equity to his collateral. The Exchange's 50 per cent of debit balance requirement is thus only a 33 per cent requirement, and its 30 per cent of debit balance requirement is only a 23 per cent requirement, when stated in the more customary way.

Prior to 1933, when a customer's margin approached the minimum established by an individual broker, the broker could either call for more margin or temporarily lower his requirement. After 1933, however, the broker had no choice but to demand additional margin if his customer's margin declined to the minimum set by the Exchange. At the present writing the Exchange requires a minimum maintenance margin of 25 per cent of the current market price of stocks to be maintained after stocks are bought. Some brokerage firms impose a higher maintenance margin than this. On short sales the Exchange requires a maintenance margin of at least 30 per cent of the current market price or $5 per share, whichever is greater, on stocks selling at or above $5 per share and 100 per cent of market value or $2.50 per share, whichever is greater, on stocks selling below $5 per share.

Initial Margin.   When the margins of many customers are close to the minimum, a small decline in prices will lead to margin calls and these in turn will cause liquidation selling and so contribute to a further unsettlement of prices. Because of this fact, a minor reaction in prices sometimes brings about a violent and disorderly collapse of prices.

To illustrate, suppose that a few traders have overextended their positions and hence are trading on margins dangerously close to the minimum. A small decline in prices occurs, and margin calls are made. Traders unable to deposit additional cash or securities are sold out, and, as a result of the forced sales, prices decline a bit further than they otherwise would. This second decline leads to margin calls on the next tier of traders, whose margins may have been quite adequate to absorb the first decline but not large enough to withstand the second. The distress selling of this tier sends prices still lower and weakens the next tier. So the process continues, tier after tier of margin traders being sold out, until the bargain prices at which securities are selling attract new buying orders into the market.

Many economists believe that excessive margin trading was one of the factors that caused security prices to rise as high as they did in the late 1920s and then decline to the depths which they did in the early 1930s.[1] Following this line of reasoning, it would seem that excessive speculation is bad for the country as a whole and that margin trading should be kept within limits. But it was clear from the outset that it would not do to control the margin requirements of brokers unless the lending by banks for the purpose of carrying securities was also controlled. Since the Federal Reserve banks already had the right to control the latter, control of the former was placed in their hands rather than left to the Securities and Exchange Commission.

Regulation T of the Securities Exchange Act of 1934 prohibits any broker from making an *initial* loan to a customer in excess of the *loan value* of his collateral. The maximum loan value of registered securities is changed from time to time by the Board of Governors of the Federal Reserve System to adjust to changes in money and stock market conditions. The maximum loan values set by the Board at various times since October 1, 1934, have resulted in the following margin requirements:

Effective date	Per cent requirement	Effective date	Per cent requirement
Oct. 1, 1934	25–45*	Jan. 17, 1951	75
Feb. 1, 1936	25–55*	Feb. 20, 1953	50
May 1, 1936	55	Jan. 4, 1955	60
Nov. 1, 1937	40	Apr. 23, 1955	70
Feb. 5, 1945	50	Jan. 16, 1958	50
July 5, 1945	75	Aug. 5, 1958	70
Jan. 20, 1946	100	Oct. 16, 1958	90
Feb. 1, 1947	75	July 28, 1960	70
Mar. 30, 1949	50	July 10, 1962	50
		Nov. 6, 1963	70

* Exact requirement on each security determined by the relation of its current price to its lowest price in the preceding thirty-six months.

In addition to the initial requirements established by the Federal Reserve System, which are expressed as a per cent of the value of the securities, the New York Stock Exchange imposes an initial dollar margin requirement

[1] It is estimated that more than 1,500,000 persons were trading on margin in 1929; see Kemper Simpson, *The Margin Trader,* New York: Harper & Row, Publishers, Incorporated, 1938, p. 9. The number of margin accounts handled by members of the New York Stock Exchange on Dec. 31, 1963, was 482,811.

of $1,000. (Some member firms impose a higher initial dollar margin of their own.) Thus a person buying securities or selling short must deposit either $1,000 or 70 per cent (at the present time) of the value of the securities, whichever is larger.

One important facet of the interworking of the Board's *initial* margin requirements and the Exchange's *maintenance* margin requirements should be noted. Regulation T prohibits brokers from making initial loans in excess of 30 per cent (at the time of writing) of the value of collateral, while the Exchange's rule requires that a minimum margin of 25 per cent be maintained at all times.

Suppose that a trader purchases stock worth $10,000, obtaining a $3,000 loan—the maximum permitted by the Board's current loan requirement. If the market value of the stock declines by 60 per cent after the purchase, the trader's dollar margin will decline from $7,000 to $1,000. But even this large shrinkage does not reduce the margin below the Exchange's maintenance margin requirement, as the following figures make clear.

	Before decline	After decline
Value of collateral	$10,000	$4,000
Customer's debt	3,000	3,000
Dollar margin	$ 7,000	$1,000
Per cent margin	70	25

This means that a broker will seldom have to sell out a customer because of inadequate margin. One of the purposes of control of margin trading is to make security prices more stable by requiring such high *initial* margins that minor reactions in prices do not create distress selling. If the Federal Reserve System required traders to maintain these high initial margins at all times, they would thereby defeat the primary purpose of their regulation.

Thus a decline in market quotations acts to curtail only the purchasing abilities of margin traders, since the regulations prohibit the execution of any order that would cause a trader's debit balance to be greater than 30 per cent of his collateral. But such a decline in market quotations would not result in distress selling unless and until margins had shrunk to the minimum set by the New York Stock Exchange or by an individual broker.

Terminology.   Certain words and expressions have a technical meaning when used in conjunction with margin trading. A registered security is a security with listed or unlisted trading privileges on a national securities exchange. Registered securities may be carried on margin. An unregistered security is a security not listed or traded on a national securities exchange. Federal Reserve regulations do not permit the purchase or sale of unregistered securities on margin unless they are "exempt securities."

An exempt security is an unregistered security which may nevertheless be carried on margin. Exempt securities are debt obligations of the United States, the various states and municipalities, and the International Bank for Reconstruction and Development. A nonexempt security is a security which comes under the regulations of the Federal Reserve System for margin purposes. For the most part nonexempt securities are corporate stocks and bonds.

An unrestricted account is an account in which the equity or margin is equal to or in excess of the required initial margin. In general such excess equity may be withdrawn or applied against new margin transactions. A restricted account is an account in which the equity or margin is below the initial margin requirements of the Federal Reserve System. As long as the margin remains above the maintenance margin requirements of the Exchange, it is not necessary to deposit additional equity. In general, when an account is restricted new transactions are permitted only if the customer deposits additional margin equal to the requirement on the new transaction.

Computing the Margin.   The margin clerk of a brokerage house is called upon frequently for an estimate of a customer's margin, perhaps by the customer himself if he is an active trader and certainly by the house in a falling market or if the customer trades in highly fluctuating stocks. Each investor should keep a careful record of his own trading so that he can quickly ascertain the margin he is carrying with his broker. He should have his own figures confirmed occasionally, perhaps frequently, depending on the market and the securities that the broker is carrying for him.

The method of computing margins in long accounts requires the following data:

> The number of shares of each issue of stocks or bonds held in the account by the broker
>
> The current prices of these securities
>
> The debit balance

Suppose that a customer is long 400 shares of Beech Nut Life Savers, 50 shares of Anaconda Copper, and 100 shares of U.S. Steel and has a debit balance of $5,120. If the market price of Beech Nut Life Savers is $29\frac{1}{2}$, of Anaconda Copper is 38, and of U.S. Steel is 60, then the customer has a dollar margin of $14,580.

400 shares Beech Nut Life Savers @ 29½	$11,800
50 shares Anaconda Copper @ 38	1,900
100 shares U.S. Steel @ 60	6,000
Market value of stock held	$19,700
Debit balance (owed to broker)	5,120
Dollar margin of stock held	$14,580

The margin as a percentage of the present value of the securities is equal to $14,580 divided by $19,700, or 74 per cent. If the customer wants to know how many more shares he can carry without putting up more margin, the answer will be found as follows:

Dollar margin now carried	$14,580
70% margin required (70% of $19,700)	13,790
Excess margin	$ 790

If margin requirements are now 70 per cent, this excess equity of $790 will permit him to increase his purchases by 10/7 of $790, or $1,128.

Margin in a Short Account.   The customer might be short securities instead of long. Suppose that he had sold short 100 shares of Control Data at $90 per share and 200 shares of Xcrox at $80 per share. The total amount of the short sale would have been $25,000 (commissions and taxes being ignored), and the customer would have had to deposit additional equity in the account of $17,500 if margin requirements were 70 per cent. Suppose now that Control Data fell to 86½ and Xerox fell to 75⅞. The account would look thus:

100 shares Control Data @ 86½	$ 8,650
200 shares Xerox @ 75⅞	15,175
Market value of stock sold short	$23,825
Credit balance in account (deposit of $17,500	
plus sale proceeds of $25,000)	$42,500
Required margin (170% of $23,825)	40,502
Excess margin	$ 1,998

It will be noted that margin requirements for short sales involve depositing the required percentage margin, say 70 per cent, of the short sale in the account. Because the proceeds of the short sale are also deposited in the account, a 70 per cent margin requirement means in effect that the credit balance in the account must be 170 per cent of the market value of stock sold short. In the case above, the account has an excess margin of $1,998, which will permit the purchase or short sale of an additional $2,854 of stock.

On occasion a customer may be both long some securities and short others, all on margin. In this case two separate accounts, designated "long" and "short," are kept; the customer's equity position is determined by the sum of the equity positions in the two accounts.

Criticism of Existing Control Methods

The Board of Governors of the Federal Reserve System has altered margin requirements a number of times since the passage of the Securities Exchange Act. Its first requirement, made effective October 1, 1934, set the maximum loan value of a share at 55 per cent of its current quotation (i.e., a margin of 45 per cent) or 100 per cent of its lowest price during the preceding three years, whichever was higher. In no case, however, was the loan value permitted to exceed 75 per cent (a 25 per cent margin) of the current price. No margin requirements were set for short sales.

At that time no one feared a runaway bull market. The Dow-Jones averages of industrial prices hovered in the neighborhood of 90. The consensus was that this level was too low rather than too high; hence a rise was wanted rather than feared. In the next fifteen months prices as measured by the Dow-Jones industrial averages rose 66 per cent. Alarmed by the rapidity of this rise, the Board of Governors raised initial margin requirements to 55 per cent of current quotations. Nevertheless, security prices continued to mount and speculative interest continued to grow. Prices reached their peak in March 1937 and then began to recede slowly until the fall of 1937, when the decline became more rapid. With the decrease in security values came a decrease in margin requirements to 40 per cent of current quotations, and, owing to the activity of short sellers, margin requirements were placed on short positions for the first time. Although the Board announced these changes without explanation, the *New York Times* referred to the hope of bolstering and stabilizing the security markets as their primary purpose.

Since 1937 the Board has changed margin requirements many times. Figure 14–1 shows the interrelationship between margin requirements, the level of the stock market, and industrial production from 1949 to 1963. Standard & Poor's composite stock price index is used to measure stock prices and the Federal Reserve Board Index of Industrial Production to measure industrial production. Shaded areas indicate economic recessions as designated by the National Bureau of Economic Research.

In general it appears that the Board's policy has been to raise margin

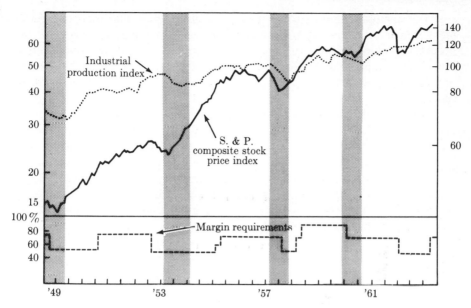

Fig. 14–1   Margin requirements, stock prices, and industrial production.

requirements after a sustained advance in stock prices and near the peak of business activity and to lower requirements after stock prices start to drop or business starts to slump.

Now, while it may be logical to justify an increase in margin requirements by saying that it will prevent an excessive amount of bank credit from being used to finance speculative purchases, it is doubtful that one ought to argue that a decrease in margin requirements is necessary because too little bank credit is being used by speculators, since the usual view is that the ideal would be for no bank credit to be so employed. Consequently, a lowering of margin requirements can mean only that those in control feel that security prices are two low. But such a view makes the Board a judge of the proper value of securities. Carried to its extreme, this would mean that, if stock prices are too low or too high, the blame is to be placed upon the Board.

If it is true, as some contend, that the price level of stocks is a result rather than a cause of changes in production and consumption, then the Board's policy is aimed at correcting symptoms rather than removing causes. The real goal of margin regulation should be, not the control of the price level of securities, but the isolation of the effect of speculation upon general business activity. Something more is required to accomplish this than a policy of lowering and raising margin requirements when prices seem to be too high or too low.

For example, there is some reason for disbelieving that margin requirements, no matter how stringent, can stop a runaway bull market once the proper psychological attitude has been created. It is equally doubtful that low margin requirements will stop investors from selling stocks if they feel that fundamental factors indicate a further decline in the investment worth of shares.

The undesirable effect of stock speculation upon the more essential economic activities of society comes, not from the highness or lowness of security prices, but from the fact that artificially high prices enable persons to borrow more funds than sound values would permit. It is impossible to stop extensive speculation or to prevent excessively high evaluations. Prices can rise too high even when all transactions are for cash. A legitimate goal of regulation would be reached if lending ability were based upon sound values rather than upon prices determined by speculative activity. Since in the long run market prices seem to depend upon earnings, some have argued that the collateral value of stocks should bear a constant ratio to earnings rather than a vacillating ratio to changing market prices.[2]

For that matter it is demonstrable that, given the proper conditions, margin trading can create its own collateral when margin requirements depend upon market quotations. The proper conditions are that prices be sensitive to small changes in demand, i.e., that supply be inelastic. To illustrate, suppose that the price level is 80 and that the floating supply is 1 million shares held on a 50 per cent margin. Suppose further that the supply and demand situation is such that the purchase of 75,000 shares would cause the price level to move up 6 points.

If those who are now holding the floating supply of stock on close to minimum margins should begin to purchase additional shares, their own activity would increase the value of their collateral faster than their purchases would increase their debit balances. While this sensitiveness of prices to purchases continued, speculators could continue to acquire additional shares on margin without putting up more cash. Thus, if 75,000 additional shares were accumulated by speculators at prices ranging from 80 to 86 but averaging 83, the following situation would result.

	Before purchasing	After purchasing
Price	80	86
Shares held	1,000,000	1,075,000
Value of collateral	$80,000,000	$92,450,000
Debit balance	$40,000,000	$46,225,000
Margin, %	50	50

[2] See recommendations of the Twentieth Century Fund survey, *The Security Markets,* New York: Twentieth Century Fund, Inc., 1935, pp. 349–353, 679, 680.

Obviously, the prevailing custom of limiting debit balances to a given percentage of market values will check excessive speculation only when excessive speculation is already restrained by the improbability of a rapid rise in prices. However, high margin requirements will act as a deterrent to the beginning of a runaway bull market, and they will restrain the tempo of the rise once it has begun. As a result, prices may require a longer period of time in which to reach the top, but that top need not be any lower than it would have been with lower margin requirements. High margins are most effective when price movements are slow; they lose their effectiveness as the speed of movement accelerates.

Dangers of Overtrading

Overtrading is a relative term, depending entirely upon circumstances. A purchase of 50 shares may be overtrading for some, while ten times that number may be quite conservative for others with more ample reserve funds. Again, a margin of 50 per cent may be quite sufficient when the trader is experienced and has plenty of time to study the changes taking place in his company and in the market for its product, as well as the changing conditions of the stock market, but 50 per cent would be overtrading for a man inexperienced in the security market and engaged in other lines of business that take his full time.

The phase of the business cycle is also a deciding factor in overtrading. At the height of prosperity a trader who does not carry heavy margins may be sold out before he realizes it, because of a rapid drop in the market. In the dullest part of a depression a relatively small margin may not indicate overtrading.

Moreover, a trader may not be overtrading when he buys on a minimum margin 200 shares of an issue selling consistently at a conservative price-earnings ratio, but he would certainly be overtrading if he bought the same number of shares of some other, much less stable stock selling at the same price. Overtrading must not be confused with overexpansion of the market. Overtrading applies to the individual and may occur in any individual case in any kind of market. Overexpansion usually refers to the market as a whole when there is great activity and stock prices are unusually high. At such times there is much unwarranted speculation and much overtrading by multitudes of persons.

An investor is overtrading whenever he buys or sells short such an amount of stock that his easily available reserve funds are not sufficient to carry the stock through any contingency that might arise without seriously impairing the customary business activity and the standard of living of the buyer or seller.

One of the first principles that should govern the trader is: Do not overtrade. Violation of this principle has probably been the cause, directly or indirectly, of more and heavier losses than any other type of bad judgment used on the market. As soon as anyone gets into the clutches of the "get rich quick" demon, he is subject to the psychology of the plunger and can save himself from disaster only with the greatest effort.

Gradually men who intend to be conservative become less and less prudent. Seldom do they limit their initial loss by studying the situation before making a commitment, as they would study any other business proposition. No one expects to succeed in any other business except by hard work and careful study. Why should one expect to succeed in the field of investment and speculation without the same diligence and care? The psychological effect of margin trading is interesting. The margin trader is especially likely to overstay the market after a rise, because another point and another and another mean so much on his investment. He hangs on, taking a chance on further and further rises because they would pay such large returns. After the tide has turned and the decline is under way, again he hangs on, hoping for a rally in the market. Finally he sells out, but long after the proper time.

15 short sales

The Securities and Exchange Commission has defined a short sale as "any sale of a security which the seller does not own or any sale which is consummated by the delivery of a security borrowed by, or for the account of, the seller." Professor G. Wright Hoffman defines short selling more simply "as the practice of selling borrowed property."[1] Thus, if a trader sells 100 shares of stock that he does not own and makes delivery with a borrowed certificate, the transaction is a short sale.

Sometimes it becomes desirable to sell a security which one does own but which one is temporarily unable to deliver because the certificate is in transit, or is held as collateral for a loan, or is unattainable at the moment for some other reason. Under such circumstances a shareowner may proceed to sell his stock and to effect delivery with a borrowed certificate. If he does this, he is legally and technically short, for he has delivered borrowed property to the seller. However, since he owned what he sold and so will be able to clear the transaction without making a purchase, he is not actually short of the issue. The Commission recognizes this distinction between a *real* and a *technical* short sale by providing that its regulations on short sales do "not apply to any sale by any person, if such a person owns the security sold and intends to deliver such security as soon as is possible without undue inconvenience or expense."

Types of Short Selling

Much of the popular criticism of short selling prevalent in the early 1930s was ineffective because it failed to distinguish between real and technical short sales. For example, a reformer declaims, "Short selling is evil because the seller is disposing of the property of other people. The practice should be abolished." To evade the issue and discredit his critic, the stock market apologist would merely ask, "And how will the odd-lot dealer continue to perform his function without short selling?" Unless the reformer knew, as is doubtful, how and why an odd-lot dealer sells short, he would lose his argument by default. It is necessary to recognize

[1] *The Security Markets,* New York: Twentieth Century Fund, Inc., 1935, p. 359.

that there are a number of reasons for selling short, only a few of which are related to speculative anticipations.

Short Selling by the Specialist.   Chapter 11 explains that one of the major functions of the specialist is to maintain a fair and orderly market and that, as part of this function, the specialist buys and sells for his own account to offset temporary disequilibriums between supply and demand. If a sudden rush of buy orders reaches the floor, the specialist is expected to sell stock from his own account in order to maintain a continuous market with price continuity. If he does not own any of the stock himself at that particular time, he sells short, hoping to rebuy later when sell orders reach the floor. Such a short sale is for technical rather than speculative reasons and serves to improve the market.

Odd-lot Short Selling.   At times odd-lot dealers find it necessary to be short of an issue by a fraction of a round lot. As is explained elsewhere, the odd-lot dealer purchases 1- to 99-share blocks of stock from small traders and disposes of them in full lots on the floor of the Exchange. Suppose that a dealer has purchased 85 shares of an issue from traders. Since he cannot sell less than a round lot on the floor of the Exchange, he must decide between continuing to hold 85 shares, which he does not want and which will cause him to lose if a decline in price occurs, or selling a full lot and assuming a net short position on 15 shares. In the latter case he will lose if the market rises. Obviously, if the market is bullish at the moment, he will decide to hold the 85 shares, and if it is bearish, he will go short the 15 shares. In either case he is merely choosing the lesser of two evils since the ideal course from his point of view would be to be neither short nor long.

It is apparent, therefore, that the short sales of an odd-lot dealer are a special type of short sale exempt from the criticism that might be entirely applicable to short sales for speculative purposes. The Securities and Exchange Commission shares this opinion. In fact, it has ruled that its regulations of short selling do *not* apply to "any sale by an odd-lot dealer to liquidate a long position which is less than a round lot, providing such sale does not change the position of such odd-lot dealer by more than the unit of trading."

Selling against the Box.   Another type of technical short selling is known as "selling against the box." In this instance the seller sells shares that he owns but, rather than deliver his own shares (which are presumed to be held in his safe deposit box), he accomplishes delivery with borrowed certificates. Occasionally this is done when the seller cannot obtain his securities from his safe deposit box in time to deliver them to his broker, but selling against the box is more frequently thought of these days as a device to preserve the amount of a capital gain without realizing it for tax purposes until the following year. Suppose that an investor owns 100 shares of a stock purchased originally at $20 per share and now selling for $40 per share. It is now October, and he is of the opinion that the stock will soon drop in price, and so he wants to take his profit. But for tax purposes he would prefer to take the profit in the next year. Both objectives can be accomplished by selling short against the box in October and covering in January with delivery of the shares already owned. The short sale preserves the amount of profit, for additional profit or loss from changes in the stock price after October will be exactly offset by profit or loss on the short sale. Yet for tax purposes the profit will be realized in the year in which the short sale is covered by delivery of the shares held long.

Short Selling for Arbitrage Purposes.   Short selling enables traders to arbitrage in securities listed on more than one exchange. If the supply of an issue happens to be excessive relative to demand on the Pacific Coast Stock Exchange at a time when the demand for the issue in New York is excessive relative to the supply, arbitragers will sell short in New York and go long in San Francisco or Los Angeles. Here again is a situation in which the trader's account in New York is only technically short since he actually owns the shares he has sold. However, the location of the certificates in California will make it necessary for him to deliver a borrowed certificate in New York. He may then deliver the shares purchased in California to the person in New York who loaned him the certificate for delivery, or, what is more likely, he may sell his California stock and cover his short position in New York by a purchase. In either event, his activity has the effect of matching the total demand for an issue against the total supply of it and so makes for a more nearly ideal market.

Arbitrage transactions also take place in internationally traded securities between various stock exchanges in different countries.

Hedging.   Perhaps an investor owns a large number of shares of stock in a company of which he is an officer, a director, or a controlling stockholder. This investor is of the opinion that the stock market in general is too high and will soon drop, but he hesitates to sell his own stock (which he expects to drop with the market), possibly because he wants to retain voting control of the company or because he would have to make a public report of his sales to the SEC, which would be taken as indicating a lack of confidence in his own company. He may hedge against the expected drop in the price of his stock by selling short the stock of other companies which he anticipates will perform marketwise about the same as the stock of his own company. What he loses in a decline of his own stock will then be approximately offset by the profits on the short sale of the similar stock.

Speculative Short Selling.   Speculative short selling involves (1) selling shares one does not own, (2) making delivery with borrowed stock, (3) purchasing the shares later at a lower price, and (4) returning the shares purchased to the lender. It is this type of short selling which most persons criticize and have in mind when they refer to short selling.

Who Sells Short?   Contrary to the opinion often held, most short selling is done by members of the Exchange rather than by the public. The 1963 *Report of Special Study of Securities Markets* provided statistics on the ratio of short sales by class of seller to total short sales for each month from January 1954 to July 1962.[2] These data, summarized below, show that on the average three fourths of all short sales were by members of the Exchange, with specialists alone accounting for over half. Motives for short sellings cannot be matched directly with each of the parties, for certainly members and nonmembers alike are involved in both speculative and technical short selling. It seems reasonable to conclude, however, that a fairly high proportion of total short sales are for technical rather than speculative reasons.

TABLE 11   Ratio of Short Sales by Type of Seller to Total Short Sales January 1957 to July 1962*

	Monthly average, %	Highest month, %	Lowest month, %
Specialists	54.4	68.9	31.7
Floor traders	5.6	10.8	1.6
Members off floor	16.5	25.2	9.1
Nonmembers	24.2	45.2	10.1

* Short sales by odd-lot dealers were not included in the data because such sales are exempt from the rules restricting short sales to plus-tick and zero-plus-tick transactions.

The Short Sale Transaction Step by Step

Suppose that Mr. Saxe is trading through an inland branch of Jones & Company, members of the New York Stock Exchange, that he keeps his account in good condition, and that it is profitable to the broker. Saxe decides that for many good reasons Anaconda Copper is too high at 48, the present market price. He calls up his broker and gives his order to sell 100 shares Anaconda Copper short at 48, G.T.C. The order is at once transmitted to the New York office, where it is relayed by telephone to the firm's telephone clerk at the Exchange, who signals for his broker on the floor by means of the annunciator. Noting the signal, the broker hurries to the telephone booth,

[2] *Report of Special Study of Securities Markets of the Securities and Exchange Commission,* 88th Cong., 1st Sess., House Document 95, 1963, part 2, pages 421–423 (hereafter referred to as *Special Study*).

where he receives the order. On reaching the post where Anaconda Copper is traded, he finds the stock bid 47, ask $47\frac{1}{2}$, whereupon he hands the order to a specialist for execution. The next day Anaconda Copper reaches 48, and Saxe's order is executed. The specialist makes a note of the sale and sends it by pneumatic tube from his post to the firm's telephone booth. The clerk calls his office, where the report of the sale is transmitted by private wire to the branch office. The next day Saxe gets through the mail a confirmation of his telephone order and also an advice of the sale, giving the number of shares sold, price, tax, commission, and the final credit to his account.

Margin Requirements.   Margin requirements are the same as in a purchase on margin. If Saxe sold 100 shares of Anaconda Copper short at 48, his broker must deliver the stock, which he does by borrowing the needed shares. If the market price should go up instead of down as expected, Saxe would take a loss. To protect himself against the possibility that Saxe could not make up the loss, which would then fall on the broker, the broker requires Saxe to deposit a certain amount of equity in the account at the time of the short sale. At the present writing margin requirements are 70 per cent; so Saxe would have to deposit additional equity of 70 per cent of $4,800, or $3,360. The New York Stock Exchange imposes its own maintenance margin requirements on short sales. They are $5 per share or 30 per cent of the market value (whichever is greater) for each stock short in the account selling at $5 per share or above, or $2.50 per share or 100 per cent of market value (whichever is greater) for each stock short in the account selling at less than $5 per share.

Stock Is Borrowed by the Broker.   Unless otherwise specified, the stock which is sold short must be delivered regular way, i.e., not later than noon on the fourth full business day following the date of sale. Since the customer has no stock, he must either buy it sometime within the day or have his broker borrow it for delivery. If Jones & Company sold Anaconda Copper for Saxe at 48 in the morning and it went down to 44 before the closing hour, Saxe might well decide to take his profits by ordering his broker to buy 100 shares at the market. If the stock is bought, Jones & Company will not need to borrow the stock, for the purchase of 100 shares will cover the sale of the same amount.

Usually, however, the short seller cannot realize a satisfactory profit so soon but must wait days and perhaps weeks before the price of the security of which he is short declines sufficiently to yield the desired profit. In this case the broker customarily borrows the stock required from someone who holds shares of the same issue of stock and is willing to lend them.

Stock may be borrowed from the margin accounts of the brokerage firm's other customers, the latter having agreed to make their stock available for lending at the time when they opened margin accounts. The stock may also be borrowed from the broker's own holdings or from other brokerage firms. Infrequently, as when a scarcity develops, securities may be borrowed from large institutional investors.

Conditions of Borrowing.   Brokers are very willing to lend stock because of the favorable conditions under which such loans are made. If the broker goes to his bank and puts up stock as collateral for a loan, he gets no more than the loan value established by the Board of Governors of the Federal Reserve System. However, if he lends the stock, he receives what amounts to an interest-free loan equal to 100 per cent of the value of the securities. This will be explained subsequently.

The conditions of a stock loan between brokers are usually as follows:

1. The lending broker receives at the time of delivery the full market price in cash.

2. Both the stock and the cash are held on a basis similar to a call loan, whereby the lender can at any time on reasonable notice call for his stock by paying back the money he holds and, on the other hand, the borrower can on reasonable notice demand his money back on delivery of the borrowed stock.

3. If the market price of the borrowed stock goes up, the borrower must deliver additional cash so that the lender always holds the full market value of his stock in cash. If the market price falls, then the borrower of the stock can demand that the lender return that part of the cash which he holds over and above the market value of the stock. Making these adjustments is called "marking to the market." The details are handled through the Stock Clearing Corporation.

4. In most cases stock is loaned "flat," which means that no compensation is paid to the lender of the shares and no interest is paid to the borrower of the shares (who is in effect lending cash). In times past, when interest rates were high and demand for collateral loans by brokers was heavy, securities were loaned "at a rate." Then the lender of the securities (who was borrowing cash) paid interest to the borrower of the securities (who was loaning cash) in the same way as a borrower of cash at a bank pays interest even though he pledges securities as collateral. The rate paid usually approximated the call loan rate and was paid for every calendar day that the loan was outstanding.

Occasionally stock is loaned "at a premium." If too many traders have the idea that a particular stock is selling too high and sell it short in large amounts, a tremendous demand for stock to borrow arises. If this demand is great enough, stock lenders make their shares available to those borrowers who offer to pay the highest premium. Premiums may also result from a "short squeeze"—a situation in which stock lenders suddenly demand a return of their shares and short sellers are sent scurrying to find shares to borrow. Premiums for borrowing shares are quoted as daily charges for borrowing 100 shares and according to the rules of the New York Stock Exchange must be in one of the following denominations: $1, $2, $3, $6, $10, $15, $20, and up in multiples of $10. These amounts are paid for each business day for which a stock loan is outstanding. Thus a short seller of 100 shares of a $10 stock loaning at a premium of $1 per day would be paying interest at a rate of 25 per cent per annum if there are 250 business days in the year.

A loan of stock can be viewed from two diametrically opposite positions. The transaction may be viewed as a stock borrower borrowing shares and depositing cash to secure his loan. From this angle the transaction is a favor to the stock borrower. But the transaction may also be viewed as a lender of stock borrowing cash and depositing shares as collateral. From this angle the transaction is a favor to the stock lender. Whether the stock borrower pays a premium to the stock lender, or the stock lender pays interest to the stock borrower, or the exchange of cash and stock is made without compensation depends upon the aggregate need for borrowed stock relative to the aggregate supply of lendable shares at the moment of the transaction.

5. The borrower of the stock, i.e., Jones & Company in our earlier example, must pay to the lender all cash and stock dividends declared and all rights issued within the time the stock is borrowed. Since Jones & Company has delivered the borrowed stock to the buyer, who has had the stock transferred to his name or whose broker has had it put in his own name, no dividends or rights come to Jones & Company. On its side, it charges Saxe's account for the amount of the cash dividend or the value of the stock dividend and rights and pays such amounts to the lender of the stock. The market compensates Saxe by a reduction in the price of the stock equal to the dividend.

"The Bull Pays Interest, but the Bear Does Not."   On all purchases of stock on margin the broker must furnish such funds for payment of the stock as are not provided by the margin. For these funds the buyer (a bull because he anticipates a rise in stock prices) must pay interest to his broker for the time he remains long in the stock. If the bull on the market finances his own transaction by borrowing at his bank, he expects to pay interest there. A short seller (a bear because he anticipates a drop in price) need pay no interest. When his broker delivers the stock which has been sold, he delivers the proceeds of the sale to the broker who loaned him the stock. In other words, the broker of the short seller does not furnish any of his own funds in handling a short sale and therefore charges his customer no interest. The short seller must reimburse his broker for all dividends and rights paid by his broker to the lender of the stock. If no dividends or rights are declared before the short sale is covered, there are no such charges.

Limitations on the Right to Sell Short

The Securities and Exchange Commission has adopted a set of rules designed to limit short selling in a declining market and thus prevent short selling from depressing prices further. Before these rules were in force, it was not uncommon for "bear raids" to occur. A group of speculators would sell short a large number of shares of a particular stock. Their selling activity would force prices down and panic uninformed investors into selling shares in the belief that the market was dropping for fundamental reasons. The speculators would then cover their short position at the lower prices and make a profit.

The first regulations of the SEC, effective February 8, 1938, required all sell orders to be marked "long" or "short" and permitted the execution of a short sale only at a price higher than the last price. If a stock sold at $48\frac{1}{2}$, $48\frac{5}{8}$, and $48\frac{3}{4}$, only one short sale could be executed at $48\frac{3}{4}$; additional short sales could be executed only at successively rising prices.

Apparently this regulation was too restrictive, for on March 10, 1939, the Commission changed the rule to its present form, which permits a short sale at the *same* price as the last sale, provided that the last sale price was higher than the last different price that preceded it. If a stock now sells at $48\frac{1}{2}$, $48\frac{5}{8}$, and $48\frac{5}{8}$, any number of additional short sales may be executed at $48\frac{5}{8}$.

In a declining market, however, the last *different* price preceding the last price will be higher than the last one. Consequently, short sales can occur only at prices higher than the last price, or, in other words, only if the market should cease declining and turn upward. Thus, if the price movement had been $48\frac{1}{2}$, $48\frac{3}{8}$, and $48\frac{3}{8}$, a short sale could be effected only at $48\frac{1}{2}$.

Implementation of the rules on short selling has led to the definition of various types of "ticks," which express the state of the market in each stock.

1. A "plus tick" indicates that the sale was at a price above the previous sale.
2. A "minus tick" indicates that the sale was at a price below the previous sale.
3. A "zero-plus tick" indicates that the sale was at the same price as the previous sale but above the last different sale price.
4. A "zero-minus tick" indicates that the sale was at the same price as the previous sale but below the last different sale price.

Short sales must be plus-tick or zero-plus-tick sales.

Certain types of short sales are exempt from the general rule that short sales may be made only on a plus tick or zero-plus tick. These include:

1. Any sale by a person who owns the security sold and intends to deliver the security as soon as possible without undue inconvenience or expense.
2. Any sale by an odd-lot dealer to offset odd-lot orders of customers.
3. Any sale by an odd-lot dealer to liquidate a long position which is less than a round lot, provided that such sale does not change the position of the odd-lot dealer by more than the unit of trading.
4. Certain sales on a national exchange made for the purpose of equalizing the price on that exchange with the current price on another national exchange which is the principal market for the security.
5. Certain types of arbitrage sales between equivalent securities or between international markets.

These types of sales are market "short exempt" when they are sent to the floor for execution.

Some Practical Points for the Short Seller

A short seller should take the same care to study an issue as he would if he were going to buy it. A purely speculative stock entails even more risk on the short side than on the long side. In a long transaction the loss cannot exceed 100 per cent of the funds committed, but in a short transaction the loss can amount to many times the amount of the commitment—in theory the loss can go on to infinity.

A short seller should not sell short when the market is oversold already. When everyone is bearish and the atmosphere is full of pessimism is no time to sell short unless one has special information unknown as yet to the general public.

One should not sell stock short unless there is a large supply of shares available for borrowing. If there is difficulty in borrowing, either the amount available for loans is small or the amount wanted is very large. In the first case the stock is in the hands of investors, and its price is not likely to decline much; in the second case there are many shorts, and the market is in a position for a rally rather than a decline.

One should seldom sell short after prices have had a long, rapid decline. At such times the market is about due for a rally of from a third to a half of its recent decline.

If one is short a stock that makes a rapid rally while other similar stocks stand still, it is likely that the issue is being manipulated to catch shorts. Unless one's short position is well margined at such times, it might be advisable to take one's losses and avoid being "squeezed" or "cornered." When stock for loaning purposes is very scarce, a squeeze, if not a corner, is always to be guarded against. A corner exists when a stock can no longer be borrowed and lenders are demanding the return of shares previously loaned. In such a situation the short seller has no choice but to go into the market and buy shares at whatever price those who hold the shares demand.

A short seller should never go against the trend. A market that is moving upward has occasional reactions of many points. The bear, by selling short just before one of these reactions and covering just before it stops, can make good profits, but the chances favor his getting caught. In a bull market the averages are weighted against the short seller, just as in a bear market they are weighted in his favor.

The question is frequently asked: How long may a short seller remain short? A short seller may remain short for as long as his broker can find someone who will lend the stock required. Suppose that Saxe, in our illustration, decides not to cover his short position because he thinks the market price will decline further; but Ryerson, from whom the stock was borrowed, calls his stock. Saxe's broker must now return the borrowed shares to Ryerson. The broker may borrow shares from Hamill for delivery to Ryerson. If later Hamill calls for his stock, the broker will borrow from Spencer to deliver to Hamill. It is evident that, as long as stock can be borrowed, Saxe need not cover his short sale, provided, to be sure, that he keeps his credit standing good with his broker by maintaining a satisfactory margin.

The Economic Function of the Short Sale

At one time there was much opposition to selling short on the stock market. It was argued by some that one could not legitimately sell what one did not own, and it was alleged that the only purpose anyone could have in a short sale was to depress the market and to destroy the value of other people's property. It was considered akin to gambling, if not worse. During the bull markets of the 1950s and early 1960s criticism tended to diminish for the most part, although after major market drops—such as that which occurred in May 1962 or on the afternoon of President Kennedy's assassination— it revived.

Others strove to justify the practice of selling short by comparing it to the practice of "selling on order" in business. For example, when a tailor takes his customer's measurements and agrees to make a suit of clothes for $120 for delivery in ten days, he sells short since he sells something not yet in existence. When a magazine publisher accepts an order for a subscription to be delivered during the ensuing year, he too is selling short. Those who argued thus maintained that short selling is a common practice in daily business affairs.

Thus far in this chapter we have been interested in the mechanism of the short sale as a means of private profit. We shall now outline the broader aspects as they affect the economic organization of society. In doing this we must be careful to distinguish between technical short selling and speculative short selling. Final judgment on the practice of short selling must depend upon the answers to the following three questions, each of which will be treated in turn. Is it morally right to sell borrowed property for personal gain? What advantages does the market as a whole gain from the ability of exchange members, investors, and/or speculators to sell short? Does speculative short selling have any adverse effect upon the stock market?

Moral Aspects.   Some say that short selling is bad because it is destructive rather than constructive in nature. They see no parallel between the practice of selling goods on order mentioned earlier and that of selling securities short. The tailor who sells a nonexisting suit does so as a preliminary to producing one. Thus the contract he makes is productive in nature. The trader who sells securities short, however, does not plan to produce anything. Rather he hopes that his short selling activity will contribute to the destruction of the value of property already in existence.

This view of short selling has a special appeal to those who are inclined to view a "good market" as one in which values are ever on the increase. Such a viewpoint is a mistake, however. From the social point of view, a good market is one in which shareowners who no longer want their shares can dispose of them to those who wish to acquire them at fair prices and without undue inconvenience and delay. A fair price is the price that would result if real buyers and real sellers who were well informed could congregate together and negotiate a price by competitive bidding. Any speculative activity that aids in the accomplishment of this purpose is economically beneficial; and vice versa, any speculative activity that acts as an obstacle to the accomplishment of this situation is economically detrimental.[3]

How Short Selling May Aid the Market.   The ability to sell stocks short helps create a good market in a number of ways.

1. Short selling is a factor in keeping market price close to real value. The bear looks ahead and foresees future disturbing events. Long before the public knows of the eventuality or is able to interpret its meaning, the bear has been selling in the market and so gradually reducing the price to a level warranted by the facts. When the event actually occurs and the public rushes to sell, the short seller begins to cover, thus supporting the market from breaking severely. The only difference between the long side and the short side is that the longs discount favorable events and when the public rushes in are in a position to sell and take their profits, at the same time stabilizing the price. Both types of operators are needed, each offsetting the other and investors in general.

Again, the longs may misjudge events, interpreting them too optimistically so that the market price is pushed above intrinsic values. The bear is less influenced by optimism and acts as a check on the judgment of the other side of the market. Similarly the bull checks the judgment of the too

---

[3] Twentieth Century Fund, *op. cit.,* pp. 283–287.

pessimistically inclined bear. In both cases the market price is kept adjusted to intrinsic values.

2. Short sales make possible a continuous market. If a banker has a collateral loan on which the margin of collateral is near exhaustion, with no further collateral forthcoming, and he must sell to protect himself against a loss, where will he turn to find a buyer? After such a decline there would be in the market a large number of short sales remaining uncovered. With odd-lot dealers, specialists, floor traders, and a fair number of commission brokers' customers short, there would be an enormous potential buying power just beneath the present market ready to assimilate offerings. Here would be the banker's market. The many longs have lost money and are in no mood to buy. Such longs as have liquidated are playing safe and are awaiting further declines in an uncertain market. In the same uncertain market the bear also is inclined to play safe, but this means to buy. Even if the market were almost sure to decline further, some one of the great numbers of shorts would be timid and not wait for further possible profits. The bear thus is, without question, a very potent factor in the maintenance of a continuous market and all that it means economically.

Registered traders and specialists are considered important in the making of a continuous market. Their methods of operation require the short sale as well as the purchase. A registered trader operates on very small margins and on occasion must reverse himself very quickly. If it were necessary for him always to buy before he dared sell, his freedom in the market would be greatly curtailed and he would be compelled to give up his business as a registered trader. With the short sale as one of his tools, he is able to buy and sell at all times.

The specialist stands at his post making bids and offers on his stocks, some active, others inactive. A broker approaches him and asks the market on, say, U.S. Steel. He says, "65 to 65$\frac{1}{8}$." The broker buys 500 shares at 65$\frac{1}{8}$. Does the specialist have this stock on hand? Perhaps so, but quite probably he does not, so he goes short. Assume that short selling is prohibited; the difficult and limited situation of the specialist is at once apparent. This is especially true of inactive stocks, for a specialist would in all probability not hold such stocks for sale. It is his business to maintain a continuous market, and to accomplish this end he must be permitted to sell short. The short sale enables the registered trader and the specialist to operate freely and contributes to the continuity of the market.

3. The short sale makes the best securities available to the small investor. The small investor or trader, in order to get proper diversification, often cannot buy in full lots because of lack of funds. He must buy in less than 100-share lots or take a much larger risk. As we know by this time, it is the odd-lot dealer who makes possible the realization of the aims of the small investor, i.e., the great middle class of businessmen, professional men, farmers, and laborers. But the business of the odd-lot dealer would be

impossible without the short sale. The odd-lot dealer stands ready to buy or sell any number of shares from 1 to 99 at $\frac{1}{8}$ to $\frac{1}{4}$ point from the price that rich men pay for their stock and with the same promptness and care that rich men receive. Now, to make this possible, the odd-lot dealer must often go short. An odd-lot dealer gets an order for 25 shares of Kennecott Copper, at the market. But he cannot carry every kind of stock to supply every want, and the only way to supply the Kennecott Copper is to sell it to the commission broker who gave the order and later to buy it to cover the short commitment. Moreover, the odd-lot dealer can operate at so small a margin only on condition that he is free to take advantage of every phase of the market on both the long and the short side. Otherwise his risk would be much greater, and he would consequently have to operate at a much larger margin than the $\frac{1}{8}$ or $\frac{1}{4}$ which he now reserves to himself. Short sales, by thus making possible the efficient operation of odd-lot dealers, give the middle classes access to the security market on the same terms as the well-to-do classes, with but a small difference in the market price.

4. The short sale encourages a national and international market. A holder of securities in a Western city can call up his broker and sell at any time. The New York office of the brokerage firm with which he does business will borrow the stock and make delivery the regular way, awaiting the arrival of the securities properly endorsed. (Such a sale, although exempt from SEC rules on short sales, is in fact a type of short sale.) An investor remote from a market is willing to put a larger percentage of his funds into securities and to pay a higher price for them because he can sell the securities he possesses in a moment's time. These facilities for the immediate sale of securities increase their collateral value. The banker accepts readily and at high percentage of their value the securities of his customer as collateral for loans, because he can always sell out without delay if his security becomes doubtful. The same thing is true of the international as of the domestic investor. He can sell his securities, and his broker borrows the stock until the arrival of the securities involved from some distant point. The broad economic effects of a wide market thus facilitated by the short sale touch all phases of business, credit, investment, and speculation.

A second way in which the short sale encourages a national and international market lies in the fact that it facilitates arbitrage in stocks between markets in different parts of the country and of the world. If the price of New York Central stock is 17 in New York and $17\frac{1}{2}$ in Chicago, a trader in New York may sell short in Chicago at the same time that he buys in New York. The difference is his profit. If London is substituted for Chicago, the trader sells short in London and buys in New York. These transactions eliminate much of the risk and equalize prices in the leading markets of the world. Moreover, the market will become more stable and continuous since many competing trading interests can make themselves felt in all the cities and markets.

5. The short sale makes possible the protection against loss afforded by hedging. The short sale can be used as a hedge against loss in various situations. Assume that a trader is long on a given stock which at the present price nets him fair profit and that he thinks the market will go higher. The market, however, becomes mixed so that the trend is no longer evident. The trader now sells short stock of somewhat similar market position so that if the market drops he will gain as much on his short stock as he loses on his long holdings. Perhaps the confused condition of the market will soon clear up so that the trend again becomes reasonably obvious. Then he can either sell his long stock and let the short sale run into profits or cover his short sale and let the long positions stand intact, depending on the trend.

6. There are other advantages in the short sale. The short sale makes possible trading in the stock of a company before it is issued. Such trading is done on a when-issued basis. A market is thus created which formulates the opinions of traders as to the merits and reasonable price of a stock before the stock is available.

Again, if directors declare a stock dividend payable at a given date a month or more in the future, the stockholder may realize on the dividend immediately by selling short the number of shares to which the dividend entitles him. When the shares are issued, he can deliver to the buyer. A stockholder may want to realize on his dividend immediately because he needs the funds or because he thinks the market is in a better position than it will be when the shares are issued.

Possibly the capital stock of the company is being expanded, and "rights" to subscribe are issued to present stockholders at a price below the market. These rights have a value and can be sold when issued. A stockholder may think the price of his stock is higher now than it will be later and may sell short the number of shares for which his rights give him a reduced price, expecting to use his rights to buy the new stock from his company and deliver them when they are issued. In the first case the stockholder sells his rights short and delivers when the warrants are issued; in the second case he sells stock short and uses his warrants when they are issued to buy the new stock of the company for delivery. The first transaction does not fully conform to all the conventional steps in a short sale, but practically it amounts to the same thing; the second transaction includes all the conventional operations of borrowing stock.

7. The short sale is an important factor in keeping the price of convertible securities in proper relation to the price of the stocks into which they are convertible. If a bond is convertible into a stock at 110 and the stock sells at 120, the convertible bond should sell at a given ratio to 120. When the stock sells above the price at which it should sell relative to the price of the bond, the stock can be sold short and bonds bought, converted

into stock, and delivered. The effect is a demand for bonds and a supply of stock, with an evening up of prices. This process will continue until the prices of the two securities have settled approximately into the relationship specified in the certificate of the convertible security. The bondholder thus sees his bonds increase in value relative to stock without the necessity of conversion to the junior issue.

Adverse Effects of Speculative Short Selling.   A good market is defined above as one in which real sellers are able to dispose of their shares to real buyers at fair prices without undue inconvenience and delay. When the buyers arrive in the market before the sellers, short sellers perform a valuable function by acting as substitutes for sellers who later will arrive *voluntarily*. However, when short selling becomes excessive in amount, it creates and brings to the market a horde of involuntary selling which may cause the price to decline far below the fair price of a good market. Thus the proper function of the short seller is to *anticipate* selling, not to *induce* it.

Induced Selling.   The detrimental effect that excessive short selling may have on the market at times can be made clearer by an example. Let us assume that the voluntary bids and offers of buyers and sellers of a given issue on a given day, if they arrived in the market simultaneously, would result in a price of 48. Let us assume, however, that on this day the buying orders tended to arrive in the market several hours in advance of the selling orders and that during this interval speculators made short sale contracts with the buyers. The closing of a deal on the floor of the Exchange removes a bid from existence. Thus in our example it would be possible for short sellers to clear the market entirely of all real bids prior to the arrival of the real sellers. If so, they could then substitute their own bids at lower prices for the bids to buy at 48 that they had previously removed. Suppose that short sellers bid 41 and that the real sellers were forced to accept their bids in the absence of higher ones. The execution of transactions at a level of 41 would have one of two results: (1) it might attract other bidders to the market and so cause the price to bound upward, or (2) it might bring liquidation selling into the market and cause further declines. In the latter event, some of those who eagerly acquired the stock at a price of 48 a few hours earlier might now be panicked into disposing of it at, say, 38.

Though we began with the assumption that both buyer and seller would have agreed on a fair price of 48, we end with a situation in which sellers got less than this price, buyers bought at the price but were forced to resell at a loss, short sellers made a profit, and the ownership of the shares in question passed to those whose bids in the first instance were so low as not to be entitled to any consideration. Such a market could scarcely be called ideal.

Thirty years ago the above example would have been considered fantastic, overdrawn, and entirely impractical. Today we know that it is an accurate description of what sometimes occurs.

Short Selling during Market Breaks.   The major purpose of the SEC's rule that short sales may be made only at a price above the last different sales price is to prevent short sellers from depressing the market by their selling pressure. While this rule may work well during times of normal trading and has apparently eliminated the deliberate bear raids of an earlier era, the SEC *Special Study* has found evidence that short selling in times of crisis often aggravates the decline in spite of the SEC rule.[4]

In its study of the market break of May 1962, the *Special Study* found that even during that sharp decline there were a large number of plus ticks, which enabled short sellers to enter the market. Because of the large numbers of short sell orders awaiting execution, every plus tick brought forth substantial selling pressure which, in turn, made it substantially harder for buy orders to push up the market.[5]

Short Selling during Market Cycles.   To constitute a stabilizing influence upon the market, short selling should increase in volume as prices rise and decrease as prices fall or approach the bottom. As explained earlier, the classical argument is that when the market gets too high short sellers sell in anticipation of a subsequent drop. Their sales create additional downward pressure on the market. When the market is too low, the classical theory holds that short sellers cover, thereby creating additional upward pressure. This theory is based on the assumption that actual or potential short sellers are able to diagnose accurately the relative level of the market.

Doubt has been cast on this hypothesis in recent years by statistical evidence that short sellers tend to be on the wrong side of market cycles more often than on the right side. The *Special Study* compared the ratio of short sales to total sales volume on the New York Stock Exchange with the level of stock prices from January 1954 through mid-1962 and found grounds to doubt the classical argument that short selling is a stabilizing force. The *Special Study* also found that short selling by nonmembers who

---

[4] *Special Study,* part 2, p. 288.

[5] *Ibid.,* pp. 288–289, this testimony of one specialist was reported:

Q. During the break in May did you feel any pressure from short selling at all?

A. There was a great deal of short selling; there can't be too much pressure because we can only sell on plus ticks.

Q. Did you . . . ?

A. They certainly lengthen the time that it took a stock to go up, probably.

Q. In other words, when you had an up tick. . . .

A. There had to be substantially more buyers to move the stock up because of the heaviness of the sell orders . . . the short orders, excuse me.

Q. So that when there was an up tick, there would be short selling. . . .

A. Right.

Q. That would take place.

A. Right. Not in every stock, just certain ones.

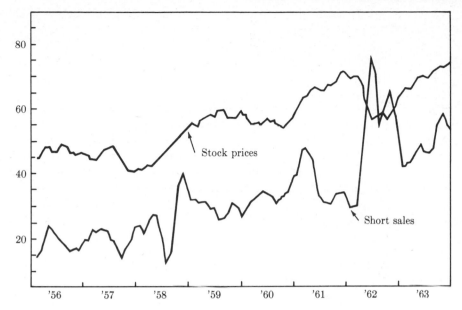

Fig. 15–1 Short sales in relation to common stock prices.

were presumed to be primarily speculators tended to increase during sharp market declines.[6]

The relationship between total short sales, expressed in terms of a three-month moving average, and Standard & Poor's composite price index for the period 1956 to 1963 is shown in Figure 15–1. When the market reached peaks in July 1957, the latter half of 1959, late 1961, and late 1963, the volume of short selling was at troughs rather than peaks. Short sellers as a group appear unable to determine when the market is at a cyclical peak and thus cannot be considered a value-correcting force at those times. When the market was at cyclical bottoms, as in late 1957 and the latter half of 1962, classical theory holds that short sales should have been low. Yet in fact these dates were periods of peak short-selling activity.

The fact that short sales are not value-correcting is well illustrated in the market rise that began in August 1960 and extended to December 1961. At first, as the market rose, short sales also rose. However, starting in March 1961, as the market passed into the top half of its cycle, the volume of short selling fell off rapidly. When the market finally reached a peak in December 1961, short selling was very low. Apparently the idea that short selling tends to diminish the magnitude of stock market cycles is more fancy than fact, for the evidence indicates that short selling in general tends to be exactly the opposite of a corrective force.

[6] *Special Study,* part 2, pp. 271, 291, 421–423.

16 puts and calls

Options were first used in Holland in connection with the tulip business in 1634.[1] At this time there was much speculation in tulip bulbs. When a seller shipped bulbs, he frequently made a contract with another grower to buy so many bulbs at such and such a price at his option. Then, if his own shipment were lost in transit, he would replace the lost bulbs by exercising his privilege; if his shipment were delivered, he would allow his privilege to expire. Writing in 1694, John Houghton described the use of puts and calls in connection with dealings in securities in London. A hundred and fifty years ago dealings in puts and calls had reached a considerable volume in Berlin.[2] Today "option contracts" are known and used in all important security markets.

In the business world options are an everyday occurrence. For example, a promoter may plan the development of a subdivision. To do so, he must *own* a tract of land, and he must arrange for the construction of the houses. If he buys the land first, his negotiations for the construction may fail, leaving the land on his hands. On the other hand, if he negotiates for the construction first, he may find himself unable to buy the necessary land. To protect himself, he will make a contract with the landowner whereby, for a small fee, he has the right with certain time limits to take or to refuse to take the land at a specified price. If he decides not to exercise his privilege, he is out and the landowner is ahead by the amount of the fee. If he exercises his privilege, he simply adds the fee paid to the cost of acquiring the land.

Operators in the stock market use the same process to limit losses and insure gains. There are two basic types of privileges—the call and the put—and in addition four variations—the straddle, the spread, the strip, and the strap. Trading in these contracts is not allowed on the floor of the Exchange. Nevertheless, there is an active business in them off the floor.

[1] Herbert Filer, "The Role of Puts and Calls in Securities," *Financial and Commercial Chronicle,* vol. 171, Sept. 28, 1950, p. 4.
[2] *Put Option and Call Option Contracts,* 3d ed., Put and Call Brokers and Dealers Association, Inc., 1964, p. 1.

At present there are close to twenty-five brokers and dealers specializing in privileges in New York City. It is possible to obtain quotations for a put or a call for practically any of the active stocks listed on the Big Board and for some stocks listed on the American Stock Exchange. Most of the dealers doing business in privileges are members of the Put and Call Brokers and Dealers Association, with offices at 19 Rector Street, New York. The chief aims of this association are to foster high standards of integrity, to prevent any practices that tend to be unfair or inequitable, and to establish trade practices that will enable the members to serve better the persons with whom they deal. Members of the association are ordinarily permitted to deal only in the options guaranteed by members of the New York Stock Exchange.

In Europe the word "privileges" is used to designate what in America are called options. The word is derived from the fact that the holder of a put or call has the privilege, or choice, of whether or not to exercise his option.[3]

Types of Options

Call.   A call is a contract, negotiable in form, giving the purchaser or holder the privilege of purchasing from the maker, for a specified length of time, a given number of shares of a certain stock at a price fixed by the contract. In other words, the maker of a call contracts to deliver to the holder, at the holder's request, a definite number of shares of a given stock at a fixed price if the request is made within a certain period of time.

Put.   A put is a contract, negotiable in form, giving the purchaser or holder the privilege of delivering to the maker, within a specified length of time, a given number of shares of a certain stock at a price fixed by the contract. In other words, the maker of a put contracts to receive from the holder, at his request, a definite number of shares of a given stock at a fixed price if the request is made within a certain period of time.

Straddle.   A straddle is a contract that combines a put and a call into one option. A straddle gives the bearer the right to buy from and/or to sell to the maker a certain number of shares of stock at a specified price within a fixed period of time. To illustrate, a straddle written when U.S. Steel was selling at $70 per share would give the bearer the right to sell 100 shares at $70 per share and, in addition, the right to buy 100 shares at $70. The holder would profit if U.S. Steel either rose or fell by an amount sufficient to offset the costs of purchasing the straddle. If U.S. Steel proved to be unusually volatile during the lifetime of the straddle, the holder might profit on both sides. For example, if U.S. Steel first dropped below, say, $65 and

[3] *Ibid.*

then rose, say, to $75, the option holder might first buy 100 shares in the market at $65 to put them to the maker of the straddle at $70 and then later call upon the maker for 100 shares at $70 to resell in the market at $75.

Spread.   A spread is similar to a straddle except that the call portion is executable at a price that is higher than the price at which the put portion may be executed. If the market price of U.S. Steel were $70, a spread might provide for calling U.S. Steel at $74 and putting U.S. Steel at $66. As with the straddle, either side or both sides of the spread may be exercised during the lifetime of the option. In recent years the use of the spread has been almost completely replaced by the use of the straddle.

Strip.   A strip is a relatively new type of option which provides that the holder may sell 200 shares and/or buy 100 shares, all at the price fixed in the option. In other words, a strip is a triple option consisting of two separate puts and one separate call, all written at the same time, all expiring at the same date, and all exercisable at the same price.

Strap.   A strap is the reverse of a strip. It is two separate calls and one separate put, all combined in one option. Thus a strap is a triple option giving the holder the right to put 100 shares and/or call 200 shares of a stock, all at the indicated price. As with the strip, spread, and straddle, the exercise of one portion of the strap does not prevent the holder later on, during the life of the option, from exercising the other portion.

In 1961 the Securities and Exchange Commission published a report on put and call options containing valuable statistics not heretofore available. This report indicated that in June 1959 a total of 1,978 options were endorsed by member firms of the New York Stock Exchange.[4] The breakdown of these options by type was as follows:

	Number of options	Per cent of total
Calls	612	30.9
Puts	344	17.4
Straddles (including spreads)	984	49.7
Strips	24	1.2
Straps	14	0.7
Total	1,978	100.0

The year 1959 ended a decade of almost continuously rising prices, and, as would be expected in such a market, calls were more in demand than puts. This relation is normal, perhaps because investors in general are

[4] *Report on Put and Call Options,* Securities and Exchange Commission, Division of Trading and Exchanges, August 1961, p. 33.

optimistic about the long-term growth characteristics of the economy and its economic units. The greater demand for calls than puts under normal market conditions is reflected in the fact that calls are normally more expensive than puts when written on the same stock for the same maturity. When market conditions are such that stock prices are falling or are expected to fall, the number of puts sold may exceed the number of calls.

The SEC figures show that more straddles were written than puts and calls together. The figures are misleading, however, because straddles are frequently divided into two sections. The call section is sold as a separate call, while the put section is "converted" into a call by a process to be explained later. Data in the above table exclude options created by this conversion process.

Option Characteristics

Option Contract. Options are written on a standard form provided by the Put and Call Brokers and Dealers Association, Inc. The association sells forms only to its members, thus virtually guaranteeing that all option transactions are effected by its members. The association requires that all options be endorsed or guaranteed by a New York Stock Exchange member firm. This endorsement plus the use of a standard option form makes put and call options acceptable anywhere as a fully negotiable instrument.

The contract forms for a put and a call are shown in Figures 16–1 and 16–2.

Size of Option. Options are usually written for 100 shares, although it is possible to write options for larger amounts or, in rare instances, for amounts of stock less than 100 shares. Of the 1,978 options endorsed by member firms in June 1959, over 76 per cent were for 100 shares, and over

New York, N. Y. ____________ 19__

For Value Received, the BEARER may DELIVER to the endorser ONE HUNDRED (100) shares of the ____________
stock of the ____________
at ____________ Dollars ($______) per share
ANY TIME WITHIN ____________ days from date.

THIS STOCK OPTION CONTRACT MUST BE PRESENTED, AS SPECIFIED BELOW, TO THE ENDORSING FIRM BEFORE THE EXPIRATION OF THE EXACT TIME LIMIT. IT CANNOT BE EXERCISED BY TELEPHONE.

DURING THE LIFE OF THIS OPTION:
1. (a) — the contract price hereof shall be reduced by the value of any cash dividend on the day the stock goes ex-dividend; (b) — where the Option is entitled to rights and/or warrants the contract price shall be reduced by the value of same as fixed by the opening sale thereof on the day the stock sells ex-rights and/or warrants.
2. (a) — in the event of stock splits, reverse splits or other similar action by the above-mentioned corporation, this Option shall become an Option for the equivalent in new securities when duly listed for trading and the total contract price shall not be reduced; (b) — stock dividends or the equivalent due-bills shall be attached to the stock covered hereby, when and if this Option is exercised, and the total contract price shall not be reduced.

Upon presentation to the endorser of this Option attached to a comparison ticket in the manner and time specified, the endorser agrees to accept notice of the Bearer's exercise by stamping the comparison, and this acknowledgment shall constitute a contract and shall be controlling with respect to delivery of the stock and settlement in accordance with New York Stock Exchange usage.

EXPIRES ____________ 19__
3:15 P. M.

The undersigned acts as intermediary only, without obligation other than to obtain a New York Stock Exchange firm as Endorser.

No. 418

PUT OPTION

Fig. 16–1 A put option.

New York, N. Y. ________________ 19__

For Value Received, the BEARER may CALL on the endorser for ONE HUNDRED (100) shares of the ________________

stock of the ________________________________

at ________________________________ Dollars ($________) per share

ANY TIME WITHIN ________________________________ days from date.

THIS STOCK OPTION CONTRACT MUST BE PRESENTED, AS SPECIFIED BELOW, TO THE ENDORSING FIRM BEFORE THE EXPIRATION OF THE EXACT TIME LIMIT. IT CANNOT BE EXERCISED BY TELEPHONE.

DURING THE LIFE OF THIS OPTION:

1. (a) — the contract price hereof shall be reduced by the value of any cash dividend on the day the stock goes ex-dividend; (b) — where the Option is entitled to rights and/or warrants the contract price shall be reduced by the value of same as fixed by the opening sale thereof on the day the stock sells ex-rights and/or warrants.

2. (a) — in the event of stock splits, reverse splits or other similar action by the above-mentioned corporation, this Option shall become an Option for the equivalent in new securities when duly listed for trading and the total contract price shall not be reduced; (b) — stock dividends or the equivalent due-bills shall be attached to the stock covered hereby, when and if this Option is exercised, and the total contract price shall not be reduced.

Upon presentation to the endorser of this Option attached to a comparison ticket in the manner and time specified, the endorser agrees to accept notice of the Bearer's exercise by stamping the comparison, and this acknowledgment shall constitute a contract and shall be controlling with respect to delivery of the stock and settlement in accordance with New York Stock Exchange usage.

EXPIRES ________________ 19____
3:15 P. M.

The undersigned acts as intermediary only, without obligation other than to obtain a New York Stock Exchange firm as Endorser.

No. 53

Copyr. 1957, Put and Call Brokers and Dealers Assn., Inc.

CALL OPTION

Fig. 16–2 A call option.

91 per cent were for 200 shares or fewer. The exact breakdown is given here.[5]

Size of option	Number of options	Per cent of total
100 shares	1,511*	76.4
200	293	14.8
300	66	3.3
400	23	1.2
500	41	2.1
600–900	23	1.2
1,000	16	0.8
1,100–1,900	3	0.2
2,000	1	Less than 0.1
Over 2,000	1†	Less than 0.1
Total	1,978	100.0

* Includes six straddles for 50 shares each.

† A put for 2,600 shares of Avco Manufacturing common at $11\frac{1}{2}$.

Length of Option. Options are normally written for periods of thirty days, sixty days, ninety days, or six months ten days. Occasionally options are written for one year or longer. In June 1959 the volume of outstanding puts and calls classified according to original length of option was as follows:[6]

[5] *Ibid.*, p. 33.

[6] *Ibid.*, p. 28.

Original length of option	Puts, %	Calls, %
30 days	0.4	0.7
60 days	5.3	4.7
90 days	14.3	14.7
6 months	64.2	65.8
1 year	15.0	12.8
Over 1 year	0.8	1.3
Total	100.0	100.0

Six-month options are by far the most popular type, followed in turn by ninety-day options and then by sixty-day options. Thirty-day options, the prevalent form many years ago, are now rather rare, as are options for one year or longer. Six-month options (six months and ten days in most cases) are popular because profits from such options may be converted into long-term capital gains, which are taxed at a lower income tax rate than are short-term (less than six-month) gains.

Exercise Price of an Option. At the present time most options are written to be exercised at the market price of the stock as of the date the option was written. This exercise price is sometimes called the "striking price." An exception is the spread, where by definition the exercise prices differ from each other and from the current market price. However, as mentioned earlier, spreads have lost their popularity in the years since World War II.

Prior to World War II, "differential options" were prevalent. In this form, the cost of the put or call was a fixed amount, $137.50 for a thirty-day option, for example, and the exercise price of the option was set at a number of points away from the market according to the stock involved and market conditions. The exercise price of the option rather than its cost was changed to adjust to supply and demand conditions.

When a cash dividend is paid on a share of stock, the exercise price of both put options and call options on that stock is reduced by the amount of cash payment on the day the stock is traded ex dividend. For example, a call option to buy 100 shares of XYZ at 40 would be reduced to a call to buy 100 shares at 39¾ on the date the XYZ goes ex dividend 25 cents.

Options are also adjusted in the case of stock splits or stock dividends. An option on 100 shares of a stock at $40 per share on which there is declared a 10 per cent stock dividend, for example, would become an option on 110 shares of stock at a total exercise price of $4,000. If there had been a 2-for-1 stock split, the option would be for the delivery or purchase of 200 shares at a total exercise price of $4,000.

When rights are offered to stockholders during the life of an option, the exercise price is reduced by the value of the right. The value of the right is determined to be the price at which rights first sell after the stock goes ex rights.

Option Premiums

The purchase price of an option is called a "premium." Premiums are conventionally quoted in $\frac{1}{8}$ point per share; thus 100-share options are sold at price intervals of $12.50.

Premiums range from a minimum of $137.50 upward, depending primarily upon supply and demand factors in the option market. The purchaser of a call option must also pay New York state and Federal stamp taxes in an amount equal to the taxes that would be paid on the sale of the stock in question in the market, but never exceeding $12 per 100-share call. No tax is charged on the sale of put options.

The amount of the premium charged for an option varies with many characteristics of the security. If the market is active, options increase in price, while in a slow market options cost less. Options on volatile stocks are higher priced than options on stable stocks. In rising markets calls are more in demand than puts and cost more. In declining markets puts increase in price as the demand for them increases.

In addition to the above general factors, an option premium varies with the length of the option and with the price of the underlying stock. The SEC found that the average premium on a thirty-day option was about one half of the premium on a six-month option, while a sixty-day option was about 56 per cent and a ninety-day option about 69 per cent of the premium on a six-month option.[7] The relation between length of an option and average premium cost is almost exactly such that each additional month in an option contract adds a fixed sum to the premium cost of the option. The additional premium per additional month is on the average equal to 20 per cent of the thirty-day premium or 10 per cent of the six-month premium.[8]

As would be expected, the premium cost of an option increases as the price of the underlying stock rises. The SEC found that premiums paid by

---

[7] *Ibid.,* p. 84.

[8] Data presented in the SEC *Report on Put and Call Options, ibid.,* p. 84, may be arranged to suggest a constant relationship between premium sizes for options of various durations such that, if the premium for a six-month option is known, the approximate premium for an option in the same stock for any other duration may be determined from the formula

$P = C(0.4 + 0.1D)$

where P = premium cost of option being considered

C = premium cost of six-month option

D = duration of option in months

Slight variations will exist, depending upon whether the option is a put, a call, or a straddle.

buyers of six-month calls amount to about 14 per cent of the value of the stock.[9] The percentage premium on low-priced stocks would probably run somewhat above this, and the percentage premium on high-priced stocks would probably run slightly below.

Premiums paid for the purchase of an option are divided among four parties: the writer, the put and call dealer, the buyer's broker, and the endorser. For the average call option purchased at the market in June 1959, the SEC found that the premium was divided as follows:[10]

Recipient	Portion of premium	Percentage of premium
Writer	$404.00	86
Put and call dealer	55.00	12
Buyer's broker	6.25	1
Endorser	6.25	1
Average premium	$472.00	100

These averages do not reflect the wide range of variation which occurs in practice among options traded at various prices.

Conversions

In the long bull market since the Korean conflict, buyers have sought call options more frequently than put options, with the result that the former have been higher priced. Writers of options usually prefer to write a straddle, for not only do they obtain a higher premium than for a put or a call alone, but they regard it unlikely that both sides of the contract will be exercised. This imbalance has been resolved by the practice of "converting" excess put options into additional call options. About two dozen New York Stock Exchange member firms are engaged in this practice.

The essence of conversion is as follows: An option dealer buys a straddle from a writer and resells the call portion on the market. He then takes the put portion to a conversion firm and asks that firm to exchange it for a call. The conversion firm (1) buys the put portion, (2) writes and sells to the option dealer a call on the same stock for the same time period and at the same exercise price, and (3) buys 100 shares of the stock on the market.

[9] *Report on Put and Call Options,* Securities and Exchange Commission, Division of Trading and Exchanges, August 1961, pp. 85–86.
[10] *Ibid.,* p. 88. The figures in the first column do not total correctly because they have been rounded off.

The conversion firm has now entered into a risk-free transaction on which it earns a rate of interest, normally about 1 per cent over the call loan rate, which is added to the sales price of the newly created call. From the point of view of the conversion firm, one of two things must happen: (1) If the newly created call is exercised, the conversion firm delivers the stock that it purchased in the market, receiving from the person exercising the call a sum of money equal to that which the firm paid for the stock on the market. If this occurs, the conversion firm breaks even on buying and selling the stock and it retains as profit the markup obtained when the new call was first sold. (2) If the call is not exercised, the conversion firm delivers the 100 shares purchased against the put which it still holds, again breaking even on the buying and selling of the stock and retaining the premium charged for the newly created call.

When a conversion firm converts a put to a call, it enters into a perfectly hedged stock transaction and charges a price which will cover the cost of buying and selling the stock and will in addition return interest on the principal amount invested in the stock during the life of the option. For example, perhaps an investor wants to buy two six-month calls on Cessna Aircraft common.[11] The option dealer finds that he can purchase these from a writer for $1,000 each, or he can buy a straddle from the writer for $1,650. The dealer purchases the straddle, good for six months ten days and exercisable at $72\frac{3}{4}$ per share. The dealer then converts the put into a call, through a conversion house, for $264.19, computed thus:

Interest at $6\frac{1}{2}\%$ for 190 days on $7,275	$249.57
Two floor brokerage fees	7.70
Transfer taxes on stock	6.92
Total conversion fee	$264.19

By purchasing a straddle and converting the put into a call, the option dealer obtains two calls for a total cost of $1,914.19. Had the dealer purchased two calls directly from the writer, the dealer would have paid a total of $2,000.

The conversion house writes a call, which it sells for a conversion fee of $264.19. The conversion fee compensates the conversion house for the cost of buying and selling the stock and returns $6\frac{1}{2}$ per cent interest on the money invested in the stock during the life of the option. This interest is earned risk-free because, as explained, the conversion house which bought 100 shares of Cessna at $72\frac{3}{4}$ will either deliver the shares against the call for $72\frac{3}{4}$ (if the stock rises in price) or deliver it against the put for $72\frac{3}{4}$ (if the stock falls in price).

If some time passed between the writing of a straddle and the conversion of the put portion into a call, the exercise price of the option might

---

[11] Example from *Report on Put and Call Options*, Securities and Exchange Commission, Division of Trading and Exchanges, p. 16.

differ from the market price of the stock that the conversion house would buy. If the market price increased, the difference would be added to the cost of the option; if the price declined, the difference would be deducted. It is possible at times to convert calls into puts by a process which is exactly the reverse. When this happens, the conversion house sells the stock short for the length of the option period.

Special Options

Options described so far are "newly made options," which are written on receipt of a specific order from a customer and are normally exercisable at the market price of the stock at the time the option is sold.

Another type of option, called "special option," is sold from the existing inventory of option dealers. These inventories exist because some dealers, usually the larger ones, buy options offered to them before expiration when the options are enough in demand and the dealers believe that they can resell them at a profit. Dealers also add to their inventories when they buy a straddle and resell only the put or the call portion. Special options are offered via newspaper advertisements or by quotation sheets sent through the mail. An example of an offering, taken from the *Wall Street Journal* of April 3, 1964, is given in Figure 16–3.

Special Call Options

Per 100 Shares (Plus Tax)

Foster Wheeler	28⅝	9/14	$225.00
Phillips Petr.	50½	6/29	250.00
Cerro	40¼	6/ 5	425.00
Reynolds Met.	42	6/15	450.00
Chrysler	44⅞	5/ 6	350.00
Bell & Howell	23¼	6/15	225.00
Vendo	17½	10/13	200.00
Vornado	22⅜	6/ 1	275.00
Bulova	26½	6/ 5	287.50
AMP Inc.	25¾	6/12	275.00
Varian	13	9/ 1	175.00
Avnet	14	10/13	312.50
Zenith	84	6/ 4	450.00
Westinghouse Electric	35¾	5/15	175.00
Pan Am World Air ..	84¼	6/ 3	600.00
Sperry	18⅛	10/12	250.00
United Air	45	8/31	500.00
Anken Chem.	16⅝	10/22	275.00
Am. Home Prod. ..	67½	5/28	400.00
Olin Mathieson	47½	9/ 3	450.00

Ask for booklet How to Use Options ESTAB. 1919

Filer, Schmidt & Co.

• MEMBERS PUT & CALL BROKERS & DEALERS ASSN. INC.

SUBJECT TO PRICE CHANGE & PRIOR SALE

120 Broadway, N.Y. 5 BA 7-6100

Fig. 16–3

GODNICK and SON, INC.

Members Put and Call Brokers Assn., Inc.

Established 1932

223 SOUTH BEVERLY DRIVE   BEVERLY HILLS, CALIFORNIA
BRadshaw 2-0271   CRestview 4-8675

We offer the following Call Options
per 100 shares plus tax
September 21, 1964

N. Y. CENTRAL	50	6 MOS	337.50
COMSAT	38 1/8	6 MOS	687.50
STUDEBAKER	6 1/2	6 MOS	162.50
REPUBLIC STEEL	51 1/4	6 MOS	487.50
CHRYSLER	66 1/4	6 MOS	625.00
IRVING AIRCHUTE	13 7/8	6 MOS	212.50
AMERADA	79 1/2	6 MOS	725.00
RAYONIER	37	6 MOS	450.00
NORTH AMERICAN	53.90	MAR 18	387.50
AMF	20 1/2	MAR 15	187.50
KAISER IND	9	FEB 24	137.50
SYNTEX	54 3/8	DEC 22	550.00
POLAROID	157 3/4	DEC 22	925.00
MACK TRUCK	44 5/8	DEC 22	350.00
GEN MOTORS	99 1/2	DEC 21	525.00
LITTON	70 1/2	DEC 21	412.50
WESTERN AIRLINES	32 1/4	DEC 21	262.50
VARIAN	14 1/4	DEC 14	137.50
U. S. STEEL	63 3/4	NOV 23	262.50
TEXAS GULF SUL	53 1/2	NOV 19	325.00
TEXAS INST	79 1/2	NOV 18	350.00

and the following Put Options

CHRYSLER	66 1/4	MAR 29	575.00
RAYONIER	34	MAR 26	212.50
MACK TRUCK	44 5/8	DEC 22	325.00
GEN MOTORS	99 1/2	DEC 21	400.00
CHRYSLER	65 3/8	DEC 22	400.00
PENN RR	34 3/4	DEC 8	137.50
RICHFIELD OIL	57 5/8	MAR 8	387.50

Subject to Prior Sale or Price Change
Call Collect for Other Quotations

Fig. 16–4

Figure 16–4 is an example of a quotation sheet printed on a rigid card and mailed without envelope.

The Filer, Schmidt advertisement indicates, for example, that a special call option on 100 shares of Foster Wheeler may be purchased for $225 plus tax. This option gives the holder the right to call 100 shares at a price of $28\frac{5}{8}$ per share, plus tax, any time through 3:15 P.M. on the following September 14. Because special options are already in inventory, the exercise price of the stock may differ from the current market price. On April 2, Foster Wheeler closed at $26\frac{1}{2}$, $2\frac{1}{8}$ points below the exercise price of the option. The cost of a special option depends, among other things, on the difference between the current price of the stock and the exercise price in the option. When option dealers are asked to quote a price for an option, they usually offer special options if these are already available. The cost of special options is not necessarily the same as the cost of newly made options.

Exercising an Option

An option is exercised by presenting the option certificate to the cashier of the New York Stock Exchange firm that endorsed the contract before 3:15 P.M. (New York time) on the date stated in the contract. Option certificates should be left in New York City in custody of a stockbroker or option dealer so that the risk of accidental nondelivery is minimized, for an option will not be honored if presented even one minute after expiration time. The option is presented together with a "comparison ticket," a written notice saying, "We have sold you 100 shares of XYZ at 50 according to the put contract presented herewith" or "We are buying 100 shares of XYZ at 50 according to the call contract presented herewith." Delivery of and payment for the actual stock are usually made on the fourth day after the trade.

An investor holding a profitable option may realize his profits in either of two ways. He may exercise the option directly, or he may sell the option to an option dealer. If the investor elects to exercise his option directly, he places the order with his broker. His profit is the difference between the price at which he buys stock and the price at which he sells stock, less commissions and taxes. The broker charges the investor one commission for exercising the option, and if the investor buys stock to deliver against a put or sells stock received as the result of a call, he pays an additional commission. (If stock already held is supplied for a put or if the stock called is retained, the second commission is avoided.)

If an investor exercises an option and on the same day buys or sells the shares of stock in the market, he need deposit a margin of only 25 per cent of the value of the stock or $1,000, whichever is higher. This lower margin requirement applies here because the transaction is virtually risk-free. The owner of a call could, if he wished, exercise his option and retain the stock. He would then have to deposit the regular (and higher) margin requirements on the stock acquired. The owner of a put could, if he wished, order his stockbroker to exercise his put and borrow the stock to deliver, thus creating a short position for himself in the stock. Again, the investor would have to fulfill the regular margin requirements against the short position.

A second way of realizing accrued profits on an option is to sell the option itself directly to a put and call dealer for a sum of money equal to the difference between the option price and the market price of the stock, less the commissions and taxes which now have to be paid by the option dealer when the dealer exercises the option. This procedure results in the same gross profit as was derived from direct exercise of the option, but for two reasons it might be a more desirable alternative.

First, by selling the option itself instead of exercising it and going through with a market transaction in the stock, the investor need put up no money to satisfy the 25 per cent margin requirement. He has avoided the purchase and sale of any stock.

Second, if the option has been held longer than six months, a sale of the option at a profit results in long-term capital gains and is taxed at a lower income tax rate. If the option is exercised, the profits are considered as coming from the simultaneous purchase and sale of the stock—a short-term capital gain. For this reason most six-month ten-day options that are profitable are sold to option dealers for execution rather than executed by the investor who holds the option.

Reasons for Buying Options

Options are employed by purchasers in many ways. The following are their principal uses.

To Make a Speculative Profit on a Small Amount of Capital.   A call on Control Data Corporation, good for six months, is bought for $587.50 when the market for Control Data is $90 per share. If at any time during the following six months the market price of Control Data rises above $95\frac{7}{8}$, the holder of the option is able to exercise it at a profit. Let us assume that at the end of four months Control Data has risen to $100 per share and the buyer decides to take his profit by exercising his call and selling the stock. He would realize a net profit of $299.70, derived as follows:

Proceeds from sale of 100 shares Control Data at $100:		$10,000.00
Less commission on sale	$48.30	
Less taxes on sale	8.00	
Less SEC fee	0.20	
Expenses on sale of shares		57.20
Net proceeds from sale:		$ 9,942.80
Price of call option	$ 587.50	
Taxes on purchase of call option	7.60	
Total cost of call option	$ 595.10	
Cost of stock called at 90	9,000.00	
Commission on exercise of call	48.00	
Total cost of option exercised		9,643.10
Net profit on venture		$ 299.70

In this case the option buyer makes a profit of $299.70 on an investment of only $595.10, achieving a return of 50.4 per cent. Had he purchased the stock outright he would have received the same net proceeds from the sale, $9,942.80, but he would have had to commit $9,048 to the venture. His profit would have been larger, $894.80, but this would be a return of only 9.8 per cent on the larger sum invested. By use of the call option the investor would be able to increase his rate of return, in this example, fivefold. In addition, he limited his maximum possible loss to $595.10, the cost of the option, since if the price of the stock declined, he would simply throw away the option and incur no added expense.

Speculative profit on a small sum invested in a put would be made in a similar fashion, the profit being derived from a drop in the price of the stock below the exercise price by an amount adequate to cover the cost of the put and the commissions, taxes, and fees involved in closing out the venture.

If, in the Control Data example above, the price of the stock rose above the exercise price of 90 by an amount adequate to cover the costs of exercising the option but not by an amount sufficient to recover also the cost of purchasing the option, it would be to the advantage of the holder to exercise his option even though he would incur a loss on the venture as a whole. Suppose that at the end of the six months Control Data sells at 93. If the holder exercises his option, he incurs a net loss of $399.59, derived as follows:

Proceeds from sale of 100 shares Control Data at $93:		$9,300.00
Less commission on sale	$48.30	
Less taxes on sale	8.00	
Less SEC fee	0.19	
Expenses on sale of shares		56.49
Net proceeds from sale:		$9,243.51
Cost of call option	$ 587.50	
Taxes on purchase of call option	7.60	
Total cost of call option	$ 595.10	
Cost of stock called at 90	9,000.00	
Commission on exercise of call	48.00	
Total cost of option exercised		9,643.10
Net loss on venture		$ 399.59

If this investor had allowed his option to expire without being exercised, his losses would have been $595.10. By exercising the option he reduced his losses by $195.51.

To Protect an Existing Security Position.   An investor who purchases 100 shares of Chrysler at 30 finds his stock selling at 50 eight months later. He does not want to sell the stock because he believes that its price will rise higher if next year's models are received favorably. Still he would like to protect the profit he has made already. He may obtain this protection by purchasing a put that does not expire until after the new models are introduced. Then, if the price of Chrysler drops, he is able to sell his shares at 50 by exercising the put. In this event his profit is reduced by the cost of the put, a cost that is small. If the price of Chrysler stock rises, he is in a position to profit from the rise because he still holds the stock. Again the benefits are reduced by the cost of the put.

The investor should consider the cost of the put as an insurance premium paid to protect against a severe loss. If the put is not exercised, the investor should still regard its purchase as having been wise, for he received the protection he wanted. A purchase of fire insurance on a building where a fire does not take place is an analogous situation.

Our investor in Chrysler could also have obtained protection against a drop in price by entering a stop order to sell the stock at, say, 45. Then, if the price of Chrysler declined as far as 45, he would be sold out. A stop order has an advantage over the use of a put in that no cost is involved unless the order is executed, whereas a put must be paid for whether it is used or not. However, a put has an advantage over a stop order in that it provides protection for a fixed time period. With a put, the investor runs no risk of being sold out on a temporary decline as he does on a stop order. With a stop order, the investor would be sold out on the first decline to 45, regardless of whether it turns out to be the beginning of an extended fall or a temporary reaction in an otherwise rising trend. With a put, the investor may bide his time and defer decisive action until the put is about to expire.

The opposite of using a put to protect an existing long position is to use a call to protect an existing short position. If the stock sold short declines, the investor covers his short position at a profit which is lessened by the cost of the unused call. The call is insurance against a price rise that does not take place. If the price does rise, the investor acquires the stock by exercising his call to cover his short position. In this event his loss is limited to the cost of the call.

To Obtain Protection in In-and-out Trading.   A variation on using an option to protect an existing security position is to use it to reduce the risk of in-and-out trading. Perhaps a speculator is convinced that U.S. Steel will fluctuate about its present price of 55 for the next six months. He buys 100 shares of the stock and also buys a put. If he is wrong and U.S. Steel declines, he delivers his shares against the put when it is due to expire. He is out only the cost of the option.

Suppose, however, that the speculator is correct. U.S. Steel rises to 62, and the speculator sells his shares at a profit, retaining the put. U.S. Steel then drops to 50, and the speculator buys. If U.S. Steel again rises above 55, the speculator again sells. During the lifetime of the option the speculator may buy low and sell high many times on repeated fluctuations. Nevertheless he is always protected against a severe drop in the stock by the ability to deliver it against the put at 55.

It would be incorrect to call such a transaction risk-free, for if the price of the stock does drop, the speculator loses an amount equal to

TABLE 12   Options Outstanding, June 1, 1959, Classified by Type of Writer

Type of writer	Volume of options outstanding, shares	Per cent of total
Domestic persons	1,921,200	70.3
Foreigners	405,200	14.8
NYSE members	203,050	7.5
Other brokers/dealers	173,000	6.3
Investment clubs	17,600	0.7
Investment companies	5,800	0.2
Other institutions	5,600	0.2
Banks	200	Less than 0.05
Insurance companies	200	Less than 0.05
Corporate insiders	0	
Pension funds	0	
Total (excluding conversions)	2,731,850	100.0
Conversions (by NYSE members)	1,003,000	
Total options outstanding	3,734,850	

the cost of the put plus the various commissions. In addition he loses if the price of the stock fails to fluctuate enough so that his trading profits offset the cost of the put. What the option does in this case is *limit* the amount of possible loss by slightly reducing the amount of potential profit.

A short-term trader may obtain similar protection against a series of short sales and covering transactions in a fluctuating stock by holding a call.

The Writing of Options

We have just seen why operators in the market buy puts and calls. But where there are buyers there must be sellers. Therefore, the questions arise why there are sellers and under what conditions options are sold.

Writers of Options.   The volume of options outstanding on June 1, 1959, classified according to type of writer is shown in Table 12.[12]

Individual investors living in the United States were the largest single group of option writers. They were primarily persons with large portfolios. The next most important group of option buyers were foreigners, who accounted for 14.8 per cent of the total. At the time of the survey, Royal

[12] *Report on Put and Call Options*, Securities and Exchange Commission, Division of Trading and Exchanges, p. 55. Of the 1,921,200 shares of stock reported as optioned by domestic persons, 99,700 shares were from out-of-town correspondents not clearly identified as to type.

Dutch Petroleum was one of the most popular stocks optioned, and foreigners accounted for almost 75 per cent of the writers in that stock. This large number of options written by foreigners in American shares of a foreign company may have been due to arbitrage activities by persons with ready access to foreign markets.[13]

Excluding their activities as converters, member firms of the New York Stock Exchange accounted for only 7.5 per cent of the options written. A mere 14 of the approximately 700 Exchange member firms wrote these options for their own account. It should be noted that various rules of the Exchange restrict the option-writing ability of members. Specialists and odd-lot dealers are prohibited from acquiring or granting options in stocks in which they are registered, and all members of the Exchange are prohibited from buying or selling for their own account any securities in which they or other members of their firm hold or have granted options.

The next largest category of option writers was "other brokers/dealers," a classification which included members of the Put and Call Brokers and Dealers Association as well as brokerage firms not members of the New York Stock Exchange. Writers in this classification were responsible for only 6.5 per cent of the options outstanding on June 1, 1959. This figure suggests that put and call brokers and dealers are primarily in the business of acting as middlemen in the option business and do very little option writing of their own.

The remaining classifications, composed primarily of institutional investors, were practically insignificant as sources of options.

Reasons for Writing Options. Options are usually written by persons who maintain a continuous portfolio of common stocks, although they are sometimes written by speculators who use them to capitalize on an expected change in the market price. A person with a continuous portfolio who writes calls is in effect making deferred sales above the current market. If he writes puts, he is making deferred purchases below the current market. By continually buying below the current market or selling above the current market, he hopes to increase the profit or decrease the loss that he would otherwise have.

To illustrate, consider the position of an investor who holds 1,000 shares of Monsanto Chemical, which he purchased at, say, 64. The stock is currently quoted at 70. At this price the investor has a profit of $6 a share, or $6,000 in the aggregate. Perhaps he is not worried about a drastic decline in prices, but he is doubtful that a further rise of more than 1 or 2 points will occur. Under these circumstances he should liquidate his holdings of Monsanto and invest the proceeds in some other issue offering better short-term prospects. Instead, he holds the Monsanto stock and sells 10 six-month calls at $600 each.

[13] *Ibid.*, pp. 55–56.

Now, during the next six months one of three things must happen: (1) the price of Monsanto will rise above 77; or (2) it will rise higher than 70 but lower than 77; or (3) it will decline below 70. The effect of each of these alternatives will be illustrated by three specific examples. In the first the price will be assumed to rise to 80, in the second to 74, and in the third to decline to 67.

If the price of Monsanto rises to 80 and the call option is exercised, the writer has to deliver shares and accept $70 per share. Because he has already received $6 per share from the sale of the call, his final position is the same as if he had sold shares costing $64 each at a price of 76 (the delivery price plus the proceeds of the call sale). This is $4 less than he would have received had he sold the shares at the price of 80 without having written the call. However, in view of the fact that he was already inclined to sell out at 70, it is doubtful that he would have held on for this top price. By writing the call in effect he sold his shares at 76 when the market price was 70, thereby changing a per share profit of $6 into one of $12. Increased profits of $6 on an investment of $70 over a six-month period is an annual rate of return of 17 per cent.

If the price of Monsanto rises to 74 (the second assumption), the holder of the call will exercise it to recoup some of its cost. This does not affect the profits of the writer of the call. The profits are still the amounts computed in the paragraph above. However, it will be noted that the call writer's profits are $2 per share greater as a result of selling the call than they would have been had he sold Monsanto at the top of the market (74).

If the price of Monsanto declines to 67 (the third assumption), the call option will be allowed to expire without being exercised. In this event the writer of the expired option holds stock worth $67 a share plus cash of $6 a share, or a total of $73, as against proceeds from an outright sale of $70. He can now sell his holdings to realize the profits; or he can continue to hold the shares and repeat the procedure of creating and selling another call option.

The SEC estimates that approximately 58 per cent of all puts and calls are allowed to expire. This means that in most cases an option writer pockets the premium for writing the option and retains the stock as well. Of the 42 per cent of options not allowed to expire, about half are exercised at a loss to the buyer. This means the option writer gains more from selling the option than he would make from selling the stock. In the remaining cases of exercised options (about 21 per cent of the total), the profit received by the option writer via the premium is less than the profit he would make from selling the stock directly. Even then the writer does not necessarily lose—he merely fails to maximize his profit.

Option writers must be percentage-minded. They forego the chance of spectacular capital gains in exchange for small repeated profits that supplement considerably the dividend income of a portfolio.

17 stock rights and warrants

Shares of stock are usually acquired in the marketplace, perhaps by sending an order for execution on an organized exchange, perhaps by a purchase from an over-the-counter dealer, or perhaps from a secondary offering of a securities underwriter. In each of these cases the purchase price is transmitted to the previous *owner* of the security. From time to time opportunities arise to acquire shares directly from an issuing corporation by exercising special privileges (rights and warrants) or by exchanging one security for another (conversion). Rights and warrants are explained in this chapter, and convertible securities are described in the next.

Stock Rights

When an investor buys 5,000 shares of the common stock of a corporation with 500,000 shares of common stock outstanding, he acquires (1) one-hundredth part of the control of the company, (2) one-hundredth part of the net earnings available for dividends on the common stock, and (3) one-hundredth part of the net worth of the corporation. To some stockholders the factor of control may not mean much, but to others it is very valuable. As time goes on, the directors of the company may build up the property by plowing back a very generous part of the net earnings instead of paying them out to the stockholders. Thus equity in the property increases in value each year. Fairness to each stockholder demands that his relative share in the control, earnings, and equity be maintained. This is what he bought, what he paid his money for, and what he sacrificed for when he accepted only a small portion of the net earnings as dividends.

As the corporation's business expands, or perhaps for other reasons, more funds are necessary. At such times interest rates may be high, and bonds cannot be sold to advantage. Perhaps the company has already assumed all the fixed charges it can reasonably carry; perhaps it is the policy of the company to issue no bonds or notes; perhaps the additions or improvements contemplated cannot be expected to pay a fixed charge on their cost for several years. In any case the decision of management may be to sell stock rather than bonds. But to sell a new issue of stock in the market at the market price may not be possible. An additional supply of the shares not only might prevent an advance in price but might even break the present price. Besides, the factors of proportionate control and equity on the part of stockholders would be reduced in each case.

The fair thing to do, then, may be to sell the stock to existing stockholders. To do this, however, the stock must be sold at a reduction sufficient to provide a guaranty against a possible decline in price and an inducement to buy more shares of this particular stock. If a stockholder does not desire to buy more stock in his company, he must be given an instrument that he can sell at a price that will recompense him for the value he will lose on each share on the issue he holds. This also means that the new stock must be offered at a reduction from the current price.

A corporation, therefore, may give its stockholders the privilege of subscribing to additional stock at a price below the current market price. Such privileges are sometimes called "privileged subscriptions" but, more commonly, "rights." In order to preserve proportionate factors in control, equity, and net earnings each stockholder must receive his proportionate part of the new issue of stock. If the common stock is to be increased by 20 per cent, then each shareholder must receive a 20 per cent increase in the number of his shares, i.e., he must be entitled to one new share for each five old shares in his name.

The number and dollar volume of new rights offerings which take place from year to year depend in part on business optimism and in part on the relative cost of debt and equity money. The annual aggregate dollar value of new rights and exchange offerings since 1952 is shown in Figure 17–1.[1] In recent years an average of about $2 million per year has been raised through the use of rights. In most years this has represented approximately 150 to 200 separate offerings. In times of rising securities prices, as during 1954–1955 and in 1961, the dollar value of new rights and exchange offerings increases. However, during the market rises of 1958–1959 and in 1963 the exact reverse happened: the value of new offerings declined. The total value of rights and exchange offerings has also dropped after each downturn in the market, such as the market declines of 1956–1957, 1960, and 1962. The largest concentration of new rights offerings in the past decade came during the period 1955 to 1958.

Procedure in Issuing Rights

Legal Requirements.   In 1933 Congress passed an act to regulate the issuance of new securities. Twelve months later it passed the Securities Exchange

---

[1] Data on rights offerings are combined with information on exchange offerings. An exchange offering reflects a company offering its own securities to the stockholders of another company, usually in return for their shares and as part of a contemplated merger between the two companies. Annual data on new offerings of securities are published in "Corporate Financing Directory," a special section of *Investment Dealers Digest,* in late January or early February of every year.

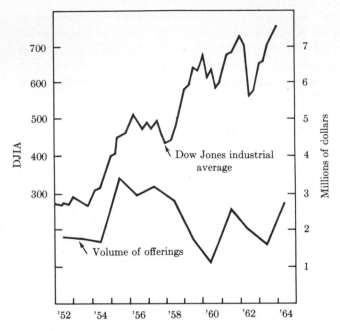

Fig. 17–1 Volume of rights and exchange offerings compared with stock price levels.

Act, the second title of which is really a minor amendment of the earlier law. In brief, the aim of the act of 1933, as amended in 1934, is to force a full and honest disclosure of every important element attending the issue of a new security and to place the responsibility for making this disclosure squarely and inescapably upon the seller of the issue.

According to the law, a business organization wanting to sell stock or bonds to the public in interstate commerce must first file with the Securities and Exchange Commission a statement containing information about the securities which it plans to offer. This statement is called a "registration statement." Its purpose is twofold: (1) to serve as a source of information for investors; and (2) to constitute a record of representations made by an issuer. Under the law, issuers are civilly liable to investors for losses resulting from their misstatements or omissions of essential facts. If the misstatements or omissions are intentional, a heavy fine or imprisonment may follow.

The registration statement must remain on file for a period of at least twenty days before the issuer sells or even makes an offer to sell a new security. During the twenty-day period, experts employed by the Commission examine the statement to see whether or not it conforms to the law. The Commission makes no attempt to pass on the merits or soundness of a security registered with it, and the law makes it a criminal offense for anyone to suggest that the fact of registration implies approval.

If the Commission finds a statement defective, it sends a "letter of deficiency" to the applicant, who then may file an amendment correcting the deficiency. The waiting period of twenty days begins with the date of the last amendment, unless the Securities and Exchange Commission permits its filing as of an earlier date.

Registration statements must be filed in one of the forms prescribed by the Commission, each of which seeks to elicit the information investors would need for that particular type of business. A registration statement consists of three parts: (1) the registration form proper, (2) the exhibits, and (3) a copy of the prospectus which the issuer will later give to prospective and actual purchasers of the issue and which contains a brief summary of the information found in the registration statement. The fee for registration is 0.01 per cent of the aggregate amount of the proposed offering of securities.

It is a criminal offense for an issuer, not exempted by the act, to use the mails or any instrumentality of interstate commerce for the purpose of conveying either a security for sale or an offer to sell a security until after the registration statement has been filed and declared effective. Even after effective registration has been accomplished, an issuer remains personally liable to investors for losses resulting from misstatements and omissions.

This liability rests (1) upon every person who signed the registration statement, (2) upon directors of the corporations even if they voted against the issue, (3) upon all experts who aided the issuer in compiling the data, and (4) upon underwriters of the issue. The only defense responsible persons may offer is that they made a careful investigation and had reasonable grounds at the time for believing that their statements were true and revealed all the essential facts.

The Securities Act of 1933 exempts certain issues from its registration requirements. In general, these are the issues which are already subject to some form of supervision so that exemption avoids double regulation, or they do not involve a public offer in interstate trade. The question arises whether or not an offer of securities limited to existing shareholders is a public offer under the act. It has been held that existing shareholders where their number is not too small are for purposes of the act the "public." Consequently, before a corporation may issue rights it must register the issue with the Commission.

Although the securities may be offered only after the twenty-day waiting period and after or at the time a prospectus is made available to the potential buyer, it is common for preliminary versions of the prospectus, known as "red herring" prospectuses, to be made available to possible buyers for their information during the waiting period. A red herring prospectus does not contain the offering price and is overprinted on the front cover in red ink with the words PRELIMINARY PROSPECTUS and with the following paragraph (also in red ink):

A registration statement relating to these securities has been filed with the Securities and Exchange Commission but has not yet become effective. Information contained herein is subject to completion or amendment. These securities may not be sold nor may offers to buy be accepted prior to the time the registration statement becomes effective. This prospectus shall not constitute an offer to sell or the solicitation of an offer to buy nor shall there be any sale of these securities in any State in which such offer, solicitation or sale would be unlawful prior to registration or qualification under the securities laws of any such State.

Issues not exceeding $300,000 in size may be offered under Regulation A of the Securities Act of 1933, which provides for the filing of a simple "notification" of the offering instead of a full registration statement. For these small offerings, information is made available to potential investors through an "offering circular" instead of a prospectus.

Steps in Issuing Rights. A rights offering of common stock to a corporation's shareholders involves many steps. As an example, consider the sequence of events preceding American Telephone & Telegraph's offer of $1.2 billion of new common stock to its stockholders in the spring of 1964.

November 20, 1963: After their regular meeting, A. T. & T. directors announced plans to offer about $12\frac{1}{4}$ million shares of stock, via a rights offering, to shareowners of record February 18, 1964, on a basis of one new share for each 20 held. The directors' press release stated that the period for the subscription would expire "early in April 1964," and that the purchase price of the shares would be established shortly before the offering at a price "somewhat below the market price of the shares when the offering price is determined."

January 2, 1964: Shareholders received their first direct notification of the rights offering in the company's *Share Owners' Quarterly,* a small newsletter which accompanies the regular quarterly dividend. The information was given in the form of a letter to shareowners from Chairman Frederick R. Kappel announcing the forthcoming offering in terms similar to those used in the November 20 press release.

January 15, 1964: The Registration Statement for the new shares, required under the Securities Act of 1933, was approved by the board of directors. The Registration Statement consisted of a 56-page booklet containing (1) a preliminary version of the prospectus, (2) a variety of additional detailed financial statements about the company's affairs, (3) information on many other aspects of the company's operations, (4) signatures of principal executive officers, principal financial and accounting officers, and directors, and (5) statements from auditing firms and law firms consenting to the use of their names in the Registration Statement.

January 24, 1964: The Registration Statement was filed with the Securities and Exchange Commission.

February 11, 1964: The board of directors set $100 as the price at which shareholders could purchase additional shares of stock under the proposed offering. This price was about $44 below the market price of the issue at this time. Amendment No. 1 to the Registration Statement, specifying the purchase price of $100 per share, was filed with the SEC and the Registration Statement as amended became effective at 5:30 P.M.

February 12, 1964: A. T. & T. rights were traded on a "when-issued" basis on the New York Stock Exchange. When-issued trading is done by means of contracts in which the seller agrees to deliver to the buyer a given number of rights for the stock when and as the rights are issued if they are issued at all. If for any reason the rights should not be issued, such contracts lapse with no responsibility by either party. If the rights are issued, delivery must be made immediately.

February 13, 1964: A. T. & T. stock was traded "ex rights" on the New York Stock Exchange. The ex-rights date is the third business day before the date of record; in this case, the date of record was Tuesday, February 18. Prior to February 13, A. T. & T. stock was traded "rights on," meaning that a purchaser of the stock also received the rights. Beginning February 13, a purchaser of A. T. & T. stock had no claim to the rights. It is normal to expect that when a stock trades ex rights (or ex dividend), the price of the stock will drop by an amount approximately equal to the value of the right (or dividend) which has been separated from the stock. In this case, the rights were trading at about $2\frac{3}{8}$ but the stock dropped only about $1\frac{3}{8}$. (Had the stock not gone ex rights, it would theoretically have risen one dollar per share.)

Also on February 13, 1964, A. T. & T. issued a press release describing the financial undertaking and noting that 4,800 mail bags weighing about 158 tons would be needed to carry the necessary mail to shareholders.

February 18, 1964: This being the date of record, persons on the record books as shareholders as of this date are determined to be the recipients of rights. It is presumed that persons buying shares of stock before February 13 would be on the record books by February 18. Persons buying shares of stock on February 13 or later would not yet be shareholders of record. Also on February 18 the company mailed its 1963 *Annual Report* to all shareholders. Among other items the report carried comments on the forthcoming rights offering.

February 26, 1964: Each stockholder entitled to receive rights was mailed (1) a letter from Chairman Kappel explaining the rights offering; (2) a prospectus, as required under the Securities Act of 1933, giving detailed information on the offering and on the company; and (3) a brochure entitled "Important Information about the 1964 A. T. & T. Stock Issue," summarizing the highlights of the rights offering. *March 2, 1964:* Each stockholder entitled to receive rights was mailed a "warrant" to serve as physical evidence of his claim to rights. The warrant was printed on both sides of an IBM data processing card, as shown in Figure 17–2. The card sets forth in a formal manner the amount of the new stock the shareholder was entitled to purchase, the subscription price, the terms of payment, and the date of expiration of the privileged subscription. It also provided space for the rights holder to specify his wishes concerning (1) the purchase of new stock, (2) the sale of the rights, or (3) the transfer of the warrant to another person. The card carried instructions that it should be returned to the

AMERICAN TELEPHONE AND TELEGRAPH COMPANY

WARRANT FOR STOCK PURCHASE RIGHTS

THE REGISTERED OWNER OF THIS WARRANT, NAMED BELOW, OR ASSIGNS, IS ENTITLED TO THE NUMBER OF RIGHTS SHOWN BELOW TO PURCHASE CAPITAL STOCK UPON THE TERMS AND CONDITIONS SPECIFIED IN THE PROSPECTUS RELATING TO SUCH STOCK.

20 RIGHTS AND PAYMENT OF $ 100 ARE NEEDED TO PURCHASE EACH SHARE OF STOCK

ACCOUNT NO. 123-4567-890 NUMBER OF RIGHTS → *100 *

JOHN DOE
191 HIGH STREET
ANYTOWN USA

TREASURER

SPECIMEN

USE THIS SPACE TO SHOW DIFFERENT MAILING ADDRESS: IF THIS IS A PERMANENT CHANGE OF ADDRESS, CHECK HERE ☐

1. TO PURCHASE STOCK, FILL IN AND SIGN BELOW:
NUMBER OF SHARES TO BE PURCHASED ________
NUMBER OF RIGHTS SUBMITTED ________
AMOUNT ENCLOSED $ ________
($ 100 PER SHARE)
YOUR SIGNATURE WILL ALSO AUTHORIZE RIGHTS AGENT (SEE ACCOMPANYING LETTER) TO BUY ANY ADDITIONAL RIGHTS NEEDED FOR YOUR PURCHASE, OR SELL ANY EXCESS RIGHTS.
SIGNATURE(S) ________
TELEPHONE NO. ________ AREA CODE

2. TO SELL ALL RIGHTS THROUGH RIGHTS AGENT
SIGN BELOW:
SIGNATURE(S) ________

3. TO TRANSFER RIGHTS, USE OTHER SIDE

THIS WARRANT WILL BE VALUELESS IF NOT USED ON OR BEFORE APRIL 6, 1964

AMERICAN TELEPHONE & TELEGRAPH CO. BELL SYSTEM AND ASSOCIATED COMPANIES

PLEASE DO NOT FOLD, MUTILATE OR STAPLE THIS WARRANT

5 224 167

3. TO TRANSFER RIGHTS, FILL IN AND SIGN BELOW:
FOR VALUE RECEIVED THE RIGHTS REPRESENTED BY THIS WARRANT ARE ASSIGNED TO:
(PLEASE PRINT NAME IN FULL, ADDRESS, AND NUMBER OF RIGHTS)
NUMBER OF RIGHTS TRANSFERRED

SIGNATURE(S) OF REGISTERED OWNER(S) ________
(IF JOINT ACCOUNT, EACH OWNER SHOULD SIGN)

IBM C67166-0

THIS WARRANT WILL BE VALUELESS IF NOT USED ON OR BEFORE APRIL 6, 1964

RETURN TO:
TREASURER
AMERICAN TELEPHONE & TELEGRAPH CO.
P. O. BOX 600
MADISON SQUARE STATION
NEW YORK, N. Y. 10010

CERTIFICATION OF ACTUAL VALUE FOR FEDERAL TRANSFER TAX: A SIGNATURE IS A CERTIFICATION THAT THE ACTUAL VALUE OF ANY RIGHTS SOLD IS THE SELLING PRICE AND THE ACTUAL VALUE OF ANY RIGHTS OTHERWISE TRANSFERRED IS THE MEAN OF HIGH AND LOW QUOTED PRICES ON DAY OF TRANSFER.

Fig. 17–2 A specimen stock right (front and back).

treasurer of American Telephone & Telegraph Company in New York City before April 6, 1964. The card was accompanied by a letter from Chairman Kappel explaining clearly the various alternatives open to a rights holder.

In former years it was customary for warrants to be printed on large sheets of paper resembling a stock certificate. However, the economies and accuracy which can be obtained by using data-processing cards and having the necessary information punched in the card for processing by an electronic computer have resulted in a widespread shift to the card form of document. To process the $2\frac{1}{4}$ million cards mailed to shareholders, American Telephone & Telegraph used seven IBM 1401 computers and a larger IBM 7074 computer. Data from the cards were transferred to magnetic tape and then processed through the computers, which in turn made out checks (whenever rights were sold), bills (whenever additional rights were purchased), and stock certificates (to be signed by the registrar and transfer agent before forwarding to the purchaser).

March 3, 1964: Rights were traded regular way on the New York Stock Exchange and trading in rights on a when-issued basis was terminated.

April 6, 1964: Rights expired on this day. Rights were traded on the New York Stock Exchange until noon and in the over-the-counter market during the afternoon.

April 15, 1964: At A. T. & T.'s regular annual meeting Chairman Kappel commented on the recent rights offering and noted that three out of five shareholders had exercised their rights, providing about 75 per cent of the total sum raised. Virtually all of the rights were exercised, and the company had raised over $1.2 billion of new capital needed to expand and improve the Bell telephone system.

American Telephone & Telegraph's rights offering differed from many rights offerings in that no investment bankers were employed to underwrite its success. A syndicate of investment bankers (underwriters) frequently agrees at the beginning of a rights offering that it will purchase at a specified price any shares not subscribed to by stockholders. During the offering period the underwriters may purchase rights offered on the market, exercise the rights, and sell the stock acquired. At the end of the offering period the underwriters "take down" the remaining unsold shares of stock and sell them on the market. The advantage to the issuing company of using underwriters is that the company is assured that it will receive the funds sought, since the risk of failure to sell all the shares rests with the underwriters. For their part, the underwriters purchase the stock at a price at which they expect to be able to resell the shares at a profit.

Another device sometimes used to ensure that the entire new offering will be sold is "oversubscription." When this procedure is used, shareholders may submit tenders to purchase shares in addition to those for which they have rights. At the end of the offering period unsold shares are allocated among those who submitted tenders for additional shares. Shareholders find this plan advantageous because the purchase price for oversubscription is the same as the price for purchase by rights.

Conditions of Success for a Rights Offering

The board of directors and the officers of a corporation issuing rights are desirous that stockholders subscribe to all the shares to which they are entitled. Stockholders are also interested in the success of the new financing. No stockholder is going to exercise his rights or even continue to hold his shares if he expects the new rights offering to depress the value of the shares. For this reason an investor or speculator about to buy shares of a company planning to issue rights should study carefully the prospects of the new issue.

For a rights offering to be successful, stockholders must believe that the company is efficiently managed so that the new capital will result in a profitable expansion of its business. They must believe that net earnings of the company will increase at least as much as if not more than the proportional increase in capital. A rights offering should state fully and frankly why the funds are sought and how it is intended that they will be used. Unless this is done, stockholders have no way of judging whether the new stock is a good or a poor investment.

The offering price of the new stock should be lower than the market price of the stock by an amount sufficient to guard against fluctuations. If the offering price is set at 38 when the market price is 40, a slight decline in market price during the offering period will ruin the success of the sale by making it possible to buy the shares cheaper on the market. If the offering price is set lower, perhaps at 35, a much bigger decline would have to take place before the offering fails. On the other hand, it is considered bad practice to make the margin too large, for to do so increases the per share dilution and increases the loss to any stockholder who through accident or ignorance allows his rights to lapse without exercising or selling them.

The stage or phase of the business cycle has much to do with the success of a rights offering. If business activity is depressed, if corporations have unused productive capacity and millions in idle cash, stockholders will be quite skeptical that a sizable issue of stock would greatly enhance growth and earnings prospects for their company. Depressed business activity is usually accompanied by a depressed stock market. If stockholders have recently suffered real or imagined losses from a drop in price of the shares they already own, they are seldom in a mood to invest more money in new shares. If the market starts to rise, however, they again show an interest in buying new securities and are more favorably disposed toward rights offerings.

Another condition favoring the success of a sale of stock to stockholders through the issue of rights is wide distribution of the stock among investors. When a relatively few large owners hold all the stock of a company, it is entirely probable that they will prefer a fairly wide diversification of their holdings and therefore will not desire to buy more stock of a company in which they own a large amount already. Thus their rights will come upon the market. On the other hand, with many holders of small lots, the percentage of those using their own rights will depend largely upon their prosperity. If these smaller holders have been getting a good return from dividends or regular appreciation in the value of their shares, they will put small emphasis on diversification and will buy what they know is good, glad of the opportunity the rights afford. It is thus entirely probable that a much smaller percentage of the rights will come upon the market when the stock of a corporation is widely distributed than if there are only a few large holders.

Computation of the Value of Rights

Presumably the value of a share of stock is equal to the aggregate value of the common stock equity of a company, divided by the number of shares it has outstanding. If new stock—issued as a result of rights financing—is sold to the general public at market price, the value of the old shares is not affected, for the purchase of the new shares enhances the aggregate value of the common stockholder's equity in the same proportion as it increases the number of outstanding shares. However, the proportionate control of the old shares would be reduced. A sale of the new shares to the public at a price lower than the market price of the old shares would diminish both the common stockholder's equity per share and his control per share. In this case the new shareholder would gain the equity that the old shareholder loses. This is one of the reasons why the right to buy new shares below market price is usually given to the old stockholders; then the old shareholder gains as much from the purchase of the new shares as he loses from the decline in value of his old shares.

If an old stockholder transfers his right to another (via a sale), he will want to be compensated for the loss he will shortly sustain on his old shares. Thus it is important to him to know the value of the right which he sells. If a corporation whose stock is selling at $110 issues one new share at $100 for each four old shares, a shareholder who purchases four old shares and then exercises his rights will find his shares costing an average of $108.

4 old shares at $110	$440
1 new share at $100	100
Total cost of 5 shares	$540
Average cost of each share	$108

If this investor holds his four shares and allows his rights to expire without being exercised, he will find the aggregate value of his four shares declining from $440 (4 shares at $110) to $432 (4 shares at $108). If he wishes to recoup this loss via a sale of the rights before they expire, he must get $8 for the four rights, or $2 for each right ($8 ÷ 4).

An investor who buys four rights acquires the privilege of purchasing a new share worth $108 for a price of $100. Thus the four rights are worth $8 to him, or $2 per right. As we have seen, this is the same amount as an old shareholder must receive from the sale of a right if he is to avoid a loss. Thus the value of rights to purchaser or seller is tied to the value of the stock. This relationship is capable of being expressed in a mathematical formula.

Value of Rights on a When-issued Basis.   The formula for determining the value of a right during the rights-on period is

$$V = \frac{M - S}{N + 1}$$

in which V is the value of one right, M is the market value of one share of rights-on stock, S is the subscription price of the new shares, and N is the number of old shares which one must hold in order to receive the privilege of purchasing one of the new shares. Applying the formula to the terms of the earlier offer, we obtain

$$\frac{\$110 - \$100}{4 + 1} = \$2$$

Value of Rights after Issue.   The formula for determining the value of a right after a stock is traded ex rights is

$$V = \frac{M - S}{N}$$

in which V is the value of a right, M is the ex-rights market value of the stock, S is the subscription price of the new shares, and N is the number of rights required to purchase one new share.

Other things being equal, the market value of a stock drops by the value of one right on the day that the stock is traded ex rights. Thus, in the earlier example, the price of the stock should decline from $110 to $108 when the issue goes ex rights. If the formula is applied to this ex-rights market price, the value of a right becomes $2, viz.,

$$\frac{\$108 - \$100}{4} = \$2$$

Actual Value of Rights.   The two formulas given above describe the theoretical value of a right. If there are no unusual circumstances in a situation, the actual market value of a right conforms to its theoretical value. However, very frequently unusual circumstances do exist, and the market value of a right may sell at a premium. For example, in a rising market where the stock is becoming more desirable the price of rights is usually above the theoretical value because of the speculative possibilities arising from the leverage characteristic of a right. Assume that 10 rights plus $40 entitle one to buy a share of stock now selling (ex rights) at $50 per share. The rights have a theoretical value of $1 apiece. Suppose that a speculator anticipates that the stock will rise to $60. If he is correct, $1,000 invested in the stock buys 20 shares (commission and taxes being ignored), which can be sold for $1,200 for a $200 profit, or a percentage gain of 20 per cent. (Margin trading could be used to magnify the results even more.) The same amount of money invested in rights purchases 1,000 rights. If the stock goes to 60, the theoretical value of a right rises to $2; the 1,000 rights are worth $2,000; and the investor has made 100 per cent profit. Obviously a speculator prefers rights to stocks if he expects the price of the stock to rise. Because of this preference the actual price of a right is higher than its theoretical value whenever speculators anticipate a rise in the price of the stock.

If speculators anticipate a drop in the market price of the stock, they avoid purchasing rights because they will decline even faster than the stock. However, rights can never sell below their theoretical value by more than the costs of executing an arbitrage transaction, for if they do, it becomes profitable to sell the stock short and protect the short position by a purchase of rights. This maneuver places a trader in a position to make a profit without possibility of loss.

The value of a right is also affected by fundamental conditions. Investors are aware that efficient operation of a company sometimes requires it to seek additional capital via a rights offering. If they interpret such an offering as arising from such a need, they look with favor upon the rights. But if they feel that the company does not really need the new capital and that it will not be able to use it profitably, they may greet the rights offering less enthusiastically. Then there are always some investors who do not wish to add to their holdings of a particular issue and who sell their rights regardless of whether or not the funds are needed by the company.

The Disposal of Rights

Suppose that a stockholder knows that his company will soon issue rights. In what different ways may he dispose of these rights? Which method of disposal will be the most profitable? There are several possibilities, each with its advantages and disadvantages.

In the first place, as soon as the official announcement of the offering is made but before the rights are issued, a stockholder may sell his rights on a when-issued (sometimes called "when, as, and if issued") basis. If he anticipates a downturn either in the general market or in the price of his stock, the value of the right is likely to be greatest at this point. In addition, the news of the offering and the publicity attracted to the stock are likely to cause the stock price (and thus the value of the right) to be high at the time the news breaks.

This theory is substantiated by a recent study of the comparative price behavior of stocks prior to, during, and after a rights offering. J. R. Nelson studied 379 rights offerings by New York Stock Exchange listed companies between January 1, 1946, and December 31, 1957.[2] His list was an exhaustive compilation of all rights offerings by New York Stock Exchange firms during these twelve years. Stock price changes were adjusted for the fractional stock split inherent in a rights offering and also deflated by the change in Standard & Poor's Industry Stock Price Index for the particular industry. Nelson's time period encompassed two recessions, two booms, a hot war, a cold war, inflation, and major bear and bull markets.

His data, shown in Figure 17–3, indicate that for both utility and non-utility (primarily industrial) offerings the price of the common stock tended to decline after the announcement date (the date on which a registration statement was first filed with the SEC). In general the data confirm the idea that the best time to sell rights is as soon as possible. The reader must be cautioned, however, that the average data of Figure 17–3 conceal a certain amount of dispersion; individual stocks may perform quite differently depending upon their unique characteristics.

Additional advantages of selling rights on a when-issued basis are the immediate use of the funds and the avoidance of the uncertainties in the rights market over subsequent weeks.

A stockholder may wait until the rights have been issued and then sell them. The traditional advice to such a seller has been "Sell early, and buy late," on the basis that the price at the time of issue will probably be highest and will probably drop during the trading period.

One reason advanced for the decline in the price of rights as the date of their expiration comes closer is the human tendency to wait until circumstances compel action. The student writes his thesis on the last day of the term; the stockholder sells his rights as the final subscription date draws near. A second reason is the anticipation of the issuance of additional shares which will be traded on a when-issued basis during the latter part of the subscription period. This addition to the old stock already on the market increases the supply while no new factor enhances the demand. Besides, at this late date stockholders and others expecting to take advantage

[2] Jack Russell Nelson, *The Role of Stock Rights in Corporate Financial Policy,* unpublished doctoral dissertation, University of California, Los Angeles, February 1962.

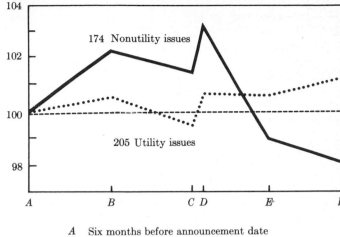

A	Six months before announcement date
B	Announcement date
C	Two days before rights trading
D	First day of rights trading
E	Last day of rights trading
F	Six months after rights trading

Fig 17–3 Comparative price behavior of 379 stocks that used rights financing. (Price of each stock six months prior to announcement date = 100.)

of the low price to acquire stock will have bought the rights they need, so that only speculators remain to furnish such support to the market as is given it. These men, however, will not buy except at a price low enough to ensure a profit later on. Hence, all the conditions of a decline obtain at the end of the subscription period.

Nelson's study, however, casts doubt on these views. As Figure 17–4 shows, stock prices tend to decline rapidly during the first part of the rights trading period and then to recover most of the decline by the end of the period. By contrast, the price of rights tends to drop faster than stock prices during the first half of the trading period and then to recover more than the loss by the end of the period. It would seem, then, that the advice on selling rights should read "Sell early or late, but do not sell in the middle of an offering period." Nelson cautions against simple generalization from his data because of the dispersion involved and suggests that investors "base their rights buying and selling on careful examination of individual cases."[3]

A third method sometimes suggested for disposing of rights is to sell long stock immediately on the announcement of the issue of rights and to buy rights on the market sufficient to replace the stock sold. The stock

[3] *Ibid.,* p. 114.

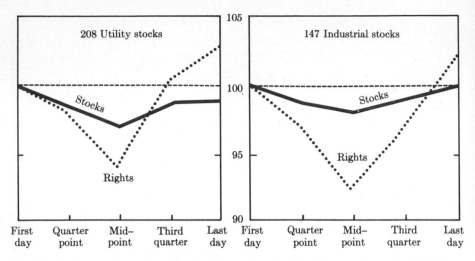

Fig. 17–4 Comparison of stock and rights prices during rights trading period. (Prices on first day = 100.)

must be sold immediately, before the depressing effect of the new stock is felt, and the rights must be purchased when their price is depressed, perhaps during the midpoint of the trading period. If the stockholder is successful, he will make a profit by selling at a relatively high price and rebuying the stock through the rights for a lesser amount. The funds realized on the sale of the old stock are available for use until needed to repurchase the shares, and no interest payments on borrowed funds need be made. The difficulty with this plan is the possibility that the rights may not drop during the trading period or that even if the rights do drop for a while the stockholder will wait too long to buy them and they will rise in price again, making reacquisition of the stock more costly than anticipated.

A variation of the above plan is to sell only as many shares as the stockholder is entitled to receive by the employment of his rights on the stock remaining after the sale. These shares should be sold immediately on the announcement of the issue of new stock on the assumption that the price will be highest at that point. The rights later received are exercised at the proper time, and the new stock replaces that sold. The investment position is then the same as before the sale of the old stock, and although a profit may have been made on only a limited number of shares, the risk of paying a high price for the rights has been avoided.

Only on or after the date on which the stock sells ex rights may a stockholder sell as many shares of the old stock as the rights on his total holdings warrant. For example, if 1 share of the new stock is issued for every 4 shares of the old and a stockholder has 1,000 shares, he may sell only 200 shares immediately. For if he sells 250 shares, the number of new shares that he is entitled to, then he will receive rights on only 750 shares, which will enable him to secure only 187.5 shares of the new stock when he needs 250 to maintain his former investment position. After the stock sells ex rights, he may sell 250 shares because he will receive rights on 1,000 shares.

Some successful speculators favor selling a stock short on or, if possible, immediately preceding the announcement of a new issue. In this case the stockholders sell short the same number of shares as they will receive of the new stock. When the rights are issued later on, the new stock is acquired at the issue price and the short sale is covered. This plan has the disadvantage that the customer must put up margin on his short sale, and if the price of the stock goes up, he will be subject to margin calls. If many speculators sell short, the demand for the loan of stock might lead to a short squeeze, with the price of the stock being driven up and shorts being forced to cover at high prices.

A stockholder may exercise his rights and secure the new stock to which he is entitled. For a long-run investor this solution holds the most promise, for by virtue of holding the original stock the long-run investor is in effect saying that he expects the long-term growth prospects of his investment to be favorable. By purchasing more shares through the rights offering he is increasing his share holding (on a commission-free basis) in what he believes to be a fundamentally attractive situation.

Short-term investors and speculators may also exercise their rights profitably, expecting to sell the stock in the near future, if the near-term price movement of the stock is upward. These investors must decide whether in the near future the price of the stock will be depressed because the additional supply has not yet been assimilated by the market or will rise because investor expectations have been enhanced by the company's plans for the future. Often the general trend of the market rather than the circumstances of the particular issue will determine the near-term price behavior of the stock.

Figure 17–3 shows that rights offerings have a good effect on the near-term price movement of utility stocks, for utility stock prices tended to rise relative to the market for similar utility stocks in the six months following the last day of trading in the rights. The average price behavior of nonutility (primarily industrial) stocks was the reverse, however. In the six months following the close of trading in rights the average nonutility stock declined in price.

Again, Figure 17–3 does not reveal dispersion. Individual stock performance depends on many variables, including whether or not per share earnings and dividends are diluted by the offering. The trend of earnings and dividends after a rights offering, in turn, depends primarily on the earning power of the new capital. In the case of utilities, new capital is virtually guaranteed an earning power equal to the average earning power of the company because of the nature of utility regulation. In nonutility industries, competition sets the earning power of new capital, which may be more or less than the average earning power of existing capital. This difference in the structure of industries may account for the differences shown in Figure 17–3.

The Parity between the Price of Rights and Stock

Whenever the price of any right declines appreciably below its mathematical value, a margin of profit awaits the arbitragers. At such times traders buy rights at the low price and at the same time sell short the stock of the corporation. After perhaps a month the new stock is issued to the holder of the rights, who then delivers it to the lender of the shares on his short sale. The arbitragers' profit is the margin between the total cost—consisting of the price paid for the rights, the price paid to the corporation for the new stock, the interest, the commission, and the transfer tax—and the selling price of the short stock.

Suppose that a corporation whose stock was selling at 110 issues rights to subscribe to new stock on a 4-to-1 basis at par. The stock is now selling ex rights at 108 and the rights at $1\frac{3}{4}$. The theoretical value of the rights is $2. A floor trader, seeing an opportunity to make a profit, buys 400 rights at $1\frac{3}{4}$ and immediately sells short 100 shares of the stock. He will deliver the stock as soon as the new stock is issued, which may be a month or two later. He has received $10,800 for the stock sold and has bought 400 rights at $1\frac{3}{4}$, costing $700. The rights give him the privilege to buy 100 shares at $100 per share. He will have a transfer tax and interest to pay plus a reserve to maintain for possible margin calls by the lender's broker in case the price of the stock should go up. These items can be estimated quite accurately; the difference between the total cost and the $10,800 received is his profit.

The effect of the buying of rights and the selling of a stock is to raise the price of rights and lower the price of the stock, thus bringing the two prices to a parity.

The importance of a continuous market has been stressed again and again in this volume. It is evident that the work of the arbitragers aids in keeping active both the outstanding stock and the rights to subscribe, and it reduces the spread between the bid and ask prices so that the variation in price from one sale to the next is smaller than it would otherwise be.

Stock Purchase Warrants

The word "warrant" perplexes many investors because of its many meanings. Earlier in this chapter the term was used to mean the physical certificate or card which a stockholder receives as evidence of his stock rights in a privileged subscription offering of new common stock. Warrants can also be used to designate long-term options to buy a certain number of shares of stock at a stipulated price. Such warrants are frequently called "stock purchase warrants."

Examples of currently outstanding stock purchase warrants are those of Trans-World Airlines and Tri-Continental Corporation. Trans-World Airlines is the third largest domestic United States airline and the second largest international American airline. Tri-Continental Corporation is a closed-end investment company. Common stocks of both companies are listed on the New York Stock Exchange; warrants of both are listed on the American Stock Exchange.

Characteristics of Warrants.   Warrants vary as to their exercise price, their expiration date, and their detachability and in many other ways. A potential purchaser should investigate each of these characteristics.

The exercise price of a warrant is the price which the holder of the warrant must pay to acquire a share of stock. Each TWA warrant permits the purchase of one share of TWA common stock for $20 per share. Each Tri-Continental warrant permits the purchase of 1.27 shares of Tri-Continental common stock at $17.76 per share. Whereas the exercise price in a rights offering is established below the current market price of the stock, the exercise price in a warrant is usually set above the market price of the stock at the time the warrant is issued. In a rights offering the company wants the stock purchased quickly. With regard to warrants the issuing company contemplates that they will be exercised at some remote time. The exercise price of a warrant may change at intervals. For example, the TWA warrants were exercisable at $20 per share through June 1, 1965, and are exercisable at $22 per share thereafter until they expire.

Some warrants expire as of a particular date, and other warrants are issued for the lifetime of the company or until exercised. The TWA warrants must be exercised by December 1, 1973, at which time they expire. By contrast the Tri-Continental warrants are perpetual; they are good for as long as the company exists.

Warrants are usually issued with preferred stock or bonds as a "sweetener" to induce investors to purchase the security at a price higher than would otherwise be possible. The warrant gives the security buyer a speculative opportunity. If the issuing company prospers, its common stock will rise above the exercise price and the warrant holder will be able to share in the good fortunes of the company without having assumed the risk of a common stockholder.

Usually warrants are issued in the form of coupons attached to the bond or preferred stock certificate. Sometimes this coupon is detachable so that the purchaser may cut it off and sell it, or he may retain the warrant and sell the security. Sometimes a warrant is not detachable, in which case it may be exercised only by the holder of the security. The TWA warrants were issued on June 8, 1961, attached to the company's $6\frac{1}{2}$s subordinated income debentures and were detachable after November 1, 1961. The Tri-Continental stock purchase warrants are completely separate and never were attached to any security of the company.

Sometimes warrants are issued directly instead of in conjunction with a bond or preferred stock offering. They may be issued directly to investment bankers, management officers, or promoters as part of the compensation for their help in starting a new business. Options issued to key officers and employees are a variation of this type of warrant. Such options resemble warrants in all respects except that they are not transferable but must be held and exercised by the person to whom issued. In rare cases warrants have been issued to "old" stockholders in a corporate reorganization to give this group, who would otherwise be wiped out, some claim on the future of the company in replacement for their original investment.

Although warrants constitute a claim to shares of common stock, they are not themselves common stock and thus they do not have a claim to earnings, dividends, or voting power. Most warrants are protected against dilution. If a warrant permits the purchase of a share of stock for $20 and the stock is split 2 for 1, the exercise terms are automatically revised to permit the purchase of the stock at $10 per share. If a 5 per cent stock dividend were declared, the purchase price of the warrant would drop from $20 to $19.05. The fact that a *warrant* is protected against dilution resulting from stock splits and stock dividends is not the same thing as saying that *common stock* is protected against dilution resulting from the exercise of warrants. This will be treated later.

The Value of a Warrant.   The basic, or theoretical, value of a warrant depends upon the value of the stock which its holder is entitled to purchase. For example, a warrant entitling its holder to purchase a share of stock at $25 has a basic value of $5 if the stock is currently selling at $30 on the market. The formula for computing this value is

$$M - E = V$$

in which M is the market price of the stock, E is the exercise price of the warrant, and V is the theoretical value of the warrant.

Warrants also have a speculative value, which must be added to their basic value. Suppose, for example, that the stock currently selling at $30 is expected before too long to rise to $60. If the price of the stock does reach $60, the basic value of the warrant is $35, ($60 − $25). If the expected rise materializes, funds now invested in stock double ($30 to $60) but funds now invested in warrants are multiplied sevenfold ($5 to $35).

Thus speculators prefer warrants to stock, a preference that causes warrants to sell at a premium over their basic, or theoretical, value.

The performance of TWA stock and warrants during 1963 and 1964 supplies an illustration of this relationship. On January 31, 1963, TWA common stock closed at $10\frac{5}{8}$. The warrant, which entitled the holder to purchase stock at $20, thus had a negative value of $9\frac{3}{8}$ ($10.625 − $20). However, TWA warrants closed at $4\frac{1}{8}$ on January 31, 1963. The fact that speculators were willing to pay a premium of $13.50 for the warrants meant that they anticipated a rise in the price of TWA common to occur before 1973 and that the rise would be large enough to make an investment in warrants at $4\frac{1}{8}$ profitable.

At the time of writing TWA common stock is quoted at 44, and the warrants are selling at $27—a premium of $3. It is interesting to note whether or not, as events turned out, speculators were justified in January 1963 in purchasing the warrants at a price $13.50 above their basic value. The answer becomes clear if we assume that there were three speculators in 1963, each with $1,062.50. The first speculator used his funds to purchase 100 shares of TWA common stock at $10\frac{5}{8}$. If he sold the shares in September 1964 at 44, he made $2,337.50 of profit—a rate of return of 220 per cent on the funds invested.

The second speculator used his funds to purchase 258 warrants. If he exercised these rights in January 1964 and sold the stock, his profits were $4,096.50—a rate of return of 385 per cent on the funds invested. Obviously it was more profitable to invest in the warrants than in the stock.

The third speculator bought 258 warrants like the second, but he did not exercise them in September 1964. Instead he sold the warrants for $27 and made a profit of $5,876.50—a rate of return of 553 per cent on the funds invested.

If a speculator multiplies his profits in a bull market by buying warrants instead of stock, then conversely he multiplies his losses in a bear market by buying warrants instead of stock. The truth of this is easily demonstrated by figuring the losses if the three speculators above had invested at September 1964 prices and liquidated later at prices equivalent to those that existed in January 1963. The movement in the prices of Tri-Continental stock and warrants between March and October 1963 affords an example. On the earlier date the stock was selling at $50\frac{1}{2}$ and warrants at $41\frac{3}{8}$. Seven months later the stock was selling at $36\frac{1}{4}$, while the warrants were selling at $25\frac{1}{4}$. Thus a decline of 28 per cent in the value of the stock was accompanied by a decline of 39 per cent in the value of the warrants.

The changes that occurred in the premium on the TWA warrants during the period January 1963 to September 1964 are interesting. The reader will recall that the warrants of this company were selling at a $13.50

premium in January 1963, suggesting that speculators were expecting a rise in the price of the stock. The expected price rise materialized. On July 9, 1964, TWA common was selling at $48\frac{1}{8}$. On this date the warrants were selling for $30\frac{1}{2}$, a premium of only $2\frac{3}{8}$. Apparently in July 1964 speculators were not anticipating a continued rise in the stock price at the same rate as they had expected in January 1963.

Dilution.   Dilution refers to an increase in the number of shares of common stock outstanding, not matched by a proportional increase in net income or in stockholders' equity. The exercise of warrants has two effects which tend to offset each other. First, aggregate earnings, dividends, and stockholders' equity must be divided among a greater number of shares. Other things being equal, the exercise of warrants results in a decrease in all three. On the other hand, the company receives new capital from the warrant holders. Presumably this new capital will be invested in such a way as to generate new earnings or to save interest expense by retiring debt. It will also lead to an increase in aggregate stockholders' equity.

The question of dilution revolves around whether or not the proportional increase in shares of common stock outstanding is greater or less than the proportional increase in net earnings and stockholders' equity. The effect on dividends depends upon changes in the future dividend policy of the company.

Dilution from the exercise of warrants can be substantial. To illustrate, compare the situation in Trans-World Airlines as it was on December 31, 1963, when there were 6,702,315 shares of common stock outstanding, with the situation as it would have been had all the outstanding warrants been exercised. The changes are summarized below:

	Actual situation	After assumed conversion
Stockholders' equity:		
Aggregate	$101,996,322.00	$155,996,322.00
Per share	15.22	16.59
Earnings:		
Aggregate	19,840,461.00	19,840,461.00
Per share	2.96	2.11

The effect of exercising the warrants would have been to increase the number of shares outstanding by 40 per cent and to reduce earnings per share by 29 per cent. Book value per share, however, would have increased from $15.22 to $16.59 because each new share brought $20 into the company. If stockholders' equity per share had been greater than $20 per share (or if it should be at some future date, when the warrants are actually exercised), stockholders' equity per share would also have been diluted.

The assumption made above that the new capital received would produce no additional income is undoubtedly too restrictive. Suppose that the $54 million received had been used to reduce corporate debt on which TWA was paying an average 6 per cent interest. Pretax income would be increased by 6 per cent of $54,000,000, or $3,240,000. Corporate taxes in 1963 were 52 per cent; so after taxes net income would be increased by $1,555,200. Earnings per share under these more realistic assumptions would fall from $2.96 to $2.28, a drop of 23 per cent.

Should Warrants Be Exercised? A general answer would be "no," at least until such time as they expire or unless their price drops below the price at which arbitragers can buy the warrants, sell the stock short, and deliver through exercising the warrants, all at a profit. At most times a warrant with life remaining will sell at a premium above its theoretical conversion value, as did the TWA warrants in September 1964. By selling the warrants, a speculator realizes the full price including the premium and pays only one commission. If he exercises the warrants and sells the stock, he loses the premium, he has to put up additional funds to buy the stock, and he has to pay a larger commission on the sale of the stock than he does on the sale of the warrants.

It would appear then that, except for arbitrage transactions, there is no reason to exercise warrants until near the end of their life. For this reason dilution is not likely until the warrants are about to expire. Prior to expiration dilution remains only as a threat, hanging like Damocles' sword over the market value of the stock. All too frequently stockholders forget this threat until dilution suddenly occurs.

18 convertible securities

A convertible security may be defined as a bond or preferred stock with a contractual clause entitling the holder to exchange it for a number of shares of common stock of the same company within a specified period of time. Most convertible securities are bonds; a few are preferred stocks. Most are exchangeable into common stock, although occasionally a convertible bond may be exchangeable into preferred stock.

The number of shares of stock obtained for a convertible bond is fixed by the terms of the original offering. For example, the Crowell-Collier Publishing Company 5 per cent convertible subordinated debentures due in 1983 are convertible at $16 per share into common stock. This means that for every $16 of par value of the bond the holder may obtain one share of common stock. Thus a $1,000 bond could be exchanged for 62.5 shares of common stock, a figure obtained by dividing the bond's par value of $1,000 by $16. (Because fractional shares of stock are not issued, the holder would receive an $8 cash adjustment for the half share due him. Two bonds would be convertible into an even 125 shares of stock.)

Conversion terms of convertible preferred stock are expressed in the same manner. Shares of the $5\frac{1}{8}$ per cent convertible preferred stock of Texas Eastern Transmission Corporation are convertible at $20 per share on or before August 1, 1966; thereafter at $22.50 per share through August 1, 1971; and thereafter at $25 per share through August 1, 1976. Because each share of the preferred stock has a par value of $100, it is initially convertible into 5 shares of common stock. As the conversion price rises with the passage of time, the number of shares of common obtainable drops first to 4.44 shares and then to 4 shares.

As can be seen from the example given, conversion prices frequently rise at prestated intervals during the life of a convertible security. There are two reasons for having an increasing conversion rate. First, it encourages early conversion by depriving the convertible security holder of some of his profit if he fails to convert. Second, it adjusts the convertible privilege to the appreciation that is expected in the market value of the common stock. This means that the convertible security holder benefits only to the extent that the appreciation is greater than expected.

Most convertible security contracts provide for a change in the conversion rate under certain circumstances. For example, the conversion price usually changes whenever a company announces a stock split, pays a stock dividend, or experiences a recapitalization, a merger, or a consolidation. If Crowell-Collier were to have a 2-for-1 stock split, the conversion price would drop automatically from $16 to $8. This change would preserve the proportional rights of the convertible bondholder, for presumably the value of the postsplit share would be half the value of the presplit share.

The holder of a convertible bond is entitled to interest, and the holder of a convertible preferred is entitled to dividends as long as these securities are held. A Crowell-Collier convertible bondholder receives $25 interest every April and October. The holder of a Texas Eastern Transmission convertible preferred stock is entitled to a $5.12½ dividend per year if declared by the board of directors. If either of these convertible security holders converts, he ceases to have any claim to the interest or dividends (including arrearage). In lieu he now has a right to receive such common stock dividends as may be declared and paid.

Convertible Bond Price Characteristics

The market value of convertible bonds and convertible preferred stocks is tied to the market value of the common stock into which they are convertible. In order to avoid undue complexity in the explanation that follows, the remainder of this chapter deals only with convertible bonds exchangeable into common stock. It is understood, however, that the principles illustrated apply to all convertible securities.

The essential elements of a convertible bond issue are frequently presented in tabular form by advisory services. The data in Table 13 are extracted from a tabulation prepared by Moody's Investors Service for its weekly *Bond Survey*. Columns 1, 2, and 3 indicate Moody's bond rating (to be explained fully in Chapter 24), the size of each issue, the name of the issuer, the coupon rate, and the maturity date. The call price for each issue appears in column 4. The call price is the price at which the company may, at its option, retire the issue. The market value of a nonconvertible bond seldom rises above its call price because of the risk of loss to the investor if the company should call the issue. An investor who paid $1,300 for a bond callable at 105 would lose $250 if the bond were suddenly called; he would certainly hesitate to pay $1,300 for the bond unless he were sure that the company would not call it.

When a convertible bond is called, the holder has an option of converting the bond into common stock before the call date. Notice of call must be issued early enough to allow a bondholder to convert if he wishes. When the market value of the common stock carries the bond price above the call

TABLE 13   Selected Convertible Securities

Rating (1)	Amount, millions of $ (2)	Issue (3)	Call price (4)	Conversion price (5)
Ba	39.9	American Mach. & Fdry., 4¼s, 3/1/81	103¼	57.68
B	4.3	Avis, 6s, 4/1/70	102½	10.51
Ba	27.9	Douglas Aircraft, 4s, 2/1/77	102½	80.45
A	8.7	Dow Chemical, 3s, 7/1/82	102¾	46.75
Ba	60.0	Olin Mathieson, 5⅜s, 11/15/82	104¼	50.00

SOURCE: Moody's *Bond Survey*, Sept. 21, 1964.

price, companies sometimes call convertible securities merely to force holders to convert. In such cases the company does not expect the bonds to be presented for redemption and frequently does not have adequate funds to pay off the bonds if presented.

Column 5 in Table 13 shows the conversion price. This is the price, expressed in dollars of par value per bond, which the holder must pay for each share of common stock. It can be determined quickly, by way of example, that a single $1,000 par value bond of Dow Chemical can be converted into 21.39 shares of common stock simply by dividing $1,000 by $46.75. An Olin Mathieson bond may be converted into an even 20 shares of common stock ($1,000 ÷ $50).

Except when the market price of a convertible bond is exactly at par, the conversion price does *not* show the price to which the common stock must rise for conversion to be profitable. The Olin Mathieson bond referred to in Table 13 is convertible at $50. A buyer of this bond at its present price of $1,180 obtains a claim to 20 shares of stock at what amounts to a price of $59 per share ($1,180 ÷ 20). For this particular bondholder the price of the common stock would have to rise above $59 per share for conversion to be profitable. The conversion price is the key to determining how many shares of common stock may be obtained for a bond, but it is not an indicator of the stock value necessary to break even or to make a profit from conversion. To their financial woe, many investors discover this aspect of convertible bonds only too late.

The remaining columns in Table 13 show the current market price of the common stock (column 6), the current market price of the bond (column 7), and the yield to maturity that would be obtained if the convertible bond were purchased at its current price and held to maturity without conversion (column 8). Note that Dow Chemical bonds would produce a loss

Market price of stocks (6)	Market price of bonds (7)	Yield to maturity, % (8)	Bond value based on price of common (9)	Common value based on price of bond (10)	Bond value if nonconvertible	
					Dollars (11)	Yield, % (12)
19	$91\frac{7}{8}$	4.98	35	50	$88\frac{1}{2}$	5.30
$12\frac{5}{8}$	119	2.35	$120\frac{1}{8}$	$12\frac{1}{2}$	$97\frac{7}{8}$	6.45
$29\frac{3}{4}$	$83\frac{1}{2}$	5.89	37	$67\frac{1}{8}$	$75\frac{7}{8}$	6.90
$71\frac{1}{2}$	$152\frac{3}{4}$	minus	$152\frac{7}{8}$	$71\frac{1}{2}$	$82\frac{3}{4}$	4.40
$42\frac{1}{4}$	118	4.08	$84\frac{1}{2}$	59	$101\frac{3}{4}$	5.35

if purchased and held to maturity, for their current price is so high that the loss of principal would be greater than the gain from interest. These bonds are profitable only if converted.

Column 9 indicates the value of the bond *in terms of its underlying stock value*. This value, sometimes called "bond conversion value," is the aggregate market value of the common stock into which the bond is convertible. Quite obviously a bond will never sell below its conversion value by more than the cost of making the conversion and selling the stock, since if it did, arbitragers would buy the bond, sell the stock short, and cover their short position with shares obtained from conversion.

Column 10 indicates the effective price paid for a share of stock if the bond is purchased at its current price. The reader will note that the price indicated for Olin Mathieson is the $59 per share mentioned earlier. The values in this column indicate the level to which the common stock must rise for conversion to be profitable if the bond is purchased at its current price. It is this price rather than that indicated in column 5 on which the investor must set his sights if he hopes to convert at a profit.

Column 11 indicates Moody's estimate of the price at which this bond would be selling if it were an ordinary nonconvertible debenture rather than a convertible bond, but otherwise identical in all respects. This price is frequently referred to as the "bond investment value" because it reflects the inherent value of the bond per se divorced from the right of conversion. The reader will note that in all cases the actual market price of the convertible bonds (column 7) is higher than their bond investment value. This indicates that the investor could buy a nonconvertible bond of identical quality and characteristics at a cheaper price. The difference between the two prices indicates the premium that the convertible bond buyer pays for the conversion privilege. An investor who buys an American Machine & Foundry bond at $91\frac{7}{8}$ when he could buy a similar nonconvertible issue at $88\frac{1}{2}$ is, in effect, paying $3\frac{3}{8}$ (or \$33.75 per bond) for the conversion privilege, i.e., for the chance that the common stock of American Machine & Foundry will rise from its present \$19 per share to over \$50 per share. Obviously the conversion privilege does not come free to buyers of convertible bonds.

Column 12 indicates the yield to maturity obtainable on a similar but nonconvertible security. The investor who buys the American Machine & Foundry bond at its current price is in fact obtaining a yield to maturity of 4.98 per cent (column 8) and is forgoing a 5.30 per cent yield on an identical nonconvertible issue. The difference of 0.32 percentage points is another way of stating the cost of the conversion privilege to the purchaser, for he is sacrificing a 0.32 per cent per annum return in the hope that the stock will rise sufficiently to make conversion profitable.

Convertible Bond Price Behavior

From the foregoing discussion the reader will have discovered that a convertible bond has two separate bases of value. The first, called bond investment value, results from the inherent value of the bond as a bond, entirely separate from its conversion characteristics. The second, called bond conversion value, arises from the value of the common stock into which the bond may be converted. The actual price of a bond in the market will be higher than either of these basic values because investors are normally willing to pay something extra for the chance, even if remote, that conversion will ultimately prove profitable. A convertible bond will sell above its conversion value because of the fact that, in case of a decline in the market price of the stock, the price of the bond will not decline lower than its bond investment value. This limits but does not eliminate the loss that would result from a drop in stock prices. The size of the premium over investment value and over conversion value depends upon investor evaluation of the conversion privilege.

The relationship of market price to bond investment and bond conversion values may best be explained graphically. In Figure 18–1 the horizontal axis indicates common stock prices, and the vertical axis indicates convertible bond prices expressed as a per cent of bond investment value. The horizontal line, labeled "Bond Investment Value," indicates the price at which a nonconvertible bond identical in all other respects would be expected to sell. The diagonal line, labeled "Bond Conversion Value," shows the value of the convertible bond viewed solely as a packet of shares of stock. In Figure 18–1 the bond conversion value line assumes conversion at 50, that is, a \$1,000 par value bond convertible into 20 shares of stock. As a result the bond conversion value line and the bond investment value line intersect at a stock price of \$50 per share.

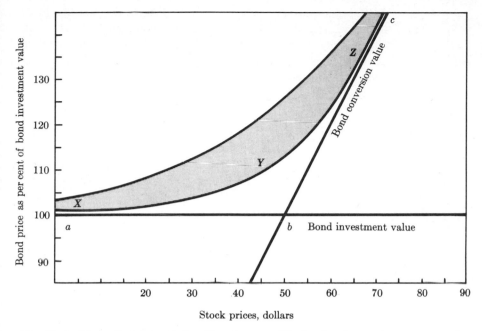

Fig. 18-1 Theoretical interrelationship of convertible bond prices and common stock prices (bond convertible at 50).

If investors could acquire a convertible bond without paying any premium for the conversion privilege, its market price would move along line *ab* when the price of the stock was lower than the bond conversion price and would rise along line *bc* when the price of the stock rose above the bond conversion price. If an investor could buy the convertible bond at a price of *b*, he would have all the benefits to be derived from a rise in price of the stock and all the safety features of a bond if the stock price should drop.

Such a happy state is difficult to achieve, for convertible bond prices do not rest on line *abc* but rather reside in an area above these minimal values. The shape of this general area is indicated in the figure by the shaded zone. If the stock were selling, say, at $10 per share, the bond price would probably be higner than its bond investment value because investors would be willing to pay something for the conversion privilege. If investors were confident that the stock would soon rise above $50, the premium above the bond investment value might be as much as several percentage points; if investors were pessimistic about future stock price increases, the premium might dwindle to almost nothing. The shaded area at *X* has width to indicate the two possibilities. The narrowness of that width indicates general agreement on the remoteness of profitable conversion.

If the price of the common stock should rise toward $50, the price of the bond would rise too. At $50 the price of the bond might be Y, even though conversion at this point is not profitable. This increase in the price of the bond occurs because investors are becoming increasingly more willing to pay a premium in anticipation of later profitable conversion. If profitable conversion appears certain but remote, the price of the bond will be near the bottom of the shaded area, but if the increase in stock prices from $10 to $50 shows signs of continuing, the price of the bond will be near the top of the shaded area. For this reason the shaded area at Y is much wider than it is at X.

Finally, if the price of the stock were to rise significantly above the conversion price, the market price of the convertible bond would continue to rise but the size of the premium would tend to diminish because at high levels a drop in the price of the stock would cause an almost equivalent drop in bond prices during the first portion of the fall. At point Z, for example, the common stock is selling at $65 per share. The bond has a conversion value of 130 and is priced somewhat higher, perhaps at 135. At this price level the aggregate value of the bond ($1,350) consists of $1,000 because it is a bond; plus $300, the value of the conversion privilege; and $50 thrown in as a premium to allow for the possibility that the stock might rise still higher. If the common stock were to start down in price, approximately a quarter of the bond's current value could evaporate.

Clearly, when a bond price has been carried way above bond investment value by a rise in stock prices, the bond no longer provides significant down-side safety against a decline in stock prices. The premium which investors would pay when down-side safety is missing would be minimal.

Figure 18–1 offers convertible bond investors a guiding principle. An investor buying a convertible bond should choose one priced in the general vicinity of Y. Bond prices at X will rise slowly in relation to the initial price rise of the common stock. If the investor seeks capital gain, he would be better off to buy the stock so as to share in the first portion of the rise. If he desires the safety of a bond, he would obtain a higher yield by buying a similar nonconvertible bond.

A convertible bond priced at Z will rise less rapidly than the common stock, owing to the tendency of the premium to diminish as the price soars. However, if the price of the stock were to fall, the market price of the bond would decline proportionately in the initial stage of the drop.

Ideally one would buy a bond priced at b, the intersection of the bond conversion value line with the bond investment value line, for at this point the bond offers complete protection on the down side and equal appreciation potential with the stock on the up side. Unfortunately bonds priced at b cannot be found. Thus a bond at Y would be the most feasible selection. A bond purchased at this price is in a position to share a major portion (but not all) of any appreciation in the price of the stock and is cushioned against most (but not all) losses that would result from a fall of stock prices.

It is also evident from Figure 18–1 that a convertible bond buyer does not acquire the conversion privilege free. Depending upon the size of the premium, he pays *both* a greater price for the convertible bond than he would pay for an otherwise identical bond that was not convertible and more for the shares of stock than he would pay if he purchased them directly.

Figure 18–2, based on data in Table 14, shows the actual price performance during the period January 1963 to April 1964 of Avis 6 per cent convertible subordinated debentures of 1970, relative to changes in the company's common stock prices. The reader will note that the actual bond-stock price relationship is essentially similar to the pattern suggested in Figure 18–1.

TABLE 14   Miscellaneous Data Relating to Avis 6% Convertible Subordinated Debentures and Common Stock, January 1963 to April 1964

Date	Market price of debentures, per cent of par	Approximate debt value of debentures, per cent of par	Market price as per cent of debt value	Common stock price
1/14/63	95	91.75	103.5	$ 8.00
2/11/63	97	91.875	105.6	8.75
3/11/63	98.5	92	107.1	8.125
4/ 8/63	104	91.5	113.7	9.75
5/13/63	112	93.375	119.9	10.75
6/10/63	114	94.625	120.5	9.875
7/ 8/63	109	94.625	115.2	9.50
8/12/63	112	95.25	117.6	11.375
9/ 9/63	117	95.875	122.0	12.50
10/14/63	120	96.125	124.8	12.75
11/11/63	118	96.375	122.4	12.375
12/ 9/63	115	97	118.6	12.375
1/13/64	120	97	123.7	12.25
2/10/64	120	97.50	123.1	11.75
3/ 9/64	124	97.50	127.2	13.375
4/13/64	135	97.625	138.2	14.375

SOURCE: Moody's *Bond Survey*.

Conversion or Sale?

Suppose that one purchases a convertible bond at a reasonable level, that the underlying common stock rises appreciably, and that the bond sells substantially in excess of its purchase price. If the investor wishes to realize

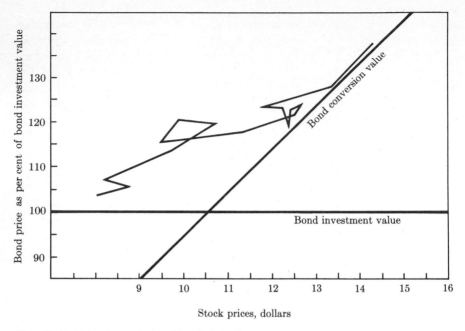

Fig. 18–2 Price interrelationship of Avis convertible debentures of 1970 and its common stock from January 1963 to April 1964.

his profit, should he convert the bond into common stock and sell the stock? Or should he sell the bond?

Usually the most profitable procedure is to sell the bond. The commission for selling a bond is almost always less than the commission for selling the shares of stock that would be obtained from conversion. For example, assume that a bond selling at $1,500 is convertible into 20 shares of stock selling at $75 per share. Selling the bond on the New York Stock Exchange would involve a commission of $2.50. If the bond is converted into 20 shares of stock, which are then sold for $1,500, the commission would be $20. The investor would also benefit from selling the bond rather than converting it and selling the shares because of the premium included in the bond price. In most cases the cash proceeds from sale of a convertible bond are greater than the cash proceeds from selling the underlying stock, regardless of the commissions.

For these reasons convertible bonds are seldom converted except when the conversion privilege is about to expire, either because the bond is maturing or because it has been called, or when the conversion price is about to be changed. At such times a sale may have no particular advantage over conversion with subsequent sale of the stock because the forced conversion tends to bring the two prices (on an after-commission basis) into line with each other.

Hedging with Convertible Bonds

The relationship between convertible bond prices and common stock prices illustrated in Figure 18–1 suggests a special type of investment operation in convertible securities, namely, hedging. If a stock-bond price relationship similar to that represented by point Y in Figure 18–1 can be found and if anticipation of a drop in stock prices is reasonable, it is possible to sell the common stock short and to buy a convertible bond as a protective hedge.

If the price of the stock does drop, a profit is made on the short sale. On the other hand, the price of the bond drops less proportionately because of the support provided by the bond's investment value plus the probability of some premium over bond investment value. Thus the gain on the short sale would probably exceed the loss on the bond purchase, and the operation would be profitable. On the other hand, if the price of the stock rose unexpectedly, the convertible bond price would tend to rise with it. Thus the loss on the short sale would be offset to a considerable extent by the profit from the rise in the convertible bond.

If convertible bond prices moved along line abc and the hedged short sale operation were undertaken at point b, the trader's position would be perfectly hedged. His assured gain would be reduced only by the amount of the commissions and other carrying charges. However, since bond-stock price relationships tend to be in the shaded zone rather than along the abc line, it must be recognized that a convertible bond is only an imperfect hedge; it protects the trader against a major portion of the potential loss, but it also offsets a small portion of the profit from a short sale.

Persons contemplating such a hedging operation must take care to find situations where the bond-stock price relationship is relatively near the Y point in Figure 18–1, i.e., where the stock is priced relatively near to its conversion price and the bond premium is not too great. A hedged short sale at point X would prove profitable if the common stock were to drop, but the hedge would offer little protection if the stock price should rise from $10 to $50. A hedged short sale at point Z would be well protected against an unanticipated rise in the stock price, but if the stock price should decline, the accompanying drop in the bond price would offset a large portion of the profit from the short sale.

Dilution

The existence of outstanding convertible securities poses a threat of dilution to the stockholders of a company. The threat arises from the fact that when convertible bonds are exchanged for common stock the number of shares of stock outstanding increases. As a result, an investor with a given number of shares may find that his proportionate interest in the company has diminished; frequently he finds that the market value of his shares drops.

There are three basic types of dilution: dilution of book value, dilution of earnings per share, and dilution of dividends. Consider a company whose capital structure is:

5% convertible debentures, cvbl. at $25	$1,000,000
100,000 shares of common stock	3,000,000
	$4,000,000

The book value per share of common stock is $30 ($3,000,000 ÷ 100,000). If the debentures were converted into common stock, the common stockholders' equity would rise to $4,000,000 and the number of shares outstanding would increase to 140,000. Book value per share would then be $28.57. This dilution of book value comes about because the new stockholders added only $25 of book value per share, which was averaged with the $30 of book value per share contributed by the old stockholders.

Of more importance to stockholders is the possibility of dilution of earnings per share. Assume that before conversion the income statement of this company revealed the following:

Net income before interest and taxes	$500,000
Less interest on convertible debentures	50,000
Taxable income	$450,000
Less income taxes (assume 50%)	225,000
Net to common stockholders	$225,000

Earnings per share are $2.25. If the bonds were converted, the net result would be

Net income before taxes and interest	$500,000
Less interest (now eliminated)	
Taxable income	$500,000
Less income taxes (assume 50%)	250,000
Net to common stockholders	$250,000

Net income to common stockholders increases by the amount of the interest saved less the tax loss on the added earnings. However, the number of shares of stock outstanding increases 40 per cent so that earnings per share drop to $1.79, a decline of almost 21 per cent.

If, as is commonly believed, market price is determined primarily by reported earnings per share, the price of the stock could be expected to decline appreciably. Yet were investors to foresee that earnings per share would soon be diluted, current prices would have discounted the dilution and the price would not drop as a result of the decline in earnings per share. On the other hand, if investors did not foresee the expected dilution, the market price of the stock would react as first noted.

Dividends per share are subject to dilution in the same manner. If a company has a policy of paying out, say, 60 per cent of earnings per share in dividends, a decline in earnings per share would lead to an equivalent percentage drop in dividends. There is a reasonable probability that the directors of the corporation would have anticipated the dilution and that their past dividends took this into account. If so, dividends per share might not be reduced as a result of conversion. Even if dividends were maintained, the increase in the number of shares outstanding means that the cash cost of paying the same dividend rate has increased. This might mean that a future increase in the dividend rate would be deferred because of the conversion.

part 4 INVESTOR ACTIVITY
IN THE MARKET

19 the long-term investor

A close examination of the movement of stock prices reveals three types of superimposed fluctuations, identified as the technical swing, the major cycle, and the long-term trend.[1] A special form of trading exists for each of these types. First it will be noted that the market advances for three or four weeks, becomes dull, and suffers a setback, usually described as a "technical reaction," after which the advance is resumed. This characteristic pattern occurs in bear markets as well as in bull markets. The pattern extends over several weeks and is of special interest to a technical trader who believes that it results from changes in supply and demand and that its direction, duration, and extent may be revealed by charts. The methods used by such traders to predict short-cycle price movements are explained in Chapter 22.

A series of minor cycles with rises greater than declines is followed by a series with declines greater than rises. The two series together constitute a major swing extending over a period of several years. It is possible to formulate a scheme of trading based upon this cyclical swing. The major cycle of stock prices is associated by many with the cycle of business activity known as the "business cycle." Many investors and speculators choose to ignore the "technical" or short-term ups and downs of the market and strive to buy shares at or near the bottom of the business cycle for sale at or near the top. These traders, or investors, are major-swing traders. The basis of their activities is explained in Chapter 20.

When stock prices are charted for a period long enough to include three or more major cycles, it will be noted that the cycles are only deviations from a trend that rises slowly and continuously. The slope of this trend and the amplitude of the deviations from it vary somewhat with the index used and for the period plotted. During the period 1898 to 1925 the trend of the Dow-Jones industrial averages advanced at a rate of $3\frac{1}{4}$ per cent per year, and deviations from the trend were contained within a range of plus or minus 25 per cent.

---

[1] Actually there is a fourth type of fluctuation not discernible in a chart of monthly highs and lows—the hour-to-hour changes. These fluctuations are of interest to floor traders, who do not have to pay commissions, and constitute the basis for the conclusions of tape readers. The activities of tape readers are explained in Chap. 22.

Confidence in the dependability of an advancing trend and in the limitations of its deviations provides a basis for trend trading. Such investors merely accumulate shares currently with an intention of holding for ten or twenty years, by which time they hope that prices even at the bottom of a major cycle will be higher than they were at the top of the cycles of previous decades. The balance of this chapter is devoted to an explanation of the techniques and rationale of this type of investment.

The Long-term Trend of Prices

The monthly highs and lows of the Dow-Jones industrial averages for the period January 1898 to June 1964 are shown in Figure 19–1. A cursory examination of this figure suggests the appropriateness of dividing the sixty-six-year period into three subperiods: (1) 1898 to 1925, (2) 1926 to 1939, and (3) 1940 to 1964.

The Period 1898 to 1925.   During this period the trend of the averages was steadily upward at a rate of 3.24 per cent per annum, with deviations limited to plus or minus 25 per cent of the trend value. Obviously the existence of this pattern could not have been known during the first part of the period in which it was established. The persistence of the pattern began to attract attention in the early 1920s and led to the formulation of what has come to be known as the "common stock theory" of investment.

This theory was popularized by Edgar L. Smith's epoch-making announcement in 1924 that in the long run a diversified investment in common

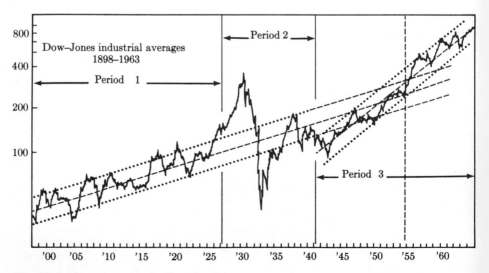

Fig. 19–1   Long-term trend of stock prices.

stocks of well-known companies is likely to prove more profitable than an investment in good bonds. Smith was not the first to make the discovery, but his book, *Common Stocks as Long-term Investments,* was published at a time when millions of persons were speculating in the market without any clear-cut plan of operation. His thesis was readily accepted by these persons as a logical explanation of what they were doing.

Smith's studies consisted of a series of tests. In each test, two funds of approximately $10,000 were invested, one in stocks and one in bonds. In some tests the investments were made in 1901, when the market was at a high point of a major cycle, and were sold in 1922, at the bottom of a major cycle. Other tests used the periods 1880 to 1899, 1866 to 1885, 1892 to 1911, and 1906 to 1922. Mechanical means were employed to select issues for investment, in order to avoid picking shares which in 1923 were known to have been profitable. For example, in one test the 10 issues with the largest volume of transactions on the New York Stock Exchange in 1900 were chosen; in another, the stocks of corporations having the most shares outstanding in 1900 were used. In all 11 tests were made. All but 1 of these showed a portfolio of stocks to have the advantage over a portfolio of bonds. Smith's findings created much interest in common stocks as a possible medium of long-term investment for a small investor and gave rise to the theory mentioned. Other studies followed, most of them confirming Smith's findings.[2]

The Period 1926 to 1939. This period is best characterized as irregular in the sense that prices during this interval did not conform to the pattern established during the preceding period. The irregularity began in 1925, when the Dow-Jones industrial averages penetrated the upper limit of their traditional range and soared to a level 300 per cent above its 1929 trend value. Then in September of that year the averages began a precipitous retreat that carried them to an unprecedented low of 30 per cent of the 1932 trend value. By 1935 the averages were back in the traditional range established in the first period, and they remained within that range until mid-1940.

The behavior of prices during this second period was disheartening to those who had acquired shares in 1928 and 1929 on the strength of the common stock theory. As might be expected, desertions from the ranks of the theory's following were many. A number of studies have been made to test the validity of the common stock theory under even more adverse conditions

---

[2]Kenneth S. Van Strum, *Investing in Purchasing Power,* New York: *Barron's,* 1925; Dwight C. Rose, *A Scientific Approach to Investment Management,* New York: Harper & Row, Publishers, Incorporated, 1928; and R. G. Rodkey, *Preferred Stocks as Long-term Investments,* Ann Arbor: University of Michigan Bureau of Business Research, 1932.

than those used by Smith. Three tests, based upon the period 1913 to 1931, were more favorable to common stocks than to bonds.[3] Other investigators extended Smith's data to the years 1931 and 1932, and these also confirmed the theory.[4] But the rank and file of investors were not impressed.

In order to test the validity of the common stock theory during the period 1930 to 1940, the following study was made by the authors. It was assumed that one investor purchased approximately $1,000 worth of each of 10 common stocks on January 11, 1930, and that a second investor purchased one $1,000 bond in each of 10 issues on the same date. Both investors held their securities for ten years and then sold.

On the date chosen to make the purchases, the Dow-Jones averages were 62 points above the low of 1929 and 209 points above the subsequent low of 1932; that is, on the basis of what is known now, January 1930 was the wrong time to buy stocks. The date chosen to sell was *exactly* ten years later, at which time stock prices were 49 points below the high for the decade.

The stocks chosen were 10 of the market leaders of 1929. The bonds were chosen from a list of the 31 most active bond issues of 1929. Those issues which were matured, redeemed, refunded, or put through a reorganization during the subsequent decade were eliminated. Then, on the basis of facts known later, the 10 best performers of the remaining lot were chosen. In other words, the portfolio of bonds was given advantages denied the portfolio of stocks. The results of the test are given below.

	Bonds	Stocks
Cost, Jan. 11, 1930	$10,041.30	$ 9,960.86
Sales price, Jan. 15, 1940	8,968.80	10,241.27
Profit (or loss)	−1,072.50	280.41
Income from interest and dividends	4,850.00	3,663.16
Net income from investment	3,777.50	3,943.57
Advantage of stocks over bonds		166.07

These figures do not prove the validity of the common stock theory. Rather they point out a fact that many investors of that era missed—that, disappointing as a portfolio of common stocks might appear, its performance was nevertheless better than that of any alternative program. Critics of the common stock theory overlooked the fact that bonds frequently default during periods of extreme adversity.

[3] J. L. Amberg, "Testing the Theory of Stocks for Long Term Investments in a Bear Market," *Magazine of Wall Street,* Feb. 7, 1931.

[4] Chelcie C. Bosland, *The Common Stock Theory of Investment,* New York: The Ronald Press Company, 1937.

The Period 1940 to 1964.   The trend of the Dow-Jones industrial averages from 1940 to the time of writing (December 1964) has been upward at an annual rate of 9.1 per cent, with deviations confir.:d to plus or minus 25 per cent of trend values. This rate of rise, it will be noted, is almost three times the rate characteristic of the first period. The reestablishment of the old pattern at an increased rate went unnoticed during the first eight or ten years of the period, but its persistence gradually attracted the attention of the public and resurrected the popularity of the common stock theory. The sharp decline of prices that occurred in 1962, even though prices did not penetrate their lower theoretical limits, shook public confidence in the reliability of the theory and led to a general exodus of many small investors from the market. Only investors with true confidence in the long-run validity of the theory resisted the tendency to flee.

Why Common Stocks Win in the Long Run.   The trends and deviations of stock prices shown in Figure 19–1 offer a clue as to why common stocks prove superior to bonds *in the long run*. During the first period, the market value of the leaders increased at a rate of 3.24 per cent per year. The maximum swing from a major top to the subsequent major bottom was limited to 50 per cent of the trend value. Thus the cumulative rise in the trend over a $15\frac{1}{2}$-year period exceeded the maximum decline from top to bottom of any major swing. For this reason the conclusions of any test in which securities are held longer than $15\frac{1}{2}$ years is predestined to prove more favorable to common stocks than to bonds even under the most adverse circumstances.

Tests beginning or ending during the period 1925 to 1934 may be an exception to this rule. But, as earlier discussion has shown, tests of the theory in this period do not prove so unfavorable to common stocks as many suppose. It is scarcely necessary to mention that all studies of long-term investment beginning after 1931 or later are predestined by subsequent events to prove favorable to common stocks.[5]

The statistical description of the market given above offers an interesting hypothesis to explain why the period 1925 to 1933 constitutes an exception to the rule of growth implied in the steady rise of the trend. Let us assume that the majority of old-time investors are inclined to sell when prices rise 25 per cent above or to buy when prices sink 25 per cent below the trend. This amounts to assuming that the great majority of investors are major-swing traders. The assumption, if true, would limit market fluctuations

[5] The reader is referred to two such studies: *Common Stock Values and Yields, 1937–1950,* by Wilford J. Eiteman and Frank P. Smith, Ann Arbor: University of Michigan Bureau of Business Research, 1953; and *Common Stock Values and Yields, 1950–1961,* by Wilford J. Eiteman and Dean S. Eiteman, Ann Arbor: University of Michigan Bureau of Business Research, 1962.

to plus or minus 25 per cent of the trend. Suppose now that after five or six major cycles some writer (such as Edgar Smith) calls attention to the historical and statistical fact that the trend rise over a period of two decades is greater than the maximum decline in any major swing. If a majority of investors are impressed by this statement, they will shift from major-swing trading to trend trading. Such a shift would remove the selling pressure that comes into the market when prices rise 25 per cent above the trend and by so doing would make possible an unprecedented rise similar to the one that occurred in the period 1927 to 1929. The sudden and drastic decline from the 1929 peak back to the 1929 trend value would occasion much financial distress and shake the confidence of investors in their recently adopted philosophy. It would also cause the downward adjustment of prices to become excessive.

The decline from the peak of 1929 to the trough of 1932 would convince long-term traders that the philosophy of the common stock theory was fallacious and would encourage their return to the fold of major-swing traders. This in turn would reestablish the conditions necessary for the smooth working of the common stock theory. That is, if everyone is convinced that stocks always rise in the long run, no force exists to prevent an unreasonable upward surge of prices. But if many traders operate on the assumption that the theory is not true, their market behavior acts as a brake to exaggerated price rises and so aids in making the theory become true. Apparently the common stock theory is valid only as long as too many persons do not believe it to be true.

The Principle of Diversification

The description given above of the movement of stock prices since 1898 clearly establishes one fact: the long-term trend of stock prices has always been upward. Declines of prices that look big at the time they occur become minor deviations when viewed in retrospect, the decline of 1929 to 1932 being an exception. No evidence contradictory to this assertion about the long-term trend is uncovered even when the period of study is extended as far back as 1865. Thus, on the basis of the historic behavior of prices over a full century, one might conclude that it is safe to invest on the basis of a "buy and hold" philosophy if the assertion is subjected to one important qualification.

The validity of the common stock theory of stock price trends rests upon the behavior of price *averages*. An individual investor does not buy averages; he buys particular issues. It is possible that the behavior of a particular issue will not coincide with that of the averages. Thus the long-term investor is confronted with two problems: (1) that of *selecting* issues and (2) that of *timing* purchases. The principle of diversification offers a solution to both problems.

Diversification Applied to Selection.   If one has confidence that the average price of a group of issues will rise through time but is not certain that the price of every issue within the group will move with the average, he assumes great risk when he invests his funds in any one issue, for he may do as well as the best or as poorly as the worst issue in the group. By investing an equal amount of funds in each of several issues or by purchasing the same number of shares of each of several issues, an investor increases the probabilities that the total outcome of his commitments will do as well as (and no better than) the average. As explained earlier, the long-term investor is confident of the outcome of the average.

It should be noted that there is a cost as well as an advantage to issue diversification. The investor who diversifies forfeits the possibility of doing as well as the best in exchange for removal of the possibility of doing as poorly as the poorest. Diversification guarantees mediocrity—that the performance of the portfolio will be average. Many long-term investors overlook this fact and register disappointment when the results of a sound program prove less profitable than an investment of all their funds in one spectacular issue.

Diversification Applied to Timing.   The second difficulty in trading successfully on the basis of confidence in a rising trend can best be described by reference to Figure 19–2. Let the curved line starting at point *A* and ending at point *I* represent the course of prices during two successive major cycles. The straight line *ACEGI* represents the trend. We are assuming that our long-term investor is confident that the trend will continue to rise but that he does not know the rate of rise nor where the price at any particular moment is with regard to the trend.

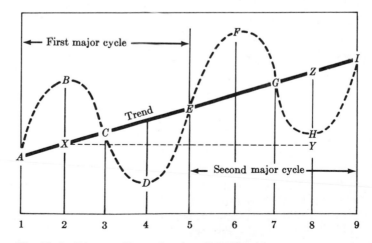

Fig. 19–2   Diagram illustrating time diversification.

In theory it would appear that one could make a profit equal to the distance YZ by investing at a price of X at time point 2 and selling at a price of Z at time point 8. But investors cannot buy at a price of X at time point 2, for the reason that the actual market price at time point 2 is B, the maximum cyclical deviation above the trend value. Furthermore, investors cannot sell at a price of Z at time point 8, since the price at this moment is H, the maximum cyclical deviation below the trend value. To buy at time point 2 and sell at time point 8 means to buy at a price of B and to sell at a price of H, with a loss thus incurred equal to the difference in the altitudes of B and H.

An investor who is going to rely upon a rising trend for his profit must find some method of making his costs and returns coincide with trend values. This is not easy to do if he is never sure how far an actual price is above or below the trend because he cannot know the trend values except in retrospect. The solution to the problem lies in *time* diversification.

To illustrate, suppose that our hypothetical investor spaced his purchases in equal amounts over time points 1, 2, 3, 4, and 5. If he were to do this, his average cost of acquisition would be slightly less than C. If he should spread the sales of his shares equally over time points 5, 6, 7, 8, and 9, the average return from his sales would be G. Thus his final situation would be a little better than if he had purchased at a price of C and sold at a price of G. However, his profit would be much less than it would have been had he invested at D and liquidated at F. But he could not have done this without knowing that D and F are the best prices at which to buy and sell. Furthermore, if he attempts to choose the proper moments at which to buy and sell, he runs the risk of investing at B and liquidating at H.

Time diversification, frequently referred to as "dollar averaging," really amounts to spreading moments of purchasing and selling over many dates because the investor is not certain as to which dates are the best. If selling dates are spread over a major cycle that is later than the major cycle in which the buying dates are spread, the certainty of the rising trend assures a profitable outcome. This profit will not be so great as that realized from a choice of auspicious dates, but for the average lay investor a happy choice of dates is a matter of pure chance.

Diversification of selection and timing does not solve all the problems facing the long-term investor in stocks. Diversification merely obviates some of the possibilities of error. It is still necessary for an investor to select issues to add to his portfolio. Obviously a diversified list of good issues can be expected to give a better long-run performance than a diversified list of run-of-the-mill issues. The problem is to separate the good from the run-of-the-mill issues. At least three schools of thought exist as to the best procedure for doing this. They are known as the growth stock theory, the margin-of-safety theory, and the random selection theory.

The Growth Stock Theory

There is no generally accepted agreement as to just what constitutes a growth stock. The concept is confused further by the loose use of the word growth. For example, one reads of a growth *industry,* a growth *company,* and a growth *stock.* A growth industry probably refers to a segment of the economy which, owing to some peculiar situation or recent development, is expected to expand more rapidly than other segments. At one time the chemical industry was considered to be a growth industry.

By contrast, a growth company is one whose strategic position within an industry (which may or may not be a growth industry) is such as to guarantee that it will enjoy unusual prosperity in the period ahead. (From an investor's point of view, prosperity relates to earnings available for the common stock equity.) However, if current quotations of a stock fully discount a company's future increased earnings, the stock is not a growth investment even though its issuer is a growth company. A growth stock is one whose market value is expected to increase faster than average, for, in the last analysis, market appreciation is what a long-term common stock investor seeks most.

Apparently the problem of practical importance is not defining a growth stock but identifying one. Investors use two widely divergent approaches to identification. The first calls for an inductive conclusion or forecast based on an analysis of the circumstances in which the company will operate, and the second assumes that a historically demonstrated rate of growth will continue on into the future.

Special Analysis Approach.   If one can find a *small* company producing a *new product* that is certain to obtain *widespread consumer use,* and that can be produced and marketed at a *satisfactory margin of profit,* and if it is possible to acquire the shares of this company at prices *based upon current earnings* per share, one has in truth discovered a really profitable situation. But there are not many such issues, and those which do exist are difficult to find.

Although every growth situation does not possess all the characteristics mentioned, there is a logical reason why these characteristics are important. To begin with, profits depend upon sales, and sales depend upon consumer use. The likelihood of a high percentage increase in consumer use is greater in the case of a new than of an old product. For example, today it is more reasonable to expect a 50 per cent increase in the use of the newly invented electric toothbrush than to expect a similar percentage increase in the use of the traditional hand model. On the other hand, the mere fact that a product is new does not guarantee that it will enjoy increased consumer acceptance.

The growth of a successful small company is almost certain to be more spectacular than that of a successful large company, but this does not mean that every small company is going to be successful. The size of the Midget Manufacturing Company might double within a year; the size of General Motors most certainly will not. Yet a growth in the earnings of General Motors may be highly probable, whereas even a small growth in the earnings of the Midget Manufacturing Company may be problematical.

Increased consumer use will not increase earnings per share of a small manufacturer of a new product if competition reduces the margin of profit to near zero. For this reason there should be something in a growth situation—patents, exclusive know-how, monopoly of supply, and such— to protect the company from the effect of ruinous competition.

Finally, it will avail a particular investor little to discover a growth company if other investors discover it simultaneously. When everyone has great expectations for a company's growth and expansion, its stock tends to be priced high by comparison with current earnings. Then, if the expectations are realized to the extent anticipated, the price remains stable; if the expectations are realized to an extent less than anticipated, the price declines. Only if expectations are realized to an extent *greater* than anticipated does the price rise. Thus it would appear that the odds are against an investor making a profit from shares of a company generally accepted to be a growth company.

It is evident that the type of information needed to recognize a growth stock in time to profit by the knowledge is the type of information available first to insiders. Because of this fact, the most fruitful (and the most dangerous) source of leads are tips from insiders. How is one to determine whether a tip is genuine, honest, and reliable? Promoters of new companies are so notoriously overoptimistic as to render their judgments regarding the future unreliable. Furthermore, some promoters are dishonest. There always remains a possibility, too, that the tip one receives did not really originate from an insider. All of this suggests that an investor is well advised to be wary of tips and to use them as a basis for investigation rather than as a basis for action.

Demonstrated Earnings Approach.   Some analysts believe that growth companies are identifiable by comparing the rate of increase in their earnings or prices over a period of (five) years with the rate of increase typical of an average company. The companies that have grown faster than average are *ipso facto* growth companies. The presumption is that in the absence of evidence to the contrary the demonstrated better than average rate of growth will continue on into the future.

Brokerage firms and advisory services constantly circulate lists of "issues that have outperformed the market." The unsophisticated investor chooses five or six of these advertised growth companies for purchase and assumes that he has a diversified portfolio of growth stocks. A number of fallacies are involved in this line of thinking. To begin with, an investigation into the history of successful companies reveals that most of them pass through a well-defined, three-phase life cycle. In the first of the three phases the company is small and struggling, lacks sufficient capital, and has difficulty securing consumer acceptance of its product. As a result the rate of growth of its earnings is average or less than average. The mortality rate of companies in this first phase of development is very high, but those which survive frequently enjoy phenomenal growth in the period which follows. Thus infant companies *destined* to survive are growth companies, but they are not identifiable by the five-year demonstrated growth test mentioned above.

The period of corporate infancy just described is followed by a period of corporate adolescence, characterized by rapid expansion, adequate financing, and earnings accretion faster than average. For many growth companies this period of rapid growth lasts for five to ten years. For a few it lasts longer; for many it endures for only a year or two. Sooner or later the period of rapid growth is followed by a period of maturity during which earnings continue to increase, but at an *average* rate. A curve of earnings typical of a company passing through all three phases of a life cycle is shown in Figure 19–3.

The existence of this three-phase life-cycle pattern confronts the seeker for growth stocks with a real dilemma. If he chooses to invest in companies while they are in the first cycle of their development, the high mortality rate works to reduce the profitability of his program. If he confines his purchases to the shares of companies that have demonstrated faster than average growth over a period of five years, he runs a risk of entering the market at just about the time when the company is leaving the second and entering the third phase of its life cycle. As will be shown, this is a hazardous moment marketwise at which to acquire stocks of growth companies.

Of two stocks having identical dollar-and-cent current earnings per share, the one whose earnings have increased faster percentagewise during the previous year will tend to sell at the higher price-earnings ratio. In the absence of evidence to the contrary, investors tend to assume that the rate of increase demonstrated in the current year will persist in the subsequent year. If this surmise proves erroneous, the price-earnings ratio applied in the following year is adjusted up or down as the occasion demands.

The risk of buying shares whose earnings have increased faster than average over the past five years can be illustrated by applying the above tendencies to the hypothetical earnings curve shown in Figure 19–3. The solid line in this diagram represents the course of earnings over a seventeen-year life cycle. From A to B earnings increased at an average rate, and a price-earnings ratio of 13 was applied. From B to C earnings increased at a faster rate than in the previous year. Accordingly the price-earnings ratio was increased gradually from 13 to 20. Beginning at C and continuing to $D,$

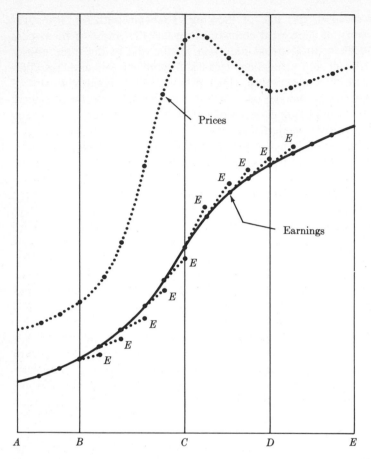

Fig. 19–3 Diagram illustrating hazards of choosing growth stocks by demonstrated earnings method.

earnings increased each year faster than average, but at a declining rate. As the rate of increase decelerated each year, the price-earnings ratio applied was reduced. From *D* to *E* earnings continued to increase, but at a rate typical of companies in the aggregate. Consequently, a price-earnings ratio of 14 was applied.

   The effect of these assumptions on intrinsic value is shown by the dotted line in the figure. During the period of rapid growth, *B* to *D,* the earnings curve on the chart was extended each year at the rate of increase characteristic of the previous year to arrive at an estimated earnings figure. The estimates arrived at by this means are shown by the series of dots labeled *E*.

   It will be noted that actual earnings were always exceeding estimated earnings between *B* and *C*, when earnings were increasing at an accelerating rate, and that actual earnings were always failing to equal estimated earning from C to D, when earnings were increasing at a decelerating rate. This is the phenomenon that causes investors to make adjustments in the price-earnings ratio applied to earnings for determining value. It will be noted that the decrease in the ratio that set in shortly after C caused prices to decline by a greater amount than the increase in earnings caused prices to rise. This is a phenomenon frequently seen in an actual market.

A growth stock investor being guided by the popular five-year demonstrated earnings test would not have been attracted to this issue until time point C, when prices were close to their zenith and were about to begin a decline. This is the hazard assumed by investors who allow themselves to be influenced by published statistical data of "stocks that have outperformed the market."

The Margin-of-safety Theory

Some trend investors select issues for inclusion in their portfolios on the basis of what has come to be called the "margin-of-safety" principle. Briefly the procedure followed by such investors is as follows: First, the investor studies available quantitative and qualitative data related to the company for the purpose of arriving at a conservative appraisal of the "proper," or "intrinsic," value of its stock. This intrinsic value is not a single figure but a range such as, say, 28 to 31. A particular issue becomes an investment only if it can be purchased at a price lower than its intrinsic range, so determined. The purchase of a stock at a price lower than its indicated value provides an investor with a cushion to absorb unfavorable developments. This cushion makes the commitment in the issue relatively safe.

It should be pointed out that the existence of a margin of safety does not by itself *guarantee* that a particular investment will not result in a loss. What it does is reduce the *probabilities* of such a loss. Obviously there is always a possibility that any one investment may "turn sour," but it is unlikely almost to a point of certainty that a diversified list of 10, 15, or 20 issues each with an adequate margin of safety could or will do so.

At this point a question of importance arises: Is it possible to find issues with an adequate margin of safety? When the market as a whole is at or near the bottom of a major swing, most listed issues are undervalued. When the market as a whole is at midlevel, most high-quality market leaders are overpriced (by reference to their intrinsic value) but many medium-quality issues of less popularity are still underpriced. These "bargain" issues are likely to be financially strong companies destined by the nature of things to stay in business and to make profits indefinitely, but at the moment they lack investment glamour. When the market is at or near the top of a major swing, most issues (even those of inferior quality) are overpriced. At such times the margin-of-safety trend investor finds it necessary to sit on the sidelines with his cash uncommitted. This is very difficult to do, but unless he can resist the temptation to buy indiscriminately at such times, he is not a true disciple of the margin-of-safety school.[6]

The Random Selection Theory

It is probably a fact that the long-run price appreciation of the majority of market leaders exceeds the long-run price depreciation of the minority. If so, then it follows that a portfolio of diversified market leaders picked at random should provide an investor with safety of principal and an adequate yield. A number of investigators have implied that such a portfolio would do as well as or even better than one chosen by the application of the accepted principles of security analysis.

Of one thing we may be certain. An evaluation of the services rendered by investment advisers or managers of mutual funds should be judged not by their reported accomplishments but by the extent to which their accomplishments exceed the performance of a portfolio chosen at random. However, it is not fair to investment advisers or to mutual fund managers to compare their portfolio performances with the movement of some well-known stock price index. It must be borne in mind that the rise of an index between two given dates measures the price appreciation that should be attained by an investment of all the available funds on the first of the two dates. Funds made available to managers of mutual and pension funds come to them in instalments and so must be committed to investment on a number of dates scattered over a period of time. No existing index of stock prices is capable of suggesting a performance standard for investment under such conditions.[7]

One of the authors has had the privilege of participating in two studies designed to discover the rate of return which might be reasonable to expect from a portfolio based upon random selection in which issues were selected at random and funds were invested on an instalment basis. The first of the two studies covered the period 1937 to 1950, during which the Dow-Jones industrial averages rose 7 per cent.[8] The second of the two studies covered

[6] For a more detailed description of margin-of-safety investigating, the reader is referred to *Security Analysis*, 4th ed., by B. Graham, S. L. Dodd, and S. Cottle, New York: McGraw-Hill Book Company, 1962, p. 431.

[7] For a precise illustration, assume that a stock price index on three successive dates was 100, 160, and 200. As a result funds invested on the first date should double in value by the third date. But an investment of $1,000 on each of the three dates would have a value of only $4,250 on the third date. Such an instalment investment would have done "as well as the market," but the fact would not be revealed by comparing the outcome with the percentage increase in the index.

[8] *Common Stock Values and Yields, 1937–1950*, by Wilford J. Eiteman and Frank P. Smith, Ann Arbor: University of Michigan Bureau of Business Research, 1953.

the period January 15, 1950, to January 15, 1961, during which the Dow-Jones industrial averages advanced 218 per cent.[9] The master list of stocks used in both studies included only the industrial issues listed on the New York Stock Exchange that achieved a trading volume in excess of 1 million shares *during the calendar year of 1936*. The list excluded, therefore, all the glamour issues of the recent bull market, and both studies ended at a stock price level considerably lower than the peak attained later.[10]

The study proceeded as follows: A hypothetical investor was assumed to invest $1,000 in each of the 91 issues included in the master list on the fifteenth day of January in each of the years of the test period. In addition he was assumed to have reinvested in the same issue all cash dividends received and the proceeds of the sale of stock rights and fractional stock dividends. Commitments in each issue were assumed to have been liquidated on January 15, 1961. Numerous test portfolios were arranged by combining the issues in ways that excluded taking advantage of hindsight. A performance index was computed for each issue, for each combination, and for each performance standard. For example, an issue or a combination would have to achieve a performance index of 2.524 to equal the performance of a portfolio made up of the issues used to compute the Dow-Jones industrial averages. The findings of the study are summarized in Table 15.

The over-all average *annual* (compound) yield on the 91 issues for the period studied was 14.2 per cent. This yield did not change significantly when portfolios were composed of fewer than 91 issues. The yield attained was higher than could have been achieved on any portfolio of bonds even under the most favorable possible assumptions. It was high enough to protect the purchasing power of the investor's commitment and in addition to yield him an annual income of 5 per cent *in protected purchasing power*. The long-term investor would have done slightly better to limit his selections to issues used in computing the Dow-Jones industrial averages.

If a portfolio of common stocks selected by such obviously foolish methods as were employed in this study shows an annual compound rate of return as high as 14.2 per cent, then a long-term investor with limited knowledge of market conditions can place his savings in a diversified list of

---

[9] *Common Stock Values and Yields, 1950–1961*, by Wilford J. Eiteman and Dean S. Eiteman, Ann Arbor: University of Michigan Bureau of Business Research, 1962.

[10] The capital gain realized from any ten-year accumulation program depends upon the extent to which the liquidation price at the end of the period exceeds the average acquisition prices during the preceding ten years. Since World War I there have been but eight years in which the Jan. 15 Dow-Jones industrial average failed to exceed the average of the 10 previous Jan. 15 indexes. These years were 1932, 1933, 1934, 1935, 1936, 1938, 1942, and 1943. Thus a study ending in any year other than these eight years is certain to show capital gains, and studies ending in four of these eight years will show a profit as a result of dividend accumulation.

TABLE 15   Performance Indexes of Various Test Portfolios Based on Varied Methods of Selection

Makeup of the portfolio	No. of issues	Performance index
All issues in master list	91	2.298
Issue in list:		
Every second	47	2.068
Every third	30	2.278
Every fourth	23	1.947
Every fifth	19	2.829
Every sixth	16	1.821
Every seventh	13	2.318
Every eighth	12	1.641
Every ninth	11	2.311
Every tenth	9	3.108
Ten best performers*	10	4.340
Ten poorest performers*	10	1.078

Standards for comparisons	Performance index
Performance required to:	
1. Equal a return of 5% compounded annually	1.326
2. Protect investor against purchasing power decline	1.085
3. Accomplish both (1) and (2)	1.490
4. Better a portfolio made up of DJIA issues	2.524

* The chance of picking this particular combination of issues by random selection is 1 in 6,419,835,006.

common stocks with some confidence that, given time, his holdings will provide him with safety of principal and adequate annual yield.

Why the Long-term Trend Rises

The success and safety of the commitments of a long-term investor depend upon the fact that the trend of common stock prices has always been upward and upon the expectation that it will continue to be upward. The risks arising from major-cycle price movements are eliminated by time diversification; the risks of making poor selections are eliminated by issue diversification. Thus the investor's situation is much the same as though he bought and sold at an average of trend values. There remains but one question: To what extent is the long-term investor justified in his expectation that the trend will continue to be upward? Or, to phrase it differently, is there a logical explanation for this upward trend?

From a purely mathematical point of view, stock prices are the product of earnings per share and a price-earnings ratio. This has to be the case, since price-earnings ratios are computed by dividing prices by earnings per share. If R equals $P \div E,$ then of necessity P equals $E \times R$. The formula is only a mathematical truism unless it can be shown that E (earnings per share) and R (the price-earnings ratio) represent independent variables in real life. This happens to be the case.

Earnings per share are an objective factor in that they are not influenced by market behavior. Fortunately an independently determined index of this objective factor exists—earnings per share of the Dow-Jones industrial averages. By contrast, the price-earnings ratio index is a subjective factor—it indicates the value that investors are placing upon $1 of earnings. An index of price-earnings ratios is also available. The two factors vary independently. Our immediate concern is with the question of whether or not the variations are tied to some level which might be considered "normal." For example, if earnings per share could be shown to have an upward trend for a logical reason and the price-earnings ratio could be shown to be tied to a fixed normal, the trend of prices should be upward at about the same rate as the trend of earnings per share. But if earnings per share could be shown to have an upward trend for a logical reason and the price-earnings ratio should prove to be erratic, then the long-term investor could place less reliance upon the permanence of the trend of prices to the extent that it is influenced by subjective factors.

The Trend of Earnings per Share.   A running average of four quarters' earnings per share of the Dow-Jones industrial averages during the period 1949 to mid-1963 is shown in Figure 19-4. The fourteen-year trend of this curve is upward at the rate of 2 per cent per year. Is there a logical reason for this upward trend? We believe there is. The real income of society is the result of labor working with the capital equipment provided by investors. By eliminating fluctuations due to business-cycle variations and by assuming that any increase in labor efficiency will be taken by labor in the form of higher wages, the trend of net income through time will depend upon the trend of total investment in capital goods. The original investment of a corporation in capital equipment is augmented from time to time (1) by new investment and (2) by the reinvestment of retained earnings. Thus, in the absence of new investment, net income should increase as a result of the reinvestment of a portion of past earnings. If there are no stock dividends, no stock splits, and no new issues, the number of a corporation's outstanding shares remains constant even though annual net income increases. An increasing net income figure divided by a constant number of outstanding shares results in increasing earnings per share even if the return per dollar of capital investment remains fixed or declines slightly.

The relationships involved in this reasoning will be illustrated by an

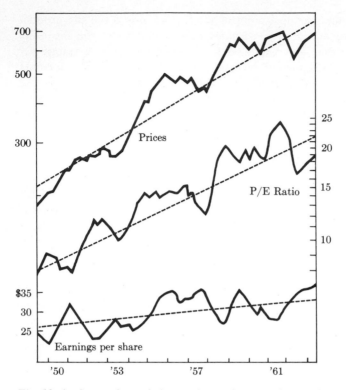

Fig. 19–4 Comparison of changes in earnings per share, price-earnings ratios, and stock prices.

example. Assume a corporation with $100,000 of assets raised by the sale of 10,000 shares of $10 par value common stock. Assume further that the company earns $20 per $100 of total investment and that it pays out 60 per cent of these earnings as dividends and reinvests the remainder in expansion of productive facilities. The outcome of this set of assumptions is reported below:

	First year	Second year	Third year
1. Total assets (at beginning of year)	$100,000	$108,000	$116,640
2. Net income (20% of item 1)	20,000	21,600	23,328
3. Dividends paid (60% of item 2)	12,000	12,960	13,997
4. Reinvested earnings (40% of item 2)	8,000	8,640	9,331
5. Earnings per share (item 2 ÷ 10,000)	20.0¢	21.6¢	23.3¢
6. Dividends per share (item 3 ÷ 10,000)	12.0¢	12.9¢	13.9¢

The rate of increase shown in item 4 will continue indefinitely as long as the assumptions are not changed. Thus it would appear that the productivity of reinvested earnings provides the explanation of the historically demonstrated upward trend of earnings per share.

The Trend of the Price-Earnings Ratios.   The price-earnings ratios of the Dow-Jones industrial averages as of the end of each quarter during the period 1949 to 1962 are also shown in Figure 19–4. The fourteen-year trend of these ratios is upward at a rate of 6.9 per cent per year. As mentioned, a price-earnings ratio is an index of subjective factors; it measures what investors think about earnings. The index of investor thinking fluctuates, but this fluctuation during the period studied did not deviate about a fixed norm. Instead, it revolved about a rising norm (a rising trend), thereby suggesting a more and more liberal evaluation. Can long-term investors rely upon a continuation of this more liberal evaluation tendency?

In prior periods the index of investor thinking has varied from 9 to 20 but has hovered about a norm of 13. The period 1949 to 1962 is the first in history in which the index has shown a tendency to fluctuate about a steadily rising norm for such a protracted period of time. This trend may represent the establishment of a new higher norm, or it may represent nothing more than an unusually long deviation from the old norm. What-

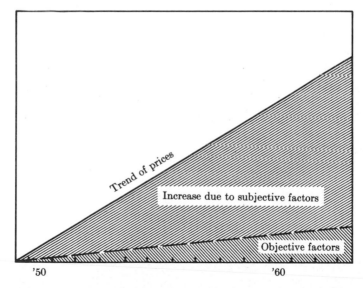

Fig. 19–5 Relative importance of subjective and objective factors as causes of stock prices. (There is no vertical scale on this chart but it is to be noted that the subjective factors in 1963 were about 4½ times as important as the objective factors.)

ever it typifies, it presents a hazard to long-term investors not existing in earlier years.

Unfortunately the risk presented by this new development is not minor in importance. As Figure 19–5 makes clear, 77 per cent of the rise in the trend of stock prices during the period 1949 to 1963 was due to the inherently erratic subjective factor, and only 23 per cent of the rise was due to the more reliable objective factor. The permanence of the present high level of the market depends therefore upon the permanence of the currently high level of the subjective factor. If this high level of the subjective factor proves to be transitory, the future experience of the long-term investor may not duplicate that of the past.

20 the major-swing trader

Thc mechanics of major-swing trading are simple. They consist merely in buying shares at the bottom of a business cycle, when prices of even the best issues are likely to be bargains, and in selling thcm at the top of the cycle, when prices of even the poorest issues are high. The principal difficulties in the procedure are (1) determining when the cycle is in its low or high phase and (2) overcoming a psychological tendency to trade as the crowd trades, it being assumed that the crowd is usually wrong at critical moments.

Three approaches exist to the solution of the two difficulties. The first is a "Forecast it yourself" program. Several of the more popular methods of forecasting are explained latcr in this chapter. The second approach amounts to asking the advice of someone else, i.e., subscribing to an advisory service or following the recommendations of one's broker. The third approach involves the use of a formula that forces one to acquire shares when they arc chcap and to dispose of them when they are dear. Several methods of such formula trading are described in this chapter.

Causal Factors of the Stock Price Cycle

The cycle that interests a major-swing trader is the cycle of stock prices. There are many other cycles, such as a cycle of business activity, a cycle of corporate profits, a cycle of interest rates, a cycle of investor attitudes, and so on. These other cycles are of interest to a major-swing trader only to the extent that they may be causal factors of the stock price cycle or harbingers of one of its phases.

Is There a Stock Price Cycle?   The solid curve in Figure 20–1 is an index of stock prices during the period 1949 to 1963 with the long-term trend removed. Three major swings, composed of three bull markets each followed by a bear market, are clearly discernible. It will be noted that the amplitude and duration of the cycles are not sufficiently regular to permit forecasting on the basis of a pattern. Yet to trade on major swings profitably, one must time the tops and bottoms of the price cycle with a high degree of accuracy.

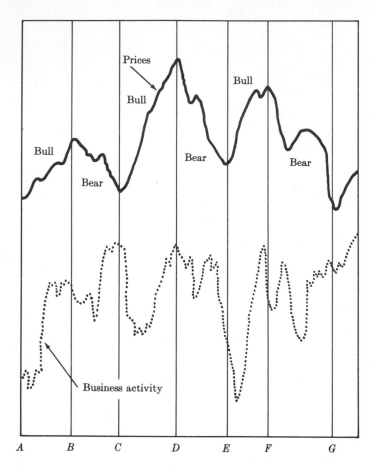

Fig. 20–1 Comparison of major swings of stock prices with an index of business activity, 1949 to 1963 (trends removed).

Unfortunately, as Figure 20–1 demonstrates, the stock price cycle does not correlate well with the business activity cycle. Obviously stock prices are related to business activity, but a careful comparison of the two cycles does not reveal a dependable correlation. The reason is obvious. If the profitability of an increase in the volume of business activity is canceled out by lower prices, higher wages, or increased taxes, nothing remains as an impetus for a rise in stock valuations.

When corporate earnings increase, most analysts expect prices of securities to rise also. If changes in earnings are the sole cause of changes in stock prices, one would find a high degree of correlation between earning and price cycles. Changes in the earnings of the 30 Dow-Jones industrial averages with the trend removed are shown by the dotted line in Figure 20–2.

The low degree of correlation between earnings and prices, so noticeable, has a plausible explanation.

If it should happen that stock prices are a resultant of *two* variable factors (instead of one variable and one fixed factor, as generally assumed), then the stock price cycle would not correlate highly with the cycle of either of its two variables unless by chance these happen to vary together. Stock prices are the product of (1) an earnings factor and (2) an investor-attitude factor. The first of these is objective, the second subjective. Although the two are interrelated statistically, they are determined independently and each possesses a characteristic cycle of its own which sometimes does coincide and sometimes does not. The extent to which the cycles of the two variables coincided during the period 1949 to 1963 is also revealed in Figure 20-2.

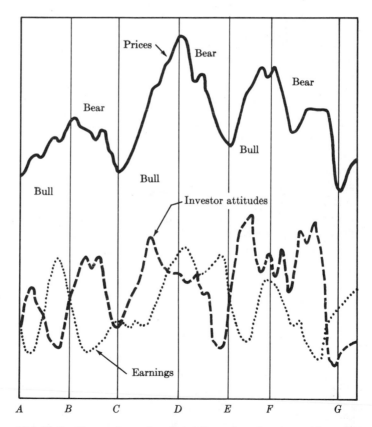

Fig. 20–2 Comparison of major swings of stock prices with cycles of an index of earnings per share and with an index of investor attitudes, 1949 to 1963 (trends removed).

During the bear market that began at *B*, it will be noted that prices declined slowly at first because the two variables moved divergently and then faster when one of the two variables deteriorated much faster than the other improved. In the subsequent bull market (from *C* to *D*), prices first moved up as a result of an improvement in investor attitude while the earnings index moved horizontally, after which the price rise accelerated as a result of an improvement of earnings while the investor-attitude index moved down slowly. The point is that, to forecast a major swing, one must forecast both reported earnings and investor responses to the current economic environment. This is not an easy task.

The problems of the major-swing trader are compounded by the fact that the profitability of this form of trading is frequently affected adversely by a rapidly rising long-term price trend. To illustrate, assume that prices have risen recently from a level of *A* in Figure 20–3 to a level of *B* and that a trader is certain that *B* is the end of the bull market and that the approaching bear market will terminate at time point *T*. If the current long-term trend is following the *OX* line and if the cycle is regular, the next bear market will reach its bottom in the vicinity of *C*. If so, leaving the market at a level of *B* to reenter it at the level of *C* will prove profitable. But suppose that the long-term trend is following the course of the line *OX'*. If the cycle is regular, the bottom of the next bear market will be in the neighborhood of *C'*, at which level prices will be as far below their trend value as they were in the earlier illustration at a level of *C*. But to leave the market at a level of *B* and reenter it at a level of *C'* will be a futile and expensive move. Recalling that the slope of the long-term trend is known only in retrospect emphasizes the difficulty of deciding how much of a cyclical decline will be canceled out by a rapidly rising trend. In an extremely strong bull market, bearish adjustments sometimes amount to nothing more than a sidewise movement of prices. Adjustments of this low magnitude are not conducive to profitable major-swing trading.

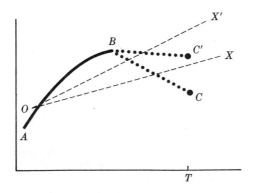

Fig. 20–3 Diagram illustrating the effect of a rapid rise in the long-term trend of stock prices upon profitability of major-swing trading.

"Forecast It Yourself" Procedures

In general a major-swing trader who attempts to do his own forecasting is forced to adopt one of two procedures. He may study market data for the purpose of discovering something that will serve as a dependable harbinger of future movements, or he may explore other (nonmarket) data for some event or combination of events that regularly precede phases of major swings.

Pattern Forecasting.   A number of price patterns, the appearance of which is believed to have forecasting significance, are described in Chapter 22 dealing with technical trading. While most of these patterns relate to short-term (technical) price swings, a number of them apply also to major-cycle turns. The patterns are discovered by keeping charts of stock prices.

The most famous of all pattern-type forecasting devices is the Dow theory. Dow theory forecasts are based upon deviations of the Dow-Jones industrial and railroad averages from their characteristic behavior patterns. In a bull market the characteristic pattern of each average is a series of short-term swings, with each successive peak and valley higher than the preceding peak and valley. In a bear market the characteristic pattern of each average is a series of short-term swings, with each successive peak and valley lower than the preceding peak and valley. A single deviation from the customary pattern attracts attention. Two successive deviations by either of the two indexes assumes significance. If both indexes deviate at approximately the same time, they are said to be *confirming* each other. Dow theorists believe that a confirmed forecast of the market is seldom wrong.

The Dow theory does not pretend to predict a major swing. What it does is to inform traders that the most recent price reversal was a major-cycle turn as well as a technical reaction. Thus its warning is always late, but not late enough to cause a trader to miss the major swing altogether. Chapter 23 describes the Dow theory in detail and analyzes its historic record for forecasting accuracy.

Simple Barometers of Security Prices.   Sometimes it is possible to discover a statistical series which, for a time at least, has a high degree of correlation with security prices. Such a series, if found, may be used as a forecasting device. Experience warns, however, that one should not place too great reliance on correlation forecasting, since one cannot be certain that the relationship between the series and prices may not cease to exist at a critical moment. The long-run undependability of correlated series is emphasized by an examination of some of the series which once enjoyed high popularity. In most instances the story is the same. First, a relationship between certain economic data and security prices is discovered. This relationship successfully predicts changes in security prices for a period of time. Suddenly it ceases to function in the expected manner. In some cases a series will reassume its predicting value after a lapse of several years; in others it remains obsolete permanently.

The relationship of stock prices to a $1\frac{1}{4}$ per cent change in the rate of prime commercial paper furnishes an example of an on-again–off-again correlated series. Many years ago some Harvard researchers found that an advance in the rate of prime commercial paper of $1\frac{1}{4}$ per cent from a previous low point indicated that stock prices were at or near the peak of a major cycle provided that the change occurred during a period of expanding business activity. Conversely, a decline of similar proportions from a previous high indicated that stock prices were at or near the low point of a major cycle provided that the change occurred during a period of contracting business activity. This relationship held during the period 1884 to 1913. It did not hold for the period 1913 to 1919, but it did hold for the period 1919 to 1924. If during the first period one had bought and sold industrial stocks on the basis of the commercial paper rate barometer, the average cost of his purchases would have been $66.10 (as compared with $61.40 at the major-cycle low) and his average sales price would have been $84.50 (as compared with $88.30 at the major-cycle high).

But a trader who blindly followed the advice of the commercial paper rate barometer during the period immediately following its discovery and publication would not have done so well. He would have accumulated shares at the low of 1924 and sold them at the high of 1925. Then he would have remained out of the market until April 1930. Thus he would have missed all the profits of the great market of 1928–1929 and would have been enticed back into the market just prior to the beginning of an 84 per cent decline in security prices. Paradoxically, if in April 1930 he had belonged to that group of misguided persons who saw prosperity just around the corner, he would not have interpreted the April 1930 decline in prime commercial paper rates as an indication to buy. As a result he would have remained out of the market until May 1932, when the commercial paper barometer would have returned him to the market at near the all-time low. Thus optimism about business activity in 1930 would have saved him from many subsequent losses.

The famous blast furnace barometer of Col. Leonard P. Ayres furnishes an excellent example of how and why certain economic events and data predict security prices accurately for a time and then suddenly cease to function in the accustomed manner. Colonel Ayres found that stock and bond prices are at or near major-cycle highs when 60 per cent of the blast furnaces of the country are in use and that stock and bond prices are at or near major-cycle lows when less than 60 per cent of the blast furnaces are in use. Suddenly, during the mid-1930s, the barometer ceased to function. There is a simple explanation of why it forecasted accurately for so long and then suddenly became obsolete.

No one would argue that the number of blast furnaces in operation *causes* security prices to rise or fall. Rather the relationship is this: during the 1920s the shutting down of a blast furnace involved relining it at a cost of $100,000. Under such circumstances, a blast furnace was never closed down until the reduced demand for steel made it necessary; and a relined furnace was never "blown in" until the improved demand for steel gave evidence of being permanent. Thus changes in the number of blast furnaces in operation were closely tied to long-run changes in the demand for a basic raw material. Since the demand for this basic raw material depended almost entirely upon general business conditions, changes in the number of blast furnaces in operation offered a reliable clue to the fundamental condition of industry in general.

During the 1930s someone perfected a method of economically banking a blast furnace fire without keeping the furnace in production. After this discovery it was impossible to tell whether a change in the number of furnaces in use reflected a temporary or a permanent change in demand. Henceforth blast furnace statistics ceased to forecast major-cycle changes in security prices.

The Confidence Index.   Each week *Barron's* computes and publishes a "confidence" index. Mathematically, this index is a ratio of the yield on high-grade bonds (as measured by *Barron's* ten highest-grade bonds) to the average yield on all bonds (as measured by the Dow-Jones index of 40 bonds). Specifically, the formula for computing the index is

$$\frac{\text{Yield on 10 high-grade bonds}}{\text{Yield on 40 DJ bonds}} = \text{confidence index}$$

When investor confidence is high, conservative bond investors grow bold and begin shifting from higher- to lower-grade bonds to obtain higher yields. This shift has a tendency to reduce the price of the high-grade bonds (the numerator of the above formula being thus increased) and to increase the price of the lower-quality bonds (the denominator of the formula being thus reduced). The mathematical effect is a rapid rise of the index. A decline in investor confidence has the opposite effect.

A small change in the confidence index is without importance, but a sharp change is believed to have forecasting significance on the theory that any change in the confidence of conservative-type investors will shortly be mirrored in a similar change in the confidence of speculative investors.

The confidence index is interpreted as follows:

1. When the index makes a sharp rise to a new high in one week and then retreats the following week, it is signaling a top of a major-swing cycle.

For example, the confidence index advanced 5 percentage points in the week ending November 6, 1936, declined 5 points the following week, and held steady at this level for six months before declining another 4 points. The Dow-Jones average reached a cyclical high on March 10, 1937, declined to June 14, rallied to August 14, moved down slowly, and then suddenly declined 49 per cent in the autumn of 1936.

2. If the index rises for only a few weeks, it is signaling a technical dip.
3. Repetitive bottoms or tops in the confidence index signal near-term lows or highs in the major swing of stock prices.

For example, the confidence index declined to 49 on May 27, 1932, rose a bit, and then declined to 49 again on July 1, 1932. The Dow-Jones average reached its depression low on July 8.

4. The confidence index speaks from two to four months in advance of the predicted events.
5. If the confidence index gives two signals, the more emphatic of the two is the important signal and dilutes the significance of the other.

Figure 20–4 compares the behavior of the confidence index during the period 1961 to 1963 with the weekly movement of the Dow-Jones average.

Multiple Correlation with Leading Series.   Almost every one is acquainted with the method of forecasting in which a prediction is based upon some event or series of events that experience has shown always to precede the event which it is desired to forecast. In recent years a variation of this method has been used by some market analysts to forecast the turning points of the major cycle of stock prices.

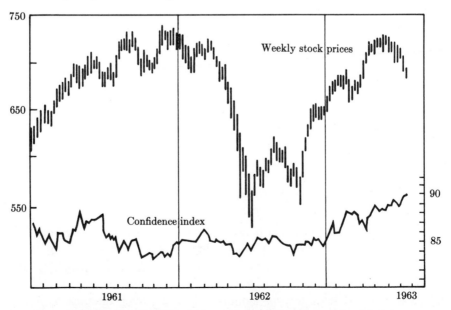

Fig. 20–4 Comparison of weekly stock prices with *Barron's* confidence index.

First, numerous statistical series are plotted on charts for comparison with the major cycles of stock prices as revealed by some suitable stock price index. Some of the statistical series cycles will correlate with stock price cycles, and some will not. Those which do not are eliminated. The forecaster then takes another look at the remaining charts to note whether the turning points of the cycles of the statistical series lead or lag the turning points of the stock price cycles. Those which lag are eliminated.

Next, the forecaster calculates the *average lead time* of each of the remaining statistical series cycles and notes whether deviations from this average are small or great. If the average deviation is large, the series is eliminated.

This leaves the forecaster with a small number of statistical series, the turning points of whose cycles regularly lead the turning points of the stock price cycle by a more or less constant time period. Detailed charts of these remaining series are maintained. If any one of the cycles turns up or down, the forecaster counts forward the number of days contained in the average lead time of that series and places a warning flag on his stock price chart. One or two warning flags are without significance, but a concentration of flags is taken as an indication of the time range within which the next turn in the stock price cycle is likely to occur. A study of Figure 20–5 will render clearer the mechanics just described.

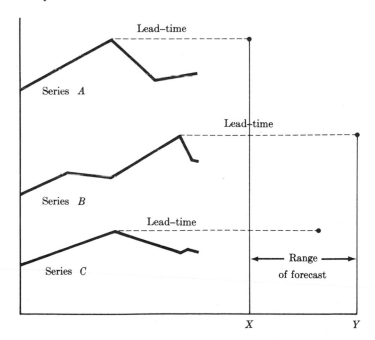

Fig. 20–5 Multiple correlation of the statistical series method of forecasting major-cycle turning points.

One professional forecaster who uses this method finds the following statistical series useful:

1. Monetary factors:
   a. A ratio of bank investments to bank loans
   b. The per cent change of demand deposits plus currency in circulation from the same data one year earlier
   c. A moving average of net free bank reserves
   d. A ratio of bank debts to bank loans (excluding figures for New York City)
2. Market data:
   a. A three-month moving average of the volume of stock trading on the NYSE
   b. Customers' free credit balances with their brokers
   c. A ratio of current monthly stock prices to a forty-six-month moving average
   d. A ratio of the average price of low-priced stocks to the average price of high-grade stocks (as revealed by acceptable indexes)
3. General economic data:
   a. Average hours worked (seasonally adjusted)
   b. A ratio of sales to inventories of durable goods
   c. A reciprocal of the liabilities of business failures

Commonsense Methods. The major-swing trader waits a long time for his returns; so he wants them to be worthwhile when they come. This means that he has to accumulate large quantities of stocks when prices are low and hold them for sale later when prices are many points above his costs. As explained, the problem is to judge when prices are low and when they are high. The systems outlined in former sections of this chapter are attempts by more or less scientific processes to pinpoint the turning points of the major cycle of stock prices. There are, however, some commonsense methods which many investors have found to give satisfactory results.

The first rule is to buy when a depression is unmistakable. This means waiting until the depression is a fact acknowledged by even the most optimistic. The major-swing trader knows that severe maladjustment in the economic organization will be followed by a period of readjustment which will give him plenty of time to accumulate his favorite stocks. Therefore he does not buy hastily.

The economic factors that indicate that a buying period is ahead are well known: (1) severe unemployment, (2) many business failures, (3) great losses by many persons and corporations, (4) iron and steel production at a minimum, (5) carloadings very low and idle cars on every track, (6) tremendous liquidation of stocks and bonds, (7) great decline in commodity prices, (8) bank loans being liquidated, (9) interest rates high but falling, (10) bank reserves accumulating, (11) debits to individual accounts at low level, (12) pessimism general, (13) the stock market inactive with volume of sales small, and (14) high yields on the best-quality stocks.

When the above conditions exist, an alert major-swing trader watches for the first signs of improvement and when these begin to appear he starts picking up stocks at low prices. Prices may go lower, but he is not discouraged if he pays 5 points more than the minimum. Having accumulated a portfolio of good stocks, he awaits the next period of prosperity. He ignores technical swings and operates on the theory that nothing is gained by trying to guess rallies and reactions.

Finally, the period of prosperity arrives, and stock prices rise. The trader watches the trend of business closely. He does not bewilder himself in a maze of statistics but picks a few essentials. He wants to know the kind of management that is behind the corporations in which he is interested and their financial condition and earnings. On these points he is alert, and if weaknesses appear he switches to another issue—otherwise he holds.

Now the degree of prosperity of the farmer, the situation of the construction industries, the course of commodity prices, the relative production of iron and steel, inventories, and credit conditions become the important elements of the economic picture. In other words, for all practical purposes half a dozen fundamentals tell the story. When these factors have made a considerable advance and the prices of stocks have reached a level that affords a satisfactory profit, the major-swing trader may put himself on the safe side by selling some of his stocks or he may wait for the period of hectic prosperity before liquidating his holdings. If he chooses the latter course, he takes a chance of misjudging the turning point of the major cycle.

One writer suggests five conditions which may be taken as dependable indications that the top of a major swing is near:

1. Stock prices standing at levels that are high by comparison with the past
2. Price-earnings ratios (of leading issues) of 20 or higher
3. Dividend yields lower than bond yields
4. Prices of low-quality stocks rising more rapidly than prices of high-quality stocks
5. Widespread acceptance of new stock issues of companies of questionable quality

When all these conditions exist simultaneously, the day of (investment) judgment is at hand for the end of the bull market is near.

Seeking Outside Investment Advice

As explained, the major-swing trader must select issues and time purchases and sales with a high degree of accuracy if his trading is to result in profit. If a trader is not prepared to make his own selection and timing decisions, he may seek the advice of investment counselors, subscribe to an advisory service, or follow the recommendations of a broker. Advantages and disadvantages are associated with each of these procedures.

Professional Investment Counsel.   Professional investment counselors are individuals who for a fee offer to supervise investment portfolios. The typical annual charge is $\frac{1}{2}$ per cent of the average value of the portfolio, with a minimum fee of approximately $500. Investment advisors tailor their recommendations to the needs of their clients. Therefore they usually analyze the investor's personal financial situation so that they can adapt the portfolio to his needs. An investment program for a widow might stress safety and yield, that for a businessman, capital gains, and so on. Sometimes an investment adviser has custody of the securities in the portfolio and is empowered to switch the issues as he deems advisable. The more usual arrangement is for a broker to hold the securities and for the adviser to make recommendations for changes. The client is free to act upon or to reject the recommendations.

Investment counselors with 10 or more clients are required to register with the Securities and Exchange Commission, but such registration does not imply competence, since anyone can register who will take the trouble to fill out the necessary forms. Obviously, therefore, firms and persons who offer their aid to investors range all the way from nationally known organizations with sizable staffs to lone individuals who become "experts" during a major-swing rise but fade into oblivion in the subsequent major-swing decline. The National Federation of Financial Analysts Societies, recognizing the investor's problem in choosing a competent advisor, has recently established a program of tests to be taken by those who wish to designate themselves as "chartered financial analysts." This program aims to establish minimum standards of professional competence.

The Securities and Exchange Commission examined 896 different pieces of literature disseminated during the week just preceding the stock market break of September 3, 1946, a break that initiated a three-year bear market. Of the 489 major-swing forecasts made in that week, 260 were bullish without qualification, 20 were definitely bearish, and 209 were so cautious, uncertain, or hedged as to make classification impossible. Ninety-five of the forecasts dealt with the current technical condition of the market, which we now know was weak. Nevertheless, 55 of the forecasts classified the market as technically strong, 6 as weak, and 34 were so vague as to defy classification.

Investment Advisory Services.   The pages of business newspapers and of financial journals abound with advertisements of organizations offering subscribers information and advice. Although such services pretend to offer long-term investment advice, the fact that they inform their clients when to enter and when to leave the market characterizes their recommendations as major-swing advice.

The recommendations issued by these agencies cannot be better than the theories upon which they are based. As might be expected, the theories used by advisory services range all the way from the ultrascholarly to the ridiculous.[1] Procedures employed by some of the better-known investment advisory services are described in Chapter 24.

It is difficult to evaluate the services of a particular advisory agency. Nevertheless it is true that, if the advice of an agency is worth the subscription price, a policy of following all its advice should prove more profitable than a policy of selecting market leaders on a random basis. Several studies of the reliability of forecasting services have been made, most of which have not been favorable to the services. For example, Alfred Cowles III examined 7,500 recommendations made by 16 services during a $4\frac{1}{2}$-year period beginning January 1, 1928. Cowles found that an investor who followed all the recommendations would have done 1.4 per cent more poorly than the market averages. Cowles also concluded from a study of the forecasts of 24 financial publications that their recommendations failed by 4 per cent to achieve a result as good as the average of the market.

On January 3, 1963, a leading advisory service recommended the purchase of nine specific issues whose recovery in its opinion had lagged in the market. On this date the nine issues were selling at 55 per cent below their 1961 peak and 43 per cent above their 1962 low. Subsequently, the individual issues rose from 12 to 52 per cent. The average of the nine rose 23 per cent above its January 3, 1963, level. Six months after the recommendation the market values of the issues varied individually from 24 per cent above to 13 per cent below but averaged 2 per cent below the price at which the agency recommended their purchase. At no time during the six-month period did the service advise its subscribers to sell any one of the nine issues. A comparison of the performance of the nine issues before and after recommendation with the performance of the Dow-Jones industrial averages is presented in Figure 20–6. As will be noted, the recommended issues did not do as well as the average of the market.

Brokers' Recommendations.   Some investors prefer to follow the advice of their brokers. Such advice is free, and since the long-run interests of a broker are tied to the profitable trading of his customers, there appears to be no conflict of interest. However, a customer's profit obtained from much trading

---

[1] In mid-1962 the attention of the authors was directed to a circular of one agency which based its predictions for the year 1963 on the following logic: The years 1929, 1937, and 1962 all showed violent declines. If one takes the last two digits of the first of these (29), reverses them (to get 92), and subtracts the first from the second (92 − 29), the difference is 63. Following the same procedure for 1937 and for 1962 yields differences of 36 both times. Reverse 36 and you have 63. Thus all the signs, they claimed, pointed to 1963 as a critical year for investors. Advice relating to specific issues based on this method could be obtained from the agency by subscribing to its services.

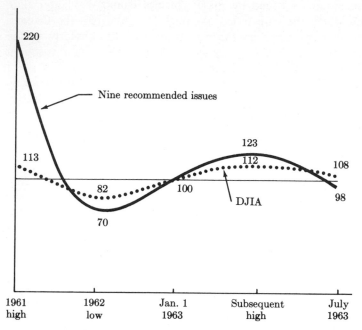

Fig. 20–6 Comparison of percentage change in average prices of nine issues recommended for purchase with the percentage change in the Dow-Jones industrial averages—before and after date of recommendation.

would be more remunerative to a broker than would the same profit obtained from little trading. Even though this is true, it is still doubtful that any broker ever gains in the long run from advising customers to overtrade. This leaves in question only the inherent competence of brokers to give wise market advice.

A study was made by S. S. Colker of all the published reports cited in the column "Market Views—analysis" in the *Wall Street Journal* between June 1, 1960, and June 1, 1961.[2] Colker found that brokers' reports are customarily worded so as to be implied and hedged recommendations to purchase. For example, "Investors interested in both income and capital appreciation *could well take note* of this company's promise" and "This stock *appears reasonably priced* in relation to its earnings" (italics supplied). In neither of these cases has the reader been advised to purchase, but this is the impression that he is likely to get from reading the opinions.

Colker found that most brokers advise buying and seldom recommend selling. He felt that the reason for this was the unconscious desire of brokers

[2] "Security Recommendations by Brokerage Houses," *Quarterly Review of Economics and Business,* vol. 3, no. 2, Urbana, Ill.: University of Illinois Bureau of Economics and Business Administration, 1963, p. 19.

to increase trading. If a broker's report suggests buying a particular issue, there is a chance of a commission from every person who reads it. If a report concludes that a particular issue should be sold, there is a chance for a commission only from readers who also happen to hold the issue. (Presumably short traders do not seek brokers' advice.)

Colker studied 1,399 recommendations and compared the performance of the recommended issues with the movement of the Standard & Poor's index of stock prices *before* and *after* the appearance of the recommendation. The object was to find out the basis and the worth of the recommendation. Colker found, for example, that brokers tend to recommend those issues which have outperformed the market during the period just preceding the recommendation. Thus, if stock A goes up this month, brokers will probably recommend it next month. He also found that the recommended issue did not, as a rule, perform as well in the month following the recommendation as the market as a whole. A year after recommendation, recommended issues were about 3.9 per cent ahead of the market as measured by the index. Apparently the unsophisticated dabbler in the market who blindly follows broker advice can expect to end up doing as well as or slightly better than the average of the market. This is sufficient for a long-term investor, but it is inadequate for a major-swing trader, since the latter incurs turnover costs and must pay normal income tax on his trading profits.

Formula Plans

Major-swing trading requires one to buy shares when the cycle of stock prices is in its low phase and to sell them when the cycle moves into its high phase. What must be done is clear; doing it is the difficult part. Earlier discussion described the various methods used by some analysts to forecast the market but stressed the risks involved. It also explained the methods used by investment counselors, advisory services, and brokers to forecast prices, though the records of these agencies are not overly impressive. Everyone knows that, when business is slow and prospects for improvement dim, stock prices are low but at such times most investors find themselves disinclined to purchase. Similarly, everyone agrees that, when business is active and investment enthusiasm runs high, stock prices are high but at such times investors find themselves reluctant to part with their holdings. Obviously success in major-swing trading requires a trader to do what he is disinclined to do, that is, buy when he is most pessimistic and sell when he is most optimistic. This is where the formula plan comes into the picture.

A formula plan is an investment-timing device designed to prevent major-swing traders from letting their "unreasoned euphoria or their dark melancholia sweep away their investment judgment."[3] Such plans operate

[3] Robert R. Dince, "Formula Planning," *Readings in Financial Analysis and Investment Management,* Homewood, Ill.: Richard D. Irwin, Inc., 1963, p. 454.

on the fundamental idea that the major-swing trader will do best to surrender his personal judgment to a mathematical formula that forces him to buy when stocks are cheap and to sell when they are dear.

Norm Determination.   Two determinations are prerequisite to the construction and operation of a formula plan. The first involves the choice of a *norm* to be used as a basis for deciding when prices are too high or too low, and the second is the formulation of a *rule* to guide and control market participation. A norm may be:

1. A predetermined level about which stock prices are expected to fluctuate. Since a predetermined level is fixed, it will be a valid norm only for a limited period of time.
2. A trend of stock prices computed from some acceptable stock-price index.
3. A figure determined by analysis of statistical data to represent the proper level of stock prices for a particular period.

The first and second of these are self-explanatory, but the third requires more detailed treatment.

A particular formula plan might accept as its norm some specific multiple of the average earnings per share of a prechosen group of stocks. For example, the group of stocks chosen might be the issues used to compute the Dow-Jones industrial averages, and the multiple applied might be, say, 15. If so, then when the Dow-Jones industrial average stands at 15 times its average earnings per share, stock prices would be neither too high nor too low. This type of norm is sometimes called a "central value norm." Professor Weston has suggested a different method of arriving at the concept of normal, or proper, level of prices.[4] He would have one compute a regression equation based upon a correlation analysis of the gross national product to the Dow-Jones industrial averages. His own computations suggested

28.20 + 0.9675 of the GNP

Once a norm has been agreed upon, the next step is to formulate the rule that is to guide market activity. This rule informs the operator when and how many shares he is to buy or sell. It does not tell him which shares to buy or sell. Obviously, the number of such rules that could be devised is legion, but all of them will be found to be variations of three basic schemes.

The Constant-dollar Plan.   Under this scheme, the investor's funds are divided into two parts: one being used to purchase a diversified group of common stocks (for purposes of identification we shall call this the "stock fund") and the other being held in liquid form (for purposes of easy refer-

---

[4] J. Fred Weston, "The Stock Market in Perspective," *Harvard Business Review,* March–April 1956, p. 80.

ence we shall call this the "cash fund"). The basic idea of the constant-dollar formula plan is *to keep the stock fund constant* by transferring sums out of or into the cash fund. This transferring process requires that the stock fund be evaluated periodically to discover whether it is over or under the limit set. Herein lies the magic secret—a rise in the market value of stocks causes the stock fund to exceed its original value and so forces an investor to sell shares. Conversely, a decline in the market value of stocks causes the stock fund to shrink and so forces an investor to buy additional shares. Thus he is always buying on declines and selling on rallies. This is exactly what a major-swing trader should do although he finds it difficult.

The necessity of periodically evaluating the stock fund introduces the question of when and how often the revaluation is to be made. One method is for the investor to predetermine a series of dates for the revaluation. He might, for example, choose January 15 of each year. Another procedure is to have the readjustment dates determined by the market prices of stocks or by changes in the value of the stock fund itself. Thus, a given percentage rise or decline in the Dow-Jones average might indicate a need for revaluation, or a given percentage change in the value of the stock fund might do the same. The latter necessitates a constant watch on the market values of the stocks held.

When the constant-dollar plan is successful, the effect is a steady augmentation of the cash fund. If the earnings are not to be put to personal uses, the cash fund will eventually become unduly large. It may become desirable, therefore, to transfer a portion of the cash fund to the stock fund, that is, to enlarge the size of the stock fund that is being held constant. In order to avoid enlarging the fund at the wrong time, it might be desirable to specify that increases shall be made only at such times as the plan calls for purchasing additional stocks.

The Constant-ratio Plan.   In this plan, as in the constant-dollar plan, the investor's funds are divided into two parts: the first being invested in a diversified list of common stocks and the second being held as a reserve of liquid cash. Again the stock fund is valued and adjusted on certain predetermined dates. In effecting this readjustment, however, the original ratio of stock to cash (rather than the original dollar value of the stock fund) is to be maintained.

Thus, if the original division is a 50:50 one and stock prices have risen, enough shares are sold to restore this ratio. If market prices are down, funds are drawn from the cash fund sufficient to restore the original 50:50 ratio. This plan also forces selling on a rising market and buying on a falling market. It does permit the dollar size of the stock fund to grow (by 50 per cent of the profits) and so tends to be more profitable than the constant-dollar plan when the trend of prices is upward and less profitable than the constant-dollar plan when the trend of prices is downward.

The revaluation dates under the constant-ratio plan can be based upon the calendar, upon a percentage change of a stock index, or upon a percentage change in the value of the stock fund.

The Variable-ratio Plan.   At a market level determined to be normal the investor's funds are divided into two equal proportions, one being invested in a diversified group of common stocks and the other being held in liquid form. As stock prices move above the normal level, shares are sold and the proceeds held in reserve; as stocks move below the normal level, shares are purchased and the relative amount of funds in reserve is reduced.

For illustrative purposes, assume that the norm is to be 180 as measured by some index. The rule determining purchases and sales might be to maintain the proportions between the two funds shown in the following table:

When level of market is	Ratio of two funds is to be	
	For stocks, %	For bonds, %
230	30	70
200	40	60
180 (normal)	50	50
165	60	40
155	70	30

A plan based on this schedule assumes that the market will continue to fluctuate above and below the index level of 180; it assumes an absence of a long-term trend.

The so-called normal level could be defined differently. For example, it could be a "moving average of a given number of the monthly mean averages," an "arithmetic trend line," or a "projected line of least squares, computed from the logs of the monthly mean prices." When a moving average or trend-line concept of normal is used, it is necessary to set up zones on each side of the trend line. Then, as the average moves from one zone to another, the holdings of stocks and cash are adjusted to the predetermined ratio of the next zone.

21 the technical position of the market

Two groups of conditions are always present in the stock market to affect the course of prices. The first of these relates to the momentary structure of the market itself and is characterized as "technical." The second relates to the adjustment of prices to economic conditions and is referred to as "fundamental."

Technical Factors. The market is made up of investors (shareholders interested in price *trends*) and traders (shareholders interested in near-term price *changes*); of bulls (those hoping for *rises*) and bears (those hoping for *declines*); of longs (those who *own* the shares they hold) and shorts (those who have sold shares they *borrowed*); of the floating supply (shares that can be purchased at prices *slightly* higher than current quotations) and investment holdings (shares that can be purchased only at prices *much* higher than current quotations). All these conditions taken together make up the technical position of the market at any one time.

For example, at a particular moment the floating supply may be in "strong hands," i.e., may be held by wealthy, well-informed traders; or in "weak hands," i.e., may be held by small, uninformed traders. Sometimes traders find that they have accumulated more shares than they are going to be able to distribute to investors at current price levels, and at other times they discover that they are short more shares than are contained in the entire floating supply. The correction of these and other technical situations has an effect upon the immediate course of quotations. One who can discover the existence of such situations and foresee the effect of their correction can profit by short-term trading. Such a person is a "technical trader." The theories he holds and the procedures he employs are the subject matter of the next chapter. Here we are concerned with the technical situation as such.

When the current situation is such as not to require a correction, the market may be said to be in "short-term equilibrium." Short-term equilibriums seldom last long. Usually the floating supply of stock is too large or too small, or short-term traders are overbought or oversold. A little disequilibrium does not matter, but as a market situation gets further and further away from its point of short-term equilibrium, the strength of the deviation forces diminishes and that of the corrective forces grows stronger until the latter overwhelm the former and bring about a reversal of the existing price movement. If the situation calls for a downward adjustment of prices, the market is said to be "technically weak." If the situation calls for an upward adjustment of prices, the market is said to be "technically strong."

Fundamental Factors.   No one knows for certain how to determine the proper value of a given stock, but most writers seem to feel that proper value depends upon such factors as (1) expected volume of deliveries (of goods), (2) prospective sales prices, (3) likely costs of production, (4) resulting earnings per share, and (5) the dividend payout policy of the board of directors. These are the so-called fundamental factors.

When the current quotation of a stock appears to be reasonably related to fundamental factors, the issue may be adjudged to be in "fundamental equilibrium." Unfortunately fundamental factors do not stay fixed but change slowly and constantly. For a while the changes may pass unnoticed and then may be realized suddenly. The slow change in fundamental factors necessitates frequent revaluations by investors, and these revaluations bring about changes in the consensus regarding the "intrinsic" value of stocks. When successive notions of intrinsic value are higher, the market is said to be "fundamentally strong." When the reverse occurs, the market is said to be "fundamentally weak."

To state the situation in brief terms, the movement of the market is made up of two distinct components: (1) a general trend upward or downward, reflecting fundamental factors, and (2) deviations above and below this trend, representing technical factors.

Four Conditions of the Market

With two variables, four situations are possible. A market may be fundamentally strong and technically weak or strong. Conversely, a market may be fundamentally weak and technically strong or weak. If the *mn* curve in Figure 21–1 represents the price movement of a given stock, the straight *xy*

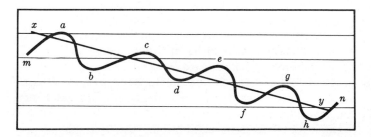

Fig. 21–1

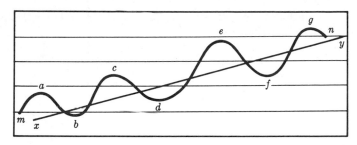

Fig. 21–2

line represents its fundamental situation. It will be noted that, although the market is fundamentally weak, it is technically weak at points *a, c, e, g,* and *n* and technically strong at points *m, b, d, f,* and *h.*

Figure 21–2 depicts the opposite situation: a market that is fundamentally strong but technically weak at points *a, c, e,* and *g* and technically strong at points *b, d,* and *f.*

Conditions Making for a Strong Technical Position

1. A large short interest in the market will lead to buying sooner or later. After a large amount of short selling, many shorts having sold on a relatively small margin and gone the limit of their credit, the market is ready for a rally. The speculators on the bull side see the position of the shorts and make an attempt to drive them to cover by buying stock. This buying arrests the decline and causes an advance. Now a bear is a timid creature, and when the element of uncertainty is injected by a halt in the decline and an advance in price, he runs for cover and the rally is under way. As short covering proceeds and prices start upward, there is a speculative rush to buy, accompanied by a rapid rise of prices. The advance is accelerated by the fact that the bulls hold the stock bought from the shorts.

Stocks of corporations that have only a relatively small number of shares outstanding may easily be sold short in volume greater than the amount of stock available for borrowing. For many years J. I. Case had only 192,000 shares outstanding, of which many shares were not for sale or available for borrowing. It was relatively easy for bears operating in this issue to sell more shares than were available for delivery, and it was relatively easy for bulls to buy as much as could be delivered to them. Frequently, the shorts borrowed shares from the longs and delivered them to buyers, who reloaned the shares to bears until the latter had sold more stock than existed. Then the bulls would call for return of their shares, and the bears were compelled to buy at any cost. Since the market was oversold relative to the available stock, the technical position of the market at such times would be described as strong.

The following clipping from the *Wall Street Journal* illustrates the effect of a large short interest:

> Without doubt much of today's improvement was due to short covering. Urgent buying of American Can, U.S. Steel, General Electric, and other leading industrials suggested that a large bear following, which had been attracted by the recent decline, was beating a hasty retreat at the first indications that the market had encountered effective support.

In other words, stock prices rose not because they were attractive investments but merely because many traders found themselves in a position where they were forced to purchase.

2. After a decline showing a profit to the short interest, a market is likely to be technically strong for several reasons. In the first place, the decline has probably eliminated a large number of weak long-margin accounts so that danger of further forced liquidation becomes slight. For example, shortly after one of the largest stock market breaks of history, a columnist wrote:

> Brokers say that the marginal situation is no longer vulnerable since the mopping up process which followed the October break greatly strengthened the situation. There are a great many accounts today which do not hold stocks on margin and many that actually have credit balances.

3. After a decline a market is frequently honeycombed with stop-buy orders that automatically become market orders to buy if prices advance slightly. Execution of these orders will induce further price rises. At the time the above paragraph appeared in the *Wall Street Journal,* the market was fundamentally weak. Nevertheless, owing to purely technical factors, prices enjoyed a three-day rally at the expense of the shorts, after which they declined to new low levels. When the decline set in, the same columnist had this to say:

> As a practical matter, the market is still trying to contend against an overwhelming array of unfavorable business statistics and hopes are not entirely sufficient to ensure continuation of the rallying movement.

4. After a period of accumulation, the technical position of the market is strong. The stock has had a well-marked decline followed by a period of uncertainty about its next movement. During this period the general public has been selling its holdings, which professional speculators have been quietly accumulating. The stock has passed from weak to strong hands; the next move will be upward. If fundamental conditions are strong, the rally will be extensive. If fundamental factors are weak, the rally will be short-lived.

The point we wish to make is that between 65 and 75 a tremendous amount of market activity has occurred in this issue and the length of time during which the price level has been maintained, together with the character of price fluctuations during the period, points quite clearly to a determined effort at accumulation. For this reason, we consider New York Central one of the most attractive purchases among the rails.

It will be noted that the newspaper writer considers New York Central to be an attractive buy not because of an improvement in its earning situation or because it is underpriced but merely because of its price stability after a decline and in the presence of great market activity.

5. Manipulation of the market of a given stock for a rise in price creates a strong position marketwise in that stock. Bull pools are formed to buy up a large amount of the stock of a corporation. Their activity attracts the attention of the public, which takes the stock off the pool's hands as its price rises. In order to win public confidence the stock must be kept strong.

Conditions Making for a Weak Technical Position

1. When the market has been overbought, a reaction may be expected at any time. The bulls have become too optimistic and have overtraded. Their margins are thin, and their credit is overextended. A large amount of stock overhangs the market, and any bad news—call for more margin or rumors of the passing of dividends—is enough to cause a rush to sell. Not only are the bulls no longer in a position to buy, but the shorts, having covered, are now ready to sell the market again. This selling activity at a time when the longs are vulnerable is conducive to a decline, regardless of fundamental factors. If the bears suspect the overextended condition of the bulls, they make drives first on this stock and then on that one, to hammer prices down. Margin calls are made, weak accounts are liquidated, and the supply of stock is increased, with no one in a mood to buy. Again the decline that occurs is unrelated to the factors that determine the intrinsic worth of stocks.

2. After the price of the shares of stock of a corporation has advanced for some time, many stop loss orders are placed beneath the market, either by longs to protect their profits or by current buyers to guard against a sudden break. A supply of stock coming into the market will force a decline. When the decline reaches the stops, these become market orders to sell. A market is technically weak when stops beneath current prices are about to be caught. Moreover, speculators on the short side, suspecting the presence of the stops, may make a concerted drive against an issue, hoping to uncover the stops, and in the decline that follows may buy in the stock to cover their short position. This is only one of the ways in which manipulation of the market may become a factor producing a weak technical position.

Eighty per cent of the experts remain bullish and see new highs ahead, but advise that you *make no additional purchases*. They feel that the market is highly vulnerable to a correction and that more lucrative buying opportunities will follow the expected decline. . . . The decline will be accelerated as a result of stop-loss orders which underlie the market at this time. After this reaction occurs the market should proceed upwards and establish new highs.

3. After a period of distribution of stocks by the strong holders who accumulated the shares at much lower prices, a market position becomes technically weak. When these large interests have completed selling at a profit and stocks have passed to weak hands and are widely held on margin, the large interests withdraw their support and the price declines. A drastic decline in the price of stocks is now in the interest of these investors so that they can again accumulate them cheaply. At the end of the period of selling by the strong holders the technical position of the market is weak, owing to the overbought condition of the public on the one hand and the lack of buying support by the large interests on the other.

4. Many short-swing traders are always operating in the leading stocks. The bull contingent buys on reactions and as the stock advances several points begins to sell out and take its profits. The higher the price goes, the greater will be the supply of stocks, for the bulls now unload all their holdings. The bears, sensing the attitude of the bulls, are encouraged to sell short. The pressure of this selling turns the market weak. As the decline makes headway, the sold-out bulls begin to buy and the bears take their profits by covering. The demand for stocks thus overcomes the supply, and the market turns strong again.

Methods of Determining the Technical Position

The factors that make a market technically weak or strong have been described. It is impossible, however, to inquire of traders and investors what they are doing and what they expect to do next. Some other way must therefore be found to determine the current technical position of the market. In practice this is accomplished by studying statistics that relate to market trading. There are no absolute criteria, but certain ascertainable facts yield clues about what is going on in the market. The more important statistical data used to judge the technical strength of a market include the following:

1. Number of advances and declines
2. Size of the short interest
3. Odd-lot purchases and sales
4. Volume of trading
5. Quality of market leadership

6. Divergencies in stock price indexes
7. Brokers' loans and customers' balances
8. Miscellaneous indicators

Obviously to gauge the technical position of the market, one must first decide on what data are significant, must obtain and statistically manipulate the data to make them meaningful, and then must interpret them by applying principles which study or experience has shown to lead to reliable conclusions. Even then a technical market analyst must be on guard constantly lest a change in circumstances destroy the validity of a relationship which research has demonstrated to be dependable in the past.

The remainder of this chapter is devoted to describing various sources of data, methods of manipulation, and theories underlying interpretation. No attempt is made to prove or disprove any of the theories, although in a few cases data are presented that will aid the reader to form his own opinion. The reader should bear in mind that there are hundreds of schools of thought on technical interpretation and that the most that can be accomplished here is to give a general idea of their stand. This means that a particular technician can always say with some justification, "But that is *not* the way I do it." Then he will probably add, "I have discovered a secret formula that reveals an important relationship that others have missed."

Number of Advances and Declines.   Each day there appears on the next to the last page of the *Wall Street Journal* a daily report of (1) the number of issues traded on the Exchange, (2) the number of issues that closed up, (3) the number of issues that closed down, and (4) the number of issues that closed unchanged from the previous day. Many technical analysts believe that a comparison of this advance-decline data with current movements of a stock price index reveals the most likely next movement of the price index. Methods of arriving at the forecasts differ, but most of them are based upon some type of application of the following four rules.

1. If advances exceed declines and the price index rises, the index will continue to rise.
2. If advances exceed declines and the price index declines, the downward movement of the index is about to be reversed.
3. If declines exceed advances and the price index is rising, the rise of the index is about to be reversed.
4. If declines exceed advances and the price index is falling, the decline of the index will continue.

The rationale of the relationship summarized by these four rules is based upon the following logic: A price index computed from the price quotations of thirty or forty issues is more representative of the movement of market leaders than it is of the movement of all the listed stocks. By contrast, any indicator based upon advance-decline data relates to the market as a whole. It is believed that the prices of market leaders cannot continue for long to move in opposition to the market as a whole. Hence, if for a day or for several days prices of the market leaders do move against the market, the direction of their movement will have to change shortly to conform to that of the market. The longer the market leaders resist the change, the more certain it is that the direction of their movement will be reversed. It will be noted that the theory makes the market forecast the leaders, and not the reverse.

Some analysts apply the rules day by day to derive a forecast of the next day's price movement. For example, there were 252 trading days in 1962. On 118 of these days the market closed up; on 132 days it closed down; and on 2 days it closed unchanged. A mechanical application of the four rules cited above to daily advance-decline data in this year would have resulted in a correct forecast of the next day's prices 56 per cent of the time and in an incorrect forecast 44 per cent of the time.

The best record that year would have been achieved in the month of March—16 successes and 6 failures; and the poorest record would have been made in the month of December—5 successes and 15 failures. In March there were 15 days in which the market continued in the same direction, and the advance-decline data indicator predicted 14 of these. There were 7 occasions on which the market reversed its direction and the advance-decline data indicator predicted 2 of these. In December the advance-decline data indicator successfully predicted 4 of the 6 continuances and one of the 14 reverses. Apparently the ability of an advance-decline data indicator to predict continuance is better than its ability to predict reversals, perhaps because there were more continuances than reversals.

Some analysts manipulate advance-decline data statistically before attempting to forecast from them. For example, the number of declines may be subtracted from the number of advances to derive a *net* advance or *net* decline figure for each trading day. If net advance-decline data are plotted on a graph, a curve that fluctuates above and below a 50-50 base line results. Some analysts reduce the fluctuation of this curve by means of a three- or five-day moving average. Short-term forecasts are then made whenever the curve deviates from its base line by some proportion which experience has shown to be significant. For example, on a rising market a net decline of 200 or more issues might be held to be significant. Of course, since there is no general agreement on the matter, each individual advance-decline data forecaster must decide for himself what constitutes a significant deviation. In Figure 21–3 the movement of the Dow-Jones industrial averages during 1962 is compared (1) with daily net advance-decline figures and (2) with a three-day moving average of net advance-decline figures.

Many technical traders, finding it difficult to interpret the fluctuations

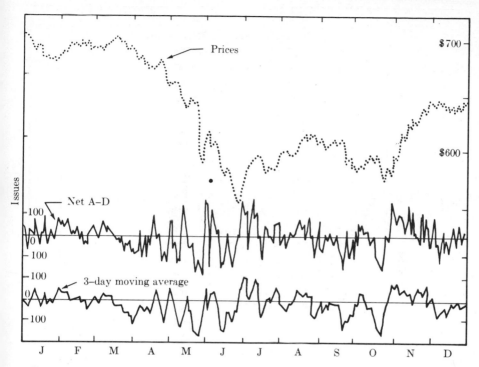

Fig. 21–3 Comparison of daily advance-decline data with daily stock prices during 1962.

of net advance-decline data, convert them into a "cumulative" index. This is accomplished by adding net advances and deducting net declines from some arbitrarily chosen initial figure, such as 20,000. In Figure 21–4 a cumulative index is compared with the daily closing Dow-Jones industrial averages of 1962. The reader cannot help noting the high degree of correlation. In fact, the correlation is so high as seriously to impair its forecasting value, as the following comparison makes clear.

Reversal dates

DJIA index	A/D index	Chart reference
Jan. 26	Following day	A
Mar. 15	Same day	B
June 26	Following day	C
Aug. 23	Previous day	D
Oct. 26	Same day	E
Dec. 5	Same day	F

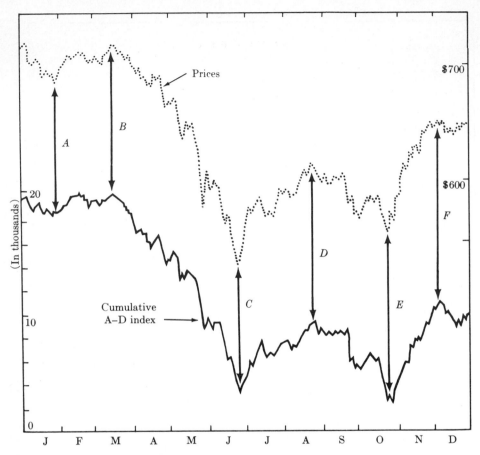

Fig. 21–4 Comparison of a cumulative advance-decline index with daily stock prices during 1962.

There are other ways in which advance-decline data may be manipulated to render them more meaningful. For example, one analyst uses the figures to derive a "resistance" index. This index is merely the percentage of traded issues which on a given day move in a direction opposite to some stock price index. For example, if 800 issues advanced and 500 issues declined, the resistance index would be 62.5 if the stock prices moved up or 37.5 if they moved down. Some analysts hold the resistance index to be predictive only when it reaches some preset level, such as 80. Other analysts derive forecasts from trend lines fitted to the index or by formations that appear when the index is charted. In Figure 21–5 a resistance index is compared with the 1962 movement of the Dow-Jones industrial averages.

Size of the Short Interest.   A short interest arises when a person sells shares that he has borrowed on the expectation that the price of the stock will be lower later. The short interest outstanding in New York Stock Exchange listed issues as of the middle of each month is reported by the Exchange. Here the interest lies not in the mechanics of executing short sales (this was explained in Chapter 15) but in interpretations frequently placed on the figures released by the Exchange. The June 17, 1963, issue of *Barron's* reported the short interest as of the previous May 15 as follows:

	Thousands of shares	Per cent of daily volume
Short interest (May 15, 1963)	5,797	1.17
Previous month (Apr. 1963)	6,002	1.37
A year ago (May 1962)	3,267	0.87

The size of the short interest as of any given moment is a measure of bearish sentiment. But the data are subject to two contradictory interpretations. A trader who is short expects prices to decline. From this viewpoint a

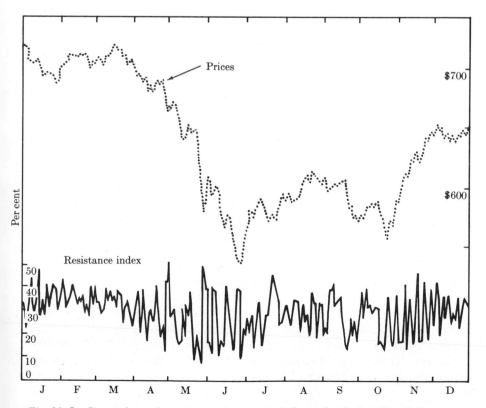

Fig. 21–5 Comparison of a resistance index with daily stock prices during 1962.

large short interest indicates widespread expectation of a price decline. But a trader who is short *must* purchase stock in the near future. From this angle a large short interest indicates a strong potential demand for stocks and justifies a forecast of a rally.

The safest plan would probably be to interpret short-interest data differently according to the current fundamental position of the market. For example: Why would a trader sell short in a fundamentally strong market? The answer is: Because he believes that prices have outrun fundamental conditions and that corrective forces are about to bring a downward adjustment of prices. If so, then a large short interest in a bull market means that professional traders are bearish at the moment but that the expected decline of prices is going to be of short duration since the shorts will be forced by the bullish trend to be satisfied with the profits derived from a 4- or 5-point decline.

The significance of a large short interest in a fundamentally weak market is different. There are two reasons why a trader might be short at such times: first, because he believes that a recent market rally overextended itself, calling for a correction; second, because prices are expected to continue their downward trend as a result of a deteriorating fundamental situation. Under such circumstances short sellers will be disinclined to accept profits from a mere 4- or 5-point decline. Furthermore, the statistics on short positions during a bear market can be deceptive. Many of the transactions that are included in the short position statistics are not sales of borrowed stock to be covered by purchases but sales to be covered by delivery of shares held in the seller's strong box. Such sales furnish no real technical strength to the market, since delivery can be made without a purchase.

In summary, a large short interest provides technical strength to a market only if a possibility exists of "squeezing" the shorts, that is, of forcing them to run for cover. This possibility exists only in a market that is fundamentally strong. In a market that is fundamentally weak, a large short interest does not provide a similar degree of technical strength, since some shorts, having sold against the box, can cover without buying and others will not panic because the market is fundamentally weak.

One aspect of the problem remains to be treated. How does one know when the short position is high enough to be significant? Short-term analysts customarily relate the short interest to average daily volume. Most of the time the short interest is less than 1 per cent of average daily volume. When the ratio rises above this figure, statistical data on the short interest assume greater importance. Figure 21–6 compares changes in the monthly short interest with the movement of the Dow-Jones industrial averages during the three-year period 1960 to 1963.

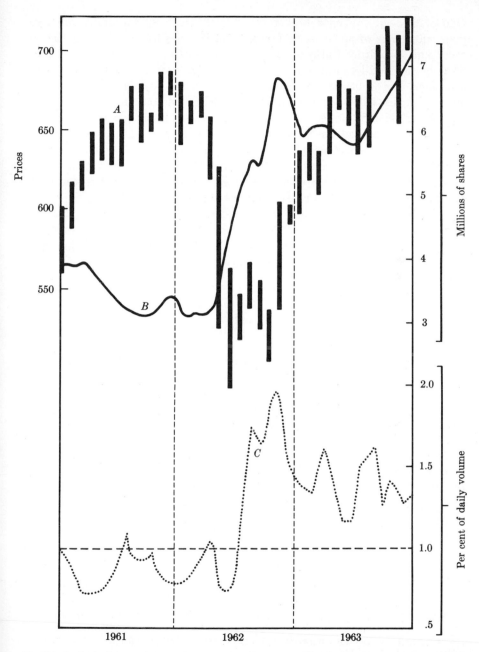

Fig. 21–6   Relation of short sales to stock prices. (*A* = stock prices, *B* = short positions, and *C* = ratio of short sales to average sales volume.)

Odd-lot Trading.   When a broker receives an order to buy or to sell fewer than 100 shares of an issue, he turns the order over to an odd-lot dealer for execution. Two firms, Carlisle & Jacquelin and DeCoppet & Doremus, execute most of the odd-lot orders received by members of the New York Stock Exchange. If one of these firms accumulates orders to buy, say, 452 shares and orders to sell, say, 353 shares of XYZ common, it would purchase 100 shares on the market and "cross" the buy and sell orders at the price at which it purchased the full lot. This would leave it with an inventory of 1 share. Thus the machinery for executing odd-lot orders is such as to cause odd-lot traders to buy and sell among themselves to the maximum extent possible. Only when there is an excess of buy or of sell orders can it be said that odd-lot traders purchase from or sell to full-lot traders.

Each day the two dealers mentioned report the total of their transactions in all issues to the *Wall Street Journal* for publication the following day. Thus readers were informed on May 21, 1963, that odd-lot transactions executed by the two firms on the previous day were as follows:

Customer purchases		351,811 shares
Customer sales:		
Short	4,236 shares	
Other	423,492 shares	427,728 shares

It is obvious from these figures that odd-lot traders sold 75,917 more shares than they purchased. Presumably these shares were sold to full-lot traders.[1]

Now some technical traders believe that a study of reported odd-lot transactions yields significant information about the inherent strength of supply and demand in the market. There are two ways of studying the published figures on odd-lot trading. In the first, one compares the volume of odd-lot purchasing and/or selling with the total volume of trading on the New York Stock Exchange. If one series of figures increases at a time when the other is declining, something significant is happening. The other method consists in subtracting sales from purchases to obtain an "on balance" purchase or sales figure for each time period. Such figures indicate whether small investors are currently entering or leaving the market in significant numbers.

In essence, conclusions drawn from odd-lot data rest upon the proposition that a majority of small investors do the wrong thing *at critical moments*. This assumption may be true or false. It could be true in the short run and not in the long run, or vice versa. It is difficult to know how to go

---

[1] Actually transactions between odd-lotters and full-lotters must have exceeded this number, since odd-lot traders may have sold more shares of one issue to full-lot traders and purchased more shares of another issue. The totals reported to the *Wall Street Journal* would make it appear that transactions in different issues were crossed or canceled out.

about proving or disproving this proposition. Presumably, if the volume of odd-lot purchases increases greatly just before a decline in prices or if the volume of odd-lot sales increases greatly just before a price rally, evidence exists to support the view that small investors as a group are inclined to act unwisely at critical moments.

Historically, odd-lot traders are purchasers; that is, most of the time their purchases exceed their sales. The extent to which this is so is made clear in Figure 21–7, where quarterly odd-lot balances are compared with the movement of the Dow-Jones industrial averages during the period 1950 to 1963.

It will be noted that odd-lot investors purchased on balance in significant quantities during the periods 1951 to 1953, 1955 to 1957, and 1959 to the middle of 1960 and that these were periods during which stock prices moved sidewise. Each of these periods of small-investor acquisition occurred at the end of a period of rising prices (proving that small investors acted unwisely) and preceded a period of rapidly rising prices (proving that small investors acted wisely). Apparently a deductive conclusion that small investors act wisely or unwisely depends upon whether one looks forward or backward.

Odd-lot traders sold on balance during the rising markets of 1950, 1954, 1958, and 1961; however, the amount of their selling was small. But the fact that they refrained from buying during these periods of rising prices

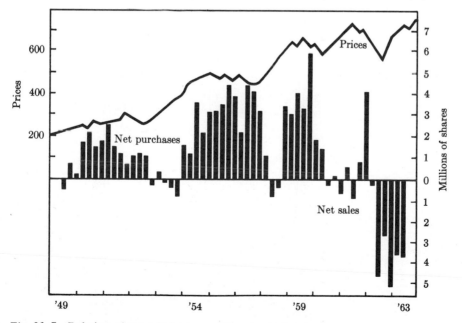

Fig. 21–7 Relation of net odd-lot transactions to stock prices.

may be significant. During the first half of 1962, when stock prices were near their historical highs, odd-lot investors acquired shares on balance in large quantities. When prices broke in May and June of that year, odd-lot investors shifted to the selling side of the market and remained there throughout the subsequent recovery. Thus it would appear that odd-lot traders purchased (on balance) during stationary or slowly rising markets and refrained from purchasing on rapidly rising markets. Whether this characteristic behavior is sufficiently reliable to constitute a basis for short-term forecasting remains to be decided.

The year 1962 is a good year for testing forecasting hypotheses. During the first four months of the year prices declined in what might well have been interpreted (at the time) as a "correction" had it not been followed by six weeks of panic selling. Following the panic, prices rose for approximately two months, then sold off for two months, after which they began a climb back to their 1961 historical highs. What were odd-lot investors doing during these periods?

During the first four months (the period of *apparent* correction) odd-lot purchases and sales both declined and odd-lot short sales were very low (see Figures 21–8 and 21–9). During the panic all three types of odd-lot trading increased greatly, but selling on balance was close to zero. During the subsequent recovery purchasing remained constant at a low level, but selling increased as the market rose. For some unexplainable reason odd-lot short selling increased rapidly during the latter half of September and

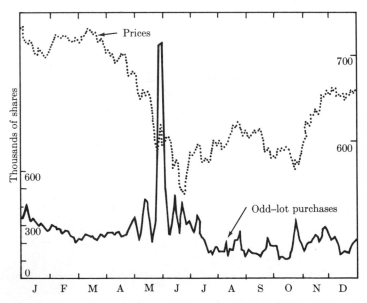

Fig. 21–8 Comparison of daily odd-lot purchases with stock prices during 1962.

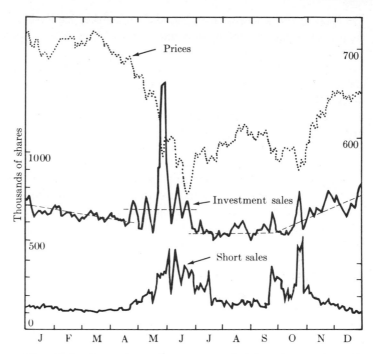

Fig. 21–9 Comparison of two types of daily odd-lot sales with stock prices during 1962.

throughout the entire month of October, just prior to the rapid rise of prices that occurred in November.

Volume of Trading. The prevailing beliefs regarding the relationship of price to volume can be summarized briefly. A rise or decline of prices *on high volume* signifies a continuation of the price movement. A rise or decline of prices *on low volume* portends a reversal of the price movement. A slow price movement (or no movement at all) *on low volume* warns of a dangerous situation. In interpreting volume data it is probably advisable to judge high and low volume on the basis of weekly or monthly data rather than to use daily figures.

Quality of Market Leadership. A box will be found in the upper left-hand corner of the page in the *Wall Street Journal* that reports the daily quotations of the New York Stock Exchange. This box contains data relating to trading in the 10 most active stocks. Under the figures there always appears a statement like this: "Average closing price of the 10 most active stocks: 40.95." Since the issues included in the list vary from day to day, the average of closing prices fluctuates greatly. For example, the average for December 16, 1963, was 39.92. The next day it was 93.41, and the following day 64.54. The highness or lowness of this average is believed by some technical analysts to reveal the *quality* of market leadership. The average is frequently used in conjunction with one of the other indicators, such as volume.

Interpretations are based upon the assumption that high-quality issues sell at higher prices than do low-quality issues. Thus on any one day the 10 most active stocks may be market leaders; on another day the 10 most active stocks may be "cats and dogs." In the beginning stages of an upswing, investors prefer and will purchase the high-quality issues, since all issues tend to be underpriced and one might as well ride up with quality. As high-quality issues move up and become less attractive, investors begin to search for bargains among the second quality issues. Sooner or later these also move up, and investors are forced to turn their attention to the low-quality issues. The continued rise of stock prices has by this time made investors bold and less discriminating. Some traders believe, therefore, that when low-quality stocks begin to lead the market the end of a rally has been reached and a reversal is about to take place.

The analysis can be made more complex. If an important stock price average is moving up but the average of the 10 most active is low or declining, a near-term decline of the important average is imminent. Similarly, if an important stock price index is declining and the average of the 10 most active issues is low or declining, the end of a bear market is in the offing. When the average of the 10 most active issues is high, a continuance of the current trend is indicated, particularly if this forecast is confirmed by one based upon volume of trading.

Comparison of Stock Price Indexes. On any single day one segment of the market may move independently of another. For example, the prices of rails may decline while the prices of industrials advance, or the Dow-Jones average of 30 industrials may not act in the same manner as the Standard & Poor's index of 500 issues. Such divergent movements are not unusual, but it is highly unlikely that they will persist for long. Consequently, if such divergences do persist, some analysts believe the situation is predictive. In general, it is believed that the weaker segment of a market precedes the stronger. Qualitywise the rails are considered poorer investment media than the industrials. Therefore during a bull market the rails should reach their peak and turn downward before the industrials, and in a bear market the rails should touch bottom and turn upward first. In this way, watching the relative performance of the two series at critical moments may reveal significant information regarding the current technical status of the market.

Another somewhat similar but slightly different comparison is frequently made by watching the relative movements of the Dow-Jones industrial averages and the Standard & Poor's stock price index. Obviously the former are more representative of the market leaders; the latter, of the market as a whole. Thus, if the two move in the same direction but the change in the Standard & Poor's index is less than ten times that in the Dow-Jones averages, a divergence has occurred. If the two indexes move together, a continuance of the current movement is predicted. If a divergence exists the Dow-Jones averages are expected to follow the course set by the Standard & Poor's index.

Brokers' Loans and Customers' Balances.   Each month the New York Stock Exchange reports the totals of customers' debit and credit balances and the aggregate indebtedness of all members of the Exchange. For example, the data released for April 1963 were as follows:

Customers' debit balances	$4,526,000
Customers' credit balances	1,201,000
Brokers' borrowings	3,362,000

If these data are viewed as constituting the current asset and current liability portion of a consolidated balance sheet of all brokers, it is possible to draw certain conclusions regarding the technical status of the market from changes in the data that occur from time to time. The absence of a cash balance figure is unfortunate but not important, since it is known that the cash balance figure is relatively small, that it does not fluctuate greatly, and that such fluctuations as occur are without analytical significance.[2]

If the floating supply of stock is more or less evenly distributed among traders, the three reported balances assume their normal relationship. If prices rise and a portion of the floating supply of stocks moves from strong to weak hands, the first effect would be an increase in *both* customers' debit and credit balances. If prices decline and some of the floating supply moves into strong hands, the totals of *both* customers' debit and credit balances would decline. Thus, a simultaneous increase in both types of customers' balances indicates a *weakening* technical situation, and a simultaneous decrease in both types of customers' balances indicates a *strengthening* technical situation.[3]

If the floating supply of stocks is being augmented by sales of investors to traders, the first effect would be an increase in both customers' debit and credit balances but this would be followed *quickly* by a decrease in customers' credit balances and an increase in brokers' aggregate borrowings. The latter situation indicates sales of stock accompanied by withdrawals of the proceeds of the sales. Since sellers who intend to reenter the market soon normally leave the proceeds of their sales with brokers (as a credit balance), a rise in brokers' indebtedness indicates that a serious market weakness is developing.

---

[2] For a more detailed analysis of the subject, see Wilford J. Eiteman, "Economics of Brokers' Loans," *American Economic Review,* March 1932, pp. 66–77; and also his article, "Economic Significance of Brokers' Loans," *Journal of Political Economy,* October 1932, pp. 677–690.

[3] The reader's attention is directed to the difference between a "strong" and a "strengthening" situation and between a "weak" and a "weakening" situation.

Usually brokers' indebtedness continues to increase after a break in prices and does not decrease until investors begin to buy stocks in quantity for cash, at which time customers' debit balances and brokers' borrowings both decline.

The chief significance of changes in the total of brokers' indebtedness lies in the clue it affords to the identity of sellers. If prices continue to move upward while brokers' indebtedness increases, investors are selling for cash. The speculative demand for stock is not lessened (as evidenced by movement of stock prices), but the floating supply of shares is being augmented. There is a limit to how long this process can continue.

If the total of brokers' indebtedness increases at a time when prices stand still or are declining, a different situation is developing. Now speculative demand is falling (as evidenced by the movement of stock prices), and at the same time the floating supply of stock is being augmented. Such a situation precedes a wholesale dumping of shares. Thus changes in brokers' indebtedness provide short-term traders with a clue to causal factors at work in a current market, but the data must be interpreted with care.

Miscellaneous Indicators.   There are a number of other rules for judging the technical position of a market, most of them based on experience and observation rather than on logic. For example, it is believed that four or five consecutive daily advances or declines heighten the probability of a reversal. There were 54 rallies and 54 declines in 1962. The longest rally in that year was 9 days; the longest decline was 7 days. The rallies and declines of 1962 and the time they lasted are shown in the following table:

Length of movement	Rallies	Declines
1 day	25	24
2 days	16	13
3 days	4	2
4 days	3	5
5 days	2	5
6 days	2	4
7 days	1	1
8 days	0	0
9 days	1	0
Total	54	54

If stock prices advance on bearish news, a strong technical position is indicated. If prices fail to rally on bullish news, a weak technical position is suggested. In the absence of overnight news, a strong or weak closing usually indicates a similar opening the following day. If the number of new highs increases daily, technical strength is indicated. If the number of new lows increases daily, the reverse is suggested.

22 the technical trader

To understand the several techniques and approaches of short-term traders, it is desirable to view them in the light of an underlying theory of market price. Necessarily this theory will appear to be oversimplified and unrealistic. Nevertheless, it will help the reader to appreciate the logic behind short-term trading procedures.

Trading Activity in a Model Market

In a model stock market every participant is assumed to be either a pure investor or a pure speculator. The first, the investor, holds shares because he *thinks* they are a good investment. In the real world investors may be insurance companies, mutual funds, pension funds, investment clubs, or any one of a million or more persons who hold stock for current income or for long-term capital gain. Presumably an investor's decision to acquire his current holdings is preceded by an investigation (adequate or inadequate) into the current and future earning and dividend prospects of the company. It does not matter whether his decision is wise or foolish; the fact of importance is that he pays attention to fundamentals and that he acquires shares with an intent to hold them for an extended period of time. This means that under ordinary circumstances an investor tends not to participate in in-and-out trading. This does not preclude him from watching daily quotations or from computing paper profits on the basis of imaginary sales. Neither does it prevent him from selling shortly after buying if, in his judgment, fundamental factors have changed. An investor is not tied irrevocably to holding for the long term; only at the time of purchase is he committed psychologically to this goal. The analysis that follows will need a label for the aggregate stock holdings of investors. Since no generally accepted term exists, the term "investment holdings" will be used.

In theory a speculator holds shares of stock because he expects to be able to dispose of them shortly at prices higher than the costs of acquisition. The speculator's decision to acquire his current holdings was probably preceded by an evaluation of the chances that future prices would be higher than current prices. Such a rise in prices occurs only if investors or other speculators are predestined by events to acquire the shares later. Thus speculators are motivated to a large extent by their anticipation of the future behavior of other persons. As long as an expectation of higher prices exists, speculators hold; when expectations of higher prices evaporate, speculators sell. They care little about fundamentals (sales, earnings, dividends, and the like) except as the fundamentals may influence the future behavior of persons.[1]

The speculative group is composed of registered floor traders, brokerage office traders, professional traders, and thousands of amateurs who buy and sell shares in the hope of making easy money quickly. From the point of view of a model market, the most important characteristic of speculators is the ease with which they can be induced to enter or leave the market and the frequency with which they change from the buying to the selling side, or vice versa. It is customary to think of speculators as being divided into the informed and the uninformed. The aggregate stock holdings of the speculative group as of any given moment is called the "floating supply." Investment holdings, as defined earlier, probably constitute 80 per cent and the floating supply 20 per cent of all outstanding shares, but this ratio obviously varies with time and with different issues.

The above discussion suggests that investors (as defined) are disinclined to participate in market activity except when current prices rise or decline to levels out of line with fundamental factors. This tendency of investors to enter the market on the buying or selling side only at certain price levels establishes the limits within which speculators can run prices up or down without interference as they barter the floating supply back and forth among themselves. If current quotations rise too high in relation to fundamentals, the floating supply is augmented by a portion of investment holdings. Conversely, if current quotations decline too far in relation to fundamentals, a portion of the floating supply is drained off into investment holdings.

Thus the major problems of short-term traders are (1) to decide at what price level investment buying and selling will dominate the price-fixing mechanism and (2) to judge what effect price changes will have upon the behavior of informed and uninformed speculators. For example, a short-term trader may feel that the high point which the price of a particular issue reached during its last rally marks the level at which investment selling dominates. As the price of the issue again approaches this level, the trader must decide whether investment selling will dominate the market again at

[1] The characteristics that distinguish investors from speculators can be described more succinctly as follows: Everyone who buys or sells stocks is in a sense a speculator. But investors are speculating in fundamentals, whereas so-called speculators are speculating in the behavior of persons. Since fundamentals change slowly, investor speculations tend to be long-term. Since human behavior is capricious at times, the so-called speculator thinks in short terms and remains on a constant alert for the unexpected.

this level and, more important, whether his fellow speculators will liquidate their holdings just short of this level in anticipation of such domination. It will be noted that the concern of the short-term trader is with the possible reaction of other traders to the price level and not with its economic justification.

Short-term traders belong to different schools of thought with regard to the best method for profiting from market situations. Each school has its technique, and each is prepared to defend the soundness of that technique by logical arguments. The remainder of this chapter will be devoted to explaining the several techniques and the theories upon which they rest. The theoretical description of the activities of pure investors and pure speculators will help the reader to understand the arguments of the proponents of the various trading techniques.

The Tape Reader

A tape reader believes that all the information essential to predicting the course of prices in the immediate future is revealed on the ticker tape. As the reader knows well, the information reported on a ticker tape is limited to the names of the issues traded, the number of shares involved in each transaction, and the prices at which each trade was consummated. By the application of rules and principles to these data, the tape reader attempts (1) to discover the current attitude of investors and speculators toward an issue, (2) to predict their subsequent buying and/or selling behavior in that issue, and (3) to forecast the effect which that buying and selling activity will have upon subsequent prices.

For example, suppose that the average size of trades in a particular issue has been 100 to 300 shares per transaction. Suddenly a 5,000-share transaction is reported on the tape. The unusual size of this transaction attracts the attention of speculators and causes them to meditate on its significance. Some traders, particularly the smaller ones, interpret the large transaction as evidence of "informed buying," by which they mean purchase by a single, well-informed large investor with special knowledge from a number of less well-informed smaller investors. There is an alternative interpretation, of course, i.e., a single, well-informed large investor *selling to* a number of less well-informed small investors. The direction in which the price moves as a result of the transaction offers a clue to whether the large trader was buying or selling. If the price moves upward, the single trader is likely to have been a buyer; if the price moves downward, he is likely to have been a seller. But the evidence is not conclusive: the market may have been rigged to give a wrong impression.

The professional tape reader does not jump to easy conclusions. He adheres to those that are obvious. In our example, a larger than ordinary order was executed. This is a fact that the tape reader cannot ignore. The execution of the large order did attract the attention of thousands of brokerage office traders. This is also a fact he does not wish to ignore. The question of major interest to the tape reader is: Did the individual who placed the large order want to attract the attention of small investors, and, if so, why? There are several possible answers. Perhaps the big buyer has been quietly accumulating the shares of the issue for some time and now holds as much of it as he desires. Now he wishes to induce the public to enter the market on the buying side so that the issue will advance rapidly on large volume and afford an opportunity for him to unload his holdings at high prices. To advertise the issue, he may deliberately purchase a large block of the stock at a slightly higher price, hoping that small speculators will interpret the act as informed buying. If the public takes the bait, the price will start moving upward rapidly.

The amateur speculator guesses at what the existing supply and demand situation is, but the professional tape reader bases his opinion on a study of the volume and course of prices prior to the execution of the large transaction. This investigation is based upon a theory that no one can accumulate or distribute large quantities of an issue on a thin market without leaving traces of his activity. The public overlooks the traces; the tape reader does not.

In one respect the behavior of the tape reader resembles that of the amateur speculator. Both want to climb on board for a ride if prices are going to move up rapidly. In another respect the behavior of the tape reader differs from that of the amateur speculator. The public buys the issue on the assumption that the current rise is due to a realization (by others) of a change in fundamental conditions. Thus they buy with the intention of holding for the long pull. By contrast, the tape reader ascribes the current run-up to technical conditions to be followed shortly by a reversal. Consequently he accumulates shares for quick resale.

The tape reader suspects that when the price of the issue has reached certain preset levels the big trader will sell his holdings and go short. As soon as the big trader's short position reaches the desired proportions, he will sell a large block of stock to knock the price down and to panic small investors into selling. As the price moves down, the insider will cover his short position by buying the shares which small investors are dumping. A large trader can do all this without revealing his activities to the public and without violating any of the rules prohibiting manipulation; but the clues revealed by volumes and prices on the tape inform the tape reader at all times about what is happening and what is going to happen next.

A tape reader has certain principles or rules to guide his thinking and to protect him from serious error. Some of these are maxims that summarize lessons learned from years of experience, and others are technical rules for interpreting ticker tape data. Among the former are the following:

1. The speculator should be a cynic. He should doubt everything and every-body. He believes nothing but factual data. Market trading is a cold, bitter game in which the object is to outsmart the other fellow. Therefore one cannot trust what another person says, nor should he expect others to trust what he says. Only facts revealed by the action of the market are reliable.

2. Since the stock market is big and broad, a trader cannot possibly follow the movements of more than three or four or, at most, five issues. There-fore, a tape reader concentrates on a few issues and records the price and volume of *every* transaction in these issues.

3. The smart trader trades alone. He pays no attention to rumors, reports, board-room chatter, or opinions of investment advisers. Such advisers are the dupes of big traders who manipulate the market. "Have no opinions and ask for none" and "He who buys on tips will sell on dips" are maxims of the tape reader.

4. The tape trader should include one giant company such as General Motors or U.S. Steel among the issues he watches. This giant issue acts as his newspaper. Its volume and price movements reflect general eco-nomic conditions. If the tape reader does read newspapers, he confines his attention to the comics, the cartoons, and the entertainment features, since to read anything else might mislead him. All the news of importance to him is reported on the ticker tape.

5. During the course of a major movement of prices up or down, everyone is an expert and likely to be right, but at the turns small investors and the majority of large investors are always wrong. Therefore, the tape reader avoids being influenced by market psychology.

It is easy to memorize and blindly to follow these maxims, but the operating principles of tape reading must be understood and applied with intelligence. The tape reader's principles are more easily retained if the reader keeps in mind that the tape reader visualizes the market for each issue as a battlefield upon which the forces of supply and demand are being pitted against each other and the tape as a series of dispatches bringing him the latest information from the fighting front. The course of prices revealed on the tape informs him which side is on the offensive and which is on the defensive. The magnitude of price changes indicates the extent to which the front line is moving backward or forward. Data on volume reveal the size of the forces committed to the fighting. From such information a tape reader draws his own conclusions about what is happening.

For example, suppose that quotations in a particular issue are inching up on low volume. Obviously small forces are involved, buyers are on the offensive, and sellers on the defensive; but the outcome will not be decisive, for the whole affair should be classified as a skirmish and not as a major battle. Nevertheless the situation is fraught with danger, for if either side were to throw in reinforcements, the other side would be forced to retreat rapidly. The question is: Which side is likely to throw in reinforcements? The odds favor the side that is currently losing. Hence the tape reader's principle:

> When prices inch up or down on low volume, a violent movement in the opposite direction is in the offing.

A wise short-term trader withdraws from such a market until a trend is definitely established.

To take another example, suppose that prices are moving up or down on heavy volume. This would be interpreted as a major battle since both sides have large forces committed. If prices are advancing, buyers are on the offensive and sellers are in retreat. If prices are declining, sellers are on the offensive and buyers are in retreat. Under such conditions a sudden reversal in direction is not likely. Hence the tape reader's principle:

> When prices move rapidly in one direction accompanied by heavy volume, a continuance of the current price movement is indicated.

The short-term trader enters such a market on the side of the offensive.

In the stock market war, neither side ever wins a final victory. The fighting rages everlastingly. For a while one side seems to be winning, and then victory changes sides. As offensive forces push on farther and farther, their lines of communication and supply become longer and their offensive punch becomes weaker. At the same time the defensive side is moving back toward its secondary line of defense (investors waiting to buy or sell shares at bargain prices). When this line of defense is reached, the battle continues to rage but the front stabilizes (little or no movement in prices). This is the sign of an impending turning point or at least of a point of temporary equilibrium. Hence the tape reader's principle:

> If, following a major advance or decline of prices, the rate of change in prices declines but volume remains high, an end of the current movement is signaled.

Obviously a wise trader departs from the market before a debacle; only the amateur remains, hoping for a miracle.

The tape reader believes that his interpretations of volume and price movements are applicable to stock price averages (such as the Dow-Jones industrial average) at the bottom but not at the top of market swings. He has an explanation for this unusual conclusion. If a majority of issues displays a trend-reversal pattern simultaneously, that pattern will be discernible in any average made up of a selected number of those issues. In such a case, a forecast based upon the pattern of the averages will coincide with one based upon the patterns of the individual issues of which the average is composed. But if the various issues display a trend-reversal pattern at different times, averaging the issues will yield a blurred facsimile of the patterns characteristic of the individual issues. The fact is that individual issues do not reach their peaks simultaneously, but they do touch bottom together. There is a logical reason for this.

As prices move up, the public becomes optimistically bullish. When the price of stock A reaches a top, bullish investors shift to stock B, and when this issue in turn reaches a top, they shift to stock C, and so on. As a result, the individual issues reach their peaks one after the other, and an index of market prices assumes a rounded-off appearance as the market approaches the top. The opposite is the case at the bottom. The more or less continuous decline of prices that precedes a bottom delights the shorts but frightens the longs. There are more longs than shorts. As the market plummets, the longs panic and dump their securities recklessly, not one after the other but all together at the moment of panic. Thus the sharply defined bottom characteristic of each individual issue is also characteristic of an average of individual issues.

The Bar-chart Trader

The simon-pure chart trader sticks to his chart even more faithfully than the tape reader hovers over the tape. Some chart men make their charts a sort of fetish. To them, chart formations are the alpha and omega, the beginning and the end of market wisdom. Among the extremists there seem to be as many systems of chart reading as there are chart traders. One school, for example, bases its predictions upon Hebrew chronology, with its signs and seasons, festivals, sacrificial days, and golden numbers. The following is a statement typical of replies that one of the authors received from various chart men: "Many people want to know what method I use to determine future indications on the markets. I keep charts of the various active stocks and also a set of averages. My charts are different from the charts kept by the average statistician because they are based on a discovery of my own. I have discovered a 'time' factor that enables me to determine important tops and bottoms months or more in advance."

Chart reading is not all hocus-pocus, however. It is undoubtedly true that the patterns which stock prices make at times do reveal essential information about the existing supply and demand situation. This knowledge sometimes helps one to determine what is about to occur. To illustrate, if the supply and demand for an issue are drying up, the volume of trading will obviously decline and the range of quotations will become narrower. On a chart this would appear as a triangle. Whenever volume is low, a sudden increase of either supply or demand causes prices to move swiftly down or

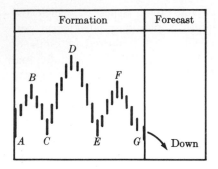

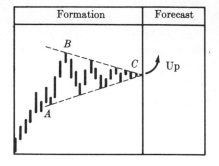

Fig. 22–1 A head-and-shoulders top.   *Fig. 22–2* A triangle, or coil.

up and justifies the chart trader's deduction that a triangle formation indicates a sharp movement one way or the other in the near future.

Chart traders, like tape readers, believe that prices as they appear on the tape represent the expectations and plans of industrial and financial leaders long before reports of such plans and expectations get into the financial and earning statements of corporations. The financial page, therefore, presents events that are of the nature of water that has gone over the dam. While this attitude holds for all chart traders, the more intelligent put considerable emphasis on fundamental statistics, particularly those which indicate trends. These traders feel that they can interpret their chart formations more accurately if they view them in the light of fundamental trends as indicated by basic industrial, financial, and psychological data.

Various chart formations are held to have predictive significance. Some forecast a continuance and some predict a reversal of the direction of current movements. A trader needs to be familiar with the numerous significant formations so as to be able to recognize them when they occur. A number of the more important are described here.

Head-and-shoulders Formations.   The head-and-shoulders formation is perhaps the best known of all. It may occur as a top (see Figure 22–1) or as a bottom. In the former, a rally starting at *A* reaches *B* and declines to *C,* thereby forming the left shoulder. This is followed by a greater rally from *C* to *D* and a subsequent decline to *E,* the head being thus formed. A third rally beginning at *E* and rising to *F* (which is about the same level as *B*) and falling back to *G* completes the right shoulder. A line joining points *C* and *E* constitutes the neckline. The signal to sell occurs when the decline from the right shoulder penetrates the neckline at *G*. A sag in the right shoulder indicates a greater decline than does a sag in the left shoulder.

Some chart traders use volume data as a supplementary aid in confirming head-and-shoulders formation forecasts. In a classical head-and-shoulders top, volume declines steadily from point *A* to *G*.

A head-and-shoulders bottom is the same as an inverted top. That is to say, the head and shoulders hang from the neckline, and the formation is interpreted to mean that the next movement will be up.

The reader should bear in mind that the illustrations for these formations are somewhat idealized. In fact, a great deal of skill (some would say imagination) is often required to recognize a pattern when it does occur. There is a logical reason for this distortion in practice of the theoretical pure patterns. For example, a historical study of price movements will reveal many head-and-shoulders tops that preceded subsequent price declines. Consequently, traders have come to place great confidence in their forecasting significance. With the passage of time the pattern and its significance have become widely known. Thus, if a head-and-shoulders top begins to form on a chart, many traders sell when the price turns down at F without waiting for it to penetrate the neckline (at G). The result may be a truncated right shoulder with a sudden increase in volume. A similar type of distortion may occur in other formations.

A Triangle, or Coil.   The triangle, or coil, sometimes called a "pennant," is the most important formation. It indicates a temporary exhaustion of both supply and demand so that the issue will respond violently to a few buy or sell orders. Unlike some of the other formations, the triangle, or coil, indicates not the beginning or end of a movement but rather an early and sharp resumption of the preceding movement. Hence, if a coil follows a decline, a continuation of the decline is predicted, and vice versa.

Ascending Bottoms or Descending Tops.   An ascending bottom or a descending top is a triangle, one side of which is horizontal. Thus, if the top is horizontal, the bottom must ascend to form a triangle and the resulting formation would be bullish. If the bottom is horizontal, the top must decline to form a triangle and the formation would be bearish.

Double Tops or Bottoms.   When prices rise to a point, decline, rise again to the first level, and then begin to decline once more, the formation is called a "double top" and indicates the beginning of a more extensive decline. If

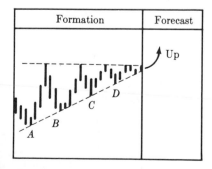

Fig. 22–3   An ascending bottom.

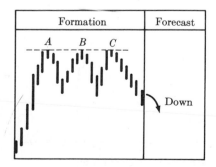

Fig. 22–4   A triple top.

the market rallies to the original top a third time, the formation becomes a "triple top." In general it is felt that the more tops the formation makes the sharper will be the future decline. Double and triple bottoms are the same formations inverted and signify the beginning of a sizable rally.

Complex Formations.   A complex formation is a head-and-shoulders formation with two heads and is interpreted in the same manner.

Broadening Formations.   This interesting and somewhat rare formation consists of five distinct reversals of direction in short order, each one going a little beyond the last one. The future movement will be in the direction opposite from the side of the formation that has the three turns. Chart traders say that this formation never misleads one.

Gaps.   The term "gap" refers to a break in the continuity of movement of stock prices and may apply to the price movement of a single stock or to the movement of an average or index of stock prices. Technically, the term is used when the price of a stock or an average of stock prices opens up or down from the close of the preceding day. Suppose that General Motors closes at $55\frac{1}{2}$ and opens the next morning at $56\frac{1}{2}$. Here is a gap of 1 point that, according to the rule of gaps, will be closed relatively soon. That is, the price may go up several points but in due time will decline to $55\frac{1}{2}$, closing the gap.

From a longer point of view and from its practical use over a period of time, the term gap applies to a discontinuity in the high and low prices from one day to the next. For example, if the high of one day is lower than the low of the succeeding day or if the low of one day is higher than the high of the following day, a gap appears in the trader's chart. Traders classify these gaps into three types: common, breakaway, and exhaustion.

If a gap occurs after an ascending bottom, a descending top, or some other formation, it is known as a breakaway gap. A gap occurring after a major rally or decline indicates exhaustion and predicts a reversal. Break-

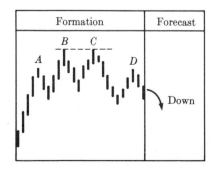

Fig. 22–5   A complex top.

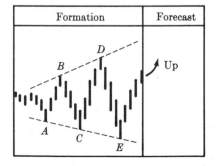

Fig. 22–6   A broadening formation.

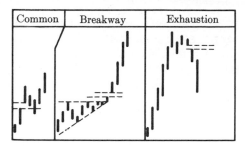

Common	Breakway	Exhaustion

Fig. 22–7   Three types of gaps.

away and exhaustion gaps are not filled later but rather indicate that the movement predicted by the previous formation is now under way. However, these gaps must be carefully studied because they may be the result of manipulation intended to catch the unwary.

Common gaps may be classified as follows: (1) up gaps in a rising market; (2) down gaps in a rising market; (3) up gaps in a falling market; and (4) down gaps in a falling market.

A study of gaps during a five-year period showed that a very high percentage of down gaps in a rising market and up gaps in a falling market were closed within two weeks and over 85 per cent within a month. Up gaps in a rising market and down gaps in a falling market were not nearly so often closed, but the percentage was very substantial.

Shake-outs.   Sometimes after a formation has clearly indicated a movement in a given direction, the market moves in the opposite direction. As a rule this contrary movement is short and is accompanied by high volume. Chart traders call these deceptive moves "shake-outs." The decline from *C* to *D* in Figure 22–8 is an illustration.

Irregularity.   Sometimes the market becomes erratic after it has enjoyed an extensive rally or decline. The price runs up a number of points, declines suddenly, and repeats. This vacillating movement following a well-defined rally or decline and accompanied by an increased volume of trading is interpreted to mean the end of the major rally or decline.

The descriptions given above do not by any means exhaust the arsenal

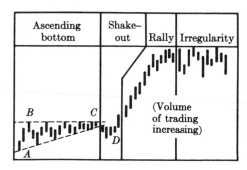

Ascending bottom	Shake-out	Rally	Irregularity

Fig. 22–8   A market formation illustrating a shake-out and growing irregularity on high volume.

of weapons with which the chart trader tackles the market. As was stated earlier, some traders rely solely upon charts. Others use charts in conjunction with the Dow theory and an analysis of investment fundamentals to forecast movements of the market. The chart trader's technique is also used by regulating authorities to detect the presence of manipulation.

Point-and-figure Charts

Many of the principles used by the bar chartist apply also to point-and-figure charting, but the technique is different. For example, the horizontal axis of the point-and-figure chart is calibrated to show alternate rallies and declines. In general the formations of a bar chart predict the direction but not the extent of a coming movement; the formations of a point-and-figure chart are believed to predict both the extent and the direction of the next movement.

Construction of a Point-and-figure Chart.   Point-and-figure charts are drawn on arithmetically ruled paper having identical vertical and horizontal rulings. The first step in preparing such a chart is to choose the vertical scale that is to be used. Each square in a vertical column on the chart may be made to represent a price change of 1, 2, 3, 5, 10, or 15 points, depending upon the chartist's objective. For example, an in-and-out trader will be most likely to use a 1-point vertical scale. An intermediate swing trader will prefer to employ a 3-point vertical scale, while a long-term investor will find a 5- or a 10-point scale more convenient. In general, stocks selling at very high prices are best charted on a 5- or a 10-point scale for short movements and on a 20- or a 30-point scale for longer-term swings. Stocks selling at prices under $20 per share may have to employ a $\frac{1}{2}$- or $\frac{1}{4}$-point scale in order to show any variation whatsoever.

The initial current price of an issue is plotted by placing an x in a square at the proper level in the first vertical column of the chart. In entering this and subsequent prices, the chartist pays attention only to full prices and ignores fractions. Thus, $35\frac{3}{8}$ and $35\frac{7}{8}$ are both entered as if they were 35. After entering the initial price in the first column, the chartist waits for the next *significant* price to appear on the tape. If the initial price is 35 and the vertical scale is calibrated on a 1-point basis, any full number quotation other than 35 will be a significant price change. If the initial price is 35 and the vertical scale is calibrated on a 3-point basis, the next significant price will be 38 or 32 (35 plus or minus 3 points). If the first significant price is higher than the initial price, an x is placed in the square immediately above the first x. If the first significant price is lower than the initial price, the x is placed in the square immediately below the first x. The chartist continues in this way to record significant price changes in the first vertical column *as long as prices on the tape continue to move in the direction first noted.*

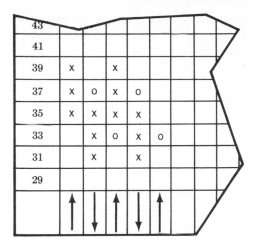

43							
41							
39	X		X				
37	X	O	X	O			
35	X	X	X	X			
33		X	O	X	O		
31		X		X			
29							

Fig. 22–9 A portion of a point-and-figure chart.

If a price reverses its previous direction, the chartist shifts to the next vertical column to the right and continues to record price changes in the same manner. An o rather than an x is used to indicate the first price entered in each column.[2] Thus, an o on top of a row of x's would indicate that the column is recording a down movement of prices; and an o at the bottom of a row of x's would mean that the column is recording an up movement of prices. This procedure causes successive columns on a point-and-figure chart to depict movements in opposite directions. The number of columns required to record a year's transactions in a particular issue will depend upon the number of price reversals occurring during that year. This may be any number from 3 to 300.

Figure 22–9 illustrates how a 2-point chart would depict the following series of quotations: $35\frac{1}{4}$ (the initial price, entered as 35); $36\frac{1}{2}$ (ignored because only rises of 2 points are significant); $37\frac{1}{2}$ (significant and entered as 37); 38 (not significant on a 2-point chart); $39\frac{3}{8}$ (entered as 39); 38 (an insignificant reversal); $37\frac{7}{8}$ (the first significant reversal and so recorded by an o in the second vertical column); $36\frac{1}{4}$ (not significant); $35\frac{5}{8}$ (significant and entered as 35); 34; $33\frac{7}{8}$; 32; 31; $32\frac{1}{2}$; $33\frac{1}{8}$ (a significant reversal and so entered in third column); 34; $35\frac{1}{8}$; $36\frac{1}{8}$; 37; $38\frac{1}{2}$; $39\frac{1}{8}$; $38\frac{7}{8}$; $37\frac{3}{4}$ (a significant reversal); $36\frac{1}{2}$; $35\frac{3}{8}$; 34; $33\frac{7}{8}$; 32; $31\frac{5}{8}$; and so on.

Interpretation of a Point-and-figure Chart. Each column of a point-and-figure chart represents a movement of prices in one direction. If the movement is up, this means that buyers are taking the initiative in market activity and, to overcome the reluctance of sellers, are offering higher and higher prices. But higher prices have two effects: they dampen the enthusiasm of

[2] Some chartists use only x's; others use x's only to indicate up movements and o's to indicate down movements; and some, as suggested above, use an o to indicate a reversal of direction.

buyers, and they decrease the reluctance of sellers. Everyone knows this to be a fact, but what point-and-figure chartists try to discover is the level at which sellers' reluctance is converted into an enthusiasm for selling and buyers' enthusiasm is replaced by a reluctance to buy further. This level is shown clearly on a point-and-figure chart at the point where an up movement ceases and a down movement begins.

When a shift in enthusiasm occurs, the sellers sell all the shares they can at the top price possible. To sell more shares, they must overcome the newborn reluctance of buyers by making concessions in price. Each concession dampens their enthusiasm for selling and reduces the reluctance of buyers to purchase. Sooner or later a level of prices is reached at which buyers again seize the initiative and prices start to move upward. The point-and-figure chartist studies the successive levels at which these reversals occur. For a while reversals occur at definite levels, but sooner or later one of the established limits will be violated. The penetration of the limit will occur when short-term holders have sold all the shares they have or short-term buyers have run out of money with which to purchase more shares. The important question is which of these situations materializes first. If, for example, buyers run out of money before sellers unload all their shares, a downward movement of prices will not regenerate buyer enthusiasm at the previous reversal level. As a result, prices will have to move to still lower levels to bring new outside buyers into the market. On the other hand, if suppliers exhaust their holdings before buyers run out of money and enthusiasm, prices will have to move higher than previously to induce other investors to enter the market and to sell some of their holdings. The chartist believes that these situations are reported on the ticker tape and revealed by his chart. He plots the tug-of-war contest, watching always for the appearance of telltale formations that inform him of the plans of speculative buyers and sellers.

Significant Point-and-figure Formations.   As explained, the point-and-figure chartist makes his predictions on the basis of distinctive patterns which show up on his charts from time to time. Each of these patterns has a name and is believed to have predictive significance. For example, if the tops and bottoms of a number of adjacent vertical columns of x's seem always to terminate at well-defined limits, the chartist will refer to the pattern as a "congested area" (see Figure 22–10). The most significant characteristic of a congested area is its horizontal width.

Sooner or later the exchange of shares within the confines of a congested area cease, either because sellers have disposed of all the shares they wish to sell or because buyers have exhausted their purchasing power. Any further inclination to trade will cause the price to move out of the congested area. A penetration of the upper limit of a congested area is called an

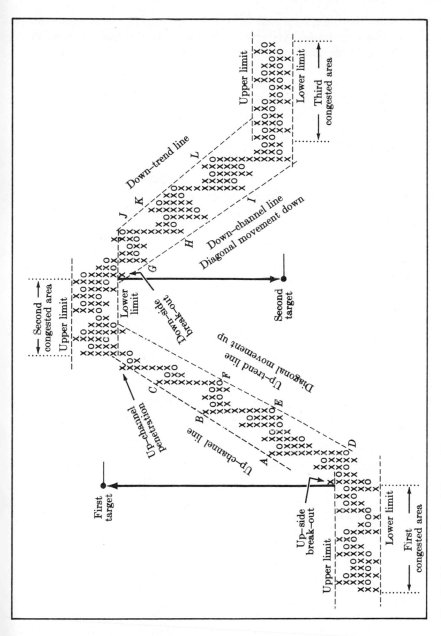

Fig. 22-10 A point-and-figure chart.

"up-side breakout" and is interpreted as a sign that buyers are anxious and sellers are reluctant to trade. An up-side breakout is a signal to buy. A penetration of the lower limit of a congested area is called a "down-side breakout" and is interpreted as a sign that sellers are anxious and buyers are reluctant to trade. Obviously a down-side breakout is a signal to go short.

Following a breakout, the x's on a point-and-figure chart can be expected to move diagonally in the direction set by the breakout. The diagonal movement takes the form of a series of short up-and-down swings with ever-higher tops and bottoms on a rise or ever-lower highs and bottoms on a decline. A line touching three rising bottoms or three declining tops in a diagonal movement is called a "trend line." Trend lines are classified into up-trend and down-trend lines. Prices are expected to continue moving in the direction of trend lines until the formation is violated by a penetration. Such a violation does not normally occur until prices reach the neighborhood of the "target," a term that will be defined and explained shortly.

A line parallel to an up-trend line and touching three successive rising tops is called an "up-channel line." Similarly, a line parallel to a down-trend line and touching three successive bottoms is called a "down-channel line." A penetration of a channel line by the x's on a point-and-figure chart indicates an acceleration of the movement under way. Such accelerations frequently herald the near approach to a major peak or valley, i.e., the end of the current movement. Thus a penetration of an up-channel line is a warning to liquidate long positions, and a penetration of a down-channel line is a warning to cover short positions.

As soon as an up-side breakout from a congested area shows on a chart, the point-and-figure chartist measures the width of the congested area and counts up a similar number of squares to determine the altitude of the target. The diagonal movement which is supposed to follow a breakout will not normally end until it reaches this target area. The rule works in reverse for a down-side breakout. Here the width of the congested area indicates the level of the target area for a down-diagonal movement. In a 1-point chart the vertical distance of the target area from the breakout point is equal to the number of vertical columns in the congested areas; in a 2-point chart the vertical distance will be twice the number of columns; in a 3-point chart three times the number; and so on. Because the public is accustomed to think in round numbers, chart traders are particularly cautious about price levels that are divisible by 10. For example, a target set at 73 might mean 70 or 80.

Point-and-figure charts must also take cognizance of "supply" and "support" areas. These are historic levels at which former diagonal movements have always terminated. A supply area is a level at which previous advances have stopped. As an up-diagonal movement gets under way, speculative buyers buy enthusiastically and speculative sellers sell reluctantly.

While this is occurring, long-term investment holders of the issue do not participate in the trading. However, if prices reach a level definitely beyond reasonable relation to earnings and dividend prospects (fundamental factors), these long-term investment holders might be enticed into the market on the selling side. No pool of speculative holders can withstand an avalanche of investment selling. If an upward price movement passes through a historic supply area without encountering the expected investment selling, the interpretation would be that an improvement in fundamentals has increased the attractiveness of the issue to long-term investors.

A support area is the level at which previous declines have terminated. This level probably represents the level at which the stock appears to long-term investors to be a bargain. Consequently, at this level enlargement of the floating supply by short-term sellers is more than offset by the purchases of long-term investors with intent to hold. If by chance a stock should penetrate a historic support area, the event would have ominous significance.

One formation of importance remains to be described. This is the "false breakout." Sometimes, after strong indications that prices will move in one direction, they inexplicably move in the opposite direction. False breakouts are the bane of point-and-figure charting. There is nothing that the trader can do about the matter except to close out his position, take his losses, and start over again.

Statistical Analysis of Technical Situations

The tape reader, the bar-chart trader, and the point-and-figure chartist concentrate on data relating to particular issues. By contrast, the statistical technical analyst studies data relating to the market as a whole. The methods and procedures employed by him rest upon the observable tendency of all issues to rally or decline simultaneously. Thus it would seem that one might learn much about the next movement of a particular issue by forecasting the probable movement of the market as a whole.

Statistical analysis of technical factors is used mostly by newspaper and magazine columnists who write articles explaining what has occurred and forecasting vaguely what is about to occur. Fundamentalists who base their decisions about what to buy on data relating to economic conditions frequently use an analysis of the technical situation in deciding when to buy. The data used by technical analysts and methods of interpreting these data were explained and critically examined in Chapter 21.

23 the dow theory

Charles A. Dow was born in Sterling, Connecticut, on November 6, 1851; he died in New York City in December 1902.[1] When he was twenty-one years of age, he took a position as reporter and assistant editor of the *Springfield* (Massachusetts) *Daily Republican,* shifting three years later to the *Star* and the *Journal* of Providence, Rhode Island. Then in 1880 he moved to New York City to become a reporter for the Kierman News Agency.

This New York news agency published what at the time was known as a "flimsy"—a sheet of tissue paper containing up-to-date financial news of importance prepared at irregular intervals and delivered to a short list of subscribers by a special messenger within a few minutes of publication. The copies were prepared by writing text material on a master sheet with an ivory stylus and transcribing the data to 20 tissue sheets by means of carbon paper. These sheets were the predecessors of modern financial newspapers.

It was while working for the Kierman News Agency that Dow became acquainted with Edward D. Jones. In 1882 Dow and Jones left the agency to organize Dow, Jones & Company, Inc., and to publish a flimsy of their own. In 1885 Dow became a member of the New York Stock Exchange and a partner of Robert Goodbody. For a period of several years he executed transactions for the firm on the floor of the Exchange. But newspaper work was more to Dow's liking, and he returned to it in 1889, the better prepared by his short period of experience as a floor broker.

The first issue of the *Wall Street Journal* appeared on July 8, 1889. From this date until the date of his death Dow served as managing editor, writing articles and editorials of current financial interest. Interspersed in his writings were brief explanations of the probable causes of financial happenings. These explanations reflect Dow's opinions and are the result of a theory of market behavior gradually evolved by him.

---

[1] The historical data contained in this chapter are taken for the most part from *Charles H. Dow and the Dow Theory,* by George W. Bishop, Jr., New York: Appleton-Century-Crofts, Inc., 1960. The reader is referred to this book for a more detailed account of the life of Dow and of the evolution of the Dow theory.

In the early years of the twentieth century, Samuel A. Nelson asked Dow to write a book presenting and explaining his theory of stock speculation. Dow refused but allowed Nelson to collect and to publish a number of his editorials in a book called *The A.B.C. of Stock Speculation*. Fifteen chapters of this book are editorials of Dow's reprinted without change. Each chapter carries a footnote explaining that it is a description of Dow's theory. The chapters discuss such diverse matters as the use of stop-loss orders, the danger of overtrading, and speculation for the decline. There is no explanation of anything resembling the present Dow theory, although fragments of it can be found here and there.

Nelson's death followed Dow's by a few years and *The A.B.C. of Stock Speculation* went out of print. Dow's successor editors of the *Wall Street Journal* were Serono S. Pratt and Thomas F. Woodlock, neither of whom were disciples of his. In the years that followed Nelson's death, the theories of Dow faded into obscurity. The name of Dow was first associated with the word "theory" in the footnotes of Nelson's book. The second time the phrase "Dow's theory" appeared in print was in 1907 in an editorial written by William P. Hamilton in the *Wall Street Journal*. During the next thirteen years the terms Dow theory and Dow's theories appeared in the *Wall Street Journal* only six times. Obviously, the Dow theory as such did not exist during the twenty-odd years following Dow's death.

Dow's Theories

As suggested, Dow theorized about stock prices but did not have a theory of stock prices as such. He was convinced that the movement of stock prices during a business cycle was controlled by values that could not be manipulated by speculators. He believed that value was a function of earnings. However, the level of stock prices at any given moment did not reflect current earnings but discounted earnings of the immediate future. Since traders could not be expected to discount future events perfectly, prices tended to run to extremes, being first too high and then too low. Whenever prices rose above value, a downward reaction would follow; whenever prices fell below value, an upward reaction was to be expected. In general the reactions would cancel about one half of the previous primary gain or loss. Thus the pattern of the market would be a primary movement in a given direction, followed by a reaction in the opposite direction of one half the amount. In a bull market the primary movements would make a series of "new tops," and in a bear market the primary movements would make a series of "new lows." Dow applied this pattern to the movements of individual issues but thought it might also be characteristic of market averages.

Dow was fond of visualizing the market as consisting of three movements all proceeding at the same time. The first was a movement up or down extending over a period of three to four years. This movement reflected the earnings of business enterprises during the business cycle and could not be manipulated by speculators. The second movement was a short-term swing of prices above and below the cycle, brought about as a result of the imperfections of the discounting process. The third movement represented day-to-day price changes resulting from speculation and was without significance.

Since the same forces—earnings and market psychology—that caused the trend and the cycle in railroad stocks also affected industrial stocks, Dow believed that it was reasonable to expect an average of the rail stocks and an average of industrial stocks to form similar patterns at about the same time. It was reasonable to expect this to occur; it was not essential for it to happen; and a failure of the two to move together did not carry the same stupendous implication to him as it did to later Dow theorists. This is as close as Charles Dow ever came to the idea of "confirmation."

Dow also spoke about "sidewise" movements as representing accumulation or distribution by insiders, but he always applied the analysis to individual issues and never to the movement of the averages. Thus the "line" concept, so much a part of the modern Dow theory analysis, was not an invention of Dow's.

If the pattern of the market as described by Dow is dependable, it becomes obvious that it (the pattern) can be used (1) to explain current market activity or (2) to predict the next movement of the market. Dow used it in the first way; the modern Dow theorist uses it in the second way.

Invention of the Dow Theory

The Dow theory as it is known today is the invention of William P. Hamilton and Robert Rhea. Hamilton was editor of the *Wall Street Journal* from 1907 to his death in 1929. Prior to 1920 his editorials mention Dow's theory six times, once each in the years 1907, 1913, 1914, 1915, 1919, and 1920. In these instances Hamilton's references are usually to the "theory of the late Dow" and not to the "Dow theory." He refers to Dow's theories four times in 1921 and seven times in 1922. It was during these two years that Hamilton was writing his book, *The Stock Market Barometer*.

In this book Hamilton codifies Dow's fragmentary ideas, assigns precise meanings to certain terms that Dow used in rather a broad sense, and adds a few innovations. The effect of the presentation is to give a reader the idea that Hamilton is describing a theory held by Dow rather than constructing a theory based upon Dow's ideas. Those who know Dow only through Hamilton therefore assume that the Dow theory was invented by Dow. It would be more accurate to consider Hamilton as the inventor of the Dow theory and to date its origin from 1922.

The pattern of stock prices in a bull market (primary movements up followed by minor down reactions) is definitely different from that of a bear market (primary movements down followed by minor up reactions). Since stock prices discount business conditions, they move ahead of economic events. Thus it is possible to forecast economic events by watching for the first signs of a shift from the pattern of stock prices characteristic of a bull market to a pattern of stock prices characteristic of a bear market, or vice versa. These first signs are a "penetration" of a previous reaction limit and a "failure" to penetrate a previous primary limit. Thus for Hamilton the Dow theory became a forecasting device.

A pure Dow theorist considers the Dow-Jones averages to be quite sufficient in themselves to do this forecasting job. It is not necessary to supplement them with statistics of commodity prices, volume of production, carloadings, bank debits, department store sales, exports and imports, and such data. If one of the averages shifts from a bull market pattern to a bear market pattern, or vice versa, and if the shift is confirmed by the other average, the course of future economic activity is clear.

With the death of Hamilton in 1929 public interest in the Dow theory went into eclipse, especially as the Great Depression of the thirties concentrated attention on economic survival. In 1932 Robert Rhea's book, *The Dow Theory,* revived interest in the Hamilton version of the Dow theory at a strategic moment of financial history. Rhea presented the Dow theory with refreshing directness and simplicity and did much to reestablish a following. Rhea's 1932 forecast of a bull market at a time when everyone was bearish and his subsequent 1937 forecast of a bear market when everyone was bullish established his reputation as a keen market analyst.

The present-day Dow theory is a synthesis of the thoughts of Dow, Hamilton, and Rhea. The theory as it now exists falls into four parts: (1) the theory of the three simultaneous movements of the market; (2) the theory of confirmation or corroboration of the two averages; (3) the theory of the line; and (4) the theory of double tops and bottoms. Each of these is explained in the discussion that follows.

Three Movements of the Market

According to the Dow theory, the market at any given moment is the composite resultant of three movements: (1) a major trend up or down; (2) an intermediate movement toward or away from this trend; and (3) a patternless day-to-day fluctuation. Some writers see in this a likeness to the level of the sea, depending as it does upon (1) the tide, (2) the waves, and (3) the ripples. This threefold aspect of the market is graphically emphasized in Figure 23–1.

The Major Movement.   Dow and Hamilton believed that a major movement of the market lasts 9 months to about 2 years and is either a bull or a bear trend. During a bull market each succeeding high point of the averages

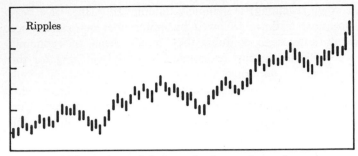

The market as it looks to the day–to–day trader

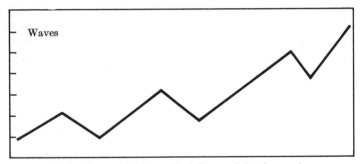

The market as it looks to the follower of the short swings

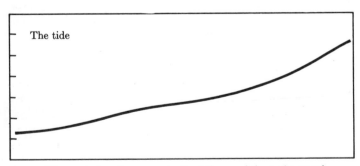

The market as it appears to the follower of the major trend

Fig. 23–1   Three market movements.

advances over the preceding high; during a bear market each succeeding low point in the averages is lower than its predecessor. From June 1900 to August 1921, Hamilton lists 6 major bull movements and 6 major bear movements. The bull markets lasted 25 months on the average and the bear movements 17 months. He sets down the following dates as the turning points of the 12 movements:

Advance   June 1900 to Sept. 1902
Decline   Sept. 1902 to Sept. 1903
Advance   Sept. 1903 to Jan. 1907
Decline   Jan. 1907 to Dec. 1907
Advance   Dec. 1907 to Aug. 1909
Decline   Aug. 1909 to July 1910
Advance   July 1910 to Oct. 1912
Decline   Oct. 1912 to Dec. 1914
Advance   Dec. 1914 to Oct. 1916
Decline   Oct. 1916 to Dec. 1917
Advance   Dec. 1917 to Oct.–Nov. 1919
Decline   Nov. 1919 to June–Aug. 1921

According to Hamilton's dates, the longest bull market lasted 3 years 4 months and the shortest 15 months. On the bear side the longest and shortest movements were 24 and 11 months, respectively. The bull markets thus averaged a longer time than did the bear movements. This was to be expected since it takes longer to build up than to tear down.

Although every major movement of the averages has its own time characteristics, the above figures seem to favor about 2 years for the completion of a bull market and to suggest 18 months for a major bear market.

It is primarily with reference to major swings that the Dow theory makes any positive claims. It may or may not be effective in predicting secondary swings. Its primary use is to indicate whether a turn up or a turn down of the cycle has come or is about to come.

The Secondary Movement.   After every primary movement has gone on for some time, a secondary movement will appear, carrying a bull market down or a bear market up for a short time, perhaps a week to two months. These reactions and rallies are a regular part of the market pattern and may be expected to retrace three eighths of the previous rise or decline of the market. The longer an advance progresses without interruption, the more imminent a reaction becomes. On the other hand, the further a decline moves, the more certain a secondary rally becomes.

The Current Fluctuations.   The market is at all times in flux, with rapid but temporary changes ever present. The averages indicate these changes from day to day, but they cannot be predicted, nor can they be used to predict anything fundamental in business.

How the Dow Theorist Forecasts

The Dow theory holds that the stock market is a barometer of business. The purpose of the theory is not to predict movements of security prices for traders but rather to call the turns of the market in order to forecast business cycles or the larger movements of depression and prosperity. In short, what a forecaster using the Dow theory attempts to do is to note changes in the economic tide by studying the height of the cyclical waves. The ripples, i.e., day-to-day fluctuations, mean little either for the market or for business.

As long as a cap is higher than the cap of the preceding wave or as long as a trough is higher than the trough of the preceding wave, it is safe to assume that the tide is rising, that is, that the trend is upward. Similarly, when caps and troughs of waves are successively lower, the conclusion is that the tide is ebbing. Once a tide has reached its maximum, the cap of the next wave is bound to be lower than that of the preceding one. This phenomenon constitutes the first sign of a change in the tide but is not by itself conclusive, since ripples and nonrecurring disturbances sometimes destroy the regular order of things. But following a failure of a cap to exceed the preceding one, if the next trough also fails to equal the preceding trough, it becomes certain that the tide has turned. Failure to realize that *both* cap and trough must penetrate the level of the preceding wave to constitute a definite signal has often caused a misinterpretation of the Dow theory at critical times.

It will be noted that the tide in Figure 23–2 turned at X but that the turning was not evident until considerably later at C. This emphasizes a point made earlier, namely, that the Dow theory predicts the trend of business and not the price of stocks. One who applies it to the stock market must bear in mind that its signal is always late. For example, when Hamilton's famous editorial "A Turn of the Tide" appeared in the *Wall Street Journal* on October 25, 1929, the Dow-Jones industrial averages had already declined 80 points. Thus the Dow theory did not give its warning until 52 days after the bear market had begun. Even at this late date, however, it warned those who heeded it of a 150-point decline yet to come.

The Dow theory predicts the turn of the tide at the bottom in the same way as at the top. While the primary trend is downward, each decline of prices will reach new lows and each rally will fall short of the level reached by the previous one. Sooner or later, however, a decline will fail to make a new low, or a rally will exceed the peak of the preceding one. When both occur, the end of the bear market is announced.

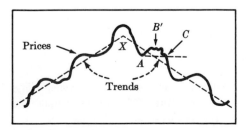

Fig. 23–2   Signaling the turn of the tide.

Supplementary Aids to the Dow Theory

It is possible to cite instances in which the Dow theory as explained above has given false signals. For this reason Dow theorists use a number of auxiliary devices in conjunction with it. Some of these are (1) confirmation, (2) volume, (3) penetration, (4) lines, or sidewise movements, and (5) double tops and double bottoms.

Confirmation.   The stock market as a whole and in its large movements represents the working of the law of supply and demand, which involves every fundamental factor in the whole financial and business situation of the nation. The averages are an index of stock market movements and thus sum up every influence that plays upon the market. In other words, the stock market is the best barometer of business, and an understanding of its movements is arrived at by an interpretation of the movements of the averages. All the fundamental forces concentrate into a supply of stock or a demand for it on the Exchange. When all the fundamental forces are bullish, both the industrial and the rail averages will advance together; and as long as these forces gain strength, new high points will be made by both averages, each confirming the other. When, however, the situation is divided so that the forces no longer act as a unit, a further advance by one average will not be paralleled by a further advance by the other average. The same reasoning is said to hold on the bear side of the market.

Thus in every primary movement the averages confirm one another. In a bull market, if the industrial average makes a new high, i.e., a high that overtops the preceding high, it is invariable that the railroad average will soon also make a new high. If either average consistently refuses to confirm the other, a major movement is probably nearing its end. Examples of such confirmation and of failure to confirm are illustrated in Figures 23–3 to 23–6.

For example, Figure 23–3 illustrates how a trader who did not wait for the rails to confirm a prediction of the industrials would have been misled in the summer of 1930. The trend of prices, as measured by the industrial averages, declined from 381 on September 3, 1929, to 202 at the beginning of 1930. By April 17 they had risen to 294. This rise was followed by a decline to 258 on May 3, a rise to 275 by May 29, a fall to 211 by June 24, and a rally to 224 by July 18. The next decline failed to penetrate the previous low and was followed by a rally that broke the previous high. Thus, according to the Dow theory, the industrial averages were clearly signaling the end of the bear market. But the average of the rails did not confirm the signal. As will be noted in Figure 23–3, the rail decline ending on August 12 did not penetrate the low of June 25, a favorable sign; but the rally that followed failed to reach the previous peak of July 18, an unfavorable sign. Thus the bull market was given three green lights and one red light; the rules require that four lights be green.

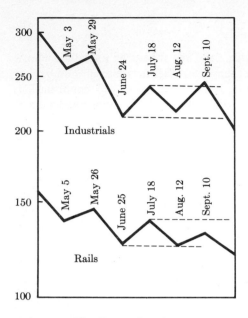

Fig. 23–3   Failure of rails to confirm industrials in 1930.

Volume.   The Dow theorist also studies volume. The principles applied are these: if the major trend is upward, dullness indicates an accumulation of buying orders; if the trend is downward, an accumulation of selling orders. Dow wrote, "In a bull period dullness runs into strength and lays the foundation for advances; in a bear market dullness runs into declines because delay brings a slow accumulation of orders to sell." However, it should be noted that Dow was speaking of individual issues and not of the market as a whole. It is the later Dow theorist who applies the principle to averages of stock prices.

Lines, or Sidewise Movements.   Frequently after a considerable rise or decline in the market, it happens that fluctuations in the averages are confined for long periods to a very limited range. If the averages are plotted, there appears to be neither an upward nor a downward trend. Prices move sidewise within a narrow area. This formation is called a "line."

A line in the market is due to an equilibrium in the supply and demand for stocks. If it occurs at the top of a major cycle, it indicates distribution by holders; if it occurs at the bottom, stock is passing from weak hands into strong hands, i.e., a period of accumulation is in progress. A line may also occur just before and at the end of a secondary swing in a primary movement of the market.

The Dow theory as developed by recent writers holds that a line signifies accumulation or distribution and that, if one of the averages breaks out on the upper side of the narrow zone of fluctuation and is confirmed by the other average, the market will make a considerable advance before its direction is reversed. On the other hand, if one of the averages, say the industrial average, breaks below the area of the sidewise movement and is confirmed by the railroad average, then the downward trend will continue for a relatively large number of points in the averages.

The line is best illustrated by the use of a chart. Figure 23–4 illustrates a line that occurred in 1924. During the spring of 1924 the two averages confined their movements to the limits shown on the chart for five weeks. In May the industrial average broke out of the range on the bottom, but the rails did not confirm this action. In June both averages broke out of the line on the upper side, indicating a somewhat prolonged rise in the market. By August 20 the industrial average reached 105.57, and on August 18 the rail average reached 92.65.

A study of a number of lines convinced Hamilton that a break by one average out of a narrow trading area, if confirmed by the other, indicates a movement of considerable extent and that in the case of major swings such confirmed movements are accurate barometers of business.

Double Tops and Bottoms.   If an average advances to a given level, recedes, and then advances to the same level and recedes again without effecting a penetration, the formation is said to be a "double top." A "double bottom" is the same formation inverted. Many Dow theorists believe that a double top or bottom signifies the end of a major movement.

Has the Dow Theory Successfully Predicted Changes?

The End of the Big Bull Market.   The test of any theory is its application. Knowing how badly the best of our business leaders misinterpreted the events of the autumn of 1929, the authors became curious to know whether the predictions of those who rely upon the Dow theory were more accurate than those of the business and political leaders of that day. Figure 23–5 shows the movement of the rail and industrial averages from May to November 1929. As will be noted, the industrial averages flashed a warning signal on October 22 which was confirmed by the rail average on the next day. Did contemporary theorists recognize these signals?

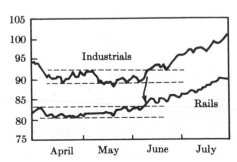

Fig. 23–4   An example of a line.

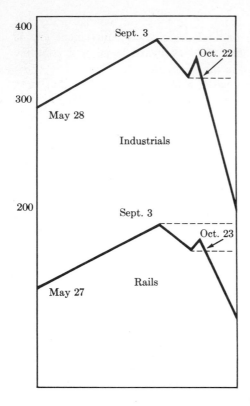

Fig. 23–5 The Dow theory signals the end of the big bull market in 1929.

On October 21, 1929, when most leaders were repeating that business was fundamentally sound, *Barron's* called attention to the crucial situation of the averages by pointing out that "if the stock market (now) takes the other direction there will be contraction in business later." Three days later Hamilton, in his now famous "Turn of the Tide" editorial, wrote:[2]

> On the late Charles H. Dow's well-known method of reading the stock market movement from the Dow-Jones averages, the 20 railroad stocks on Wednesday, October 23, confirmed a bearish indication given by the industrials the day before. Together the averages gave the signal for a bear market in stocks after a major bull market with unprecedented duration of almost six years.

The End of the Big Bear Market.   Figure 23–6 shows the intermediate movements of the Dow-Jones industrial and rail averages during 1932 and the first part of 1933. When would these movements have informed a trader who was depending upon them that a turn in the major trend had occurred? The industrial average established a new low on July 8, 1932. This low

[2] *Wall Street Journal,* Oct. 25, 1929, p. 1.

proved later to be the all-time low, but nothing at the time indicated this. The next rally carried the average to 79.93, a level lower than the high of March 8. Then began a decline which lasted until February 27, 1933, and which failed to break the low of the previous July. However, in February 1933, it could not have been known with certainty that this decline was not to continue. Not until the March 31 to June 12 rally carried the averages above the September 7 figure of 79.83 could the end of the bear market have been predicted by the Dow theory. The industrials indicated the end on April 10, 1933, and the rails confirmed the industrials on April 24.

The End of the 1932 to 1937 Bull Market.   The bull market which began on July 8, 1932, came to an end on March 10, 1937, but was not announced by the Dow theory until six months later. Figure 23–7 presents the essential data. The fact that the rally which began on June 14 failed to cross the 194.40 level reached on March 10 constituted the first warning. But the real indication came on September 7, when the industrial average penetrated the 165.51 resistance level established on July 14. This confirmed the bear market predicted by the rail averages on July 27. The market then continued downward unchecked until March 31, 1938. While the duration of the little bear market was relatively short—one year and three weeks—its decline as measured by the Dow-Jones industrial averages amounted to more than 49 per cent. Editorials and articles published in *Barron's* during the first three weeks of September 1937 called attention to the warnings issued by the averages. However, other conditions at the time seemed so favorable that

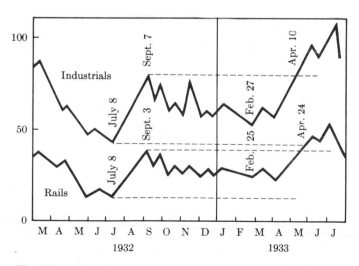

Fig. 23–6 The Dow theory signals the end of the big bear market in 1933.

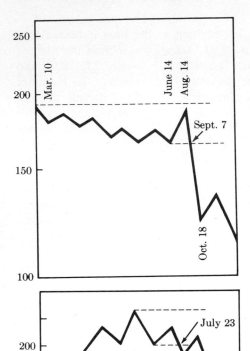

Fig. 23–7 The Dow theory forecasts the end of the 1932 to 1937 bull market.

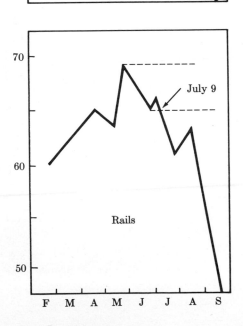

Fig. 23–8 The Dow theory signals the end of the World War II bull market in 1946.

most persons chose to interpret the stock market's difficulties as technical in nature rather than as indicative of a change in trend.

The End of the World War II Bull Market.   On the day of the attack at Pearl Harbor, the Dow-Jones industrial average stood at 110. By April 1942 it had declined to a low of 92.29, after which it began a long, steady climb that culminated in a high of 212.50 on May 29, 1946. As will be seen from Figure 23–8, the Dow theory gave its first indication of a change in the trend when the rails closed at 68.02 on July 9, 1946. This indication was confirmed by the industrial index on July 23, when it broke through the 200.65 resistance point. Then began a downward trend that lasted for thirty-six months. The interesting fact about this decline was that it took place in spite of increased per share earnings.

The End of the 1946 to 1949 Bear Market.   The Dow theory did not signal the end of the 1946 to 1949 bear market with the definiteness that is desirable. The industrials declined from 178.39 on March 29 to 173.24 on April 21, then rose to 176.63 on May 4, and fell off to a low of 161.60 on June 13. On August 18 the industrials rose to 182.02, going through the previous high of 176.63 on August 1. The average then began an eighteen-month climb to a level above 250. The Dow-Jones signal of August 1 was not confirmed by the rails until October 10, and then in a manner that must have left Dow-theory disciples in doubt as to its interpretation. This fact is brought out in Figure 23–9.

The End of the 1949 to 1956 Bull Market.   The bull market that began in 1949 lasted eighty-one months, coming to an end in the spring of 1956. The averages of the rails reached their peak on May 9 at 181.23, promptly declined to 161.60 on May 28, rallied to 171.37 on July 25, and declined to 156.75 on September 13, giving a clear indication that the bull market was over. The industrial average reached its peak sooner (April 16) at a level of 521.05; declined to 468.81 on May 28; and rallied (on August 2) to within $\frac{1}{10}$ point of its previous high before declining to its November low of 466.10. This last level amounts to a 2.70-point penetration of the previous low.

Thus, in a technical sense the industrial averages did confirm the forecast of the rails, but not until the 554-day bear market was 236 days old and not until after prices had lost 54 per cent of the amount they were predestined to lose. Only a Dow theorist who possessed great faith in the theory would have been willing to attach significance to a failure of 0.1 point and a penetration of 2.70 points.

The End of the 1956 to 1957 Bear Market.   An orthodox Dow theorist would have experienced difficulty interpreting the action of the industrial averages in 1957. As will be seen in Figure 23–10, the industrial average established a low at D and a subsequent high at X. Following the pattern of the typical

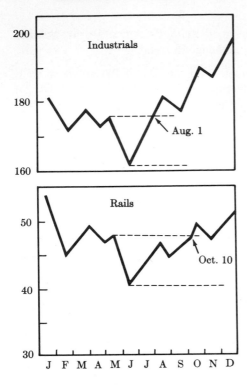

Fig. 23–9   The Dow theory signals the
end of the bear market in 1949.

bear market, the next decline was to *F*. From *F* the market rallied to *E*,
thereby penetrating the previous *X* high. Furthermore, the next decline
stopped at *Y*, thereby failing to penetrate the previous low. This was a clear
signal that the bear market which had just begun was at an end. However,
an orthodox theorist would have rejected the signal because it was not
confirmed by the rail averages. The end of the bear market was signaled
when the averages penetrated the *H* level in April 1958 and was confirmed by
the rail averages.

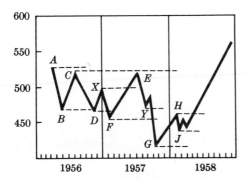

Fig. 23–10   The Dow theory signals the
1957 bottom.

The End of the 1957 to 1961 Bull Market. The industrial average rose to 734.91 on December 13, 1961; declined to 689.92 on January 29, 1962; and then on the next rally, which terminated on March 15, failed to reach its previous high by 10.37 points. On the subsequent decline the industrial average penetrated its January floor on April 11. Meanwhile the rail average reached its peak of 152.92 on October 11, 1961; declined to 140.66 on December 20; rallied to 149.83 on February 2, 1962; and penetrated its floor on April 26.

The End of the 1962 Bear Market. The 1962 bear market was unique for its shortness. The industrial average touched bottom on June 26. The rail average did not reach its lowest point until October 1, 1962. The industrial average was signaling the end of the bear market on July 18 (point *J* on Figure 23–11) but the rails did not confirm the forecast until November 12.

Criticism of the Dow Theory

Two criticisms of the Dow theory are possible. The first is that it does not warn an investor that the tide has turned until several weeks or months after this has occurred. Thus, at best, the theory is a tardy forecaster. The answer to this criticism is that it gives a trader a warning, even though tardy, to get away before complete disaster strikes. As the "Dow Theorist" writing in *Barron's* once stated:

> A man does not have to be smart to get off a railroad track when he sees an express train coming, and the Dow theory focuses his atten-

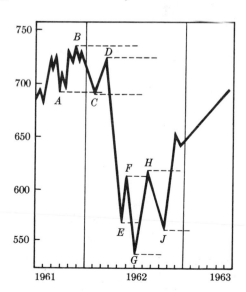

Fig. 23–11 The Dow theory signals the 1961 top and the 1962 bottom.

tion on the fact that an express train *is* coming notwithstanding time-tables, guidebooks, and the testimony of the local half-wit that the line has been abandoned.

The second criticism is that the signals given by the theory are not easily recognizable at the time they occur even though in retrospect they seem to have been quite clear. One who chooses to be guided by the theory must decide whether to apply its tenets literally or liberally. If the movements of the two averages are interpreted strictly, there will be many occasions when the investor will be misled by trivia. If the movements of the two averages are to be interpreted broadly, one must continually be deciding whether a recent signal is or is not significant.

In the final analysis, all that the Dow theory really does is to furnish an investor with a means of distinguishing between a technical readjustment of stock prices and a reversal of the trend of market values. Since the method is to observe the early stages of the actual reversal, the Dow theory of necessity reveals the truth *after* rather than *before* the event.

24 informational and advisory services

Investment services are of two types—those which provide an extensive array of factual information and those which offer advice on the purchase and sale of specific securities. The non-advisory informational services are independent, research-oriented firms that collect and distribute financial data to their subscribers. However, since most banks, public libraries, and brokerage houses subscribe to one or more such services, the information the services publish is available to almost anyone who wishes to use it. The type of information published by the services is indispensable to an investor who wishes to do his own analytical work and make his own investment decisions.

Investors who seek advice along with factual information can obtain it free from brokerage houses or on a subscription basis from independent advisory firms. Agencies that sell investment advice to the public must register with the Securities and Exchange Commission under the provisions of the Investment Advisors Act of 1940. Advertisements for many such advisory services appear regularly in the pages of the *New York Times, Wall Street Journal, Barron's,* and other financial journals.

If one can obtain free investment advice from a brokerage firm, why should one pay for the investment advice of an independent advisory service? This question was rather fully investigated in the Securities Exchange Commission's *Special Study.*[1] In general, information disseminated by brokerage firms is oriented toward sales promotion. Almost always the recommendations of brokerage firms are to buy, and thus they serve to assist securities salesmen in their selling efforts. One has only to ask a broker for his latest sell recommendations to demonstrate the truth of this statement. New buy recommendations supersede previous buy recommendations, but sell recommendations as such are hardly ever forthcoming because they do not lead to increased involvement in the stock market. The research departments responsible for brokerage house recommendations run the gamut from highly

---

[1] *Report of Special Study of Securities Markets of the Securities and Exchange Commission,* 88th Cong., 1st Sess., House Document 95, 1965, chap. III, part C, Research and Investment Advice, pp. 330–387. (Hereafter referred to as *Special Study.*)

qualified staffs, with professional chartered financial analysts doing the research and writing, to completely unqualified departments staffed by clever journalists. The sole purpose of the latter is to turn out a continuing stream of sales material as ammunition for the firm's commission-generating salesmen.

The same degree of conflict of interest is not found in the subscription investment advisory services, because these agencies do not depend upon trading activity to cover their costs. Nevertheless it seems to be a fact that investors prefer services which produce an abundance of buy recommendations accompanied by "how to get rich quick" hints to those which present a carefully thought-out and well-balanced investment program.

Nevertheless there are a number of competent, well-staffed investment advisory organizations whose research is intended to stimulate reason rather than emotion. Four of these are described in this chapter to acquaint the reader with the type of material disseminated by these agencies and to illustrate the various philosophies about and approaches to the task of evaluating the state of the economy and of forecasting the effect it will have on the fortunes of individual corporations.[2]

Methods of the Babson Organization

Roger Ward Babson was one of the first to systematize the analysis of major movements in business. His pioneer work in this field is recognized as of very great value to businessmen, who have learned from him the need for carefully collected and interpreted information. The theories and philosophies he formulated are the basis of the advice given out today by Business Statistics, Inc., and by Babson's Reports, Inc. The essentials of the Babson system are summarized here.

Comparative and Fundamental Statistics.   Babson divides data on business matters into two classes—comparative and fundamental. Comparative statistics are those figures which relate to the internal situation of a particular company. They are useful for the purpose of getting a picture of the financial structure of a company, and they help in comparing one company with another. On the other hand, fundamental statistics refer to the conditions outside any particular plant or business. They describe the environment within which an individual firm must operate.

Comparative statistics include such items as investment in plant and equipment, sales revenue, operating expenses, interest charges, and the like. Fundamental statistics include such items as the price level, wage rates, interest rates, political conditions, and foreign affairs. When the fundamental forces are right, business generally is improving; when they are poor, business generally is declining.

The Babson organization has classified many fundamental factors into

[2] The addresses of all the organizations mentioned are listed at the end of this chapter.

three main groups. The particular items in each group given in the accompanying listing are intended only as examples and not as a complete tabulation. In addition to the three groups listed, there are psychological factors such as the confidence of investors, businessmen, and consumers which must be considered. These psychological factors affect each of the items listed in the three main groups, yet do not belong exclusively to any one.

Business conditions	Monetary conditions	Investment conditions
Steel production	Commodity prices:	Corporate policies
Auto and truck output	Wholesale	Manufacturing and distribution
Food processing	Retail	bution
New building and construction:	Foreign trade	Earnings estimates
struction:	Foreign exchange rates	Stock market conditions
Contract awards	Domestic money rates:	Bond and stock prices
Construction put in place	Bank rates	Research and development
Sales and inventories:	Federal Reserve policy	policies
Manufacturers	Treasury policy	Competition
Wholesalers	Fiscal and tax policies	Government regulation
Retailers	Wage policies	
Consumer spending		
Failures		
Unemployment		

The Babsonchart.   An important statistical tool used by the Babson organization as an aid to its analysis of business and investment is the Babsonchart, a copy of which is shown in Figure 24–1. (The original chart appears in two colors.) The outstanding features of the chart are the comparatively regular X–Y line, the shaded areas above and below this line, and the irregular line that bounds the shaded areas. This irregular line is the curve that results from plotting Babson's index of physical volume of business.

Babson's index comprises 56 items of productive activity that can be classified under seven headings: (1) Manufacturing: butter, ice cream, cattle and hog slaughter, wheat flour, sugar meltings, malt liquors, cigarettes and cigars, textiles, shoes, rubber, cars and trucks, coke, gasoline, fuel oil, lubricants, pig iron and steel, aluminum, glass containers, cement, paper and paperboard, newsprint, newspaper and magazine advertising. (2) Minerals: bituminous and anthracite coal, crude petroleum, natural gas, iron ore, copper, zinc, lead. (3) Agricultural marketings: receipts of cattle, hogs, sheep, poultry, eggs, corn, oats, wheat, barley; carlot shipments of apples, oranges, potatoes. (4) Building and construction. (5) Electric power. (6) Railway freight. (7) Foreign trade.[3]

[3] Agricultural marketings and foreign trade are given weights equal to their importance in business channels on a value-added basis rather than on the basis of the total value of products handled.

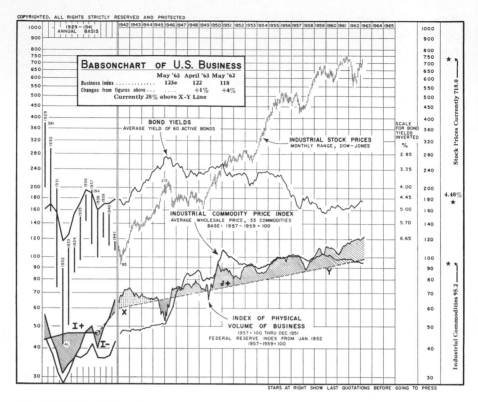

Fig. 24–1   The Babsonchart.

Before these component indexes are combined to form the composite index, the seasonal movements of each of the series are removed and each series is weighted on the basis of its economic importance.

The Law of Equal Areas.   When the business volume curve has been plotted, it shows a more or less regular wavelike motion. The problem is to interpret these up-and-down swings with reference to the future. Roger Ward Babson noted that the science of physics has Newton's law that action and reaction are equal. He noted similar laws existing in chemistry. He noted that philosophers talk of a law of rhythm or a law of compensation in operation throughout the universe. Why should this law not hold in the field of business? In Babson's opinion, it does. The law of action and reaction is fundamental; it is so accepted without statistical proof. It supplies the key to an estimate as to what constitutes average, or "normal," business.

This law also gives the key to the interpretation of the swings of business. The best method of representing the law on a chart is to draw a line through the business curve so that the areas above and below are equal. That is, the law of action and reaction is best represented by equal areas above and below a normal line, the boundaries of the areas being the business curve. The method of drawing the normal line is the next problem.

The X–Y Line.   The X–Y line on a Babsonchart represents the trend of business and industry as measured by the Babson index of physical volume of business. In technical terminology the line is the secular trend. Economists and statisticians would disagree about how the position and the slope of such a line should be determined. Most statisticians would probably fit a line of least squares to the index figures for a very long period of time. The line they would obtain would be a straight line running through decades.

The approach of the Babson organization is different. Although its X–Y line represents the basic rate of growth of the economy, it is not a straight line, for the rate of growth varies in each cycle. For this reason the X–Y line is calculated separately for each cycle so that on a chart for a very long period of time it appears as a series of straight lines joined at their ends. That portion of the X–Y line indicating the rate of growth characteristic of past cycles is shown as a solid line. Since the most recent cycle is almost always incomplete, the growth line for this period is shown in dashes to indicate that its position and its slope are tentative.

Expansion in population, advances in technology, and increases in industrial output all indicate a continuous growth. Even a setback in activity such as occurred in 1957–1958 did not cause the Babson index to decline below the secular trend as measured by the X–Y line on the Babsonchart, although it did come close to the line. Subsequently the index continued its upward trend so that the actual current rate of growth is far higher than suggested by the X–Y line. However, this does not invalidate the principle of the law of action and reaction, for sooner or later this current growth period is expected to be followed by a period of readjustment and consolidation during which the economy will mark time and rest in order to evaluate gains made previously. At this time the index will decline below the X–Y line. Just when this will happen and to what degree cannot be known in advance. In other words, several questions remain to be answered. When will actual production fall below the estimated average rate of growth as indicated by the X–Y line? How long will the index remain below the X–Y line? How far below the line will the index go? Only *after* a cycle has been completed can the X–Y line be definitely drawn through the midpoints of the cycle to become a final line.

The reader cannot help noting that the Babson index in Figure 24–1 has been above the X–Y line for a very long time. This fact suggests that perhaps the line should be raised. To raise the line merely to obtain equal areas above and below it would cause many periods which are acknowledged to be periods of rapid growth and prosperity to appear as periods of depression. For example, the World War II period would appear as a depression, whereas it was really a period of rapid advance and induced prosperity. If the line were to be elevated, portions of the postwar boom period would sink below it and become classified as depressions. Inasmuch as these years were really prosperous, changing the position of the line would be misleading. On the basis of observation the current position of the X–Y line is considered to be an accurate estimate of the *level* of the country's basic growth although there are no areas below the line.

The slope of the X–Y line indicates the rate at which business activity is increasing. From 1933 to 1938 the X–Y line was flat, denoting the lack of economic growth during the Great Depression. From 1939 to the end of 1941 the X–Y line climbed steeply, reflecting the rapid rate of growth resulting from the renewed economic activity stimulated by the international situation. Since 1941 the rate of rise has been much more gradual. Actually the X–Y line shown in dashes which appears straight is a curved line. This curvature results from the fact that the slope has not been constant throughout the period but has changed slightly from time to time. The changes that occurred before 1941 are easily visible, but the changes that have occurred since then are only mathematically perceptible. Currently the rate of rise is approximately 2 per cent per year, a rate of growth that corresponds with the generally assumed growth rate of the economy.

Interpretation of the Babsonchart.   As we have seen, the tentative X–Y line is drawn, not so as to make areas above and below the line equal, but so as to conform with what is known to be occurring. Since in the long run areas above and below the line must be equal, it follows that, if an area develops *above* the line, an area of equal size must sooner or later develop *below* the line. By noting the characteristics of the area above the line it is possible to draw certain conclusions about the characteristics of the anticipated area below the line. For example, each area is the product of intensity multiplied by duration. Thus, if in the beginning stages of a depression that follows a period of prosperity the index falls far below the X–Y line, a severe depression of short duration is indicated. But if the index declines only a short distance below the X–Y line, a less intense depression of longer duration is forecast.

It should be emphasized that the Babsonchart is a statistical tool of value for presenting a pictorial concept of business conditions but is not intended to forecast with great accuracy the size and timing of future periods of prosperity and depression without reference to other influential factors such as credit and monetary conditions.

The Babsonchart enables one to compare the current area as it develops with other areas already completed. It is not intended to enable one to forecast the size of areas above the line (such as J+ in Figure 24–1). When the J+ area is completed, however, the J– depression area is expected to follow and to endure until its area is equal to that of the J+. As this J– area approaches the area of J+, we may surmise that the K+ area is about to begin; but the actual beginning of the K+ area, its duration, and its intensity must be determined by means other than the Babsonchart. Nevertheless, it is well to appreciate the circumstances whereby the most reliable period of estimate of the Babsonchart coincides with the forecast most needed by businessmen, i.e., how long activity is to remain depressed and when recovery is to occur.

During the long J+ span of time, there have been periods in which the degree of prosperity has waned; at such times the "plus," or prosperity, areas have receded, occasionally to such an extent as to become "minus," or depression, areas. These setbacks have been short and mild, however, and cannot be said to have brought the economy below the expected rate of growth as indicated by the X–Y line. Many reasons have been advanced to explain this unusual phenomenon. The most likely is that the current practice of controlling fluctuations by economic and political policies have cushioned and shortened slowdowns in the economy. As a result traditional economic relationships may have become distorted. An important question is whether this distortion is temporary or permanent.

Because the J+ area has been of such long duration, the Babson organization is confronted with a serious dilemma similar to one that it faced in the late 1920s. In spite of the absence of minus areas it is maintaining the position and slope of its tentative X–Y line. It sees little point in altering its position to give an impression of completed cycles even though *some* of the characteristics of low business activity have appeared at various times (high unemployment, numerous business failures, and the like). The result has been a plus area of great magnitude. Is this plus area to be followed by a minus area of equally great magnitude, as in the early 1930s? If so, will the minus area be severe and of short duration or mild and of long duration?

The Babson organization is inclined to believe that the J– area, when it comes, will be a moderate but prolonged depression and that it will appear on the Babsonchart as a long, shallow, negative area during which hardship and suffering will be a relative matter and scarcely noticeable.

Other Indicators Shown on Babsonchart. As will be noted from Figure 24–1, the Babsonchart contains much factual information other than the X–Y line and the shaded areas. Specifically it contains four monthly indexes: an index of commodity prices, an index of bond yields, an index of stock prices, and, of course, an index of the physical volume of business activity.

The first of these, commodity prices, reflects average inventory costs. The second is the average yield of 60 high-grade and medium-grade bonds plotted on an inverted scale to make it appear similar to an index of bond prices. Stock prices are shown by a series of vertical lines, each line representing the monthly high and low of the Dow-Jones average of industrial stock prices. The Babson index of the physical volume of business has been described. Since fluctuations in this index in recent years have paralleled those of other production indexes, the Federal Reserve index of industrial production has been used on the Babsoncharts since January 1952.

The Babsonchart is printed on semilog graph paper so as to make comparable changes in the several curves and changes in the same curve in different time periods. Thus the Babsonchart gives a clear composite "weather" picture of the United States economy. The organization also publishes a similar chart for Canada through its subsidiary, Babson's Canadian Reports, Ltd. A Babsonchart extending back to 1871 is also available. This chart contains the index of physical volume of business for the entire ninety-four-year period and is believed to be the only monthly index of this type that goes so far back.

Babson's Reports (and Business Statistics Organization) do not aim to forecast any but the major cycles. In their opinion it is a mistake for either businessmen or investors to attempt to operate on the short swings, which cannot be forecast with any degree of assurance. The Babson organization is always experimenting with economic theories that can be proved statistically, with a view to constant improvement. As these newer methods are found to give better results, the public is given the benefit of an improved service. The use of the theory of action and reaction, so helpful in diagnosing the progress of business conditions, does not exclude the use of other guides of a dynamic nature. The "continuous working plan" and constant supervision of a long list of securities give the investment service its additional framework.

The Investment Advice of Moody's Investors Service

Moody's gives as much weight in analysis to evaluation of risks and of selective investment values as to prediction of business and market fluctuations.

Moody's separates itself sharply from those who follow any one simple system in analyzing and forecasting general economic conditions and stock market trends. It feels that such an approach is far from the needs and requirements of the average investor, who is controlled by many points of view instead of by the single one of connecting his stock buying and selling with the presumed stage of the business cycle. The typical investor, Moody's believes, is interested in steady, growing income and in the individual companies and particular industries which will provide that result, with growing capital values as well. Consequently, the approach used by Moody's in its analytical work is one which takes account of long-term secular trends of industries and segments of industry as well as the cyclical movements of business as a whole and which finds many of its answers by analyzing income and dividend prospects.

General Economic Conditions.   In analyzing and trying to project the trend of general business activity, Moody's does not rely on fixed forecasting devices. It claims that too many forces in society and in nature or those having to do with human psychology or political conditions defy measurement and cannot be fitted into formulas. Moody's employs, however, a great many time series, both factual and interpretative, which assist in a quantitative understanding of the economic situation in its many details. This is in addition to close contacts with Federal agencies and with business managements. A cross-sectional analysis of information so acquired and interpreted serves as a basis for any forecasts or projections, which are seldom made for more than a few months ahead. Occasionally the service puts out tentative extensions of the longer trends. The shift in emphasis toward longer trends—both for the economy in general and for individual industries—has been the result of the changing nature of the business cycle and of the requirements of the institutional type of investment.

The method of historical analogy is used by Moody's infrequently and with reservations. Typically its reports contain a pragmatic interpretation of the main current economic and political forces and an estimate of their effect on industrial production and on corporate earnings and dividends.

Among the topics most often mentioned are businessmen's intentions regarding plant and equipment expenditures, residential construction, changes in inventories, and government expenditures—in short, factors affecting new investment, both private and public. These are usually judged in the light of supply-demand studies and fiscal, monetary, and credit conditions, including government policies regarding mortgage and other credit. In the field of consumers' goods, Moody's uses its own specially constructed indexes of consumers' goods production and keeps current comparisons of its estimated retail value with the Department of Commerce series of consumers' expenditures for goods. This throws light on inventory formation. Productivity and technology are other subjects frequently mentioned in connection with estimates of wage rates, unit labor costs, and profits. Productivity also enters in as one of the elements of a calculated normal trend for industrial production for civilians. The effects of monetary and other factors on commodity prices are given considerable attention, and the behavior of "sensitive" commodity prices is watched through Moody's own indexes. Prospects for costs and for margins of profit are studied and appraised, not only in connection with the stock market, but also as over-all indications of incentives to businessmen in connection with plant expansion. Inflation and expectations of "potential" inflation enter into every calculation having to do with businessmen's and investors' decisions.

The Stock Market.   The most important (but not the only) force behind the stock market is believed to be the trend of earnings and dividends, and therefore Moody's relies on the above methods of analyzing and projecting earnings trends for anticipating any major movements of stock prices. These anticipations are modified by conclusions regarding (1) broad risks in the level of production and earnings, (2) corporate taxation, (3) financial and other conditions affecting dividend payout, and (4) the movement of stock yields. The latter are studied extensively as to their cyclical behavior, longer deviations from past averages, and relationships with bond yields. Such factors as political environment and sentiment, rates of individual taxation, competition of tax-exempt bonds, changes in nature and sources of demand, new supply, general credit conditions, and margin control are all given weight. Parallel comparative studies are made of stock prices, in relation both to their calculated trends and to the changing components of earnings and dividends. Measures of purchasing power of stock prices and dividends, in terms of wholesale commodity prices and the cost of living, also play a part in the appraisal of market position. Moody's service gives no emphasis to so-called technical analyses, although it admits that such analyses may help reveal some invisible causes of human behavior that otherwise escape measurement. A logical interpretation of the forces behind the market is preferred and is ordinarily used.

For purposes of analysis and interpretation of market movements, Moody's employs for the most part its own measurements, viz., homogeneous series of prices, earnings, and dividends per share, as well as yields of 200 common stocks, including 125 industrials. These are available back to 1929 by months and are extended still further back by means of other series. Through the use of comparable series of sales and main elements of corporate costs, the attempt is made to tie in the above earnings and dividend series, quantitatively, with broader economic measures behind them such as production, prices, wages, productivity, and the like. This procedure is of assistance in extrapolating earnings and dividends as used in market studies. But studies of averages are merely a background for analysis and projection of individual groups and issues. These individual projections in turn provide a check on projections of averages.

The Bond Market.   Having developed its own averages of bond yields by different rating groups, Moody's has contributed to a more analytical approach to bond market movements. Before World War II Moody's relied on the more orthodox group of forecasting devices, those generally relating to factors of demand and supply of investment funds, including the influences of the business cycle. During and since World War II the immeasurably increased influence of the Federal government in controlling and influencing interest rates has given primary importance to continuous analysis of forces shaping government monetary policy and operations.

Standard & Poor's Investment Advice

In formulating conclusions about the major trends of business and security prices, Standard & Poor's Corporation places considerable reliance on the "industry approach method," a procedure long promoted by this organization through its published industry surveys and stock price indexes.

In analyzing the current position and outlook for every important industry, all the salient factors affecting the specific line of business are studied, and their effects on the operations and earnings are appraised. As the whole economy is a sum of its parts, the conclusions reached about what is happening in each important part of the economy—and, more important, what is likely to occur in the months and years ahead—are then weighed in order to appraise the future trends of business and equity values as a whole. Standard & Poor's industry approach method, therefore, consists in inductive reasoning from the specific to the general.

After the general policy is formed, the survey conclusions regarding the individual industries are restudied, and definite forecasts and advices are formulated. Standard & Poor's takes the position that there are usually a number of stock markets operating within the orbit of the broad general list. Economic pressures and other influences bear unequally on the various groups at any given period, resulting in dissimilar and often divergent market action. Some groups rise or decline faster than the general list, and some frequently run counter to the general trend.

Individual industry groups are graded as to their relative market appeal, with such important factors taken into account as the earnings and dividend outlook and position of each group, pricewise, in relation to the general market. Four broad classifications are used—most favorably situated, defensive, average, and least attractive. Selected securities in the favored groups are recommended for purchase and retention, and switches out of less promising groups are advised.

It is obvious that the use of this industry approach method requires a considerable organization, because all the details affecting each important industry must be watched constantly to keep the method functioning. In the matter of staff, there are four groups: (1) The statistical staff, whose duties are to collect and compute all pertinent data affecting industries and keep this information up to date. (They collect data on production, consumption, inventories, prices, employment, wage rates, and such for the economy as a whole and for each important line of business.) (2) The industry analytical staff, consisting of specialists who forecast trends in individual industries. These men, through their training and experience, are experts in the industries assigned to them. In their analyses they weigh the economic, political, social, and international developments that are constantly affecting the operations and earnings of each industry. They prepare surveys of their industries and keep them always up to date. (3) A field staff, located in all the important business and financial centers of the country, to report the plans and current activities of corporations and to obtain the prevailing opinions and sentiment of the executives of the leading industries. A large part of the information obtained by these trained field analysts is confidential in nature and is extremely helpful in formulating opinions about the prospects of the companies studied and of the relative appeal of their securities. (4) The investment policy committee, which draws the general conclusions about basic policy after studying the conclusions of the industry specialists and the field staff. Thus, if there is a strong preponderance of evidence that the majority of important industries can expect higher levels of activity and earnings, the basic policy determined by the investment policy committee will be constructive.

While Standard & Poor's places chief emphasis on the industry approach method, its reliance on this approach is by no means total. Trends in the economy as a whole, as foreshadowed by the movement of cyclical leading indicators, by monetary and credit developments, and by government policy generally, are under constant survey. The technical position of the stock market is constantly appraised, and so are other factors that might influence the market psychology of the investing public. Market indexes are watched closely. In this connection, Standard & Poor's has one of the most comprehensive series of stock price indexes, broken down to show the market performances of more than ninety leading groups.

The Value Line Investment Survey

The Value Line Investment Survey was formed in the early 1930s by Arnold Bernhard, an investment counselor, who came to realize the need for systematic evaluation methods that would make it possible for investors to compare stocks objectively in order to determine which were overpriced and which were underpriced.[4]

Thus Value Line is dedicated to the goal of introducing a rational discipline into the field of stock evaluation. By so doing it hopes that the madness of the high prices of 1929 or of the low prices of 1947 to 1950, both of which were sanctioned by nearly all economic authorities at the time, can be avoided in the future. Value Line believes that the acceptance of illogically high or low prices at various times in history takes place because most observers of the scene rationalize whatever level exists. The tendency to rationalize the current level of stock prices occurs because investors lack objective standards with which to compare current prices of

---

[4] A complete description of the methods and philosophies of the Value Line Investment Survey is given in Arnold Bernhard, *The Evaluation of Common Stocks,* New York: Simon and Schuster, Inc., 1959. However, Value Line has made many improvements in its methods since 1959.

stocks. Value Line attempts to create such standards by quantifying both historical performance and future expectations. Its organization rates more than 1,100 individual stock issues and ranks them with regard to each other on the basis of four attributes. These attributes are:

Quality
Probable market performance
Appreciation potential
Estimated dividend yield

Having done this, it provides a method whereby each person may choose stocks for purchase on the basis of his own preference ranking of the four attributes.

The Concept of Quality.   Quality refers to the general safety of a stock and is judged by the growth of cash earnings and by the price stability of the stock over the past ten years. This makes it necessary for Value Line to have a growth index and a stability index for each of the 1,100 stocks surveyed. The growth index is based upon year-to-year percentage changes in per share cash earnings for each of the last ten years, as well as for successive three-year and five-year periods. Code numbers are assigned for varying growth rates of cash earnings, and a composite growth number is derived for each stock. The stability index is based on the spread of the annual high and low prices of a stock during the most recent ten-year period. The annual spread is divided by the yearly average price, and the resulting ratio is adjusted to remove the effect of the secular price movement over a ten-year period.

After growth and stability indexes are computed, the quality grade of each issue is determined by comparing its rating with that of a control group of issues. This control group is made up of 10 high-quality stocks, 25 medium-quality stocks, and 10 low-quality stocks—the stocks in each classification being those which would be generally accepted as belonging there. The final result is a stratification of the 1,100 stock issues into nine quality groups labeled A+, A, A−, B+, B, B−, C+, C, and C−. Index weights are then assigned to each group as follows:

Group	Characterization	Index
A+ and A	Highest quality	10
A− and B+	Above average	8
B	Average quality	6
B− and C+	Below average	4
C and C−	Lowest quality	2

The Concept of Market Performance. Market performance refers to the probable price behavior of each stock relative to all other stocks during the next twelve months. Performance is measured by the ratio of average price during the past fifty-two weeks to Value Line's "normal average value." Normal average value is the organization's projection of value one year hence on the basis of its estimates of earnings and dividends for the next twelve months. The estimate is derived from a mathematical formula based on a twenty-three-year correlation analysis of earnings, dividends, and prices of five groups of stocks of descending order of quality and applied to the past ten-year history of each stock in a particular quality group.

Thus a high-grade stock has a different normal multiplier for its earnings from a speculative stock. The formula indicates the normal average value of the stock during the next twelve months if market psychology as a whole is normal and if earnings and dividends are accurately estimated.

The 1,100 stocks surveyed are then ranked into five groups and assigned these market performance indexes:

Group	Composition	Characterization	Index
I	Top 20%	Highest	10
II	Next 20%	Above average	8
III	Next 20%	Average	6
IV	Next 20%	Below average	4
V	Lowest 20%	Lowest	2

The Concept of Appreciation Potential.   Appreciation is not a forecast of price but is a measure of potentiality for the next three to five years. Because of the hazards of estimating economic activity three to five years in the future, the potential is based upon a plausible hypothesis of what conditions might be at that time. This hypothesis is based on projections of gross national product, the Federal Reserve Board's index of industrial production, disposable income, and on certain assumptions regarding war and peace, taxes, and commodity prices. The hypothesized economic environment is then used as a basis from which to estimate corporate sales, earnings, and dividends for individual companies. If the hypothesized economic conditions fail to materialize, the appreciation potential might not be reached but the potential is there nevertheless.

This is a method for projecting the future price expectancies of all stocks so that the relative values are logically appraised within the framework of a single economic environment. An analyst working on a rail stock, for example, should not be free to forecast in terms of a $700 billion gross national product, while a utility analyst in another part of the service bases his estimates upon a hypothesized $750 billion economy. It does not follow that if the economic environment is incorrectly hypothesized the relative values will, nevertheless, be correctly appraised in the projection. A lower than expected economic environment could affect a railroad stock more adversely than a utility. But the method does assure at least a measure of consistency.

In 1964 Value Line modified its ranking for three- to five-year appreciation potentiality by introducing a risk factor for each stock. A stock's risk is defined as being a function of its price stability, its relative price performance during the past five years, and the yield level of the market as a whole. The effect of this adjustment to appreciation potentiality is to favor safe (stable) stocks when the market yield is low and stocks in general are overpriced. Conversely, the adjustment favors lower-quality stocks when dividend yields are high and stocks are undervalued.

In determining the potential value of each stock three to five years hence, the multipliers that have normally been applied to earnings and dividends over a long period of time are applied to forecasted earnings and dividends. The potential value for each stock is then divided by its current price to give a ratio of appreciation potential. Each stock's ratio of appreciation potential is next combined with its own risk factor to produce a number which allows the 1,100 issues to be ranked thus:

Group	Composition	Characterization	Index
I	Top 20%	Highest potential	10
II	Next 20%	Above average	8
III	Next 20%	Average potential	6
IV	Next 20%	Below average	4
V	Lowest 20%	Lowest potential	2

In determining what multiplier has been normal over a long period of time, the annual average price-earnings ratios of the stock are first divided by the average annual price-earnings ratios of a representative average of all stocks. This treatment has the effect of removing from the trend of a particular stock's price-earnings ratio the influence of general market sentiment. If the result shows a persisting secular trend in the price-earnings ratio of the subject stock that is clearly not the product of a short-term cyclical thrust, the thirteen-year median of the stock's price-earnings ratio—the basic standard of normalcy—is adjusted for this trend *to a degree*. Furthermore, a cross-sectional control is introduced; that is, the multiplier is brought as closely into line with the multipliers applied to other stocks in the same industrial group and of roughly the same quality as historical experience adjusted for trend permits.

In an effort to find a consistent earnings series over a long period of years, Value Line falls back upon *cash* earnings rather than *reported* earnings as the criterion of the normal price-earnings relationship. By "cash earnings" is meant reported earnings plus depreciation and depletion. Because depreciation regulations have been greatly modified in recent years, the reported earnings series of recent years is no longer consistent with the reported earnings of earlier years. Two dollars of earnings after $3 of depreciation, for example, is clearly a different factor from $2 of earnings after only $1 of depreciation. It is Value Line's belief that over a long period of years the level of dividends will conform more closely to the level of cash earnings than of reported earnings, although it is probably also true that in any single year a change in the direction of the dividend payment will be more closely related to the direction of change in the reported earnings.

Estimated Dividend Yield.   The last of the four general concepts upon which Value Line bases its systematic appraisal system is the estimated dividend yield of each issue during the next twelve months. Probable percentage yield is computed by dividing the expected dividend payment by the current price. Individual issues are then assigned indexes on the basis of the following classification scheme:

Group	Expected yield, %	Characterization	Index
I	5.1 and up	Highest	10
II	4.2 –5.0	Above average	8
III	3.1 –4.1	Average	6
IV	2.2 –3.0	Below average	4
V	0.02–2.12	Lowest	2

Combining the Four Attributes.   As explained, within each attribute Value Line places each stock into one of five categories and assigns each category a weight of 10, 8, 6, 4, or 2. For example, the Value Line *Investment Survey* in September 24, 1964, classified Corn Products as follows:

Attribute	Rating	Index
Quality	A	10
Market performance	II	8
Appreciation potential	IV	4
Yield	3.0%	4

Each subscriber is expected to arrange the four attributes in the order of their importance to his portfolio and his philosophy of investment. Thus a conservative investor might arrange the attributes in this order: quality, yield, appreciation potential, and market performance. A more speculative investor might arrange them in the order of market performance, appreciation potential, yield, and quality. Whatever the order, the most important attribute is always to be given a weight of 4, the second most important a weight of 3, the third a weight of 2, and the least important a weight of 1. Then by means of the indexes assigned to each issue by Value Line and the weights given to each attribute by the investor, it is possible to arrive at an index of suitability for each issue to be included in an investor's portfolio. Two examples will make this computation process clear.

The conservative investor mentioned would compute the suitability index of Corn Products as follows:

Attributes (in order of preference)	Attribute weight		Value Line index		Suitability score
Quality	4	×	10	=	40
Yield	3	×	4	=	12
Potentiality	2	×	4	=	8
Performance	1	×	8	=	8
Total					68

The speculative investor mentioned would derive a suitability index of 62 computed as follows:

Attributes	Attribute weight		Value Line index		Suitability score
Performance	4	×	8	=	32
Potentiality	3	×	4	=	12
Yield	2	×	4	=	8
Quality	1	×	10	=	10
Total					62

For the conservative investor Corn Products would be preferable to any stock whose suitability score is lower than 68 and less desirable than any stock whose suitability score is higher than 68. The speculative investor would judge the relative suitability of Corn Products in the same manner except that the issue's suitability score to him is only 62.

Value Line recommends that a portfolio hold at least 10 stocks with a suitability score of 75 or higher.

Nonadvisory Information Services

Frequently investors want financial or descriptive material about a company or industry in order to make their own analysis or to use in a supplemental check on a recommendation already received. The following services are among those most widely used for this purpose. In most cases they provide factual material alone, but on occasion they make limited recommendations.

Moody's Manuals.   Five large annual volumes, each supplemented with a loose-leaf binder containing up-to-the-minute data, are published annually. They deal respectively with industrials, transportation companies, utilities, financial firms, and governmental securities. Descriptions cover the type of business, properties owned, corporate history, charter provisions, bond industries, officers and directors, brand names, financial statements, financial ratios, dividend record, stock price history, and so on.

Standard & Poor's Corporation Records.   Six semi-loose-leaf binders are periodically updated, a portion at a time, throughout the year. An additional binder carries daily news. Material covered is similar to that in Moody's Manuals, except that little space is given to state or municipal bonds. Coverage is good on smaller companies.

Walker's Manual of Pacific Coast Securities.   A bound volume is issued annually and is accompanied by a monthly supplement. The manual provides detailed information, similar to that covered in Moody's Manuals, on companies with headquarters in the Far West.

Standard & Poor's Trade and Securities Service.   Three loose-leaf binders are issued. Volumes I and II (Standard & Poor's *Industry Surveys*) contain annual descriptions of 66 industries (such as steel, petroleum, tobacco), plus a quarterly updating of the annual review. Each industry's income, expense, profit, and dividend outlook are reviewed, and comments about the industry and its leading companies are included. Volume III (*Statistics*) contains a 14-section statistical review of many aspects of economic activity and of securities prices, updated monthly. The Security Price Index Record within this volume provides complete historical records of all Standard & Poor's stock and bond indexes, as well as of the Dow-Jones averages.

Standard & Poor's Stock Reports.   This loose-leaf service, which is constantly revised, covers several hundred leading stocks. One page is devoted to each company. A brief description of the company and its stock, the history of the stock's prices, earnings, and dividends, and a brief summary of financial statement data are given. Editorial advice and opinions are also presented, and lists of stocks recommended for income or for market gain are included. Four volumes cover listed stocks, and four volumes cover unlisted stocks.

Standard & Poor's Bond Reports.   This service is basically similar to the *Stock Reports*. Several hundred actively traded corporate bonds are reviewed, one to a page. All reports give Standard & Poor's appraisal of the quality of the bond through its bond rating and written opinion. Two volumes cover regular corporate bonds, and one volume covers convertible bonds.

Moody's Handbook of Widely Held Common Stocks.   A paperback volume is issued quarterly, containing charts of monthly price ranges, volume for the past fifteen years, and summary financial data for the past eleven years. The service, which covers approximately nine hundred stocks, contains concise analytical comments on the characteristics of each company.

Financial World **Stock Factograph Manual.**   A paperback volume is issued annually, containing a brief summary of statistics of stocks listed on the New York and American Stock Exchanges, plus a short description of each company's activities and a brief discussion of the outlook for each stock.

Methods of Rating Securities

Attempts at rating securities by investors are as old as the investment business itself, but carefully conceived systems of rating are a phenomenon of the twentieth century. In 1909 John Moody began a rating system that would make it possible for an inexperienced investor to know the relative rank of securities. At first Moody undertook to rate railroad bonds only; later he added corporate bonds as well as municipal bonds and common stocks. In 1935 Moody's dropped its common stock ratings owing to the growing tendency to confuse the ratings of bonds with the ratings of stocks.

Many agencies now rate stocks and bonds. Among these the most important are Value Line, *Financial World,* and Standard & Poor's Corporation.

No service claims to be able to rate securities in an absolute sense. All ratings are more or less relative. The facts are that some securities are better than others and that those which stand at the head of the list are considered to be of the highest quality, while others are placed as nearly as possible in their proper relative position. Stocks or bonds within any given rating are not of absolutely equal quality, for only a limited number of rating steps are used, while there are possibly thousands of fine shadings of quality between various securities.

Furthermore, securities may be rated from different points of view. In one case security of principal and income may be selected as the basis of rating. In another case a major criterion may be marketability, or rate of yield, or future profit expectations, or exemption from taxation, or some other quality.

The current phase of the business cycle is not of primary importance in establishing ratings. Rather, an effort is made to look at the worst possible economic environment which might occur and to judge the status of a security under such conditions. Thus a rating is not a statistical measure of past performance alone but is, rather, the informed judgment of the rating organization about how the security will perform in the future.

The Rating of Bonds.   Bond ratings are supplied by both Moody's Investors Service and Standard & Poor's Corporation. The rating symbols used by both are given in Table 16. These systems of rating bonds use three or four general classes represented by A, B, C, and possibly D. Within each class there are three grades.

Major class A for both services includes only sound investment issues. Assets must have a liquidating value ample to cover the securities; average earnings must exceed interest by a suitable margin so that changes in earnings will have no effect on the price of bonds of this class. With few exceptions, changes in the price of class A bonds are determined by the interest rates and credit conditions.

Class B securities are sometimes designated as "businessmen's investments." These securities yield a higher rate of income than those of class A, but they also contain many elements of uncertainty not found in the higher major class. In the highest group the investment features outweigh ·the speculative elements, but speculative factors are not entirely absent. In the lower class B group speculative factors predominate. The upper groups in

TABLE 16   Symbols Used in Rating Bonds

Moody's Investors Service		Standard & Poor's Corporation	
Rating	**Meaning**	**Rating**	**Meaning**
Aaa	Best quality	AAA	Highest grade
Aa	High quality	AA	High grade
A	Higher medium quality	A	Upper medium quality
Baa	Lower medium quality	BBB	Medium grade
Ba	Possess speculative elements	BB	Lower medium grade
B	Lack characteristics of desira-ble investment	B	Speculative
Caa	Poor standing	CCC⎫ CC⎭	Outright speculations
Ca	Speculative in a high degree		
C	Extremely poor prospects	C	Income bonds on which no interest is being paid
		DDD⎫ DD⎬ D⎭	In default, with rating indicating relative salvage value

this class may be said to be fairly safe investments, but the lowest group is merely a better grade of speculative issues.

Class C securities are definitely speculative. No true investor would be interested in even the highest grade. They often have possibilities for the future, but the risks are great. The lowest grade is uncertain as to present position and as to future prospects. Little of substantial earning power is found in this grade.

The D group used by Standard & Poor's indicates bonds which are in default.

Market price is not considered in determining bond ratings, and thus the rating alone cannot be construed as a recommendation with respect to attractiveness. Because bond prices change with changes in both the level of interest rates and the term structure of interest rates, the desirability of any particular bond for any particular investor must take into account portfolio needs and bond prices relative to their quality ratings as well as the quality rating itself. In general it may be said that the first four grades for each rating service (Aaa through Baa or AAA through BBB) are investment-quality bonds of the type considered acceptable for bank investments.

Moody's Method of Arriving at Bond Ratings. In the half century since John Moody began rating securities, a phenomenal increase has occurred in both volume and quality of statistics and other factual information relating to corporations and to debts of every kind. This has permitted a great improvement in the standards by which bonds are rated and in the methods of rating by Moody's. The strictness of Moody's requirements so far as statistical data is concerned has increased; at the same time its method has been revised so that the weight given to statistical as against nonstatistical material has been decreased. Ratings have become less the result of mere statistical tests, but insofar as they do rest on statistical evidence, that evidence is sounder and more complete than ever before.

In the rating of corporate securities, Moody's customarily starts with the Securities and Exchange Commission statements (Interstate Commerce Commission statements in the case of railroads; other basic data in other cases). From such data certain statistical tests are made, the tests varying widely according to the industry. Obviously depreciation and depletion policies may be vitally important considerations in the case of a given industry; so the statistical tests in such a case would give important weight to these factors. But, equally obvious, depreciation policies may be relatively unimportant in another industry, in which case this test would be given small weight or might not be included at all. The same may be said of other statistical tests, such as those concerning the trend of operating and selling costs, research expenditures, cash income in relation to property expenditures, and so on. In rating utilities, a good deal of weight is likely to be given tests concerning rate structures, depreciation policies, property valuations, and so on. In the case of railroads, much importance is attached to tests of ability or inability of a railroad to retain traffic.

This list of examples provides no more than a good general idea of statistical tests but is sufficient to indicate that Moody's does not believe in or employ an approach to the rating of bonds by any simple formula. Moody's holds, rather, to the idea of tests devised to reveal the weaknesses that may be peculiar to or even inherent in the individual company.

The statistical tests are then compared with similar tests on companies in the same or comparable industries, to obtain a comparative statistical judgment. Following this course, the instrument or contract itself is meticulously examined for items of weakness—the security which has been provided, sinking fund provisions, the existence of a "hereafter acquired" clause, restrictions on further debt creation or payment of dividends, and the like. Finally, the intangibles, both of management (as judged by past policies) and of the broad outlook for the industry (its trends and peculiar characteristics, its stability or instability), are considered and a rating arrived at.

An effort to attain or approach uniformity in ratings is constantly made, although Moody's agrees that ratings as between various fields (industrial, utility, railroad, municipal, etc.) will never be completely uniform or comparable. The effort is centered in a rating committee, which reviews complaints and examines all new ratings to see that they are as closely consistent as possible with the existing ratings. It is furthered by the fact that all Moody experts engaged in making ratings undertake their work with identical objectives in mind, such as (1) making the rating as final and as unchanging as possible under all reasonably conceivable conditions; (2) expressing in the rating a protective judgment, i.e., a judgment concerning the risks of loss.

Standard & Poor's Bond Quality Ratings. A bond quality rating, according to Standard & Poor's, is a measure of the indicated ability of the obligor to pay interest and principal promptly when due. Inasmuch as long-term bonds are involved, the rating is a measure of the prospective credit standing of a company over the long term in contrast to its short-term commercial rating. From this it is apparent that there is much more to classifying a bond than substituting figures for symbols in a formula. Determination of a long-term rating involves an intensive study of those factors which make for continued profitable operations, maintenance of sound financial resources, and corporate longevity.

Benchmark ratios are employed, of course, but they are merely the starting point and are most useful for making comparisons of one issue with another. Each ratio must be evaluated in the light of those factors which permit long-term appraisals. The rating must be equitable at all times. A liberal appraisal penalizes the purchaser of the bond; a harsh one penalizes the obligor.

Standard & Poor's analysts break down their rating studies into four broad classifications: earnings, financial resources, property protection, and indenture provisions.

Earning power is given the most weight. Without earnings the obligor has practically nothing to offer. But the term "earnings" does not mean merely the past earnings record in relation to interest charges. It also means the ability to earn money indefinitely; this requires an accounting of all factors which contribute to earning power.

For an industrial company, Standard & Poor's analysts go beyond earning power and make a close study of the company's products and the position of the concern in its trade, as well as the character of its business. They examine the quality of the management as evidenced by its ability to keep up with changes in trends and in the general economy, the course of sales, the operating ratio, other sources of income, and money spent for research and plant expansion over a period of time. There are other earnings items to look for; these are the highlights.

Analyzing a public utility bond does not present the same problems. A utility company almost always has a monopolistic position in supplying a particular service in a stated area. This makes long-term projections easier. Whether an issue is rated AAA (highest) or C (lowest) depends upon demonstrated earning power in relation to fixed charges, type of service, character of the territory served, and operating efficiency. Operating efficiency is related to the amount of funds spent in modernizing the system. The debt in relation to plant investment is also important.

Railroad bonds, too, have tests applied to them which are peculiar to themselves. The character of the territory served, the breakdown of the type of goods hauled, the amount of traffic originated and terminated, and the volume of freight received from connecting lines are important. The trend of freight volumes over a period of years compared with other roads in the region and with all Class I roads is a good test of the management's ability to meet competition from other roads and other means of hauling freight. The physical condition of the road, maintenance expenditures, operating ratios, and efficiency as measured by gross ton-miles per freight-train-hour are given careful consideration.

Liquid resources are important. They indicate an ability to carry on a normal business, to finance larger sales without borrowing, to provide new capital needs, and to withstand temporary declines in times of economic stress. Depreciation and dividend policy are considered, in the sense that they influence financial strength. Current finances, however, are excluded as a test for electric power companies. Their earnings are relatively stable, and they operate profitably in good or poor economic periods. Their business, moreover, is on a cash basis. Normally power companies have little or no working capital.

Property protection involves three ratios for an industrial issue: debt in relation to property and fixed investments; working capital in relation to debt; and combined assets in relation to debt. Property involves more than merely noting the net plant figure carried on the balance sheet. Depreciation policies must be scrutinized. Plant expenditures tell a great deal about the modernity of plant. The plant account must be examined to see whether or not there has been a change in the character of the business and to ascertain that the assets do not include dead wood.

Standard & Poor's regards indenture provisions as least important in their rating since such provisions are designed to be protective rather than to promote earnings. They are studied because they deter management from making deleterious moves in such areas as excessive dividends, stock purchases, or assumption of additional senior, *pari passu,* and junior debts. Limitations on the right to incur additional debt are important, since industrial companies now finance almost exclusively through the issuance of unsecured debentures.

It is apparent that the determination of a quality rating involves a close study of all factors that affect the obligor. The price of the bond has no place in these deliberations. Recognizing its responsibility in setting up ratings, Standard & Poor's management has designated its principal bond men to act as a committee in arriving at a proper quality rating.

This committee is made up of a rating specialist, a trade analyst who becomes a member only when a bond in his particular trade is involved, and the managing editor of Standard & Poor's bond advisory services. A study of each situation is made independently by the rating specialist and the trade analyst, and they present their studies and recommendations to the committee sitting as a whole. Thus a check is made on each analyst. The rating specialist has a broad bond viewpoint, and his recommendations are related to all corporate bonds. The trade analyst makes his study from a trade angle, and his recommendations are related only to bonds in his particular area of expertness.

The Rating of Stocks.   Common stock ratings are issued by several statistical organizations and preferred stock ratings by only one. The ratings used by four services are shown in Table 17.

By their very nature common stock ratings cannot be so precise as bond ratings. Bond ratings are essentially defensive. How much assurance is there that bondholders will receive their interest and principal as scheduled without interruption even during declines in business activity? The chance of loss for stockholders, however, is offset by the possibility of large gains,

TABLE 17   Symbols Used in Rating Stocks

Standard & Poor's common stocks		Standard & Poor's preferred stocks	
Rating	Meaning	Rating	Meaning
A+	Excellent	AAA	Prime
A	Good	AA	High grade
A−	Above average	A	Sound
B+	Average	BBB	Medium grade
B	Below average	BB	Lower grade
B−	Low	B	Speculative
C	Lowest	C	Submarginal

Financial World common stocks		Value Line quality rating common stocks	
Rating	Meaning	Rating	Meaning
A+	Investment grade with greater earnings consistency	A+ A A− B+	Highest quality
A	Investment grade with lesser earnings consistency		Above average quality
B+	Upper medium grade		
B	Medium grade	B	Average quality
C+	Semispeculative	B− C+	Below average quality
C	More speculative		
D+	Highly speculative	C C−	Lowest quality
D	Unsuited for average investor		

which makes the rating of stock by any one scale a more difficult task.

In general, stock ratings are intended to indicate the investment quality of each issue rather than to forecast its market behavior. In most cases ratings are based upon the stability and growth of earnings and dividends. Past and expected performance are studied for both company and industry in order to judge security of earnings and dividends in the future. Since current price is not a part of the rating scale, a stock rating by itself cannot be regarded as advice to buy or to sell.

Addresses of Investment Agencies

The addresses of the various investment services referred to in this chapter are:

Babson's Reports, Inc.; also Business Statistics, Inc.
Wellesley Hills, Mass.   02181

Financial World
17 Battery Place
New York, N.Y.   10004

Moody's Investors Service
99 Church St.
New York, N.Y.   10007

Standard & Poor's Corporation
345 Hudson St.
New York, N.Y.   10014

Value Line Investment Survey
5 East 44th St.
New York, N.Y.   10017

Walker's Manual, Inc.
333 Kearny St.
San Francisco, Calif.   94108

25 financial statement analysis

The principal source of a stockholder's information about the condition of his company is two financial statements published as a part of the company's annual report. These are the "balance sheet" and the "income statement." Most companies supplement the two statements with less detailed quarterly reports. Unfortunately balance sheets and income statements are presented in stereotyped form and are couched in technical terminology, with the result that the average lay investor is often more confused than informed. This confusion is not really necessary. Facts of importance about a company could be presented in simpler language. Alternatively, an amateur analyst could easily master the technical jargon.

The object of the present chapter is to define some of the terms employed by professional accountants, explain some of the fundamental principles of accounting theory, and suggest ways and means of finding and interpreting the facts that are believed to have a bearing upon the market value of stocks and bonds. Obviously the chapter is intended not for accountants and others who understand the fundamentals of accounting but for laymen who already are or who are about to become stockholders in a corporation.

The Balance Sheet

The lay investor should view a balance sheet as a report of a company's total investment at a particular moment, classified first on the basis of location of the funds and second on the basis of source of the funds. The first classification is reported under the heading of "Assets," and the second is labeled "Liabilities." Traditionally, assets are reported on the left-hand side and liabilities on the right-hand side of the page. An alternative form, frequently found in published reports, places assets at the top and liabilities at the bottom of the page. Since assets and liabilities are merely two aspects of total investment, it follows that the two sides balance—hence the name of balance sheet.

A balance sheet for a hypothetical firm is given on the following page (Table 18). Note that the total investment of this firm is $12,450,000. The present situs of the funds is reported in

TABLE 18   Balance Sheet of a Hypothetical Company, as of the Close of Business on Dec. 31, 1966

Assets (location of investment)

Current assets		
Cash (in the bank)	$ 950,000	
Investments in marketable securities	1,500,000	
Accounts receivable from customers	2,550,000	
Investment in inventories of goods	1,127,000	
Total current assets		$ 6,127,000
Fixed assets		
Original investment in land	$ 200,000	
Original investment in buildings	5,000,000	
Original investment in equipment	4,000,000	
Total original investment	$9,200,000	
Less reserve for depreciation (this is the amount of the original investment which has been recovered to date from the firm's customers)	3,000,000	
Total current investment in fixed assets		$ 6,200,000
Miscellaneous assets		
Prepayments (of future expenses)		123,000
Total assets		$12,450,000

Liabilities (sources of funds)

Current liabilities		
Accounts payable (to trade creditors)	$ 563,000	
Notes payable (to banks and other lenders)	1,000,000	
Accrued income taxes payable	530,000	
Total current debts	$2,093,000	
Long-term obligations		
Bonds (5%, $1,000 par, due 1975)	4,000,000	
Total debt-type investment		$ 6,093,000
Equity-type investment		
Preferred stock (10,000 shares)	$1,000,000	
Common stock (200,000 shares)	1,000,000	
Capital surplus	500,000	
Total equity-type investment		$ 2,500,000
Internally generated investment		
Accumulated past earnings retained	$2,857,000	
Reserve for contingencies	1,000,000	
Total internally generated funds		3,857,000
Total liabilities		$12,450,000

great detail on the left-hand side of this statement. Accounting reports frequently contain more information than is of use to the investor. For this reason the first step in analyzing a statement should be to combine the details under a few meaningful headings so that significant comparisons can be made. If this is done for the assets of the hypothetical company, something like the following results:

Assets		
Location	Amount	Per cent of total
In short-term commitments	$ 6,127,000	49.3
In long-term commitments	6,200,000	49.8
In miscellaneous commitments	123,000	0.9
Total	$12,450,000	100.0

Next, the investor might simplify and summarize the liability side of the balance sheet as follows:

Liabilities		
Sources	Amount	Per cent of total
Borrowed:		
On a short-term basis	$ 2,093,000	16.8
On a long-term basis	4,000,000	32.2
Permanently invested:		
By preferred stockholders	1,000,000	8.0
By common stockholders	1,500,000	12.1
Earnings retained:		
For reinvestment	2,857,000	22.9
For contingencies (i.e., to cover possible losses)	1,000,000	8.0
Total	$12,450,000	100.0

The handling of reserves presents a problem when combining balance sheet items as suggested above. Valuation reserves (such as depreciation) should be subtracted from the items to which they apply. Liability reserves (such as accrued income taxes payable) should be added to short-term borrowings. Contingency reserves are earnings retained for reinvestment in the business but are labeled as contingent because management considers that they are almost certain to be lost in the future. Until such funds are lost, however, they should be treated as accumulated past earnings and merged with retained earnings.

To facilitate understanding, balance sheet data are frequently stated as percentages of total investment. Viewed in this manner, the total investment of the hypothetical company is half in current assets (short-term commitments) and half in fixed assets (long-term commitments). The investment in prepayments is too small percentagewise to be significant. Viewing investment from the angle of sources, the $12,450,000 could be said to be derived 49 per cent from borrowing, 20 per cent from the commitments of owners, and 21 per cent from retained earnings. Whether deriving funds from such sources and using them for such purposes is advisable is one of the judgments which an analyst must make.

The data revealed on a balance sheet can be used by an analyst in several ways. First, it is a source of factual information. For example, the hypothetical company has $950,000 of cash in the bank and has committed $1,127,000 to the purchase of inventory. Whether these sums are excessive or inadequate for their purposes is difficult for an outside observer to decide. On the other hand, an analyst may get a clue to their adequacy by making certain comparisons.

For example, a comparison of the current assets with the current liabilities on the illustrative balance sheet reveals that the company has 2.92 times as much money invested in short-term assets as it has short-term debts. This ratio is known as the "current ratio." A current ratio may be compared with a similar ratio computed a year ago to note improvement. It may be compared with a similar ratio of a competing company to judge relative liquidity. Or it may be compared with a ratio accepted as a standard of adequacy by analysts. A later section of this chapter lists a number of ratios, shows how they are computed and comments on their analytical significance.

The Income Statement

A simplified income statement for the hypothetical company is exhibited on page 487 (Table 19). If an income statement of an actual company contains more detail than this one, the investor may find it convenient to reduce the details to the fewer headings shown on this statement.

It will be noted that an income statement divides itself quite naturally into two parts, the upper portion offering an explanation of the derivation of distributable income and the lower portion reporting on the disposition of distributable income. Both are of interest to a common stock investor.

One of the principal concerns of an investor is the way in which a change in economic conditions may affect items reported on future income statements. He is especially interested in how two particular items may be affected—the operating profits and the earnings available for common stock equity.

TABLE 19   Income Statement of a Hypothetical Company,
            for the year of 1966

(Part I—reporting derivation of income)

Gross Revenue (from sales)		$10,000,000
Operating Costs		
Cost of the goods sold	$6,760,000	
Depreciation	1,380,000	
Selling and administration	760,000	8,900,000
Operating Profit		$ 1,100,000
Other Income (dividends on investments)		160,000
Distributable Income		$ 1,260,000

(Part II—reporting disposition of income)

Interest Expenses	$ 200,000
Taxable Income	$ 1,060,000
Income Taxes (rate assumed to be 50%)	530,000
Earnings Available To Equity Investors	$ 530,000
Preferred Stock Dividends	60,000
Earnings Available to Common Stock Equity	$ 470,000
Common Stock Dividends	240,000
Earnings Retained For Reinvestment	$ 230,000

The Principle of Leverage.   The basic profit and loss formula—gross revenue minus operating costs equals operating profit—is axiomatic. The effect on operating profits of a possible increase or decrease in gross revenue depends upon what happens to costs of operations. Two situations are possible. First, a given per cent change in gross revenue might be accompanied by a similar percentage change in costs of operations, in which case the change in operating profit would be *proportional* to the change in gross revenue and the situation would be described as without leverage. But if any portion of the costs of operations is nonvariable, then the percentage change in costs of operations will be less than the percentage change in gross revenue and the change in operating profits will be in the same direction but *more than proportional* to the change that occurs in gross revenue. When such a relationship exists, the situation is said to contain a degree of leverage.

Leverage arises as a result of the existence of nonvarying costs: the greater the proportion of nonvarying costs, the greater the degree of leverage. Obviously, an investor will want to examine an income statement carefully to determine the amount of leverage existing.

Operational Leverage. The first column of the accompanying table repeats the essential data of the operational portion of the income statement given in Table 19. In this table the traditional classification of operating costs has been abandoned in favor of a twofold classification of "fixed" and "variable." The second column of this table shows the effect upon costs and profits of an assumed 10 per cent increase of gross revenue; the third column gives the same information for an assumed 10 per cent decrease of gross revenue. It will be noted that the change in operating profit and in distributable income is more than proportional to the change assumed to occur in gross revenue. This magnification of effect is due to the presence among operating costs of $2,140,000 nonvarying expenses.

| | As reported for 1966 | Assumed change in revenue | |
		+10%	−10%
Gross revenue	$10,000,000	$11,000,000	$9,000,000
Operating costs			
Fixed	2,140,000	2,140,000	2,140,000
Variable	6,760,000	7,436,000	6,084,000
Total	$ 8,900,000	$ 9,576,000	$8,224,000
Operating profits	$ 1,100,000	$ 1,424,000	$ 776,000
Other income	160,000	160,000	160,000
Distributable income	$ 1,260,000	$ 1,584,000	$ 936,000
Percentage change		+25.7	−29.8

Financial Leverage. Operational leverage arises when one or more of the costs of operations is nonvarying. Financial leverage arises when one or more of the claims to the distributable income is fixed in amount. The principal difference between operational and financial leverage results from the fact that the former frequently arises from circumstances beyond managerial control, whereas the latter is deliberately introduced by managerial decision. Nevertheless, an investor will want to be informed concerning the potential effect of each type of leverage present in a situation.

    The following table illustrates the effect upon earnings available to common stock equity of the financial leverage that results from the capital structure of the hypothetical company. It will be noted that the percentage change in earnings available to common stock equity is greater than the percentage change in distributable income.

	As reported for 1966	Assumed change in earnings	
		+25.7%	−29.8%
Distributable income	$1,260,000	$1,584,000	$936,000
Interest payments	200,000	200,000	200,000
Taxable income	$1,060,000	$1,384,000	$736,000
Income taxes (50%)	530,000	692,000	268,000
Available to preferred stockholders	$ 530,000	$ 692,000	$268,000
Preferred stock dividends	60,000	60,000	60,000
Available to common stock equity	$ 470,000	$ 632,000	$308,000
Percentage change		+34.4	−34.5

Summarizing the Leverage Situation.   The easiest way to obtain a clear concept of total leverage is to prepare tables like those above and then to summarize the findings thus:

Change in gross revenue (assumed)	+10.0%	−10.0%
Resulting change in operating profits	+29.4	−34.6
Resulting change in distributable income	+25.7	−29.8
Resulting change in earnings available to common stock equity	+34.4	−34.5

On the basis of summaries like this, it is possible to classify a company as having high leverage, moderate leverage, low leverage, or no leverage.

Ratio Analysis

A good common stock investment is one which offers (1) safety of the principal sum committed, (2) an adequate annual yield on that sum, and (3) a chance for a reasonable capital gain. Unfortunately, data of the type given on a company's financial statements do not offer much guidance in these respects. All the information reported on balance sheets and on income statements is factual in nature and relates to the present or the past, whereas the factors that make for a good common stock investment have to do with the future.

By comparing facts revealed on financial reports with each other and with similar facts reported on earlier statements, an investor may discover important relationships and significant trends of value to him in estimating the direction of probable fluctuations, their extent, and their effect.

The remainder of this chapter is devoted to explaining some of the ratios which security analysts have come to consider significant. The list of ratios considered here is by no means exhaustive. An able analyst will invent additional ratios to reveal other trends and relationships which he believes to be significant. A particular ratio of great value in one situation may prove useless in another. For this reason the average analyst finds himself computing many more ratios than he actually uses.

Capitalization Ratios. Capitalization ratios summarize the financial structure of a company and aid an analyst in judging the probable effect upon earnings of fluctuations in gross revenue. The easiest way to compute the many capitalization ratios is to classify all the items on the liability side of a balance sheet under the five headings given below and then to reduce each to a percentage of the total. Numerous ratios can then be derived merely by adding the proper percentages. If this procedure is followed with regard to the hypothetical company's capital structure, the following results:

	Amount	Per cent
Short-term debts	$ 2,093,000	16.8
Long-term debts	4,000,000	32.2
Preferred stock equity	1,000,000	8.0
Common stock investment	1,500,000	12.1
Retained earnings	3,857,000	30.9
Total capitalization	$12,450,000	100.0

Here the bond ratio is 32.2; the debt ratio is 49.0 (16.8 + 32.2); the total equity ratio is 51.0 (8.0+ 12.1 + 30.9); the leverage capital[1] ratio is 57.0 (16.8 + 32.2 + 8.0); and the nonleverage capital ratio is 43.0 (12.1 + 30.9).

A stockholder is interested primarily in income available for dividends. If the amount of leverage capital is too great, a relatively small decline in gross revenue will cause a relatively large reduction in net income available to common stock equity and may lead to the passing of dividends. Corporations whose gross earnings are liable to fluctuations of substantial amounts should have low leverage capital ratios and high total equity ratios. Most industrial companies fall into this class. Public utility companies can have much higher leverage capital ratios without increasing the risk exorbitantly.

[1] Leverage capital includes all liabilities of a company which promises to pay the claimant a fixed annual sum. Thus they include short-term and long-term debts and outstanding preferred stocks.

The Current Ratio.   This ratio is the best known. It is computed by dividing current assets by current liabilities. The current ratio of the hypothetical company is 2.9 ($6,127,000 ÷ $2,093,000).

Since in the ordinary course of business current assets are the first to be converted into cash and current liabilities are the first debts that must be paid, the current ratio offers a rough measure of the ability of a firm to meet its near-term debts as they mature. Some analysts say that the current ratio of a company should always be 2 or better. However, the investor should consider a ratio of 2 as a minimum and not as a standard of adequacy. A proper standard for a particular company varies with circumstances. For example, a company with a small, fast-turning inventory and easily collected accounts receivable can "get by" on a smaller current ratio than could a company that sells a slow-turning product on a monthly instalment basis. For this reason, establishment of a standard current ratio should wait until something more is known about the collectibility of accounts receivable and the salability of the firm's inventory.

Frankly, the current ratio is more revealing to a short-term creditor who wi .es to gauge a company's credit rating for trade purposes than it is to an investor whose interest lies in the long-run profitability of the company's operations. Nevertheless an intelligent common stock investor hesitates to acquire the stock of a company with an unsatisfactory current ratio and is not easily misled into believing that a high current ratio is a sign that a stock is a good purchase.

The Collection Period.   The collection period is the amount of time *normally* required to convert accounts receivable into cash. The formula for estimating the length of this period (in days) is:

$$\text{Accounts receivable} \div \frac{\text{annual sales}}{365}$$

Here is the logic of the formula: annual sales divided by 365 gives average daily sales. If a typical balance of accounts receivable is divided by average daily sales, the dividend indicates the number of days' sales that are waiting to be collected at each given moment. This collection-waiting period indicates how long each dollar of sales lingers as a claim against customers before becoming a dollar of cash. In the hypothetical company, the length of the collection period is 93 days [$2,550,000 ÷ ($10,000,000 ÷ 365)].

The period of time required to collect funds can be converted into a turnover of accounts receivable rate by computing the number of collection periods in a year. Thus, a collection period of 93 days amounts to a turnover of accounts receivable rate of 2.99 (365 ÷ 93).

Inventory Turnover Period.   An inventory turnover period is the number of days normally required to convert raw material into finished goods or to convert finished goods into accounts receivable. The formulas for computing the length of the two periods are:

For raw material,

$$\text{Raw material inventory} \div \frac{\text{raw material put into production}}{365}$$

For finished goods,

$$\text{Finished goods inventory} \div \frac{\text{cost of goods sold}}{365}$$

The logic of the two formulas is similar to that for computing the length of the collection period. If the amount of material devoted to a particular use (such as being put into production or being delivered to customers) is divided by 365, the dividend is the average daily use. A mathematical comparison of daily use with the stock of material carried (inventory) indicates the length of time (in days) that the stock on hand could sustain use at the average daily rate. This, of course, is the length of the turnover period, and the number of such periods in a year is the inventory turnover rate.

The balance sheet of the hypothetical company reports only one inventory. By using this inventory figure and the cost-of-goods item reported on the income statement, the length of the inventory turnover period is determined to be 61 days [$1,127,000 ÷ ($6,760,000 ÷ 365)]. A period of this length converts to a turnover rate of 6.0 annually (365 ÷ 61).

Cash Turnover Period.   The method used to compute the length of the collection period and the length of the inventory turnover period may also be used to compute the length of the cash turnover period. The cash turnover period may be defined as the length of time that cash inflows remain in the bank before being disbursed again. The formula for computing this is

$$\text{Typical cash balance} \div \frac{\text{total cash expenditures}}{365}$$

The total cash expenditures item in the formula includes all the expenses reported on the income statement that involve cash outflows made periodically during the course of the year for purposes of sustaining operations. Thus the list does not include depreciation or outlays that are made only once or twice a year. Dividing this total cash expenditure by 365 gives average daily cash outflow, which when compared with the average cash balance indicates the length of time that each dollar of inflowing cash lingers in the bank before being reexpended. The length of the average cash turnover period for the hypothetical company is 42 days [$950,000 ÷ ($8,250,000 ÷ 365)]. The turnover of cash rate is 8.69 (365 ÷ 42).

Working Capital Turnover Period.   The term "working capital" is not clear. Some persons define it as current assets. Others define it as current assets minus current liabilities. Still others define "capital at work" as expended funds to be recovered (with profit) during the current accounting period.[2] Regardless of how the term is defined, the operation of a business enterprise consists in expending cash to obtain a product that is to be delivered to a customer in exchange for a claim which will ultimately be converted into cash. The length of time required to complete this cash-to-cash cycle is the length of the working capital turnover period. Obviously the length of the period is the sum of the lengths of its components—the cash turnover period, the inventory turnover period, and the collection period—described in the paragraphs above.

One hundred and ninety-six days were required by the hypothetical company to complete its cash-to-cash cycle (61 days + 93 days + 42 days). If a single turnover of working capital requires this number of days, then the process can be repeated 1.8 times a year (365 ÷ 196).

Some books on ratio analysis suggest that an investor compute the working capital turnover rate by dividing sales revenue by current assets. This procedure is mathematically indefensible, for the numerator of the formula is expressed in sales dollars while the denominator is expressed partly in sales dollars (accounts receivable) and partly in cost dollars (inventories). The result is mathematical nonsense.

Gross Revenue per Dollar of Assets.   This ratio is computed by dividing a company's total sales by its total assets. A comparison of this ratio with the same ratio of prior years and with the same ratio of other companies is revealing. If the ratio is below that of other concerns and perhaps shows a downward trend where the industry trend is upward, the investor is warned of danger ahead. Shortly after earnings or the proceeds of sales of stock and bond issues are disbursed to acquire fixed assets, the ratio of gross revenue to assets may decline for a time. Sooner or later, however, the ratio should return to its former position or to an improved one. If this does not happen, then there are reasons for suspecting that too much capital is being invested in the company considering the amount of business available to it.

By itself the ratio suggests that the amount of investment in assets is somehow responsible for or the cause of the volume of a company's revenue. The implication is that increased investment would augment sales more or less proportionately. This is partly true. Technical factors—more engineering than economic—create a degree of correlation between total investment and gross revenue.

For example, an investment of $1 million in a generating plant might be necessary to produce the 10 million kilowatthours of electricity demanded by a community. If regulating authorities allow a rate of 2 cents per kilowatthour, the company's gross revenue would be $200,000 and its ratio of gross

---

[2] For a more extended discussion of this concept of working capital, see "Working Capital Management," by James N. Holtz and Wilford J. Eiteman, in *Essays on Business Finance,* 4th ed., Ann Arbor, Mich.: Masterco Press, Inc., 1963.

revenue per dollar of assets would be 0.2. By comparison with other similar companies, this ratio would be normal. But in such a case the $200,000 of sales revenue is due not alone to the investment of $1 million but also to the community demand for electricity and to the rate allowed. It does not follow that if more funds are invested in plant the company will experience proportionally more revenue.

In the hypothetical company, $10.9 million of investment in assets (the investment in marketable securities was omitted) was accompanied by gross revenue of $10 million. This is a ratio of 91.7 cents of revenue per dollar of asset investment. Whether it is safe to assume that one more dollar of investment would produce an additional 91.7 cents of revenue is questionable.

Earnings per Dollar of Asset Investment.   This ratio is computed by dividing earnings before interest and taxes by total investment in assets. It is useful for comparing the profitability of investing dollars in one industry with the profitability of investing them in some other industry. Also, by noting the trend of this ratio for an individual company over a period of years, one can obtain a rough measure of its earnings growth. However, when the ratio is used by an investor to gauge the profitability of expansion, it is subject to the same criticism as the ratio of gross revenue per dollar of assets.

Earnings for a particular year are only partly a function of the amount of investment. They are affected also by such factors as the level of general prosperity, the productive efficiency of the company, the ability of its sales force to get a proper share of the market, and happenstance. The ratio of earnings per dollar of assets for the hypothetical company is 10.12 ($1,260,000 ÷ $12,450,000).

Operating Ratio.   An investor wants to know that operating expenses do not consume an unreasonable share of gross revenue. The percentage of gross revenue used to defray expenses is an essential statistic. It is commonly called the *operating ratio* and applies alike to industrials, railroads, and public utilities.

The operating ratio is very closely related to two other ratios—the margin of profit and the markup. If one recalls the basic profit and loss formula—gross revenue minus operating costs equals operating profit— then the so-called operating ratio is the ratio of costs to revenue; the margin of profit is the ratio of profit to revenue; and the markup is the ratio of profit to costs. It will be noted that the three ratios are merely different ways of expressing the same relationship.

The operating ratio of the hypothetical company is 89.0 per cent ($8.9 million ÷ $10 million); the margin of profit is 11.0 per cent ($1.1 million ÷ $10 million); and the markup is 12.3 per cent ($1.1 million ÷ $8.9 million).

Times Interest Earned.   This ratio is valuable to bond investors and rating agencies as a measure of the safety factor involved in any investment calling for the payment of a fixed sum quarterly, semiannually, or annually. The formula for computing the ratio is

$$\frac{\text{Earnings before interest and taxes}}{\text{Interest charges}}$$

The hypothetical company earned its interest charges 6.3 times ($1,260,000 ÷ $200,000), and on the basis of this ratio its bonds would be entitled to a high rating. Most analysts feel that an industrial company should earn its interest charges a minimum of three or four times if its bonds are to be considered safe investments. The ratio of times interest earned is of less importance to a common stock investor than it is to a bond investor. Nevertheless, a common stock investor should hesitate to purchase shares of a company with a low ratio of times interest earned since a low ratio is a harbinger of financial trouble.

Times Preferred Dividends Earned.   This ratio does for preferred stock what the ratio of times interest earned does for bonds. When applied to preferred stock the computation is made more difficult because of the necessity of considering the effect of the income tax and of making allowance for the prior claim of bondholders. Since interest charges take precedence over preferred stock dividends, it follows that a preferred stock issue of a company can never achieve the degree of safety achieved by a bond of the same company. For this reason it is necessary to add interest charges to preferred stock dividends to obtain a true measure of the safety factor of the preferred stock. To state this in a different way, the preferred dividend payment is only as safe as the preferred dividend plus the interest payment.

There is a further complication. Earnings must provide for income tax before a dividend on preferred stock may be paid. Unfortunately this situation cannot be met by adding the income tax payment to the preferred stock dividend (as is done with regard to the interest payment) because the income tax payment varies with earnings. Therefore, the preferred stock payment must be multiplied by a correction factor to adjust for the income tax payment.[3] For example, if the preferred stock dividend is $6 and if the income tax rate is 50 per cent, the company would have to earn $12 (after interest) to pay the dividend once. It would have to earn $24 to pay the dividend twice, and so on.

The *easiest* way to compute the ratio of times preferred dividends earned is to compare earnings before taxes and interest with the amount of earnings required to pay the preferred dividend once. This last amount for the company in our example would be computed as follows:

[3] The formula for computing the correction multiplier is $1 ÷ (1 - R)$, in which R represents the applicable income tax rate.

Amount needed to pay interest charges once	$200,000
Amount needed to pay preferred stock dividend once	60,000
Income tax that would have to be paid in order that $60,000 would be left for dividends	60,000
Total minimum earnings necessary to pay interest, preferred dividends, and income taxes	$360,000

If $360,000 is required to pay interest, income taxes, and preferred stock dividends with nothing left over, then distributable income of $1,260,000 is sufficient to meet these payments 3.5 times ($1,260,000 ÷ $360,000).

In the above computations the income tax rate was assumed to be 50 per cent. If the income tax rate had been 52 per cent, $61,224 would have to be earned for income taxes. If the income tax rate had been 48 per cent, the amount required to pay income taxes would have been $57,680.

Some writers advise investors to compute the ratio of times preferred dividends earned by dividing earnings after interest and taxes by the amount of the preferred stock dividend payment. If this formula is applied to our hypothetical company, the resulting safety factor is 8.8 ($530,000 ÷ $60,000). According to this computation the bonds of the company are more risky than the preferred stock because the safety factor of the bonds is only 6.3. That this cannot be so is obvious. For example, a reduction of 84 per cent in distributable income would wipe out every cent of the earnings available for preferred stock dividends but would not disturb the interest payment to bondholders.

The Payout Ratio.   This is the ratio of dividends paid on common stock to earnings available for common stock equity. The payout ratio for the company in our example is 51 per cent ($240,000 ÷ $470,000).

The payout ratio for the Dow-Jones industrial stocks during the period 1953 to 1963 averaged 63.4 and varied from a high of 71.5 in 1958 to a low of 56.8 in 1963. In five of the eleven years the ratio deviated from 60 by less than $\frac{1}{2}$ per cent. This tendency of the payout ratio to cling to the 60 per cent level is due to the existence of the Federal tax on unreasonably retained earnings and to the policy of the Internal Revenue Department of accepting a 40 per cent retention as not unreasonable. Thus a company may avoid argument by merely paying out 60 per cent of its earnings as dividends.

A low payout ratio is regarded by some investors as an indication of a growth company. There are two reasons for this conclusion. First, it is argued, a board of directors of a company would have paid out a higher percentage of earnings as dividends if they had not considered it profitable to use the funds for expansion. Thus a low payout ratio indicates the availability of profitable opportunities to the company. Second, only a real growth company can present a good argument to the Internal Revenue Department that its low payout ratio is not for the purpose of aiding wealthy stockholders to avoid a high tax rate on their personal incomes.

Earnings per Share.   Earnings per share is a concept rather than a ratio. In theory it represents the portion of aggregate earnings "owned" by a holder of a single share of stock. The amount is computed by dividing earnings available for common stock equity as reported on the income statement by the number of shares of stock outstanding. For our hypothetical company earnings per share are $2.35 ($470,000 ÷ 200,000).

Much depends upon the *trend* of earnings per share. A company earning $2.35 per share with improvement likely is to be preferred over a company earning $6.35 but displaying a downward trend. An important factor in evaluating stocks is the price-earnings ratio to be applied to current earnings per share. Most analysts believe that the rate of rise in the trend of earnings per share is the factor that determines the applicable price-earnings ratio. The matter is discussed in much greater detail in Chapter 27.

A good procedure for studying earnings per share is to make a chart with a curve representing dividends paid in each year, another indicating earnings per share, and a series of bars showing monthly high and low stock prices. Such a chart should stretch over a period of seven to ten years. With a chart of this nature available, an investor can tell at a glance the relationship of prices to earnings per share and to dividends and so be in a position to judge the probable effect on prices of changes in earnings and dividends as they are reported. One such chart is shown in Figure 25–1.

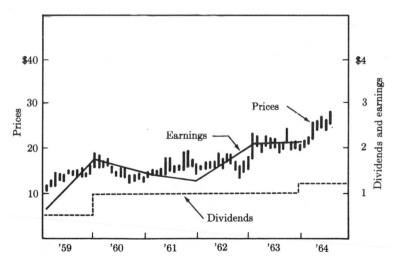

Fig. 25–1   Prices, earnings per share, and dividends of Udylite Corporation, 1959 to 1964.

The Price-Earnings Ratio.   The relation of price to earnings can be stated as a ratio computed by dividing the price of a share by its earnings. Thus a share earning $6 and selling at $72 would have a price-earnings ratio of 12. In a sense the price-earnings ratio of a corporate stock represents the amount investors are currently paying for $1 of that company's earnings. In the example just given, the price-earnings ratio of 12 suggests that purchasers are paying $12 and sellers are accepting $12 for the ownership of $1 of the company's earnings.

The search for a *normal* price-earnings ratio is a search for the normal price of a dollar's worth of earnings. Obviously, no such normal price exists. The current earnings of a corporation whose business is expanding rapidly command a higher price on the market than an equal amount of the earnings of a corporation whose business is on the decline. Even if it were true that investors are willing to pay the same price for earnings of all companies regardless of their prospects, it would still be possible for such a "normal" price-earnings ratio to change from time to time as investors changed their minds as to what is the proper price to pay for a dollar of earnings. For example, on June 29, 1951, the stocks included in the Dow-Jones industrial averages were selling at 7.6 times their earnings. Twelve years later, on November 27, 1963, they were selling at 18.3 times their earnings.

The student of prices and earnings is confronted with a contradictory situation. In the first place, the trend of the market as a whole follows the trend of earnings, making for stable price-earnings ratios. Yet the price-earnings ratios of individual companies are found to fluctuate within such wide limits as seemingly to deny the relationship of price and earnings that is known to exist. This confusion is partly explained by the fact that the relationship about which we are certain is the relationship of *trends,* whereas the computation of the price-earnings ratio for any given issue at any given moment is based upon price and earnings figures that may be, and probably are, deviations from the trend. Then, to confuse the matter further, the average price-earnings ratio itself has been moving steadily upward for a period of twelve years.

With these reservations in mind, certain generalizations about price-earnings ratios are possible.

1. There is no normal price-earnings ratio applicable to all industries. The price trend of one industry may be eighteen times its earnings trend, that of another eight times its earnings trend. As a rule the stocks of companies supplying the basic needs of society as well as the stocks of the older established industries have a lower ratio than do the stocks of companies engaged in supplying the newer wants of society. When a corporation engaged in one of the older lines of activity enters a new field, its ratio level rises.

2. Stocks of companies whose earnings do not show extreme fluctua-

tion from quarter to quarter or from year to year sell at more or less constant price-earnings ratios. This is natural, since their earnings do not deviate so far from their trend. An increase in the earnings of such a company enhances the market value of its stock without effecting much change in the price-earnings ratio.

3. A sudden increase or decrease in the earnings of a company accustomed to violent fluctuations in earnings may or may not cause a change in prices, depending on whether investors feel that the latest earnings report represents a change in what is to be expected henceforth or merely a temporary deviation from normal. If the consensus favors the latter, an adjustment will be made in the current price-earnings ratio and not in the price.

4. With the passage of time, the average price-earnings ratio may increase. There is no way of ascertaining whether this increase is permanent or transitory.

According to the principles outlined above, the price-earnings ratios of stocks during periods of depression should be high. Stock prices at such a time are low, but earnings, if they exist, are still lower, resulting in a high price-earnings ratio. As business slowly emerges from its slump, both prices and earnings rise, but the latter at a faster rate than the former so that price-earnings ratios are lower. The lag of prices behind earnings at this point in the cycle may be due to the timidity of investors who lost money in the preceding panic (a psychological factor) and to the general lack of funds for investment purposes (the economic effect of the preceding depression).

Then for a time prices and earnings move upward together, and price-earnings ratios remain at a more or less constant level. Toward the peak of the cycle, speculative enthusiasm carries the prices of securities to abnormally high levels and thus increases the price-earnings ratios just at the time when they might be expected to be lower. This last move accentuates the violent readjustment that occurs when earnings fail to confirm the high prices set by speculators. After a panic, prices and earnings gradually decline until the bottom of the depression, when the cycle starts over again.

In the long run the market prices of stocks depend upon the earnings of corporations, and a rise in the latter is accompanied by a rise in the former. There exist in this relation, however, a lead and a lag, which cause the level of price-earnings ratios to vary at different phases of the business cycle. Thus the trend of prices is fundamentally based upon the trend of earnings, but prices lead or lag behind earnings as a result of psychological and economic conditions.

The discussion above assumes that the price-earnings ratio for individual stocks is constant except for the changes that occur at the peaks and in the troughs of the business cycle. If this were true, then changes in the market prices of securities would correlate much more closely than they do with changes in earnings. Actually the average price-earnings ratio itself changes. Hence, instead of there being one variable (earnings), there are two (earnings *and* the price-earnings ratio). When the two variables move in opposite directions, they exert counteracting influences upon prices. Therefore, the direction in which prices move depends upon which variable has exhibited the greater change. As was mentioned in Chapter 19, this is an important factor to be considered by the investor who seeks growth stocks.

The Sophisticated Price-Earnings Ratio.   A good argument can be advanced to the effect that the price-earnings ratio is a mathematical expression of the relation of the trend of prices to the trend of earnings. Thus, since the actual price at any one moment and the actual earnings in any one year may be deviations from their trends, there is little point in paying too much attention to ratios computed from actual prices and recently reported earnings.

To illustrate, let us suppose that the trend of earnings per share of a company is the XY line shown in Figure 25–2. Let us assume that the slope of this line is such as to justify a price-earnings ratio of 15. If so, then the XY line should also be the trend of prices as read on the right-hand vertical scale. (This right-hand scale is calibrated at fifteen times the scale on the left.)

Now at any particular moment, such as M, actual price and earnings may deviate from their true trend value. Perhaps earnings per share are lower than normal because of a four-month strike, and market quotations are higher than normal because of a temporary increase in market orders to buy brought about by a rumor that the strike is about to be settled. If so, a price-earnings ratio computed from the actual price and reported earnings would be very high and without significance; but the relation of the normal price of the issue to its normal earnings, as indicated by trend values, would not be affected.

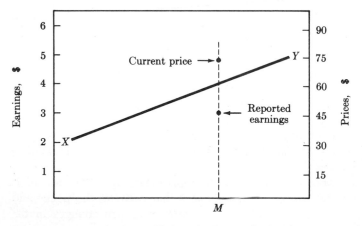

Fig. 25–2   Concept of a sophisticated price-earnings ratio.

Book Value of Common Stock.   The net book value of a share of common stock is the amount of money each share would receive if (1) the company's assets were to be sold at their balance sheet values; (2) the creditors, the preferred stockholders, and all others holding claims having priority over those of common stockholders were to be paid off in full; and (3) the residual funds were to be distributed equally among the outstanding shares of common stock. Since none of these things is going to happen, it is obvious that book value is a rather visionary concept.

Nevertheless, the book value of the common stock of our hypothetical company would be computed as follows:

Proceeds to be derived from a sale of assets at their balance sheet values	$12,450,000
Proceeds required to liquidate the claims of creditors and preferred stockholders	7,093,000
Residual proceeds available for distribution to common stockholders	$ 5,357,000

Amount each of the 200,000 shares would receive: $26.78

It was once widely believed that book value set a price floor below which the market value of a stock would not decline. The theory was that, if market price did decline below this figure, stockholders would sell the company's assets, liquidate its liabilities, and withdraw the residual in cash. The idea is left over from the thinking of the old-fashioned small merchant, who could and frequently did sell his merchandise, pay off his creditors, and retire from business. But funds invested in a large modern corporation are irrevocably committed to a particular productive use and so cannot be sold easily or transferred to some other use. The assets must be abandoned, sold for practically nothing, or continued to be used with a revamped capital structure. Under such circumstances book value ceases to have much significance.

Even if assets can be sold at a reasonable price, it is still doubtful that the prices received would coincide exactly (no more, no less) with balance sheet values. If not, then computation of book value in the traditional manner is totally without meaning.

The Cash Flow Controversy.   The most popular current theory of stock values holds that the investment worth of a stock is a multiple of its earnings per share and that prices vary about this investment worth. Recently some of the members of this school have substituted the concept of cash flow for earnings per share. (Cash flow is earnings plus noncash expenses.) This substitution has given rise to much controversy. A great deal of the unnecessary confusion resulting from the arguments has been due to a careless definition of terms. If the present discussion is to avoid this error, it must be very careful to assign specific meanings to five terms—"cash flow," "real earnings," "reported earnings," "depend upon," and "correlate with"—and then never to use the terms interchangeably.

Accordingly, we begin with the definitions.

Cash flow is what is left of income after every expense except depreciation and every distribution except common stock dividends have been deducted. The amount of cash flow in a given situation is most easily computed by adding depreciation expenses to earnings available for common stock equity. Aggregate cash flow in the case of our hypothetical company is $1,850,000 ($1,380,000 + $470,000). Cash flow can and usually is expressed on a per share basis. The per share figure is computed by dividing aggregate cash flow by the number of shares of common stock outstanding. In the case of this company cash flow per share is $9.25 ($1,850,000 ÷ 200,000).

Real earnings refers to the amount that would be available to common stock equity if accountants strove to determine the amount accurately. Reported earnings is the amount which the published income statement states to be available.

Now the astonished layman may ask: Do not accountants always strive to report real earnings? The answer is: Not if the object is to minimize income taxes. And how do accountants minimize income taxes? By overstating expenses. But is not overstating expenses tax evasion? The answer is: Not if the income tax law specifically authorizes such overstatements, as it very definitely does with respect to one particular expense—depreciation.

To illustrate, assume that a corporation has cash flow during a five-year period as indicated in the following table. Assume further that the company uses up fixed assets of $150,000 during the five-year period and that accountants agree that this amount was consumed evenly during the five years. In this event real earnings would be the amounts shown in the last column.

Year	Cash flow	Depreciation	Real earnings
1	$ 60,000	$ 30,000	$ 30,000
2	61,500	30,000	31,500
3	63,250	30,000	33,250
4	64,912	30,000	34,912
5	66,658	30,000	36,658
Total	$316,320	$150,000	$166,320

Assume now that the accountants are instructed to employ whatever accounting procedures bring about a postponement of income tax payments.

(There are certain advantages to the corporation in achieving such post-ponements.) Accordingly, the accountants decide to distribute the deprecia-tion expense among the five years in accordance with the ratios 5:15, 4:15, 3:15, 2:15, and 1:15. (This is the so-called sum-of-the-digits method.) The result of such an allocation of depreciation on reported earnings is shown in the following table:

Year	Cash flow	Depreciation	Reported earnings
1	$ 60,000	$ 50,000	$ 10,000
2	61,500	40,000	21,500
3	63,250	30,000	33,250
4	64,912	20,000	44,912
5	66,658	10,000	56,658
Total	$316,320	$150,000	$166,320

Although aggregate earnings for the five years are not altered by the method of allocating depreciation, a stockholder would conclude from the reported earnings that the profitability of operations is increasing by leaps and bounds, whereas the truth is that real earnings are increasing at a rate of 5 per cent a year (see preceding table).

In the discussion that follows the term "depend upon" is used to mean that a causal relationship exists between two factors—one factor is a cause and the other a result. The expression "correlate with" is used to mean that two statistical series move in parallel paths without implying that either is the cause of the other's movement. With these connotations clearly in mind we are ready to list a series of propositions.

1. *Real* earnings and *reported* earnings are not necessarily correlated. For proof of this proposition, compare the figures contained in the last columns of the two tables.
2. Investment worth *depends* upon *real* earnings. This proposition is axio-matic to the disputants.
3. In the above tables the correlation of cash flow to *real* earnings is greater than the correlation of cash flow to *reported* earnings.
4. Investment worth does not *depend* upon cash flow.

The following conclusion emerges from the four propositions:

When accounting procedures aim at minimizing income taxes rather than computing earnings accurately, investment worth which depends upon real earnings will correlate more closely with cash flow than with reported earnings.

Here is the heart of the so-called cash flow controversy. Opponents of the cash flow theory have interpreted proponents as saying that investment worth depends upon cash flow, and proponents of the cash flow theory have failed to call attention to the difference between "depends upon" and "correlates with."

Inherent Limitations to Financial Analysis

A purchase of common stock is a good investment if (1) it offers safety of the principal commitment, (2) it promises the investor an adequate dividend yield, and (3) it holds prospects of a satisfactory capital gain. The potential stockholder is the judge of what constitutes an adequate yield; his problem is determining probable dividend payments. This is not difficult, since the dividend policies of corporations tend to be stable and, if they vary at all, the variance is in the upward direction.

But judging safety of the principal commitment and chances for capital gain is very difficult, for these two characteristics depends upon the *future* price of the issue, and this in turn depends upon two factors: (1) the financial condition of the company in the future and (2) the behavioral response of investors to its future condition.

Now it becomes clear at once that even the most penetrating analysis of a company's past financial statements is going to reveal very little information about either of the two factors that determine future prices. Thus the investor who expects statement analysis to guide his investment decisions is asking too much.

What financial analysis does do is to make an investor intimately acquainted with the company's past operations and its present financial condition. This acquaintance may warn him of dangers already in sight. It may also uncover trends which he can extend on into the future and may thereby reveal something of what is yet to come. However, the existence of a trend in the past is no assurance that it will continue. Thus forecasting future conditions is at best a hazardous task; but predicting investor response to the conditions forecast is even more uncertain. This being so, no method of forecasting stock prices can consistently surpass good judgment.

26 projected income statements

Current market quotations may be compared with actual current earnings or with expected future earnings. During prolonged periods of business optimism most common stocks are either reasonably priced or overpriced in comparison with their current earnings. At such times only a few issues appear to be undervalued. Some security analysts follow the policy of seeking out the undervalued issues—a procedure that taxes one's patience. But most common stock investors are satisfied with issues whose prices are reasonably related to current earnings but low by comparison with expected future earnings. A search for these issues necessitates a forecast of future conditions.

Some investors attempt a forecast of the future only in general terms. They buy shares at prices reasonably related to current earnings that are expected to improve with the passage of time. In other words they want the future to be better than the present by an indeterminate amount. Other investors try to measure the *extent* of the expected improvement. These are really choosing issues that are undervalued on the basis of specifically expected earnings. To do this, a projected income statement is essential.

The first step in constructing such an income statement is to predict gross revenue. In general there are two methods for doing this—extending a past trend or relying upon a dependable correlation. An estimate of gross revenue having been arrived at, the remainder of the income statement is constructed from ratios taken from past earnings statements. The goal of the forecaster is to estimate earnings available to common stock equity so that he can compute an expected earnings per share figure for some future year. This figure then becomes the basis of an estimate of future investment worth by application of the security analyst's favorite stock price theory.

Chapter 25 showed how to compute the numerous ratios needed to project an income statement. The present chapter will explain the procedures for constructing the projected statement. Chapter 27 will describe four stock price theories by means of which expectations are converted into a price forecast.

Forecasting by Trend Extension

A trend is a *pattern* of change observed as typical of a series of statistical data. The usual procedure is to plot the series and then to study the plotted data to discover a discernible pattern. Patterns found to exist can usually be represented on a chart by a straight line or a regularly shaped curve marking the general path of the plotted data. Such a line or curve may be sketched freehand, or it may be located precisely by the method of least squares. An explanation of this method is given in every textbook on elementary statistics.

The straight line or curve mentioned above is the *trend* of the statistical series. The value at a given date as indicated by the trend line is accepted as the normal value for that date. Thus an extension of a trend line is supposed to indicate the normal values for future dates on the assumption that the forces responsible for the line in the past will continue to control it in the future.

If a statistical series is plotted on a chart, it is important that the proper type of chart paper be used. For investors there are two types of chart paper: arithmetic and semilog paper. Horizontal and vertical distances are calibrated on arithmetic paper in multiples of uniform size. On semilog paper horizontal distances are calibrated arithmetically, but vertical distances are laid off according to the logarithms of the digits 1, 2, 3, and so on (see Figure 26–1).

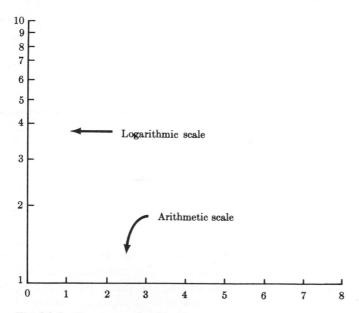

Fig. 26–1   Two types of calibration.

Which type of chart paper is appropriate for a particular statistical series depends upon the nature of the increments and the decrements of the series. An "increment" is an increase in magnitude that occurs between two successive statistics of a series. A "decrement" is a decrease in magnitude that occurs between two successive statistics of a series. Thus, if the fifth item of a series is 1,200 and the sixth item is 1,450, the increment is 250 (1,450 − 1,200). If the sixth item of the series is 1,450 and the seventh item is 1,200, the decrement is 250 (1,450 − 1,200). When the absolute amounts of the increments or decrements of a statistical series are substantially constant, the series should be plotted on arithmetic chart paper. When the absolute amounts of the increments or decrements tend to increase or decrease by a constant percentage, the series should be plotted on semi-logarithmic paper.

Even when a statistical series is plotted on the proper type of paper, the plotted points seldom fall exactly on the line that represents their pattern. Hence a trend line is an *idealized* rather than an exact representation of the pattern. If the figures of the past deviated from the line, the figures of the future can be expected to deviate similarly, though it is legitimate to assume that the future deviations will be no greater than those of the past. Thus a forecaster must have an index of past deviations to indicate the probable error of his estimates of the future. There are two such indexes: the "average" deviation and the "standard" deviation.[1]

To summarize, the procedure for forecasting by trend extension involves the following steps:

1. Plotting of past data on the proper type of chart paper to determine whether or not change has occurred according to a discernible pattern
2. Derivation of the mathematical formula of the line that best represents the pattern of change characteristic of the past
3. Computation of an index of past deviations to be used as a measure of the possible error in a forecaster's estimates
4. Extension of the trend line to obtain a specific estimate for a particular year
5. Application of the index of probable error of estimate to obtain the possible range of the estimate

The several steps listed above will become clearer by their application to the gross revenue of a hypothetical firm.

---

[1] The average deviation is the sum of the deviations divided by their number. The standard deviation is computed by adding the squares of the deviations, dividing the sum by the number of deviations, and extracting the square root of the quotient.

Example of a Regular Arithmetic Progression. The following table gives the gross revenue of a hypothetical company for a period of five years and the increments computed from the data reported:

Year	Gross revenue	Increments
1961	$11,455,000	
1962	14,530,000	$3,075,000
1963	17,605,000	3,075,000
1964	20,680,000	3,075,000
1965	23,755,000	3,075,000

The absolute amounts of all the increments in the above table are identical. Hence the series is regular and arithmetic, and if it is to be plotted, arithmetic chart paper should be used. If the data are properly plotted, it will be found that all the plotted points fall in a straight line and that there are no deviations (see Figure 26–2). The formula that represents the relationship of this company's gross revenue to time is

$$GR = A + BX$$

in which GR is the gross revenue for a particular year, A is the gross revenue in the year designated as the base year, B is the annual increment, and X is the number of years by which a particular year is removed from the base year. On the basis of this formula, the 1966 gross revenue of our hypo-

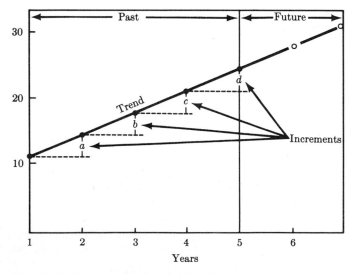

Fig. 26–2 An example of an arithmetic trend.

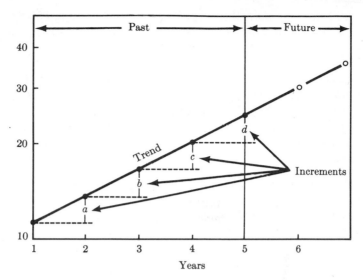

Fig. 26–3 An example of a geometric trend. (Note the vertical calibration.)

thetical firm (five years away from the base year of 1961) would be $26,830,000, viz.,

$11,455,000 + (5 × $3,075,000)

Since there were no deviations from the pattern in the past, the probable error in the estimate is zero.

Example of a Regular Geometric Progression.   The first and fifth items of the following table are identical with those of the preceding table; but the second, third, and fourth items are different, and the absolute amounts of the increments are not identical.

Year	Gross revenue	Annual increment	Per cent increase
1961	$11,455,000		
1962	13,747,000	$2,292,000	20
1963	16,497,000	2,750,000	20
1964	19,796,000	3,299,000	20
1965	23,755,000	3,959,000	20

However, it will be noted that the annual percentage increase in the increments is constant at 20 per cent. Thus the series is geometric and, if the data are to be plotted, semilogarithmic chart paper is used as in Figure 26–3.

The formula that expresses the relationship of this company's gross revenue to time is

$$GR = A \, (1 + R)^x$$

in which GR is the gross revenue for a particular year, A is the gross revenue for the year designated as the base year, R is the annual per cent increase in revenue, and X is the number of years by which a particular year is removed from the base year. On the basis of this formula, the 1966 gross revenue of our hypothetical firm (five years away from the base year of 1961) would be $28,506,000.

Example of an Irregular Arithmetic Progression.   The first and fifth figures of the following statistical progression are identical with the first and fifth figures of the preceding tables, but the second, third, and fourth figures are different. Neither the absolute amounts of the increments nor their rates of increase are constant. However, an average of the four increments is $3,075,000, and none of the four varies from this average by more than $300,000. If a deviation of this amount could be classified as unimportant, the increments might be characterized as *substantially* constant in absolute amount and the statistical series might be ruled to be *approximately* arithmetic.

Year	Gross revenue	Annual increment	Per cent increase
1961	$11,455,000		
1962	14,455,000	$3,000,000	26.1
1963	17,830,000	3,375,000	23.3
1964	20,630,000	2,900,000	16.2
1965	23,755,000	3,125,000	15.1

Whenever the deviations of increments from their average are small enough to be unimportant, it is permissible to smooth out the irregularities by computing a line of least squares to represent the ideal relationship of gross revenue to time (see Figure 26–4). In the example at hand, the formula for this line is

$$GR = \$10,765,000 + (X \times \$3,167,900)$$

in which GR represents the gross revenue for a particular year and X is the number of years by which the particular year is removed from the year chosen as the base year (1961 in the present instance). By this forecasting method, the estimate of gross revenue for 1966 becomes $26,604,500 with

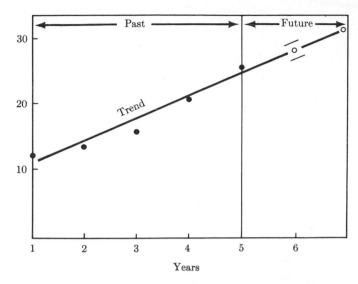

Fig. 26–4 Trend line for an irregular arithmetic progression. The parallel lines above and below the hollow circle indicate the range of probable error.

betting odds of 2 in 3 that the actual figure for the year will fall between $26,144,000 and $27,064,500 (plus or minus one standard deviation).

Example of an Irregular Geometric Progression. The first and fifth figures in the following table are the same as the corresponding figures of the preceding tables, but the three intermediate figures are different. It will be noted that neither the absolute amounts of the four increments nor the annual percentage increase is constant.

Year	Gross revenue	Annual increment	Per cent Increase
1961	$11,455,000		
1962	13,860,000	$2,405,000	21.0
1963	16,494,000	2,634,000	19.0
1964	19,940,000	3,446,000	20.9
1965	23,755,000	3,915,000	19.2

However, the *average* annual percentage increase in the increments is 19.9 per cent, and the maximum variation from this rate of growth is very slight. If such a small variation in the rate of growth can be held to be unimportant, the progression may be classified as irregularly geometric, which means that the data must be plotted on semilogarithmic paper (see Figure 26–5).

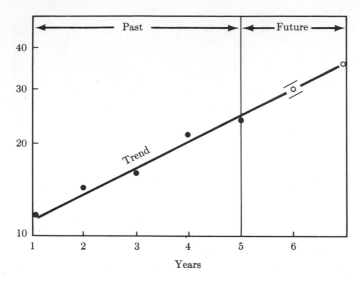

Fig. 26–5 Trend line for an irregular geometric progression. The parallel lines above and below the hollow circle indicate the range of probable error.

The trend line shown in Figure 26–5 is fitted by the least-squares method to the logarithms of the annual gross revenue figures. The formula for this line is

$$\text{log of } GR = 3.05830 + (0.08015 \times X)$$

where GR represents the gross revenue (in millions of dollars) for a particular year and X represents the number of years by which the particular year is removed from the base year (which in this case is 1963). By this formula $28,780,500 becomes the most likely gross revenue for the year 1966, with a likely variation of less than $102,600.

Forecasting by the Correlation Method

Sometimes the magnitude of an item to be forecast depends upon the magnitude of some other factor which either regularly precedes the item to be forecast or which is capable of being estimated in advance. For example, the gross revenue of a firm may be believed to depend upon the gross national product of the economy. If so, the item to be forecast (the gross revenue of the firm) is said to be the "dependent" variable, and the controlling item (the gross national product of the economy) is said to be the "independent" variable.

The first step in forecasting by this method calls for plotting past data of the independent and dependent variables for the purpose of determining whether or not a relationship actually exists. As an example, Figure 26–6 plots the gross revenue of the National Dairy Products Company during the period 1952 to 1962 against the gross national product for the respective years. The fact that the plotted points fall in an approximate line rising to the right suggests that the gross revenue of this company is imperfectly related to the gross national product of the economy. The relationship is best expressed by the line of regression shown in the figure. The formula for this line is

$$GR = 44 \times (X - \$61,000,000)$$

in which GR is the gross revenue for the year in which X is the gross national product.

It will be noted that the 11 points plotted in Figure 26–6 do not fall exactly upon the regression line of the chart but, rather, are scattered above and below the line. This suggests that the line is not a perfect representation of the discovered relationship. The standard deviation of these variations is $46,100,000.

The basic idea of forecasting by correlation is that the *most likely* value of the dependent variable in the future is indicated by the regression line. For example, if the gross national product of 1963 is expected to be $585 billion (as it was estimated in 1962 that it would be and as it later turned out to be), then the best estimate of National Dairy Products' gross revenue for 1963 would be $1,951,000,000 with a possible error of $46,100,000.

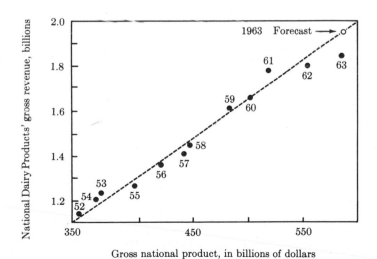

Fig. 26–6   A forecast of 1963 made by the correlation method.

The gross revenue of National Dairy Products in 1963 was $1,839 million. This is $158 million short of the amount estimated above. The error in the estimate is three times the index of probable error. Thus, in addition to illustrating the method of forecasting by correlation, the example emphasizes the possibility of an occasional error greater than the standard deviation.

Completing the Income Statement

Gross revenue having been estimated by one of the two available methods, the next step is to fill in the other items reported on income statements. This is usually accomplished by means of dependable ratios derived from past income statements. For example, the operating costs of National Dairy Products during the period 1952 to 1962 varied from 91.7 to 92.6 per cent of the company's gross revenue, with the lower ratio characteristic of the earlier years and the higher ratio characteristic of the later years. One might therefore decide that 92.2 per cent was a reasonable ratio to apply to the gross revenue figure forecast for 1963.

If the gross revenue of this company in 1963 is estimated by extending the line of least squares fitted to the gross revenue of the company during the preceding eleven years, if operating costs are estimated by the 92.2 per cent operation ratio, if prior claims to operating revenue other than income taxes are estimated to be the same in 1963 as they were in 1962, and if 1963 income taxes are estimated to be 52 per cent of estimated taxable income— then a projected income statement would be as follows:

	Estimated	Actual
Gross revenue	$1,876,000,000	$1,839,000,000
Operating costs	1,729,000,000	1,693,000,000
Operating income	$ 147,000,000	$ 146,000,000
Interest and depreciation	40,000,000	41,000,000
Taxable income	$ 107,000,000	$ 105,000,000
Income taxes	56,400,000	56,000,000
Residual earnings	$ 50,600,000	$ 49,000,000

Estimated earnings per share on the basis of this forecast would be $3.51, as compared with actual earnings per share of $3.40. It is interesting to note that in early 1963 a prominent forecasting agency was predicting 1963 earnings at $3.65 per share.

A Short-cut Method of Forecasting

It is now common practice for companies to make quarterly announcements of sales revenue and earnings per share. Financial writers and security analysts use these announcements as a basis for short-term forecasts of annual earnings per share. In doing this they unconsciously rely upon the dependability of the ratio of earnings available to common stock equity to gross revenue. Their methods and their logic will be made clearer by an illustration.

Suppose that earnings per share of a company during the preceding year were:

First quarter	$0.79
Second quarter	0.88
Third quarter	0.80
Fourth quarter	1.17
Total for year	$3.64

In early April of the current year the company announces first-quarter earnings of $0.88, up 11.6 per cent from first-quarter earnings of the previous year. If this percentage improvement persists for the remainder of the current year, annual earnings will be $4.05. This figure becomes the April forecast for the current year.

Then in July the company reports second-quarter earnings of $1.02, up 15.3 per cent from second-quarter earnings of the preceding year. The analyst reasons that if third- and fourth-quarter earnings show a similar improvement and are added to the first- and second-quarter earnings already announced, annual earnings should be $4.17. This becomes the July forecast.

In October third-quarter earnings are reported to be $0.94, up 18.4 per cent from third-quarter earnings of the previous year. Earnings during the first three quarters of the current year have totaled $2.84. If fourth-quarter earnings also increase by 18.4 per cent, annual earnings for the current year will be $4.23. This is the October forecast. Recapitulating the forecast, we have the following:

April forecast	$4.05
July forecast	4.17
October forecast	4.23

The above figures are not hypothetical. Actual earnings for the year turned out be $4.11. The error in the October forecast was due to the fact that the 18.4 per cent increase characteristic of the third period was not characteristic also of the fourth period. Actual earnings in the fourth period were $1.27, an increase of only 8.2 per cent over the fourth quarter of the previous year.

27 stock price theories

The market price of an issue at a given moment is the result of the volume of buy and sell orders that have been placed with brokers for execution. However, an explanation of the process by which a given volume of orders results in a particular price is not an explanation of the level of stock prices. To really understand prices, one must know something about the factors that induced traders to create the volume of orders executed by brokers.

The solution to the price riddle will be found in the answer to the question: What causes persons to decide to place buy or sell orders with brokers for execution? One school of thought answers: Prospective dividends. Another says: Forecasted earnings per share. A third suggests: Both earnings per share and dividends. Still another offers an answer based upon a supply and demand analysis. The present chapter will describe the four schools of thought without indicating a preference.

The Present Value Theory

The present value theory holds that the investment worth of a share of stock is the sum of the dividends which it is expected to pay, discounted at an appropriate yield rate. To determine the investment worth of a stock in this way, it is necessary to complete two steps: (1) estimating future dividend payments, and (2) determining and applying the appropriate discount rate. The discount rate to be applied is the minimum rate which an individual investor expects to obtain on his commitments.

Assuming that an investor is satisfied with an annual return of 4 per cent and that he expects a particular company to pay a dividend of $2 a share in perpetuity, he would value the stock at $50 ($2 ÷ 0.04). If the stock is selling on the market at a price below $50, he would be inclined to purchase, provided that he has funds for investment and that no other issue offers a better bargain. If the price on the market is above $50, he would refuse to purchase and, if he already possesses the issue, would be inclined to sell. Investors' orders to brokers to buy or to sell stocks are supposed to originate from thinking of this type.

If all investors are assumed to be in agreement regarding the stream of future dividends and the appropriate discount rate, the resulting flow of orders would be such as to confine fluctuations of prices to a range approximating investment worth. In this event, the market price of the issue would change only if and when investors' expectations of future dividend payments changed or when their notions of what constitutes an appropriate discount rate altered.[1]

Some critics argue that investors cannot and do not estimate the stream of future dividends in the manner required by the theory. Admittedly this is true if one means *accurately* estimating future dividends. But the theory does not require estimations to be accurate; it only requires investors to have expectations, accurate or otherwise, and to base their concepts of investment worth upon these expectations. The object of the theory is to explain how investors behave in the market, not how they should behave. The theory simply says that investors act on the basis of dividend expectations.

A question may be raised about what happens to market prices if investor expectations differ radically. For example, suppose that one group anticipates future dividends to be $2 indefinitely and that another group expects them to be $1.75 indefinitely. Assuming that both groups agree on 4 per cent as an appropriate discount rate, the first group would value the stock at $50 and the second group at $43.75. If so, the market price of the issue would vacillate back and forth between the two values until the ownership of all the shares was concentrated in the first group. But this is nothing unusual. The ownership of shares is constantly passing from those with conservative valuations to those with liberal valuations.

It is not necessary for an investor to assume that a given dividend will be maintained unchanged throughout the future. The theory is adaptable to changing dividends. To illustrate, assume that an investor has the following dividend expectations (a 4 per cent discount rate is assumed):

Dividend expectation	Present value
$1.80 was paid this year	$ 0.000
$2.00 will be paid next year	1.923
$2.20 will be paid two years hence	2.034
$2.50 will be paid three years hence	2.222
$2.90 will be paid four years hence	2.479
$3.40 will be paid annually after that	67.176
Total present value of these payments	$75.835

Five years hence the stock should have a market value of $85 (the present value *then* of a $3.40 dividend to be paid in perpetuity). If the investor can

---

[1] If the majority of investors are inclined to sell an issue at a price of 51 or higher and to buy it at a price of 48 or lower, supply and demand would tend to limit speculative fluctuations to the 48 to 51 range.

acquire the stock now at a price of $75.875, if he collects dividends as expected, and if after five years he sells the stock at a price of $85, he will then have earned a return of exactly 4 per cent on his original commitment.[2]

Some advocates of the present value theory do not believe that investors evaluate stocks with the mathematical precision suggested but that they arrive at somewhat identical evaluations by a much looser application of the principles. Thus, an investor may expect a company to pay a minimum annual dividend of $2 that will increase gradually over the next four or five years to the neighborhood of $3.40. The $2 minimum justifies a valuation of $50. Five years from now the stock should be worth $85 if it is then paying $3.40. Without engaging in any intricate computations the investor may conclude that the stock is a good purchase if he can get it at a price around $70 or $75. This is a loose application of the principle of present value. It will be noted that the investment worth of the issue *was based* upon dividend expectations even though the value was not determined with mathematical precision.

It is much easier to explain and illustrate a rigid application of the principle of present value. It is possible that the rigid theories advocated by textbook writers are applied loosely in practice. In any case, exponents of the theory do not hold that the value of a stock is a mathematical function of its stream of future dividends, but only that concepts of investment worth are based upon dividend expectations.[3]

The Multiple-of-earnings Theory

The multiple-of-earnings theory bases investment worth upon earnings per share rather than upon prospective dividend payments. The relationship of investment worth to earnings is expressed by the formula

$$I = E \times M$$

in which I is investment worth being sought, E is normal current earnings

---

[2] In this example expectations regarding dividends have them increasing for five years and then stabilizing. A more realistic expectation would be to have them increasing at a very rapid rate for a period of definite length and then increasing at an average rate. W. Scott Bauman has calculated a series of present value tables for every possible rate of growth and for different periods varying from two to thirty years. See *Estimating the Present Values of Common Stocks,* by W. Scott Bauman, Ann Arbor, Mich.: University of Michigan Bureau of Business Research, 1963.

[3] The reader who desires to pursue the logic of the present value theory further is referred to *Theory of Investment Value,* by John B. Williams, Cambridge, Mass.: Harvard University Press, 1938.

per share, and M is the multiplier considered the most appropriate for the situation. The first step in applying the theory is to determine the values of E and M.

Normal Current Earnings. The E in the formula represents normal current earnings and may be ascertained by fitting a line of least squares to reported earnings per share for a period of years. Seven is a convenient number of years to use for this purpose. The value of E to be used in the formula is then the value of the trend line in the last year of the series.

Seven years of reported earnings per share of a well-known company are given in the accompanying table. A line of least squares has been fitted to the logarithms of the earnings, and the trend value for each year is shown. Normal current earnings in 1962 are $3.297. Normal earnings for future years are ascertainable by extending the trend line.

Year	Earnings per share	
	Reported	Normal
1956	$2.04	$2.056
1957	2.27	2.224
1958	2.38	2.407
1959	2.51	2.604
1960	2.92	2.817
1961	3.14	3.047
1962	3.20	3.297

Choosing an Appropriate Multiplier. The multiplier appropriate for use in a specific application of the $E \times M$ formula depends upon the annual rate of growth characteristic of earnings. This growth rate is revealed by the slope of the trend line fitted to the earnings data. In the illustrative case above, the annual rate of growth of normal earnings is 8.9 per cent.

An analyst chooses the multiplier appropriate to a given rate of growth by reference to his concept of a basic multiplier. A basic multiplier is the multiplier appropriate to a group of stocks which an analyst uses as a base for comparison. For this purpose he may use stocks in general, or stocks of companies whose earnings are not expected to increase or decrease in the immediate future, or shares of the companies used to compute the Dow-Jones industrial averages. Presumably he has chosen a multiplier appropriate for his base group. Basic multipliers suggested by three well-known analysts are given here.

Suggested multiplier	Applicable to
0.50 ÷ current yield on AAA bonds	Stocks in general
15.3	Current normal earnings of stocks of type used to compute Dow-Jones industrial averages
8.5	Stocks of companies whose earnings are not expected to increase or decrease in the foreseeable future

In addition to possessing a concept of a basic multiplier, an analyst must have a means of converting his basic multiplier into one appropriate for a given growth rate. For example, it is suggested that the 8.5 basic multiplier above be converted to a specific multiplier by adding 1 to the 8.5 for each $\frac{1}{2}$ per cent growth potential. Thus a proper multiplier for a stock with an annual growth potential of 3 per cent would be 14.5, that is, $8.5 + (2 \times 3)$. By the same formula, a proper multiplier for a company with an 8.9 per cent growth potential (the illustrative case) would be 26.3, that is, $8.5 + (2 \times 8.9)$.

Another writer suggests that a multiplier of 15 be applied to earnings having an annual rate of growth of 3.5 per cent, that a multiplier of 41.5 be applied to earnings having an annual rate of growth of 20 per cent or higher, and that multipliers for rates of growth between the two extremes be determined by interpolation. Such interpolation would give a scale of multipliers similar to those in the following table.

When the annual rate of growth is	Apply a multiplier of
4.0%	15.8
5.0	17.4
6.0	19.0
7.0	20.6
8.0	22.2
9.0	23.8
10.0	25.4
12.0	28.6
14.0	31.8
16.0	35.0
18.0	38.2
20.0	41.5

On the basis of these figures, a proper multiplier for the hypothetical company with an annual growth rate of 8.9 per cent would be 23.64.

Computation of Investment Worth.   Once an analyst has determined normal current earnings per share for a company and has chosen an appropriate multiplier, he has only to substitute the values in the $E \times M$ formula to arrive at an estimate of investment worth. The investment worth of the stock used in the illustrative case given earlier would be $86.75 by the method using a basic multiplier of 8.5 and $78 by the method using the above table of multipliers.

Some analysts prefer to let the *E* of the formula represent average earnings of a future period and the *M* the multiplier applicable to future earnings. In this event it is necessary to convert one's scale of current multipliers into a scale of future multipliers, a not too difficult step. For example, if 15.8 is the multiplier appropriate for earnings having an annual growth potential of 4 per cent, then 13.5 is the multiplier appropriate for the *average* earnings of the company over the next seven years. Both multipliers give exactly the same results. If current earnings per share are $1 and the annual rate of growth is 4 per cent, average earnings of the next seven years will be $1.17. One dollar multiplied by 15.8 (the current multiplier) is $15.80, and $1.17 multiplied by 13.5 (the future multiplier) is $15.79. In fact, the two multipliers must give the same result, for a table of current multipliers is converted into a table of future multipliers by finding the figures that do give the same result.

Dividends and Earnings per Share[4]

The present value theorist maintains that an investor's concept of investment worth stems from expectations regarding the stream of future dividends. The multiple-of-earnings theorist has investors ignoring dividends and concentrating upon estimated earnings per share during the next five to ten years. Both theories contain an element of truth. We all know someone who purchased stocks for the purpose of receiving dividends; and we all know someone who purchased stocks that pay no dividends or very small ones. These observations have given rise to a third theory—one that stresses both dividends and earnings per share.

Advocates of this third theory divide stocks into three broad categories: (1) growth issues, (2) below-average issues, and (3) a middle group of issues. They define a growth issue as stock of a dynamic company that is expected to experience an unusual earnings growth. Such a stock, they say, is entitled to a high multiplier. The investment worth of growth stocks is decided on the basis of earnings prospects, with little or no regard to dividend yields.

Below-average issues are those whose book values exceed their values based upon earnings. The middle group includes shares whose value based upon earnings exceeds their book value but whose growth potential is not

[4] For a more detailed exposition of this theory, see Benjamin Graham et al., *Security Analysis,* 4th ed., McGraw-Hill Book Company, New York, 1962, chap. 38.

sufficient to classify them as growth issues. The investment worth of below-average and middle-group stocks is determined by the relationship expressed in the following formula:

$$I = M\left(D + \frac{E}{3}\right)$$

In this formula, I is the investment worth being sought, M is the multiplier determined in the manner explained earlier, D is the current dividend payment, and E is the normal current earnings per share as previously defined.

The formula is based upon an assumption that a below-average company *should* pay out two thirds of its earnings as dividends. If the company does this, the right-hand side of the equation becomes $M \times E$, since D is equal to two thirds of E. To make this clearer, assume that 11 is a proper multiplier for an issue that has earnings of $6 and that pays a dividend of $4. Thus its investment worth by the formula would be $66, that is,

$$11 \times [\$4 + (\$6 \div 3)]$$

This is the same as eleven times its earnings per share.

If the company pays out more than two thirds of its earnings as dividends, its investment worth is enhanced by the formula. For example, if it pays a dividend of $5, its investment worth according to the formula becomes $77, that is,

$$11 \times [\$5 + (\$6 \div 3)]$$

This value is the same as though its earnings had been multiplied by 15.6 instead of 11. The general idea is that a company with poor growth prospects should pay out more of its earnings to stockholders as dividends and that when it does so stockholders will value the issue more highly.

If the company pays out less than two thirds of its earnings as dividends, its investment worth deteriorates. For example, if a company with earnings of $6 pays a dividend of only $2, its investment worth according to the formula becomes $44, that is,

$$11 \times [\$2 + (\$6 \div 3)]$$

This value is the same as though earnings had been multiplied by 7.3. The suggestion is that investors, feeling that they will never receive a return on the major portion of earnings withheld for reinvestment in the company, will base their value of the stock mostly on the dividend portion of earnings.

Advocates of the theory suggest not that the formula is actually used by investors to determine investment worth but that values computed by the formula will come close to approximating values unconsciously set by investors in similar circumstances.

The formula is applied to stocks in the middle group in the same manner as to the below-average group, except that E is divided by a number less than 3. This change is based upon a belief that retained earnings become more important as an issue becomes less like the below-average group and more like a growth stock. If so, then it becomes important for an analyst to determine the significance of a change in a payout ratio. For example, an increase in a payout ratio might herald a slowing down of the rate of growth in earnings, and a decrease in the payout ratio might indicate an acceleration in the rate of earnings growth.

Demand and Supply Analysis

Demand as used here means orders to buy shares *actually placed* with brokers for execution, and supply refers to orders to sell *actually placed* with brokers. As explained in Chapter 1, only orders placed with brokers play any part in determining market quotations. But as suggested at the beginning of this chapter, a real explanation of price levels must deal with the factors responsible for the volume of placed orders rather than with the mechanical process by which exchanges convert the orders into prices.

To explain these causal factors, it is convenient to divide shareholders into three categories on the basis of the environmental forces that most influence their market behavior. In the absence of formal terminology, the three classes will be called (1) "inert investors," (2) "price-conscious investors," and (3) "speculators." The terms will be used in a special sense to be defined later.

Outstanding shares of the stock of individual companies and of corporations in the aggregate may be divided into investment holdings and the floating supply. These terms are frequently employed by investment analysts and financial writers, but they are seldom defined with care. "Investment holdings" will be defined as shares held by inert and price-conscious investors and floating supply as shares held by the speculative group. Investment holdings plus the floating supply equal total outstanding shares. This axiomatic statement applies to shares of an individual company and to stocks in general.

The principal difference between the theory being outlined here and the three theories described earlier lies in the factors held responsible for the market behavior of participants. The earlier theories ascribe all market behavior to investor response to expected earnings and dividends, whereas the present analysis has each of the three classes responding to a different environmental stimulus. The reader will find the supply and demand analysis more useful in post-mortem analysis than in predicting events, but, because it contributes to a better understanding of market activity, it is included here as a theory of price determination.

Behavioral Characteristics of Inert Investors. The principal characteristic of persons classified as inert investors is their disinclination under ordinary circumstances to engage in market activity. Some members of the group have inherited their shares and have never given serious thought to selling them. Others are too absorbed in their respective professions to bother with stock market matters. Still others do nothing because they do not know what to do. Some are long-term investors convinced that selling one issue to buy another is unprofitable. The reasons for inaction are not important. What matters is that there are stockholders who are disinclined to engage in market trading and that their number is large enough to have importance. The significance lies in the fact that shares held by the group are not a part of the floating supply.

In 1948 one of the authors conducted a study to ascertain the relative size of investment holdings and the floating supply of some representative market leaders. The findings of this study suggested that *more than* 79.4 per cent of the outstanding shares of Bethlehem Steel were held by inert investors. Similar percentages for Sears, Roebuck and Eastman Kodak were 94.5 and 95.0, respectively, while that for Coca-Cola was 99.0. Admittedly the size of the floating supply varies with the issues and with time, but the exact size is not important. The important fact is that the floating supply of stocks is *always small by comparison* with the size of investment holdings. A market in which trading is limited to a very low percentage of total outstanding shares is said to be "thin."

In a sense thinness denotes stability of stock ownership, for if every stockholder were entirely satisfied to hold his shares, market activity would cease altogether. But stability of ownership is apt to be accompanied by unstable prices, for when a majority of investors refrain from trading, prices become increasingly sensitive to small changes in the floating supply. For example, in 1948 less than 1 per cent of the stockholders of Coca-Cola placed sell orders. Had another 1 per cent decided to sell, the market supply of the issue would have doubled and the downward pressure on prices would have been tremendous. Herein lies the significance of investment holdings— the larger its size, the smaller the size of the floating supply and the more sensitive prices become to small changes in market supply and demand. It is the relative size of investment holdings and floating supply that causes a minor change in the former to become a major change in the latter. Inert investors are responsible for this relationship.

Members of the inert investor group are not entirely absent from all buying and selling activity. In fact, if the size of investment holdings is large enough, the law of probability will assure a small but steady flow into the market of orders originating from within the group. When inert investors sell shares, however, they do so because they want the proceeds of the sales for some noninvestment purpose such as buying a new car or financing a trip around the world; and when they buy shares, they do so because they have funds for investment and it is their established policy to invest in common stocks for long-term holding. The point of theoretical importance is that the behavior of inert investors is motivated by factors other than prospective earnings and dividends. For this reason it is likely (1) that the number of buy versus sell orders normally originating within the group balances in any given period (or if not, the imbalance is not due to economic factors such as are generally believed to motivate investor activity), (2) that the volume of inert investor trading does not vary much with time, and (3) that the short-term effect of this constantly balanced trading upon the relative size of investment holdings and the floating supply is negligible.

There is no law that says, "Once an inert investor, always an inert investor." A single member of the group or a large number may defect at any moment. Obviously a mass exodus, if it occurred, would have a tremendous influence upon market supply and/or demand and might lead to a buyers' or sellers' panic. A sudden surge of inert investors into the market as a result of a declaration of war, an assassination of a political leader, or a great national disaster is a possible explanation of the sudden rise or fall of prices that occurs occasionally.

Behavioral Characteristics of Price-conscious Investors.   Price-conscious investors are persons who hold shares of stock as investors but who are aware that market prices do not always coincide with investment worth. This awareness is coupled with a willingness to part with a portion of their holdings when market prices grossly overvalue shares or to acquire additional shares when market prices grossly undervalue shares. This typical response to under- and overevaluation is the force that causes a portion of investment holdings to become a part of the floating supply, or vice versa.

As long as prices approximate investment worths, price-conscious investors are inclined to remain inert and their shares are a part of investment holdings. If prices drop below investment worth, the group tends to increase its purchasing and decrease its selling and the floating supply is diminished. If prices rise above investment worth, the group increases its selling and decreases its purchasing and the floating supply is augmented. The search of analysts for a normal price-earnings ratio is really a search for the price-conscious group's momentary standard of the proper relation of prices to earnings. Like all concepts, it is subject to variation.

Up to this point the analysis presented resembles the typical textbook treatment of normal price determination. Inert investors are playing the role of extramarginal suppliers. Price-conscious investors correspond to marginal buyers and sellers. The relative size of investment holdings and floating supply suggests that the supply curve is very elastic at prices far above investment worth. Since a small change in price is sufficient to cause price-conscious investors to shift from the buying to the selling side, and vice versa, demand and supply are very inelastic at prices near investment worths.

Behavioral Characteristics of Speculators.   Speculators are persons who buy shares because they expect prices to rise and who sell shares because they expect prices to decline or not to rise further. Their market behavior is the result of their expectations regarding price changes. It does not matter to them whether the price changes are justified by earnings and dividend prospects; it is sufficient that they expect changes to occur.

Speculators are the temporary owners of the floating supply. For this reason transactions between them do not affect the size of the floating supply. But a transaction between a speculator and a price-conscious investor does have an effect upon the size of the floating supply. Since speculators are not interested in becoming permanent owners of the floating supply, they purchase shares only when they anticipate selling them shortly at higher prices. This means that an increase in the size of the floating supply indicates speculative confidence that price-conscious investors will be repurchasing the shares at higher prices in the not too distant future.

For this reason speculators are constantly on the alert for information that forecasts the future behavior of investors. Knowing that investors are guided by earnings and dividend prospects, some speculators make a study of business fundamentals, not to determine investment worth but to anticipate investor thinking. Others seek similar information from tips on earnings about to be reported and pending dividend changes. Still others try to deduce investor behavior by noting the market activity of corporate officers and large stockholders who are believed to be acting now on facts that will be known to investors later.

Speculators are not adverse to profiting at the expense of other speculators. Thus many study the formations shown on bar charts and point-and-figure graphs for purposes of determining the technical position of the market. The market is technically weak if speculators have purchased more shares than they are going to be able to sell to investors at existing price levels, and the market is technically strong if the floating supply contains fewer shares than investors will be demanding later. The first speculator to discover the technical condition of the market can profit at the expense of another who is slower.

Speculators share profits and losses by transactions between themselves. The aggregate profit of the group depends upon their ability to dispose of their holdings to the price-conscious investor group at prices higher than the shares were acquired. Speculators buy when investors are uncertain about the future and sell when investors are again certain. Their success hinges upon their ability to guess how uncertainty will be resolved.

How Successive Price Levels Are Determined. The level of prices existing at any one moment is merely the average price at which the floating supply of stock is being augmented by sales of price-conscious investors to speculators, or is being diminished by sales of speculators to price-conscious investors, or is being maintained by sales between speculators.

Since the floating supply of stocks is owned by the speculative group, changes in its size can occur only with the approval of the group. This approval is granted or withheld on the basis of speculators' expectations regarding future prices. If speculators are willing to buy what investors are trying to sell, or vice versa, an exchange can take place without a change in prices. But if either group is reluctant to trade, the insistence of the one and the hesitancy of the other are modified by a change in prices. Each group views the existing price level in its own accustomed manner and determines what buy and sell orders it wishes to place with the broker. The flow of these orders into the market results in the next price level, which may be the same or different from the previous one.

Today's price is yesterday's price modified by the trading public's estimate of changes in conditions. Fundamental, seasonal, technical, and incidental forces are constantly influencing the thinking of persons and groups and leading them to place orders with brokers for execution. The fundamental forces arise out of business conditions and establish the trend of prices. The other forces modify this trend to produce temporary rallies and reactions. Analysis of corporate reports will reveal some of the forces at work, but the psychological response of traders to the forces is equally important.

28 the portfolio of a small investor

Wealthy persons have always invested a considerable portion of their funds in common stocks. Should a small investor do likewise? Conservative advisers usually answer in the negative and support their conclusions with one or more variations of the following arguments:

1. The portfolio of a small investor should be considered an emergency fund. Since there is no certainty that funds invested in common stocks can be recovered in full, they should be placed at interest in government bonds or in savings banks.
2. Brokerage commissions, odd-lot differentials, transfer taxes, mailing charges, and other overhead costs render trading in small lots expensive.
3. A small investor does not know how to select issues or how to time purchases and sales. The cost of expert advice is too high to be borne by the owner of a small portfolio. Furthermore a small portfolio cannot achieve a satisfactory degree of diversification.
4. Investment in common stocks is inherently risky and should be avoided by those who cannot afford to lose any portion of their meager savings.
5. The slightly higher yield that may be earned on a portfolio of common stocks is not great enough to warrant the added risks.

Events of the past do not support these arguments. Before attempting to refute them, however, it is necessary to come to some agreement as to how a "small" investor is to be defined. To some a small investor is a person with $1,000 to invest, others would put the sum at $5,000 or $10,000, while still others would set it at $25,000 or $50,000. In the discussion that follows a small investor will be considered to be one who might have as much as $3,000 available for immediate investment in common stocks *or* one who expects to accumulate savings at a rate of $600 a year. Thus the question at issue is: Should such a person place his savings in common stocks?

Analysis of Objections to a Small Portfolio

Common Stocks as an Emergency Fund. Securities listed on the larger exchanges can be liquidated quickly at their *market* price; but there is no assurance that this price at any given moment will be equal to the original cost of acquisition. Thus the argument advanced against using a portfolio of common stocks as an emergency fund is valid. However, this means not that small investors should avoid purchasing common stocks but that funds which might be needed in an emergency should not be so committed. Even then a portfolio of high-grade listed issues is not so deficient as an emergency fund as is generally assumed. Most banks are willing to make short-term renewable loans for amounts up to 50 or 60 per cent of the market value of well-known issues listed on leading stock exchanges. Still, small investors are probably well advised not to place emergency funds in common stock investments.

Overhead Costs of Small Stock Transactions. Many persons assume that brokerage fees, transfer taxes, and other charges add a sizable amount to the cost of acquiring shares in small quantities. First the odd-lot differentials and brokerage fees must be added to the cost of acquisition. Then the odd-lot differentials, brokerage fees, and transfer taxes must be deducted from the proceeds of a sale. All these items considered together reduce the liquidation value of a small commitment to something less than its cost of acquisition at the moment of purchase. That is, a small investor has a loss to recoup right from the start. It must be borne in mind that a large investor has a similar loss to recoup, but an impression prevails that because a large investor deals in full lots his loss percentagewise is much less.

Just how large is this immediate loss that must be recovered by a rise in the market price? To illustrate, consider the total outlay of a small investor who orders his broker to purchase 10 shares of an issue currently quoted at $29\frac{7}{8}$. The amount of his outlay would be $307.45 made up of the following charges.

Cost of 10 shares at $29\frac{7}{8}$		$298.75
Add: Odd-lot differential	$1.25	
Brokerage fee	7.00	
Mailing charge	0.45	8.70
Total outlay		$307.45

The immediate realizable value of this commitment would be $289.96 computed thus:

Proceeds from sale of 10 shares at 29⅞		$298.75
Deduct: Odd-lot differential	$1.25	
Brokerage fee	7.00	
Transfer taxes	0.54	8.79
Realizable value		$289.96

Thus at the moment of purchase the realizable value of the shares is $17.49 less than their cost of acquisition, and to break even, the market price of the shares must appreciate 6.03 per cent.

Since it is generally known that overhead costs of market transactions do not increase proportionately as the amounts involved increase, it is believed that the rise in the market price required to recoup the overhead costs is materially greater for small than for large transactions. The tabulation below indicates the extent to which this is so. As will be noted, the small investor (as defined)' does not trade at a much greater disadvantage than the large investor.

Number of shares purchased at 29⅞	Rise of price required to recoup initial loss
10	$1.75
20	1.50
30 ⎱ 40 ⎰	1.25
50 ⎱ 60 ⎱ 70 ⎰ 80 ⎰	1.125
90	1.00
100	0.75

Diversification of a Small Portfolio.   The discussion in Chapter 19 suggested that an investor who does not know what to buy should spread his purchases over a number of issues and that an investor who does not know when to buy should make his purchases at different times. A small investor who can commit only $600 a year to stock purchasing has no timing problem, since he is forced by circumstances to employ time diversification. But the problem remains of deciding how many issues constitute minimal diversification.

Obviously a portfolio with $600 invested in a single issue is not diversified. When the second $600 is invested in a second issue, the portfolio is twice as diversified. An investment of a third $600 increases the degree of diversification but not by as much as the second did. So it goes—each addition increasing the diversification at a diminishing rate. Eventually a point is reached where the addition of still another issue advances the safety of the portfolio by an imperceptible degree. Thus there must be a point of minimum acceptable diversification, a point of optimum diversification, and a point of excessive diversification. The authors are inclined to believe that for a small investor 5 issues are minimal, 10 issues are adequate, 20 issues are optimum, and 30 issues are excessive. If so, an investor saving $600 a year can obtain minimal diversification in five years. However, he is not without some diversification before this. In the second year he is 50 per cent diversified, in the third year 33 per cent diversified, and so on.

If a small investor does not know which issues to select, it is suggested that he confine his purchases to public utilities and/or the issues used to compute the Dow-Jones average of industrial stock prices. Any reputable broker can aid a small investor to choose wisely from such a list of issues. While this approach is something less than scientific, it is not likely to lead to a loss in the long run, particularly if the purchases are scattered over a period of five to ten years.

Inherent Risks of Common Stock Investment.   The average small investor has an exaggerated notion of the amount of risk involved in owning common stock. A number of lay investors, all of whom had expressed a distrust of common stock investment, were asked to list the reasons for their views. The replies are summarized in these two statements:

> The market value of common stock is insecure; one can lose all of his savings in a short time as a result of a decline in values.

> There is no certainty of receiving dividends; one must invest without assurance that he will receive any dividends.

It will be noted that both objections relate to a lack of certainty —concerning the principal amount invested and the annual yield.

It would be well to point out that there are two types of security. The first stems from a contract; someone is legally obligated to do something. The second inheres in a situation and is known only from experience. For example, there is no law that requires an automobile engine to start when one turns the ignition that engages the starter. Nevertheless, when this act is performed, the engine usually starts. Although a driver lacks legal or contractual assurance that his engine will start, he possesses experimental confidence that it will do so. Common stocks lack the first type of security; they do not lack the second.

There is a third type of safety which common stocks have but which preferred stocks, corporate bonds, savings accounts, and government bonds do not have. This third type, of great importance to a small investor, is protection against a decrease in the value of the dollar, or, to put it more plainly, protection against inflation.

A person who saves $500 a year and places it at 4 per cent compound interest will have $6,243.20 at the end of ten years. But if a 25 per cent increase in the price level should occur during the period, all the compound interest received would be required merely to maintain the purchasing power of the original savings. If the price level should rise more than 25 per cent, a portion of the principal would also be required. Between 1940 and 1950 the price level rose 42 per cent; during the next decade it rose another 6 per cent; and during the twenty-year period 1945 to 1965 it increased 45 per cent. Who is to say that history will not repeat itself?

There is reason to believe and ample evidence to prove that when the purchasing power of the dollar declines the market value of common stocks rises *more* than enough to offset the loss of purchasing power. An example will make the reason for this tendency clear. Assume that the earnings of a particular corporation are predestined not to increase as a result of increased volume of sales or decreased cost of production. Assume that the price level rises 30 per cent. If stock prices move in conformity with the increase in earnings, it will be found that they rise faster than the assumed rate of increase in the cost of living. The following figures support this conclusion:

	Before the rise		After the 30% rise	
Gross revenue		$100,000		$130,000
(1,000 units @ $100)				
Production costs:				
Variable	$40,000		$52,000	
Fixed	20,000	60,000	20,000	72,000
Net profit:		$ 40,000		$ 58,000
Increase in net profit				45%
Increase in price level				30%

The more than proportional increase in net profits in this case is due to the existence of fixed expenses. If prices of stocks maintain a constant relationship to earnings, they too should advance faster than the price level.

One might ask: Who loses most from inflation? Those investors who are afraid of the inherent risk of common stocks and who to avoid this risk place their savings in bonds or in savings institutions.

Yield on a Small Stock Portfolio.   The short-run yield to be obtained from a small investment in common stocks is not impressive, but its cumulative effect over a period of time is important. To illustrate this truth, five test investment programs were worked out. In each case the investor was assumed not to know how to choose issues intelligently and to limit his periodic purchases to one public utility and four issues taken from the Dow-Jones industrial stocks. The issues chosen were:

American Tel. & Tel. (public utility)
Anaconda (extraction)
General Motors (manufacturing)
Sears, Roebuck (merchandising)
U.S. Steel (raw material processing)

The investor's first purchase was an investment of $600 in the first issue in the list. His second purchase was made in the second issue in the list, and so on. His sixth purchase was in the first issue, the seventh in the second issue, and so on. Each purchase involved a commitment of $600 plus the dividends received from the portfolio during the previous year.

Five tests were made. The first and second involved 10 annual purchases made at January high prices, followed by liquidation in January of the eleventh year. The first test covered the period 1937 to 1947, and the second test covered the period 1947 to 1957. The third and fourth tests involved similar programs started in January 1958 but interrupted by the 1962 decline of prices. One investor liquidated at the 1962 decline and the other hung on until January 1963. The fifth test was the short-run program of a veteran of the Korean Conflict. The young man was commissioned into the army just in time to be assigned to Korea at the outbreak of hostilities. Each six months he sent $500 home for his father to invest. The fifth test assumed that the father invested the funds in January and July of each year in accordance with the program described and that the veteran on his return liquidated the portfolio in July 1953 in order to continue his schooling. The results of the five programs are summarized here.

	Test 1	Test 2	Test 3	Test 4	Test 5
Cash committed	$5,994	$ 5,994	$2,975	$2,975	$2,999
Dividends reinvested	1,879	2,746	268	268	210
Cost of purchases	$7,873	$ 8,740	$3,244	$3,244	$3,209
Liquidation value	9,832	16,709	3,490	4,514	3,746
Capital gain	$1,959	$ 7,968	$ 246	$1,270	$ 537
Dividend income	2,336	3,523	249	423	301
Total increase	$4,295	$11,491	$ 545	$1,693	$ 837
Equivalent to an annual return of	9.9%	18.1%	4.9%	12.1%	13.2%

The movement of the market averages during each of the five test periods may be observed in Figure 28–1. Those inclined to ascribe the results attained to a happy choice of a time period might try to find any ten-year periods that would have given different results. Note that the yield on each of the test portfolios greatly exceeded the yield that could have been obtained by depositing the funds in a savings institution.

Conclusion.   Common stocks lack legal security as to principal and yield. For this reason many consider them to be an inappropriate medium of investment for the small investor. However, common stocks do possess *de facto* security of principal and yield and in addition give a high degree of protection against inflation. As a result, the small, uninformed investor can build a fundamentally sound program of long-run investment in common stocks if he religiously follows four rules.

1. He should buy only the shares of high-quality market leaders listed on the New York Stock Exchange.
2. He should diversify his portfolio by spreading his commitments over at least 5 (preferably 10) different companies, each in a different industry.
3. He should buy shares periodically so that some of his stocks will be purchased at low prices to average down the cost of those purchased at high prices.
4. His basic investment philosophy should be to buy and hold; he should sell only when convinced that a given issue is a poor investment.

Past experience indicates that a program based upon these principles will yield the small investor better than 10 per cent compounded annually.

The Importance of a Plan

Some readers might interpret the previous discussion to mean that the authors advocate purchasing stocks without careful analysis. This interpretation is not correct. The purpose is to establish confidence in common stocks

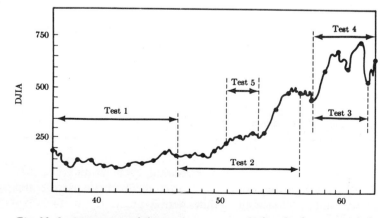

Fig. 28-1   Movement of the market averages during the five test periods.

as a medium of investment for small investors by pointing out that a purely mechanical program based on the four rules cited will do more for them than any program of committing funds to fixed income contracts (such as bonds, mortgages, savings accounts, and the like). If so, then the application of analytical techniques to the problem of selecting issues and timing purchases should cause small investors to do even better.

Earlier chapters have called attention to certain characteristics of the market prices of stocks. For example, Figure 19–1 suggests that the long-run trend of stock values is upward. It is possible to base an investment program on this fact alone. Such a program would require only a periodic purchase and retention of a relatively small number of shares of a diversified list of companies. There is reason to believe that such a program would be highly successful over a long period of time.

The reader cannot have failed to notice the cyclical swing of prices about the trend line of Figure 19–1. This cyclical swing offers an opportunity for a different type of investment program, one in which the investor buys at the low points and sells at the high points of the cycle. The difficulty lies in determining low and high points. As mentioned elsewhere, a strong psychological pressure exists to encourage an investor to enter and to leave the market at exactly the wrong time. Inability to resist this pressure has led to the invention of formula plans.

It is not the object here to argue for formula-plan investment. Rather, the existence of formula plans emphasizes the importance of having a plan and of adhering to it. Whatever the plan may be, it should be fundamentally sound; that is, its underlying principles should be based upon known characteristics of the market. But even the most soundly constructed plan is without value if an investor does not adhere to it. The long-term investor who shifts to cyclical trading and the cyclical trader who cannot resist the temptation to trade on the technical swings are both doomed to disappointment.

Security Analysis

A good investment program by itself is not enough. Individual issues must be picked for purchase. One may have devised a method of determining when to buy and when to sell, but it is still necessary to decide what to buy and what to sell. Selecting issues wisely calls for an analysis of security listings.

The first step in security analysis is to *collect facts*. The problem at this point is to know which facts are important. Obviously one can go on collecting facts about a company ad infinitum, but the point of diminishing returns is quickly reached. Most analysts agree that facts about the following are essential:

1. What is the nature of the company's business? (Is it a public utility, a mining company, a manufacturer, a department store?) What is the probable future demand for its products?
2. What is the financial plan of the company? (Is it trading on its equity, or is it financed entirely by common stock?)
3. What is the company's record of earnings per share?
4. What is the company's dividend record?
5. What are the high and low price-earnings ratios for the company's common stock for the past decade?
6. What is the current price of the company's stock, and how does it compare with past high and low quotations?

This list does not exhaust the important questions; it merely mentions a few which every analyst considers essential.

The collection and tabulation of this material imposes a task upon the lay investor. A number of organizations, however, sell services that provide such data. For example, the Securities Research Corporation of Boston issues a series of three-trend security charts; and F. W. Stephens, Newfoundland, New Jersey, publishes *Graphic Stocks* monthly (see Figure 28–2). The

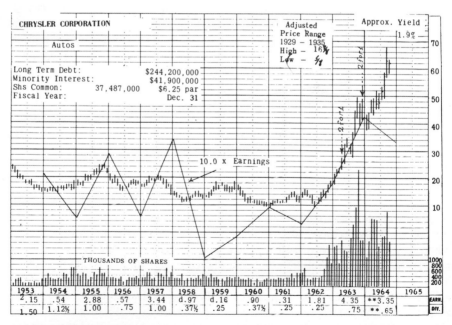

Fig. 28–2 Illustration of data published in *Graphic Stocks*. (*Chart reproduced by permission of F. W. Stephens, Newfoundland, N.J.*)

Financial World, New York, publishes *Factographs,* which presents the essential data in convenient tabular form.

The second step in the analytical program is to *interpret the facts.* For example, from the list of annual high and low price-earnings ratios the analyst may decide that the stock of a particular company tends to sell at seven to nine times earnings. From the data derived from the first three questions, he probably arrives at a reasonable estimate of probable future earnings. Multiplying this reasonable earnings estimate by the typical price-earnings ratio gives the probable future market value of the issue. By comparing this value with the current quotation and with past quotations, the analyst may decide that the stock at its current price is grossly undervalued or overvalued.

Unfortunately there is a tendency for many investors to act as if the mere collection of numerous statistical data means security analysis. The investor must bear in mind that all the facts and figures he collects must ultimately be resolved to one of the following three words: buy, sell, or hold. This reduction of a number of data to one word is accomplished by the *application of investment principles.*

To some extent the principles to be applied depend upon the theory of stock prices held by the investor. One investor, for example, may believe that dividends are the most important factor to be considered; another may emphasize estimated earnings; still a third may rely upon book value. By the use of one theory or another, each investor must convert the statistical data he has assembled into a decision to buy, to sell, or to hold.

The Theory of Investment Analysis

The person who purchases a hundred shares of an issue chosen at random from all listed stocks takes a chance that the market value of his issue will increase, remain constant, or decrease. Expert mathematicians could no doubt compute the probability of picking winners by such a method, in which case the odds could be stated as 1 to 2, or 1 to 10, or whatever they might be.

If it is true that analysis improves one's ability to pick winners and avoid losers, then it would be expected that the record of professional investment counselors would prove better than the average of the market. Yet Alfred Cowles, after examining 7,500 recommendations made by 16 financial services during the 1930s, discovered that the performance of the recommended issues was poorer than that of the market. A decade later the Securities and Exchange Commission found that during the week preceding the break which occurred on September 3, 1946, and which was followed by a thirty-three-month bear market, 260 out of 489 investment advisors were bullish, 209 were uncertain, and only 20 were bearish. Figure 20–6 gives a chart comparing the performance of nine recommended issues with the performance of the Dow-Jones averages before and after the date of recommendation (January 1963). The chart shows that the recommended issues did poorer than the market.

The discussion here is not intended to disparage analysis. Certainly an investor should not buy stocks without investigation, but he should bear in mind the limitations upon which it is based. It is highly probable that a sound, long-run, intelligent program contributes more to eventual success than an ability to pick the issues which at the moment appear to offer the best prospects for a rise—a rise that often proves temporary.

Earnings Basic to Value. If a small investor is going to engage in security analysis, he must keep one principle foremost in his thinking and that is that market value, in the long run, depends upon earnings. Some investors put the value of assets first and earning power second. This may be the true relationship for a creditor of a corporation who has the right to foreclose a mortgage and wants to be sure that his principal is safe when earnings are no longer adequate to pay charges. In the case of stock, however, the order of importance must be reversed and earning power put ahead of the value of the assets. The return to stockholders is contingent on net earnings per share. If earnings decline greatly, the value of the assets will so diminish that bond issues will absorb them all in case of bankruptcy. Though the stockholder does consider the liquidating value of the assets in case of failure, the primary purpose of his analysis is to avoid buying issues of businesses that are likely to fail.

Although the ratio of market value to earnings is not the same for all companies or even constant for one company, nevertheless the trend of prices is to a high degree dependent upon the trend of earnings. This is true of stocks individually and of the market as a whole.

The stock market's valuation of the shares of a company takes into consideration the past, the present, and as far as possible the future. The student of stock values must use present and past earning records, but the future prospects of a company are of greater importance. If the inventories of a company are accumulating and the price of its product is becoming uncertain, the price of its shares will discount the expected reduction in income regardless of present high earnings.

Future Demand. There can be no prosperity in any industry unless there is to be a large demand for its product. In times of depression the most essential test for an investor to apply to an industry is his estimation of the probable future demand for its goods. An industry that has been considerably weakened during a depression will recover rapidly only if demand for its products is forthcoming. The ability to estimate future demand is therefore one of the essentials in judging future prospects.

Overcapacity. During the prosperity phase of the cycle some industries overbuild, usually those which are enjoying the greatest profits. The cement industry offers a recent example of tremendous productive capacity built up to meet a temporary demand during a single period of profitability. When this temporary demand was satisfied, the huge productive capacity remained to plague the industry. As revenue declined, costs increased, profits decreased, and prices of cement company stocks dropped to one third of their previous highs. The small investor must consider the effect of expansion of productive capacity on future earnings, especially in those industries where companies produce similar products.

Investment in New Industries

Almost every small investor has been urged by a stock salesman to invest money in the shares of a new company. The salesman argues that great profits are probable and that the only way to share them is to "get in on the ground floor." New industries are usually based on an invention, a patented process, or a secret formula that may or may not prove successful. Even if the new company is successful, it may take a long time to develop a market for the new product. It took the automobile business many years to become a great industry, and of the hundreds of companies that went into the business, only a few survived to make large profits for their owners. On the other hand, some of the companies organized to exploit recent photographic inventions prospered quickly.

Nevertheless it is not the province of the small, conservative investor to take part in the financing of new industries. He can find plenty of opportunities among well-seasoned companies. On the other hand, the progress of the economy depends upon risk taking. But the financing of this progress is the function of the man of wealth, who can lose a million in an honest venture and still have enough money left to try again and again.

Investment in Growth Stocks

The small investor is often advised to build a portfolio of growth stocks. This is excellent advice if it can be followed, but to avoid pitfalls, it is necessary to know something about the economics of growth.

The demand for the products of an industry is of two types: (1) new demand, i.e., the demand of those who have never used the product before, and (2) replacement demand. When a new industry first comes into being, its capacity to produce is likely to be inadequate to supply the immediate demand for its products. At such time expansion leads to lower costs, larger volume, and greater net earnings. This rapid increase in earnings during the growth period provides a basis for breathtaking advances in the market value of its shares. Then, as some of the products first marketed wear out, replacement needs further augment demand and cause profits to mount and stock prices to soar.

When the demand of the first users reaches the saturation point, the expanded industries have only to supply replacement demand. Since it takes less productive capacity to supply replacements than it does to supply both replacements and new demand, a period of stiff competition follows, during which many of the weaker companies fall by the wayside. The travel trailer industry furnishes an excellent example. During the years 1933 to 1937 this industry was in its growth period, but this period proved to be short. Managers of the industry mistook the purchases of those who had never owned a trailer for a permanent, recurring demand and expanded their plants accordingly. The sudden exhaustion of new demand in 1937 before replacement demand could take up the slack left the industry in a precarious earning position.

Companies that survive the "killing-off" period become matured industries. By this time their production is adjusted to replacement needs plus whatever new demand may be created by increases in the population. Over a period of years their earnings become stable or else increase slowly as new techniques lower their costs of production. Sometimes, after a company has reached the matured status, it enters a new growth period owing to the discovery of a new product or marketing method or to the finding of a new use for an old product. Thus in picking growth industries an investor must differentiate between age in years and maturity with reference to markets.

Following the period of maturity comes the period of decadence, during which the demand of the public for the product actually declines. The railroad industry supplies an excellent example of a decadent industry. It is not always easy, however, to recognize the beginning of a period of decadence, since the beginning is likely to coincide with a cyclical decline in business activity. For example, was the decline in automobile production which came after 1929 a cyclical decline—or did it herald the beginning of a period of decadence? The fact that automobile production in 1937 failed to equal the pre-Depression peak would suggest the latter. But the growth in automobile production that has taken place since World War II contradicts this suggestion. It is also possible for an industry as a whole to enter a period of decadence and yet for some one company by strenuous efforts to stave off decadence by obtaining more than its proportionate share of the declining aggregate demand.

The small investor inclined toward accumulation of growth stocks is referred to the discussion of growth stock theory in Chapter 19, where some of the risks involved are described in greater detail.

Low-priced Stocks

Some small investors believe it to be good policy to accumulate a well-diversified holding in a large number of issues selling at prices below $10. If a stock acquired at $6 rises to $7, the investor realizes a profit of 16 per cent less expenses, whereas a stock selling at $60 would have to rise 10 points to net the same percentage gain. A rise of 1 point may occur in one or two days, but a rise of 10 points ordinarily requires a much longer time. Small investors are also advised to accumulate "bargain" stocks, meaning shares with lower than average price-earnings ratios.

When the public is not interested in the market, such speculative activity as exists is likely to be concentrated in market leaders. As a consequence, the stocks of the leading corporations will sell at higher price-earnings ratios than will those of the less well-known companies. However, when corporate earnings increase and interest in the market revives, the prices of all issues rise but differences in their price-earnings ratios diminish as activity increases.

On the assumption that the rate of increase in earnings of two companies is the same, that issue which sells at the lower price-earnings ratio in dull times can be expected to show the greater market appreciation in times of great activity. This being so, the wisest policy would seem to be that of accumulating shares with low price-earnings ratios when market prices lack a definite trend. While this theory can be demonstrated to be true of groups of stocks, it is not always true of specific issues.

The likelihood and probable extent of an increase in earnings are factors that must be considered along with low price-earnings ratios. To illustrate, consider the case of two issues both with earnings of $1 per share during a depression but the first selling at twenty times earnings and the second at ten times earnings. Assume that during the ensuing period of prosperity both companies experience an equal increase in earnings, say an increase of 200 per cent. If so, their price-earnings ratios will probably coincide, perhaps at 18. This means that the price of the first issue rises from $20 to $54, while that of the second issue rises from $10 to $54. This is a price rise of 170 per cent compared with a price rise of 440 per cent.

But the high price-earnings ratio of the first issue during the depression probably represents an expectation that its earnings will increase faster than those of the second issue when prosperity returns. Suppose that this expectation is justified and that earnings of the first issue increase 300 per cent, while those of the second issue increase only 100 per cent. In this event the price of the first issue might rise from $20 to $72 ($18 \times $4), while that of the second issue rises from $10 to $30 ($15 \times $2). Some companies are more likely to have a 300 per cent increase in earnings than others are to have a 100 per cent increase. This possibility must be taken into consideration in judging the advisability of accumulating stocks merely because they are selling at low price-earnings ratios.

Summary

The small investor who has neither the time nor the inclination to engage in extensive study is probably well advised to hold to a simple program of periodically acquiring shares of large, well-known companies listed on the New York Stock Exchange. His portfolio should be diversified according to industry, and he should buy stocks with the intention of holding them for long periods of time. In most cases he should select issues having a record of growth in earnings per share and of paying dividends regularly. He should avoid glamour issues and stocks selling at price-earnings ratios above 18. To whatever extent possible he should apply the principles of security analysis; but he need not worry if his knowledge in this respect is limited. If he consistently follows these rules, he can expect his portfolio to do as well as or slightly better than the average of the market—a performance that many professional security advisers would be happy to achieve.

29 manipulation and the securities exchange act

The great stock market crash of 1929 occurred more than thirty-six years ago, and the Securities Exchange Act has been law for more than three decades. Persons fifty years of age today (1966) were in elementary school in that fateful month of October 1929; they were high school students when President Roosevelt signed the regulatory act in 1934. Since most of the piratical practices of pre-1934 traders no longer exist, it is difficult for the contemporary generation to understand the necessity for many of the regulatory powers granted to the Securities and Exchange Commission. After all, a rule outlawing wash sales or touting cannot be understood by one who does not know what the terms mean. Since most investors of today were too young during the 1920s to know what was happening, their knowledge of the old trading practices must come to them through a study of history.

Accordingly, the approach of this chapter is historic. It reviews the nondesirable market practices of bygone days and explains how various powers enabled the SEC to cope with and outlaw many of them. The chapter describes manipulative methods and conspiratorial activities, which, although now obsolete, are nevertheless amazingly ingenious and not without a certain degree of romantic appeal.

The 1921 to 1932 Price Movement

A long, sustained rise of stock prices breeds the optimism necessary for a wild bull market. Just such a rise began in August 1921, when the Dow-Jones average of industrial stock prices stood at 63. During the next twenty-six months the average rose to 105 and then fell back to 85. Then, after a lull of several months, prices began a long, steady climb that did not end until they reached a peak of 381 on September 3, 1929. At the time this high level was accepted as heralding the arrival of a new era of permanent prosperity and abolishment of poverty.

During the later part of this exciting period public participation in stock trading became enormous. Persons from all walks of life, many of whom had never before owned a single share of stock, were actively accumulating shares on margin—as low as 20 per cent—and were pyramiding their holdings as prices rose. Confidence in the integrity of financial leaders and in the honesty of professional speculators and tipsters was unbounded. But this rush of the trusting public into the market brought about a fundamental change that was not immediately apparent. Prior to 1928 stock exchanges were considered to be the private hunting grounds of professional speculators. By encouraging widespread participation in market activity, the exchanges charged themselves with a public interest that made absolutely indefensible certain manipulative practices that might have been excusable had speculation been confined to professionals.

As explained, the Dow-Jones industrial average reached its high of 381.17 on September 3, 1929. There followed a decline that extended through forty-two trading days and carried the average down to a level of 305.85 on Wednesday, October 23. The next day prices dropped 40.44 points and recovered 26.86 points in a single trading session on an unprecedented volume of 12,895,000 shares. On Friday and Saturday, October 25 and 26, prices held steady on high volume; but on Monday, October 28, they dropped another 38.33 points on a volume of 9,213,000 shares. The public, frightened by such huge volumes and rapid price changes, panicked. On Tuesday, October 29, prices dropped another 48.31 points but rallied 27.64 points to close the day at 230.07. Volume was 16,410,000 shares.

Two weeks later, on November 13, the average reached its low for the year—198.69. Then a five-month rally carried the average up to 294.07 (reached on April 17, 1930), and investors regained a measure of confidence. Prosperity, it was said, was "just around the corner." But the corner was apparently far away, for a long, steady decline of prices started in April 1930 and did not end until July 8, 1932, when the Dow-Jones industrial average reached the unbelievable low of 41.20—one ninth of the 1929 high and 30 per cent lower than the low of 1921. Thus ended the new era.

Indictment of the Old Market

Earlier, in 1928 and 1929, when stock prices were skyrocketing, everyone knew about but was not concerned over certain manipulative practices that were taking place in the securities markets. Instead of condemning the deceptions, the general public welcomed tips so that they could participate in the activities and share in the illegitimate profits. When the market began its descent, exposure of the malpractices led to a popular clamor for their elimination. As a result of this reaction, the Securities Exchange Act was signed into law by President Roosevelt on June 6, 1934. The declared purpose of the law was to create a market of a type that would best serve investors although the "old guard" professed to see it only as an attempt to completely destroy the efficient operation of the market.

If a formal indictment were to be drawn up against the pre-1934 type market, it would probably contain the following specific charges.

1. Excessive speculation during a bull market greatly exaggerates the extent of demand, and so causes prices to soar far above sound values. This in turn renders the market vulnerable to attack by sellers and magnifies the amplitude of price swings. The excessive speculation is made possible by low margin requirements, which also cause an undue quantity of bank credit to become absorbed in the speculative market at the expense and to the detriment of legitimate business.
2. In a bear market short selling is demoralizing and makes an already bad situation much worse.
3. Certain manipulative practices, formerly employed by pools and professional speculators and winked at by exchanges, are inconsistent with just and equitable principles of trade.

Margin trading is the subject of Chapter 14. The pros and cons of short selling are listed in Chapter 15. In those chapters the reader is given a complete explanation of how regulatory authorities now control the practices. The remaining portion of this chapter will describe the manipulative practices that are "inconsistent with just and equitable principles of trade."

The Securities and Exchange Commission

The act places the control of national securities exchanges in the hands of a Commission of five persons to be appointed by the President with the advice and consent of the Senate. It denies the use of the mails or any instrumentality of interstate trade to any broker, dealer, or exchange for the purpose of effecting a transaction in a security unless the exchange (1) is registered with the Commission or (2) has applied for registration and has been exempted by a decision of the Commission.

A stock exchange achieves registration by filing a registration statement with the Commission in which it agrees: (1) to enforce the regulations which the Commission may adopt and (2) to inform the Commission of any changes in its own rules. In addition, the exchange must provide the Commission with all the data which it may request, including among other things copies of its constitution, bylaws, and rules of procedure. These rules of procedure must include provisions for the expulsion, suspension, or disciplining of members for conduct inconsistent with just and equitable principles of trade.

The powers given the Commission are far-reaching. They extend not only to the exchanges but to the members of those exchanges, to the companies whose securities are listed thereon, to the officers of the listed companies, and finally to the customers who trade with brokers. Each regulatory power given the Commission is the direct outgrowth of an abuse that once existed. To the extent that the act has been successful, the abuse no longer exists and the powers of the Commission seem to be more extensive than is necessary under the circumstances. Only those who are able to recall the situation when the abuses existed are in a position to gauge the degree of wisdom employed in framing the act. In the exposition of the various powers of the Commission which is to follow, the authors first describe an abuse and then point out the procedure that the law takes to prevent a reoccurrence.

Manipulation Defined

The word "manipulation" is a sort of blanket term that covers many kinds of operations to be found in the market for commodities as well as in the stock market. Whenever a sudden rise or a sudden drop of prices occurs in any market, the term manipulation affords an easy if somewhat vague explanation. Specifically, however, manipulation may be defined as any activity by a person or group of persons designed to make the market price of a security behave in some manner in which it would not behave if left to adjust itself to uncontrolled or uninspired supply and demand. Manipulation may take place on the bear side as well as on the bull side. It always implies the use of special powers and ingenious methods in handling the market for the manipulated stock.

Conditions Favoring Manipulation

Manipulation of one sort or another exists in every market at all times. Some of it is helpful; some of it is harmful. At times it is confined to a relatively few issues, while at other times there may be artificial stimulation or depression in a broad list of stocks. However, there are certain circumstances that make manipulation possible. If these conditions do not exist, manipulative efforts will fail.

A Major Advance in Prices.   No one man or set of men has enough power to influence the price of the billions of shares and thousands of issues traded on the exchanges. The forces of supply and demand alone determine the trend of the values of these securities. For this reason no sensible manipulator ever goes against the trend for long. What he does during a bull market is to cooperate with public optimism by temporarily retarding and then exaggerating that enthusiasm to his own advantage.

A Major Decline in Prices.   The manipulator on the short side of the market takes advantage of the fear psychology of the public. He knows that rapid declines in prices frighten the public into selling and breaking the price further. Therefore, when fundamental factors favor a decline of prices, the manipulator initiates the downward movement and seeks to accelerate it by activities designed to scare investors.

Easy Credit.   Manipulators on the bull side must have large amounts of liquid funds at their command in order to buy and hold stock until the public can be brought into the market. Also, large amounts of funds must be available to the public so that when they come into the market they can purchase the holdings of the manipulators at high prices. Thus the manipulator for the rise finds it easier to act during times of easy credit. It must be said, however, that manipulation for a rise can reach great heights with dear money if the other factors are strong enough to overcome the check which dear money provides.

The bear manipulator prefers tight credit conditions. Speculators on the bull side and the general public find it difficult to carry stock on margin when money is dear. Therefore tight money, which checks buying and encourages selling, is desired by the bear operator.

A Large Floating Supply of Stock.   While a stock whose floating supply is small may be marked up easily, the process of accumulation and distribution is difficult. When there is but a small supply of stock, a relatively small demand advances the price quickly. When the pool tries to accumulate it, the price goes up and the stock costs the pool a relatively high price. Because the number of shares available is small, the stock must be distributed at a large margin above the buying price to make the manipulation worthwhile.

Stock is distributed under cover of activity, but when only a few shares are involved, each share must be turned over frequently. Again, a little selling by outsiders will cause wide fluctuations in the price. The unusually high price of the stock, the extreme turnover of the floating supply, and the rapid, wide fluctuations in the price will indicate distribution so clearly that brokers will not advise purchase and traders will be tempted to sell short and thus smash the pool.

On the other hand, when there is a large floating supply, accumulation will not put the price up rapidly, a large number of shares can be accumulated, a good profit will accrue with a relatively small markup, activity in the stock can be created, and the stock can be distributed with much less danger from the professionals and without loss of confidence by the public.

A Hidden Value.   The manipulator has much more difficulty in stirring the emotions of the public when all the essential factors in the case are out in the open and their value is a matter of common knowledge than when there is some mystery connected with the assets and earning power of the company. The hidden possibilities in oil in distant fields can be used to fire the imagination of the speculatively inclined. Again, a secret process or formula, by carefully handled fact and rumor, can be made to appear of extraordinary earning power and to provide a pool manager with a basis on which to build a pyramid of manipulated prices. A new invention upsets values and introduces conjectured factors. In a rising market the dreams of the promoters of the invention can be magnified into possibilities and then probabilities in the minds of the optimistic public by carefully managed publicity and statements of large potential earnings.

What has been said of the factor of mystery on the bull side of the market is equally true of the bear side. In a declining market, an injection of the unknown quickly scares the public into an avalanche of selling. Oil companies with large interests in tidewater wells have felt the effect of the "saltwater" scares again and again. Into such psychology the manipulator can gear his machinery and get results if he does not miscalculate.

On the whole, manipulation for a rise is more successful than for a decline. The public goes long on stock but seldom sells short. This favors the operator on the constructive side as against the manufacturer of artificially low prices on the bear side.

Technical Position of the Market.   When the market is technically strong—for example, when it is oversold—the operator for a rise finds the stage set to his purpose and, unless the fundamental condition of the market is too unfavorable, the shorts can be driven to cover, resulting in a rapid rise in prices of the stocks involved.

On the other hand, when the market is in a weak technical position, the operator for the decline can break the price by planned drives against stocks vulnerable because they have been overbought or because the support beneath them has been withdrawn. At such times numerous stop orders have been placed just below the market, and drives against selected stocks will uncover the stops and break the price for a number of points.

Manipulative Organizations

In the 1920s it was common practice for a group of men to band together in a pool for the purpose of manipulating the price of a particular company. If the object was to put the price up, the organization was known as a *bull* pool; if the object was to put the price down, it was known as a *bear* pool.

Sometimes the members of a pool were professional traders, but very frequently they were large stockholders, officers and directors, or prominent bankers. A temporary or a lasting organization would be formed, participants would agree to contribute cash or shares, and arrangements would be made for the division of profits and control. Usually safeguards were needed to prevent members from leaking the secrets of the pool to the public. It was customary to hire an experienced operator to direct the pool's buying and selling activities and to manage its public relations in accordance with a planned course of action.

A Blind Pool.   If the manager of a pool is given power to operate in the market without informing members of his operations, the organization is known as a "blind pool." In a blind pool each member contributes cash or shares and promises not to trade in the issue to be manipulated. He has nothing to say, he knows nothing of what is going on; but he has a right to share in the profits of the pool if it is successful.

Daniel Drew, after making $7 million from his corner in Erie stock, was invited by Gould and Fisk to join in a blind pool. As Clews puts it, "In plain terms, he was coolly requested to go into a blind pool in Erie, to deposit four millions of dollars, to shut his eyes and open his mouth, leaving the Erie sharpers to put taffy or candy into it, just as they pleased." When Drew discovered that "he was to be one of the puppets that should dance to the music of Gould and Fisk and let them pull the wool over his eyes," he withdrew from the pool at a cost to him of $1 million.[1]

A Sucker Pool.   Sometimes in the old days owners of large blocks of stock, foreseeing financial difficulties, would form a pool for the purpose of unloading their shares on unsuspecting investors at inflated prices before disaster struck. In such cases they would hire a manager and turn their stock holdings over to him for disposal. Frequently the manager would form a pool with "regular" and "associate" members. The regular members were the stockholders who hired him to dispose of their shares. The associate members would be brokers "from the sticks" who had never had any experience with pools but who had heard a great deal about their profit possibilities. The game was to bring the associate members to New York to meet the members of the pool and to be fed propaganda about the wonders of the company, the abilities of its officers, and the big profits which the members of the pool were certain to receive. The difference between regular and associate members was not one of the matters explained to them.

The associate members, flattered by the attention given them, would return to their cities enthusiastic about the pool. They would call in their clients and tell of the honor to the firm of being let in on the inside and of the big profits that this would mean to themselves and to their favorite clients. The clients would be informed of the price to which the issue was to be run. Meanwhile dozens of firms in as many cities would be doing the same thing.

The buying of the associate members and their favorite clients would cause the price of the stock to rise, as forecasted by the pool manager. As

[1] Henry Clews, *Twenty-eight Years in Wall Street,* New York: Irving, 1888, p. 142.

the price rose the associate members and their clients would purchase still more shares. When the price reached a level slightly lower than the goal announced by the pool manager, the pool would dump its holdings on the market. This would stop the upward movement and cause the price to sag slightly. The associate members would continue to wait for the reaction that was to run the price up to the announced goal. This price, of course, would never be reached, since the pool manager was no longer manipulating the market. As the price then declined further, the associate members and their clients would have to liquidate their holdings for whatever they could obtain.

A Regular Pool.   The objective of this type of pool was to accumulate holdings in a particular issue at a low price and to sell them to the public later at a high price. The first step involved tying up the floating supply. To do this, the largest holders of the issue would be brought into the pool and asked to promise not to sell their shares. One pool operator, James R. Keene, is said to have made a record of the number of all stock certificates held by members of the whisky pool so that if any one of them cheated by selling his shares while the price was being put up his action could be detected from the numbers on the certificates circulating in the market.

The next step involved accumulating shares by purchases on the market without causing the price to rise. To induce investors to part with their holdings at low prices, the pool would circulate rumors of financial difficulties, reduced dividends, small earnings, and the like. If the price ran up a few points, the pool would sell short and cause the price to sink below its former level. Newspapers would call attention to the false starts, followed by setbacks, with no progress being made. The pool's program would be continued week after week until holders of the issue would become disgusted and sell out their stock.

As soon as the pool accumulated the desired number of shares at low prices, it would begin the marking-up phase. Since the floating supply was now small, the price would tend to advance quickly on little buying. The pool would buy a few shares, the price would advance sharply, and the public would await the customary reaction, which of course in this case would not materialize. After the stock had been active for some time and the price had been marked up many points, the public would rush in to buy and the pool would unload its holdings.

The process of distributing the pool's holdings at a high price required first-rate generalship. The machinery of publicity was accelerated, and rumors of extra dividends, melon cutting, stock splits, and hidden assets were broadcast. The whole gamut of tricks was run if necessary. Directors were kept busy with interviews, favorable earnings statements were disclosed, and hints of mergers were circulated. Everything came from "people on the inside," "authoritative quarters," or "large banking interests."

The period of distribution was followed by a period of disillusionment. Newspapers continued their glowing reports; nevertheless the stock declined. Officials of the company or even the pool manager would give out interviews condemning the "destructive element of bear raids and manipulators." An occasional rally would revive the hopes of the public, but the stock would continue to decline. As prices slowly slipped, the public would begin to unload. Suddenly an avalanche of sell orders would plummet the price below its intrinsic value. If the pool functioned continuously, it could now accumulate stock again and prepare for a repeat performance.

A Legitimate Pool.   There is nothing essentially evil about forcing prices up or down. The harm, if any, results from hiding the manipulative activities with intent to deceive investors. The real question is: Would an investor have purchased or sold the manipulated issue if he had known that the price quoted on the Exchange was an artificial one not derived from the free interplay of the forces of supply and demand?

An example of manipulation that seems quite legitimate is found in the support which an underwriting syndicate gives to a new issue of stock by employing a broker to buy shares if the market price goes below the issue price and to sell shares when the price goes above. Without these operations, the price would drop or rise. Clearly this is an artificial price due to the planned activities of the syndicate.

Section 9A (5) of the Securities Exchange Act makes it unlawful for any person to stabilize the price of a security other than in a manner approved by the Commission. The rules of the Commission require that persons seeking to stabilize a security must send a notice of their intention to stabilize with full particulars to the Commission and to the Exchange upon which it is intended to effect stabilizing transactions. Then they must report all transactions to the Commission. Prior to selling a stabilized security off the Exchange, the stabilizer must give the prospective purchaser a written notice similar to the following:

> TO FACILITATE THE OFFERING, IT IS INTENDED TO STABILIZE THE PRICE(S) OF . . . .
> Identify security(ies) in which stabilizing transactions will be effected
> ON . . . .
> . . . .
> Identify exchange(s) on which stabilizing transactions will be effected
> THIS STATEMENT IS NOT AN ASSURANCE THAT THE PRICE(S) OF THE ABOVE SECURITY(IES) WILL BE STABILIZED OR THAT THE STABILIZING, IF COMMENCED, MAY NOT BE DISCONTINUED AT ANY TIME.

Thus it will be noted that the law does not prohibit stabilizing a security but requires only that the stabilizer refrain from using stabilized market quotations to deceive investors.

Methods of Manipulation

A history of stock speculation reveals a great variety of devices for creating artificial values. Most of these methods are no longer permitted, either by law or by the rules governing the practices of the Exchange. Some of the more important of the prohibited devices will be explained.

Options. Most of the professionals whose services were available for manipulative purposes in 1928 and 1929 protected themselves from risk by options. A manipulative option is different from the put and call contract described in Chapter 16. A call is a right to demand delivery of 100 shares of a stock at a specified price and is purchased in the market. A manipulative option was a right to call for the delivery of shares, but it was usually for 10,000 or more shares, and it was given away, not sold.

An example of just how an option was used by a manipulator will make the distinction clearer. In the 1920s the chairman of the board of the Kolster Radio Corporation owned 250,000 of the 830,000 outstanding shares of the company. At that time only a few shares were changing hands on the market, at approximately 74. Obviously it would be impossible for him to sell 250,000 shares in such a thin market without breaking the current price. The services of a professional were engaged. He was given an option for 100,000 shares at 72, an option for 50,000 shares at 74, and an option for 100,000 shares at 84.

The usual custom in such a case was to go short immediately. Then, if the manipulator failed to put the price up he profited from his short sale. At the same time his short sale rendered the stock technically strong and so laid the groundwork for a rise designed to attract attention and draw public support. If this support should come too quickly, the manipulator's short position was protected by his option at 72 and he could still profit by his options at 74 and 84. Thus, no matter what happened, he would not lose. In this case demand was inspired by the manipulator's purchase of large blocks of stock from himself at ever-increasing prices. By this means he was able to attract the attention of the public, to force the price of the stock as high as 96, and to dispose of 250,000 shares at a profit of $1,351,152.50 to himself. Within several days of the completion of the deal, the quoted price of the issue declined to 66. Two years later the stock for which the chairman of the board received $19,300,000 was valued by the market at $500,000.

Wash Sales. Manipulators do not themselves put the price of a stock up or down. Supply and demand do that. What the manipulator does is to execute a series of deceptive transactions or disseminate false information designed to cause others to augment supply or demand as they would not if they were acquainted with the facts.

Nothing excites the speculating public as much as increased activity in an issue, accompanied by mounting prices. Knowing this, manipulators sometimes create artificial activity by buying and selling shares to themselves. Such transactions are called "wash sales." Wash sales are fictitious transactions in which no change of ownership takes place. For example, an operator who is long on stock or is hired to create a market for a given stock agrees with other operators on a price above the market at which the holder will sell and at which his confederate shall buy. No change of ownership takes place, and the buyer by agreement incurs no financial obligation to the seller. The sale is purely fictitious; but it creates market activity in the stock, keeps the stock on the ticker and the financial page, and makes it appear in a strong position because of its activity and advance in price. The purpose is to deceive buyers who become interested and take the stock off the tricksters' hands at an artificially high level.

For years every reputable exchange throughout the country prohibited wash sales. In the Senate investigation of stock exchange practices, officials of the Exchange vehemently denied that wash sales took place.[2] But during the period 1928 to 1934 traders were acquainted with a number of stratagems by means of which wash sales were executed in fact but not in appearance. Evidence exists to show that members of the Exchange knew of these practices and often cooperated with the manipulators.

One method used by professionals was to open accounts in dummy names and then to trade with themselves via these accounts. For example, the chairman of the board of Anaconda Copper Mining Company had an account with a New York Stock Exchange firm under the name of Greene and another account called Greene Account No. 55. On March 20, 1929, shares of Anaconda Copper were accumulated in the morning for both accounts. At 2 P.M. an employee with discretionary privileges for these accounts placed an order to buy 35,000 shares with one broker and an order to sell a similar number of shares with another. The execution of such a large order attracted attention and ran the price of the issue up 4 points and a fraction, at which level the two Greene accounts were liquidated at a profit. After the close of the market it was decided that the 35,000-share order was an error and the transaction was canceled by a reversing entry, but the broker nevertheless charged a $1,700 commission for the erroneous execution of a nonexisting order.[3]

On another occasion a pool manager entered buying and selling orders as he thought necessary in order to control the price of his stock and left the distribution of these orders among the various dummy accounts in which

[2] *Stock Exchange Practices,* Report of Committee on Banking and Currency, U.S. Senate, 73d Cong., 1934, p. 25.

[3] *Ibid.,* p. 814.

he operated to the clerks in the brokerage office. Their task was to assign the orders to the various accounts in such a way as to avoid the appearance of wash sales. When questioned by the Senate committee later on the question of a purchase charged to his wife's account, the following conversation took place.[4]

Attorney: What do you mean by a "thousand shares in the air"?

Pool Operator: A thousand shares that they bought that somebody don't own and they would say, "Have you got some place to put it?" The clerk says, "Yes." And then they put it in my wife's name.

Attorney: Well, was your wife buying from the syndicate?

Pool Operator: I don't remember that particular transaction. It might have been so that the stock would not meet there. So that there would not be a wash sale.

Attorney: Well, who gave the clerk in the office instructions?

Pool Operator: I don't know who gave the instructions.

Attorney: Well, who would? Who had the authority to?

Pool Operator: A thousand shares—*any clerk* in the office could have done that. (Authors' italics.)

The evidence presented to the Senate committee brought out the fact that both traders and members of the exchanges were more concerned with obeying the letter than the spirit of the law prohibiting wash sales. Thus a pool operator testified that in his opinion it was not a wash sale if he got one broker to buy for him what he sold through another.[5] Neither was it considered to be a wash sale if individual purchase and sale orders varied by eighths but balanced in the aggregate or if a trader sold to one person at the identical price at which he was buying the stock at that moment from another.

The Securities Exchange Act ignores these fine distinctions altogether. It declares it to be unlawful for any person directly or indirectly to effect a transaction that involves no change in *beneficial ownership* if the purpose is to create a false or misleading appearance of active trading. It is also unlawful for any broker to accept an order for the purchase or sale of a security if he has knowledge that an offsetting order of substantially the same size, time, and price has been entered with a different broker either by the trader or by someone acting in collusion with him. Finally, it is unlawful for anyone to effect a series of transactions in a security designed to induce others to purchase or sell it.

In other words, the intent of the law as it now stands is to allow freedom of trading as long as purchasers buy because they want to acquire shares or

[4] *Ibid.,* p. 483.

[5] *Ibid.,* p. 479.

sell because they no longer want to keep the shares, but any purchase or sale intended or designed to influence the market behavior of others automatically becomes manipulative in character. It is almost as if the law applied to a trader's motives rather than to his behavior.

Touting.   As was mentioned above, the efforts of a manipulator are bent toward influencing the public to act in the market in a way that will be beneficial to the manipulator's interest. Wash sales are one method often used to accomplish this end. Touting is another. It consists for the most part in disseminating tips and rumors designed to bring the public into the market at the proper moment.

In May 1925, when Baldwin Locomotive was down to 110, the air was full of tips to sell Baldwin. Soon, however, the price began to advance rapidly, and when it got to 120, the tips were reversed and the purchase of Baldwin was strongly urged. Of course a steep decline followed. Rumors of stock dividends and melon cutting at the next meeting of the board of directors; of interviews by leading directors or men having the ear of leading directors, hinting of large earnings and stock split-up or extra cash dividends; of the success of new processes and of patents already proved or about to be proved of extraordinary earning power—all are put afloat at the psychological moment to stimulate enthusiasm and send the market up. Rumors of mergers have always been fruitful of results. Rumors of large hidden assets, immense coal holdings all undeveloped, tremendous oil potentialities, and so forth, stimulate dreams of quickly realized gains in enormous amounts. Plausible tips as to the operations of the insider or the "big interests," properly intermingled with one or more of the kind of rumors mentioned above, help to make the artificial stimulus situation more palatable.

Operators for the decline have a number of methods similar to those of their friends on the constructive side of the market. Rumors of passing dividends, of accumulating inventories, of strikes, of bankruptcy, of earthquakes, of salt water breaking into oil wells, of the spread of radical sentiment, of unfavorable foreign political disturbances—all provide the basis for drives against the market and the destruction of values.

The art of disseminating false information reached its peak in the hectic days of 1928 and 1929. No opportunity to deceive the investing public was overlooked by the tricksters. Even the most innocent-appearing news items were revealed later to be the result of undercover activity or of some manipulator. For example, this item appeared in a New York newspaper and was reprinted by thousands of others:

> A 7-million-dollar power laundry merger of companies in New York and New Jersey is in the process of formation. According to interests identified, it is one of the largest laundry corporations in the country. It is understood that companies in other Eastern states will be

included at a later date which will bring the total capitalization to above $10,000,000.

Few who read it suspected that the article was prepared by men who planned to manipulate the stock and that the reporter who sneaked it into his paper as news was paid $1,800 for doing so. During the course of the Senate investigation, Representative LaGuardia presented canceled checks purporting to show that financial writers of the leading newspapers often accepted bribes from manipulators for advising their readers to invest in the shares being manipulated. He presented stories used 605 times in 228 newspapers, with a combined paid circulation of 11,248,000, published in 157 cities whose aggregate population was 32,399,000. One man went into this publicity business as a profession and in a few months paid out more than $289,279 to editors for printing his rumors.[6] All the largest and most reliable newspapers employed writers who accepted money from this man at one time or another.

One New York daily ran a column under the heading of "The Trader" in which rumors and tips about pools were repeated. The writer of this column was a friend of a free-lance trader. The *modus operandi* was this: The free-lance trader would reveal his plan of operation to the writer, who would then recommend in his newspaper column the purchase or sale of the stock, whichever was to the interest of the trader. The manipulator would open an account with a broker in the writer's name, buy shares of the issue for this account at low prices, and sell them after the tips published in "The Trader" column had brought public support to the issue and forced the price up. Profits were sent by the broker direct to the newspaper columnist, but losses, if there were any, were taken care of by the free-lance trader. Between May 3, 1929, and March 1, 1930, the columnist earned profits of $19,063.44 on the shares which he touted in his column for the trader.[7] When the trader was questioned later, he denied the collusion. He explained why he surrendered $19,063.44 profits to the newspaper writer as follows:

> I got to know him [the writer] and I liked him. He was desirous of moving up in the country where I lived and I tried to do everything I could to help him. My way of helping him was to make this money for him.

In the Indian Motorcycle case, the company gave a brokerage firm an option for 100,000 shares at 5 at a time when the company was facing bankruptcy and when a few shares were selling on the market at 4. The following transcript of testimony offered to the Senate committee brings out

[6] *Ibid.,* p. 457.
[7] *Ibid.,* p. 605.

the fact that all participants in this deal, including the company president, knew that the company was on the verge of failing.[8]

> *Attorney:* Your financial condition was such that you could not carry on?
>
> *President:* Yes.
>
> *Attorney:* Now as a matter of fact, he marketed these 40,000 shares and afterward another 60,000 shares.
>
> *President:* That is right.
>
> *Attorney:* He knew that you were in this bad financial shape when he took the 40,000 shares from you and put it on the market to the public?
>
> *President:* Yes.
>
> *Attorney:* No question about that?
>
> *President:* None, whatsoever.

In this case the stock of the bankrupt company was run up to 17 by disseminating information about the acquisition of the rights to a worthless engine invented by an Englishman.

Touting is now rendered dangerous by the Securities Exchange Act of 1934, which makes it unlawful for a broker or dealer to make a statement that is false or misleading in the light of the known circumstances for the purpose of inducing a purchase or sale of a security. It is also unlawful for a broker to disseminate information, even if true, that the price of a security will rise or fall because of the market operation of some person or group of persons. Finally, another section makes it unlawful for a person to employ any manipulative device or contrivance in contravention of rules of the Commission.

Inside Collusion. In the pre-Commission days, customers sometimes complained of collusion between manipulators and members of the exchanges. Allegations that members frequently engaged in practices that were detrimental to the interests of their own customers were of course strenuously denied by officials of the New York Stock Exchange, who pointed out that its business conduct committee was constantly alert to discover and punish any such activities by its members.

One customer, however, sued a prominent New York Stock Exchange firm for an accounting. The case was carried to the Supreme Court, where a justice in giving his opinion stated that the pleadings, at the election of the plaintiff, might have been amended to conform to proof of fraud. The brokerage firm settled with its customer for $16,000. But when the same evidence that drew the strong condemnation of the jurist was presented to

[8] *Ibid.,* p. 593.

the business conduct committee of the Exchange, that committee reported that its investigation had "failed to indicate any conduct on the part of the firm involved that would warrant disciplinary action by the Exchange against it."[9]

Pool operators also testified to the Senate committee that it was possible to get access to the specialist's books even though this was a violation of an Exchange rule. In one instance a professional pool operator stated that a pool could not operate "very well without the aid of the specialist."[10] In the famous RCA pool, the wife of the specialist in that issue was herself a participant in the pool, and orders to buy or sell for her account were issued by the specialist.[11]

The Securities and Exchange Commission is now amply provided with the powers needed to cope with all such abuses. It is given the right to prescribe such rules and regulations as it deems desirable (1) to regulate floor trading and (2) to regulate specialists and odd-lot dealers. If a broker participates as a member of a selling syndicate, he may not sell any of the securities of the syndicate to his customers on credit, and if he sells for cash, he must give the purchaser a written notice of his interest in the syndicate. The first of these requirements prevents a dealer from aiding his customer to buy securities which he has obligated himself to distribute to the public. The second serves warning on the customer that any advice which the broker has given about the securities in question may be prejudiced owing to his self-interest. Finally, if it becomes desirable to control some practice not covered by any of these provisions, the Commission has the right under the law to require that an exchange alter or supplement its rules and regulations. It would seem, therefore, that the powers of the Commission are sufficiently flexible to enable it to formulate specific remedies for almost any imaginable abuse.

Manipulation of Fundamentals. Four decades ago the standards of business permitted boards of directors and officers of corporations to manipulate earnings, dividends, and the property of their companies in such a manner as to cause great fluctuations in the price of the stock of the concern. A railroad or industrial corporation was made to appear very prosperous, extra cash dividends were declared, and stocks were split. The price of the shares rose and the insiders sold out. After they were sold out, earnings were made to appear small, rumors of distress were floated, the cash available was meager in amount, dividends were passed. When the price of the stock declined to a bottom figure, the officials and the board and large stockholders bought

[9] *Ibid.*, pp. 1128–1131.
[10] *Ibid.*, p. 386.
[11] *Ibid.*, p. 498.

it back, knowing that earnings would again show a gain and that the cash saved the previous year would enable large dividends or extra dividends to be paid. The price then went up, and the stock was again distributed.

It is difficult to say that these men did wrong. They paid out liberally when earnings were large and conserved when earnings were small. No one can be brought into court for doing this sort of thing, for no one could pay dividends when earnings were small. On the other hand, when earnings were large, the stockholders were entitled to the product of their capital investment. This kind of dividend policy alone tended to produce extreme fluctuations in prices, to say nothing of the effect of the manipulation of statistics, balance sheets, and income accounts and the manufacture of rumors intended to deceive. Business standards along these lines have made a great advance. Executives of large corporations now feel a responsibility to the community to minimize fluctuations in the company's securities and to stabilize business activities. Manipulation such as went on in the railroads, oils, coppers, steels, and other lines because of the attempts of men in positions of executive power to accumulate great wealth can no longer be tolerated.

Chapter 10 gives a description of the information that a company seeking listing must file with the New York Stock Exchange. There the reader's attention is called to the requirement that an issuer explain fully its accounting policy in regard to such matters as depreciation, depletion, and inventory valuations. Although the requirements described there are those of the New York Stock Exchange, many of them are mandatory by Section 12(b) of the Securities Exchange Act. Section 13 of the act then goes on to say that every issuer of a security registered on a national securities exchange shall file periodically such information as is necessary to keep reasonably current the information and documents filed at registration. The Commission is the judge of what is reasonably necessary.

Chapter 5 points out that certificates of stock represent the ownership of a corporation. If this is so, then officers are merely persons chosen by the owners to be entrusted with the management of the corporation. Corporate officers have not always viewed their relationship to the organization in this way. In many instances, officers have assumed that the corporation in their control was their personal property and that it existed solely for their personal profit. Imbued with this philosophy, some officers have not hesitated to make glowing reports to stockholders about a company's future at the same time as they were secretly disposing of their own shares in it or even selling them short. The case of the Indian Motorcycle Company cited earlier is an example. At other times officers and directors bought up shares in advance of a directors' meeting, with full knowledge that a melon was to be cut, or else sold them short, knowing that a dividend was about to be passed. In most such cases directors and officers preferred that stockholders remain uninformed about their personal trading in the shares of the company. For this reason they would sell short "against the box" so that the transfer would not appear on the company records.

All this is now a thing of the past. Every person who is the beneficial owner of more than 10 per cent of any security listed on an exchange and every person who is an officer or director of a company whose shares are listed must now report monthly to the Commission every change in his ownership. Furthermore, for the purpose of preventing the unfair use of information that one may have obtained by virtue of his relationship to the company as principal owner, director, or officer, all profits realized from the purchase or sale of shares held less than six months must be surrendered to the company. Selling short against the box is now unlawful, since the act requires officers and directors to deliver all securities which they sell within five days of the sale. Short sales by officers and directors are prohibited altogether.

Corners.   Corners are of historic interest only, since their occurrence under modern conditions is very improbable. Corners in the stock market may be of two kinds: natural and manipulated. In a natural corner a group of persons, through the regular course of investing and trading, find themselves in control of the stock of a given corporation. Without planning or intention, the regular chain of circumstances puts control in their hands. But once conscious of holding control such persons begin to utilize it and force a corner.

One of the most notable natural corners in the history of the New York Stock Exchange occurred May 9, 1901, when the Hill-Morgan interests on the one hand and the Harriman interests on the other were attempting to get control of the Northern Pacific Railroad. The Hill-Morgan interests represented the Northern Pacific and Great Northern railroads and the so-called Harriman–Kuhn, Loeb syndicate represented the Union Pacific. Each group wanted a controlling interest in the Chicago, Burlington, & Quincy Railway in order to get an outlet into Chicago for their own systems. The Hill-Morgan interests won out by buying practically all the Burlington stock and refusing to allow the Union Pacific people participation in stock ownership.

The next move on the part of the Harriman group was to buy control in the Northern Pacific, which owned half of the stock of the Burlington. Here the fireworks began. The two most powerful financial groups in the country were pitted against each other. As the price advanced, a large short interest was built up. Since there were no reasons in respect to fundamentals for an advance in the price of Northern Pacific, many traders sold the stock heavily, thinking that the bubble must soon burst. During the latter part of January 1901 the stock was selling around 77 and 78; April 2, at somewhat above 100; May 3, at 115; May 6, high 133; May 7, high 150 and low 127; May 8, high 180, low 145; and May 9, high 700 and low 160.

Without any intention on the part of the contending interests to manipulate a corner, one had actually come into existence as the result of the chain of circumstances arising out of the contest between the two powerful groups. When the extended short interest realized their situation and began to cover, they found that the two groups had all the stock and also the contracts calling for delivery. Out of a total of 800,000 shares of common stock outstanding, about 636,000 shares were sold during the week of the corner; and on the day of the corner, May 9, at a quotation of 700 few shares were to be had. The story runs that the shorts were offered settlement at $1,000 per share.

The effect of the corner was to demoralize completely the prices of stocks. The short interests were compelled to liquidate large blocks of their long stocks in order to buy Northern Pacific. Such stocks as Pennsylvania Railroad dropped from 147 to 137; New York Central, 153 to 140; Delaware & Hudson, 165 to 105; U.S. Steel, 47 to 24. Total sales for the day of the corner amounted to over 3,281,000 shares, a record that stood for twenty-five years. Support came into the market on May 10. While on May 9 the average high price of eight leading rails was 134.75 and low 108.63, a decline of over 26 points, on the next day the highs for the same rails averaged 133.70.

The manipulated corner is, as its name implies, one that is deliberately, maliciously planned and executed with all the ingenuity at the command of the manipulators. The method of procedure in carrying through a manipulated corner involves three stages: (1) the accumulation of the floating supply of stock; (2) the stimulation of a large short interest; and (3) managing the lending of stocks to the short interest.

If the majority of shares of an issue are closely held, the floating supply will be small. Knowing the number of shares outstanding and the probable potential floating supply, the manipulators buy additional stock from the bears until they hold a preponderant amount. To encourage the short interest, the manipulators lend stock freely through different brokers so that the floating supply appears large and the technical position weak. Rumors, publicity, and a declining market do the rest. After many more shares have been bought than actually exist, the final step in the process is reached. That many more shares might be sold short than exist has been made possible by relending under cover shares that have just been delivered. For example, A sells 100 shares short to B. B's broker loans B's stock on the exchange to A, who then delivers it back to B's broker. Next, C sells short, and B's broker buys for B's account. Now, C borrows the same 100 shares from B that A had borrowed from B and then delivered back to B. Thus, the same 100 shares serves as delivery for short sales amounting to 200 shares. This process can be repeated as long as there is short selling. Meanwhile, B has accumulated contracts for the delivery of the 200 shares of borrowed stock and also holds the 100 shares. After he has contracts for much more stock than the floating supply can amount to at the most liberal estimate, or perhaps after he has contracts for much more stock than exists, he refuses to lend further and calls on the shorts for the stock he lent them. When the shorts order their brokers to buy in the market, no stock is offered. In an effort to buy stock the brokers of the shorts bid the price up and up. B has all the stock and holds it for the highest price he can get. Nothing is left for the shorts to do except to break their contracts or to attempt some kind of compromise with the parties who hold the contracts and the stock.

Commodore Vanderbilt in the 1860s engineered three corners. All were carried through in defense of his property against the attacks of un-principled speculators. The Commodore had been operating steamboats most of his life and had made a lot of money. In 1863 as an investment he bought some Harlem Railway stock around 8 and 9. He became interested in the enterprise and began to develop the property. The stock soon climbed to 30 and then to 50. Traders began to suspect manipulation. In April 1863, an ordinance granting Vanderbilt the right to build a streetcar line the length of Broadway was passed by the New York City Council. Since such a grant meant much to the railway, the stock soon advanced to 75. The council now conspired to make large profits by selling Harlem Railway short and then repealing the ordinance passed in April. The council members tipped off their friends, and total short sales amounted to much over the 110,000 shares outstanding. The great bear operator, Daniel Drew, had a share in the attempted raid. The ordinance was repealed on schedule but, instead of a decline in price of 20 to 30 points as expected, the decline amounted to only 3 points. Vanderbilt had learned of the conspiracy and had bought up all the stock. When the members of the council and their friends became frightened because the price did not decline and began to cover, they had to buy from the Commodore. The price was bid up rapidly. The council settled at 179, while the Commodore profited to the amount of $5 million or more.

The next year, 1864, Vanderbilt wanted to consolidate the Harlem Railway and the Hudson River Railroad, the control of which he had obtained by purchasing its stock. He and his lobbyist in Albany had won the Governor and a safe majority of the state legislature to his side, and a bill was to be passed granting the right to consolidate. While the Com-modore was in New York buying stock in expectation of a rise after the passage of the bill, his lobbyist in Albany learned of a conspiracy by the legislature to sell Harlem short and defeat the bill and so informed his principal. The stock under Vanderbilt's guidance had advanced from 75 to 150. Thousands of shares more than existed were sold short by the members of the legislature and their friends. Vanderbilt, knowing exactly what was going on, rallied several friends to his aid and bought all the stock offered. The first Harlem corner was repeated. The solons of the great state of New York settled at $285 per share.

The third Vanderbilt corner took place two years later in the stock of the Hudson Railroad. Vanderbilt was out of New York on a vacation when bear cliques began to hammer the stock of the Hudson Railroad down. Its sponsor being away, the price declined rapidly. A messenger brought the news to the Commodore, who immediately returned to New York and ordered his brokers to buy all the stock offered. To give the bear cliques the impression that the takers of the stock were financially weak and had to have help to carry so much stock, Vanderbilt through his brokers approached the leading bear houses, requesting them to take the stock and pay cash. The broker's principal, however, was to have the right to buy the stock back at his own option. The bears immediately took the bait, bought the stock, and threw it on the market. The proper impression was created, and more selling followed. All the stock was at once bought by the great manager of the corner. When the bears began to deliver, the stock went from 112 to 180 in a few days. While the bears were buying cover, Vanderbilt was selling stock quietly at 140 and thus avoiding the difficult situation of being left with a large amount of stock on his hands and no market for it.

Conclusion

The securities market is a place where buyers and sellers of stocks and bonds meet to acquire or dispose of their holdings at prices determined by the interaction of uninspired supply and demand. This is the ideal to which organized exchanges have always pledged allegiance, although of course individual members of the exchanges have not always taken the pledge seriously. Then, too, the vision of those in control has not always proved equal to the inventive genius of those who promoted the abuses. When viewed in this way, the Securities Exchange Act is only another step toward the ideal to which exchanges have been slowly but steadily progressing.

The philosophy of the act is exceedingly simple, though its machinery is complex. Its primary objective is to enforce honesty in security dealings. It does not prevent one from doing anything that he can reasonably argue he has the right to do. If one has shares to be sold, he may still sell them, but his right to sell shares that he does not have is now limited. If one wishes to purchase shares, he may buy all that he has the money to pay for, but if he does not have the money to pay, he may not buy as much as he once could. All buying and selling, however, must be for the purpose of acquiring or disposing of shares and not for the purpose of deceiving others or influencing their behavior. Under no circumstances is one permitted to sell and lie to the buyer or buy and lie to the seller. What one says and writes about the shares handled must be true. Officers and directors of corporations may buy and sell as before, but they must reveal the nature of their trading to those who have entrusted them with the management of the corporate property. While paid to manage that property, they must surrender to its owners any profits they are able to make by virtue of their position. Finally, corporate organizations are no longer permitted to deceive their stockholders by use of unrevealed accounting tricks. It may be that some of the rules and regulations imposed upon the markets by the Commission are more stringent than is necessary. If so, one might legitimately criticize the administration of the law; but it is difficult to see where one could sincerely oppose its purpose.